Praise for
Is That All There Is?
The Strange Life of Peggy Lee

"A killer biographer . . . Gavin makes you understand [Lee's] disillusionment and gift."

—Tim Appelo, *The Hollywood Reporter*

"Absorbing . . . the meat of *Is That All There Is?* is Gavin's adroit music writing and the dimension he brings to the details of Lee's life. His command of the artistry and musicology in the worlds of jazz and Lee's contemporaries is first rate. . . . Gavin keeps focus on what Peggy Lee was doing musically even as everything else in her life was sensationally spiraling out of control."

—Lew J. Whittington, *New York Journal of Books*

"Probing, perceptive."

—David Freeland, *The Wall Street Journal*

"Comprehensive and immensely readable."

—David Munk, *The Huffington Post*

"Gavin numbers among that rare breed of biographer capable of tremendous style and substance, meticulous about detail and accuracy yet blessed with exceptional storytelling élan. What emerges is a masterwork of balanced reporting, unflinchingly honest yet eminently respectful."

—Christopher Loudon, *Maclean's* (Canada)

"A penetrating portrait . . . of a troubled and talented woman."

—*Booklist*

"Nobody writes as eloquently, knowledgeably, and page-turningly about the midcentury music heroes who sang—and lived—our American story as James Gavin. His biography of Peggy Lee immerses us in a singular life of radiant self-invention. Peggy Lee patented the unlikely: she was the first white girl who sang (and felt) black. She sounded cool and soft and ironic and understated, making you lean in. This elegant, confident book does that, too."

—Sheila Weller, bestselling author of *Girls Like Us*

"My dad, Nat King Cole, was very friendly with Peggy Lee, his label-mate at Capitol Records. Her mysterious glamour made quite an impression on me. Peggy was a trailblazer—not just as a performer but as a song-writer, at a time when it wasn't very common for singers to write their own songs. James Gavin has captured the essence of the rich musical era that people like my dad and Peggy defined. In his keenly observed, scrupulously researched biography he has also illuminated something very true and touching about the woman behind the glamour. I highly recommend this book."

—Natalie Cole

Praise for
Stormy Weather:
The Life of Lena Horne

"[E]ventful and suspenseful . . . a thorough and fluent biography."

—*The New York Times Book Review*

"Magnificent, gripping, marvelously written. . . . [It] may just be one of the best biographies about show business, race, love, sex, and music ever written."

—Liz Smith, *Variety*

"A fascinating study of a complicated woman and the complicated times that shaped her."

—*USA Today*

"In Gavin's capable hands, Lena Horne's story is both uniquely her own and an integral part of a larger cultural story."

—San Francisco Chronicle

"Sympathetic and tough."

—The New Yorker

ALSO BY JAMES GAVIN

Stormy Weather: The Life of Lena Horne
Intimate Nights: The Golden Age of New York Cabaret
Deep in a Dream: The Long Night of Chet Baker

Is That All There Is?

The Strange Life of

Peggy Lee

James Gavin

ATRIA PAPERBACK

NEW YORK   LONDON   TORONTO   SYDNEY   NEW DELHI

For Zuza Homem de Mello and Ercília Lobo
a minha família brasileira
Thank you for giving me a new world

ATRIA PAPERBACK
An Imprint of Simon & Schuster, Inc.
1230 Avenue of the Americas
New York, NY 10020

Copyright © 2014 by James Gavin

All rights reserved, including the right to reproduce this book or portions thereof in any form whatsoever. For information, address Atria Books Subsidiary Rights Department, 1230 Avenue of the Americas, New York, NY 10020.

First Atria Paperback edition October 2015

Unless otherwise noted, photos are from author's collection.

ATRIA PAPERBACK and colophon are trademarks of Simon & Schuster, Inc.

For information about special discounts for bulk purchases, please contact Simon & Schuster Special Sales at 1-866-506-1949 or business@simonandschuster.com.

The Simon & Schuster Speakers Bureau can bring authors to your live event. For more information or to book an event, contact the Simon & Schuster Speakers Bureau at 1-866-248-3049 or visit our website at www.simonspeakers.com.

Interior design by Paul Dippolito

Manufactured in the United States of America

10 9 8 7 6 5 4 3 2 1

The Library of Congress has cataloged the hardcover edition as follows:

Gavin, James, date.
    Is that all there is?: the strange life of Peggy Lee / James Gavin.
        pages cm
        Includes bibliographical references and index.
1. Lee, Peggy, 1920–2002.   2. Singers—United States—Biography.   I. Title.
    ML420.L294G38 2014
    782.42164092—dc23
    [B]   2014010307

ISBN 978-1-4516-4168-4
ISBN 978-1-4516-4179-0 (pbk)
ISBN 978-1-4516-4180-6 (ebook)

Introduction

*I*F THEY'RE WAITING for me to die ... good luck!"

So said Miss Peggy Lee, age seventy-two, to her startled audience at the New York Hilton's Club 53 in 1992. "They" meant the Walt Disney Company, her foe in a legal war for unpaid royalties on the top-selling videocassette of *Lady and the Tramp*, the 1955 cartoon classic. Lee had contributed four character voices and cowritten the songs. In court, the mythic songstress had looked like no match for the mighty Disney; she entered in a wheelchair that held an oxygen tank and seemed to be at death's door. She won the case—but Disney kept fighting. So did Lee. It was her nature. In her theme song, "Is That All There Is?," she smilingly declared, "I'm not ready for that final disappointment!"

Nearly all the fans inside that packed cabaret were old enough to remember the Peggy Lee of legend—the blond seductress with a mermaid's figure and a vixen's smile, who held out a snapping hand and sang "you give me *fever!*" in a tough purr. Now she sat enthroned like a bizarre fallen angel—a shapeless blur of ghostly, gleaming white, from her snowy Cleopatra wig to her feathered silk robe. Critic Rex Reed compared her to "an intergalactic Mae West"; according to Gerald Nachman of the *San Francisco Chronicle*, her voice had changed from "warm and sexy" to "cool and eerie." The air in her presence felt thick, slow-moving, as though one were in a dream. Offstage, Reed found her "strange to the point of madness."

Even so, Lee retained an almost magical ability to touch the heart. According to pianist Mike Melvoin, her conductor in the 1960s, "there was no way you could escape her spell. There was no way you couldn't believe every word she said." Pop star k.d. lang saw Lee at the Hilton. To lang, Lee had "an aura of majesty about her. It was like there was a vacuum in that room except for this one piercing ray of light, which was her voice and her presence. It doesn't happen frequently, when people channel the universe like that." Peggy Lee had never had to shout to make her point; in her musical language, silence spoke as loudly as sound. Hers was the sweet, husky voice in the bedroom, beckoning you to pull in closer. "When I get very quiet and very intense," she explained, "the power goes right through."

She controlled the stage like a puppeteer. Characters materialized one by one: a barroom vamp on the make, an indomitable and still-sexy housewife, various faded women whose last chance at love had passed them by. Wispy as it seemed, her voice could drive a whole orchestra—even that of the "King of Swing," Benny Goodman, who had discovered the awkward young singer in 1941 and made her a star. Other band vocalists had to belt to be heard; Peggy Lee made audiences lean forward. To Rob Hoerburger of the *New York Times*, Lee had formed the blueprint for the sexualized cooing of Eartha Kitt, Diana Ross, and Madonna. "I knew I could never sound like her, but I wanted to," said Dusty Springfield.

To many black musicians, including Count Basie, Lee sang the blues like no other white woman could. "Are you sure there's not some spade in you?" joked the bandleader. Grady Tate, her longtime drummer, placed Lee on the same pedestal as Billie Holiday. "Peggy had that nasty, laid-back, demented, sultry, incredibly funky sound that Lady Day had," he said. "But it was Lady with another Lady on top of it." Lee's influence reached beyond pop and jazz: Julius Baker, the renowned classical flutist, copied her airy, confidential tone; the operatic mezzo-soprano Marilyn Horne, known for her plush sound and technical bravura, grew up trying to imitate Lee.

But no one could capture the aura that radiated from behind that placid façade and riveted audiences before she had uttered a note. "In singing, it's all in the mind," she noted. "I just sort of go into my own little universe." Impressionist Jim Bailey, who channeled Lee so uncannily that it shook even her, had found the singer much harder to capture than Judy Garland and Barbra Streisand, his two most famous subjects. "Barbra and Judy projected to the back of the house. But Peggy made you come and find her. She made you *very* curious. I would be on the edge of my seat. I wanted to get into her head."

Inside it lurked a misty storybook world where truth and fantasy blurred. Peggy Lee, of course, hadn't been born Peggy Lee; she was really Norma Deloris Egstrom, a name as flat as the desolate North Dakota landscape that had created her. "She came up out of nowhere," said Artis Conitz, her closest childhood friend in Nortonville, population one hundred. "She made a lot out of nothing." Lee never doubted that her mind was the gateway to miracles. She carried her credo around on a sheet of paper: "Whatever you vividly imagine, ardently desire, sincerely believe, and enthusiastically act upon . . . must inevitably come to pass."

By the late 1940s she was *Miss* Peggy Lee, star. In her favorite song, "The Folks Who Live on the Hill," a couple ascend, hand-in-hand, to the oasis of their dreams—a "home on a hilltop high." Around 1980, Lee acquired her own: a villa in Bel Air, the exclusive gated community in west Los Angeles. Along the side of the house grew a profusion of pink Peggy Lee roses, named for her by the American Rose Society. A staff was on hand to treat her like a queen. But she lived alone. The love of her life—guitarist Dave Barbour, the first of her four husbands—resided there only in her mind; he had died years earlier, and divorced her well before that.

In January 1999, when I visited her home, Lee's own time seemed to have run out. A whopping stroke had left the singer incapacitated and barely able to speak. I had made arrangements with *Vanity Fair* to write what would likely be a memorial profile. Her daughter, Nicki Lee Foster, had moved in, and had agreed to see me. Virginia Bernard, the uniformed black wardrobe mistress and cook who had worked for Lee since the 1960s, greeted me at the door. I walked through a regal foyer with a chandelier and passed a grand staircase, the kind descended by Gloria Swanson in the movie *Sunset Boulevard*.

Ushered into the living room, I met Nicki, a large woman of fifty-five with a brown shag hairdo. Her weary movements and sad air suggested that life as the child of Peggy Lee had not been easy, even in better times. Her stories confirmed it. Like most stars, Lee had demanded and received constant attention; her career came before all. In the 1970s, Foster had left her mother as well as a marriage, and taken her three children far away to Idaho. Now Lee's illness had brought her back.

As I stood with Foster, Peggy Lee was just steps away, behind the closed door of a bedroom off the living room. "I can't take you in there," Foster warned.

For the next two hours I couldn't get my mind off that door. I imagined Peggy Lee inside, wondering: "*Who is he? What are you telling him?*" I remembered her Oscar-nominated performance in *Pete Kelly's Blues*, the 1955 crime drama in which Lee played an alcoholic torch singer of the Roaring Twenties who goes insane. In her first appearance, she stands in the background while her mobster boyfriend and a bandleader talk business. Silent and out of focus, Lee dominated that scene; now, invisibly, she was ruling this one.

Gone were her low, hearty laugh and the risqué jokes she loved to tell; now her pretty home had the frozen quality of a museum. Foster showed me the office. On its walls were twelve Grammy nominations—Lee had scored one award, for "Is That All There Is?," and another for lifetime achievement—along with signed photos and letters from the likes of Albert Schweitzer, Frank Sinatra, and the Dalai Lama. The father of jazz, Louis Armstrong, had written this to Lee on a picture of his grinning face: "The greatest ever since I heard her chirp the 1st note."

Nearly the whole house was painted peach, a color Lee thought soothing. But according to friends, the queen of laid-back minimalism couldn't find much comfort in anything. Lee had spent most of her adult life in bed, nestled in a cocoon of fluffy pillows and sheets; it was the only place she seemed to feel safe. Bottles of tranquilizers were tucked away in the bedclothes. Hints of an obsessively controlling nature—some called it perfectionism—appeared in the crowning feature of her living room: a wall of cabinets that housed her career's worth of orchestrations by some of the greatest arrangers in jazz. All were guarded in numbered plastic envelopes, alphabetized, and notated in a binder.

French doors looked out on a pool Lee had seldom used. A pair of Peggy Lee puppets, with huge eyelashes and red-painted lips, lay slumped together on a chair. Her daughter's hazy watercolor paintings hung in various places, a reminder that she, too, had creative gifts. But Nicki had long ago abandoned the call of art. "I didn't want to ever have to try and follow in my mother's footsteps," she told me. "That's too big a shoe to fill."

Well into our discussion, we were joined by Holly Foster-Wells, Nicki's vivacious daughter. For all the trouble she had caused them, both women clearly adored the sleeping figure in the bedroom. So it was with most of the people who knew her, including many of the ones she had burned. Lee sang, and all was forgiven.

In her last months of lucidity I had gotten my own moment with the star when I interviewed her by phone for the liner notes of a reissue of *Mink Jazz*, her 1963 album. Speaking to me from bed, Lee could offer little more than a weakly murmured "I don't remember." But when I mentioned a song she had cowritten, "Where Can I Go Without You?," Lee's voice turned to steel. "*Will I be given credit for that?*" she asked with an imperiousness that chilled me.

Robert W. Richards, an illustrator who had worked with her in the 1970s, offered some insight. "Peggy operates on anger," he said, "and the minute you can get her angry you've got her attention."

Anger. It was a product of her childhood, and it had seen her through the pressures of every show; surely it had also helped her survive a series of near-death experiences. Lee had weathered so many, she had come to feel she would never die. Her friend Phoebe Jacobs didn't doubt that Lee had a special line to the beyond. "Peggy was a very spiritual person," she said. "I saw what she could do to an audience. That's not just talent. It's gotta come from something else."

Others who knew her felt the turmoil within. Jazz singer Mark Murphy, her fellow artist at Capitol Records in the late 1950s, picked up on it. Murphy was infatuated with her talent, and when he met her he expected to find the Peggy Lee he had seen on TV: "like a jazzy Myrna Loy—the coolest, sweetest, most down-home." Instead he saw the dichotomy common among artists who create a persona apart from their real selves. "She was a woman horribly not at peace with herself," he said. "When she was Peggy Lee, not so many problems—but when she was Norma it was problem city."

"When she wanted me to play bluesy she'd say,
'Trains,'" recalled one of Lee's musicians. A train
depot at Jamestown, North Dakota, c. 1910.

Chapter One

To DRIVE THROUGH the Dakota plains is to feel the numbing sameness of a place where nothing ever seems to change. "North Dakota was forever," explained Peggy Lee, "and it was flat." As the landscape flies by outside a car window, one has a strong sense of going nowhere. According to Frank Sonnek, a retired Los Angeles accountant who came from South Dakota: "The Dakota prairies just roll on and on—they can make you sick. You feel like a sailor in the middle of the ocean."

But Dakota life was all about reaping fruits from the soil, turning emptiness into riches. Peggy Lee did the same. She recalled herself as "a weird little child with a tremendous imagination . . . I had some very strange thoughts. I used to daydream my way through some of the more difficult things." Fantasy became so crucial to her survival that it permanently altered her view of reality. Lee developed intense powers of visualization; she could escape into far-off points in her mind when she sang, envisioning them in such detail that listeners could see them, too.

Her father, Marvin Egstrom, worked on the railroad, which gave her a sense of the world beyond. To see an approaching train excited her. A deafening mechanical clamor, a huge cloud of hissing steam, and there it was, chugging rhythmically toward her, car after car. The whistle blared melodiously, so loud that it seemed to sound from the heavens. For Norma Deloris Egstrom, trains meant a way out. "I knew where they came from, and where they were going to, and I made up my mind at an early age that I was going to go to all those places."

Getting there, though, could seem impossible at a time when life was a daily struggle. Work dominated prairie life, but the elements waged war at every step. In 2011, Artis Conitz, Norma's best friend, looked back at her childhood in tiny Nortonville: "You will never understand what it was like if you didn't live it—those horrible days of very, very severe winters and very, very dry summers and very, very poor people."

Rhiannon, a jazz singer and educator, grew up in the 1950s on a farm in South Dakota. In a recorded monologue, "Love of the Land," she evoked the battles that all Dakotans faced.

> There is a cruelty to this life. A loneliness. A separation from the rest of humanity. You have *got* to fit in here. It's cultural monotony! . . . These flat cornfields, the endless squares of crops growing, the cows . . . *standing*. The men in their silage-smelling bib overalls with their big heavy shoes, sucking their teeth. Big chests, red faces, rough hands. And the women in their plain cotton-print dresses with children hanging off them. Busy with their hands all the time. Big hands. Plain hair, plain features. They were built kind of low to the ground like *they* were crops coming up out of the earth. Miraculous people. Sturdy. You've gotta be: there is *no* mercy from the wind that blows out of that big sky.

Cold was the ultimate hardship. Winter winds of thirty to forty below seemed to scorch the skin; each breath, wrote North Dakota's Lois Phillips Hudson in *Reapers of the Dust: A Prairie Chronicle*, "was like strong hot smoke in my nostrils, so that for one confused instant I thought I was going to suffocate with the cold that was so cold it was hot." Before leaving the house, Dakotans layered on long underwear and wool garments, then braced themselves for the opening of the front door. Some parents wrapped their children in buffalo-skin coats. Blizzards buried the town in towering snowdrifts. If school wasn't canceled, parents took their children there on sleighs or by horse and buggy. Plows that looked like monsters roamed the streets, their toothy, gaping mouths scooping up mountains of white, but no machine could match a Dakota snowstorm.

Sometimes a blizzard made it too dangerous for kids to walk to school. On blustery nights, while the Egstrom children sat around the pot-bellied stove, their father, Marvin, kept them riveted with accounts of a legendary Midwestern catastrophe, the Schoolhouse Blizzard of January 1888. For two days it swept the plains states—Nebraska, Minnesota, Montana, Wyoming, Idaho, and the Dakotas—with deadly results.

The story began on an unseasonably sunny weekday morning. Children walked casually to school; grown-ups ventured out as well, rejoicing in the odd wave of warmth.

Around noon, snow began to fall. Within an hour it had buried everything in sight. Whipped about by fierce winds, the snow blew horizontally, destroying visibility and making driving—and walking—impossible. Panic spread, for children were stranded at school. Some teachers fetched rope and strung the students into a chain, then attempted to lead them home one by one. Most of the time, children and adults froze to death. In one schoolhouse, teachers tore up the floorboards and burned them, along with chairs and desks, for heat. By the time the storm had ended, 235 people—mainly children—had died.

Dakotans faced other attacks. Modern medicine had far to go; disease and accidents cut short many lives, and infant mortality was high. Death records from the teens and twenties report countless premature demises, from tuberculosis, pneumonia, scarlet fever. Blue-collar labor brought its own hazards. Alfred Nash, who married Norma's aunt Hannah, was buried alive in a mining accident. On his first railroad job, Marvin Egstrom dropped heavy freight on his foot, crushing two toes.

Home life brought its own challenges. Indoor plumbing was rare; families drew well water through a cistern pump into a bucket. When the wells froze, they melted snow on the stove. Many pots of water had to be boiled to fill one bathtub, which bathed the whole family. Clothes were hand-laundered on scratchy metal washboards or in primitive hand-operated washing gadgets. This was also the age of the makeshift toilet known as an outhouse: a backyard shed with a hole dug in the ground. Coarse pages from the Sears or Montgomery Ward catalogs served as toilet tissue.

Houses were not necessarily safe harbors. The wood-frame, weatherbeaten structures were prey to kerosene lanterns that tipped over, primitive gas stoves that exploded, early and hazardous electrical wiring. Many towns had no fire department; houses burned to ash in minutes. But townspeople helped one another out of tough binds. When fire leveled Artis Conitz's house, neighbors brought them replacements for almost everything. The same was done for the Egstroms, two of whose homes burned.

But as Russell Duncan wrote in his Dakota memoir *I Remember*, people didn't complain: "The work had to be done so they did it." They and their immediate ancestors, most of them Scandinavian, had grown up amid long, dark winters and harsh conditions; stoicism was in their blood.

Still, they had to vent somehow, and many men reached for the bottle. Alcoholism wore down Marvin; his brother Milford, who drove a cab in Jamestown, drank, too. "So did most of the males I was aware of," said Milford's son, Glen Egstrom. They kept their disquiet to themselves. "In that culture, you're not allowed to show much emotion," said Frank Sonnek. "Big boys don't cry. Angry means, I'm a bad person. With Peggy Lee, the feeling came out in her music. When she performed you didn't see a lot of emotion, but you could feel it."

Lee couldn't exist without drama, though. Insanity figured in many of her family stories. In her autobiography, Lee tells a fanciful (and almost completely unsubstantiated) tale of how her Swedish-born paternal grandfather, Jan Magnus Eriksson Ekström, moved to Norway and then, in his attempt to leave, nearly died in a shipwreck. He and five fellow sailors built a raft, Lee explains; they floated on it for a month. Only Jan and one other man survived, rescued by a passing ship bound for New York. The tragedy peaks as Jan goes temporarily mad and winds up in a Manhattan psychiatric ward. Once recovered, he saves enough money to send for his Norwegian wife, Berthe, and Erik, a son he didn't know he had until he had reached America.

The truth was much less cinematic. Jan was a ship's carpenter who impregnated his girlfriend Berthe in his adopted home of Norway. He married her, then lived there with her and their son Erik until they emigrated to the States. After a brief stay in New York, they settled in Wisconsin, where another son, Ole, was born on November 23, 1874. Five more children followed. A few years later the family moved to the Dakotas, whose wealth of fertile farmland was attracting hordes of Scandinavian immigrants.

Of the Eriksson brood, Ole grew up to be the standout: over six feet tall, lanky, and good-looking, with a brisk stride and a ladykiller's charm. By seventeen he had relocated to Minnesota, where he won a then-prestigious job as a railroad telegraph operator. That, combined with his rakish charisma, helped him land a beautiful dressmaker, Eva G. Williams. The couple married, and in 1896 became the proud parents of a baby girl, Zelda.

Thereafter, something went terribly wrong. Eva took Zelda and fled to her family home in Iowa; Ole returned to his parents' home in South Dakota. No proof exists that they divorced. In a 1900 census form, either Eva or her family listed her as a widow; a year later she remarried. Ole blurred his own past by changing his name to Marvin Olaf Egstrom.

His checkered marital history resumed in 1903, when at twenty-eight he scored another teenage beauty. Selma Anderson was a petite Norwegian, just eighteen, and born in Volga, South Dakota. She looked like a dainty porcelain doll: a bow adorned her dark, upswept hair, and hanging curls framed an alabaster face. As Peggy Lee recalled her, Selma was almost too good to be true—she played piano beautifully, cooked and sewed to perfection, and showered her family with love.

In truth, neither Selma nor her family were paragons of goodness. Her parents had divorced, a scandal at the time; her mother, who ran an inn, had borne children by two men, one of them probably illegitimate. According to the *Volga Tribune*, Marvin and Selma married in October 1903—three months after the birth of their first child, Milford.

Sexual impropriety was then more common than one would assume. "What else was there to do?" remarked Artis Conitz. But Marvin's wild days were behind him. Just around the time he married Selma, he won his most prestigious job, as superintendent of transportation at the Sioux Falls headquarters of the South Dakota Central Railway. Children kept coming—Della (1905), Leonard (1908), Marion (1913), Clair (1916).

The pressure mounted, and soon, people who spoke of Marvin tended to describe him as Conitz did: "He was a sweet, sweet man who loved to drink." Sloppiness with the railroad's finances cost Marvin his job. In 1918 he moved to Jamestown to manage the depot there for a junior line, the Midland Continental Railroad. His new job was a comedown. The Midland was originally meant to stretch from Canada to Texas, but World War I had wreaked havoc on the financing, and only sixty-eight miles of track were laid. Locals laughed off the Midland as "puny." A freight train carried farm goods and supplies; the passenger train came and went just once a day.

At least Marvin had wound up in a real city. Jamestown was North Dakota's fourth largest, with six thousand residents. Instead of the state's habitual flatness, it lay in a valley surrounded by hills; the James River, which connected the Dakotas, ran through it. There were farms on the periphery, but the street names—Milwaukee, Wisconsin, St. Paul, Washington—gave the town a worldly air. Aside from being the county seat of government, it boasted a college, an opera house, and a theater.

Still, the place epitomized small-town America. Few people locked their front doors. Clip-clopping horses pulled carriages down Fifth Avenue South—a dirt road that contained a general store, a barbershop with a peppermint-stick pole outside, and other essential businesses. Men strode down the street in dour three-piece suits; women wore neutral-colored dresses and overcoats and church-lady hats. There was no room for stylishness, just prim practicality. Mary Young, who lived in Jamestown, recalled big nights out: "You'd park your car downtown and watch the people window-shop. Folks would buy popcorn and hot peanuts from Mr. Wheeler's cart. That would be a big deal for me, to have a bag of popcorn. Everybody was poor. We'd go to the ball games, and if I got a bottle of pop, oh, that was incredible."

Each Sunday residents gathered in Jamestown's many churches—Lutheran, Methodist, Presbyterian, Episcopal. The tall, pointy steeples aimed at the heavenly paradise they hoped someday to reach; church bells resounded through the town on Sunday, suggesting that something larger was looking out for them. But darkness radiated from the city's largest business, known as "the Nuthouse." The North Dakota State Hospital for the Insane stood on a hill that overlooked Jamestown. A hamlet unto itself, the Nuthouse had its own farm, power plant, and general store. Marvin Egstrom knew the place well, for the Midland carried its supplies.

The hospital was proof of the staggering degree of mental illness that plagued the region—another byproduct of the grim pressures of the Dakotas. By 1950, the Nuthouse's population had ballooned to almost 2,500—nearly a quarter of Jamestown's population. A 1915 report told of rooms overcrowded with lice-infested cots, of patients doped into oblivion. Outbreaks of smallpox and tuberculosis there were deemed "almost impossible to prevent." Even in the fifties, a doctor brought in to overhaul the institution talked of finding "cages, strait jackets, leg irons, stern guards, malnutrition." Inmates were so neglected they could wander out freely.

Before she left Jamestown at the age of eight, Norma Egstrom had seen some of the patients, with their vacant stares and strange behavior, and had heard many stories. These memories came in handy in 1955, when the movie *Pete Kelly's Blues* costarred Peggy Lee as a woman who ends up institutionalized, her mind nearly blank.

But only sweetness was apparent in the face that greeted Selma and Marvin Egstrom at Trinity Hospital on May 26, 1920, the day their sixth child, Norma Deloris Egstrom, was born. Norma had extremely fair skin, light brown hair, and hazel eyes; soon she became Marvin's little angel.

In her early years, the Egstroms thrived. They had settled into a spacious house on Pennsylvania Avenue between Second and Pacific Streets; Marvin, meanwhile, was promoted to vice president of the Midland Continental. The family lived simply; they sang together, played cards with neighbors, went to church socials and barn dances, and ice-skated on the frozen creek in winter. As the temperature climbed—sometimes to 115 degrees—they picnicked along the James River. Farm kids walked around barefoot, partly to save on shoes; boys fished or hunted gophers. "We were satisfied with very little as far as entertainment," said writer Connie Emerson, who grew up in Valley City, North Dakota, in the thirties.

Selma and Marvin continued to indulge in the pastime that kept wives perennially pregnant. For Selma, it was proving dangerous. Buried in Jamestown records is the fact that Selma had developed diabetes while carrying Norma. No longer was she a petite, doll-like beauty; a family portrait from that time showed a woman worn down by motherhood—bloated, with a weary face and a short, messy hairdo of convenience. Just sixteen months after Norma's birth, Selma was pregnant again. The baby, who arrived on June 21, 1922, and was named Gloria, emerged stillborn.

Just over a year later, Selma was expecting again. According to Peggy Lee, her mother feared for her life, and spent the last months of the pregnancy making clothes for the children—"so we'd be dressed for a long time."

Selma returned to Trinity Hospital, where on April 23, 1924, she bore Jean—a fair-skinned child with the whitest of blond hair. Jean looked like an angel fallen from heaven; and indeed, congenital ill health made her not long for this world. Neither was Selma. "Following her return," the *Jamestown Daily Alert* would report, she was "confined to her bed and her life despaired of many times." A bed was set up in the living room and a nurse engaged. Jean was entrusted to Selma's sister; the other Egstrom children took turns sitting vigil with their mother.

After three months, Selma lapsed into a coma. She died of diabetes-related causes on August 7, 1924, at four in the morning. She was thirty-nine. By the next afternoon, a coffin had replaced the hospital bed. Friends and neighbors filed past, while a reverend from the Scandinavian Lutheran Church intoned a grave funeral service. Even though she was only four at the time, Peggy Lee would claim vivid memories of that day. "There they were, standing all around with the sweet-smelling flowers, the eyes of everyone focused on the casket. They had on hats and sad faces . . . Why was everyone so serious?" She recalled asking: "Can I see my Mama?" Someone picked her up and sat her in a chair alongside the casket. There lay Selma "looking so tiny and beautiful . . . I thought she'd just gone to sleep."

The casket lid was closed, and a fleet of pallbearers carried Selma out. "I was so puzzled," recalled Lee at seventy-two. "So I asked Daddy, 'Where did they *take* Mama?' He said, 'To heaven, with God.' And *that* answer set me on a search that has never ended."

As she heard her siblings recalling their mother, Selma became Norma's fantasy ideal. Selma seemed like an angel, wrenched from her for reasons she couldn't comprehend. Gone were the unconditional love and safety her mother symbolized. In their place came the gnawing sense that her gestation and birth might have pushed Selma to her demise.

Alone, Norma went walking by a nearby stream. Spotting stones and flowers, she paused to pick them up; maybe her mother lay in the ground beneath them. At other times, Norma stood in the backyard and stared at the sky. "I always thought she was going to appear someday and look over a cloud and wave at me," recalled Peggy Lee. "Sometimes I really thought I saw her."

During childhood, she kept the longing locked inside; Artis Conitz couldn't recall her ever mentioning Selma. Many years later, though, Lynn Ringuette, one of Marion Egstrom's sons, knew that his aunt Peggy "grieved terribly; all her life she kept a photograph of her mom on her dresser."

As for Marvin, his wife's death "really tore his guts out," said Glen Egstrom. Marvin's drinking increased, and his fatherly attention shrank. With no mother to look after them, some of the children were scattered around. Grown-up Della married and moved to another part of Jamestown; neighboring families took in Clair, Marion, and Norma. The younger Egstroms still needed their father, and he wanted them back.

Marvin hired a local widow to housekeep and tend to the children. She had midwifing and nursing skills; according to one report she had even helped care for the dying Selma. Minnie Schaumberg Wiese was a full-blooded German, age thirty-one, whose parents had settled in Jamestown. "Min," as she was known, moved into the Egstrom house with her eight-year-old son, Edwin. To the Egstrom brood, Min was unnervingly different from their beloved mother. Tall, hulking, and stern, with waist-long hair braided and tied in a bun, she epitomized cold efficiency. Lee described Min in monstrous terms: "Bulging thyroid eyes. Extremely obese, but light on her feet, fast and violent. Spent time with *True Romance* [a magazine] and boxes of chocolates. Came from rather nice background, but her taste was imitation oriental rugs and mohair sofas. Nostrils flared a lot. Wore percale. Full lips, gold tooth in front."

Her granddaughter, Janice Wiese Duffy, recalled a "warm and loving" side to Min, who could laugh at a joke until tears ran down her face. But Min wasn't there to charm anyone; she had work to do, and Marvin was relieved to let her take over. All the children resented her presence, but Norma had the most violent reaction toward Min—"because of all the evil she seemed to represent."

Some of that darkness surely stemmed from a tragedy too painful to discuss. In 1916, Min and her first husband, farmer Emil Wiese, were living with Edwin, then a toddler. A week before Christmas, the family had gone to visit Min's parents. The Wieses returned home later that day. While Min busied herself in the house, Emil did farming tasks outside. He needed gas, and about a gallon remained in a sealed barrel. The bitter cold had frozen the nozzle. Using a piece of wire and a rag soaked in oil, Emil designed a makeshift blowtorch. He lit a match and held the rag to the nozzle to thaw it.

Min heard an explosion so strong that it shook the house. She ran outside to find her husband's body some distance away, crumpled on the ground in flames. The near-empty gasoline barrel had exploded like a bomb; according to a detailed report in the *Jamestown Daily Alert*, it had blown off the top of Emil's skull and shot it clear over the house. In shock, Min grabbed the baby and ran to the nearest farm, which was about a mile away. No one was home. Bolting farther, she found a schoolhouse with a church service in progress. She screamed for help. A doctor was called, and he rushed to the house with Min; but her husband, of course, had died instantly. He was thirty-three.

Emil had known all about the dangers of farm equipment. The violence of his exit suggested a Dakota prototype: an unhappy man in an environment he longed to escape. But no one, except perhaps Min, would ever know his motives.

Too little of her husband remained to display in a casket. Min's parents took in her and Edwin. For eight years she struggled to survive, working whatever domestic jobs she could find. But on the afternoon of December 27, 1924, Min was ensconced at the Egstrom home, serving as midwife for Della and her husband Paul Rudrud's first baby. By midnight most, if not all, of the Egstrom family was asleep. The temperature outside dipped to thirty below zero.

Marvin had lingered at the depot. He returned home around one in the morning to find smoke seeping out of seams in the walls. A fire had erupted in the chimney. Marvin quickly notified the fire department—how wasn't clear, for the house had no phone. Milford ran from room to room to rouse his siblings. Two firemen carried Della and her newborn son into the bitter cold and dropped them off with neighbors. Others doused the house or hauled out furniture. By the next morning, the Egstrom house was a charred and sodden mess. Min's parents and her former in-laws divided up the children and sheltered them while Marvin and Min looked for a new house. Peggy Lee talked about that fire for the rest of her life; for her it was one more symbol of displacement, of warmth and safety removed.

———

THE EGSTROM SIBLINGS WERE aghast when, just a year after their saintly mother's death, their father told them of his plans to marry Min. No one in town could fathom why this still-handsome and charming man would want to replace Selma with a battle-ax like Min. Nevertheless, the wedding took place on August 15, 1925, at Min's parents' home.

It was a practical choice for Marvin and for Min, too, who had struggled as a single mother for years. Their failure to produce any children suggested a sexless marriage. "I never saw him touch her or her touch him in a loving fashion," said Artis Conitz. But Min grew to care about

Marvin very much, and was unfailingly devoted to him. All the while she faced the constant challenge of being compared to Selma, whom her husband had adored, and whose shoes she would never manage to fill.

Min couldn't possibly feel secure, so she retained her tough shell. After the marriage, the Egstroms moved into a house at 215 Milwaukee Street East, three blocks from the Midland Continental depot. Min, said Janice Wiese Duffy, "absolutely took care of business. Early to bed and up at the crack of dawn." In the autumn of 1926, Norma entered Roosevelt School, a block away from home. But her day didn't begin there. Min expected the children to rise by at least six and perform household chores. "It was just normal that you worked from the time you were little," said Jeannette Loy, Norma's future high-school classmate. In years to come, Peggy Lee recalled baking bread, milking cows, churning butter, and—to her revulsion—butchering animals, a technique taught by Min. All these tasks, she said, were enacted behind the house on the family farm, where Lee remembered spending untold hours in indentured servitude.

Those memories clashed with the ones that Marion Egstrom passed on to her son Lee Ringuette, Lynn's brother. "There was really no family farm as such," said Lee. "Given that era, it could be that you had your own animals and a garden, but I don't know this." Artis Conitz doubted that the Egstroms had *ever* had a farm. "Norma had quite an imagination," she said with a laugh.

No one would inflame it like Min, the villain who had torn her storybook home life asunder. "Where were the tender smiles and happy laughter . . . the feeling of fresh linen and the smell of flowers?" lamented Peggy Lee in the 1980s. She envisioned her mother "baking delicious cakes and cookies, singing and laughing, playing games with us, playing her prize possession, a Circassian walnut piano. And then she was gone, and there was this ominous heaviness and anxiety everywhere."

It's unlikely that Lee could have recalled so many details of a mother she lost at four; the portrait was probably a collage of her siblings' recollections and her illusory Paradise Lost. For now she kept her hatred of Min hidden, but in the years to come it would flare up with mounting intensity if the wrong buttons were pushed. Dona Harsh, Lee's secretary and traveling companion in the late 1940s and fifties, recalled entering the singer's bedroom once on a late morning to wake her up. "I said, just kidding, 'Are you gonna sleep all day?' She practically clawed me. She said, *'That's what Min used to say to me, and don't you dare ever say that again!'*" Lee's secretary of the 1970s, Betty Jungheim, told of a Christmas season when someone sent Lee a beautiful arrangement of yellow poinsettias, a flower Min had loved. "Peggy nearly went bonkers. *'They remind me of Min! Just get them out of my house!'*"

Lee didn't speak much of Min publicly until after her death in 1971. But from then on she attacked her stepmother with a vengeance, charging her with the beastliest of brutalities. Lee's most damning recollections of Min begin, chronologically, right after the marriage. Washing dishes was one of Norma's duties; she was so little she had to stand on a box to reach the sink. "If the water was not hot enough," asserted Lee, "she would pour boiling water over my hands." At the house, she said, she was held captive at the washboard, "scrubbing the shirt collars and cuffs with Fels Naptha Soap"—a lye-based laundry cleaner—"until my knuckles were bleeding."

Min, she said, had once whipped her so hard on her back that she drew blood—just because the child had slipped in a puddle. Atrocities mounted: Min bashed Norma on the head with a frying pan, hit her in the face with a metal-ended razor strap, grabbed her hair and dragged her around by it. The stories took a high place in Lee's personal mythology, and her stepmother became known to the singer's fans as the all-oppressive pinnacle of evil in her life.

What was the truth? Betty Jungheim recalled working late into the night at Lee's home with Marion (now known as Marianne), her sister's occasional girl Friday. The two women spoke of Lee's obsession with Min. "Peggy went on and on about how horrible Min was," said Jungheim. "Marianne said, 'You know what's funny? I was there and I don't remember any of this!'" Dona Harsh, who was close to both Marianne and Della, couldn't remember either sister saying a bad word about Min. "But Peggy exaggerated everything," said Dona.

Certainly Min was no stranger to corporal punishment, then the norm in childrearing. According to Janice Wiese Duffy, Min had been raised with it, and practiced it toward her own son. Lynn Ringuette recalled hearing about Min punishing his mother Marianne for some indiscretion by whacking her on the back with the dull edge of a knife.

It took Artis Conitz to give the most authoritative word on the matter.

Norma was eight when she met Artis, and they were inseparable for the next six years—the prime time of the alleged violence. "Min *never* abused Norma physically," she insisted. "I think if Min had beat Norma like she implied, her father would have killed her. He loved that girl to death." The children used to skinny-dip together in a creek that ran through the Conitzs' pasture. "I saw a lot of her body," explained Artis. "I never saw her with a black and blue mark or a scar or a scratch or a Band-Aid." Still, she said, "Min did everything she could to make Norma's life miserable. For some reason she hated Norma with a passion. It was obvious to everybody." One of Min's key weapons was to ignore the child, which had an effect as painful as any beating. "Min made her feel unnecessary," said Artis. "Invisible."

Lee recounted her version of Min's abuse in such searing terms that one wondered if she actually believed it were true. Paul Pines, a jazz-club owner, psychologist, and poet, was fascinated by Peggy Lee, and he had his own theories. "I think that one has to make a distinction between the literal truth and the psychological truth. The story she told was the reality of how she felt about her experiences. One of the things that children often suffer from is not being seen. They feel like they exist in a landscape where they are lost, where nobody knows them. If they translate the emotional beating into literal, physical terms, their experience can be rendered the way they felt it. It's a cry for attention."

But as Lee's assistant in the nineties, Robert Strom, observed: "There are two sides to every story. It's clear that whatever Min did had this lifelong, unforgettable impact on Peggy." The furor of their clash nurtured Lee's fighting spirit. All the while, she clung to her sense of abandonment and rejection and carried it into nearly all her relationships. As a girl, Norma learned about emotional abuse from Min; as Peggy Lee, she often wielded it against her loved ones.

And against her stepmother. Norma detected Min's weak spots, which gave the child the ammunition she wanted. She brought up Selma whenever possible, while stressing the fact that *she* was her father's favorite. The emotional war escalated. Lee told of a time when Min found her in the attic, looking through old family photos in hopes of seeing her mother. Min, she claimed, retaliated by burning all the pictures. The older woman also ridiculed Norma's hands, which were oversize. The child felt terribly self-conscious and kept trying to hide them. Later, as Norma began to show an interest in singing, Min belittled that, too.

The businesslike German couldn't help but resent daydreaming Norma. Instead of working, the child talked to a fictional playmate named Green Cida, and pretended to feed imaginary chickens. She identified with lost souls, such as the hobos that passed through town. Some of them traveled for free by climbing on top of railroad cars. When a wanderer crossed her path, the child would say hello, then invite him home for a meal. Inevitably Min and Marvin found out and put an end to Norma's hospitality. She would have preferred the company of her father, but the more he drank, the more distant he seemed. Maybe because she saw him as another of Min's victims, she forgave him everything. "He was a dear man, but very private," she explained later. "I don't think I ever knew him very well." Still, she recalled him romantically: "He had light-brown hair, which never turned gray; he had beautiful gray eyes and a beautiful smile." His touch, she said, was magic. "If I had a toothache he'd put his hand on my face and the ache would go away." He sometimes stayed downstairs at the depot until past midnight, drunk and singing songs to the train tracks. When he finally came home, Marvin found Norma sound asleep at the dining room table, where she had waited up for him.

Through it all, Norma was an excellent student. In school, she said, "I could get away from Min, so I studied hard and got good marks." When class let out, she went to the Jamestown depot, where her father gave her small tasks. She preferred to playact the role of mistress of the depot. She waited excitedly for the train to pull in, and when her father let her run aboard, she pretended that the passenger coach was a restaurant car and she was in charge. Norma ran down the aisle, waited on imaginary people, then yelled the orders at a nonexistent chef.

Her search for her mother continued. She recalled standing under a tree and talking to God, asking him where Selma was. No answer came, but the one-sided conversations eased her longing. Later, when she heard about a Bible school in nearby Nortonville, Marvin let her ride the train a number of times to attend. Maybe she would find her mother there, she thought. She recalled sitting on the floor and piecing together what she later called the first lyric she ever wrote; it began, "Mama's gone to dreamland on a train."

Music may have struck her as a way to bond with Selma, who had loved to play the piano. Talent began to appear in Norma around the age of six. Her first-grade class had a percussion band, and a teacher held a rhythm class. In a 1993 interview with the record producers Ken Bloom and Bill Rudman, Peggy Lee remembered twenty children clapping in an effort to keep time. "There were only two of us that could do it. I thought, how strange that is. I wonder why they don't know how much to measure between their hands so it'll come out even. Obviously that's something that comes with the genes."

With onstage microphones rare at that time, singers often performed with their mouths pressed to megaphones and bellowed with all their might. Recordings were made "acoustically" then; artists poured hefty volume into a big horn, which channeled the sound through a needle and cut sound waves into a spinning wax disc. Seventy-eight-rpm records were pricey, as were machines to play them on. But the Egstroms had somehow found the means to acquire a luxury item, an Edison Victrola with a huge metal horn for a speaker. What blared out sounded tinny and hissy, but the invention seemed miraculous. The record that Peggy Lee remembered best was "When the Red, Red Robin Comes Bob, Bob, Bobbin' Along," a chirpy number-one hit from 1926. The song promised brighter days, and little Norma could sing all the words.

It was a huge hit for superstar Al Jolson, a Russian Jew whose nasal bray could almost shatter glass. But Norma preferred the happy robin's tale in a competing hit version by "Whispering" Jack Smith, a star vaude-villian. Smith had an unusual style for the time; he spoke-sang breathily, as though whispering secrets. Smith hit his peak in the mid-1920s, near the dawn of "electrical" recording, which employed a microphone. That revolutionary breakthrough enabled singers to tone it down. The mike could pick up gentler vocal contours and nuances, paving the way for an age of subtler, more refined popular singing. Smith's style was an accident; as a World War I soldier he had inhaled poison gas, which destroyed his old lung power. His amiable plea to "Wake up, wake up, you sleepyhead/ Get up, get up, get out of bed" sounded much sweeter to Norma Egstrom than Min's impatient bark. Having come from a stoic Scandinavian tradition, where lids were kept on emotions of all kinds, Norma connected instantly with soft voices that expressed strong feelings.

Her talent continued to reveal itself in small ways. Jamestown was full of accents, German and Russian as well as Scandinavian. She could mimic them with ease. But the sound that captivated her most was the blowing of the train whistle. In 1942, she told the *New York Post* about how "the sad whistle of the engines at a crossing" was the first music she had ever heard.

Trains inspired a lot of songs, few of them happy. Their *waaAAAHHH, waaAAAHHHs* carried for miles throughout the empty prairie. That sound signaled the loneliness of the itinerant life, with pained good-byes at stations; it could echo like a wail in the night or a scream for help. "A freight train whistle taught me how to cry," went "Freight Train Blues," which Bob Dylan recorded on his first album.

There were all sorts of whistles. Those on steam locomotives were sounded by a pull cord, which the train operator could manipulate to vary the pitch and duration, as though he were singing. He could create a bluesy slur, the kind heard in the singing of Bessie Smith and other blues pioneers. Some trains had several whistles, and clever operators could play chords or make choral sounds.

Norma absorbed the vibratoless tone of the train whistle; once she became Peggy Lee, she used it in her singing. "When she wanted me to play bluesy she'd say, 'trains,'" said Steve Blum, her guitarist in the late sixties.

But Norma's attraction to the dark side went far deeper than that. Ever since her mother's mysterious demise, she was obsessed with what lay beyond. According to one grisly recollection, she and her Jamestown pal Everold "Ebbie" Jordan were out picking beans on a summer day. Wandering through a field, the two children spotted a snazzy Model A Ford parked off the road amid tall grass. They recognized it as the car of Fred Bitz, a man from the neighborhood. Moving closer, they peeked inside. There sat Fred at the wheel, maggots crawling all over him, his head slumped over amid a cloud of flies. Apparently he had sealed himself inside and left the engine running until the exhaust fumes suffocated him.

Death seemed to be everywhere. She and Ebbie went to the wake of an acquaintance who had accidentally shot himself in the face. The two children stared down into the man's open casket. "You could see all the black marks," she recalled. Ebbie himself was still a child when he met a fate almost as grisly: the horse he was riding stepped into a gopher hole and fell, crushing him to death. When her dog, Rex, was mauled by a neighbor's pack of hounds, Norma carried the dying animal up to her bedroom, then buried him beneath the railway bridge. She added spookier details in a story she jotted down for William Luce, the playwright enlisted to write the script for her 1983 Broadway show *Peg*. Wrote Lee of Jamestown: "Hank Schmidt—town drunk—wife killed herself. Came to get me and showed me how it happened—5:00 AM. Town thought he killed her." So much early exposure to dying made her feel she had a direct rapport with the afterlife.

But other brutal realities faced the Egstroms. In 1928, the general manager of the Midland Continental uncovered an embezzlement scheme among a few employees; Marvin was counted among the guilty.

It was a grievous charge, but Marvin's employer chose not to let him go. Instead, he transferred Marvin about twenty-six miles south to the depot in Nortonville, the least important stop on the Midland. A town of one hundred inhabitants, Nortonville was so minor that a mention of it could bring a smirk to anyone living in Jamestown or Bismarck. It was just a few blocks long—so small that the streets had no names, and the fifteen or so houses lacked numbers. There were dirt roads, three tall grain elevators, a lumberyard, a schoolhouse, a hotel where almost no one stayed, and—significant in that tiny but arduous town—two churches and two bars. Marvin became a regular in both saloons—no surprise, for apart from the blow to his ego, the demotion had brought a drop in salary from $175 to $100 a month.

The Egstroms would live upstairs from the depot, which was decorated in drab Midland style, orange-yellow with green trim. The apartment had no phone, indoor plumbing, or electricity; kerosene lamps and candles provided light. Min worked as a train dispatcher at the same depot. Marion and Milford had left home, but Clair, Norma, and Edwin remained; Min enrolled them in the little Nortonville School.

Norma got attention. "I envied her," said Pearl Hickey, a local farmer's daughter. "I always thought she was so pretty. I was a shy little gal from the country. Coming from Jamestown, she was a city gal." Another classmate, Mattie Foy, recalled Norma as "just a new girl that we all came to like. She took part in everything that was held in our little Nortonville Town Hall. They used to have roller-skating and dances and movies and community plays. Her father was always in them, because he was quite an actor."

It was in Nortonville that Norma met her best friend, Artis Conitz, one of eight children born to a farmer and his wife. The Conitz home became her refuge, and she stayed overnight with the family whenever possible. Norma saw Artis's mother as a beacon of kindness, her house as a peaceful place without anger. Mrs. Conitz ended up making most of Norma's clothes, a task Min had no time to do. The children amused themselves by hiking in pastures, bending down to pluck wildflowers, and cutting out paper dolls and pictures from catalogs.

On October 29, 1929, the stock market crashed, plunging America into the Great Depression. But survival in North Dakota had already been pared down to bare-bones essentials; cows still produced milk, chickens kept laying eggs, the land yielded its harvest, the train rolled on no matter what. As the Jamestown professor Katherine Stevenson observed in 2010: "When you're already dirt-poor, how do you know what the Depression is?"

Having been branded a crook in Jamestown, Marvin now held the mantle of Nortonville town treasurer. His First Lady was seen as an upstanding community leader who could "be as sweet as apple pie," according to Artis. Min hosted meetings for the local ladies' club; the *Edgeley Mail* was rife with reports of her "delicious lunches" and of a stream of visiting houseguests given shelter by the Egstroms. But in the mornings there was work to do; all had to pitch in. And every day, Norma and Min crossed swords over it. When Min roused her brusquely at dawn to do her chores, the child seethed. "Min was strict, and very critical," said Artis. "Norma would have to wash the kitchen floor. Min would make her do it again. She would keep Norma at home working in the morning, trying to make her late for school, so she'd get in trouble." The principal found out and took sympathy on her. From upstairs in the schoolhouse, he could see the Egstrom home. He waited until she came out the door before he started ringing the bell.

Norma never showed she was upset. "I think she was very, very strong-willed, and probably pugnacious and argumentative," reflected William Luce. The girl began to purposely come home late from school, breaking a cardinal rule of Min's. "She knew she wouldn't get spanked because her dad wouldn't allow it," said Artis. "All Min could do was make her wash more dishes or whatever, work harder, longer." Pearl Hickey saw

Norma's revenge: "She and Clair would tease Min and pick at her. Then Min would get mad and hit 'em."

On Sunday morning, January 5, 1930, Norma watched in glee as fate dealt Min a nasty blow. The young girl and her father had gone to church. In the middle of the service, someone made a chilling announcement: the train depot was on fire. Mattie got in the car with the Egstroms; everyone else rushed over on foot.

Approaching the depot, they saw smoke billowing out of the upstairs windows. A crowd had gathered. Moving closer, Norma, Marvin, and Mattie spotted Min on the ground, sprawled out and moaning in pain. Only minutes before, Min had lit the gas range to start dinner. Then she went downstairs into the barn. She heard an explosion—a sound she knew too well. Min grabbed a bucket and ran to the cistern pump. "She was gonna get some water and take it back up there, thinking she could do something for the fire, but she couldn't, of course," said Mattie. "It was winter, and there was a lot of ice." Min slipped, and her weight took her down so hard she broke her leg.

By the time a fire crew came, the depot was almost completely razed. Min was brought to the doctor in nearby Edgeley, whose newspaper wrote sympathetically of her plight: "Her many friends hope to hear that she will soon be back with them again." A kindly local family took the Egstroms in until they found a home on the east end of town; the Midland hauled a small freight house to serve as temporary depot.

Min's accident gave Norma wicked satisfaction long after she had turned into Peggy Lee; in 1983 the singer included it in "One Beating a Day," a comedy song about her stepmother's evilness. For now, though, Norma was uprooted yet again, and the atmosphere inside their new home was almost as cold as the weather. She and Artis kept their distance from Edwin—the child whom Min naturally favored—and he from them. More than ever, Marvin found his solace in the bottle. Prohibition was on, and he brewed bootleg beer in the basement; after work he stopped at one of the local bars to keep imbibing. Spirits brightened, he would shuffle home, and the entertainment began. "He could tap-dance like nobody you ever saw in your life," said Artis. "He only did it when he'd had too much to drink." Marvin loved to sing an Irish jig about McGinty, whose wife Mary Ann took him out for a grand night of burlesque. Marvin belted out the song's big finish: "He said, 'Mary dear / Why did you bring me here? / I can never love you, you know / The way I used to . . ."

Sadness in music touched Norma deeply, and it baffled Marvin to see tears falling from her eyes. "That's a funny song, honey!"

"No, it isn't," she said, sobbing. "He doesn't love her anymore."

Norma escaped whenever she could. In the summer she and her siblings did local jobs to help support the family. One year, barefoot and clad in overalls, she went to work for a poor mother with a single infant, handling farm duties for two dollars a week. Joined by Artis, Norma traveled to a farm outside Jamestown to visit their friend Ruby Savage. Ruby suffered from a severely infected knee that had left her bedridden, but Norma diligently coaxed her onto her feet and even got her up onto a horse. To Ruby's sister, Rose, Norma worked magic; she "*made* her walk."

As far as Artis could tell, music was just a hobby to Norma. The girls sang together in church, or while walking along dirt roads. "She didn't sing any better than I did," claimed Artis. "And I wasn't talented." But other friends saw a budding songbird in their midst. "She used to sing a lot," said Pearl Hickey. "When we'd have a high-school play and they needed a singer in it, they'd let her sing with us even though she was a grade behind. We didn't mind, because she had a pretty voice." In her bedroom, she sketched out song lyrics, but didn't dare show them to anyone. Norma yearned to take piano lessons, but the rigidly practical Min dismissed that as nonsense. Still, the teacher let Norma occasionally sit in on other students' lessons. Just by listening and watching, then by practicing at whatever piano was available, she learned to play in a rudimentary way.

For most of her friends, and certainly for the grown-ups in town, little existed outside their daily small-town grind. But Norma was getting a sense of the world outside. Movies entranced her, as they did all of America. The Nortonville Town Hall had occasional screenings, but the closest theater was in Edgeley, and on the rare occasions when Norma managed to go, she was dazzled. To small-town girls like her and her friends, films showed them women who looked and acted nothing like the ladies of North Dakota. Even back in Jamestown, show business had excited her. A top celluloid sweetheart gave Norma her first Hollywood thrill. "This man came to Jamestown with Janet Gaynor's bra. He had worked in some Hollywood studio. He put it in a window on Main Street, and we all filed by to look at it. I was so impressed. I wanted desperately to be a part of show business."

Norma took special notice of Clara Bow, the silent-screen superstar known as the "It Girl." Born in poverty to an abusive and mentally unstable mother in Brooklyn, Bow had bucked the odds to become Hollywood's number-one box-office draw. A defiantly liberated flapper with a mop of short curly hair and a saucy glance, she exemplified the scandalously freewheeling sexuality of the Roaring Twenties. "They yell at me to be dignified," said Bow. "But what are the dignified people like? They are snobs, frightful snobs." Having the nerve to be herself, she said, made her a "big freak" in their eyes.

Bow was everything that Norma longed to be. With her broad shoulders, thin eyes and lips, and extremely pale skin, the child hardly looked like a budding glamour queen. But she had started to learn how women could get attention. Starting around age twelve, said Artis, "there wasn't a shy bone in her body. She *made* you recognize her. Whenever we went anywhere, she loved to be the one whom everybody looked at. She loved to tell stories and to exaggerate, and she told them so convincingly that people believed her. I wonder if she didn't believe them herself half the time."

In 1932, Norma began traveling every Saturday to Jamestown to begin the two-year process of classes that prepared children for confirmation. She and twenty-five other pubescent youths sat in St. John's Lutheran Church and listened to Reverend W. W. A. Keller expound solemnly upon the Bible and Christian behavioral ideals. Russell Krueger, a farm boy from nearby Eldredge, never forgot Norma Egstrom: "She was a big gal for her age, and she was loud. Quite a talker. Before class started, you knew she was around." The other girls wore plain floral dresses and flat, austere hairstyles; Norma teased hers out into a modest facsimile of Clara Bow's. As Reverend Keller spoke, Norma sat in her pew sketching movielike femmes fatales. Her flappers had furs, blond Marcel waves, bright lipstick, and brassy names—Trixie, Babe, Bumps. Meanwhile, popular song continued to seduce her. When Keller was out of earshot, another girl stood watch while Norma committed the sinful act of playing current tunes on the church organ. Dreams of fame began to fill her

Confirmation day at St. John's Lutheran Church in Jamestown, 1934. Norma Egstrom sits third from right in the front row; others include the Reverend W. W. A. Keller (*front row, center*), Elga Woodell (*front row, far right*), and Russell Krueger (*middle row, third from left*). (COURTESY OF KATE STEVENSON)

head. "I remember standing at the cistern pump," she said, "and looking out across the wastes of North Dakota . . . and thinking, *One day I'll get out of here. And I'll come back in a big car with presents for everybody. I'll drive down Main Street, passing out gifts. When people thank me I'll say, 'Oh, it's nothin', it's nothin'.'*"

A serious illness yanked her down to earth. In September 1932, the twelve-year-old's appendix burst, and peritonitis set in. Her brother Clair drove her to the nearest hospital, above a bank in Edgeley. Norma was carried up a long, steep flight of stairs and laid on a table. A nurse anesthetized her with ether. The surgery was risky, but it worked. On October 13, during the two-week recovery time, a report in the *Edgeley Mail* suggested that Min wasn't as uncaring as Peggy Lee would claim: "Mrs. M. O. Egstrom and son Ed visited at the Edgeley hospital Sunday."

But in years to come, that appendectomy formed the basis of Lee's favorite tale about Min's viciousness. Before she was hospitalized, said Lee, Min had coldly ignored her fever, nausea, and vomiting. After her appendix had burst, she was doubled over in pain, but Min tried to hold her captive at home. "I'm quite sure she hoped I would not pull through," declared Lee in her memoir. Clair, she wrote, had to threaten Min with a shotgun in order to get her to let him drive the child to the hospital.

Her recuperation time spawned another morbid childhood memory: "Each day I would walk to the window and stare at an enormous tumor they had removed from some woman. They had placed it in a pan and put it out on the roof of the annex building. It started out as large as a small watermelon, and the last time I saw it, it was like a small cantaloupe." How she could have recognized a tumor was mysterious, but the horror had just begun. Immediately upon her return home, she said, Min ordered her to scrub the floor. As she crawled on her hands and knees, brush in hand, Min supposedly began kicking her so savagely that her stitches broke. According to one of Lee's accounts, she ran for bandages to close the wound; another version has her rushing to her father for help. Then Min beat *him* up, after which he fell to the floor and broke a rib. The child ran out of the house into a blizzard, as did her father. Min followed them, waving a fireplace poker.

Back home, a traumatized Norma came close to poisoning herself by drinking Lysol. "You may well ask, 'Where was your Daddy?' Well, he was probably out trying to drown his sorrows, and, besides, I tried to hide everything from him. He was troubled enough on his own." Apparently he was also powerless to prevent Min from hiring her and Clair out as day laborers—another of Lee's claims. Their nephew Lee Ringuette doubted it: "Clair never said that, and he would have." Lee's story grew. From dawn to sundown, she worked for a threshing rig, shocking grain, driving the water wagon, and cooking for the crew. Years later, neither Artis nor other friends of Norma's could recall any such thing.

Over time, Lee strung those episodes into a *Cinderella*-like fable. It starred the idealized mother snatched away by the Grim Reaper and the wicked stepmother who forces the daughter into domestic enslavement. The girl tolerates the abuse, afraid to tell her father. Each night she retires in fear to her cold room, crying for her mother.

Rage, pain, and victimization were the themes, all inspired by Min. "I often thought that if there had been no Min, maybe there would have been no Peggy Lee," said Paul Horner, her composing partner of the 1980s. Added Horner, "Peggy never got past being four years old."

PEGGY LEE

Friends, we'd like to have you meet Miss Peggy Lee, the newest addition to our entertaining staff. Peggy hails from Jamestown and has been with the station about four months. Of course, you know Peg is single. Guess she hasn't any hobbies, all we know is that she's rather sing than eat. On her broadcosts she is heard along with the Four Jacks. She sang with orchestras before joining the staff of entertainers.

Chapter Two

AFTER SIX YEARS in the bleakness of Nortonville, Marvin Egstrom got a slight reprieve. In the summer of 1934, the Midland Continental transferred him to the last stop on the line, Wimbledon, population three hundred. The town had abundant trees and a pretty park, but Edith Lockett, daughter of the local druggist, recalled it as "just plain." The Egstroms set up house on the second floor of the depot, a drab wooden box.

At least they had a furnace, plumbing, and electricity, new additions to all depots. And for a few weeks Marvin could revel in his freedom from Min, who had stayed in Nortonville to close up the house. She too seemed to enjoy the single life; the *Edgeley Mail* reported her adventures as the town's social doyenne, along with her shopping trips and vacations in bigger cities, away from Marvin. "Daddy took advantage of that," claimed Peggy Lee in her memoir, leaving the implication clear.

By now all of Norma's siblings had gone; at last she had her father to herself. But his drinking continued, and with Prohibition now repealed, Marvin could drink at the neighborhood bar until past midnight. In bed, Norma would hear him dragging himself up the creaky wooden stairs, almost too drunk to walk.

She busied herself with high school, which she began on September 10. Fellow student Ginny Lulay spied Norma for the first time as she walked near the two-story, red-brick schoolhouse. She wore a drab skirt and a sweater that accentuated her broad shoulders. To Connie Emerson, who met her later in Valley City, she looked nothing like the glamorous songstress to come: "She wasn't a real blonde; she was kind of a dishwater blonde. And she was stocky." Still, recalled Ginny, "there was something exciting about her. Us girls stood there gawking. We thought, 'Who's the new girl?'"

Under their scrutiny in an unfamiliar town, she lost the bravado she had developed in Nortonville. After that first sighting, Edith and a couple of her friends passed Norma on their way to choir practice. They asked if she wanted to come. "Oh, I can't sing," she told Edith despondently.

During Norma's second week of school, Marvin, who was sixty, took ill. Back he went to Nortonville and Min's care. In years to come, local legend—fueled by Lee's claims—held that the young girl valiantly ran the depot in his absence. But the story seems like one more figment of her imagination. The *Wimbledon News* reported that E. E. Kelleran, Marvin's predecessor, was "back on the job at the depot at this time"; what's more, if it had so incensed Norma to have to rise at six to do mundane household chores, it seems unlikely that she would have awakened even earlier to work harder at a train station.

Worried as she was about her father, she thrived without him. Her schoolmates had nicknamed her Eggy, and now, feeling less self-conscious, she made her first attempt at public singing. At a PTA meeting that October, she and three other schoolgirls "sang two numbers which were enjoyed very much by everyone present," wrote the *Wimbledon News*. The "something exciting" about her was starting to flower. "She could write stories, she could write poetry; she was very talented," said Edith Lockett. As a child in Jamestown, she had seemed as straitlaced as any of her elders; school principal Ella Fetcher had proudly jotted down little Norma's statement that people who "say bad words" would wind up "where they have to shovel ashes." Now she was an adolescent of fourteen, and the *Wimbledon News* printed her saucy exchange with a pal:

JEANNE: I know that fellow awfully well, in fact we've broken bread together.
NORMA: Well, I know him even better than that. We've broken davenports together.

Forbidden things attracted her, be they the sexual charms of boys or, increasingly, the Negro race. There in Wimbledon, as in all of North Dakota, a black person was a rare sight. Virtually the only ones in view were porters, dressed in livery and treated like servants. The show-business custom of blackface thrived in North Dakota. A few years earlier, Marvin had joined the all-white Nortonville Dramatic Club. In a play called *Two Days to Marry*, he played Simon P. Chase—"as black as his race," quipped the wag who wrote the program notes. (Another character, Emily Jane Pink, was listed as "blacker than ink.") Added the *Edgeley Mail*'s reviewer: "A little darkey boy and girl furnished music between acts." Norma joined in on the fun. Pearl Hickey, her Nortonville classmate, recalled a "musical contest" in Edgeley, where father and daughter "dressed as minstrels and blackened their faces, and they sang Negro spirituals."

Norma meant no disrespect. To her, blacks were special; perhaps she identified with them as fellow maligned outcasts.

Soon they would alter her world dramatically, via an innovation that was opening up American households to worlds unimagined. Marvin, who had returned to Wimbledon on New Year's Day 1935, celebrated by buying a luxury item: a handsome floor-model radio produced by Atwater Kent, the most popular brand in America. He had splurged on a top-of-the-line model, priced at $165—a handsome piece of polished-wood furniture with lacy woodworking and five knobs.

Careful twisting of the one on the top right made clouds of static part, revealing crystal-clear voices. They gave national and local news in comforting tones; they sang Verdi and Puccini at the Metropolitan Opera in New York. By day, radio kept housewives company with soap operas like *Ma Perkins* and *The Romance of Helen Trent*. At night, it made families laugh with the antics of Fibber McGee and Molly, a cornpone couple surviving creatively amid the Depression; or chilled the blood with *The Witch's Tale*, hosted by the cackling "Old Nancy, witch of Salem, and Satan, her wise black cat."

Parents and children sat in semicircles around the magical talking box. Radio was the theater of the mind, and it conjured scenes more vivid than anything Hollywood could dream up. In his book *Raised on Radio*, Gerald Nachman recalled the impact the medium had on him in the forties: "Radio made me want to see the places I kept hearing about each night, sparking a wanderlust the way a passing train and paddle-wheeler might have for a boy a century before."

More and more families were finding the money to acquire these costly devices, the popularity of which signaled the start of financial recovery in America. In 1935, President Franklin D. Roosevelt launched the W.P.A. (Works Project Administration), the latest phase of his New Deal program to combat the Depression. It provided construction jobs for millions of the unemployed. To buy a radio after years of monetary fear was to see a way out of the dark.

For Norma Egstrom, radio had one overwhelming asset. It was the key accelerant of the swing era, which was unfolding just as her father bought that Atwater Kent. Clarinetist Benny Goodman, the bookish son of Russian-Jewish immigrants, had burst on the scene with his big band, which made swing a household word. Played by groups of twelve to eighteen men, it had a kinetic, syncopated swagger that made toes tap and shoulders sway.

To Depression-weary Americans, swing was the rallying cry to get the lead out of their shoes and start dancing. The *New York Times* called it "more than a form of music-making; it is a social phenomenon." Swing brought the white mainstream face-to-face with black musical culture, primarily the blues, which was its foundation. And it brought Norma Egstrom an epiphany. Dialing the tuner late at night, she happened upon WX9BY, an experimental station. She heard a broadcast from the Reno Club, a hangout for black jazz fans in Kansas City. Until now, Norma had only heard music made by whites—solemn hymns sung in her Lutheran church or her mother's prim piano playing. Nothing in her young life had prepared her for the hot sounds of the Reno Club's resident nine-piece, all-black swing band, led by Bill (soon to be known as Count) Basie, a young pianist from Red Bank, New Jersey.

He and his bandmates had swing in their souls. Someone would play a riff (a short repeated phrase), and the others would follow. In this freewheeling fashion, the Basie band created its theme, "One O'Clock Jump." Within that rollicking twelve-bar blues was a low-down, midnight feel. "We kept late hours," said Basie. "The hours when the spooks came out."

His music worked on Norma like a drug. The rhythm conjured up her exhilaration when a train sped by; the bluesy wail evoked the train whistles she'd heard all her life. Basie's piano defined the minimalism for which Peggy Lee would become famous. His gently touched, perfectly placed notes were all the band needed to set it swinging. Tenor saxophonist Lester Young's silky playing was light, lyrical, and full of feeling, qualities that Lee's singing would share. Later to join that orchestra was the first swing guitarist she had ever heard, Freddie Green, whose quarter-note, strumming technique swung hard. Green triggered her lifelong infatuation with the guitar and the men who played it.

Basie's men had lived the hard-knock life, and it came through in their playing—a connection to hurt and struggle that would later be termed "soul." But their prevailing spirit was joy—even if the band worked in a joint that, in sax man Buster Smith's words, was "nothin' but a hole in the wall." Call girls lingered in the stairwell, pimps and thugs at the bar; cigarette smoke permeated a room that felt "hot as hell," according to trumpeter Buck Clayton. Black patrons were confined to the balcony and a small space behind the bandstand.

The Reno Club altered jazz history nonetheless. One of its broadcasts reached John Hammond, a wealthy white producer who would play a crucial part in launching many of the music's greats, including Billie Holiday. Hammond heard the Basie band on his car radio as he passed through Chicago. He took Basie under his wing and set him on the road to stardom.

Norma liked the gruff, nasal blues shouting of Basie vocalist Jimmy Rushing, but she didn't try to imitate it. She related much better to a white singer who was bridging the gap between white and black music, while conquering Hollywood and selling millions of records. In 1935, Norma saw *Mississippi*, a movie musical set down South. It starred Bing Crosby, a superstar crooner whose voice caressed the ears of the scuffling masses. A discovery of the so-called King of Jazz, bandleader Paul Whiteman, Crosby was revolutionizing popular singing by turning it from declaiming into confiding.

His art lay in his ease. Crosby's rise coincided with the emergence of the microphone; before him, a singer's key aim was to be heard. In vaudeville or on Broadway, performers had to belt loudly enough to reach the last row of the balcony. This left little room for nuance; bluster was the trademark of most popular singers then, including two giants, Al Jolson and Sophie Tucker. Pop singing still bore the trappings of operetta and European art song, which employed formal diction, strict adherence to the written note, a "produced" sound, and artily rolled *r*'s.

Now, with the microphone, singers didn't have to shout; they had a tool capable of hearing and amplifying a sigh. A world of interpretive possibilities opened up for vocalists, many of whom were touched by black music, which was invading almost every corner of show business. The star black singers of Crosby's youth, notably Louis Armstrong, Ethel Waters, and the "Empress of the Blues," Bessie Smith, freed pop of its musty formality and brought it to sassy, syncopated life. Waters and Smith pounced on sexual innuendos with glee; trumpeter Armstrong colored his singing with the same growls, slurs, and freewheeling swing phrasing that poured out of his horn.

Their white vocal peers—Mildred Bailey, Connee Boswell, Lee Wiley, and most of all Crosby—learned much from them, just as they did from the white jazz innovators of the day, including honey-toned cornetist Bix Beiderbecke and the "Father of Jazz Trombone," Texas-born Jack Teagarden, who played with a bluesy swagger. Crosby distilled all these influences into a style that had a laid-back flavor of jazz. His buoyant rhythm made his singing sound off-the-cuff and light as air. He sang words as though he were speaking them. "When I'm asked to describe what I do, I say, 'I'm not a singer; I'm a phraser,'" he explained. "That means that I don't think of a song in terms of notes; I try to think of what it purports to say lyrically. That way it sounds more natural, and anything natural is more listenable."

Even in his thirties, Crosby had a paternal air; and Norma, who clung to father figures, was hooked. "I literally saved pennies to go to see his movies," she explained. "Tears rolled down my cheeks if the leading lady didn't treat him right." A hymn to lost love that he sang in *Mississippi*, "Down by the River," haunted her: "Once we walked alone, down by the river/All the world our own . . ." His intimate delivery profoundly inspired her sense of how a song should be sung.

Until then, singing for Norma had been an amusement. Now it became her reason for being. The fifteen-year-old saw it as her ticket out of North Dakota, and perhaps as a way to show Min—who had long since moved into the Wimbledon depot—that she *wasn't* invisible. "She just went hog wild to make a name for herself," said Artis Conitz. "She would have done anything to become famous."

Thus began the fierce drive that would spur her for the rest of her life. Norma was obsessed with swing; she heard it in the rhythmic chugging of trains as they pulled out of the station and in the gentle trot of the horse that carried a young suitor to her home. She couldn't get enough of the jazz of the day. Norma and a high-school classmate, Lillian Wehler, would "lie on the floor by the radio and listen to music," said Wehler. "She was singing then. She was very good. And very ambitious."

Even when she wasn't singing, she craved attention. In September of 1935, at the start of her junior year, Norma was voted class president. She began writing lofty editorials for the school paper; in one of them, she piped out a rallying call to her own generation, heralding the news that "someday the torch of democracy will be ours to bear." But Norma had her eye on the stage. Two months later, in Valley City, the Kiwanis Club held its seventh annual one-act play contest. Wimbledon Public School entered with *At the Stroke of Twelve*, a "mystery comedy" about a young couple haunted by a ghost. Norma wasted no time in auditioning. The *Wimbledon News* soon reported that the key role of "Liza, colored girl servant" had gone to her. Her part would require her to don blackface, but that, of course, didn't bother Norma.

At the Stroke of Twelve lost the competition. Undeterred, Norma joined a school committee that mounted further shows. That December she starred in *The Little Clodhopper*, a comedy about a poor girl who meets a tycoon from the big city and winds up an heiress.

It broke Norma's heart to stare out at a nearly vacant auditorium, the result of a nasty storm. But the *Wimbledon News* gave Norma her first rave review. Lauding her as "our comical and talented Norma 'Eggy' Egstrom," the paper reported that she had "very splendidly" played her part. In between acts, the six-girl Wimbledon High School Glee Club, featuring Norma, offered a musical interlude. Norma soloed on "Come, Sweet Morning," a turn-of-the-century French ballad. The song itself didn't matter; singing, to Norma, "was the only time I ever felt important. . . . I could get thoughts out of my system that I didn't dare express."

In the spring of 1936 she mostly felt sad, for her beloved father had moved away. The Midland Continental's assistant president, who worked in Jamestown, had taken ill, then died; Marvin was sent there to fill in. Min took over as Wimbledon depot agent. Except for brief visits, Marvin never returned; semi-estrangement from Min suited him fine.

To Norma, he had always seemed an elusive father, emotionally unavailable and frequently too drunk to give her the attention she needed. Now he had left her alone with Min—one more painful desertion. But her ambition saw her through. Norma became editor-in-chief of the class newspaper, while speeding ahead on her quest for stardom. She was excited to learn of a statewide talent contest that took place every May in Grand Forks. Over a thousand students vied for honors in everything from sports to homemaking to music. Norma competed in the "low voice solo" category and lost. Quickly she set her sights on another competition, the May Festival, which happened annually in Fargo. This one focused on domestic skills, a subject that didn't remotely interest her. But according to contestant Jeannette Loy, Norma plotted a trip to Fargo anyhow.

Once there, she went to a local dress shop and had herself fitted for a big, showy gown, the kind a singer would wear. Back in Wimbledon, Jeannette was asked to address the high-school student body about her experience. During her talk, she got her first sense of Norma's hunger for attention. "She got up and said that I was waving at all the truck drivers. It was a big lie! Everybody laughed. I could have killed her. I guess that's how she got where she did. I didn't like her very much, but I admired her."

September 7, 1936, found Norma back at Wimbledon High for the first day of senior year. After her recent disappointments, she tore into the semester more determined than ever to stand out. That November, Valley City again hosted the Kiwanis Club's one-act play contest. Wimbledon's entry, *The Man Who Came Back*, echoed Norma's life; it told of a damsel pining for her absent father. But Norma didn't play that role; once more she confirmed her affinity with the black race by darkening her face to portray "Mammy Jinnie, Negro servant." The play won first place in the dramatic category, and Norma luxuriated in praise. "I remember the kids in high school telling me, 'Norma, you'll wind up in Hollywood,'" she said later. "In my secret heart, I knew it, too." She started planning ahead. In Home Economics class, her classmates sewed shawls and aprons; Norma made herself a silk bra.

For now, she earned survival funds by waiting tables in Wimbledon. As usual, she had put herself in the right place. A customer informed her that Valley City had launched a radio station, KOVC, that was scouting for talent. Its programs formed a mosaic of North Dakota life: *Livestock Market, Lutheran Seminary Quartet, Valley Radio's Kiddie Revue*. She made up her mind that one of the vacant slots would be hers.

Learning of her plan to audition, Min typically dismissed it as foolish, and forbade her to go. But at sixteen, Norma wasn't so easily intimidated anymore, and the townspeople of Wimbledon were poised to help. A depot agent on the Soo Line arranged for her to hop a drive with the station's resident singing duo, the Fehr Sisters. One Saturday, Norma and the Fehrs trekked twenty-five miles into Valley City, and pulled up near the Rudolf Hotel, which housed KOVC. The tiny street-level station was causing daily excitement; a glass exterior allowed pedestrians to peer into the control room at the people talking on the radio.

Inside the studio, KOVC pianist Belle May Ginsberg greeted a fleshy sixteen-year-old in hayseed clothes. Belle led her to the piano. This was Norma's first professional audition, and whatever moxie she had shown in the past deserted her; she sang in a small, sweet, but quavering voice. Touched by her determination, Belle arranged for the girl to come back and sing for the station director.

To her astonishment, Norma won a Saturday-afternoon slot—3:45 to 4:00 PM. The pay was five dollars a show, plus a meal. Her show debuted on November 27, 1936. Norma sang four tunes, accompanied primly by Belle, and made some shy remarks. The *Wimbledon News* reported: "Miss Egstrom sang over KOVC for the first time and her program was enjoyed very much by her listeners. We are very proud of our home girl."

The next Saturday, a Lutheran minister drove Norma to KOVC. Thereafter, she hitchhiked—"The truck drivers all knew her," said Jeanette Loy—or rode the train. Once there, she stood in front of her microphone and sang proudly to the gaggle of townspeople who had gathered outside the glass partition, waving and smiling.

Back at school, word spread about Norma's success. "All us kids were excited," said Ginny Lulay. "We thought, 'Wow, someone from Wimbledon is singing on the radio!'" In a place where girls' ambitions seldom reached beyond marriage and home, Norma was a rarity. Previously her aspirations had seemed quaint, not like anything that might make her famous. Now, said Edith Lockett, "we thought, gee whiz, she's really gonna do something."

Norma maximized her big break. That New Year's Eve, she served as featured singer at a dance thrown by the Eagles, a high-flown social club. Her performance betrayed her inexperience, starting with her corn-pone appearance. After she had become Peggy Lee, the *Valley City Times-Record* recalled that early appearance: "Some of the girls snickered at her evening dress. Peggy had the voice, alright, but not the clothes to go with it, and her outfit was a honey. . . . It was black, with an artificial flower of some kind hanging on her back."

Even if she couldn't afford to dress like the sirens she saw onscreen, Norma still identified with them. She hoped her charms would melt Lyle "Doc" Haines, KOVC's star bandleader, whose "orchestra" consisted of him and six of his fellow college boys. Each weekend they hauled their instruments in a trailer and played barn dances and social functions to earn tuition money.

"To Doc Haines and his buddies," wrote a reporter, Norma "was just a cute little girl with precocious vocal chords, and they treated her like a baby sister." But Norma had other ideas. Photos of Haines reveal a pleasant-looking young man with spectacles and a shock of wavy hair. But Norma looked at him as though he were Clark Gable or Cary Grant. To her Haines was "dark and handsome"; even his glasses looked sexy to her. As a college man, he had the mature authority she liked, but it was his musicianship that made him irresistible. Haines became her first in a lifetime of crushes on jazzmen; for Norma, they possessed a magical connection to a higher force, the same one she had sensed in her piano-playing mother.

Haines offered her fifty cents a night to sing with his band. She jumped at the chance. The school superintendent at Wimbledon, Ivar Knapp, came to her aid. Norma had maintained a near-perfect attendance record and high marks, and Knapp told her that if she completed all her homework by Friday morning, she could go straight to Valley City to sing with Haines.

Those stints on the road testified to how desperately she longed to sing. Norma and the band sat stuffed in a freezing truck, trailer dragging behind as they plodded through treacherous snowstorms. None of the dance halls and recreation rooms they played had microphones. Norma tried in vain to sing over the band, but her voice was too soft to battle a brass section. Finally she took a cue from Rudy Vallee, a crooning idol of the day, and used a megaphone. Singing such close-dancing ballads as "Moonglow," Norma was supposed to appear starry-eyed and winsome. Instead she trembled visibly. A musician saw how scared she was and offered her a cigarette, explaining that it would calm her down. She never forgot her first drag; as promised, it eased her stage fright. "I was so busy coughing that I guess I forgot to be nervous," she said. With that, the singer began a thirty-five-year smoking habit of such intensity that it nearly killed her.

Jittery and green as she was, Norma performed nicely. Doc tagged her his "little blues singer"—proof of how she could make listeners feel when she sang a sad song.

Winter turned to spring, and she counted the days before each of those weekend trips. Though not quite seventeen, she was already a local celebrity, and Min seemed determined to put her in her place. Ginny Lulay recalled Norma's downtrodden greeting as she arrived at Wimbledon High: "I had to scrub the floor before I got here!"

Whether or not Haines called her, she vowed to spend as much time away from home as possible. Each weekend she hung around KOVC, hoping to score extra airtime by subbing for absentee guests on other programs. Norma caught the eye of Connie Emerson, a seven-year-old Valley City girl who sang "On the Good Ship Lollipop" and other age-appropriate tunes on a kiddie show. Even at that age, Connie saw that Norma was "*extremely* determined." Connie's dad, a jeweler, served on the Junior Chamber of Commerce, and he roamed the state, seeking out cultural events to bring to Valley City. In various dance halls, he and his wife spied Norma. "She would be sitting very close to the bandstand, waiting for the opportunity to sing a song," recalled Connie.

That bullheadedness had taken Norma far, and she set her sights on the next Grand Forks talent contest. For the Valley City preliminaries,

Norma chose a formal art song, "Clouds," introduced by lyric baritone John Charles Thomas, a radio star. The song interested her, maybe because she'd spent so much time looking heavenward for her mother's face: "Clouds that drift in the sun of sky / Resemble life as they wander by . . ."

It was a demanding song for an untrained singer, full of extended notes that required strong breath control. Whereas Thomas sang "Clouds" operatically, Norma thought it needed "a soft sound." Astutely she realized that "it wouldn't make sense to bellow, 'Clouds that drift . . .' You'd break the cloud."

Two finalists from Wimbledon were announced—a trombone player, Ernest Kupka, and Norma Egstrom. The youngsters starred in a benefit concert at the school gym in order to pay for their trip. Frances McConn, Norma's school music teacher, borrowed her father's car to drive them to Grand Forks. Other ladies pitched in with clothes and food.

Norma competed on a Friday. Later the first- and second-place contestants for Girl's Low Voice Solo were announced: Elsie Heiberg of Fargo and Marian Walker of Minot. Norma went home heartbroken, feeling she had let everyone down.

On May 27, 1937, she had one last chance to emerge as the star of Wimbledon High. Graduation day had come, and an assemblage of proud families, dressed in their Sunday best, sat politely inside the school auditorium. Among them were Marvin, Min, Min's son Edwin, and his wife Lorraine. The ceremony was a small affair; the graduating class had only eight girls and three boys. Norma had lost out on special honors; Donald Evans, the school track star, was valedictorian, Edith Lockett salutatorian.

But Norma managed to steal the ceremony. The class motto was "Success Awaits at Labor's Gate," and Norma had penned an epic poem that could have been uttered at the start of war. She intoned it passionately: *There's work to be done and a place to acquire / There's a road to be blazed with ambition's fire . . .* After reciting stanza upon inspirational stanza, she came to the rousing final lines: *Strive hard till your goal's reached, for our motto doth state / That success awaits at labor's gate!*" She won a huge ovation. The poem appeared complete on the front page of the *Wimbledon News*. At a gathering after the ceremony, Marvin and Min presented Norma with a graduation watch.

Now old enough to be on her own, Norma couldn't bear the thought of living in the depot with Min. She had always felt safest near her father, whose health, worn down by drinking and smoking, had grown weak. A month after graduation she returned to Jamestown to be with him. She took a waitressing job in the coffee shop of the three-story Gladstone Hotel, the city's most fashionable downtown dwelling. Norma rented a one-room basement apartment nearby. It had no windows, and the furnishings consisted of a bed and an orange crate. No matter; Min was out of her life.

On June 5, Norma had given her farewell show at KOVC. But she made sure she wasn't off the air for long. She could have waitressed anywhere; but as she had known before she took the job, Jamestown's main radio station, KRMC, operated from an upstairs floor of the Gladstone. Norma rushed to make friends with a secretary there, who helped her get an audition. By July, the teenager—now dubbed "The Sunshine Girl"—had a fifteen-minute show, three mornings per week.

After singing, she walked downstairs to the coffee shop, put on her white uniform, and spent the rest of the day delivering scrambled eggs and burgers to customers. Off time, local celebrity Norma scored herself a trophy beau. Floyd "Red" Homuth was the curly-haired, redheaded captain of a Jamestown football team. Though just a teenager, Red struck her as one more manly protector figure of the kind she liked. Her casual dating of the much-coveted jock made her self-conscious of her "excess poundage," as she called it in a letter to Red. She joked uncomfortably about the summer temperatures: "You know how heat bothers those who are afflicted with a need for a diet!"

Peggy Lee's memories of Homuth suggest she pursued him with a vengeance. One night she insisted on borrowing his mother's car and taking the two of them for a spin. Driving down a dark road, she crashed into a crossing herd of horses. Miraculously, the teenagers survived, but one of the horses died, and the car was mangled. "I guess I better get out and see what I did," said Norma sheepishly. Answered Red: "I don't have to get out to see what you did." Any chance of a future with him ended then.

One day at the Gladstone Coffee Shop, she waited on a tableful of players from a visiting baseball team, the Fargo-Moorhead Twins. They flirted with her playfully. One of them, Bill Sawyer, told her he had heard her sing on the radio. If she could get herself to Fargo he would introduce her to Ken Kennedy, program director of WDAY, North Dakota's premier station. Sawyer said it half-seriously; the offer may have only been a come-on. But Norma insisted that Sawyer make that connection for her. Once he did, she made him drive her to WDAY.

This was her first trip to Fargo, the Manhattan of North Dakota. From outside the car window, a *whoosh* of big-town sights sped past her eyes: office buildings taller than any she had seen, department stores almost the size of a city block, a fur salon. On Broadway, she and Sawyer passed the Fargo Theatre, a first-run movie house; and a posh restaurant where a string quartet played amid potted palms. "Luxury" Plymouth and Ford cars crossed paths on the roads. Everything Norma saw revealed a rising national prosperity; the economy had regained its 1929 levels, and employment had jumped nearly seven percent since the year before.

At 118 Broadway stood Fargo's crown jewel: the Black Building, which locals called the Cathedral of Business. At eight stories, it towered above every other structure in town. The Black Building was actually white; the name came from its developer, George M. Black. He rented out the lower floors to Sears, Roebuck & Co.; WDAY filled the penthouse level. Throughout town, one couldn't walk a block without hearing the station's beloved voices booming out of shops and cars.

In early September, Sawyer took Norma inside the WDAY reception area. There she encountered a "beehive of activity," as a station brochure termed it. The waiting room had an Art Deco checkerboard floor, just like the ones in Fred Astaire and Ginger Rogers movies. People filed in and out briskly—announcers, comedians, singers, members of the resident staff orchestra. The walls were hung with pictures of the station's star entertainers: the Gals in Gingham; the Texas Ranger; hillbilly bandleader Lem Hawkins and his Georgie Porgie Breakfast Food Boys; and Ken Kennedy, who not only ran the station but starred as Uncle Ken in a hit kiddie show.

Norma, in her prairie garb, knew she was in the big time—at least by North Dakota standards—and fear paralyzed her. "Bill literally had to shove me toward the door," she recalled. Still, Kennedy encountered a driven young woman. He, in turn, struck her as dazzlingly worldly, even though he was only in his twenties. Tall and lanky, he wore a pinstripe suit and wire-frame glasses; his slicked-back hair and thin mustache seemed patterned on Clark Gable's.

As a favor to Sawyer, Kennedy allowed her to audition on the spot. A minister's daughter played piano for her. She sang a ballad, and Kennedy stunned her by offering, in his sonorous radio voice, to put her on the air immediately. "But I told her that I couldn't pay her enough to justify her making the move from Jamestown," he explained.

Two weeks later, Norma phoned him. She had found a waitressing job right down the street from WDAY, and was all ready to start broadcasting. Fine, he said, but there was another problem: her name. It had to go. Before WDAY, he had been Kenneth Sydness; Norma Egstrom sounded like a dowdy girl from the sticks. "He sat and looked at me for a minute and said, 'You look like a Peggy.' He thought a little longer and said a couple of names as his choices for my last name, and then he said, 'Lee—that's it—Peggy Lee.'"

Unlike the soft, sluggish sound of Norma Egstrom, "Peggy Lee" had rhythm; it popped, like a drumbeat. She accepted it without argument. But the young woman pictured in WDAY's next ad brochure looked anything but hip; she was chubby and wore a floor-length dress with puffy short sleeves, suitable for a Dakota housewife. The accompanying bio noted: "Guess she hasn't any hobbies, all we know is that she'd rather sing than eat." A cryptic aside—"Of course, you know Peg is single"—made one wonder if her age or her looks had kept her unhitched.

Kennedy took her out for some decent clothes and a more flattering hairdo. Initially he placed her on the *Noonday Variety Show*; then he added her to *Hayloft Jamboree*, a small-time forerunner of *Hee-Haw*, the 1960s TV show that brought hillbilly humor and song to a mainstream audience. Kennedy emceed the *Jamboree* and appeared in it as ragtag farmer Ole Anderson, who clowned with Tekla, a Norwegian comedienne with a comically thick accent. Lee became Freckle-Faced Gertie, a hick who sang hillbilly ditties. In between shows Lee earned extra cash by donning a straw hat and gingham dress and making live appearances with the cast.

All this exposure earned her a dollar-fifty per fifteen-minute show— too little to survive on, even in 1930s Fargo. Kennedy steered her to Regan's Moorhead Bakery, a bread factory. For thirty-five cents an hour, Lee sliced and wrapped bread on the graveyard shift. "In the bakery I used to slide these big bread racks around," she recalled, "and I would sing when I did it, and they didn't seem heavy at all. You get a rhythmic thing going and it's sort of fun." By day she did secretarial work at the station. All the while, she begged Kennedy for her own series.

On October 16, 1937, only a month after she had first set foot there, WDAY premiered *Songs by Peggy Lee*, a ten-minute recital. At 7:45 in the evening, just as housewives had finished washing the dinner dishes and joined their families around the living-room radio, a cooing voice wafted from the speaker. Lee had been warned that radio microphones didn't have limiters, which cushioned loud sounds. So she held back, which felt natural to her. "I think basically I was born with that timbre in my voice," she said years later. "My mother was a soft-spoken woman. It's just the way that I feel about music." Singing, she decided, was "almost like giving someone a kiss."

So it was with a newcomer who captivated her. Maxine Sullivan was a black jazz singer, nine years Lee's senior, who had burst into the big time. Sullivan sang with the lightness of a falling leaf, yet she made everything swing—even "Loch Lomond," the traditional Scottish air that had made her famous. The hit had won her a show on CBS radio; for the next few years her lilting voice permeated the airwaves. In an age of frenetic swing bands and their eager-to-please songsters, Sullivan stood out. Her elegant delivery, with never a wasted note or cheap effect; her way of dancing blithely on the surfaces of deep emotions, rather than spelling them out—all this left a mark on Peggy Lee. "I liked the way she phrased, the way you would conversationally," she remarked. And while Lee would learn to probe the darkest layers when she sang, she held on to Sullivan's cool, minimalist approach. It had taught her that she didn't have to shout or emote in order to make her point. Given her innate reserve, Lee found that notion very appealing.

But the allure of Hollywood kept calling her. With the Fargo Theatre right down the street from WDAY, she spent countless afternoons and evenings sitting in the air-conditioned dark, watching her idols act out melodramatic scenarios about love. She rushed to see *Stage Door*, in which her first screen idol, Ginger Rogers, and Katharine Hepburn costarred as a pair of aspiring actresses in a boardinghouse. Lee, who was still living in one, could relate.

North Dakota friends were tempting her with tales of Southern California, where many of them had gone, either on vacation or permanently, to escape the brutal cold. As the autumn thermometer dropped, rhapsodic letters about orange trees and balmy breezes arrived in her mailbox. Around the time she had met Lee at KOVC, Connie Emerson's family took its first trip to Los Angeles. Crossing San Bernardino on their way to Hollywood, the Emersons drove down a boulevard lined with swaying palm trees. A sunny, shimmering blue sky was their roof. "This must be like entering the gates of paradise!" exclaimed Connie's dad. In Hollywood, she and her mother stood near posh hotels and watched chauffeurs drop off and pick up ritzy-looking people. When Connie turned eighteen, she and her family moved to California.

Lee received a letter from a North Dakota friend, Gladys Rasmussen, who now lived in Los Angeles as well. Gladys raved about the city's sundrenched splendors, and urged Peggy to join her. Gladys promised her a job at the Circus Café, where she worked as a cashier. For Peggy, who would one day recall "practically no sun for the first twenty years of my life," L.A. "became like the promised land."

All winter long, she teased her friends with the wishful announcement, "I may go to California." But she never named a date. The more they egged her on, the more jittery she became. In February, with Fargo's weather at its most bone-chilling, Lee finally said, "I think I'll go next month." When her landlady and fellow boarders threw her a surprise going-away party, she knew she had to go.

But the seventeen-year-old decided on a compromise. She would visit L.A. briefly, then try her luck in Chicago. When she told her father of her plans, he got her a railroad pass with which she could travel anywhere in the U.S. As for how to eat along the way, Peggy, who had no savings, sold her graduation watch to her landlady for thirty dollars.

In March 1938, an excited but very nervous Peggy Lee boarded a train in Fargo. The long journey would take her to Valley City and to Butte, Montana; then to Salt Lake City, Utah; then finally to L.A. Some Dakota ladies gathered on the platform to see her off. As they waved goodbye, she disappeared inside a railroad car.

After several days, she stumbled onto a station platform with her suitcase and felt the balmiest air she had ever felt—and winter wasn't even over. Gladys waited there with a group of friends. But as they took off for her rooming house in Hollywood, she gave Peggy the bad news. A heavy rainstorm had flooded the Circus Café, which was below street level, and the place was shuttered.

For the next several mornings, Peggy waited on line at an employment agency downtown. The streetcar cost ten cents; that, combined with daily peanut butter sandwiches—the cheapest meal she could find—was erasing her tiny nest egg of cash. In her desperation, she accepted the first temp job offered her: that of a substitute short-order cook and waitress on Balboa Island in Newport Beach, fifty miles southwest of Los Angeles. She thumbed the lengthy ride; once there she managed to find a spare bed in a beachside cabin occupied by several girls. As her two-week diner stint ended, Peggy panicked. But her boss—a retired sideshow lion tamer—told her there were many jobs available at his old place of employment, the Balboa Fun Zone, the mini amusement park alongside the beach.

Off she went, on foot, to the Fun Zone. The park was nothing special: a few rides, some concession games, a penny arcade. Peggy applied for any job she could get. On the spot, she was hired as a barker. A manager fed her the line she would use to coax passersby into pitching balls at a target: "Three for a dime, you break one, you win!" It made for a laughable scene—a Dakota bumpkin trying to shout over clanging bells and carnival music with "the softest voice you ever heard," as she put it later. "You couldn't hear me unless you were standing on top of me."

Feeling lost and far from home, she identified with every outcast she saw. In one attraction, Hit the Wino with the Baseball, a "poor old soul" sat on a little bench above a glass tank of water. Whoever pitched a ball at a bull's-eye watched the seat collapse, dropping the "wino" into the tank. The sight of it broke Norma's heart.

Still, she knew she had come far from North Dakota, and the energy of the Fun Zone seduced her. So had the sexiness of the Strong Man. "He let me touch his tattoo," she said, adding cryptically, "Oh, I was so young and trusting of everyone."

She probably didn't work there for more than two weeks, but as always, she used the time to advance her career. One of her roommates had a guitarist boyfriend. Late at night, he and the girls convened on the pier. Learning that Peggy sang, the guitar player picked up his instrument and invited her to do a song. "'The Man I Love' in A-flat," she said. Once she had finished, he asked her why she wasn't singing more. He urged her to audition at the Jade, a new Hollywood nightclub that often hired unknowns.

On her next free day, Lee set off for the Jade. It stood on Hollywood Boulevard a few blocks away from the Pantages Theatre, one of L.A.'s grandest movie palaces. Late at night after a film, Pantages customers and others drifted into the Jade to enjoy some Chinese food and vaudeville-style entertainment. Occasionally the customers included such boldface names as Hedy Lamarr, James Cagney, and champion prizefighter Jack Dempsey, who would arrive with a gaggle of pretty girls.

The place inspired some of Lee's most fanciful tales about her hard knocks on the way up. She claimed she had hitchhiked to the Jade, but apparently her driver had let her out too soon; she spoke of trudging along Hollywood Boulevard, her threadbare platform shoes falling more apart with each step. She tried a quick repair with the sash from her dress, but arrived at her destination barefoot. Later, Chuck Barclay, the Jade's emcee and talent booker, told a different story: that Lee had "spent her last money on carfare to come see us."

However she got there, the young woman walked past a bar adorned with a huge carved dragon, then entered the main space, the Dragon Room. There she met Barclay, whose height and looks made her swoon. She asked him for an audition. Barclay let her sing. Owner Larry Potter took a bemused look at Lee: "corn-fed, milk-cheeked, and with hay practically falling out of her hair." A hard-boiled old-time restaurateur, he wasn't impressed. "Larry said we had plenty of singers," recalled Barclay. "But I hired her anyway." For two dollars a night plus dinner, she would sing a song or two per set amid a parade of performers. Quitting time was two AM.

Lee found the Jade tantalizing and mysterious. She recalled "the smell of the gardenias and Chinese food, the waitresses in their satin coats and satin pants moving silently about on the thick carpet." On the wall hung a giant painting of a nude blond goddess worshipping at the feet of a pot-bellied, Confucius-like figure.

Over time the Jade would evolve into a haven for black performers, including a forefather of jazz, trombonist Kid Ory; and the "Sunburnt Sophie Tucker," blues singer Lillian Randolph, later known for playing radio's most famous black housekeeper on *Beulah*. But in 1938, customers saw a raucous grab bag of mostly white oddballs, including "midget entertainer" Yvonne Moray; "head-balancing act" Bill and Dotty Phelps; and Jabuti, an Amazonian beauty with a mane of flowing red hair and a trombone.

Out wandered Peggy Lee in an evening gown loaned to her by Potter's wife. She couldn't hide her almost comical awkwardness. Potter, she recalled, "thought it was charming, or so he said, the way I clenched my fists and left my thumbs stuck up in the air when I sang."

She stayed for weeks, despite the presence of a more seasoned songbird, Mary Norman. And she gained some poise. "Both girls know their showmanship," wrote *Billboard*'s critic. "While neither one is what could be termed sensational, still they are adequate for a place of this kind. Both gals are lookers." Norman took an interest in Lee, giving her clothes and helping her choose songs. The Jade wound up dropping Norman and keeping Lee.

Phil Moore, the club's hulking young black pianist, accompanied Lee. Over the next few years Moore, who looked like a smiling bulldog, would land an arranger's job at MGM and serve as coach and conductor for Bing Crosby, Lena Horne, and Marilyn Monroe. He and Lee hit it off, and before or after work he took her to one of the few spots in town where a black man could accompany a white woman without risking violence. Moore drove her to Central-Alameda, a black neighborhood in South Los Angeles, to eat at Father Divine's Peace Mission and Truth Center. The budget hotel-restaurant was part of a chain founded by the controversial minister, who preached a daring stance of total desegregation. His cult-guru charisma and slick way with words inspired a pop standard in 1944, when Johnny Mercer, Lee's future boss at Capitol Records, attended one of Divine's flamboyant sermons. The minister had declared, "You got to accentuate the positive and eliminate the negative!" Mercer spun that line into one of the biggest hits of the World War II years, "Ac-cent-tchu-ate the Positive."

No harm befell Lee with Moore at her side, but one of the most bizarre episodes in her 1989 memoir concerned the Jade. One night after work, she claimed, an acquaintance of Potter's offered her a ride home. He drove her not to her rooming house but to a dark, seedy club whose door had a peephole. Inside, they joined a group of shady drinkers. A stranger watched Lee with alarm; suddenly he told her to run for her life. The two of them made a hasty getaway in his car, at which time the kindly gentleman informed her that she had narrowly avoided getting sold into white slavery.

Lee had evidently heard tales of the U.S. white slave trade of 1912–1913, when women were kidnapped, held prisoner, and forced to work as prostitutes. By 1938, the FBI had long since stamped the problem out. But even Lee's most preposterously delusional stories held glints of emotional truth. She had already gone far on sheer bravado; many who knew her during her ascent were surprised to hear her describe herself as "shy," for to them she seemed anything but. But the fast-lane Jade chilled the blood of a seventeen-year-old who had grown up amid country streams and grain elevators. At any moment, someone, or something, might snatch her from that microphone and send her back to North Dakota to scrub more floors.

Psychosomatic illness was Lee's key expression of fear, and it may have begun at the Jade. The crowd talked through her singing, and she took that as rejection. One night in July she did something that grabbed their attention as no song had: she fainted at the microphone. Lee awoke in a hospital bed. The doctor, she recalled, showed no sympathy. "Why don't girls like you go back home where you belong?" he snarled. Lee needed a tonsillectomy. "I didn't want to go back, but I had to go back," she explained later. "I was ill. I wanted to be close to my family."

The railroad pass that had taken her west had expired, and she couldn't afford the trip. "We'd all grown to love her so much that all the bartenders, waiters—everyone who worked at the club—chipped in to get Peggy home," recalled Chuck Barclay. Hubert Sweeney, an old boyfriend from North Dakota, picked her up at the Jamestown station. She moved in with her father, but the experience was painful. Min had finally left the Wimbledon depot and rejoined Marvin in Jamestown, and she looked upon her vagabond stepdaughter with all the disapproval of old. Once settled, the teenager called Artis Conitz and asked her to visit. Lee's once-closest chum found the singer more depressed than she'd ever seen her. "We sat on the porch," said Conitz. "She told me the trip was a total loss."

By August, Lee had moved to "a small town that looked all gray to me"—Hillsboro, North Dakota, where she settled into a crowded cottage presided over by Marion Egstrom, her hard-working sister. Marion was taking care of a brood that included brother Clair, a hard-drinking drifter who was continually unemployed and broke; another sibling, the now-divorced Della, who was recovering from tuberculosis; Della's son Paul; and family friend Ossie Hovde, one more lost soul.

Peggy was the neediest of all. Her tonsillectomy was overdue, and as she lay on an operating table in Hillsboro her throat began to hemorrhage. She had to be rushed to a bigger hospital in Grand Forks for another operation. "I nearly died," she insisted. This surgery seemed to work, however, and Lee rallied. Back home, she stared out the window from her bed. "I watched a sparrow hop around chirping happily as he pecked away at some horse manure. I remember thinking, 'If that little sparrow can make it, I can make it, too.'"

But more sadness lay ahead. Just before Thanksgiving, her ailing sister Jean—born months before their mother's death and adopted by their aunt in South Dakota—died at fourteen. One obituary blamed "cancer of the blood," which might have meant leukemia; another reported long-term heart troubles. Jean's aunt and uncle had taken her to specialists all over North Dakota, to no avail. The adolescent girl knew she was going to die, and had even arranged her own funeral.

Marvin, Min, Norma, and Marion had visited Jean in the hospital; now they were reunited alongside her coffin. One more piece of Selma Egstrom had vanished, and Peggy stayed depressed for weeks. But nothing could squelch her ambitions, and she was anxious to get back to the big city.

Another good word from Ken Kennedy got her a singing job at one of Fargo's smartest dwellings, the Powers Hotel. Situated near the trolley tracks in the heart of downtown, the five-story, red-brick building attracted scores of locals with the Powers Coffee Shop, a bustling, black-and-chrome, Art Deco café. It seemed patterned on the dining room of New York's Hotel Algonquin, where such 1930s literati as Dorothy Parker, Robert Benchley, and George S. Kaufman traded lunchtime barbs at a fabled roundtable. The Powers acquired one of its own, and invited the town's smart set to gather there. But the clientele leaned more toward students from North Dakota State University, who sat at the soda bar, sipping Cokes and munching burgers.

The Powers supplied live music from an organist, Frank Norris, who worked on a riser near the entrance. Starting on December 1, 1938, evening patrons walked in to find a singer standing by the organ. Many of them had heard Peggy Lee on WDAY; now here she was in the flesh, a gawky five-foot-seven teenager in a white prom-style dress, a sausage curl atop her forehead. As diners talked and china clattered, she crooned through a strained smile and tried to seem sophisticated. The Powers had booked her for seven nights a week; on three of them, WDAY broadcast her and Norris for fifteen minutes. An announcer made it known that this was not just some run-of-the-mill songbird; he introduced her as *Miss* Peggy Lee, the title she would favor for a lifetime. Lee liked its ring: the "Miss" slowed down her name, giving "Peggy Lee" more space to be heard; moreover, it implied a woman who deserved respect.

Mary Young, a student from the university, often walked a mile with three or four classmates to see her. Young was a farmer's daughter from Jamestown, but those outings made her feel like a woman of the world. "Us girls thought it was cool to go down to the Powers Hotel in Fargo to order a cherry Coke, and Peggy Lee would sing for us," she said. Young heard a "soft style" that "masked a lot of confidence, I thought. Sometimes she'd just lift her eyebrow during a song. It was amazing, what those tiny little moves added."

In the spring of 1939, she moved on to another major North Dakota town, Grand Forks, where her brother Leonard managed the YMCA. Lee quickly found herself a new showcase at another restaurant, the Belmont Café, on fashionable North 3rd Street downtown. Guests drifted in from the Hotel Dacotah across the street after they'd heard the hotel's resident act, the Clark Sisters, four North Dakota girls-next-door. In a few years, the Clarks—who changed their name to the Sentimentalists—would score two enormous dreams come true: a job with one of the most adored bandleaders in the country, trombonist Tommy Dorsey, followed by a big hit record with his orchestra, "On the Sunny Side of the Street."

Between sets at the Dacotah, the Clark girls would check out Peggy

Lee, who sang with the resident band, the Five Collegians, on a tiny platform in back of the Belmont. Her sotto voce style had continued to evolve. "She always sang in tune," recalled Peggy Clark, "and her words meant a lot to her, you could tell that." To sister Ann, Lee "sang very quietly, gently on the notes." A friendship formed, with Lee and the Clarks crossing the street to hear each other. They sat together and made "little-girl talk," as Ann called it. "We thought she was really darling," said Peggy Clark. "But she was kind of quiet. I think she felt insecure. She was just getting her feet wet, trying to figure out how to do this."

The Clark Sisters were broadcast nightly; Lee wanted the same. And she got it—a half-hour each Sunday on KFJM. Newspaper ads proclaimed the "popular, pretty songstress" as "one of WDAY's outstanding entertainers" one more indication of the Fargo station's prestige throughout North Dakota.

Her summer job ended in September when the Belmont's usual singer, Jane Larrabee, known professionally as Jane Leslie, came home from vacation. The Powers Coffee Shop welcomed her back, and by year's end Lee had taken on a grueling six-night-a-week performance schedule, sweetened by more live broadcasts. This time her organist was Lloyd Collins, a professorial lad who also played in church. On radio nights, the public was invited to come in and make its presence heard over the airwaves.

They didn't hold back, and Lee took their chatter as indifference. Offstage she chewed her nails and sulked, certain she was bombing. When she saw an ad for a course by Dale Carnegie, the self-help guru whose books and classes had taught millions how to face crowds with aplomb, Lee signed up. She learned a key point of Carnegie's fear-conquering technique; it involved dredging up anger and using it to help one conquer an unruly audience. Thoughts of Min had always made her blood boil, and Lee used that rage in her shows for many years to come.

But at the Powers she learned how to hide it behind a Mona Lisa smile; to mask it with sexiness or other emotions. It gave her singing a mysterious spark, and more eyes turned her way. She and Collins kept the audience involved by taking requests.

Lee taught herself to memorize the names of regulars and their favorite tunes, which she sang as they entered. No music pleased her more than torch songs, and the 1939 airwaves and jukeboxes were packed with

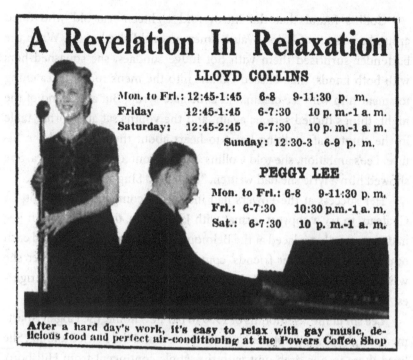

A Revelation In Relaxation

LLOYD COLLINS

Mon. to Fri.: 12:45-1:45   6-8   9-11:30 p. m.
Friday   12:45-1:45   6-7:30   10 p. m.-1 a. m.
Saturday: 12:45-2:45   6-7:30   10 p. m.-1 a. m.
Sunday: 12:30-3   6-9 p. m.

PEGGY LEE

Mon. to Fri.: 6-8   9-11:30 p. m.
Fri.: 6-7:30   10:30 p.m.-1 a. m.
Sat.: 6-7:30   10 p. m.-1 a. m.

After a hard day's work, it's easy to relax with gay music, delicious food and perfect air-conditioning at the Powers Coffee Shop

(COURTESY OF RICHARD MORRISON)

them. "In my solitude, you haunt me/With memories that never die," sang Lee in Duke Ellington's "Solitude." "Deep in a Dream," a smash hit for the Artie Shaw orchestra and his singer Helen Forrest, found Lee wallowing in imagery as ethereal as a cloud from a cigarette: "The smoke builds a stairway for you to descend/You come to my arms, may this bliss never end . . ."

A song had become Lee's most cherished escape. She discovered the exhilaration of stepping inside a lyric and "living it." Whether or not the story had happened to her, she could make an audience feel that it had. The Powers advertised her as "A Revelation in Relaxation." On Sundays, after Fargoans left church, they could go to the Powers for lunch and hear Lee and Collins perform a matinee of art songs, including "I'll Take You Home Again, Kathleen," an Irish-style ballad about an immigrant couple's longing for the old country. Many of the Powers's Sunday customers had moved to North Dakota decades earlier from Scandinavia or Germany; during "Kathleen," many brushed tears from their eyes.

Collins found that the introverted eighteen-year-old who toted around a volume of Ralph Waldo Emerson could also be silly. When the bartender surprised them with hot fudge sundaes, she squashed hers with both hands, then chased Collins into the men's room, threatening to smear him with ice cream and chocolate syrup. But at the end of the night, things turned serious again, and the youths sat at a corner table in the empty café, talking heart-to-heart about their lives and the future. Lee's ambition, she told Collins, was to front a swing orchestra. She showed him a lyric she had written, "If I Could Sing with a Band."

Her success at the Powers had inspired a competing nightspot, Le Chateau, to try a copycat format with Jane Leslie, the singer whom Lee had temporarily replaced at the Belmont Café. The women resented each other; Lee relished her friends' comments about how much better she was. But once she felt sure that Jane was no threat, they became the tightest of friends.

Lee spent the last months of 1939 in her new home, the Hogan Apartments, right down the street from the Powers and the Black Building. She lived there in one drab unit with the whole contingent from Hillsboro. Marion had mild showbiz ambitions herself; she had adopted the more glamorous name of Marianne and posed for Hollywood-style headshots, one of which showed her as a dramatic beauty with upswept curls. According to Artis Conitz, both Marianne and Della sang at least as well as Peggy. But Marianne was employed as a doctor's receptionist; someone had to pay the bills. Sickly Della couldn't work; Clair earned a pittance as a grocery-store clerk. Ossie barely contributed. Lee wrote optimistically to an out-of-town girlfriend: "Sometimes we are a little low on food, but we've always got beds to sleep on."

Lee's singing and waitressing had netted her a decent salary that year, but most of her income went toward dresses and other accoutrements for her career. Everyone in the house, especially Marianne, felt sure that Peggy Lee was a star in the making. "My mother was Peg's one true friend, the one person she could count on through life," said her son Lee Ringuette. "She very much wanted Aunt Peggy to have her opportunity to sing." While Marianne stitched her gowns, others showed up to dote on Lee, such as Johnny Quam, a young admirer "who was *really* important in my life," noted the singer in her memoir. "Not just because I liked him, but also because he worked in a dry-cleaning shop and could keep my 'other dress' clean."

Paula Ringuette, the sister of Marianne's future husband, Leo Ringuette, lived behind the Hogan in the Jackson Apartments. "We would sit on the front step at night and wait for Peggy to come home from the Powers Hotel," she said. Ten-year-old Paula couldn't wait to see what the glamorous songbird was wearing. The grown-ups, she noticed, "were all excited about what Peggy was doing." They seemed to know she wouldn't stay in North Dakota for long.

"I had the feeling I was being run down by a steam engine," said Lee when Benny Goodman put her in the spotlight. (COURTESY OF RICHARD MORRISON)

Chapter Three

*I*N THE SUMMER of 1940, true-blue Ken Kennedy got Lee her first job with a serious swing band. Kennedy had raved about her to his cousin Severn "Sev" Olsen, a college boy whose orchestra played for dancing at the Radisson Hotel, the premier hotspot of downtown Minneapolis. Olsen needed to hear Lee before he could hire her, so she set off on a two-hundred-mile train trip to the hotel. The twenty-year-old auditioned with "Body and Soul," the most gut-wrenching torch song of the previous decade. "You know I'm yours for just the taking," she sang into the face of "Minneapolis's most personable bandleader," as *Down Beat* called him.

Lee found him irresistibly attractive and witty. He returned her interest—and she embarked on what she would call her "first big romance." It was messy, though, for Olsen had a wife. "I just couldn't help it," protested the singer. Word spread throughout the orchestra that Olsen's prairie-girl find was on the verge of breaking up his marriage.

Wracked with conflict, Lee cried on the shoulder of Jane Larrabee, who lived in Minneapolis. But the affair continued. On the bandstand Lee took care to keep her Scandinavian mask of control in place. Jeanne Arland, a pianist and singer whose future husband, Willie Peterson, played piano with Olsen, saw nothing but smiling restraint whenever Lee opened her mouth on the bandstand. "It was a sweet voice," said Arland, who noted admiringly that Lee had "nice control" and "knew how to deliver a song"—all this with no formal training.

But her offstage role as the "other woman" was torturing her, and in November 1940 she wrenched herself out of it. Lee grabbed the next job offer that came along, with a more famous (if less sexy) conductor at a rival hotel, the Nicollet. Before anyone had heard of Bing Crosby, Will Osborne had reigned as the first star crooner on radio. His whispery style, backed by the sticky-sweet strains of his dance band, was all over the airwaves in the 1930s.

But by the time he hired Lee, his band had gone to seed, and he announced his upcoming tour as his last. Osborne was carting a bus-and-truck vaudeville show around the country; it included a hillbilly fiddler, a black baritone who sang "Ol' Man River," a buxom bombshell who turned cartwheels, the "fire-eating comedian" Chaz Chase, and a singing jokester, Dick "Stinky" Rogers. *Variety* singled out Peggy Lee: "The gal trills 'Body and Soul' and had to come back to do 'Exactly Like You' before the customers would cease the palm-pounding."

Just before the band went on tour, Lee spent five days at the Minneapolis Auditorium, guesting in the traveling version of what had been the most breathtaking show of the 1939 World's Fair. *Water Follies* was a low-rent version of *Billy Rose's Aquacade*, a flashy spectacular in which balletic swimming and diving met vaudeville. The road show had held onto its star, Buster Crabbe, the Olympic gold-medal swimmer who had played Tarzan and comic-strip hero Flash Gordon onscreen. The backup cast had been slashed from five hundred–plus to twenty-three. Water athletes dived into an Olympic-size glass tank and wriggled around like mermaids; scaffolding on the left held a stage, an orchestra, some clowning comics, and Peggy Lee. By the time she sang her one song, "God Bless America," her gown was soaked. On press night, the loud splashing of the divers threw off her timing so badly that she came in two bars late and never found the beat.

Variety mocked the "amateurishness and crudeness" of the show, which flopped at the box office. Lee was glad to rejoin Will Osborne in St. Louis for a holiday engagement. During the run, however, she felt a blockage in her throat. After all the vocal problems she had incurred at the Jade, Lee was terrified of losing her voice forever. She rushed to a doctor, who sent her to the hospital for one more operation. Newspapers reported her ailment as a "badly infected throat," but Lee's growing hypochondria took over. Four decades later she described the anesthesiologist as "mentally ill," declaring, "He slammed me down on the table and started pouring ether down my throat. While I was asleep, I dropped off the table and my teeth cut loose my tongue and went through my lip."

During her recovery, Osborne turned his band over to Stinky Rogers and moved to Hollywood to become a producer. Lee was fired. "I cried," she told a reporter. "Then it seemed I was steel inside." Once the hospital had released her, she "set out to meet the right people." The place to find them, she decided, was back in Movieland.

Shortly after New Year's Day 1941, she hitched a ride to L.A. with some musicians. The Jade rehired her briefly for the same two-dollar-a-night salary. A songwriter she met there told her she could do better at the Doll House, a restaurant in Palm Springs that hired singers as dinner music. A tiny renovated cottage, the Doll House stood in a desert town that offered Hollywood folk a tranquil escape from the fast lane. Early in 1941, some of the most recognizable stars in America—Jack Benny, Franchot Tone, Peter Lorre—glanced up from their dinner plates and conversations to see a callow blonde singing love songs with a strained smile. A moment later, they resumed their chitchat.

This time, apparently, her Dale Carnegie anger technique didn't suffice; this crowd was far more blasé than any she'd encountered in Fargo. The Doll House became the site of a fabled (if probably exaggerated) breakthrough in her development. "I knew I couldn't sing over them," she said later, "so I decided to sing under them. The more noise they made, the more softly I sang. When they discovered they couldn't hear me, they began to look at me. Then they began to listen. As I sang, I kept thinking, 'softly, with feeling.' The noise dropped to a hum; the hum gave way to silence. I had learned how to reach and hold my audience—softly, with feeling."

Lee had sung that way for years, but finally, it seemed, she had learned its power. "By that accident, I discovered that if I could really find my way into a song itself, people would listen more readily. I began to think about meaning, about words, rather than just singing."

One night her listeners included Freddie Mandel, who owned the Detroit Lions. He returned that week with Frank Bering, a Chicago hotel mogul. One of Bering's properties, the Ambassador West, had a lounge, the Buttery, that offered entertainment; Mandel had told Bering that Lee might make a pleasant addition. It was late, and the Doll House musicians had gone home, but Lee took Bering to another nightspot and sat in with her preferred audition song, "The Man I Love." He wasn't that impressed, but out of faith in Mandel, he offered her a job at the Buttery.

"I'm hiring you more because of your enthusiasm than anything else," he told her.

Even though she would once more serve as background music, Lee wove visions of grandeur around her debut at this big-time hotel in Chicago—the town that had launched many a jazz great, including Louis Armstrong and Benny Goodman. With the extravagance that would nearly ruin her when she acquired real money to lose, Lee spent what little cash she had to buy a new wardrobe at a Palm Springs boutique. The splurge left her without enough money to eat or pay her way to Chicago. She wound up borrowing the funds for the trip.

In May 1941, Lee embarked on a long set of connecting rides to Chicago. Once there, she found her way to the "Gold Coast" neighborhood—one of the most affluent in all the U.S.—and to the Ambassador West at 1300 North State Parkway. The hotel wasn't as posh as its partner across the street, the Ambassador East. Yet to Lee's eyes, the place was a palace. She had invited Jane Larrabee to come and share her room. Soon, as the Buttery's new singing star, Lee would be earning the unfathomable windfall of seventy-five dollars a week. But her first paycheck was days away, and both girls were broke; no one had told Lee that her contract included free room service. "There I sat in this fancy suite," she recalled, "feeling like a fairy princess in my new clothes, but starving in the lap of luxury."

She and Jane survived on cookies, vending-machine crackers, and peanut butter. Returning to her quarters one afternoon, Lee found a surprise outside the door: a tray of food she hadn't ordered. The same thing happened the next day, and the next. She viewed this miracle as further proof that if she concentrated hard enough, she could manifest whatever she needed. Soon, though, she figured out that the magic had been wrought by two resident angels, Tillie and Ivy, the black housekeepers who worked her floor. Years later, when a by-now-famous Lee stayed in the same hotel, she spotted Tillie. Lee asked her how they had known she was hungry. Explained Tillie: "We didn't see no grub coming in nor any bones going out!" Whenever they found leftover food on a room-service tray, they saved it for Lee.

All over town, nightcrawlers had their pick of smoky lounges where demure songbirds sang amid a din of chatter. The Buttery was a casual alternative to the Ambassador East's Pump Room, a swanky restaurant with dancing. Instead of indulging in that tuxedo-and-evening-gown scene, one could stroll inside the Ambassador West, make a sharp right, and spend an hour drinking and enjoying the lounge acts that performed in the Buttery's rear corner. They included Lon Sax & His Saxonaires, the Noteables ("those hilarious kids who play such cute music," wrote the *Chicago Tribune*), and hoity-toity songstress Maggi McNellis, a future New York socialite and radio host.

On May 7, Peggy Lee wove her way through the noisy crowd to give her first show. Backing her were The Four of Us, a perky all-male singing band. Lee smiled gamely as she crooned "Body and Soul" and "These Foolish Things," two of her usual showstoppers, to a barely responsive crowd. One customer who took notice was Jean Enzinger, a blond, pretty Vassar graduate and local society columnist. Later she would marry TV producer Bob Bach and move to New York, where, as Jean Bach, she became known as a jazz-crazy party-thrower and the producer of radio's *The Arlene Francis Show*.

Though just twenty-two at the time, Jean was already a jazz connoisseur, and she wasn't too impressed by the Buttery's new vocalist. "Peggy's singing was OK," said Jean. "She didn't have any particular style." Lyricist Johnny Mercer also dropped by. To him she sounded out of tune, in keys that were obviously wrong for her. But no matter how unnerving the din, Lee wouldn't raise her voice. "You had to really pay attention when she was on," Jean said.

Lee was determined to learn, and she soaked up knowledge from her elders. Chicago had a feast to offer. After work, she trekked to Rust Street in the city's jazz-laden South Side—an area known as Bronzeville, and not a place for unescorted white girls. She kept returning there nonetheless to hear her new discovery, Laura Rucker, a fixture of Chicago blues since the twenties. Rucker held forth like a haughty grande dame, but there was nothing pretentious about her voice, a cool, salty wail edged with sarcasm. She played piano and sang songs, sometimes original, about the two-timing men she had known. Rucker kept her phrases short and clipped, as though dishing with a girlfriend over a glass of gin. Her art reminded Lee that less could be more, and could swing just as hard. Back at the Buttery, she tried to phrase the way Rucker did.

The management kept extending Lee for months. One August night, a smartly dressed and coiffed brunette sat at a table, "gaily puffing her cigarette," as a reporter noted. Alice Hammond Duckworth—known as Lady Duckworth—was both the estranged wife of a member of British parliament and a descendant of Commodore Cornelius Vanderbilt, the magnate who spawned a historic American family.

The next night, Alice came back with two men. One was Mel Powell, a lanky blond wunderkind of the jazz piano; the other his boss, Benny Goodman. As soon as her divorce came through, Duckworth and the world-famous King of Swing were set to marry. Goodman's band had come to town to play the College Inn, the ballroom of the Sherman House hotel. There, and virtually everywhere else they appeared, so many swing-crazy jitterbuggers fought to get in that police had to be called. Goodman was a shining American success story—an immigrant couple's son who had triggered a musical revolution. A virtuoso clarinetist, Goodman had brought swing to every major ballroom in America and even to Carnegie Hall.

From her microphone, Lee spotted him—a thirty-two-year-old, bespectacled egghead in a tweed suit. She froze. Like most of America, she worshipped the Goodman band; at the Fun Zone in Balboa, she had fed hard-earned nickels into a jukebox to play "Don't Be That Way," Goodman's bouncy number-one hit.

At the Buttery, Lee didn't know that Helen Forrest, Goodman's celebrated singer, had just quit in disgust. Forrest would recall that twenty-month stint as a "life sentence." Goodman, she said, was "by far the most unpleasant person I ever met in music"; she had loathed his bad manners, his cheapness, his egocentrism. At the Sherman, Goodman, true to form, had driven her crazy by distractingly "noodling" on the clarinet throughout her vocals. After the set, she had stormed off and told him, "This is it. Find another singer, and find her fast."

Her departure had left Goodman in urgent need of a replacement. Alice had suggested Lee as a convenient and adequate substitute, and the bandleader reluctantly agreed to give her a listen. The Four of Us were ecstatic over Goodman's presence. Lee tried not to stare, but through the darkness and smoke she couldn't take her eyes off him—a glum, fidgety figure, glaring in her direction while chewing his tongue. Lee was experiencing the fabled Goodman "ray," a stare of seeming disapproval that "went right through you," as his previous singer, Martha Tilton, recalled. Some who knew him claimed that this was his perverse way of listening intently, but Lee felt sure he hated her. Out came her worst insecurities, rooted in all the times when Min had told her she was wasting her time trying to sing.

Goodman neither smiled nor applauded. After one set, he and his companions left without greeting her. Lee told one of The Four of Us sadly, "I wish he would have enjoyed it."

She hadn't thrilled him, but as he later put it, he heard "character in her voice." A day or two later, Lee came home to her suite to find Jane Larrabee beside herself with sisterly glee. Larrabee sputtered out the news that Benny Goodman had called, asking for Miss Lee. Peggy insisted that someone was playing a cruel joke. "I know he didn't like me!" she said.

"What can you lose?" asked Jane. "At least call."

Lee waited a day before dialing the number. "It was a very short conversation," she recalled. "He just said, 'Would you like to sing with the band?' and I said, 'Well, y-yes.' " He wanted her to join immediately at the Sherman, and he would match her seventy-five-dollar salary at the Buttery. "I was in a state of shock," admitted Lee. Mel Powell later told her that, during her Buttery set, Goodman had murmured half-heartedly to Alice: "I guess we've got to get somebody for Helen."

———

LEE'S NEW JOB PLACED her in the eye of the hurricane known as swing; if she lasted with Goodman, fame was guaranteed. But she would have to learn how to bend to the quirks of one of the most maddening personalities in jazz. Benjamin David Goodman was a towering example of what could happen when gut determination met talent. Goodman and his eleven siblings had grown up poor in a Chicago ghetto with their parents, Jewish émigrés from Eastern Europe. David, the father, shoveled lard in a stockyard. He vowed to give his kids a better life; to that end, he sent several of his sons to music school. David bought Benny a clarinet and found him a classical teacher, but the budding art of jazz stole the boy's heart. By sixteen, he was already good enough to win a spot in the pioneer jazz orchestra of drummer Ben Pollack, a Chicago idol. Soon thereafter, David was mowed down in a car accident. For years, Benny would struggle to live up to his father's exacting dreams for him.

Black musicians struck Benny as the authentic voices of jazz, and he vowed to work with them, although the racism of the day made that a risky prospect. At the same time, he had inherited David's goal of upward mobility, and burned to join the upper crust. In 1933, one of its members took up his cause: the lawyer and Columbia Records producer John Henry Hammond II, the man who introduced his sister Alice to Goodman.

A Yale graduate, Hammond had sprung from a family tree that included a Civil War general, the U.S. Ambassador to Spain, and a Vanderbilt. He was a moneyed snob to the manner born; but whereas most people of his class associated only with the blacks who cleaned their homes and served their meals, Hammond—a know-it-all hipster with the high-flown speech of an aristocrat—insisted upon the "Negro's supremacy in jazz," and wanted the world to share his obsession. His discovery of Count Basie was one example of his canny ear. In another, he teamed a still-obscure Goodman with an unknown Billie Holiday on a 1933 single, "Your Mother's Son-in-Law." Hammond became Goodman's trusted advisor; it was he who urged the clarinetist to hire four incomparable black musicians: pianist Teddy Wilson, vibraphonist Lionel Hampton, guitarist Charlie Christian, and arranger Fletcher Henderson.

In 1934, Goodman launched his first big band. He landed a regular spot on an NBC radio program, *Let's Dance*, but nobody yet knew how to dance to swing, and a ballroom tour nearly bankrupted him. His fortunes turned in 1935 when Victor Records signed him. Critics and deejays raved about his new singles; that August, at the Palomar Ballroom in Los Angeles, the orchestra—and swing itself—exploded. Fans had devised a frenetic new dance, the jitterbug; by year's end, they had dozens of swing bands to dance to.

Goodman piled up number-one hits. In January 1938, mobs waited in the cold outside New York's Paramount Theater for the ten AM show on his opening day. When the leader strode onstage, clarinet under his arm and a self-satisfied half-smile on his face, "bedlam broke loose," according to the *Herald-Tribune*. Jitterbugging couples jammed the aisles, "and during a jam session a group of addicts invaded the stage and began to dance the Big Apple. Ushers stood by helplessly." Twenty-nine thousand people came that weekend, breaking attendance records at the hottest theater in Manhattan.

That same month, Goodman brought swing to Carnegie Hall for a sold-out concert that lives on in legend. Conducting from resident maestro Arturo Toscanini's spot, Goodman gave jazz and swing the prestige of concert music. The high point was "Sing, Sing, Sing," a furious ten-minute tour de force that built into ever-rising crescendos until it drove fans to a near frenzy. Drummer Gene Krupa sat hunched over his tom-toms and cymbals, wild-eyed and dripping with sweat as his sticks flew in a blur.

For the older generation, Goodman's music, like most of swing, was a dangerous sign of youth run amok—perhaps in the throes of marijuana, the most feared drug of the day. The jitterbug was as threatening to the establishment as the future sights of Elvis Presley's gyrating hips, the Beatles' long hair, and Jim Morrison's leather pants and numbed doomsday prophesies.

The 1930s equivalent of those hurricane figures was an owlish professor-type with a white jacket, bow tie, and a vacant gaze. His playing revealed nothing of his heart; for Goodman, swing was the thing. Offstage he was a fierce taskmaster, both toward himself and others. His early vocalist Helen Ward couldn't remember seeing him offstage when he wasn't practicing. He made his band rehearse songs ten, fifteen, twenty times through, as he pushed for an elusive dream of perfection. "If something went wrong," explained his singer of 1939, Louise Tobin, "all he had to do was lower his glasses and look. That was devastating to whoever was at the end of that look. There were very few guys who were not intimidated by Benny. Because of his accuracy, his fluency, everything."

To his daughter Rachel, "this self-absorption enabled him to go where he needed to" musically. "It also drove everybody else crazy, because it shut the rest of the world out." Goodman's eccentricities became jazz legend. The leader made no attempt to learn musicians' names; he called them all Pops, including girl singers like the Clark Sisters, who sang with him briefly. Peggy Clark told of one memorable rehearsal. "The guys complained, 'Gee, Benny, it's so cold in here.' He said, 'Oh, OK. I'll be right back.' He went out and came back in with a sweater on."

Ed Shaughnessy, one of his drummers, saw Goodman torture his musicians, intentionally or not. "I think he liked to keep people off balance. He was a weird man." Arranger-composer Johnny Mandel, who emerged in the swing era, also knew Goodman's ways: "He'd break down the confidence of first-line players, and demoralize them, and they'd quit."

Benny Goodman, New York, 1946
(PHOTO BY WILLIAM F. GOTTLIEB;
COURTESY OF LIBRARY OF CONGRESS)

Bizarre as his methods seemed, few could question the results. "Benny made musicians play better than they could," explained Tobin. "They never wanted him to be disappointed in them, because they were so thrilled to be in that band. These guys were at the very top of their profession with him. Most of them could never hope to get any bigger."

On her opening night at the Sherman House, Peggy Lee, age twenty-one, sat on the bandstand between two other singers, Tommy Taylor and Helen Forrest. The latter remained silent and glum; she had quit a month before her contract expired, and Goodman had forced her to stay—though he didn't permit her to sing—until it ended. If anyone asked, he said she had laryngitis. Meanwhile, the maestro had given Lee no rehearsal; she didn't know where to come in on her songs, and relied on Mel Powell to cue her. The singer took her place at a center microphone that faced the one enormous spotlight that lit the band. "I had the feeling I was being run down by a steam engine," she said later.

Backstage, Forrest was frigid to Lee, who was singing her arrangements. Lee would complain for years of having had to sing in Forrest's keys, but in fact they were close to her own; her strained, wavery vocalizing had another cause: "I had a psychosomatic cold from being terrified to be with Benny Goodman. Benny really wasn't crazy about singers."

Neither John Hammond nor another of Goodman's advisors, George Avakian, cared much for this one. Avakian, a producer at Columbia Records, Goodman's current label, heard her for the first time at a rehearsal. Fear had kept the young woman hiding in an aloof shell, and she struck Avakian as "ice-cold—very reserved and austere looking and quiet," with a "certain artificial quality."

Hammond dismissed her more bluntly. It happened at Lee's first recording session held in Chicago on August 15, 1941, a week after Goodman had hired her. The song was a light but catchy novelty, "Elmer's Tune," whose author, Elmer Albrecht, was allegedly an undertaker. "What puts the kick in a chicken, the magic in June? / It's just Elmer's tune," went the silly words. Glenn Miller, Goodman's runner-up as the hottest bandleader in the country, had just recorded the ditty, and Columbia had pushed Goodman into competing.

In an interview with Goodman biographer Ross Firestone, engineer Bill Savory recalled the session as extremely tense. During the first take, said Mel Powell, Lee "stood at the mike with the sheet music in her hands—I'm pretty sure she couldn't read it—and it shook so badly it sounded like a distant forest fire." As usual, Goodman kept calling for more takes. Lee felt sure she was failing. Hammond, there to supervise, began deriding Goodman's judgment in a loud voice: "Benny, she can't sing. She just can't sing." Goodman did not like to be challenged. Finally he picked up a chair and hurled it at Hammond.

This war over her singing mortified Lee, and it left her feeling that Hammond was right; during playbacks, the sound of her voice made her heartsick. According to Down Beat, Goodman wanted the disc shelved, but Columbia refused. In fact, the record betrays no backstage drama. Inexperienced as she was, Lee sounds relaxed and swinging, with a cool touch that set her apart in the "hot" arena of swing. But the jazz press, which had grown hypercritical of the King of Swing, brushed off his singer. Lee, complained Down Beat, was no Helen Forrest. Hammond aired a stinging public opinion: "Miss Lee is a lady whose attractiveness occasionally makes the listener forget that she has no vocal or interpretive talent." Lee's debut single died more swiftly than almost any recent Goodman release. She was shattered. "I'd like to stomp on it . . . break it . . . smash it to bits!" she declared.

Before she and Goodman left Chicago, the leader gave her another chance when they recorded a lightweight love song for dancing, "I See a Million People (But All I Can See Is You)." Defying Hammond, he had her lead off the record rather than just sing the second chorus, as band vocalists typically did. Calmer now, Lee sang with dulcet purity, and Goodman was pleased. But *Down Beat*'s Dave Dexter, Jr., called her the bandleader's worst singer ever. "Miss Lee," he wrote, "should be selling discs behind a counter instead of on the grooves."

All the potshots convinced her that this dream hiring was a hopeless thing. Columnist Frank Farrell recalled the sight of her onstage: "She couldn't sing a line without gripping the mike as if it were a baseball bat she was clinging to in mid-ocean after a shipwreck." Even in her fifties, Lee looked back upon that time as a marathon of rejection. *Down Beat* ran a photo of her with the header, "Never Been Hissed." In Lee's mind, the pun metamorphosed into a painful and illogical putdown that she misquoted for years: "Sweet Sixteen and Will Never Be Missed."

She decided to quit before Goodman fired her. The man who in Helen Forrest's words "never said one kind word to anyone about anything" stunned Lee by refusing her resignation. She offered to take singing lessons; Goodman told her not to. "He said, 'I've heard you sing, I know you can. I believe in you.'"

Lee's conviction returned. "She's one of the gals who way, way back said, 'I'm gonna make it, I'm *determined* to have a singing career,'" observed Helen Ward. To give up would mean that Min was right—she really *was* wasting her time. Still, Goodman kept her neurotic. He liked to play with his band members' heads, perhaps as a way of keeping them in line. Dona Harsh, Lee's later secretary, recalled the singer's account of a panic-stricken day when she woke up late for work. Goodman was a stickler for punctuality, and Lee jumped into her clothes and ran all the way from the hotel to the theater. "All the way she thought, 'He's gonna kill me, he's gonna fire me!' She got there. All he said was, 'Hello, Peg.' That was it."

THE BIG BANDS SURVIVED by maintaining a grueling itinerary—a night here, a week there—that took them all over the country, with spouses and lovers left behind. For Lee, life on the road "was like boot camp, tremendously tough to endure. But if you come through it, you'll be in shape for anything that comes along."

The job was such a grind, however, that visions of glamour faded fast. As Helen O'Connell, the beautiful blond songbird from the Jimmy Dorsey orchestra, later joked: "If I'd known it was going to be an 'era,' I'd have paid closer attention!" Goodman's earlier pianist, Jess Stacy, recalled a schedule of fifty one-nighters in a row. When the Clark Sisters traveled with the Tommy Dorsey band, each stop in their haphazard agenda seemed "a million miles away," said Peggy Clark. Everyone tried to sleep in stiff bus seats as cars traveled bumpy unpaved roads and turned hairpin corners. Finally they stumbled off the vehicle and into the lobby of some hotel or motel whose rooms they would pay for themselves. "They were all dumps—grim, grimy, just awful," said Helen Ward.

Sometimes band personnel had time for a quick nap and a shower before the gig; more often they drove straight to the venue. Wolfed-down diner food or drugstore sandwiches would have to do. Lee applied makeup in ladies' rooms and pressed her gowns in any nook of the venue that had a flat surface and an electrical outlet. With a curling iron, she rushed to create the sausage curls that hung on her neck and forehead.

At theaters like the Paramount, where a musical act alternated with a film, bands played as many as eight shows per day. In ballrooms they performed several sets per night, with short breaks. "I used to average about two hours' sleep a night," said Lee in 1986. "I'm glad I was young enough to take it." Sometimes they barely could, and doddered through their paces on numbed autopilot. "We were like those little Swiss toys in a cuckoo clock," she observed.

Off they sped to their next destination. Wildly disorganized agendas, backroad paths, and dark, wet nights comprised many an itinerary. *Down Beat's* pages held hair-raising accounts of cars and buses that crashed, skidding over embankments or sliding on ice. Many musicians died in transit. Ballroom fires were not uncommon then; numerous bands found their instruments melted and gnarled and their music in ashes.

Yet for all the hazards, almost every jazz musician and aspiring pop

singer in the country longed to work in a big band. It meant employment
with the swing idols of the day, and the chance to perform songs that made
millions of Americans sigh or sing along. On the bandstand sat fifteen
to twenty-one musicians, neatly arranged and wearing jackets and bow
ties. Vocalists stayed in chairs to the side, smiling frozenly as they waited
for their turn to sing. They looked out at a sea of jitterbugging youths—
girls in bobby sox and sweaters, hair tied demurely with a bow; clean-cut
boys with Brylcreemed hair. The show-offs wore zoot suits, the flamboyant Harlem look known for its wide, padded shoulders, high waist, and
billowy legs. Starry-eyed couples stood near the bandstand, swaying in
embrace as the singers sang of eternal love. No matter how tired she was,
Ann Clark recalled the experience of singing with a big band as "the biggest thrill in life. It energizes you; it gives you so much strength."

That was something Peggy Lee had, however timid she seemed. "I
was strong," she said in 1982. "You can't believe how strong." North Dakota life—including Min's iron hand—had made her that way. Pianist
Hal Schaefer, who accompanied her later in the forties, caught her dual
nature as he watched her from the piano. "My God, she had shoulders
on her," he said. "From the back she looked like a man." Face to face, Lee
appeared sweet, with a ready smile, but in her own inscrutable world.
Autobiographical jottings about her Goodman days, written years later,
give a sense of the dark and foggy creature he had hired. In a reference to
the band's Manhattan headquarters, Lee notes without elaboration, "New
Yorker Hotel—all the suicides falling by my window."

But the public saw a princess: five foot seven yet seemingly taller,
with sunshiny blond hair (lightened by peroxide) and a winsome sexiness. Lee had upped the band's box-office appeal, but to Goodman and
most of his peers, singers were an attention-stealing necessary evil. Few
had dared to withdraw into themselves, as Lee did, and make an audience
come to them.

Goodman may have discovered her, but he wasn't eager to give her
too much of his spotlight. His band, she said, was "better to listen to" than
to sing with; he demanded swing, and he liked it loud. Her heart sank
when she heard the first run-through of the George and Ira Gershwin
tearjerker "But Not for Me," arranged for her. "He had it roaring," she re-

called. Boldly, Lee spoke up: "Benny, that's not the way I would sing that." Rather than slow it down, he scrapped it altogether.

Yet Goodman allowed his new arranger, Eddie Sauter, to give her what she wanted. "He didn't like singers either," said Lee. Still, he realized her potential, and began building sophisticated charts around her. A baby-faced, brainy twenty-six-year-old with a degree from Juilliard, Sauter had given swing arranging a new degree of finesse. He loved the French Impressionist composers such as Debussy and Ravel, and sought to bring their dissonant colors and dreamlike atmospheres to the band.

In the fall of 1941, during a long Goodman engagement in New York, Sauter showcased Lee dramatically in Duke Ellington's "I Got It Bad (and That Ain't Good)." She, not Goodman, was the star of this side; breaking with big-band tradition, her chorus came first. Sauter's moody sonorities, combined with the heartbreak of the song, had their effect on her. As Lee begged God to make her man stop mistreating her, flickers of pain shot through the poised, glassy surface of her singing. Mel Powell pushed her furthur into the spotlight with an arrangement of Cole Porter's risqué come-on, "Let's Do It (Let's Fall in Love)." Lee sang the politically incorrect words—"Chinks do it / Japs do it / Up in Lapland little Laps do it"—with the blunt phrasing of a gum-chewing floozy on a barstool; she had copied it from Laura Rucker. Her improvisations on the tune could have come out of Goodman's horn.

"I Got It Bad" rose to number twenty-five on the charts—Lee's first hit. In *Down Beat*, Dave Dexter, Jr., offered a mea culpa: "It's with a double-swallow of guilt and with utter frankness that Miss Lee's attempts can now be described as really good—judging from her 'Let's Do It' and 'I Got It Bad,' she may shortly develop into Goodman's best canary of all time."

Lee passed one more test when the band played the Paramount, whose intimidating size—it held 3,664—made her gasp when she first walked in. In spaces that cavernous, singers tended to belt from the bottom of their lungs. But not Lee. On a few songs, Goodman featured her with just six of his sidemen, a configuration he called the Benny Goodman Sextet. In Rodgers and Hart's "Where or When," Lee sang of romantic déjà vu as a celeste twinkled like a child's music box. Ignoring the multitudes out front, Lee held her delivery at a near-whisper. "She sings with feeling in a pleasantly sleepy sort of way," wrote a reviewer. *Metronome*'s George T. Simon, who had recently called her cold, marveled at how Lee had grown. She "hushed the house completely," he wrote.

The more attention she got, the more Goodman cut her down. "He had a profound effect on her life by giving her that opportunity, but he also made her pay dearly for it," said Brian Panella, who became her manager in the late 1960s. Lee could end a song to a roar of approval, and Goodman would merely glare, making her wonder what she had done wrong. During one rehearsal, he held his clarinet to her ear and shrieked out a measure he didn't feel she had sung properly. When Goodman muttered a vague criticism of her phrasing, Lee hadn't a clue what he meant. Later, she asked one of his graduates, trumpeter-bandleader Harry James, to translate. James advised her to change nothing—but to tell Goodman she understood him completely, and from then on would sing exactly as he wanted. Lee followed his advice. The next time Goodman heard her, he grinned in her direction.

———

LIFE FOR THE CREW remained a treadmill of bus trips, rehearsals, record dates, and shows; no one had much time to contemplate the worldly dangers that crept ever closer. War had broken out in Asia and Europe; it seemed just a matter of time before North America would be dragged in. On December 7, the Imperial Japanese Navy shocked the world by bombing Pearl Harbor, the U.S. naval base in Hawaii. The attack left 2,402 Americans dead, 1,282 wounded.

A day later, the United States declared war on Japan. And on December 18, just as Columbia Records was pressing copies of Peggy Lee's latest Goodman showcase, a show tune called "Not a Care in the World," World War II officially began.

For Goodman and other leaders, the post-Depression frivolity ceased; now their main job would be to lift wartime morale. Finding good sidemen would soon become a chore, for the draft would rob every leader of invaluable players. Many maestros themselves were drafted. But Goodman suffered from painful sciatica, and the draft board classified him physically unfit for service. Even so, he panicked, for the war was chipping away at the artistic perfection he had fought so hard to achieve.

With men at their most vulnerable, girl singers acquired a new-found power. Nobody would draft them; and overseas, the sound of a warm, sexy female voice, broadcast on the Armed Forces Radio Service, soothed many a lonesome soldier. In the winter of 1942, Columbia released Goodman's months-old recording of a lightweight ballad of lost love, "Somebody Else Is Taking My Place." With the war at full tilt, nobody needed a sad song; Lee stayed cheerful as she chirped, "my heart is aching, soon will be breaking" in swing tempo. Both she and Goodman were stunned when the disc hit number one.

Lee's girlhood ambition had come true; now she was a star. But she couldn't help but feel like an imposter. "You know, I'm not really Peggy Lee of Benny Goodman's band," she told the *New York Post*. "I'm really just Norma Egstrom of Fargo, North Dakota." Jane Larrabee, with whom she roomed in Greenwich Village while the band played New York, could see that success had not taken the prairie out of Peggy Lee. "Instead of buying six potatoes, she'd buy a twenty-five-pound bag. And she'd make bread and put the dough to set in a warm closet—and run down to Washington, D.C., to see a boyfriend."

Lee and her Greenwich Village roommate, singer Jane Larrabee (aka Jane Leslie), in 1943. (COURTESY OF LORRAINE FEATHER)

Lee, of course, was a much more conflicted personality than the innocent some people saw. She craved a career, while pining for a strong man to take care of her. Meanwhile, she thrived on drama. It was no surprise when rumors sprang up about her relationship with the man who confounded and intimidated her, yet to whom she was professionally bound. The *Valley City Times-Record* posed a juicy question: "Are wedding bells soon to ring for Peggy Lee, the former Norma Egstrom of Wimbledon and present songstress with Benny Goodman in New York City?" When the squib ran on February 27, 1942, Goodman and Lady Duckworth were soon to marry, so he would not have been available for anything more than a fling. Lee herself was dating a string of swains: George T. Simon; personal manager Peter Dean, uncle of the yet-to-be-born singer-songwriter Carly Simon; and two World War II flyers, one of whom, according to Lee, shot himself in the head after they met.

She and Goodman occasionally hit the town after work, and musicians gossiped about the assumed liaison for years. If it happened, the affair would have been halted not only by Goodman's marriage but also by the appearance of "the man of my life," as Lee termed her new paramour. Years later she scrawled in some autobiographical notes: "Met David—love at first sight."

In June of 1942, Goodman had hired a new guitarist, David Michael Matthew Barbour, better known as Dave Barbour. A thirty-year-old Italian from Queens, New York, Barbour had played with Artie Shaw, Maxine Sullivan, Teddy Wilson, and Mildred Bailey. But what Goodman liked the most about him was that he sounded much like Charlie Christian, a former star of the band. The black, Texas-born electric guitarist had performed with Goodman for nearly two years, and later died of tuberculosis. Christian's single-note lines kept the orchestra swinging, and his harmonic wizardry looked ahead to the era of bebop, which was three years away. "He played like a horn," said Steve Blum, Lee's guitarist in the sixties.

Christian had quit Goodman in 1941. The next year, when he took ill, the clarinetist ignored him completely. Now he had hired Barbour to bring back Christian's sound. To his close friend, pianist Hal Schaefer, Barbour was "a very good guitar player, not one of the best. But he was good enough for Benny Goodman."

And for Peggy Lee. "There was a depth of feeling in his playing, a sadness that always draws me," she recalled. "I always had the feeling that wherever he went I should run after him and tell him it was OK. I don't know if he really felt that way or not."

In fact, Barbour seemed perpetually cheerful and easygoing. But he had a problem. In 1941, the composer Alec Wilder attended a rehearsal at the Greenwich Village apartment of Mildred Bailey. Barbour arrived so drunk that everyone wondered how he could play. "He managed to get the guitar up in his arms somehow and get his fingers up on the frets," recalled Wilder. "He was in terrible shape, but so cute about it that Mildred didn't get mad at him."

Almost no one did, because Barbour was lovable, especially to Lee. With his dark, wavy, slicked-back hair, rugged features, and masculine air, he was attractive, though not unusually handsome. And he had a touch of mystery. "There was a presence about the man," observed Lee's later pianist, Gene DiNovi. "He was very quiet." When Lee looked at the guitar-plucking charmer, she saw the father-protector she had grown up longing for, and a man who played the blues as soulfully as she felt them. To her he was nothing less than a Prince Charming of jazz—but it was she who played the aggressor. She "watched his every move," Lee admitted later. "You know, I had to chase him for a year! He is the type who wouldn't admit he was attracted to me, but at night after the shows he was always there to drive me home. We never had any dates and he always acted very disinterested. He was extremely serious about music and marriage and just a touch cynical."

His indifference made her all the more determined to snare him. Finally Barbour succumbed. At first they kept their affair a secret for fear of inflaming Goodman, who forbade his sidemen from fraternizing with the girl singer. But the love songs she sang in that period—"The Way You Look Tonight," "All I Need Is You," "You're Easy to Dance With"—now had someone dreamy to inspire them, even if Barbour was treating the relationship as a lark.

It was an odd time for Lee to become obsessed with one of the bitterest outcries to have appeared in the previous year's R&B jukeboxes. But in her dressing room at a Chicago theater, she couldn't stop playing a 78-rpm disc about a woman who was sick of playing the victim. Each time the worn, crackly platter came to an end, Lee lifted up the needle on her windup phonograph and started the record again. She heard a black woman slowly, defiantly tearing into her no-account lover for blowing his money and leaving her bereft: "I fell for your jivin' and I took you in / Now all you got to offer me's a drink of gin." Twenty-one-year-old Lil Green didn't have the walloping belt of the Empress of the Blues, Bessie Smith, but her soft, drawling voice still held the punch of an iron fist. Through minimal emoting, she conveyed all the stinging disapproval and eye-rolling sarcasm the song needed. Green sang "Why Don't You Do Right?" with just piano and guitar; its intimacy conjured up a tenement bedroom and a woman who had downed plenty of belts before putting her spineless man in his place.

The writer, Kansas Joe McCoy, had sung with the Harlem Hamfats, an R&B group who crooned of reefer, booze, and sex. "Why Don't You Do Right?" was a cleaned-up version of the Hamfats' "Weed Smoker's Dream," which sounded like a pimp's sales pitch to a potential whore: "Sittin' on a million, sittin' on it every day / Can't make no money givin' your stuff away."

Lil Green couldn't have sung that, but the rewrite tickled her. An orphan from the Mississippi Delta, Green had grown up with foster parents in Chicago, then sung her way to local fame in clubs on the city's South Side. She also wrote a lot of her own songs—common among blues singers but still rare in the pop world.

Green had gone farther than most of her peers; she recorded for Bluebird, which released Glenn Miller's discs. "Why Don't You Do Right?" charted in a segregated category called "Race Records," where all but the most commercial black artists such as Count Basie and Duke Ellington were placed. The Race section housed many embattled black women who cried for attention, lashing out at the men who had wronged them. Far from making them sound weak, the blues empowered them; through it they could demand what *they* wanted, especially in the bedroom. "Ooh-WEE! Good to the last drop!" purred Green in her lascivious "Love Me."

Bronchial pneumonia would kill her in 1954. But she had gained a small stake on immortality thanks to "Why Don't You Do Right?" On that record, Green's voice stirred up feelings that had gnawed at Lee since childhood—a rage to fight back, a reclaiming of the power that Min had stripped from her. So far, almost everything Lee had recorded sounded neat, clean, and white; now she had found a song that connected with her darker side.

For hours on end, Goodman heard "Why Don't You Do Right?" seeping out from beneath the door of Lee's adjacent dressing room—"until he couldn't stand it anymore," recalled Lee. "After a week, Benny finally noticed and made some profound remark like, 'I guess you like that.'" Yes, Lee answered, she did. Goodman made a vague offer to have the song arranged for her. She perked up. For the next several weeks, she felt emboldened enough to pester him.

Finally Goodman asked Mel Powell to write a chart. Lee wanted to sing "Why Don't You Do Right?" with Green's slow-burning intensity, "but Benny wanted it faster," she rued. "He liked everything faster."

Lee begged him to let her record the song. He kept putting her off. This game was nothing new; that year, when Lee had given him her first published work as a lyricist, "Little Fool," Goodman had let her sing it with the band, then broken her heart by omitting it from his many recording sessions. Finally, by accident, Lee got her chance with "Why Don't You Do Right?" The musicians' union was set to go on strike against the record industry in a fight to secure royalties for airplay. Until the issue was resolved sixteen months later, the union barred members from recording. Panic-stricken labels scrambled to amass product. "Benny ran out of things to record," explained Lee, "so he recorded 'Why Don't You Do Right?'"

On July 27, 1942, five days before the ban started, she and the Goodman men waxed the song in New York. Powell's arrangement was big and bombastic. But it swung, and in its toughness it shook off any traces of Lee's meek air. Pitted against icy stabs of brass, she sounded hard, bluesy, and sarcastic, with a sting of anger as she faced down the man who had failed her. "Why don't you do *ri*-ight?" became an in-your-face threat.

Producer Morty Palitz, who headed Columbia's jazz department, was startled by what he heard. Lee had united white and black music more authentically than almost any band singer; even she was thrilled with how she sounded. Looking back, though, she wasn't surprised. "I'm not really a *white* singer," she told writer Shaun Considine in 1974. "I sing black. I always have."

But while subsequent Goodman singles hit the market within weeks, "Why Don't You Do Right?" stayed on the shelf. Having given her the gift she wanted most, Goodman had seemingly taken it back. Certainly he had the clout to demand the disc's release, but he didn't. Lee felt broken-hearted and angry. She was sure he didn't like the record, or maybe was punishing her for some unnamed sin.

By December, Columbia had exhausted most of its Goodman back-log; at last, "Why Don't You Do Right?" was released. On January 2, the song premiered on the *Billboard* pop chart. Later that month, it peaked at number four. For the first of several times in her recording career, Lee had found a song she loved, encountered resistance, fought it, and won.

That winter she basked in glory. *Metronome* called Lee's vocal a "big surprise," adding in its hard-nosed music-biz slang, "The lass really chews it right off." *Look* magazine displayed Lee in a full-page photo. The text declared: "You can hear her electric-blue voice from every juke box in America . . . And, only a few years ago she was just a corn-fed waitress in Fargo." Lee even became the subject of a cutout book for little girls, who snipped out drawings of glamorous gowns and pasted them onto paper figures of Benny Goodman's blond goddess.

Hollywood—Lee's girlhood dream town—now beckoned. With "Why Don't You Do Right?" still on the charts, United Artists Pictures released *The Powers Girl*, in which she made her film debut. A wartime trifle about a girl who yearns to make it big with a famed modeling agency, *The Powers Girl* features a cast of second-rung stars of the 1940s (Carole Landis, Priscilla Lane, George Murphy). The film is mainly a showcase for the Goodman band, which appears in several dance-hall sequences. In a less-than-two-minute cameo, Lee sings a fluff novelty, "The Lady Who Didn't Believe in Love."

She certainly believed in it off-camera, though. Jane Larrabee had vacated their rented flat in Greenwich Village, and Lee got to spend her New York nights there with Dave Barbour. At the start of 1943, her fame took one more leap when she appeared with the Goodman band in *Stage Door Canteen*, an all-star wartime extravaganza for RKO Pictures. It recreated the recreation halls in which stars entertained and hobnobbed with homesick soldiers. Lee shared the screen with dozens of stars, including

Tallulah Bankhead, Jack Benny, Katharine Hepburn, Helen Hayes, Ethel Merman, and George Raft. Her moment onscreen was again short—a truncated version of "Why Don't You Do Right?" Nervous and too eager to please, she smiled her way through the bitter song, arms glued to her sides. "I didn't know they were filming," she claimed later. "I thought it was a rehearsal. As a matter of fact I stepped on one of the extra's feet."

In February 1943, some startling news spelled a halt to her ascent; she was pregnant.

Lee confided later in the young singer Margaret Whiting about that bombshell moment. "She was elated," said Whiting. "And she was terrified. This was the forties. She wasn't married. And she knew Benny would be furious." But it didn't matter. To Lee, the pregnancy was a gift from God—proof that she had found true love in the arms of Dave Barbour. "Nothing, not the hit records, not the cheering fans, not the new stardom I'd achieved, nothing was as important to me as David and what *we* had together," she wrote in her memoir.

Dave was less enthusiastic. Whether he had planned to do so or not, he saw only one choice, and proposed marriage. He suggested they both leave Goodman and set up house in Hollywood.

After they had finished *Stage Door Canteen,* Lee broke the news to Goodman. He was furious—but professional worry was the main cause. Goodman remained the King of Swing, but critics had begun pricking holes in his golden armor. He was still smarting from a pan by *Metronome's* Barry Ulanov. "Never before, in this reviewer's experience, has Benny's band sounded so bad. In four numbers not one shred of distinction was uncovered, while every kind of humiliation and mistake and lapse was displayed. . . . This reviewer hopes he never again has to go through the humiliating experience of hearing such a performance from the great man."

Such jabs made Goodman more neurotic than ever. He went on a firing binge and dropped several sidemen; others, including Mel Powell, lost patience with his behavior and quit. Eddie Sauter left to recover from tuberculosis. Now Goodman was losing his star singer.

The thought of escaping him gave Lee enormous relief. More important, every romantic ballad she had sung since her teens had come true.

On March 8, 1943, the couple had a shotgun wedding at Los Angeles City Hall. Lee's sister Marianne was her maid of honor; Goodman saxophonist Joe Rushton served as best man. *Billboard* inadvertently leaked the truth—"Miss Lee was forced to leave the Goodman organization because of approaching motherhood"—but no one, at least not in print, noted that her pregnancy had preceded the marriage. Goodman gave them a gift that made their eyes roll: an ashtray.

In years to come, some of Lee's accompanists traded a rumor that Goodman was the true father of her child; a few swore that Benny and Nicki looked alike. Early on in their association, Lee *had* been hitting the town with Goodman. But given her longtime allergy to her prickly boss, the paternity theory seemed far-fetched. And now, Goodman's only concern was to replace her. A parade of songbirds passed through the band; none of them pleased him. Because Lee's contract hadn't ended, he made her come back whenever he needed her.

For Goodman, a sour glimpse into the future appeared in *Billboard*'s Sixth Annual College Poll, published on June 5, 1943. Lee scored more votes than he did; among female band singers, only Helen Forrest and Helen O'Connell outranked her. Frank Sinatra topped the male singers' poll, but he, too, had left his employer, Tommy Dorsey, and was zooming toward a zenith of stardom that eclipsed every bandleader's. Most of them had showcased their singers lavishly—and in so doing, had inadvertently groomed them to steal the spotlight.

By the time World War II had ended on September 2, 1945, the swing craze had faded. Reunited lovebirds wanted to hear their ardor expressed in words, not in the frantic instrumental sounds of Glenn Miller's "In the Mood" or Goodman's "Sing, Sing, Sing." In any case, most leaders were buckling under the cost of carting an orchestra around the country. By the late forties, Count Basie was presiding over groups of six or seven; Goodman and the majority of his fellow leaders had disbanded.

For the rest of her life, Lee weighed her public words about him carefully. Goodman, she said, had taught her the value of rehearsal and of painstaking discipline. But to friends like Dona Harsh, Lee admitted "what a horror Benny was to work for." In 1951, the two of them reunited on a Los Angeles TV show, *Kreisler Bandstand*. The once-trembling singer bounded out, full of fire, to sing "Why Don't You Do Right?" The King of Swing had become nostalgia, as he well knew. He reminisced sadly to a reporter: "Only yesterday, jitterbugs were dancing in the aisle of the Paramount to my band."

In 1973, when the TV series *This Is Your Life* honored her, Goodman appeared on video with a breezy salute. "You know," he declared, "I remember so clearly the night that Alice and I went down to hear you at the Buttery in Chicago. I was so impressed that I hired you on the spot." As he showered her with the praise that he had doled out so stingily before, Lee glared, let out a chortle, then lowered her eyes.

"I'm retired," said Lee to a record producer. "I don't care to sing anymore." That didn't last. (PHOTO BY GENE HOWARD)

Chapter Four

*T*HE BARBOURS RENTED a love nest at 4239½ Monroe Street—"a little ole beat-up apartment," Lee called it, on a side street in a dingy Hollywood neighborhood. It cost thirty-five dollars a month, an average rent for the mid-forties, yet the couple could barely afford it. "Those were our really lean days," said Lee. Barbour awaited his L.A. musicians' union card, the license to work legitimate jobs; for now he played in bars for a few dollars a night. But Lee was so much in love with him, and so excited about her impending motherhood, that anything short of starvation seemed romantic to her. For the rest of her life, Lee would remember this time as the happiest she had ever known.

But as her pregnancy wore on, ill health plagued her. She developed preeclamptic toxemia, a condition marked by high blood pressure and swelling of the feet and ankles. On November 10, 1943, labor pains set in, and Barbour drove her to Hollywood Presbyterian Hospital. Her birth canal proved too narrow for natural childbirth, so in the early-morning hours of November 11, Lee delivered a girl by Caesarian section. She and Dave named her Nicki Lee, after Barbour's father, Nicholas.

Soon after the birth, pneumonia, uremic poisoning, and dangerously high blood pressure threatened Lee's life. But in two weeks, the new mother was healthy again and ensconced in her humble apartment, where she breast-fed Nicki or beamed down at the chubby little girl in her crib.

For now, Barbour wasn't much of a provider. Even after he had received his union card, he barely earned enough to support his small family. His prewar, two-seater Ford was falling apart. Often he went to bed drunk. But nothing could puncture Lee's bubble of domestic bliss. Friends who visited echoed a reporter's idyllic assessment of the scene:

"It's the kind of marriage you read about in storybooks, but rarely see." Margaret Whiting, whose 1942 hit, "My Ideal," had made her a teen-age star, dropped by often. "They were very simple kids," she recalled. "Peggy was a darling girl, loved her baby, *adored* David. He was a beauti-ful, soulful man. I remember her cooking a lot and taking care of Nicki. Complete opposite of what she became." When the Clark Sisters (by now the Sentimentalists) came to town, Lee invited all four to dinner. "She was just a housefrau then," said Peggy Clark. "Dave was a neat guy, real friendly. You couldn't not like him." While Lee did housework, Barbour painted pictures for fun; he taught his wife to do the same, thus starting her on a lifelong avocation as a painter. Better still, he was trying to cut back on his drinking.

Whenever they could afford it, Dave and his "Pegalah" hired a baby-sitter and hit the town to hear music. But for now, motherhood and new-lywed life seemed to fulfill her completely; singing stayed far from her mind. "It was strange to see Peggy changing the baby with one hand and refusing fabulous offers over a telephone held in the other," said her sister Della to a journalist.

One of those offers came from a new label that had squeezed inside the near-monopoly that Victor, Decca, and Columbia had on the record industry. Capitol was the idealistic brainchild of two songwriters with money to burn, and a music-store owner who had tired of just peddling other people's 78s. In 1942, when the three united, Buddy DeSylva was an executive producer at Paramount Pictures and a former member of DeSylva, (Ray) Brown, and (Lew) Henderson, the trio who had penned a host of wildly popular tunes, including "The Best Things in Life Are Free" and "You're the Cream in My Coffee."

DeSylva had recently hired Johnny Mercer to cowrite the score for a war-themed movie musical, *The Fleet's In*. Five more hits, including "Tangerine" and "I Remember You," tumbled from the mind of one of America's most bankable tunesmiths. A genial, portly Southerner from Savannah, Mercer had the nondescript air of a small-town banker. Mer-cer had a knack for turning the common man's vernacular into lyrics that millions of Americans couldn't get out of their heads—meticulous yet seemingly off-the-cuff, playful but full of heart. At the start of 1942, Mer-cer and his composing partner Harold Arlen had reached the top perch of the *Billboard* pop chart with "Blues in the Night," a panoramic tale of American manhood's most formidable foe: "A woman's a two-face/A worrisome thing who'll leave you to sing the blues in the night."

Mercer's favorite hangout was Music City, a bustling record, sheet-music, and radio shop on Sunset Boulevard in Hollywood. In the back office, liquor flowed as he spent hours dissecting the business with Glenn Wallichs, a radio repairman who had founded the store with his father and brother. He and Mercer decided that they could run a better label than anybody's—one that would make ample room for the black music that Mercer loved.

Mercer and DeSylva pooled some seed money; Wallichs took on the job of treasurer and creative advisor. Their little start-up had a mom-and-pop-store quaintness. It made its first office above a tailoring shop on Vine, and rented outside recording studios and pressing plants. In June 1942, the company made what should have been a prestigious debut with a new single by Paul Whiteman, the venerable though faded "King of Jazz." It bombed. Soon thereafter, the partners learned that shellac, the material used to press those fragile 78-rpm platters, was growing scarce due to wartime rationing. Worse still, the American Federation of Musicians was about to launch its strike against the record industry. The label seemed doomed.

Nonetheless, recalled Mercer, "we forged ahead with the undaunted enthusiasm of young men to whom nothing is impossible." Just before the AFM ban, the label released "Cow Cow Boogie," a loping cowboy tune crossed with boogie-woogie and sung by Ella Mae Morse, an unknown teenager from Texas. "Cow Cow Boogie" stunned everyone by reaching the top ten. Within a month, magic struck again, this time with a naughty-for-its-day Mercer novelty, "Strip Polka," sung by the lyricist himself. It reached number seven. Capitol was saved.

Mercer and his colleagues didn't forget their goal of diversity. They signed the King Cole Trio, whose leader, Nat King Cole, was an Alabama-born preacher's son. Billie Holiday and the Texas bluesman T-Bone Walker took their place among the white canaries Connie Haines, Martha Tilton, and Kitty Kallen, all of them newly sprung from the big bands. Margaret Whiting—daughter of the late Richard Whiting, a grand name of 1930s movie songwriting—became the label's princess.

Largely because a lyricist helmed it, Capitol was mainly a singer's house. The company's first jazz album, a four-disc set entitled *New American Jazz*, wouldn't have seemed complete without a vocalist. By December 1943, the recording ban was ending, and work on the project could start. Its producer was Dave Dexter, Jr., the former *Down Beat* critic and new Capitol staffer. Dexter was a smart-alecky white youngster with a swatch of wavy hair and enlightened racial ideas. To him, "new American jazz" was a biracial fraternity. Dexter's project aimed to advance a revolutionary notion: that desegregation was the American way.

He enlisted a black clarinetist (New Orleans–born Jimmie Noone, a Dixieland pioneer) and a white one (Barney Bigard, who had spent fifteen years with Duke Ellington); a black piano player from Kansas City (boogie-woogie master Pete Johnson) and a white one from Chicago (Joe Sullivan, a pillar of the city's jazz in the 1920s). Trombone great Jack Teagarden was a white Texas boy whose blues feeling enchanted Louis Armstrong.

Having branded the young Peggy Lee "no bargain" in *Down Beat*, Dexter now felt she belonged in this aristocracy. Just after New Year's Day, he phoned her and asked her participation. Lee had not forgotten his painful snub, and her response was tinged with smug revenge. "I'm retired, Dave," she said. "I don't care to sing anymore."

Dexter tried again later, and found that Lee had had a change of heart. "What does the job pay?" she asked. Dexter offered a hundred dollars for two songs. She admitted that she and Dave were hurting for cash. "If you can get me in and out of the studio in a couple of hours, I'll be there," she said.

On January 7, Barbour drove her to the C. P. MacGregor recording studio in Hollywood. Two months after Nicki's birth, the singer was still plump but "smartly dressed," said Dexter, and clearly happy to be there. He gave Lee her songs on the spot. "Ain't Goin' No Place" was a simple twelve-bar blues about a woman who was "hopin', prayin', waitin' for my no-good man to show." The musicians ad-libbed an arrangement in raunchy bordello style, with Shorty Sherock's growling trumpet.

Everyone was surprised at the sounds that came out of the fair-skinned white housewife. The glassy, vibratoless tone and demure remove of her Goodman days had vanished; now she had a huskier sound and, away from Goodman's withering glance, a newfound confidence. Dexter recalled a bandmember's comment: "This chick sounds like a drunken old whore with the hots." Lee surprised them again in a downtrodden torch song, "That Old Feeling." Here she sang like a lovelorn teenager, shattered at having seen her former beau dancing in another woman's arms. "I saw you last night and got that old *feeling*," sighed Lee, making that pivotal word sound like a swoon.

Lee knew she had done well. Most of the airplay for *New American Jazz* went to Lee's sides. Hearing herself on the radio repeatedly, she got even more excited; so did Capitol's executives, who tried to talk her into a full-fledged comeback.

But she couldn't bring herself to plunge into one quite so soon. Baby Nicki needed her, and the notion of surrender to a manly man still appealed. For most of 1944, Lee avoided professional singing. But amid warming baby food on the stove, changing diapers, and chatting on the phone with friends from her big-band days, she thought increasingly about music. Lee had toyed with writing lyrics and poetry for years, and she knew she had a flair for it. One day while Barbour was out at a record date, she was "standing at the kitchen sink," she recalled, washing dishes "and thinking about how much I loved David." Afterward, she scratched out the naïve stanzas of "What More Can a Woman Do?," a portrait of wedded bliss. "If he told me that I should steal / I guess I would, the way I feel . . ." went the words. She showed it to Barbour, who worked out a simple tune on his guitar.

For a time, the finished song sat untouched. Meanwhile, memories of *New American Jazz* and what fun it was had stayed with her. Mercer had vowed to sign her; and that year, Lee accepted several invitations to drop by Capitol. On one of those outings, Lee watched a driver hit another man's car in a nearby parking lot. Someone yelled to the latter that he'd been hit; he stuck his head out the window and said, "You was right, baby!" At home, Lee turned that phrase into an "I done him wrong" lyric in which a woman, not her man, was the lying cheater who gets thrown out into the cold.

Meanwhile, "the best (and best-liked) personal manager in America," as singer Mel Tormé called him, was hot on her trail. Carlos Gastel was a hulking, black-haired, gin-guzzling Honduran who had forged a close relationship with Capitol. Many of the label's stars—including Nat King

Cole, Tormé, and bandleader Stan Kenton—were shepherded to stardom by Gastel's Hollywood office, General Artist Corporation. According to another of his clients, the jazz singer Anita O'Day, Gastel "was on an artistic rather than monetary kick. He'd hear a sound, fall in love with it and go after the artist."

Soon he was sitting in the Barbours' living room as Dave played guitar and Peggy performed "What More Can a Woman Do?" and "You Was Right, Baby." Gastel marveled at the fact that Lee wrote her own lyrics—an extreme rarity among pop singers of the day. And he knew that vocally, Lee sang like no one in the business, especially at Capitol. Margaret Whiting sang with a forthright clarity that composers loved, but she steered clear of the darker places. Ex–Tommy Dorsey vocalist Jo Stafford had a trombonelike tone along with flawless pitch and breath control, but not much warmth. Ella Mae Morse could swing the blues, but she was blunt and lusty, not subtle. Outside Capitol, sunny-voiced, singing girls-next-door proliferated; they reminded young American women to wait chastely until their men came back from war.

In that company, Lee had an enticing sense of the forbidden. Her vocal caresses evoked the bedroom, not the nursery or kitchen. Mystery lay in the silences between her phrases; her eyes shone with secrets.

It was Gastel's challenge to pry her out of retirement, but Lee's reluctance was fading fast. On Sunday afternoon, December 10, 1944, she took part in a jam session at the Philharmonic Auditorium in downtown Los Angeles. The cast included the 1920s cornetist Red Nichols and his band, the Five Pennies; guitarist Les Paul; and Joe Sullivan. Afterward, Lee agreed to talk business with Capitol.

Two days after Christmas, with the tree still up in her living room and presents for Nicki scattered on the floor, she showed up at a Hollywood recording studio for her first solo session. Barbour played guitar and led the band.

There was nothing white-bread about the fair Scandinavian singer's sound. Weeks later, a *Billboard* critic deemed "You Was Right, Baby" and its singer's "heated pipes" to be "geared mostly to the race locations." In Harlem, Steve's—which billed itself as the "Most Outstanding and Complete Race Record Shop"—advertised the disc alongside new singles by Duke Ellington, Count Basie, and Lil Green.

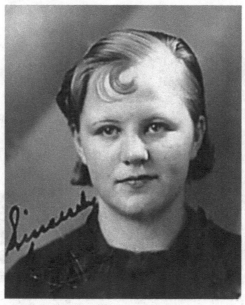

Prairie girl Norma Deloris Egstrom at
Wimbledon School, ND, 1936. (COURTESY OF
KATE STEVENSON)

To Norma, Minnie Schaumberg
Egstrom—her stepmother, Min—was
the fairy-tale embodiment of pure
evil. Millarton, ND, ca. 1952. (COUR-
TESY OF RICHARD MORRISON)

Fargo, ND, March 1938: Norma leaves for the
"promised land" of Los Angeles, California.
(COURTESY OF RICHARD MORRISON)

The recently renamed Peggy Lee and organist Lloyd Collins entertain at Fargo's hot spot, the Powers Coffee Shop, 1939. (COURTESY OF RICHARD MORRISON)

Lee's first glamour head shot, inscribed in 1941 to a member of The Four of Us, the quartet that backed her at a Chicago lounge. (COURTESY OF RICHARD MORRISON)

Cinderella at the ball: Peggy Lee as vocalist with the King of Swing, Benny Goodman, in 1942. (COURTESY OF RICHARD MORRISON)

A staged moment of serenity in the grueling life of a band singer, 1942. (COURTESY OF RICHARD MORRISON)

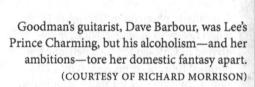

Goodman's guitarist, Dave Barbour, was Lee's Prince Charming, but his alcoholism—and her ambitions—tore her domestic fantasy apart. (COURTESY OF RICHARD MORRISON)

Carlos Gastel, a gin-guzzling Honduran, managed the cream of the Capitol Records stable in the 1940s. (*Left to right*) Gastel, Nat King Cole, June Christy, Mel Tormé, Lee, Stan Kenton. (PHOTO BY GENE ROLAND)

Lee (*right*) and her indispensable Girl Friday, Dona Harsh, ca. 1950, on Horseshoe Bay in Vancouver, BC—a rare outing for the star, who stayed in bed as often as possible. (COURTESY OF DONA HARSH HUTCHINSON)

A motherly photo op in December 1950, when Lee, with daughter, Nicki, in tow, arrived in Chicago to join a patriotic but doomed touring revue, *Red, White, and Blue*. (COURTESY OF RICHARD MORRISON)

Success had not brought much happiness to Lee, who in 1951 was bloated, drinking, and facing divorce. (COURTESY OF RICHARD MORRISON)

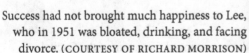

In the arms of married actor Robert Preston at Manhattan's Stork Club, July 14, 1951. (STORK CLUB WIRE SERVICE; COURTESY OF RICHARD MORRISON)

Newly signed to Warner Bros. in 1952, Lee dreamed of Hollywood stardom. (AUTHOR'S COLLECTION)

"I think I shouldn't go through with this," said Lee to bridesmaid Dona Harsh on January 4, 1953, when she married movie tough guy Brad Dexter. (*Left to right*) Lee's spiritual guru, Ernest Holmes; Harsh; Hazel (Mrs. Ernest) Holmes; Nicki Lee Barbour; Lee; Dexter; his mother and brother; unknown. (PHOTO BY GENE ROLAND; COURTESY OF DONA HARSH HUTCHINSON)

As Doris Day's replacement (and Danny Thomas's costar) in *The Jazz Singer* (1953), Lee made little impression. But in *Pete Kelly's Blues* (1955), her portrayal of Rose, an alcoholic gun moll and sometime singer, scored her an Oscar nomination. Director and star Jack Webb played bandleader Pete Kelly. (*Below, left to right*) Webb, Ray Sherman (mostly hidden), Herbert Ellis, Lee, George Van Eps, Matty Matlock, Wallace Ruth, Joe Graves. (ALL PHOTOS FROM THE AUTHOR'S COLLECTION)

Jack Webb guides a nervous Lee on the set of *Pete Kelly's Blues*. (COURTESY OF RICHARD MORRISON)

"We are Siamese, if you please": Lee gave voice to two mischievous cats (as well as a dog and a human) in Walt Disney's 1955 cartoon classic *Lady and the Tramp*. (AUTHOR'S COLLECTION)

Rehearsing at Ciro's, the Sunset Strip playground of the stars, 1960.
Musicians include drummer Bill Richmond and harpist Stella Castellucci.
(AUTHOR'S COLLECTION)

At the first annual Audience Awards, Lee was named most promising new
female personality in the movies—yet she never made another film.
(*Left to right*) Lee, Tab Hunter, Natalie Wood, Warner Bros. president
Jack Warner, Jennifer Jones. Beverly Hilton, Los Angeles, December 6, 1955.
(AUTHOR'S COLLECTION)

It caught the attention of Sarah Vaughan, the rising black jazz singer with a near-operatic instrument and a dazzling flair for bebop. "I like those nice breathy tones Peggy gets on her low notes," said Vaughan, who went on to record "What More Can a Woman Do?" Lee's version captivated Joe Williams, who went on to sing the blues with Count Basie and in an enduring solo career. Williams first heard the song in a black record store in Chicago, a fact that would have pleased Lee.

A housewife's life was no longer enough for her—especially now that her honeymoon paradise had started to cloud. Years later, some biographical jottings by Lee identified 1944 as the year when Dave "began to drink again."

For now she preferred to look the other way. As Nicki lay sleeping in her crib, Lee kept writing song lyrics. In July 1945, she and a quintet led by Barbour recorded "Waitin' for the Train to Come In." On the surface, it was a laid-back plea for the man she hoped would step off a locomotive and into her arms. But when Lee sang, "I'm waitin' for my life to begin / Waitin' for the train to come in," she touched on the monotony that had marked her first seventeen years, and may have hung over her as a housewife. A drummer simulated the dull clacking of train wheels; Lee, by accident, sounded bluesier than ever. She was tired and hoarse from a cold, and couldn't hold onto notes. Mercer told her to touch them lightly, then slide off them. That hint of a slur felt so right to her that she used it for the rest of her life.

Late in 1945, while Nicki was taking her first steps, "Waitin' for the Train to Come In" climbed to number four. Lee was back. Gastel and the Capitol brass knew they had a golden goose. With the holidays approaching, the Barbours performed their newest tune for Mercer. In "I Don't Know Enough About You" she adopted yet another face—that of a coy, baby-doll temptress—as she chided a man for playing hard-to-get: "Just when I think you're mine, you try a different line." She told a reporter that she was "thinking about how a fellow plays hard to get, the way David did. He's the only fellow I ever chased."

Mercer had helped her with her lyric-writing considerably, as he would in the future. "He made me go back and rework the whole thing," she recalled. "He said, 'Put this here, and this here, and switch this around . . .'"

The day after Christmas, Lee stood at a microphone in a West Hollywood studio and delivered her words in a breathy purr that presaged Marilyn Monroe. Her spoken tag proved the most memorable line: "I guess I'd better get out the encyclopedia and brush up on *schmerr* to *schmoo* . . . *hmmmmm?*" Lee's hairdresser, Faith Schmerr, had found her way into the song. The public, of course, hadn't a clue what the line meant. But it got a laugh.

"I Don't Know Enough About You" became her second top-ten solo hit.

Now that she had scored on record, Lee gave Carlos Gastel full license to book her for radio and shows. Watching her perform, Margaret Whiting saw a rainwater blonde who had found her bliss. Lee, she said, "was singing a song as if she loved every word, every note of it. She was a young woman who was coming into maturity and trying things, telling jokes and talking, having fun, free as a bird. The sophistication came later."

Offstage, she often seemed in a fog. An interviewer visited Lee in her dressing room before an appearance. In the course of their chat, he asked if she dreamed of singing in Europe. "No," said Lee. "I don't want to see anything that was touched by war. . . . Do you smell gas escaping?"

"No."

"I'm sure there's gas escaping."

He tried changing the subject: What was her favorite song? "Happiness Is Just a Thing Called Joe," she said. "It's about a man and I guess it says more than anything else about how women feel about men. You're sure you can't smell gas? Would you call someone and ask them to find out if there's gas escaping? Oh, good heavens! I've forgotten to find out the list of what I'm singing tonight and I have to go on now!"

Her ambitions, at least, were crystal-clear. "She always seemed a career girl, never a wife," observed Dave Dexter. On July 6, 1946, *Billboard* published the results of its eighth annual poll of college music fans. Lee ranked third in the female vocalist category, after Jo Stafford and Dinah Shore. Six days later, she returned to Capitol to record another of the twenty sides she made that year. In a new anthem she had written with Barbour, "It's a Good Day," Lee proclaimed the world a sunny place, vibrating with possibilities: "It's a good day for shining your shoes and it's a good day for losing the blues!"

"It's a Good Day" reached the top twenty. It was the anthem of a young woman who had reclaimed her raison d'être, yet it also captured a time of dizzying postwar optimism, when the country had triumphed over its enemies and the future seemed like a yellow-brick road to success. Employment rates and the economy had boomed; technology, medicine, and science were turning corners every month. War-torn couples had reunited, sending marriage and pregnancy rates skyrocketing. Nothing seemed more romantic than to settle down and start a family—the postwar recipe for eternal fulfillment.

The Barbours had wanted another child. According to an article printed at the time, Lee had written "It's a Good Day" after learning that she had just become pregnant. "I looked out the window and said to myself, 'It's a good day,'" she explained.

Lee wound up miscarrying—and a doctor gave her the sad news that she would never bear another child. But to most appearances, Lee was much more a star than a mother or a wife. According to her publicist at the time, Fran Jackson, the singer was "just tasting the wine of success" and "loving every moment of it, for everything was new to her. Being famous. The money pouring in. She was pixieish and kind of witty and amiable and having such a good time with her first mink coat and her first white convertible, a three-hole Buick, and she adored shopping and buying jewelry and furniture and clothes."

The label of "It's a Good Day" billed her accompaniment generously as Dave Barbour and His Orchestra. Barbour was no leader; he preferred to pluck his guitar and let others do the hard work. In this case it fell to Lee's new arranger, clarinetist Henry J. "Heinie" Beau. On the record, Barbour played a tricky instrumental refrain, written by Beau in the language of a revolutionary new sound called bebop.

But henceforth, he would be known first as Peggy Lee's husband, then as her conductor, and finally as a guitarist. Lee couldn't imagine he was any less happy than she.

For now her group needed a firm guiding hand, and Gastel found one. Hal Schaefer was a boy wonder who, at eighteen, had played piano for an esteemed saxophonist and bandleader, Benny Carter; soon he would launch a dozen-year stint as singing coach for some of Twentieth Century–Fox's brightest stars, including Marilyn Monroe. Schaefer had a shock of dark wavy hair and a broad, toothy grin, but he was a sophisticated accompanist; and as Lee sang, concentration shone on his face. Most vocalists, he observed, held the last note of every phrase in a formal, trained manner. But Lee rarely sang a line that she wouldn't have spoken the same way. In her case, silence meant as much as words. Schaefer punctuated her spaces discreetly, while still giving her a breezy lift. "Nobody could swing more than Peggy!" he said. "She would snap her fingers and it was already cooking."

Her ears astonished him. "She wasn't like me, who was raised in New York and went around to little jazz joints and heard a million people. For her it was instinctive. Her intonation was perfect. Her time was impeccable." Lee showed a "feeling for orchestration," he found, when she directed the drummer to use brushes instead of sticks, or asked the other players to pull back or to build.

Awards rained down on her. At the end of 1946, a readers' poll in *Down Beat* named her the best female singer not with a band. The woman who had turned down almost every offer in 1944 was eagerly saying yes to anything that sounded interesting. Apart from her growing output of commercial discs, Lee cut a mammoth seventy-two jam session tracks for Capitol's radio transcription service, which supplied music for broadcast. She acted and sang in *Midnight Serenade*, a short dramatic film for Paramount Pictures. Having once lain on the floor with her ear pressed to her family's Atwater Kent radio, Lee was now all over the dial; she guested frequently on the shows of Jimmy Durante, Frank Sinatra, and Bing Crosby, three of her superstar idols. But mainstream stardom hadn't diminished her appeal in the "race" market. A year earlier, a black musical variety show on NBC, *Jubilee*, had invited her on, reaffirming her belief that she was "not really a white singer."

"She felt she had a black soul," said Leata Galloway, an African-American backup singer who supplied backup vocals for Lee in the 1970s. "She connected to the pain that black people go through. The blues."

Proof of that came in 1946, when she lent her voice to an odd cartoon character—a harp that comes to life as a black chanteuse. *Jasper in a Jam* was one in a series of "Puppetoons"—animated shorts, made by filmmaker George Pal, in which clay figures were photographed in stop-motion, moving around in dollhouse settings. This short, set to the swing of bandleader Charlie Barnet, featured Puppetoon favorite Jasper, a black boy with oversize pink lips and huge pop eyes. Jasper embodied the racist depictions in countless cartoons of the day, from Warner Bros.'s *Coal Black and de Sebben Dwarfs* to Walt Disney's *Fantasia*. But Pal softened the clichés by giving Jasper a humanizing sweetness, and the Lee character brought it out further. In *Jasper in a Jam*, the little boy runs into an antique shop to escape a rainstorm. When a cuckoo clock strikes, musical instruments come to life and start to play. The singing harp—a busty, bronze nightclub vixen in a gold gown—belts a Louis Armstrong hit, "Old Man Mose," for a dazzled Jasper. Lee did nothing to "blacken" her delivery, yet it fit her character so closely that no reviewer questioned the casting. Black activist groups were incensed over Jasper, though, and he made his last appearance in this cartoon.

As she toured a circuit of grand movie houses that alternated film showings with live music, Lee left male critics as awestruck as she had Jasper. At the State Theater in Hartford, Connecticut, she reminded a local scribe of Mae West. It wasn't just her voluptuous figure and her near-platinum-dyed hair; to him, Lee possessed "that certain something . . . I wish there was another word for it than sex."

Lee's earnings had enabled the Barbours to move from their Monroe Street apartment to a small house on Blair Drive in the Hollywood Hills—not a glamorous abode, but a definite step up. Their lives had become a rush of deadlines to meet and planes to catch; songwriting for Dave now meant work more than fun. "He was not driven," recalled Nicki. "I don't think life in the limelight was for him at all."

Mundell Lowe observed the Barbours at work. The drawling Mississipi-born guitarist was a discovery of John Hammond, who had launched him on a career that teamed him with Charlie Parker, Billie Holiday, Charles Mingus, Sarah Vaughan, and eventually Peggy Lee. But few people knew Lowe in 1947, when he played in the cocktail lounge of the Warwick Hotel, where Lee often stayed. She and Barbour used its ballroom to rehearse, and Lowe enjoyed eavesdropping. He saw which partner held the reins. "Peggy was a very strong woman," said Lowe. "Dave was kind of mild and quiet. Things went the way she wanted them to."

Any complaints Dave may have had stayed between them, but his drinking—which had burgeoned into full-blown alcoholism—implied that he wasn't nearly as content to be Mr. Peggy Lee as he appeared. He swilled his preferred bourbon both at home and in clubs, where he closed out the night by sharing adjacent barstools with Carlos Gastel and Hal Schaefer.

Invariably, Barbour went to sleep drunk. He began to suffer a severe burning in his stomach. Lee hadn't a clue why he seemed so intent on destroying himself. She blamed Gastel for keeping him drunk, while begging Barbour to cut back. But he didn't in the slightest—nor did she reduce a performing schedule that was taking a toll on her husband's well-being.

On a night at home in early 1947, Barbour suddenly doubled over, delirious with pain. Lee rushed him to the hospital. At thirty-five, Barbour had hemorrhaging ulcers, kidney damage, and acute nephritis. As he lay in the hospital awaiting emergency surgery, his health kept imploding; Barbour went into convulsions, and for a time couldn't see. The fantasy that Lee had spun around him teetered in the balance, and she was hysterical with fear. But even as he faced potential death, his sense of humor didn't fail him. As assistants wheeled him toward the operating room, Lee walked alongside the gurney, sobbing uncontrollably and blubbering, "I love you, I love you!" From under a sheet, Barbour quipped, "Stop nagging me!"

A surgeon cut away a portion of his stomach. Barbour survived, but stayed in critical condition for days. Lee drew comfort from her girlhood idol Bing Crosby, who had hosted her numerous times on his radio show and in turn become her friend. Crosby called her each morning to check that Barbour had made it through the night. He offered money, blood, even his babysitting services.

But Lee was inconsolable. Death had haunted her childhood; now here it was again, hovering over the man she loved. A neighbor urged her to read the sermons of Dr. Ernest Holmes, minister of the Science of Mind philosophy—a nonsectarian, metaphysical movement he had founded in 1927. Holmes's religion combined Eastern sacred wisdom, positive thinking, and a tinge of Hollywood glamour; Cecil B. DeMille and Cary Grant swore by his teachings. Holmes was a small man with snow-white hair and a sagely calm about him. In his handbook, *What We Believe*, he wrote: "We believe . . . that all people are incarnations of the One Spirit . . . that the Kingdom of Heaven is within us . . . that anyone may become a revealer of Truth who lives in close contact with the indwelling God." The soul, he declared, was immortal; and as for the body, any adverse conditions, including sickness, could be healed through the power of the mind.

For Lee, who already lived by the force of her imagination, Holmes's edicts seemed heaven-sent, the confirmation of all she wished to believe. According to a 1955 profile in *Redbook*, Lee sought him out "for spiritual reassurance," then rushed back to the hospital. There she received the shattering news that Barbour had died. "I refused to believe it. A path stretched before me down the hospital hall—like a great shaft of light. I walked it in faith." It led her to his room. By the time she arrived, his heart had resumed beating.

With that, she adopted Holmes as her surrogate father. "She *loved* Papa, as she called him," said her future assistant, Dona Harsh. "That religion took over her life. Peggy thought it brought her comfort."

Within weeks, Barbour was home, but confined to bed. As soon as he could manage it, the couple took a two-and-a-half-hour drive to the coast of Mexico, where they camped out in the beach town of Ensenada. The warm, dry climate would do Barbour good. Lee was anxious for him to mend, and not just because she loved him; on April 15 she was set to open at a new Hollywood nightclub, Bocage, with his quartet. Though still frail, he made it.

For the rest of the year, she didn't leave him much time to rest—especially when she learned that one more recording ban would stymie the industry on January 1, 1948. Labels rushed their artists into the studio to stockpile product. In November and December, Peggy Lee recorded thirty-two sides—flimsy novelties that had lain around on company desks, dashed-off originals that she and Barbour had written, an updated "Why Don't You Do Right?"

Knowing that Capitol was desperate for product, Lee slipped in a couple of unknown art songs that had caught her fancy. "Don't Smoke in Bed" was a chilling domestic drama by Willard Robison, a forgotten tunesmith from the infancy of jazz. "While We're Young," by the obscure, elitist composer Alec Wilder, reflected on the cruel race of time. Both Wilder and Robison were troubled men; and as a young woman who had grown up feeling unwanted, Lee responded instinctively to their songs, although she couldn't quite explain why. "They're sort of like poems, little character sketches," she told *Metronome*'s George T. Simon.

Lee had met Wilder through Benny Goodman. Thirteen years her senior, he became a stern but loving father figure who unflinchingly told her the truth when even her closest friends wouldn't dare. Wilder was the chain-smoking, intellectual black-sheep son of a wealthy banking family in upstate New York. A graduate of the Eastman School of Music in nearby Rochester, he wrote arty café ballads that the record industry usually snubbed, operas and classical works that went largely ignored. Wilder had found commercial success once, with the Mills Brothers's hit version of his song "I'll Be Around." Otherwise, despite the support of Frank Sinatra—who went so far as to conduct some of Wilder's classical works on a Columbia album—Wilder deemed himself "the eternal loser." He certainly looked the part, with his rumpled tweed suits, food-stained ties, and a beaten-down expression on his craggy face. He sneered at commercial success, but seemed agonized by the lack of it.

Cranky and judgmental as that made him, he believed passionately in maintaining the highest possible artistic standards. Lee thought him a "lovable eccentric"; he, in turn, took a near-obsessive interest in the singer, whose complex psychology held endless fascination for him. Some in her inner circle felt sure he was in love with her, but Wilder's sexuality was unclear, and he never married. Still, he cherished Lee's friendship and the "sweet sadness" in her.

She was the first to record "While We're Young," his acknowledged masterpiece, written with Morty Palitz (who had produced the Goodman version of "Why Don't You Do Right?") and lyricist William Engvick. Hal Schaefer taught her the lilting but rangy waltz, and she recorded it with just him and Barbour, who played the music as formally as if it were Schubert. Singing about the preciousness of youth—"none can refuse, time flies so fast / Too dear to lose and too sweet to last"—Lee lingered over each phrase as though determined to slow the clock.

But the disc proved too esoteric to sell, and when Wilder heard it he was incensed. Schaefer had taught Lee an incorrect note, and she had flubbed a word. The fussy composer "really gave her hell about it," said Engvick; Lee, in turn, lashed out at Schaefer for his mistake. Subsequently Wilder hurt her feelings by ignoring the fact that she had introduced "While We're Young" to the public, if a small one. More painful still was an oft-repeated story about a letter he bragged of having written her: "Dear Peggy, when you get to the bridge, jump off." But Lee couldn't stay mad at him, and when she recorded another of his wistful ballads, "Goodbye John," his caustic mood swung the other way. In a letter to Lee, Wilder wrote: "How absolutely dear and loving that record was! Every word you uttered I believed and every note you sang was definitive."

If Wilder never remotely became a household name, Willard Robison at least had a halcyon past. Born in Missouri, Robison was a once-thriving stride pianist and bandleader who, in the twenties, had employed Bix Beiderbecke, the fabled jazz cornetist who had drunk himself to death by the age of twenty-eight. Robison recorded dozens of his own songs; they spoke fondly of the Midwest that Lee knew well—a land of tumble-down shacks, small-town train depots, and backwoods oddballs.

But Hoagy Carmichael had covered much of the same ground; and while Carmichael's "Star Dust" had made him a superstar, Robison never had a comparable hit. By the 1940s he was living in New York amid boxes of yellowed music; the proceeds from his two most popular songs, "A Cottage for Sale" and "Old Folks," helped keep him alive, although he drank to excess. "He was extremely weird," said Dona Harsh. "I remember him telling Peggy, 'I was coming to see you in California. And I got off the train in North Dakota. I went to Jamestown, where you were born, and I just sat on a curb and thought about you. And then I went home.'"

Lee so loved the heartbreaking "A Cottage for Sale" that she chose it for one of her first Capitol sessions. Now she was obsessed with Robison's bleakest song. It was the first-person confession of a woman who leaves a predawn note for her husband—"Good-bye, old sleepyhead / I'm packing you in, like I said"—along with her wedding ring; then she flees. Her letter explains nothing, but ends with some advice: "Remember, darling—don't smoke in bed."

Often in her career, Lee had to fight to record daring songs she believed in. Capitol producer Lee Gillette argued that "Don't Smoke in Bed" was sure to bomb. The singer bargained with him. She would record a trite potential hit he had picked if he would let her do "Don't Smoke in Bed." Gillette agreed.

In later years, out of ego, self-delusion, or both, Lee claimed doggedly that she had written certain music credited to her collaborators. After Robison's death in 1968, she insisted that the composer had come to her with a line or two of a song that he was too drunk to complete—and that she and Barbour wound up writing nearly all of "Don't Smoke in Bed." But Hal Schaefer, who had rehearsed the song with her from the start, then played it on her Capitol single, swore the allegation wasn't true. "She and Dave may have contributed something," he said, "but they never mentioned it to me."

As they pored over the ballad at her home piano, however, Lee told Schaefer she was determined to "own it." For a woman in denial over the truths of her married life, "Don't Smoke in Bed" was a peek over a dark precipice. Before recording it, Lee sang the song over and over in clubs, accompanied only by Schaefer. She phrased and rephrased lines, stressing one word then another, determined to make it all ring true.

The record marked a dramatic breakthrough for Lee. A breezy, purring songbird with a hint of the blues had now entered the shadowy underside of "It's a Good Day." In three minutes and ten seconds, Lee conjured up all the intrigue of a film noir—those dimly lit, postwar crime dramas that exposed the threats and sexual tension that smoldered within a supposedly picture-perfect, triumphant America.

Arranger Harold Mooney lent irony to that tortured tale by placing it in a stark classical setting—an icy string quartet, an English horn wailing mournfully, a piano whose florid runs and arpeggios seemed disconnected from the plight of a woman who had just made the toughest choice of her life. As she sings the contents of the letter, Lee's voice swells with defiance, fear, and finally resignation. An echo chamber blurs her parting words, making it sound as though Lee had vanished out the door.

Jazz singer Mark Murphy was a sixteen-year-old living in Syracuse, New York, when he heard "While We're Young" and "Don't Smoke in Bed" on his car radio. "You had to wonder, what were these songs about? Peggy liked to do that to people; she wanted to be serious, to think of herself as a far-out artist. She was the first singer of her level to go into slightly abstract songs." The daring paid off: "Don't Smoke in Bed" hit a surprising number twenty-two on the *Billboard* pop chart. Chicago deejay Dave Garroway began using it as a sinister closer for his midnight radio show. Decades later, Carly Simon and k.d. lang were so entranced by Lee's performance that they mimicked it in their own versions of the song.

"Don't Smoke in Bed" gave America an unsettling look at an all-

American sweetheart of song. But as always, she kept people guessing, for the same group of sessions included a politically incorrect spoof sung in a vaguely Mexican accent. "Mañana (Is Soon Enough for Me)" had been born in Ensenada, Lee claimed, as she nursed Barbour through his recuperation. "It was so relaxed in Mexico," she explained, and the folks there had a "wonderful attitude—do it mañana." The Barbours whipped up a satire of a lazy Mexican: she lives in a falling-down shack with relatives who, like her, are jobless and snoozing; she's housebound because her money's gone and she can't fix the car; a friend borrows what cash she has left and blows it in a horserace; rain pours in through a broken window and nobody cares. After each chorus comes the carefree refrain, "Mañana, mañana, mañana is soon enough for me!"

Lee showed the song to Johnny Mercer, who typically suggested improvements. (She told columnist Sidney Fields that the songwriter "wrote special lyrics" for "Mañana"; he never received credit, though.) As for who would play on the record, Lee needed a Latin sound, and she went straight to the top. She had recently met the "Brazilian Bombshell," movie star Carmen Miranda, who had conquered Hollywood with her "tutti-frutti hat," piled with tropical fruit, and her flirty songs and wisecracks that played every South American stereotype for laughs. "Mañana" did the same, and even though they were Brazilian, not Mexican, Miranda recommended her accompanists, the Bando da Lua.

On November 25, 1947, they joined Barbour, his band, and Lee at a studio in Hollywood. The arrangement was a hodgepodge of samba and rumba; Barbour and the other available males chanted the refrain. Lee used the Brazilians on two more novelty tunes: "Caramba! It's the Samba," another Latin lampoon; and "Laroo Laroo Lilli Bolero," which wasn't even about South America ("That's a magic saying that I heard one day in Napoli," went the illogical words).

But "Mañana" was the standout. Capitol released it in December. By late January, the song had jumped into *Billboard*'s top ten. It climbed to number one, where it stayed for a staggering nine weeks—a record-breaker at Capitol. Though Lee had meant no harm, the song's ethnic parodies set off a wave of controversy. Naïvely, Lee seemed thunderstruck at the brickbats that "Mañana" sent hurtling her way. "It was never meant to be in any way degrading to the Mexican people at all!" she insisted.

But at the posh West Hollywood supper club Ciro's—many of whose well-to-do customers surely employed Mexican help—the song unleashed so many cheers that Lee sometimes had to sing it twice. "Mañana" had helped pave her entry into that room, which became her Los Angeles headquarters from February 1948 until it closed in 1957. The Sunset Strip nightspot had a drab charcoal-gray exterior with a tiny marquee. Outside it, said Hal Schaefer, "these gorgeous limousines would pull up, and the doorman would lead people in." The procession was eye-popping; on various nights it included the likes of Marilyn Monroe, Ginger Rogers, Joan Crawford, Ava Gardner, Betty Grable, Humphrey Bogart, Cary Grant, Bette Davis, and Clark Gable. The headliners were equally stellar: Judy Garland; Frank Sinatra; Mae West; Sammy Davis, Jr.; Dean Martin and Jerry Lewis; Nat King Cole; Jimmy Durante.

Inside, Ciro's looked "like some great movie set," recalled Schaefer. Xavier Cugat, Hollywood's favorite Latin maestro, waved his baton on a raised stage; just in front of it, a small dance floor was awhirl with revel-

(PHOTO BY JESS RAND)

ers in tuxedos, fur stoles, and diamonds. At the tables and booths, which seated about 450, martini glasses glimmered and cigarettes glowed; a fog of smoke hung in midair. Photographers scurried around with bulky press cameras, snapping "candid" photos of the stars.

For a North Dakota girl who had sat in so many darkened movie houses and wished she could step inside the screen, Ciro's was a living dream. Lee wanted her friends to see her there; during that first engagement, she put so many on her guest list that their drink tabs wiped out her earnings.

Onstage, though, she typified less-is-more. Except for the goofy fun of "Mañana" or the feistiness of "Why Don't You Do Right?," Lee still seemed as tranquil and enigmatic as the Mona Lisa. In truth, Ciro's and its boldface-name clientele struck fear in her heart. "She was *always* scared to death before she went on," said Virginia Wicks, the lovely blond press agent who handled several of Carlos Gastel's clients, including Nat King Cole, Mel Tormé, and Peggy Lee. Wicks stuck close to Lee in the terror-fraught moments before showtime. Then she watched the singer float from the wings into the spotlight. Lee stood almost motionless at a microphone, a red curtain behind her, and said hardly a word between songs; the club's hypercharged ambiance made her seem like an oasis of calm. Beside her sat Barbour on a stool in the crook of the piano, legs crossed, electric guitar in his lap, lost in the music.

Minimalist though she was, all was thought out in advance. The better she prepared, the less likely it was that she would make some embarrassing mistake. She couldn't afford that; important people were watching her. The discipline she'd learned from Benny Goodman served her well. "Most of the time, she worked with the musicians until she drove them nuts," said Dona Harsh. "Nothing was ever done properly enough to suit her. She was the most ambitious person I know. She had to know every single thing. That's why she was so good. She made herself understand music. Technically she was as smart as any good musician."

But a singer as restrained as she needed more than just musicianship to get her points across. At Ciro's she began to experiment with lighting, one of the future keystones of her shows. The club had almost as many spots and gels as a movie set, and Lee discovered the magic that dramatic illumination or a sudden blackout could add to a song.

Lee Ringuette, her nephew, went to Ciro's as a child. He remembered his sense of awe as he sat "among the elite, in that completely adult setting of contained decadence and glamour." Up front stood his aunt Peggy in her shimmering white dress. Ciro's was a setting of "smoke and noise," he recalled, yet when she sang, "the whole house was transfixed." Maxine Sullivan had taught Lee the power of a light touch, while Lil Green had shown her how to convey defiance. But another singer was giving Lee the courage to dig deeply into her pain. "I used to listen to Billie Holiday every chance I got," she confessed. "I idolized Billie."

Mel Powell had turned her on to this most influential of female jazz singers, and Lee saw her every chance she got, whether at the tiny Famous Door in New York or at the Tiffany Club or Billy Berg's in Los Angeles. Sometimes Margaret Whiting joined Lee. Whiting saw the worship on her friend's face as Holiday stood on the bandstand, hardly moving—an elegantly gowned beauty with a gardenia in her pulled-back hair. Holiday's small, wailing voice revealed a woman who lived for love and would possibly die for it. She both luxuriated in her suffering and gave it dignity, even in "My Man," in which she sang: "He isn't true / He beats me too / What can I do?"

Holiday's singing was pure autobiography, tied to stylistic quirks that are copied to this day: seductively bent notes that sounded like sighs; a thin, brassy edge that evoked a muted trumpet; a languid delivery that could drag perilously behind the beat yet never fell out of time. Her life was cloaked in tabloid scandal, much of it involving her addictions to heroin and abusive men. She lived her saddest songs to such a reckless degree that she died at forty-four.

Lee's bitter childhood memories had left her feeling like a victim, and she identified with the downtrodden Holiday. She made mental notes of songs her heroine sang indelibly: "Easy Living," "Trav'lin' Light," "Them There Eyes," "You're My Thrill," "Crazy He Calls Me," "God Bless the Child." Lee went on to sing them all. They told of women hopelessly, often senselessly in love, willfully surrendering their power to men. As Lee studied Holiday's every move and sound, key phrases from the great singer's repertoire jumped out: "For you, maybe I'm a fool but it's fun" . . . "Nothing seems to matter, here's my heart on a silver platter" . . . "If he wants it, so shall it be."

At home, Lee played a Decca 78 of Holiday's "Good Morning Heartache" almost as often as she had spun Lil Green's "Why Don't You Do Right?" She marveled at how vividly Holiday could evoke beleaguered women, shiftless men, and scenes of domestic embattlement, coloring them "with all kinds of little facets." Raved Lee to *Metronome*: "I honestly feel that I understand what she sings because *she* understands what she's singing."

In several of her recordings of that period, notably "Stormy Weather," Lee sounds so much like Holiday that she seems at risk of losing her identity. Critics noticed. In his review of a Holiday concert, Larry Douglas of the *Atlanta Daily World* noted how "singers like Peggy Lee try to copy her every move." Onstage, Lee adopted not only Holiday's vocal mannerisms but her body language—the sly sidelong glances and the saucy half-smile; elbows tucked in as the hands moved daintily. At certain parties or as an encore in the occasional late show, Lee would imitate Holiday so precisely that she seemed to be channeling her.

She never got to know her idol well, but it wasn't for lack of trying. After Holiday's shows, Lee would ask the jazz star to sit at her table or appear at her dressing-room door. Holiday stayed aloof. Although Lee's close friend, jazz critic Leonard Feather, quoted Holiday as saying that she had "always loved Peggy," the former proved less charitable on other occasions. In her 1956 memoir, *Lady Sings the Blues*, Holiday told of reluctantly accepting Lee's invitation to a party she was throwing at Bop City, the San Francisco jazz club. There, Lee presented her with an adoring lyric about the gardenia Holiday wore in her hair. The book left little doubt that Holiday thought the song was awful.

Years later, her biographer Donald Clarke cited a line about Lee that had been cut from Holiday's book, apparently for legal reasons: "She stole every goddamn thing I sing." Bassist John Levy, who played for Holiday, recalled her disdain for the young white songstress. "When Peggy Lee came around," he said, "Billie would say, 'Look, bitch, why don't you find some other way to sing?' . . . Peggy Lee wouldn't take offense. She'd say to Billie, 'It's because I love you. I love everything you do.'"

Holiday may well have resented the amount of money and fame Lee was acquiring through a style that owed her a debt. In a publicity photo, Lee posed amid tall stacks of "Mañana" 78s, a confident smile on her face. A three-page spread in *Life*, "Busy Singer," profiled her as a beacon of achievement. Not only did she sing hit songs, she wrote them. Lee appeared frequently on radio and toured the country, guitarist husband in tow. In a forward-thinking business move, Capitol and Carlos Gastel helped her to found Denslow Music, a publishing company for the songs she wrote with Dave.

Lee had gotten almost everything she had ever wanted, but it wasn't enough. "She was always needy," said Dona Harsh, the ultraefficient young blonde who worked both in Carlos Gastel's office and as Lee's assistant. Harsh found it unnerving that, at twenty-eight, her celebrated boss spent most of her nonperforming hours in the safe cocoon of her bed—a suggestion of how fearful and depressed she was. At night, with Dave asleep or passed out, Lee couldn't bear to be left alone; Harsh often had to keep her company until she drifted off, close to dawn.

So much self-obsession left minimal time for Nicki. A magazine photo showed the singer kissing her goodnight, but *Life* suggested that Lee's conquests as a prefeminist career girl had trumped her efforts at motherhood. "Miss Lee sees as much as she possibly can of her four-year-old daughter," explained the reporter. "When she cannot, Nicki plays herself to sleep with one of her mother's records." According to Kathy Levy, Lee's later confidante, daughter, like mother, had experienced depression "from a very early age." Food became the child's key source of comfort, and she had grown quite plump. Other troubles marred her life, including serious farsightedness, the reason she wore thick glasses.

Undoubtedly, Lee cared. Before a Canadian appearance, she told a reporter that she had traveled there by train. Asked why she hadn't flown, Lee explained, "I never fly. It's not that I'm scared for myself. I'm scared for my four-year-old daughter, Nicki. If anything should happen to me— poor little Nicki. I'm all nervous even at being away from her."

Yet she had left the job of raising Nicki mostly to Alice Larsen, a North Dakota friend whom Lee employed as housekeeper and nursemaid. The chasm between Lee and Barbour was also widening. To Hal Schaefer and other friends, Dave had never seemed as much in love with her as she was with him; increasingly he appeared trapped, and sought escape the best way he knew how. "Dave was drunk half the time," said Harsh. "He'd just sit there and mumble."

Lee knew that much around her was going wrong, but took no re-sponsibility for it. Everything in the household revolved around her needs. Although Barbour earned royalties as his wife's writing partner, he was mainly her accompanist.

Success had also changed the face of Capitol, which was now rolling in wealth. "Mañana" had contributed handsomely to making 1948 the label's all-time financial bonanza. Three other Capitol hits that year—Nat King Cole's "Nature Boy," Dixieland trombonist Pee Wee Hunt's "Twelfth Street Rag," and Margaret Whiting's "A Tree in the Meadow"—had tow-ered at number one for weeks on end. In 1949, the company became the first to issue singles both as 78-rpm platters and as 45s, a new, smaller vinyl format. Capitol also helped launch a revolution in the industry: the long-playing, 33⅓-rpm album. The innovations kept coming, as Capitol adopted the groundbreaking technique of high-fidelity recording onto magnetic tape, rather than onto a spinning wax disc.

Mercer's dream of a boutique label, devoted solely to his hand-picked favorites, had vanished. Busy with his own career, he left daily operations to Glenn Wallichs, who had replaced Buddy DeSylva as president. Capitol had acquired stockholders who expected payback, and it was Wallichs's job to see that they got it. "Glenn Wallichs didn't fit in with all the creative people down there," said Kay Starr, a country-blues belter whom the label had recently signed. "He was the machine that ran the business and kept the money coming in." Dave Dexter compared his fussy, eagle-eyed new boss to a computer. Wallichs defended himself in *Billboard:* "Contrary to the belief of some folks in the entertainment field, a record company *is* a business with responsibilities to employees and stockholders, just like a manufacturer who makes steam turbines or cuts glass ashtrays."

Mercer watched in dismay as Capitol issued a rash of blatantly com-mercial sides and "covers"—competing versions of other labels' hits. It was everything he had never wanted. After 1948, he kept his distance from the company he had helped conceive.

Lee was still floating on a cloud from the success of "Mañana," but on July 1, 1948, some upsetting news brought her crashing down to earth. She and Barbour, along with Capitol, were getting sued for plagiarism. A million-dollar suit had been filed in Los Angeles Federal Court by folk singer Harry Kirby McClintock, better known as Haywire Mac; and Sterling Sherwin, a San Francisco publisher of folk songs. They charged that the Barbours had stolen the music for "Mañana" from "It Was Midnight on the Ocean," a tune allegedly written by McClintock and published by Sherwin in 1932. Haywire Mac, then in his sixties, had a colorful history as a menial laborer and hobo troubadour from Tennessee. Throughout his travels he had collected many traditional songs, tinkered with them, and copyrighted them under his own name.

The practice was common in the folk world, which viewed songs as evolving diaries of the common man; some of Bob Dylan's early "originals" were recognizably based on folk chestnuts. But Lee's accusers had only one American tradition in mind: the acquiring of money. McClintock had successfully claimed authorship of a beloved old children's tune, "Big Rock Candy Mountain," but had tried and failed to do the same with "Hallelujah, I'm a Bum," a huge hit for Al Jolson in 1928. Sherwin published and took credit for an entire folio of borrowed tunes, which he titled *Sherwin's Saddle Songs*.

In the case of "Mañana," however, the Barbours had cause for fear. Its singsong, nursery-rhyme tune *was* undeniably similar to that of "It Was Midnight on the Ocean," a retitled version of a song that McClintock had recorded for Victor in 1928 under the title "Ain't We Crazy." But in a preliminary investigation, the court judged the melody to be in the public domain. By December of 1949, McClintock and Sherwin had dropped their suit.

Before they withdrew, two other songwriters piped up, claiming that the music for "Mañana" was theirs. In February 1949, Luis Fronde Ferrazzano tried to sue Lee and Barbour on grounds that the couple had pilfered his 1929 composition "La Rifa." He couldn't gather enough evidence, and the case fizzled. But in July, the Barbours faced their most stubborn foe. Vaudevillian Walter C. McKay—better known as Hats McKay—filed suit in New York Supreme Court, claiming that "Mañana" plagiarized his "Laughing Song," a ditty he had sung internationally, he said, since 1919. As evidence of the tune's resemblance to "Mañana," McKay's lawyer produced several manuscripts of "Laughing Song," which the troubadour had neither published nor recorded.

Yet the tune in those manuscripts did sound almost identical to that of "Mañana"—and unlike McClintock and Sherwin, McKay wasn't backing down. The Barbours' attorney set out to argue that the tune in question was public domain, and that McKay couldn't claim he owned it.

The couple would have to wait over a year for the trial, and Lee refused to let anxiety halt her career. She intended to keep living like a star; never could she return to the threadbare existence of Norma Egstrom. In 1949, Lee learned that the married movie stars Ronald Reagan and Jane Wyman were divorcing and selling their home in Westwood, an affluent community on the west side of Los Angeles. The two-story house stood on a tree-lined hill. Its price was steep, but Lee didn't care. Using the "Mañana" windfall, she bought it.

She hired a decorator, Charles Hagerman. Under her direction, he made 167 Denslow Avenue as frilly as a little girl's bedroom. Hagerman filled the rooms with chintz, pink plaid taffeta, and ruffles. There was a large living room with French provincial furniture; a music room with a candelabrum on the piano; and a dark backyard pool that, according to Dona Harsh, looked "like a mountain lake." Rock gardens surrounded the house. Above the garage was a small apartment that Lee turned over to her sister Della and her second husband, Jack.

The Denslow home, said Harsh, was Lee's "big sign of success." But when Jean Burden of the *Los Angeles Times* dropped by, she noted that the couple had separate bedrooms. Barbour didn't like the house; he much preferred their humbler Blair Drive abode and the Peggy Lee he'd known there. A *Redbook* reporter made a terse observation: Lee's attention-grabbing had turned her husband quite "morose."

On May 26, the day of her birthday, he tried to even the score. Lee and Barbour were performing that night, and after the late show a few friends, including Hal Schaefer, came to their suite to celebrate. As ever, Barbour had stocked up the bar. He proposed a birthday toast, and insisted his wife join in. Until then, Lee's friends had known her as a nondrinker; as she waited in the wings to go on, Virginia Wicks would hand the singer her preferred preshow beverage, ice water.

Barbour had attempted before to coax her into drinking, and at her birthday party he stepped up the effort. "Peggy said, 'No, no thank you, I don't want to drink, I don't like the taste,'" recalled Schaefer. "Dave said, 'Come on, sweetheart, it's your birthday!' She said, 'I really don't want to. I don't like alcohol.' He answered, 'Aw, come on, how many times a year are you gonna have a birthday?' Peggy said, 'Okay, okay.' And she had a drink."

Gradually Lee developed a liking for brandy, then for cognac. "I had to be there to hand her a little snifter when she came back for the encore," said Dona Harsh. As Lee discovered its relaxing effects, her intake grew. "Peggy drank a lot; we all drank too much in those days," admitted Harsh. "But she was so much fun when she drank. She went to parties and enjoyed life. We'd sit around the house at four in the morning singing. I really loved her then. She could tell a joke better than anybody on this earth. She had the most wonderful laugh."

Steve Allen, the future TV variety-show host, met Lee around that time. "I never knew whether she had a drinking problem," he said, "but her attitude was harmonious, shall we say, with people who do—I don't mean the real alcoholics, but the ones who've maybe had one too many at lunch. There was always a momentary slowness, a second-and-a-half behind the beat in conversation. All her friends noticed that."

It was certainly perceived by Hal Keith, who directed one of TV's first variety spectaculars, *Star-Spangled Revue*. The show, which starred Bob Hope, Frank Sinatra, Beatrice Lillie, and Lee, aired live over NBC on May 27, 1950. Posed in white satin and chiffon on a love seat, Lee gave a drawn-out, internalized rendition of Rodgers and Hart's "Bewitched," the confession of an older woman turned into a "simpering, whimpering child again" by lust. In a sketch, Lee played Hope's philandering fiancée.

During the rehearsals, she sounded so tentative and woozy that she threw off Hope's brisk timing. In the *New York Times*, critic Jack Gould called her "out of her element" on the infant medium of TV; he echoed a complaint she had heard in her Goodman days when he tagged her "easy to look at" but "impersonal" and cold.

She was certainly stone-faced in November, when Harsh accompanied her to New York Supreme Court to face down Hats McKay. Lee had hired Frank Gilbert, lawyer for one of the richest songwriters in America, Irving Berlin. McKay, recalled Harsh, was "this little funny guy," over seventy and wearing a big hat. Judge Isidor Wasservogel sat at the bench in his black robe, projecting the requisite pomp. But as the trial proceeded, he didn't seem to be taking the case too seriously. An upright piano had been wheeled in for McKay to demonstrate his would-be plagiarized tune. He performed "Laughing Song" repeatedly; sometimes it resembled "Mañana," other times less so.

One of the defense's key witnesses, Lee's friend Jimmy Durante, took the stand. There to prove that the tune of "Mañana" was as old as the hills, the star comedian played and sang a similar song from memory, inserting schtick in his Lower East Side accent and gravel tones. Everyone howled. McKay's attorney, Julian T. Abeles, shouted, "Objection!" Wasservogel overruled—"in view of the fact that we have such a distinguished entertainer in court." Even Abeles succumbed to the fun. "I withdraw only on the occasion that Mr. Durante do not one but three songs for the court," he announced. Things were so clearly not going McKay's way that he resorted to emergency measures. According to *Variety*, he "suffered a slight heart attack in court as a result of the emotional stress."

As her next witness, Lee had enlisted Deems Taylor, the esteemed classical music critic and original president of ASCAP (the American Society of Composers, Authors and Publishers). Taylor, who presumably knew more about songs than anyone, testified that "Mañana" was a samba—and that the form hadn't been invented yet in 1919, the year McKay wrote "Laughing Song." His testimony was accepted—but Taylor, in fact, was wrong. The first known samba, "Pelo Telefone," had been published and recorded in 1916.

On November 22, 1950, court reconvened. Wasservogel read the decision. McKay's performances in court, he declared, were blatant attempts to copy "Mañana," and his manuscripts of "Laughing Song" looked doctored. Furthermore, it seemed highly unlikely that the Barbours had ever heard McKay perform the song—he had barely entertained in twenty years—nor could they have found sheet music for it, because there wasn't any. No recording existed, either.

The case was dismissed. Barbour celebrated with Hal Schaefer by getting drunk. Lee joined them.

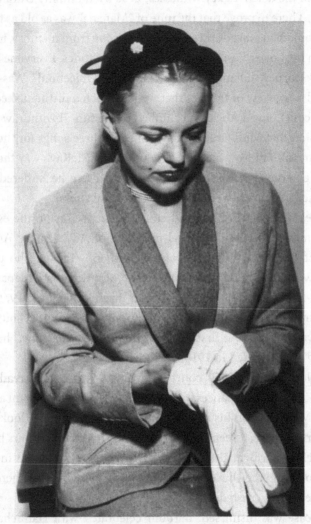

"He said he didn't love me anymore," sobbed Peggy Lee.
Santa Monica divorce court, May 15, 1951.

Chapter Five

NOW LAWSUIT-FREE, the Barbours resumed touring. But gone were the carefree lovebirds that Margaret Whiting remembered. Out of the public eye they walked around looking haggard, cigarettes in their hands. Lee's weight ballooned, while Barbour grew so skinny due to constant drinking and not enough food that his legs looked like sticks. In later years, Lee spoke freely about her husband's descent into alcoholism. "She didn't tell you that she was pouring two drinks," said her friend of the 1970s, Robert Richards.

More than ever, Lee seemed like a fragile soul floating in a cloud of her own design. Her vulnerability won almost everyone's heart, as did her charming daffiness. For a short time, Lee was the resident singer on Steve Allen's lunchtime CBS radio show. In one episode, Allen polled viewers by phone, querying them as to which noises or visual eyesores made them jump out of their skin. He used fingernails on a blackboard as an example. Allen asked Lee what jolted her.

"Teabags," she said.

"Um . . . What about teabags?"

"Well, I just hate it when people leave wet teabags around."

Meanwhile, echoes of Ernest Holmes's teachings worked their way into her interviews, in terms that left reporters perplexed. "When you see unloveliness in others," she informed one writer, "it's because you have some unloveliness in yourself."

Such pontification made it all the more jarring when the iron butterfly in her leapt out. Harold (Hal) Jovien, an agent at GAC (General Artists Corporation) and her former neighbor on Blair Drive, watched her become "a very demanding person. Saying this has got to be and that has got to be.

People had always known her as acting very nice, saying 'thank you very much.' Now she was getting a *lot* of attention, and it had gone to her head."

At the same time, Kay Starr saw a young woman who had become almost paranoid about what people thought of her. Starr, who was born on an Indian reservation in Oklahoma and whose mother raised chickens, had never seen anyone act like Lee. "I think I was kind of put off by her attitude," said Starr. "She knew who she was and how important she was. She had gone with half the guys who ran Capitol. Johnny Mercer was one of them. She had her tiptoes in the door and all around the house!"

Inebriated as he was, Barbour had a dead-on sense of how she had changed. "Dave used to cut her down all the time for being the princess," said Harsh. "She had started to turn into Miss Peggy Lee. And the sweet girl he married was no longer." In a typewritten, all-lower-case letter to Harsh, he scored a lot of laughs at his wife's expense. He asked Harsh to give "Miss Lee" a song he wanted her to learn, even though he knew that stars as big as she were "too busy swimming in their pools, riding around in jaguars and eating rich food."

Barbour took a jab at Lee's growing penchant for rewriting her own history—"i suppose now she says she was born in switzerland daughter of a ski instructor or something"—but he didn't spare himself, either. "i hear her husband is a manishevitz wine addict," cracked the guitarist. "i know how that can be." He cited *A Star Is Born*, the 1937 film in which an actress's faded actor husband sinks into depression and alcoholism, then kills himself by walking into the ocean. Barbour signed the letter Hats McKay. His sense of humor seldom left him.

For the first time, he took steps to fashion a separate career. Columnist M. Oakley Stafford cheered him on: "Dave's a modest man who shines in reflected glory, when he has plenty of what it takes to shine alone." In 1949, he put his wife's needs aside and went to Cuba to play with the Woody Herman band. Capitol encouraged Barbour by letting him record as a leader. He gave them some clever novelty sides, including "Forever Nicki," a jaunty instrumental salute to his daughter; and "Little Boy Bop Go Blow Your Horn," an ambitious pastiche of bebop, Latin rhythms, Russian-style guitar, and klezmer trumpet. When the press took interest, Barbour became more vocal about his plans. He told George T. Simon of his "big ambition" to lead a twelve-piece Afro-Cuban band; soon a Capitol single of his, "The Mambo," became a modest hit. *Metronome* generously reported that Barbour was "breaking into the bandleading game with a vengeance." He became musical director of radio's *The Curt Massey Show*, which starred a popular Capitol baritone. Barbour even acquired a manager, Marty Melcher, later famous as Doris Day's husband and producer.

Dave was less available now, and his wife wasn't pleased. She certainly had never expected him to beat her in scoring something she had wanted all her life: a dramatic role in a feature film. The Barbours had become friendly with Mel Ferrer, a budding movie actor and director with a bright future in store; it included roles in *Lili* and *War and Peace* and a marriage to Audrey Hepburn. Ferrer had been signed to direct *The Secret Fury*, an RKO film noir. Claudette Colbert would play a classical pianist and heiress who, at her wedding ceremony, is suddenly accused of bigamy by a stranger. Evidence stacks up against her, but she can't remember a prior marriage. She locates her would-be husband, a guitar player. Minutes later he is mysteriously shot, and detectives blame her. Initially Ferrer had planned to cast a professional actor as the musician. Then he thought of Barbour. "It occurred to me that it might be easier to make an actor of him than to make an actor look and act like a guitarist. We gave him a screen test and—well, he's great!"

Hedda Hopper, the crotchety Hollywood gossip doyenne, reported the casting of "Peggy Lee's husband" in a Claudette Colbert film. Mel Ferrer, she wrote, "thinks Dave is star quality." Barbour saw a new life unfurling before him, and he liked it. Small as his part was, he proved utterly believable as an arrogantly cool jazzer in on an evil con game. "After the first couple of days I got over the twitches and kind of enjoyed it," he observed. "I worked about ten days altogether—and may I say there's a very large amount of money in that type of work. . . . I'd like to do some more pictures."

But Hal Schaefer, who played piano in the Barbour character's onscreen band, thought a film career unlikely for his alcoholic friend. "I don't think he was ever entirely sober," said Schaefer. "But he kept his drinking down enough during the shooting schedule so that it didn't interfere."

The Secret Fury opened in June 1950. *New York Times* film critic Bosley Crowther dismissed it as "cheap and lurid twaddle," and didn't even mention Barbour. The guitarist received no further film offers. Likewise, his short-lived Capitol solo career had gone nowhere. Three years earlier, his alcoholism had nearly killed him; now, with only a portion of his stomach left, Barbour began drinking even more ferociously. "It was sad to see him disintegrate like he did, because he had really become a screaming alcoholic," said Dona Harsh. "And Peggy couldn't take it." Her father, of course, had been one, too; certainly the danger signs had been there for Lee to spot in Dave before she married him. But like many children or spouses of alcoholics, she had unconsciously perpetuated the cycle of codependency in her life. At the same time, she continued to drag Dave around the country with her while ignoring his own needs.

Now she had to tend to those of her ailing father. Marvin Egstrom's career as a depot agent had ended in another tiny North Dakota town, Millarton. When he retired in 1944, Min—well into her fifties but as tough as ever—took over his job. Glen Egstrom occasionally paid his now-aimless uncle a visit. "He was beaten down. He was thin, his face was a little gaunt, and he was stooped. His face was pretty animated when he was talking to strangers, but there was definitely unhappiness there." As a small child, Norma Deloris had been the apple of his eye—at least in her perception. From there she grew up with an emotionally unavailable father, tied to the bottle. Marvin seemed to know it. In a 1948 profile of Lee, the *Minneapolis Sunday Tribune* reported that her father spent "much time at the barber shop telling about his famous daughter."

But he hadn't seen her since the early 1940s. As freely as she talked about her North Dakota roots, Lee wasn't keen to revisit them; her home state held bitter memories. Lee had stayed in touch with almost none of her old pals—not even Artis Conitz, who had since married and moved to California. "I saw her a few times, because I made the effort," said Conitz. "She was familiar to me, but she didn't act like she used to act. She was somebody I grew up with, who grew away from me."

Ginny Lulay, her girlhood friend from Wimbledon, had sensed Lee's resentment of her father for having married Min. But in her memoir, Lee detailed a sentimental surprise visit from Marvin, who suddenly appeared, rail-thin and with a hacking cough, at her Denslow Avenue home. His words, as Lee detailed them, revealed a man who knew little about his daughter beyond what he'd read in the papers. It thrilled him to see how high his little girl had climbed. The reunion ended, said Lee, when Min phoned to demand his return.

Her stepmother remained an ogre to her. Marianne's son Lee Ringuette could sympathize. In the late 1940s, Min and her son Edwin had come to Los Angeles to visit the Ringuettes. "Her appearance scared the hell out of me," he recalled. His description of her evoked Miss Almira Gulch, the mean spinster who turned into the Wicked Witch of the West in *The Wizard of Oz.* "She had gray hair worn in that braided kind of bun that we remember from that era, and those oddly heeled shoes that older women wore, and an inappropriately loud dress. Everybody was trying very hard to be polite, but I could feel the strain."

Having been widowed once, Min now faced the imminent loss of her second husband. Early in 1950, she phoned Peggy with the bad news: Marvin, a lifelong heavy smoker, was home in Millarton, dying of lung cancer. If Norma (as she still called her) wanted to see her father again, she had better come now.

Coincidentally, Lee had agreed to serve as Grand Marshall of the annual North Dakota Winter Show, an agricultural festival in Valley City, and to give four concerts. Thousands were expected to attend the March event, which would showcase prize livestock and include a rodeo. Afterward, Lee could go to Millarton. She dreaded the prospect. It would mean facing Min again, and seeing her father for probably the last time.

She and the Dave Barbour Quartet flew to Fargo on the Sunday before their shows. As they descended the stairs of the plane, a blur of flashbulbs greeted the return of a homecoming queen. Barbour himself went nearly unnoticed. A driver took the couple to Valley City. Soon nearly everyone in town was packing Central Avenue for a ticker-tape parade in Lee's honor. Marchers led with a big sign that read, WELCOME HOME PEGGY LEE! Behind them came a brass band dressed in blue, baton-twirling little girls, and boys in farm clothes.

The "glamorous Hollywood star," as a town newspaper called her, rode along in a convertible driven by Dean McConn, the brother of her Wimbledon High teachers, Frances and Edith. Lee sat perched on the backrest of the rear seat, bundled in a mink coat; she waved and smiled broadly to the cheering crowds. Her husband wasn't there. McConn, who chauffeured him around without her, saw how impatient he was with all the festivities: "It was like, he had to be there." Locals recalled Dave's sarcastic remark that they probably hadn't seen many mink coats.

By contrast, Lee went out of her way to treat everyone graciously, and struggled to recall the names of childhood acquaintances. But stardom and its perks had carried her far from the prairie lifestyle; no longer could she relate to it. Later she told the *New York Post*'s Earl Wilson that going home was painful—"because the people work so hard. They seem to get so little pleasure. You wish you could send them all on a cruise."

As Millarton loomed on her agenda, Lee panicked. She repeated Ernest Holmes's texts to herself and to anyone who would listen. "Closer is He than breathing and nearer than hands or feet," went her credo. God, she chanted, was "within me, working through me"; so long as she let His love flow through her, no harm could come.

Lee's brother Milford had offered to drive her there immediately after the last show on Tuesday, March 6. Barbour refused to accompany her; he went home to California. As a blizzard raged, Milford showed up in Valley City, behind the wheel of a farm truck. Joined by her road manager, Joe Cancelleri, Lee embarked on a forty-mile journey over snow-blanketed and unpaved roads. Finally they reached the Millarton depot. Min ushered them upstairs; there, they found a seriously ill Marvin in bed. Father and daughter exchanged loving words. Handing her a Bible, he asked her to read him Psalm 23, the passage recited by priests at funerals or as a form of last rites: "The Lord is my shepherd; I shall not want . . . Yea, though I walk through the valley of the shadow of death, I will fear no evil: For thou art with me . . . and I will dwell in the House of the Lord forever."

Lee could hardly keep from crying, but the visit was short; she flew home immediately to California, where she launched a tour. On the road, Alice Larsen was there to play nursemaid to Nicki; Dona Harsh did the same for Lee. Luxury suites and star treatment greeted the singer everywhere. Barbour wanted none of it. After a heated argument with his wife in St. Louis, he abruptly went home, leaving her to scramble for a replacement.

On April 27, 1950, the *Jamestown Sun* reported that Marvin O. Egstrom, "father of Peggy Lee," had died that morning. He was seventy-five. Lee had felt a premonition on the flight to Los Angeles: "Something told me very clearly that my Daddy was making the transition." She flew back to North Dakota for the funeral, which Min organized. After visiting briefly with her siblings, Lee fled. Twenty-five years would pass before she set foot in North Dakota again.

The rest of 1950 brought her mostly disappointment. Lee's dream of motion-picture stardom had flared up again in July 1950, when MGM screen-tested her for a remake of *Show Boat*, the classic Jerome Kern-Oscar Hammerstein musical. Lee was one of many contenders for the pivotal role of Julie, the story's mixed-blood heroine. Ava Gardner got the part.

Her nightclub career went on as before. Lee had hired a young promotional director, Dick LaPalm, to travel with her and interface with deejays and the press. LaPalm witnessed the continued unraveling of the Barbours' marriage. He recalled a heated scene in Lee's dressing room at the Cocoanut Grove, the palm-tree-adorned supper club inside the Ambassador Hotel in Los Angeles. Show time was delayed as everyone awaited the arrival of Louella Parsons, one of the most powerful gossip doyennes in the country. Barbour wasn't impressed. "Screw Louella Parsons!" he barked. "Let's do our show. Who the hell is she?" Lee pleaded with him to be patient. Gloria DeHaven, MGM's pretty singing starlet, had come backstage to say hello; she knew the couple, and managed to explain Parsons's importance to Barbour and calm him down.

But his impatience with his wife's professional needs continued to explode; at times it seemed as though he were determined to sabotage her. During one of Lee's trips to New York, her publicist, Virginia Wicks, arranged a press party for her at the Royal Roost, a popular jazz club near Times Square. The celebrity turnout astonished Wicks—especially the presence of Billie Holiday and Tallulah Bankhead, who were invited separately but turned up together. Holiday and the flamboyant Southern actress-comedienne had met in New York and become close friends; rumors had spread that the two were lovers.

The next day, Wicks got a phone call from Barbour. "You're fired!" he snarled, adding that he didn't want her to have anything to do with his wife again.

Wicks was stunned. "I said, 'What did I do?' He said, 'You knew very well when you invited Tallulah Bankhead and Billie Holiday . . . you knew what they were!' I protested, and he just said, 'Don't contact us. We'll send you whatever we owe you.'" Later on, Lee called Wicks to apologize for Barbour's behavior and to thank her for doing a wonderful job. But she didn't offer to rehire her.

The distance between the Barbours kept growing. Lee confided in friends that she had begun an affair with comic Hal March, one of her fellow performers at the Jade in 1938. March was now famous as the host of TV's hottest game show, *The $64,000 Question*, but his career would crash amid the notorious quiz show scandals—the revelation that several of those programs, notably March's, had been rigged by the producers.

In the 1970s, Lee told her assistant Magda Katz of a mess that her fling with March had triggered. Somehow Barbour had heard of his wife's philandering. She and the guitarist were home with the TV on, and March appeared on the small black-and-white screen. According to Lee, a drunken Barbour picked up the TV and hurled it through the window. "Whether this is true or not I don't know," said Katz.

Evidently Barbour had his own wandering eye. Just before an engagement in Las Vegas, Lee invited Dick LaPalm and his wife, Jean, to spend a week with them in the sun. They encountered a painfully drunk Barbour. One night Jean returned, shaken, to their hotel room. Dave, she said, had made a pass at her. According to LaPalm, this wasn't the only time Dave had seemed eager to stray.

Those in the know detected the marital strain in the ten songs the couple filmed for Snader Telescriptions, a company that supplied musical filler for early TV. "Snaders," like "soundies" before them, were cheap precursors of the music video, with shabby sets, kitschy premises, and awkward camera work. Nonetheless, they provide early sightings of Nat King Cole, June Christy, Sarah Vaughan, and other pop and jazz greats.

Lee's Snaders, made in September of 1950, serve as snapshots of a waning marriage. The selections span their songwriting history, from "You Was Right, Baby" to "Mañana"; in the latter song, Barbour wears a sombrero and sits cross-legged at his wife's feet. Incongruously, Lee performs "What More Can a Woman Do?" on a nightclub set, where, garbed in an off-the-shoulder black sequined gown, she sings of a housewife's contentment. In "I Don't Know Enough About You," Lee is a prim schoolteacher at her desk; Barbour sits on a stool with legs crossed, lost in his guitar. Throughout the Snaders, Lee turns to him with longing eyes; he barely looks at her.

With most of their chemistry gone, Lee withdraws into a private world where songs had become dialogues with herself. Conversely, her rapport with the camera had blossomed. When she stares at the lens, she lures viewers into her dreamland.

Just before Christmastime, audiences caught one of their last glimpses of the Barbours together. Bing Crosby had thrilled Lee by recommending her for a cameo in his latest film, *Mr. Music.* At a penthouse party, surrounded by revelers, she and Crosby, accompanied by Dave's combo, sing Johnny Burke and Jimmy Van Heusen's homespun slice of philosophy, "Life Is So Peculiar." Lee had grown in confidence since her nervous appearances in *The Powers Girl* and *Stage Door Canteen,* and she and Crosby prove a perfect match—a rising minimalist alongside the king of nonchalance. At a break in the song, Marge and Gower Champion, the Hollywood dance team, twirl gracefully throughout the room and even up on the terrace ledge. Barbour stays on the sidelines, barely visible.

Mr. Music opened during the 1950 holiday season to pleasant reviews. It was a minor entry in the Crosby filmography, and earned Lee only passing mentions. But that December her hopes rose again when she was invited on short notice to join the national tour of a lavishly hyped, hugely budgeted stage spectacular. Produced by the American Legion, *Red, White and Blue: All American Revue* was an evening of patriotic propaganda, with a cast of 123 and twenty-five sets. The show trumpeted a message of nationwide prosperity; proceeds would benefit veteran rehabilitation and child welfare. But the lead performer, Hollywood singing siren Gertrude Niesen, had quit, hence the urgent need for a bankable substitute. Lee's job was easy: amid flag-waving sketches and songs, she and her husband's group would present a chunk of their club act.

The show's true intentions eluded Lee, at least initially. It opened in the heat of the Red Scare—the rampant fear that Communist infiltration would overturn U.S. capitalism and replace it with socialism, thus destroying the bedrock of American society. Newspapers carried almost daily reports about Republican senator Joseph McCarthy, who was on a rabid witch hunt to ferret out Communists, real or imagined, from the federal government and the broadcast media.

Thus the need for *Red, White and Blue,* a caravan of squeaky-clean, anti-red American values. The Legion had declared that each local production would feature one of America's most beloved household names—Bing Crosby, Bob Hope, Milton Berle. But far-right legionnaires shot down many of the proposed headliners, simply because they "didn't find their political associations pure."

Peggy Lee passed muster. A corn-fed blonde from the heartland, she had seldom, if ever, made a public statement about politics. On the face of it, Lee was a happily wedded wife and mother. Her sex appeal crossed no offensive lines; and if her biggest hit, "Mañana," made shameless fun of Mexicans, that didn't concern the American Legion.

The organization wasn't counting on the bombshell dropped on December 31 by gossip columnist Sheilah Graham. She wrote: "Peggy Lee plans to divorce Dave Barbour after the first of the year, when she goes to Chicago to replace Gertrude Niesen in 'Red, White and Blue.' That is when she will make the announcement." Barbour had "told her he wanted his freedom."

Lee wasn't fired; the Legion didn't dare lose her after a newspaper had reported "little or no interest" in the show. The bloated, critically panned five-hour spectacle was "limping across the country," a reporter wrote. Lee's presence had sold far fewer tickets than hoped. Claudia Cassidy reviewed *Red, White and Blue* in the *Chicago Tribune*. "The actors, brave souls, did what they could despite material you wouldn't believe . . . Much of it sounded as if it had been mistakenly retrieved from wastebaskets." Cassidy was no kinder to the star: "Peggy Lee, a shiny blonde, sings (a) briskly and (b) like a juke box slowed to a crawl."

Red, White and Blue closed in Chicago on January 20. *Variety* called it "the second biggest flop in show biz history"; the other was an obscure 1920s musical kept afloat by an oil magnate. For Lee, *Red, White and Blue*'s demise had made the future seem even emptier. Ever since the age of four, when she lost her mother, Lee had lived in fear of desertion. Now the love of her life was about to depart. Barbour still lived in the house on Denslow—"her" home, as he called it—but the early weeks of 1951 were fraught with screaming arguments, crying jags from Lee, and some of Barbour's most hostile drunken binges. Finally, on April 5, 1951, Lee permitted her publicist, Fran Jackson, to send out a press release announcing an imminent divorce. On April 28, Dave moved out.

All of Lee's friends had their own theories as to what had gone wrong. To Dick LaPalm, Barbour "was tired of being Mr. Peggy Lee." Marian Collier, the actress who became his second wife, felt that Barbour had run for his life: "I think he just wanted to sober up." Dona Harsh had the simplest view: "It was just a marriage that was over. I think there was still affection between the two of them, but they grew apart." In her most candid moments, Lee had to agree. "Getting along became impossible," she told a reporter in 1953, adding that the relationship had been souring "over a longer period of time than anyone realizes . . . We really weren't right for each other at all." They had tried to hold it together for Nicki's sake, she said, "but it was no good. I think we had outgrown each other." Only in 1974, to a *National Enquirer* reporter, did Lee admit any responsibility. "I loved him dearly but eventually we began to come up against the problem of my career. You see, it is always very difficult for a man to be married to a career girl. She's the one who gets all the attention."

At first, Lee had announced plans to go to Las Vegas and obtain a fast, "friendly" divorce, but second thoughts overwhelmed her. The day after Barbour had left, Lee slowed things down by filing in Santa Monica. According to Southern California divorce law of the time, husband and wife had to wait out a one-year "interlocutory" trial period, giving them time, if need be, to change their minds. Then, if they still wanted to part, the court would grant a final decree.

On May 15, 1951, Lee arrived at Santa Monica Superior Court for the preliminary hearing. Her outfit—a somber black suit and hat and white gloves—would have befitted a funeral. As the family breadwinner, Lee wanted no alimony, only custody of Nicki. Lee had charged Barbour with "cruelty," a standard claim then in women's divorce filings. Yet a more truthful charge would have been rejection, and the weight of it had hit her hard. "He said he didn't love me anymore," blubbered Lee to a reporter present.

She didn't add that she had already found a new Mr. Right. But the news broke the next month when a house photographer at Manhattan's Stork Club, a nighttime playground for celebrities and society, snapped Lee dancing cheek to cheek with Robert Preston, a rugged Hollywood supporting actor. Debonair and mustachioed, Preston had played utility roles in island movies, westerns, and crime dramas, while never quite becoming a star. That wouldn't happen until 1957, with his Tony Award–winning run as the star of the Broadway show *The Music Man*. For now he was appearing as José Ferrer's replacement in the play *Twentieth Century*, but his still-minimal name value couldn't sustain the show for long.

Friends of Lee's were startled at how swiftly she had moved on from Dave. But she couldn't bear to be alone, and the attentions of the swaggering Preston were enough to restock her head with fantasies. The blurb that accompanied the Stork Club photo had announced that the romance might "shortly lead to the altar"—a tidbit that Lee had supplied. She willfully ignored the fact that Preston was a well-known philanderer with a wife, though an estranged one, screen actress Catherine Craig. Lee felt sure that Preston would divorce Craig and marry her. For now, he didn't discourage her illusion.

She identified Preston as "Roger" in her memoir. Her remarks suggest a needy woman who had happily let delusion run amok. According to Lee, she had met him in Las Vegas the year before—"and when I first saw that face," she wrote, "I knew it meant trouble." No one but Dave had ever made her feel quite that way. Preston had just come home from the Army Air Corps, and he told Lee that when he had heard her records overseas, he thought she was black. She liked that.

No romance ensued until 1951, she claimed, when he showed up in her dressing room at the Copacabana. "By now I was really on my own," she asserted in her book. But the two-week engagement at the Copa began on March 15, 1951, and she hadn't even filed for divorce yet.

That night after the Copa, Lee wrote, Preston offered to take her home. They took a moonlit stroll as snowflakes fell. Lee was renting an apartment in Manhattan, and Preston stayed there a lot; quickly she began grooming him as the full-time father her seven-year-old needed. When Nicki professed approval, one more Peggy Lee daydream took flight.

As Preston wined and dined her all over Manhattan, she felt he was hers forever. She begged him to divorce Catherine Craig, but he told her that was impossible, because she was Catholic and would never agree to it. Lee persisted—and the affair crashed to a close that October.

Many years later, she made the dubious claim that, before he died in 1987, Preston had phoned to say he had never stopped loving her. But he stayed with Catherine Craig until the end. Lee couldn't bear to acknowledge that another man had walked out on her. When friends asked what had happened, Lee told them that she had "sent him home to his wife."

———

SHE STILL HAD HER career, but by the early 1950s her record sales had dipped. Lee's sound and demeanor had darkened considerably, and Capitol tried lightening her up. Commercial pop had entered its most puerile age; ditties like "Come on-a My House" (Rosemary Clooney), "If I Knew You Were Comin' I'd've Baked a Cake" (Eileen Barton), and "Sparrow in the Treetop" (Guy Mitchell) became mass-consumed sugar pills at a time of grim realities—the Korean War, the atom bomb, McCarthyism—that threatened to burst the pretty pink bubble of postwar contentment.

Now Miss Peggy Lee found herself recording such titles as "Don't Give Me a Ring on the Telephone (Until You Give Me a Ring on My Hand)," "Ay Ay Chug a Chug," "If You Turn Me Down (Dee-Own-Down-Down)," and "Pick Up Your Marbles (And Go Home)"—Capitol's choices, not hers. All of them flopped, and the label strained to point Lee in a different direction. "For her latest release, 'Yeah! Yeah! Yeah!,' " reported *Billboard*, "the diskery used an all-Negro jazz group, headed by Jim Wynn, in an effort to set off her pipings with a rough 'n' ready backdrop."

But in all of 1951, only one of her singles—"I Get Ideas," a cover of a kitschy tango hit by Tony Martin—made the charts. Her recorded casualties of that year had included two duets with Mel Tormé, a Capitol golden boy whose sales had also waned. Like Lee, Tormé had the rare distinction of writing many of the songs he sang; one of his originals, "The Christmas Song (Chestnuts Roasting on an Open Fire)," became a seasonal blockbuster. But neither singer's career gained much from *TV's Top Tunes*, a fifteen-minute CBS series that starred both of them but left Lee mostly in the dark. The show was a poor man's *Your Hit Parade*, a radio phenomenon that had moved successfully to TV; it featured a resident company of singers who covered the favorite songs of the week. *TV's Top Tunes* found Lee looking uncomfortably posed amid potted palms and hawking Chesterfield cigarettes to the monster TV cameras. None of that fazed the cocky Tormé. At twenty-five, the so-called Velvet Fog was a showbiz veteran, with MGM film appearances, major nightclub engagements, and a 1949 number-one hit ("Careless Hands") to his credit. Tormé viewed *TV's Top Tunes* as his show, and grabbed the best songs, leaving Lee with "Come On-a My House" and other trifles.

Various singing stars, including Patti Page and Dinah Shore, were succeeding as television hostesses, but no one offered that job to Lee. Instead,

With Mel Tormé on *TV's Top Tunes*, 1951. (COURTESY OF RICHARD MORRISON)

she returned to the now-fading medium of radio. Starting on Christmas Day of 1951, Lee starred in a twice-weekly, fifteen-minute recital on CBS. "You've got a date with Peggy Lee!" exclaimed the announcer of *The Peggy Lee Show*. Now free to sing whatever she wanted, Lee snubbed most of her current singles, which didn't endear her to Capitol.

Since 1943, she had blossomed under the guidance of Carlos Gastel. But their relationship was faltering. Gastel found her bossy and temperamental; she viewed him as a key culprit in the downfall of Barbour, his perennial drinking buddy. Lee fired and rehired Gastel; he kept threatening to quit. In September 1951, they had a screaming fight in a Chicago dressing room. Gastel stormed out the door, while Lee shouted behind him that he would never work for her again.

Even Dick LaPalm, who loved her, had to admit that Lee had grown "*very* difficult to work for"—demanding, moody. Louis Berg of the *New York Herald Tribune* profiled her revealingly in "Life of a Canary," an article that gave Lee a painful look in the mirror. "Nobody could be more assured than Peggy when she steps before the mike," wrote Berg. "Behind the scenes it's another story. This canary reveals herself to be as nervous as a cat. Her hands tremble, she puffs incessantly on a cigarette, holds herself under control with visible effort." Another journalist proclaimed her "Our Lady of Sadness."

Lee consulted her *Science of Mind* handbook for lessons in positive thinking, and applied them in odd ways. Before her shows, recalled Hal Schaefer, Lee "had these séances" in which she enjoined her musicians to sit with her on the floor in a circle and "think good thoughts." She corraled LaPalm and other bystanders to hover in the wings and send her "rays of love" as she sang.

Barbour needed them too. On May 20, 1952, two policemen found him staggering down a Hollywood street, obviously drunk. He denied it, and kept protesting as they arrested him and drove him to the station. When they tried to take fingerprints and a mug shot, Barbour loudly refused; he would "stay here forever," he shouted. Finally he cooperated, and paid a token sum of bail for his release.

Many saw him as a sad case—the former Mr. Peggy Lee who had fallen flat on his own. In 1952, Gastel took him to Europe, hoping the change of scene would help him start anew. Also rooting for Dave was Leonard Feather, the *Down Beat* jazz critic. Years earlier, Lee had introduced Feather to her friend Jane Larrabee, and the two had married. Lee considered him family, and it inflamed her to read a Feather column that seemed to incriminate her in Barbour's self-destruction. "Here is a guy who, after years surrounded by leeches and phonies, living in a world where your only friends can be those who are as wealthy or successful as yourself . . . knew that he wanted to turn his back on what Artie Shaw has called the $ucce$$ story, and get some kicks out of music again."

Depressed as Lee was, nothing could sap her creativity. The singer had devised a torrid reconception of "Lover," a Rodgers and Hart waltz that Jeanette MacDonald, a Hollywood soprano, had sung daintily in a 1932 film, *Love Me Tonight*. Lee was left cold by MacDonald's version, but not by the song, which she heard as pure sex. A new approach to it popped into her mind as she watched *La belle équipe* (The Good Crew), a 1936 French film in which Jean Gabin played a Foreign Legionnaire. As he galloped on a horse, Lee thought of Latin rhythms. "I also decided to change keys every chorus, which gives the illusion it is going faster and faster—from trotting to cantering to galloping." She explained all this to her combo, and they worked out an arrangement.

"Lover" became the hit of her club act. "They just, as they say, ate it up," she recalled. Lee asked Alan Livingston, now Capitol's head of Artists and Repertory, if she could record it. He turned her down. Guitar virtuoso Les Paul, one of the proudest additions to the company stable, had already recorded the song, said Livingston, and Capitol didn't want any competition.

But Paul's "Lover" had come out three years before, argued Lee, and hers was completely different. Livingston wouldn't budge—proof of how her label had cooled on her.

Lee was doing brisk business at the Copacabana, the nightclub that hosted the top headliners in the country: Frank Sinatra, Dean Martin and Jerry Lewis, Jimmy Durante, Carmen Miranda. In February 1952, several Decca Records executives came to hear Lee, hoping to woo her from Capitol. She performed "Lover," and as usual, she recalled, "the audience went crazy." When Milt Gabler, the head of Decca's pop division, offered to sign her, Lee eagerly consented—but only if they let her record "Lover." Gabler agreed.

Her Capitol contract had months to run. But when she asked Livingston to release her, he didn't protest. Lee would do one last session for the company that had nurtured her as a risk taker, a lyricist, and a singer who now seemed as troubled as the times she lived in.

On February 18, 1952, she and conductor Sid Feller teamed at Capitol's New York studio to cut six sides. Except for "Goin' on a Hayride," a clip-clopping tune from *Three Wishes for Jamie*, a new Broadway musical for which Capitol held recording rights, Livingston didn't care what she recorded; Lee chose the other songs. Only "Hayride" and a smoldering love song, "Ev'rytime," were released at the time; the other songs sat on the shelf for years.

The singing set the tone for the Peggy Lee of the 1950s—a torch balladeer for whom heartache was second nature, but who could latch onto moments of pure joy, swinging all the way. Her accompaniment, a jazz trio with muted trumpet, looked ahead to *Black Coffee*, her bluesy milestone LP of 1954; a string quartet added pathos when needed. "Oh, Baby, Come Home" was one of the last songs she had written with Barbour;

in it she smiled through tears as she bemoaned the single life: "Tried to build a fire in the fireplace / I wound up with nothing but soot upon my face." On a swing novelty, "Whee Baby," Lee shared songwriting credit with Alice Larsen, Nicki's nursemaid, who had voiced the title. The singer became a red-hot mama in "Louisville Lou," a 1920s hit about a "vampin' baby" with "no more conscience than a snake has hips."

All turned serious in "Let's Call It a Day," written by Lew Brown and Ray Henderson for *Strike Me Pink*, a forgotten Broadway revue of 1933. Lee's recording stands as one of the saddest she ever made. As she sings about bravely moving forward—"Let's have no regrets, or a word of blame"—she trembles audibly on the brink of tears.

On June 6, 1952, her divorce from Dave Barbour turned official. Lee was alone again and drinking to excess—this after growing up as the daughter of an alcoholic, then marrying one. But for her, reality had become too hard to face without anesthesia.

"He was too calm for Peggy," said Dona Harsh of the singer's second husband, Brad Dexter (*right*). With radio host Larry Finley at the premiere of *The Jazz Singer*, Fox Beverly Hills Theater, December 30, 1952. (COURTESY OF RICHARD MORRISON)

Chapter Six

*L*ONG AFTER THE 1950s had ended, Lee summed up the richest creative decade of her life as "years of romance and suffering." Barbour dropped by the house frequently—to pick up Nicki, not so much to see Lee. He regarded his ex-wife and musical partner with a deep fondness, but nothing more. Lee remained in denial. When an interviewer quoted her tearful divorce-court assertion—"He said he didn't love me anymore"—she demurred. "He did say that once," Lee insisted, "but he didn't mean it."

She scrambled to fill the vacant space in her life. Columnists couldn't keep up with her romances, rumored or real. For a time in 1952, she focused on one of Hollywood's trophy-boy bachelors, attorney Greg Bautzer, whose office handled her legal affairs. Wavy-haired and debonair, Bautzer was "easily one of the most handsome men I've ever seen," said Lee. He took advantage of that, doing double duty as lawyer and bedmate to some of filmdom's most fabled women, including Ginger Rogers, Lana Turner, and Joan Crawford.

Like most of Lee's affairs, this one lasted just a few months. Ultimately, no amount of male companionship could ease her sense of emptiness. In her singing, less was always more; but in all else she did, from applying makeup to decoration to sex, more was never enough. Aside from her chain-smoking and excess drinking, she binged on food; one of her weaknesses was Van Camp's canned beans, a comforting treat from her childhood. As her waistline grew, gowns didn't fit properly, compounding her panic before engagements. "She was *always* on a diet when she was young," said Dona Harsh. Lee's weight-loss schemes alarmed her friends. She tried an all-buttermilk crash diet and lost not a pound; before meals she gobbled an over-the-counter appetite suppressant.

Her public face had stayed soft-spoken and endearingly fuzzy, with a delivery so full of pauses that people tended to hang on her every word, wondering what would come next. But the calm hid a volcano. "I tried to bury myself in my work and I almost got a nervous breakdown as a result," said Lee. She came home from shows and couldn't fall asleep, so she sat in bed until dawn writing poems, drafting song lyrics, and drawing faces. "She was restless," said Harsh. "She wanted to sing and she wanted to paint and she wanted to write and she wanted to sculpt. She had a small amount of talent in certain things and a lot in others."

Lee's whole future, she feared, rested on her Decca contract, which she signed on March 28, 1952. Her first singles session was a compromise. Lee performed two dreamy standards she loved, "You Go to My Head" and "I'm Glad There Is You," in exchange for recording a pair of saccharin ballads, "Forgive Me" and "Be Anything (But Be Mine)." Gordon Jenkins, one of Decca's resident maestros, draped the latter tunes in a blanket of weeping violins and solemn choral *aaaah*s. "Be Anything" charted at number twenty-one; the other sides were mostly ignored. In a *Down Beat* Blindfold Test, in which an artist commented on unidentified records, Dick Haymes, who had sung alongside her briefly with the Benny Goodman band, heard "You Go to My Head" and thought of the singer Lee most adored. "It could be Billie," said Haymes. "She scares me a little at times, when she gets so far behind the beat that I'm afraid she'll never quite wind up at the end of the bar, but she makes it every time."

At that time, Holiday herself was just barely hanging on. *The New York Age*, a small newspaper, reported a bittersweet incident in which Peggy Lee once more crossed paths with her great inspiration, if only in spirit. It was two AM at Connie's Inn, a Harlem nightspot that had once rivaled the Cotton Club. Into that cellar establishment walked a broken Lady Day, wearing dark glasses. With one arm, she held onto a friend; in the other she clutched two white Chihuahuas.

To Sonny Murrain, a reporter, Holiday reminisced of how she had gotten her start in Harlem. But drug infractions had cost the singer her cabaret card, the license to perform in New York clubs. Holiday had maneuvered without success to get it back. "I even went to Cardinal Spellman, being a Catholic, but it's no deal," she said in her cracked, raspy voice.

As she spoke, someone dropped a coin into the jukebox. Out came the voice of Peggy Lee, the rival who had climbed much higher than she, and whom Holiday had bitterly resented. The song was "You Go to My Head." Murrain was startled by her response. "Almost without knowing, Billie Holiday joined in with that harsh, oddly sensual voice which no one can imitate."

The moment was a truce of sorts between two women for whom happiness did not come easy. But if Holiday was on a long gangplank with no turning back, Lee had found safe harbor at Holiday's former label, Decca. The timing seemed just right for Lee to record her Latin version of "Lover." Just then, the campy "Kiss of Fire," an ersatz tango, was sweeping the charts in six hit versions. As orchestrated by Jenkins, Lee's "Lover" was an Afro-Cuban fantasia—a cacophony of bongos and congas that turned a maiden's love call into a cry of lust.

On April 28, Lee arrived at Liederkranz Hall, Decca's Manhattan headquarters, to record "Lover." Jenkins had written a similar arrangement for the second song on the day's agenda, Cole Porter's "Just One of Those Things." Lee wanted everything big and brassy. She hadn't had a major hit in years; this was no time for moderation. In that sprawling studio, Lee stood amid a sea of string and brass players, a rhythm section, a chorus, and eight percussionists. Even that wasn't enough Latin fury for her, so she asked Ed Shaughnessy, her drummer, to play a conga, a tall Cuban drum with a hypnotic, tribal sound. Two top Decca producers, Morty Palitz and Milt Gabler, plus assistant conductor Russ Case, were on hand to manage the unwieldy session.

Jenkins raised his arm and struck the downbeat on "Just One of Those Things." Violins and cellos sawed away over a teeming bed of percussion, while Lee's voice sailed above the orchestra at half the tempo. Despite the bombast, the engineer caught a perfect take.

"Lover" was even noisier. It opened with a frantic whirlwind of cellos; then came the rush of percussion and the moans of four choral singers. The arrangement could have kicked off the chariot race in the movie Ben-Hur, but its clamor overpowered Lee. "They couldn't hear one note of me," she rued afterward. False starts and rejected takes piled up. After hours of failed efforts, Palitz had to admit defeat. Lee went home and cried, sure her recording career was over. "Oh, it's just another dream gone wrong!" she thought.

But Palitz hadn't given up. According to Lee, he phoned her in the middle of the night from Liederkranz Hall. His engineer had come up with a possible solution. Would Lee do one more session? "*What time?*" she blurted out.

Three days later, everyone reassembled. Palitz placed her far from the orchestra in an isolation booth—a rare device in 1952. With headphones piping the band into her ears, Lee sang "Lover" again. To her huge relief, the experiment worked. But she wasn't taking chances. Instead of confiding Lorenz Hart's erotic plea in a hushed bedroom voice, she grew louder and more heated with each chorus and key change. By the end, she was shouting Hart's words—"*Lover, it's immoral, but why quarrel with our bliss?*"—in a blast of female sexual aggression scarcely heard on record since Bessie Smith. Determined to make herself heard, Lee pounced upon certain words and repeated them like mantras—"Softly, softly in my ear / You breathe, you breathe, you breathe a flame!"

Her instincts proved dead-on. In June, "Lover" became the number-three single in the country. Male critics rhapsodized over it. In the *Los Angeles Times*, Philip K. Scheuer raved over Lee's "orgiastic" performance: "While the ensemble beats out a furious tempo, the Lee gal moans, gasps, and shivers in ecstasy." Orders for product piled up. Lee hadn't felt such affirmation since "Mañana." Yet her heart sank when she learned that her take on "Lover" had appalled Richard Rodgers. "I suppose this recording is about as far as you can go in the way of distortion and still have the nerve to use the title," he groused. In *A Fine Romance*, a study of Jewish-American popular songwriters, author David Lehman cited a saltier quote by Rodgers: "I don't know why Peggy picked on me; she could have fucked up 'Silent Night.'" Her liberties with Hart's words didn't seem to bother him; Rodgers—a notorious stickler for note-perfect treatments of his songs—was offended that Lee had thrown away his lilting waltz meter and sung "Lover" like a panther in heat. Friends of Lee's recalled an encounter she had with the composer at a party. "By the way, Miss Lee, it's a *waltz*," said Rodgers coldly.

Only in 1968, when Lee sang "Lover" in a salute to him at New York's Lincoln Center, did Rodgers seem to have come around. He sent a conciliatory letter to be read onstage: "In the years since I wrote that song, 'Lover' has been played by everything from calliopes to symphony orchestras, and I am happy indeed to let Miss Peggy Lee have her way with it." But Rodgers's daughter and fellow musical-theater composer, Mary Rodgers Guettel, doubted the change of heart: "I do not remember his *ever* forgiving her."

In this case, the record-buying public didn't care. The unbridled libido of Lee's singing was heady stuff in 1952, when soda-shop juke-boxes spun such chaste platters as Patti Page's "I Went to Your Wedding" and Doris Day's "When I Fall in Love." Day, the sunshiny blonde whose movie musicals had depicted an idyllically wholesome America, sang, in lyrics rife with implication, of a "restless world" where boys bestowed "moonlight kisses" with no strings attached.

But outright sex had begun invading commercial pop, a field of such sterile blandness that it soon sparked a youthful backlash in the form of rock and roll. A few months after "Lover," Karen Chandler caused a minor scandal with her number-five hit, "Hold Me, Thrill Me, Kiss Me." In it, the singer extolled those magic moments "in the dark" with the beau whose embrace, she declared, could "drive me slowly out of my mind." And there wasn't an altar in sight. Nineteen fifty-two saw the emergence of Eartha Kitt, a black singer, dancer, and recording artist whose serpentine writhing, combined with a voice as prickly as a cat's tongue, flung open the bedroom door. The next year, Marilyn Monroe's fame would skyrocket when she costarred (with Jane Russell) in *Gentlemen Prefer Blondes*. Monroe had seen Lee at Ciro's, and although she never acknowledged it, the boudoir intimacy of her singing seemed patterned on Peggy Lee's.

Both women knew what sex appeal could get them. Yet Lee was no submissive plaything; her allure seemed tough around the edges, wounded at the core, and a bit dangerous. "Peggy is not the girl you'd run into at a high school prom," observed the DJ and columnist Eddie Gallaher. "Her voice is more that of the girl in the smoke-filled room at a truckline café or at a juke joint along a Texas highway." While Doris Day was hired to plug Lux soap and Royal Crown cola in commercial ads, Lee endorsed other kinds of products. "Chesterfield is my cigarette—has been for years," she proclaimed in one ad. Another paired a photo of her with the quote, "My beer is Rheingold—the Dry beer!"

Her publicity machine exploited this brazen image. "Peggy puts more sex into a song than most girls could into a strip tease," exclaimed one press release. Wire services reported that the eight thousand marines in attendance at a Los Angeles Rams football game had voted Lee the girl they most wanted to date; surely few of them envisioned a night ending with a good-night kiss on the cheek.

A year or so after "Lover," Arthur Hamilton, one of Lee's songwriting pets, got a hint of how disconnected she felt from her public persona. As she sang in the darkness of Ciro's, he glanced around at a sea of sweaty-faced men. "They were intrigued and moved in every way you could see," said Hamilton. "She was like the other woman in every couple." Late that night, Lee took him back to her house. As the cognac flowed, her defenses melted away. The temptress stepped aside, allowing Norma Egstrom to peep through. Like so many who met her, Hamilton found Lee's timid charm and easy laugh irresistible; her vulnerability inspired protectiveness. She and Hamilton talked heart-to-heart until deep in the night. She recited her original haikus; he read her some unfinished lyrics. Laughter and jokes punctuated their exchanges. Around three AM, Hamilton decided to make her night by telling her about the mesmerized fans who looked as though they had wanted to jump into bed with her. Lee abruptly froze. "I don't want to talk about *her* anymore," she declared curtly.

———

TWO MONTHS AFTER THE release of "Lover," "Just One of Those Things" had reached number fourteen on the *Billboard* pop chart. Lee certainly wasn't the first American artist to use Latin percussion; but following "Lover," bongos became a staple sound in the pop music of that era. At her fabled Carnegie Hall concerts of 1961, Judy Garland earned screaming ovations with "Come Rain or Come Shine," arranged by Nelson Riddle in a format almost identical to that of "Lover."

Lee never had another Decca hit to equal it, but she had won the reverence of everybody there. From then on, she had complete freedom to let her imagination roam. Other star songbirds, notably Rosemary Clooney, would grumble or laugh for years at the junk they had recorded in search of a hit; but at Decca, Lee was often defiantly noncommercial. Shortly after "Lover," she and Sonny Burke, a fatherly Decca producer and arranger, teamed to write "Sans Souci," one of the most outré singles of her career. The title is French for "carefree," but Lee's words, set to a throbbing bolero rhythm, spin up a whirlwind of exotic melodrama. An evil siren scandalizes a remote island; a choir chants, "Go, boat, go, go!" Surreal images abound: "Oh, the mountain starts to giggle when the springtime waters wiggle down the mountainside," sings Lee in a voice that bends as sinuously as a snake charmer's flute playing. She sounds, in turn, like a purring kitten and a witch. "I've tried to figure out why I was so angry when I wrote that," reflected Lee in 1990.

More and more, she was learning how to mine a wealth of texture and nuance from a seemingly meager instrument. "People say my voice is thin or small, but I have a lot more voice than I ever use," she explained. Belting wasn't in her plan. "I start with a small amount of volume, and sometimes I'll sing softer and softer, and that gives me a long way to go."

"Sans Souci" didn't sell well, but her reigning place on the nightclub circuit was assured. Twice a year she returned to Ciro's. "It was a very exciting gig," said Gene DiNovi, Lee's Brooklyn-born pianist, who accompanied her from 1951 to 1955. "You looked out, and every star you'd ever heard of was out there listening to you. It put a lot of intensity into the performances."

This was an era of "smoking, drinking / Never thinking of tomorrow," as Mitchell Parish wrote in his lyric for Duke Ellington's "Sophisticated Lady." Ciro's general manager George Schlatter recalled the endless imbibing of the period: "You'd have two drinks before you went out to dinner, then a cocktail or two at the restaurant before dinner, then you'd have wine with dinner, a little brandy after dinner, then you'd have one more for the road, then maybe a nightcap."

Even with all that swilling, Lee commanded rapt attention. Most of her shows sold out, and Herman Hover, who owned Ciro's, treated her like a queen. "Anything that Peggy wanted, she got," said Schlatter; that included a repainting of the dressing room in pink before each engagement.

Her June 1952 engagement was special. "Lover" had peaked, and the reservation book filled up weeks before the opening. Feeling even more jittery than usual, Lee hired a director: Mel Ferrer, who had cast Dave Barbour in *The Secret Fury*. Ferrer revamped her presentation aggressively, then discussed Lee with the press as though she were an old Jeep in need of a tune-up. "It seemed to me that Peggy was singing too long, talking too much between songs, and not singing the right songs," he told *Down Beat*. "Every musician liked her, but not the general public. Another thing, she was too fat. Right away I put her on a high-protein diet and trimmed her down."

Blunt as Ferrer was, his ideas worked. He made Lee wave a chiffon scarf for dramatic emphasis, and helped her create a dreamlike flow by bridging together certain songs with a few mysterious words, delivered over a musical segue. Ferrer brought in a Hollywood lighting wizard, Jimmy Neilson; from him, Lee learned even more about how light cues could enhance her art. As she sang heatedly of sexual intoxication in "You Go to My Head," a pinspot cut a gray beam through the smoky room and lit on her face. Her fair skin and white-blond, short-cropped hairdo shone like a jewel against black velvet. But as columnist Sidney Skolsky observed: "She is in a world of her own and is oblivious to everything else when she is singing."

On several nights, a corner table at Ciro's was occupied by Michael Curtiz, director of such Warner Bros. classics as *Casablanca* and *Mildred Pierce*. Curtiz had discovered Errol Flynn and John Garfield, and had launched Doris Day as a movie star in *Romance on the High Seas*. Curtiz knew how to elicit magic from actors, yet he considered many of them phonies. Day, who had never acted before he found her, was an exception. As he told her in his thick Hungarian accent, "I sometimes like girl who is not actress. Is less pretend and more heart."

For now, though, Curtiz was angry at Day, who had dropped out of his long-planned Technicolor remake of *The Jazz Singer*, the breakthrough talkie of 1927. Danny Thomas, a soft-sell nightclub comic, had been cast in the role created by Al Jolson—that of a Jewish cantor's son whose heart is in the theater, but whose father is pressuring him to inherit his job. Day and Thomas had just costarred in a big moneymaker, *I'll See You in My Dreams*, and the studio wanted to keep cashing in on the partnership. But according to the *New York Daily Mirror*, Day had decided that her second-fiddle role in *The Jazz Singer*—as Thomas's girlfriend, a star singer who urges him to follow his heart—"wasn't up to her, shall we say, stature?"

Warner Bros. needed a replacement. Studio president Jack Warner had heard Lee at Ciro's, and he urged Curtiz to go. The director studied her laser-beam focus, her low-burning intensity. "I felt that anyone who could put so much feeling in a song could do just as well with the spoken word," he explained.

After the show, he appeared at Lee's dressing-room door. Curtiz's steel-gray hair and expensively tailored suits gave him an imposing look; so did a demeanor so heated that sweat soaked his silk shirts. Faced with that intensity, Lee could barely speak. Curtiz found her reticence a refreshing change from the blowhard egos of other actors. He mentioned *The Jazz Singer*, and asked if she would be willing to screen-test for the female lead. She hesitated. As much as she had yearned for movie stardom, Lee was worried. She confessed to Curtiz that she hadn't liked her performance in *Mr. Music*, and that she knew nothing about acting. Doris Day had voiced similar misgivings in 1948, but Curtiz had changed her mind, and he changed Lee's.

Following her closing at Ciro's, she arrived—"scared to death," Curtiz recalled. As he, a cameraman, grips, and makeup and hair designers hovered around her, Lee panicked. Retreating into her shell, she stammered through her script. Curtiz urged her to pretend that her lines were the words of a song. Her reading improved. Lee was no innately gifted actress like Day, but Curtiz sensed enough potential to sign her for *The Jazz Singer*.

That July, with much fanfare, Warner Bros. announced its exciting find. Lee, spouted Curtiz, was a "great actress" who was sure to become "one of the biggest stars." From the start, it seemed clear that her casting was, in part, the studio's revenge against Day. Curtiz made no secret of his ire. "He's still mad that Doris Day turned him down," announced *Variety*. Knowing good publicity when they saw it, Warner Bros. didn't discourage the spreading gossip of a feud between the singers. Day tried to do damage control. "When I saw her in the makeup department one morning," she told Hedda Hopper, "I said, 'All this is a lot of junk and I hope you're not upset.'" Lee was not, insisted Day.

Still, Curtiz was clearly grooming her in Day's image, which included giving her a similar poodle-cut hairdo. "Peggy Lee is gonna look an awful lot like Doris Day when Mike Curtiz finishes having her teeth and hair fixed,'" wrote the *Hollywood Reporter*. Curtiz delighted in comparing the two young women, quite insightfully. "Doris is an extrovert, happy-go-lucky about every turn of fate," he told a reporter. "Peggy is an introvert—a dogged analyst, tenacious, moody, sensitive, and shy almost to the neurotic stage."

Those qualities made Lee an odd choice for a role custom designed for Day: that of Judy Lane, America's vivacious queen of musical comedy, full of can-do optimism. Lee's role was far from deep, but fear of failure seized her. Danny Thomas got a hint of what lay beneath her detached façade when he complimented her on her economy of movement at Ciro's. "I thanked him and said I just stood there because I was too scared to move," admitted Lee.

Shooting began on August 1, 1952. Following Curtiz's advice, she analyzed her lines as though they were lyrics; when the camera rolled, she tried to envision herself singing instead of speaking. But the strain showed. Curtiz didn't like her early scenes, but Thomas was sensitive enough to spot the "inner sadness" in Lee. "Michael Curtiz saw that, wanted to get it from her, but I don't think she wanted to explore it," said the comic. Though it had nothing to do with her character, Lee sang her arrangement of "Lover" in a nightclub scene. As though compensating for her tentative acting, she shimmied self-consciously in the crook of the piano.

Lee on the set of *The Jazz Singer,* performing her hit "Lover."

All the while, she leaned doggedly on her Ernest Holmes–inspired positive thinking. Lee had offered to write a song for Judy to share with Jerry Golding (the Thomas character) when they appeared together, through Judy's machinations, in a Broadway show. "This Is a Very Special Day" was a naïvely cheerful tune for the lovebirds to sing aboard a carousel. The ride wasn't just a prop; Lee had spotted it in a Los Angeles playground where she'd taken Nicki. The eight-year-old was enchanted, and Lee convinced Warner Bros. to rent it for the film.

Later on she tried, unsuccessfully, to buy it for Nicki—a wildly extravagant gift from a largely absentee mother. Around the time she was filming *The Jazz Singer*, Lee enrolled Nicki in the Westlake School for Girls, located in the fashionable Holmby Hills section of Los Angeles. At home, Nicki's parenting was shared by Alice Larsen; Lillie Mae Hendrick, Lee's cheeky black housekeeper, cook, and wardrobe mistress; Dona Harsh; and Dave Barbour, whose minimal work load left him ample time to spend with his daughter.

As far as Lee was concerned, her daughter had the best of several worlds. But all this pampering couldn't keep Nicki from feeling lonely. She dreamed of becoming a ballet dancer; but more than anything, she craved her mom's attention. "Peggy was typical of these show-business mothers," said Harsh. "They spoiled their kids rotten, prepared them for nothing, and they weren't there for them. In a sense, they couldn't be. Peggy was earning the money to keep the whole show afloat. She had to travel, and she took Nicki with her when she was little. But then Nicki was in school, and she couldn't go on the road."

No one doubted that Lee adored her little girl. That year, she wrote a poem about her:

> *She's so wise*
> *For one so small . . .*
> *Hard to understand at all*
> *It's almost as though she had lived before*
> *And returned to show me heaven's door*

But with work continuing on *The Jazz Singer*, Lee remained career-driven above all else, and no amount of fatigue could slow her down.

"Whenever I go to do anything, I go all the way," she told the *Los Angeles Times*. "I knock myself out. It has to be that way. Do it or don't do it." At the end of many exhausting days of filming, Lee taped her twice-weekly CBS radio show; stayed up most of the night penning poems; then reported to Warner Bros. at dawn.

Now another glamorous task would add to the consumption of her time. Walt Disney Productions had hired Sonny Burke to compose a handful of songs for an animated feature already in production. It concerned the midwestern romance between Lady, a high-class cocker spaniel, and Tramp, a mutt from the shady side of the tracks. Burke asked a thrilled Peggy Lee to collaborate. Somehow he sensed that the reigning femme fatale of pop-jazz could look through a child's eyes into the film's small-town Victorian world, where animals were as human as people, and capture it in lyrics.

Disney's thin mustache, graying hair, and patient voice made him ideal as the father of children's entertainment—"a charming man, full of enthusiasm," as Lee remembered him. Along with his brother and business partner Roy, he had brought children all over the world some of their dearest imaginary friends: Dumbo, Bambi, Donald Duck, Pinocchio, and most of all Mickey Mouse, for whom he had supplied the voice. In 1950, a thirty-year-old Lee had sat in a darkened movie theater, dazzled by Disney's adaptation of *Cinderella*. She had always identified with the title character of that ancient fairy tale; now she, too, was about to become the belle of a heartwarming cartoon ball.

On June 28, 1952, Hedda Hopper announced that Lee and Burke had begun the score for *Lady and the Tramp*. Before they had signed their contracts, Disney had shown them around his labyrinth studios in Burbank, California. He introduced them to the members of his creative team, including the Nine Old Men, as he called his chief animators. Their work on *Lady and the Tramp* hadn't progressed far beyond storyboards; Disney showed them to his new songwriters and asked them to look for places to insert songs. Lee had lots of suggestions. "He liked every idea—I don't remember being turned down on anything," she said.

The plot mirrored both of their early lives. Disney had grown up in Marceline, Missouri, a railroad town that inspired the one in *Lady and the Tramp*. As depicted in the film, it suggested Lee's various addresses in

North Dakota. Like her, Disney loved trains, which is why he had Tramp live by the railroad tracks. Having grown up feeling closer to animals than she did to most people, Lee was enchanted by the film's truer-than-life canine characters. Lady, a tawny seductress, had ears that draped down like flowing hair and lashes that accentuated her batting eyes. Tramp's trusting gaze, goofy grin, and hanging tongue made him the storybook image of Man's Best Friend. Lady's kindly human mother, Mrs. Darling, reminded Lee of her dear lost Selma. Throughout the animation process, Disney kept real dogs at the studio as a reference point for his artists.

Lee's head spun with ideas. That summer, she and Burke worked on the songs. Shooting on *The Jazz Singer* stretched through September, but Lee's spell of happy prolificacy fell prey to exhaustion. Erskine Johnson of the *Daily News* reported that a "sudden glandular illness" had stricken the singer, alarming everyone on the set. "Peggy's doctors are deeply concerned about her condition," he warned. She began having vocal problems, and her physician announced that she needed throat surgery. Lee's imagination took a dark turn; she decided she was dying.

Even so, she seemed incapable of cutting back. Upon finishing *The Jazz Singer*, Lee plunged into a demanding engagement at the Capitol Theatre in Washington, D.C. In between showings of a film, she headlined a variety show that played five times a day. Onstage she revealed no hint of illness. "She moves around stage in her slow, sultry style, and socks her tunes across with almost no visible effort," wrote a critic. "This is an act which deserves the almost hysterical response it gets from the Lee devotees."

But each night after work, no matter how late it was, she phoned Ernest Holmes in tears over her anticipated death. "Papa," as Lee called Holmes, didn't buy it. More than once he had seen her think herself ill through worry, and her favored opiates—alcohol, cigarettes, promiscuity, and overwork—weren't helping. The minister thought that a stable man in her life might make all the difference. In September, Holmes and his wife showed up at her house for dinner. With them was Brad Dexter, a film actor, then thirty-five, who specialized in playing tough guys. Born Boris Malonovich of Serbian roots, Dexter was a tall, rugged, round-faced man with thinning hair and a friendly smile—not exactly the menacing sort. "He wasn't a great actor," said Lee's friend and future secretary, Betty Jungheim. "But he was a nice guy."

Lee had seen him in *The Asphalt Jungle,* director John Huston's 1950 film noir. She remembered a bit part played by the still-unknown Marilyn Monroe, but couldn't recall Dexter. At the dinner table they made polite small-talk. Dexter was attracted to her, but when he phoned repeatedly in coming weeks to ask her out, she wouldn't commit. Holmes prodded them both, and eventually Lee began to halfheartedly date the actor. Dexter went out of his way to act paternal toward her daughter, a gesture that helped melt Lee's reserve. "Brad's wonderfully kind and generous and good and Nicki saw that," she told an interviewer. After a short courtship, he asked Lee to marry him. The singer hesitated. She didn't love him, yet nearly everyone close to her—Dona Harsh, Dr. and Mrs. Holmes, Nicki, even Dave Barbour—tried to talk her into it.

Lee wouldn't give Dexter an answer, but the pressure to do the right thing for Nicki's sake weighed on her. Lee still believed she hadn't long to live, and she wanted her daughter to have a full-time dad. On December 27, three days before the Los Angeles premiere of *The Jazz Singer*, Hedda Hopper broke the news about Lee and Dexter's impending marriage.

There were other tidbits to report. Warner Bros. had offered Lee a nonexclusive contract with an option for two more features. Recently she had donned a black wig to screen-test for the starring role in *The Helen Morgan Story*, a biopic about the tragic torch singer of the speakeasy era. The studio announced plans to reteam Lee and Thomas in two new films: a remake of *Wonder Bar*, another early Jolson vehicle; and *Everybody Comes to Rick's*, a musical spinoff of *Casablanca*.

On December 30, 1952, *The Jazz Singer* was unveiled at the Fox Beverly Theater in Beverly Hills. Warner Bros. had arranged a glittering premiere. Bleachers were built on the street to hold a huge crowd of Korean War veterans; they and mobs of civilian fans cheered as one luminary after another stepped out of limos and waved: Joan Crawford, Tony Curtis, Jeff Chandler, Greer Garson, Dean Martin, Jerry Lewis, Mary Pickford, even Salvador Dalí. Lee's arrival, on the arm of Dexter, brought a comparable roar of approval.

The movie did not. In *Cue,* Jesse Zunser called the remade classic "modernized, glamorized and excessively sentimentalized." Though Thomas had mimicked Jolson's flamboyant body language and cantorial mannerisms, he came off as stiff and bland. Lee fared no better. Instead of exuding the ebullience of a reigning Broadway star, she seemed distant and unknowable, and mumbled her lines. As in her Benny Goodman days, fear read as aloofness. "Peggy Lee performed adequately, but hardly sensationally, in the feminine lead," wrote one critic. "All the ballyhoo whipped up over Miss Lee is scarcely justified. She certainly doesn't come across as a 'warm' personality."

But Hedda Hopper and her fellow dowager gossip queen, Louella Parsons, took pains to shower Lee with praise—a possible slap at Doris Day, whose refusal to kowtow to journalists would provoke the Hollywood Women's Press Club into giving her their "Sour Apple Award" for uncooperative actors.

As her marriage to Dexter loomed, she supplied gushy tidbits to columnists, perhaps to convince herself that she'd made the right choice. Lee told Betty Craig of the *Denver Post* that Brad was "one of the handsomest and most talented men I have ever met," and that she would stand by him "until death do us part." Brad's more sincere comments invoked giggles among Lee's friends; Dexter, wrote Parsons, "says his mother is crazy about Peggy because she can bake bread and is so sensible."

On the afternoon of Sunday, January 4, 1953, Lee prepared for a lavish wedding in her backyard. Bridesmaid Dona Harsh helped her squeeze into a pink taffeta gown with matching coat. But Lee felt no joy. "I think I shouldn't go through with this," she murmured into a mirror.

An A-list Hollywood crowd had begun streaming into her garden, which was sheltered by a tent. Lee's doubts hadn't curbed her extravagance; the original guest list of two hundred had swelled to nearly twice that many. Bing Crosby, Bob Hope, Jane Russell, and Victor Mature mingled with the throng, as did Lee's collie, Banjo. "It was a storybook wedding," wrote a reporter, "with scores of movie and television 'names' milling about in Peggy's beloved rock gardens, happily consuming seventy-one cases of imported champagne."

Several glasses were consumed by Dave Barbour, who seemed not at all wistful about his ex-wife's new marriage. "Either that or he was loaded," recalled Nicki, who served as flower girl. With no father to give her away, Lee had recruited Michael Curtiz. He walked her to the altar, a bouquet in her hands, and brought her face-to-face with Dexter. Holmes performed the ceremony. After he pronounced them man and wife, Lee tossed her bouquet to the women present. A reporter picked up on the wedding's undercurrent when she wrote of Lee as "sometimes tense and moody despite her relaxed air in public."

With the words "I do," Dexter stepped into his role as Mr. Peggy Lee. On January 7, 1953, the couple took the train to Manhattan for a three-week honeymoon that was all about Lee. The couple attended the New York premiere of *The Jazz Singer* at the Paramount; it was raining, and photographers snapped Dexter carrying his wife over the watery curb. Lee was scheduled to sing "This Is a Very Special Day" on January 20 at the inaugural ball of President Dwight D. Eisenhower, but according to a news report, illness led her to cancel.

According to Betty Jungheim, one aspect of the honeymoon lingered: "Brad said that she wouldn't let him out of bed." Otherwise, Lee found him far less exciting than Greg Bautzer, her recent glamour beau, who had stayed in her life as a friend and lawyer. That year, Bautzer paid for a vanity publication of a Peggy Lee book of poetry, which she titled *Softly—with Feeling: A Collection of Verse*. The forty-page volume, printed on off-white parchment, had a generic cover and looked more like a pamphlet. Most of the poems were wispy musings, jotted while Lee lay woozily under her blanket. Her frequent use of ellipses pointed to the spaciness of her thoughts. "I write in a very odd free form," she explained.

The book serves as a window into Lee's nonmusical concerns at the time. Some of her verse ponders the psychology of mice, spiders, and her pet canary; time and again she channels her inner prairie girl:

> We have a new milkman
> I guess we'll get to know him . . .
> He leaves the wrong amount of eggs . . .
> I guess we'll have to show him . . .

Storm clouds keep passing over the book's sunny landscape, however, as Lee writes of "memories faded . . . lost and jaded" and of "great love / Obscured by mortal fear." She talks to her own body ("You're nothing but a fat shadow . . . you tell me lies . . .") and exposes her fear of death ("the mortal me / Thinks it must / Be dying . . .") There are rambling passages of what would later be called New Age philosophy: "But then, the peace that comes of leaving judgment to a wiser judge . . . the selflessness that leaves a love free to grow like the strongest, most beautiful tree you ever saw . . . to give to love, so that love can be given, to say, in effect, 'Here I am . . . breathe upon me.'"

If nothing else, her poetry is sincere, and both it and she touched Lea Sullivan, Bautzer's secretary. The two women had never met, and when they finally crossed paths in the lobby of Bautzer's office building, Sullivan blurted out, "Oh, my God, it's Peggy Lee!" The singer took Sullivan's hand, smiled broadly, and said, "And I'm glad to see you, too!" Lee could make a stranger feel like her new best friend, and so it was with Sullivan. She asked the young woman's name, then suggested they sit together in the lobby to chat some more. "Do you like what I do?" asked Lee.

"Of course I do!" answered Sullivan.

"OK, I'd like to give you something to remember me by." Lee reached into her purse and pulled out *Softly—with Feeling*, which Sullivan still hadn't seen. "We talked about the book, and she read a few pages for me," said Sullivan.

Lee's enigmatic manner gave even her most simplistic verse a between-the-lines profundity. So it was at the cavernous Hollywood Bowl, the outdoor bandshell where stars ranging from Louis Armstrong to the titans of classical music performed for up to eighteen thousand people. Two-thirds that many listened under the stars as Lee, accompanied by the Los Angeles Philharmonic, recited and sang her epic poem, "New York City Ghost," from *Softly—with Feeling*. The conductor was Lee's sometime songwriting partner, Decca maestro Victor Young, the short, cigar-chomping composer whose stately music for such films as *For Whom the Bell Tolls* and *Samson and Delilah* would earn him twenty-two Oscar nominations. In black tie and tails, Young waved his baton before an army of musicians; out came an atmospheric soundscape that evoked Manhattan in the wee hours. Lee was the soul of stillness as she stood near Young and sang "I'll be a ghost and fly from the coast . . ." Then she intoned, as though in a trance, her poem about the music of the dark city streets: "It came up from your subways and climbed up high; it circled your buildings and swept on with a sigh . . ." Albert Goldberg of the *Los Angeles Times* noted how she had "successfully established a nightclub atmosphere" in the mammoth space.

More and more, the public Lee seemed like an ethereal figure, not of this world. On TV's *The Colgate Comedy Hour*, she sang "Johnny Guitar," her somber title song (written with Young) for a Joan Crawford western. Posed in a Mexican-style gown with a hood, Lee caressed a prop guitar, gazed out into the eyes of an unseen man, and reflected yearningly: "I was always a fool for my Johnny / For the one they call Johnny Guitar."

Johnny, of course, was Dave. Lee had continued to romanticize their parting; the two of them could have been Romeo and Juliet, ideally matched lovers wrenched apart by fate. The woman who had grown up on daydreams now sang from inside them, and the results, according to Mark Murphy, were "hypnotizing." On television, observed the jazz singer, "you thought she was singing only to you. It was as though she knew you. Her face in those days was made for TV; it was a beautiful thing." In her book *America's Child: A Woman's Journey Through the Radical Sixties*, Susan Sherman shared a youthful memory of attending a telecast of *The Colgate Comedy Hour*, which her stepfather booked. When Lee drifted before the camera, Sherman beheld a woman unlike any living being she'd ever encountered. "She was dressed in a gauzy white dress and I felt like I was literally seeing an angel—the closest image my child's mind could conjure up."

Lee's innermost feelings radiated through her songs, but acting was another matter. *The Jazz Singer* hadn't scored at the box office. Certainly Lee was no threat to Doris Day, yet the *Hollywood Reporter* hinted that Day wanted Lee out: "Warner's decided Peggy Lee ain't Doris Day and is giving in to Doris' demands." Certainly the studio's enthusiasm for Lee had cooled. *The Helen Morgan Story* went to raven-haired Ann Blyth, an Oscar nominee for her role as Joan Crawford's vixen of a daughter in *Mildred Pierce*. *Wonder Bar* and *Everybody Comes to Rick's* were shelved. That fall Danny Thomas found his niche on the small screen in the long-running sitcom *Make Room for Daddy*; as for Lee, Warner Bros. canceled her option "by mutual agreement," giving her a $20,000 payoff.

It was a crushing blow to Lee, and in years to come she seldom mentioned *The Jazz Singer*. But over at Disney, *Lady and the Tramp* was showing great promise. In a string of meetings with Walt, Sonny Burke and Lee presented their new songs in character. From there they made cleverly produced demo recordings. For "The Siamese Cat Song," the duet of two mischievous felines named Si and Am, Lee dubbed one part over another, singing "We are Siamese, if you please" in a faux Thai accent. On piano, Burke plunked out a regal tune that could have greeted the King of Siam. Lee was all maternal warmth in "La La Lu," a lullaby sung by Lady's human owner, Darling, to her newborn baby. Another canine character, Mame, was a mangy, one-toothed old showgirl from the dog pound. For her, Lee and Burke wrote "He's a Tramp," a torch song with a stripper's bump-and-grind rhythm.

The voices of Si, Am, Darling, and Mame had not been cast. Disney had rarely asked a star of her level to do voiceovers, but he offered all four roles to Peggy Lee. She was ecstatic. To perform in a Disney film meant universal prestige; now her mark would be all over *Lady and the Tramp*. Her joy took one more leap when Disney renamed a character after her. He had intended to call the vamping pound dog Mame, and to show her wearing bangs, a fashionable style for the woman of 1952. Then Eisenhower became president, bringing with him a wife, Mamie, who had bangs. Disney couldn't risk insulting the First Lady, so he asked Lee if they could call the dog Peg instead. "*Of course!*" she exclaimed.

Her influence on the character didn't stop there. "Peg" had to strut as sexily as a stripper. Animator Eric Larsen searched for inspiration at a burlesque house, but all he saw were tired women going through the motions. Lee, he recalled, "knew what we wanted—the biggest vamp we could get without being vulgar." In his office, Lee sashayed back and forth as her "He's a Tramp" demo played in the background. Larsen and his assistants sketched her moves. "Peg" came to life in those drawings—an over-the-hill but still sexy minx who brandishes her tail and rolls her eyes like Mae West.

According to the script, Old Trusty, a wise, elderly bloodhound, would die under the wheel of the dogcatcher's wagon. But Lee, who had once carried her beloved dog's dead body up the stairs of a train depot, couldn't bear the thought. "Walt, please don't let that dog die," she pleaded. "Children won't be able to stand that." Disney argued that the story needed dramatic tension, but he proposed a compromise: "I will let him live, but the rat stays." The rat was a snarling creature who sneaks into Darling's house and waits at the crib, ready to devour the baby, until Tramp bolts in and kills the toothy rodent in the nick of time.

As for Si and Am and "The Siamese Cat Song," Disney let Lee poke around in the sound-effects department for gadgets that could lend spice to the recording. A set of finger cymbals gave it just the right ancient, Far-Eastern sound.

Everyone at the studio agreed: Lee's participation in a Disney film was an event. A company photographer trailed the star, snapping pictures of her in discussion with various members of the creative team. By now Lee had signed five contracts, four for the songs and one for six days of vocal work. She would receive $3,500 for the voices and $1,000 to split with Burke for cowriting six songs—respectable fees for the time, and Lee accepted them willingly. Because she was under exclusive contract to Decca, Disney added the provision that it retained no rights to "make phonograph records and/or transcriptions for sale to the public." "Transcriptions" was the industry term for audio discs produced strictly for radio and not for sale; its inclusion in that phrase seemed like a careless slip by the legal department. Twenty-five years before the creation of home video, nobody at Disney could have foreseen the weight that the word "transcription" would one day hold.

With Disney animator Gerry Geronimi during the production of *Lady and the Tramp*, 1953.

———

ONSCREEN, LEE WAS but a single cog in a vast machine; in nightclubs, she controlled her whole production as deftly as a puppeteer. Her marriage went on hold as she flew to New York to launch a lengthy engagement. She took her sister Della as assistant but left behind Dexter, who struggled to advance a slow-moving Hollywood career.

Lee's newfound Manhattan headquarters was tonier than anything she could have envisioned in her North Dakota youth. La Vie en Rose stood on an upscale block—East Fifty-Fourth Street between Lexington and Park Avenues—but it aimed for the minimalist chic of a boîte on Paris's Left Bank. Stylishly printed menus listed costly French cuisine; abstract wire sculptures hung on the walls. During her shows, Lee gazed out at a sea of shadowy faces, lit faintly from below by the candles on the tables.

La Vie en Rose was a departure for its owner, Monte Proser. For years, the British-born impresario had worked as a producer amid the sweat and greasepaint of Broadway. In 1940 he hopped in bed with the mafia when he and mob boss Frank Costello launched the Copacabana. By decade's end, Costello's thuggish front man, Jules Podell, had forced Proser out and taken over as manager. Proser was ready for some class, and in 1951 he opened La Vie en Rose.

The club lasted only three years, but it set a high bar of taste. Virginia Wicks described it as "an elegant nightclub where elegant people could go and hear usually well-known stars, who were always sophisticated." They included the Portuguese *fado* singer Amalia Rodrigues, the beautiful black supper-club singer and film actress Dorothy Dandridge, Ella Fitzgerald, Pearl Bailey, and Nat King Cole. La Vie en Rose also hosted the Manhattan cabaret debut of a still-unknown Eartha Kitt. With her humming voice and exotic, multilingual repertoire—Spanish, French, Turkish, English—Kitt struck that worldliest of audiences as weird, and she flopped.

But they adored Peggy Lee, and not just because of her singing. As a performer, Lee's innovations lay in her presentation. "I wanted to make it as close to a Broadway performance as I could," she explained. Increasingly she calculated every effect, from her precisely timed hand gestures to the subtlest vocal nuances. Unlike Billie Holiday, Lee seldom improvised vocally; she preferred to deliver tunes as written while adding a dose of swinging rhythm. To have every detail in place before showtime freed her from worry, and allowed her to escape into a song's essence.

Before the La Vie en Rose opening, Lee employed an arranger who was just as obsessively probing as herself. Gil Evans was revered for his work on a set of recordings that had launched Miles Davis and the art of cool jazz; he went on to arrange several of the trumpeter's most celebrated albums. Evans wrote with a moody, cerebral richness inspired by his love of Kurt Weill and of French and Spanish impressionist composers. Exactly which of Lee's songs he worked on isn't known for sure, but he made a permanent impact on her taste—"not just musically," she said, "but from the man's thinking. That's a key, I believe, in all fields of art . . . A musician must start to *think* before he can become great."

As for who would play piano for her, Lee went back to the top. Jimmy Rowles was the hard-drinking, foul-mouthed, but exquisitely sensitive accompanist for many of the greatest singers in jazz; throughout the years they included Holiday, Ella Fitzgerald, Sarah Vaughan, and Carmen McRae. Rowles typified Lee's best pianists—white men who played with a laid-back funkiness. Songwriter Dave Frishberg, who also played piano, was in awe of his touch. "Rowles could milk sound from the bass clef register that was almost organlike. He splashed chords down with a rolling, blurry attack that was his alone." No singer intimidated him; with Lee he amused himself by muttering expletives out of her hearing range: "Wait till you hear this intro, you bitch!"

Aside from Rowles, Lee shared La Vie's tiny bandstand with Ed Shaughnessy, future drummer for the *Tonight* show orchestra, as well as bassist Joe Mondragon and trumpeter Pete Candoli, two fixtures of West Coast cool jazz. Lee took them all over the musical map. She sang "Good Morning Heartache," the Billie Holiday trademark about a woman whose closest companion is grief; dipped into vaudeville with "Hard Hearted Hannah," the tale of a "vamp from Savannah" who "loves to see men suffer"; and unearthed a mystical English folk ballad, "The Riddle Song." On the night when *Down Beat*'s critic came, Lee's scaled-down arrangement of "Lover" caused such excitement that she had to sing it twice at the first show, three times at the second. "Being very cautious about overstatement," wrote the reviewer, "we will only say conservatively that Peggy gave the greatest performance we have seen delivered by any singer in a Manhattan club in the last five years—and that includes everybody, from Lena Horne and Sinatra on down."

Shaughnessy glanced out at a sea of spellbound listeners as Lee stood in a pinspot and sang "(Ah, the Apple Trees) When the World Was Young," a worldly Frenchwoman's lament for her lost innocence. The song was a gift from Johnny Mercer. In 1953, a music publisher had asked the lyricist to craft an English adaptation of an Édith Piaf favorite, "Le Chevalier de Paris." A French female poet, Angèle Vannier, had written the song with composer Marie Philippe-Gérard, a protégé of Maurice Ravel. Vannier's words detailed an old knight for whom a "round and sweet" apple sets off as many recollections as Proust's madeleine.

With Lee in mind, Mercer feminized the protagonist into "la grande femme fatale, the belle of the ball." Wealth, fame, and countless men are hers, but love is not, and she yearns to recapture "the schoolgirl who used to be me."

That spring, Lee recorded the song just as she had sung it at La Vie en Rose. Pete Candoli begins "When the World Was Young" with a bit of "La Marseillaise," the French national anthem. In comes Lee, singing coolly about the brittle glamour of her nights. As distant memories of true happiness take over—"On our backs we'd lie, looking at the sky"—Norma, the vulnerable child, and Peggy Lee, her conquering creation, come face-to-face.

The performance captivated Charlie Cochran, a cabaret pianist-singer who emerged later in the 1950s. He noticed "a kind of scrim between her and the listener—some kind of interruption between her and reality. She was blurred in the most beautiful kind of Cézanne-ish ways."

"When the World Was Young," along with much of her La Vie en Rose repertoire, appeared on an eight-song, ten-inch Decca LP. *Black Coffee* marked Lee's breakthrough as a torch singer of utmost refinement—yet one who ventured fearlessly into the dark corners of the heart. At Decca's studio in midtown New York, Lee and her quartet recreated the midnight jazz-club ambiance of her late shows. She always preferred to record late, and with her favorite vocal relaxant at hand—cognac spiked with honey—she entered the somber world of *Black Coffee*.

Just like saxophonist Lester Young on Billie Holiday's 1930s recordings, Candoli served as Lee's shadow voice. Sometimes brassy, sometimes muted and distant, his trumpet commented wryly as she sang; he added vinegar to her sweetness. Rowles played with such restraint that at times he was almost imperceptible, but he gave *Black Coffee* the pulse of the blues. At least some of the charts were his; they flirted with bebop, but Lee had made it clear that everything her band played had to enhance the drama. She asked Shaughnessy to "sprinkle a little with the cymbals" on one song and to "get a darker rhythm going" on another. Producer Milt Gabler mostly sat back and left the music in the artists' hands.

The record that emerged is a portrait of addiction—to a man, to illusion, to the past. Its title song, written in 1948 by Sonny Burke and the movie lyricist Paul Francis Webster, is the plaint of a dead-end victim of love, alone at home. Candoli's wailing horn helps conjure up a seedy apartment in half-light, a figure in a nightgown sprawled on the sofa. A Holiday-like cragginess coarsens Lee's voice as she mourns a woman's fate—to "drown her past regrets in coffee and cigarettes" while waiting for her "baby to maybe come around." In a *Down Beat* Blindfold Test, Leonard Feather played "When the World Was Young" for bandleader Raymond Scott, a Juilliard-schooled pioneer of electronic music. Scott, who was known for his brilliant ears, couldn't discern Peggy Lee from her idol. "It must be Billie Holiday," he said, "but it's so accurate and so precise, it's so artistic that I can't believe it. That's the best I have ever heard her."

Throughout the album, the fragile flower and the dominatrix in Lee collide. In "Easy Living," she melts in the arms of the lover she lives for; the arrangement starts with a quote from a classical piece she loved, Ottorino Respighi's *The Pines of Rome*. Cole Porter had written "My Heart Belongs to Daddy" as the coy boast of a kept girl who loves to tease her swains. Lee's version strips away the cuteness; against Shaughnessy's frantic double-time drumming, she sings as a mature woman in tough control of her heart. "Love Me or Leave Me" was a wilting torch song from the twenties; on *Black Coffee*, Lee barks it out in syncopated rhythm to a man playing hard to get: "I want no one unless that someone is *you*!"

The armor falls away in "A Woman Alone with the Blues," written by Willard Robison. Lee's performance starts and ends with the sound of tolling church bells. In between is a saloon song about lost love and self-pity, sung at a crawl that evokes the last slouching, tipsy figure at a bar. "I would make Pete Candoli go way to the end of the studio and play against the wall," explained Lee, "because I was trying to make him sound like a French horn."

On the LP's lilac-tinted cover image, items on a table suggest a woman in waiting: a cup of coffee, a cigarette holder leaning against an ashtray, a faded rose. But it was the music that dazzled Mark Murphy. The jazz singer was twenty-one when *Black Coffee* appeared; he studied every note. "That record was her catalytic arrival," he said. "Everything finally came together. She emerged as one of our great singers. The rhythm, the ability to do the ballads in such a communicative way—that album opened up a whole new world for her."

Down Beat awarded it five stars, a rating reserved for instant classics. "Here, we suspect, is the true Peggy," wrote the reviewer. "Warm, personal, Holidayish, sexy, and as un*Lover*like as you could wish. Or, when the occasion demands it, fiery, swinging, with a beat few can beat."

In years to come, *Black Coffee* would leave its mark on a wide array of female artists. Joni Mitchell loved it; Petula Clark called the album "my Bible. I knew every note she sang, every note of the orchestrations. I did record the song 'Black Coffee' eventually, but I really shouldn't have touched it." k.d. lang did, on her first solo album, *Shadowland*. Marianne Faithfull pronounced Lee's rendition so "virtuoso" that she didn't dare study it before recording the song, lest she end up copying Lee. Seventies pop star Helen Reddy, who grew up in Australia, found a copy of *Black Coffee* and played it "to tatters." Reddy told the columnist David Noh that "The problem arose when someone said, 'You sound just like her,' and I thought, 'Uh-oh,' and began to develop my own style."

To Lorraine Feather, the jazz-singing daughter of Leonard Feather, Lee was "pretty well perfect. I never heard her rush a note or sing out of tune. She had a sense of humor; she knew how to pull the audience in and make them laugh with her, care about her. She had that gift that some performers have of being alluring to the audience yet keeping them at a bit of a distance without their realizing it. And Peggy had a very distinctive instrument; you couldn't mix her up with anyone else. It was sweet yet kind of smoky. There was something poignant about the way she sang even when she was happy. There was a vulnerability. She was soft and ultra-feminine, but it was combined with a steeliness you had to have in order to forge a career in show business."

Black Coffee scored critically, but it was a far cry from commercial pop, and at a time when LPs were just starting to catch on, the album didn't sell much. What's more, it seemed as though Lee were living under the same black cloud as the woman she had embodied in the title song. Late in June of 1953, while onstage at Ciro's, she was suddenly racked with abdominal pains. She made it through the show, but afterward she went straight to St. John's Hospital in Santa Monica. Doctors found nothing, but she canceled the next four nights' shows. Once more, her friends pointed to exhaustion as the cause.

Just as likely, the pain was a manifestation of emotional duress. Offstage, Ed Shaughnessy sensed a conflicted woman. "I really loved her as a person," said the drummer. "She was very kind and very dear. But I used to think there was an innate sadness in her." Lee had felt for months that she was living a lie in her marriage to Brad Dexter, and their union was on the brink of collapse. "It was a big mistake," she admitted later. As much as she had encouraged Lee to marry him, Dona Harsh had to agree. "I liked Brad a lot," she said, "but he was too calm for Peggy." Dexter had tried to persuade his wife to cut back on her travel for the sake of the marriage and Nicki; Lee flat-out refused. She had no intention of sacrificing any part of her career; she'd fought too hard for it. Alice Larsen still served as live-in housekeeper and nursemaid; Lee tended to avoid housework. "I don't have time," she declared.

While Dexter sweated out jobs, Lee's earnings reached a hefty $250,000 a year. Someone, she argued, had to be the breadwinner. Yet much of that income went toward supporting her grandiose lifestyle, which included a staff. "With such disregard for the money she earns, Peggy has kept little," wrote *Redbook*. Funds kept running low, which sent Lee into a tailspin. On the road she covered Dona Harsh's room-service bills, but forbade her to order steak, "because it was too expensive," said Harsh. "We ate a lot of ground round."

Meanwhile, every week Lee gave her five hundred dollars as a not-so-petty expense fund. Harsh was so rock-solid reliable that Hedda Hopper saluted her in print as a model of efficiency; yet panic over money made Lee's trust crack. "We had a fight about something," recalled Harsh. "We were standing out in her driveway, and she said, '*Where's my five hundred dollars?*' I said, 'You think I want to steal it, Peggy?' She said, 'I don't know!' So I took it out of my purse and threw it on the driveway. And it started blowing around. She went after it, let me tell you."

That September, her luck crashed. In a notice sent to Warner Bros., the Internal Revenue Service announced that it had filed a levy against her wages in the amount of $8,315. She and Barbour had underpaid their 1949 taxes. Lee blamed "Dave's business mistakes," but the IRS took no excuses.

Within the same week, Brad Dexter moved out of Lee's house on Denslow. Divorce proceedings began quickly. Nicki was disappointed, for she'd grown fond of her kindly stepfather. Dexter was even sadder, but he knew that nothing would change; in the course of nine and a half months of marriage he had metamorphosed from "husband to help," as Lee Ringuette observed. Friends had watched Dexter standing in the wings of theaters, holding his wife's glass of cognac. "This was a proud, good man," said Ringuette. "He wanted no part of that."

Back she went to the Santa Monica courthouse where just two and a half years earlier Lee had gone for her divorce from Barbour. She seemed embarrassed as she murmured a vague set of grievances to the judge. Dexter, she said, "didn't like my friends or business associates"; pressed for details, she had none to offer. Her lawyer alleged that Dexter had "interfered with business transactions . . . and had argued with her business manager." Lee added that Dexter had worked only three weeks since the wedding. "He asked me to restrict my career to local engagements," she complained. "But that was impossible. I had to earn some money."

An interlocutory divorce was granted on November 3, 1953; the final judgment sailed through on both sides.

Dexter went on to act in a few notable films, notably the 1960 western *The Magnificent Seven*, where he appeared alongside Charles Bronson, Yul Brynner, and Steve McQueen. Four years later, while in Hawaii to film the role of a World War II marine sergeant in *None but the Brave*, Dexter earned his true claim to fame. The director and star, Frank Sinatra, had gone swimming with Ruth Koch, wife of the film's producer, Howard Koch. The two of them were swept out to sea by a ferocious undertow. Dexter, who had accompanied them to the beach, lunged into the tide; aided by lifeguards, he rescued them. The actor had saved Sinatra's life; after that, his short marriage to Peggy Lee seemed immaterial.

"Sometimes she wakes up sad, and then her name is Deloris."
Peggy Lee, as Rose Hopkins, clutches her "baby" in *Pete Kelly's Blues*. (COURTESY OF RICHARD MORRISON)

Chapter Seven

*I*N HER PRIVATE life as in her songs, Lee required drama. Following her separation, Lee sold the house in Westwood at a loss. She found another in Coldwater Canyon, the hilltop region that lies between Beverly Hills and the San Fernando Valley. Once moved in, Lee began to hear strange noises. She decided the house was haunted. A ghost, she believed, kept ringing the doorbell; and when her sister Della entered the basement through a trapdoor and it closed on her head, Lee blamed the ghost. She told *Cosmopolitan* of the sinister goings-on: "One day my manager was sitting alone in the living room, and all the cornices fell down." By the time Lee published her memoir in 1989, the haunted-house tale had grown; Alice Larsen, she claimed, had seen a stool "walk" across the kitchen floor, while Della "tripped on absolutely nothing and broke her leg."

For a woman who at age five had imagined seeing her dead mother's face in the clouds, brushes with the paranormal, real or delusional, weren't rare. In this case, Lee's far-flung powers of visualization might have leapt out of a story she'd heard about that house. Allegedly it had belonged to actress Olivia de Havilland in 1948, the year she filmed *The Snake Pit*. De Havilland played a woman who is trapped in an insane asylum with no clue how she got there; unexplainable voices and sounds threaten to push her permanently over the edge.

Lee decided it was best to move. In between shows at Ciro's, a friend informed her of a beautiful vacant home, also in Coldwater Canyon. Deep in the night after work, they drove to the address—2345 Kimridge Road—and investigated it by flashlight. Some of its ten rooms offered panoramic mountain views, and Lee detected no evil spirits; she fell in love with the house on sight. The next day she made arrangements to buy it.

Almost immediately Lee, who had just been in hock to the IRS, began an expensive renovation. The house's entrance had a black gate with a Chinese motif; Lee extended the Asian theme by planting a Japanese garden out back. She added a thirty-foot goldfish pond with a bridge over it, birch trees, stone tiling, and a kidney-shaped swimming pool. Assisting her in the design was handsome, dark-blond Eduardo (Eddie) Tirella, a decorator, landscaper, and hatmaker. Tirella and Lee scampered about like children, buying goodies at nurseries and antique shops. Lee told *TV Guide* of walking on the beach and scavenging a cartful of colorful rocks and pebbles. Tirella turned them into a rock garden that Lee could see from her bedroom window. "She wanted every single pebble to be illuminated by the moonlight," said Tirella's friend, actor Jack Larson. "They were busy covering them with some kind of coating to pick up the light."

When guests came, Lee pointed out such rare items as an Egyptian libation pitcher, a Dresden hinged box that came (she said) from Marie Antoinette's castle, and a fourteenth-century bronze lamp from the mansion of automobile mogul Henry Ford. The white living-room carpet "was like Pekingese fur," recalled Lorraine Feather. "It literally had long hair. People were always snagging their heels in it."

The singer's king-size, pale blue bed rested on an elevated white platform, like a horizontal throne. The push of a button made a filmy white curtain surround the bed. Elsewhere in the house were crystal chandeliers, Louis XIV chairs, and other accoutrements suited to the grandest of stars.

Lee often greeted the press at home, but her comments could leave them scratching their heads. She told a writer from the *New York Journal-American*: "I get my ideas from odd little things. Birds in the garden. Trees. Trees always make me think of patience. If I write a song, I suppose it's a kind of prayer."

Lee seemed grateful for company—especially now, after two failed marriages. "She hates to be alone," observed Jimmy Rowles. When they rehearsed in her soundproof home music studio, he said, "You would be lucky to get away before dawn." Even for a man as hard-boiled as Rowles, though, Lee's charm was hard to resist. She could make almost anyone feel like her new best friend; from then on, she expected round-the-clock availability.

One day Lee phoned Gene DiNovi in Brooklyn and commanded him to fly to her home to spend some days rehearsing. He wound up staying for weeks. "I was more or less a captive on the top of Coldwater Canyon. She would wake me up at three in the morning and say, you know that arrangement we're doing on such-and-such? When we get to the bridge, could you give me a star? I said, 'Sure, Peg. Can I go back to sleep now?'"

Lee's sister Marianne lived in the San Fernando Valley with her sons, Lee and Lynn, and her daughter, Merrilee. But the singer kept her on Kimridge as often as possible to serve as girl Friday; Lee also phoned her at the last minute when she needed assistance on the road. "Aunt Peg was at ease until there was an engagement looming," said Lee Ringuette. "At that point she turned into a she-lion. She had trouble keeping help. She'd give them lists and lists of things to do. She'd be getting down to the wire and mom had to go along. In my mother's over-selflessness, this is something she would do, but it was really difficult for her and she didn't enjoy it."

In 1953, another angelic figure flew into Lee's inner circle. Probably no singer besides she would have thought to add a harp to her jazz combo, but the instrument's wafting, sugar-spun tones comforted a woman in perpetual need of soothing. Frequently at the house Lee played a recording of Ravel's pastoral chamber work, "Introduction and Allegro," built around the harp. She had a keen ear for instruments that would complement her ethereal quality, such as oboe and French horn; now she sent Pete Candoli in search of a harpist. The trumpeter thought of Stella Castellucci, who had worked with him in the ABC radio orchestra. Then twenty-two, Castellucci was a shy Italian girl from a religious family. She had never played jazz or even gone to a nightclub; one of Lee's friends likened her to a Catholic nun.

Candoli invited her to a rehearsal, and the harpist's fear turned to bedazzlement. "Peggy could swing her head off and really be a jazz singer, and at the same time she was a profound singer of ballads," she said. Lee invited her to "jump in whenever you want." The singer hired Castellucci on the spot. For the next seven years, her graceful, billowing glissandos swathed Lee's voice in a celestial cloud. "She's a complete musician," said Lee. "The sweetest girl. I think she's devoted her whole life to music."

Further balm to Lee's frazzled nerves was the spiritual counsel of Adela Rogers St. Johns, who worked under Ernest Holmes as a minister for his Institute of Religious Science and Philosophy. Then nearing sixty, St. Johns was one of the most accomplished women of her time: a pioneering screenwriter of the silent era, the author of numerous novels and stories, and a journalist whose reporting on crime, politics, society, Hollywood, and sports would help earn her the Presidential Medal of Freedom. Both worldly-wise and down-to-earth, she struck Lee as an oracle; in years to come the singer couldn't go onstage without phoning her nightly.

Lee needed bolstering, for she kept working at a neurotic pace, staying up all night and sleeping little. On November 2, 1953, she collapsed at home. A doctor diagnosed her with severe exhaustion and ordered her home to her powder-puff bedroom to rest out the year. Lee followed his advice for less than a week. In the first month of her recuperation, wrote Hedda Hopper, Lee "wrote three new songs, finished eleven oil paintings, and completed the booking arrangements for her 1954 tour . . . Contracts already signed will bring her in $380,000."

The singer didn't fully heal for months. But by the spring of 1954, she had rebounded enough to plunge what columnist Dorothy Kilgallen termed a "torrid romance." Young Don Cherry did double duty as a pro golfer and a best-selling pop idol; when Lee met him he was in between two big hits, "Thinking of You" and "Band of Gold." Cherry sang in an ardent baritone, but between songs audiences saw a bashful, drawling lad from Wichita, Texas. Lee had met him in Washington, D.C.'s Capitol Theater, where Cherry appeared on a bill she was headlining. Before the opening, Lee had spent hours rehearsing onstage with Jimmy Rowles; she paid no attention to anyone else's scheduled rehearsal time, and Cherry was furious to learn that she had used up all of his.

At the first show, she heard him singing his latest single, "I'm Just a Country Boy." Afterward, Cherry overheard her asking Rowles in a testy voice, "Why would they book a country singer to sing with *me*?" That night, Rowles approached him and conveyed an invitation from the star to attend a party in her honor. "Tell Miss Lee to go shit in her hat," Cherry said.

When he arrived in his dressing room the next day, he found a rose in a small vase. Alongside it was a note from Lee: "The hat is full."

Lee had no trouble acting the aggressor, and she promptly asked him out to dinner. Their late-night meetings became a ritual. Cherry fell under her spell. "Nobody in my life had ever happened to me like this!" he exclaimed in a golly-gee tone that proved he *was* just a country boy. Lee, he added, was "the greatest talent I ever met"; if anyone had asked him to name his dream woman, "it would have been her."

In her hands, the Texas lad grew up fast. He watched her gulping cognac before the first show; by the time the two of them walked back to her hotel, Lee was feeling no pain. On their walks they passed White Castle, the fast-food chain restaurant famous for its small, square-shaped burgers. One night Lee commanded Cherry to go in and buy eight. He obeyed. Up in her suite, Lee ordered him to "take them to the bed and shake them out" as though they were playing cards. "Shuffle 'em!" she said. He obeyed. Then she said, 'Deal!'" He tossed four of the greasy hamburgers on the bed in front of her, and Lee picked them up. "She said, 'I am going down with one pickle!' I said, 'That's no good. I've got to have the piece of lettuce.'"

Early in their brief liaison, Lee arranged for Cherry to open for her at her Las Vegas base, the Copa Room of the Sands Hotel. The Nevada gambling town would become the source of her heftiest earnings for the next many years. Lee began singing there just as Vegas was burgeoning into the most garish entertainment hub in the world. All along the fabled Las Vegas Strip of resort hotels, neon signs trumpeted the presence of Frank Sinatra at the Desert Inn, Liberace at the Riviera, Marlene Dietrich at the Sahara, Dean Martin and Jerry Lewis at the Flamingo, and countless other stars, all of them enshrined in the desert within castles of glass, chrome, and steel. The British theatrical legend Noël Coward, Vegas's most high-flown headliner, marveled at the bizarre allure of his surroundings. "I am simply mad for all this plush and honky tonk," he told Gilbert Millstein of the *New York Times*. "I am fascinated by the mountains looking like peach-colored cardboard. I love this curious, artificial vividness plunked down in the midst of the most primitive part of the world."

In fact, the Strip was a shrewdly designed, mafia-run money machine. It lured in tourists with free chips, cheap booze, and glamorous but inexpensively priced shows, then seduced them into dropping every dollar they had, or didn't have, in the gambling casinos. The gangster financiers could well afford to pay twenty-five to fifty thousand dollars a week to their headliners—staggering fees at the time. And if Nat King Cole, Sammy Davis, Jr., and other black stars were barred from using the pools or even sleeping in the hotels where they performed, few of them turned down the money. In some hotels, blacks were forbidden from crossing the casino floor, lest they offend racist but deep-pocketed whites. As George Jacobs, Sinatra's black valet, wrote in his memoir, *Mr. S: My Life with Frank Sinatra*, "Vegas was a Wild West cowboy town back then, and these cowboys didn't cotton to colored dudes."

Lee certainly did. But given her heartfelt devotion to black music and its creators, it seemed odd that she employed so relatively few black musicians in her rhythm sections. Her groups may have hinted at the "hot" sound of rhythm-and-blues and Harlem swing, but they looked cool, California, and white, which suited the needs of Vegas. Attention spans in the showrooms tended to run even shorter than the town's racial tolerance; but Lee didn't compromise her art, even if entertainers were told to wrap it up in less than an hour.

Her boss at the Copa Room was Jack Entratter, ex-manager of the Copacabana. Under his auspices, the club played host, in the 1950s and '60s, to Judy Garland, Ella Fitzgerald, Jimmy Durante, Bobby Darin, Bob Hope, Milton Berle, Bing Crosby, Tony Bennett, and most famously the Rat Pack, the summit of five stars—Frank Sinatra, Dean Martin, Peter Lawford, Joey Bishop, and Sammy Davis, Jr.—who carried on like frat boys. They and their colleagues looked out into a vast, low-ceilinged showroom whose rows of neatly arranged tables for two, covered in white tablecloths, seated seven hundred and fifty. The stage, behind a rail, was large enough for an orchestra. Between shows, the dancing "Copa Girls" kicked and smiled in their scanties.

Still, Lee's shows there were barely less subtle than the ones she had performed at La Vie en Rose. "She didn't adjust to the audience; they adjusted to her," explained George Schlatter, who managed Ciro's. "I don't remember us ever having an inattentive audience," said bongo player Jack Costanzo, who worked with Lee in the mid-fifties. The Sands, he said, "had security you wouldn't believe"; noisemakers were brusquely silenced or thrown out.

Lee sometimes ran into a top Vegas attraction, the glamorous Polly

Bergen, whose career skyrocketed after she won an Emmy Award for her TV portrayal of the tragic torch singer Helen Morgan. As Bergen noticed, the sexy, confident Lee of the stage could seem lost without a song to escape into. "She struck me as strange," said Bergen. "She had this kind of blank look on her face all the time."

Her enigmatic nature fascinated Jack Webb, the actor who played the most famous fictional detective of the 1950s—stern, deadpan Sergeant Joe Friday of *Dragnet*, the hit crime series of radio and TV. Lee was one of Webb's favorite singers; now he had devised a project that he hoped would bring them together. Webb had launched a production company, Mark VII, in order to create a film inspired by *Pete Kelly's Blues*, a Dixieland radio show he had produced in 1951. Now, in counterpoint to the slap-happy sound of 1920s traditional jazz, Webb had developed a tale about a cornet-playing bandleader thrust into a maelstrom of gangsters, insanity, and murder. Warner Bros. had agreed to distribute the film, to be shot in Cinemascope, the new widescreen format. Webb would direct, star, and invest much of his own money in this labor of love.

Early in 1954, Lee answered her phone and heard the grave voice of Joe Friday on the other end. True to the reputation of that character—who told witnesses, "Just give me the facts"—Webb leveled with Lee. He said he had a "wonderful yet unglamorous part" for her: that of Rose Hopkins, an alcoholic Prohibition-era gun moll and sometime speakeasy singer who loses her mind. Lee was intrigued. Webb promised to send her the script by Richard Breen, who had just won an Oscar for *Titanic*; prior to that Breen had written the script for *Niagara*, which gave Marilyn Monroe her first starring role.

Rose clearly mirrored Peggy Lee, whose blurry, distant quality suggested a woman not quite in touch with real life, but intimate with pain. Once the script arrived, Lee pored over it. The role both attracted and disturbed her. "She drinks too much and sings a little," she said of the abused Rose. For obvious reasons, the part spoke deeply to her. Onscreen Lee would have to lose control, singing drunkenly out of tune and cracking under pressure—daunting prospects for an artist who only wanted audiences to see her at her most disciplined, edited best. But in her work, at least, Lee remained willing to confront even her darkest sides. Rose spoke to her. She accepted Webb's offer.

His instincts about Lee were shared by Arthur Hamilton, Mark VII's resident songwriter. A former delivery boy for a drug company in Seattle, Washington, Hamilton had come highly recommended by Webb's ex-wife, the sultry singer-actress Julie London, Hamilton's date at the high school prom. In 1955, his song "Cry Me a River" would make London a star.

Through Webb, he got to know Peggy Lee. "It was like meeting the Mona Lisa," he said. Hamilton caught her attention with one tune, "Bouquet of Blues." Its heroine—"the girl of great regret"—lives with the ghost of a vanished man who haunts her thoughts. Hamilton's memorable description of her—"Misery in high-heeled shoes / Holding a bouquet of blues"—summed up every downtrodden dame ever mistreated in a film noir.

For "Bouquet of Blues," the composer had envisioned "a beautiful woman walking the streets alone, no place to go, thinking about what brought her to where she is. You could hear the echo of her footsteps." On May 26, 1954, Lee became the first major artist to record a Hamilton song. She performed "Bouquet of Blues" at Decca's Los Angeles studio, where a jazz quartet spun an ambiance as chilling as any on *Black Coffee*. Benny Carter's alto sax wove icily around Lee's voice, which shivered with a sense of impending doom.

"Bouquet of Blues" failed to make even the bottom of the *Billboard* pop chart. But the disc became a staple on many a late-night disc-jockey show. According to Mark Murphy, it became "a kind of hit among the bopsters and the hipsters. Peggy *was* the girl of great regret."

Yet she presented so many masks to the public that it was hard for them, or her, to know who the real Peggy Lee was. On her recordings that year, the cool, swinging Lee and the tragic one alternated with several others. She joined the Mills Brothers, the suave black vocal quartet, to record her own "Straight Ahead," a hand-clapping gospel tune about rocking down the road to salvation. Lee wrote the flamenco song "The Gypsy with Fire in His Shoes" for a Tony Curtis western, *The Rawhide Years*; she sang it in a faint Spanish accent while her coauthor, Brazilian guitarist Laurindo Almeida, plucked away tempestuously and Sammy Davis, Jr., tap-danced in rhythm.

In a package tour set to play a month of one-nighters that fall, Lee traveled with a largely black cast—all of them stars at New York's Apollo Theater including jazz crooner Billy Eckstine, doo-wop quartet the Drifters, and comic George Kirby. But luck was against them. During the first week, their bus passed through towns hit by Hurricane Hazel, a tropical storm that had blown from Haiti to the U.S. and Canada, causing many fatalities and wreaking devastation. The cast escaped harm; but whether through fear of Hazel, mismanagement, overbudgeting, or simple lack of interest, *The Biggest Show of '54* bombed. Several shows were canceled, and halfway through, Lee and Eckstine bowed out. The promoters had no choice but to halt the tour; they blamed an "illness that befell Peggy Lee."

Lee wasn't the sole culprit, of course, but the claim did seem to hold some truth. On December 18, the *Boston Globe* noted that she had undergone "major surgery" for removal of a benign tumor. It forced her to cancel all engagements until after the New Year. Once more, Lee felt she had escaped death. Thereafter she entered a short phase of "almost Zenlike peace," as Lee Ringuette described it. On the surface, at least, her anxiety seemed lifted as she reveled in the comforts of family and home. The Ringuettes came over for barbecues, and joined her in the kitchen to do dishes while they all sang. Lee spent hours tending her garden and discussing philosophy and metaphysics with such friends as scientist Jimmy Marino, who worked with Albert Einstein and J. Robert Oppenheimer, the father of the atomic bomb.

Marino had a timely job; the Cold War was raging, and many Americans feared an atomic Armageddon. But Lee seemed little aware of such earthly concerns. Instead she treated Marino to a lengthy explanation of her theory that music emitted healing waves. The perpetually ailing singer was no case study for her own thesis, but she swore she was right, and asked Marino to tell Einstein. He dutifully reported back that the founder of twentieth-century physics thought it might hold some truth.

In February 1955, Lee channeled her "Zenlike peace" into the most uncommercial LP of her career. To Bill Rudman, one of her later producers, *Sea Shells* was "a New Age album in the Fifties." Lee's manager Ed Kelly had given her a book entitled *Music of Many Lands and People*; it filled her thoughts with centuries-old images of fair-haired maidens, heavenly birds, and verdant fields of plenty. With that, she began gathering fanciful verse and folk songs—"The White Birch and the Sycamore," "The Happy Monks," "The Gold Wedding Ring," "The Wearing of the Green." A poem by Ernest Holmes, "Of Such Is the Kingdom of God," tells of heaven's mystical splendors; in a "Chinese Love Poem" Lee speaks calmly of desertion, a subject that haunted her:

> *I am alone in my room*
> *I have put out the light*
> *And I am weeping*
> *I weep, because you are so far away*
> *And because you will never know how much I love you*

Stella Castellucci was on hand to spin celestial clouds on the harp strings. Gene DiNovi, the only other musician, arrived at Decca's studio on Melrose Avenue in Hollywood to learn that he would be playing harpsichord, not piano. "I had never seen a harpsichord in my life," he said. It looked like a small antique piano, but had two rows of keys, and the metallic tones it produced had formed the basis of much Renaissance and Baroque music. That was the ancient sound Lee wanted.

Her tranquility throughout the album could coax a child to sleep. "Peggy said, 'You know, these songs are such small, delicate little things; why don't we call them sea shells?'" recalled Castellucci. Decca's willingness to record such an esoteric disc suggests how highly the company thought of Lee. Hearing the finished product, however, they weren't so eager to release it; *Sea Shells* wouldn't see the light until 1958, after "Fever" had made Lee a hot seller again.

Throughout the sessions, Lee had summoned up a mental oasis she could never maintain for long. In the album's most revealing piece, the Victorian-era "I Don't Want to Play in Your Yard," a little girl scolds her playmate:

> *I don't want to play in your yard*
> *I don't like you anymore*
> *You'll be sorry when you see me*
> *Sliding down our cellar door*

The song evoked the petulant child in Lee who had never died, and never would; near the age of sixty she was still singing it. Anyone who had known the soft, spacy Lee would have been shocked at how brusque and bullying she could turn, especially with underlings. Her book of poems, *Softly—with Feeling*, contains the oblique line, "You pick up little habits from those BIG people and not all of it is good." The "BIG" person was very likely Min. Although she would never have acknowledged or perhaps even perceived it, Lee had absorbed her stepmother's powers of intimidation, and she wielded them in almost every relationship she had.

Secretaries suffered some of her harshest treatment. Just as Min had made her scrub the floors over and over, Lee forced assistants to redo tasks—such as typing letters and lists or vacuuming her plush carpeting—until she'd pushed them to the brink. Ignoring the fact that her employees had lives of their own, she kept them working as late as she could, evoking all the days when Min had done that and made her late for school. Della and Marianne maintained their almost saintly willingness to help, and still Lee wasn't happy. "Marianne was the sweetest woman that ever lived," said Dona Harsh. "They were both very loyal to her. And Peggy worked them half to death." Harsh quit Lee around 1955. "My father was ill, but I would have had to leave because I was ready for a nervous breakdown, I was so tired. I had no sleep on the road for three years."

By now the singer's sunny California prettiness had hardened. Lee had adopted a short, coiffed, silver-blond hairdo "which is unlike any natural hair on anybody," wrote columnist Sidney Skolsky. It made her look tough, and older than she was. Certainly she had lost her onetime country-girl charm, the sort that had made Dinah Shore second only to Doris Day as America's premiere blond songbird. Born in Tennessee, Shore had emerged on the eve of World War II as a soothing symbol of home. Her drawling voice—whose confidential softness predated Peggy Lee's—had a tinge of Southern blues, but it was her cheerful earthiness, free of dark undertones, that had made millions of people welcome her into their homes as TV's foremost singing hostess.

Harsh recalled the night when Lee and Shore were on the same roster at the Hollywood Bowl. Lee's dressing room was a bees' nest of nervous activity. Assembling the "Peggy Lee doll," as Mark Murphy termed her elaborate public persona, had become a trial. Lee's broad shoulders, wide hips, shapeless legs, and fluctuating weight made her hard to dress; and years of peroxide use had thinned her hair, which required buns and falls to fill it out. Backstage at the Bowl, recalled Harsh, "somebody was doing her hair, and Peggy was doing her own makeup, and I'm fluttering around doing this and that, and the musicians are consulting with her." In walked Shore to pay her respects. "She says, 'Hello, everybody!' She's carrying this gorgeous gown over her shoulder. She jumps into the dress and says, 'Honey, would you mind zipping me?' I zipped up her dress. She runs a comb through her hair. Makeup is fine. And on she went. Peggy sat there for three hours getting ready."

Yet all of Lee's subliminal tension gave her singing a mystique that Shore's would never have. Jack Webb drew on it for the tortured character of Rose. The spring of 1955 found *Pete Kelly's Blues* in the heat of production. The cast had fallen into place. Recent Oscar-winner Edmond O'Brien would play Fran McCarg, the thug who muscles in on Kelly. In the role of Ivy Conrad, a society flapper in love with Pete Kelly, Webb cast Janet Leigh, future costar of *Psycho*. Martin Milner, later famous for his roles on TV's *Route 66* and *Adam-12*, would play Kelly's drummer Joey, whom McCarg's henchmen rub out to intimidate Kelly. Movie tough guy Lee Marvin would appear as Kelly's clarinetist; the still-obscure bombshell Jayne Mansfield took the small role of a cigarette girl. Webb adored Ella Fitzgerald, and although she had never done any serious acting, he cast the jazz great as Maggie Jackson, a roadhouse singer.

He and his team sought to recreate, with pinpoint accuracy, the Kansas City of 1927. His research crew pored over that year's issues of *Vogue* and *Ladies' Home Journal*; they searched for period cars, liquor bottles, furniture, clothing, songs. Only items that had existed in 1927 were allowed. Webb was just as obsessed with authenticity of character. Casting a party scene in a dance hall, he hired a hundred nonprofessional couples to frenetically dance the Charleston and the Black Bottom. "I did not want them to be perfect in their steps," he explained. Real musicians would dub for Webb and the actors who played his bandmates; still, the star spent months mastering the correct fingerings on the cornet.

Filming began in February. Webb and over fifty cast and crew members flew to Louisiana to shoot the prologue: a black cornetist's funeral, set on a plantation near LaFitte, a small bayou village. Costly as it was, Webb had refused to film the scene on a soundstage; he wanted the action to unfold amid swaying oak trees, draped with moss, and riverboats that drifted lazily by. Webb engaged the gospel choir from the nearby Divine Spiritual Church to sing a funeral dirge, followed by a ragtime brass band to perk things up. He hired locals to play a gravedigger, a plantation worker, and other mourners. At the scene's end, an antique hearse transports the coffin to its destination. Someone places the dead man's cornet on top of it. As the hearse rolls away, the horn falls onto a mud road. Picked up by a stranger and pawned, the horn is won years later in a crap game by Pete Kelly, a returned doughboy from World War I.

From there, shooting moved to the Warner Bros. soundstages in Burbank, California. The center of the film's action is a replica of a Kansas City speakeasy, with a dance floor, a stage, and tables. Pete Kelly and His Big Seven entertain. Mob boss Fran McCarg moves in on the band, demanding a fat cut of its take in return for bookings and protection. The hotheaded but righteous Kelly resists, and a war ensues. Throughout the film, Webb, as director, uses the group's jubilant traditional jazz ironically, as a backdrop for murder and mental collapse.

Between takes, Webb rushed around, as dead serious as Joe Friday. "The only time I saw Jack sit down during the entire shooting was when he had lunch and when he posed for still pictures," recalled Janet Leigh. During rehearsals, a stand-in did his part while he directed; Webb placed mirrors on the set that enabled him, literally, to see behind his back. He wore a grave, hangdog expression, his probing eyes heavy with concern.

But Webb wasn't cold, especially when it came to Peggy Lee, whom he saw as fragile on several levels. Just before she began shooting in April, she received some troubling news: the State of California had once more liened her Warner Bros. earnings for unpaid back taxes. The amount, $1,410.14, was considerably less than her previous IRS lien, but for a woman who spent as recklessly as she did, the news was a rude awakening. Throughout the filming, anxiety dogged her, and she drank more than usual. Whether or not it affected her behavior during production was unclear. To pianist Ray Sherman, an onscreen member of Pete Kelly and His Big Seven, Lee "seemed the same as any actor—just as professional as anyone I had ever been around." But Webb conveyed a hint to the contrary to Reva Youngstein, the wife of Max Youngstein, head of promotion and marketing for United Artists Pictures. Reva knew Lee slightly, and she asked Webb how it had been to work with her. "Reva," he said, "you don't have enough time for me to tell you."

For *The Jazz Singer,* Michael Curtiz had tried to draw from Lee the same magical connection with her lines that she had with lyrics. Like Curtiz, Webb soon learned that Lee had no acting technique at all, but she certainly had soul. He tried to help her to build emotionally by shooting her scenes in the order of the script. Otherwise, recalled Lee, Webb left her alone, telling her to trust her own feelings.

His instinct hit the mark. Lee's identification with Rose is palpable and riveting—even in her first scene, in which she speaks not a word. Upstairs in the speakeasy's office, McCarg and Kelly are butting heads over the gangster's insistence on "representing" him. Rose, his mistress, waits uneasily in the background, wrapped in mink. Standing still without a close-up, Lee dominates with her eyes, which exude all the fear, dejection, and weariness in Rose's broken heart. Those emotions had lived in her since childhood; *Pete Kelly's Blues* suggests how close to the surface they remained.

With each of Lee's scenes, the unwanted child at the heart of Rose merges more closely with the abandoned, belittled Norma. Rose doesn't resurface until the film's forty-three-minute mark, when McCarg has had the band's drummer rubbed out as an intimidation tactic and pressured Kelly into hiring Rose to sing. "She comes free," he rasps. Rose responds in a tone of chilling resignation: "Ten years he's known me and all he can say is, 'She comes free.' But I guess that covers it." When McCarg finds his alcoholic mistress with a drink, he grabs it from her and hurls the glass at the top of the wall. Rose murmurs her defining line: "Don't worry, Fran— I can't climb that high anymore."

Some of Rose's poignancy stems from the fact that she does have talent; it emerges at a rehearsal, when she is neither drunk nor scared. Yet while preparing to go on for the first time, Rose empties a bottle of gin and her reserve shatters. Upstairs at the club, she tells Kelly of her sad past and sadder present. Dead drunk, she insists on performing anyway. The rowdy crowd ignores her. McCarg shouts at them, "She's gonna sing, you're gonna listen!" But by now Rose is a confused, incoherent mess, and she stumbles offstage and runs upstairs. McCarg follows her. Moments later, the office door opens and there stands Rose, dazed, with a bloodied gash above her left eye. She faints and tumbles down the stairs. Kelly is so incensed that he vows to fight McCarg and get to the bottom of who killed his drummer.

The filming of that sequence shook Lee profoundly. "I remember that as being a very tense day," said her daughter Nicki. "She was really within herself, sort of withdrawn." Lee had brought Stella Castellucci to the set for moral support; as the harpist watched her, she felt that Lee was reliving the horror of her years "with that stepmother of hers."

All this nuanced characterization gives proof of Webb's and Richard Breen's sensitivity. Kelly is both hotheaded and high-minded; McCarg turns to violence and even murder as a reflex, yet he loves Rose and wants her to succeed. The film's sole anachronism is the singing of Ella Fitzgerald, whose boppish swing far postdates 1927. Yet in her small role as a timid roadhouse singer who becomes privy to dangerous information, darkness clouds her normally sunny façade. The childlike songstress had never done any serious acting before, and she felt painfully self-conscious as the principles filed out of their dressing rooms to hear her. "I was bothered by all the movie stars watching," she said later. "Mr. Webb gave me my cue, and all I could answer was, 'Huh?' I kept thinking, 'Here I am doing a scene with Joe Friday.'"

Elsewhere on the Warner Bros. lot, one of the watershed movies of the 1950s, *Rebel Without a Cause*, was in production. A melodrama about tortured suburban youths and their clueless parents, *Rebel* captured all the festering teenage angst that would soon tear the generations apart. The film's twenty-four-year-old star, a leather-jacketed James Dean, was already the poster boy for every lost, angry, misunderstood son in America.

Peggy Lee's age—nearly thirty-five—placed her on the elder side of the generation gap. But Dean was drawn to her nonetheless, and one day a surprised Lee found him sitting in her dressing room "like a friendly cat." It happened more than once. "Our conversations were mostly silent, but he would stay for quite a while. He smiled a lot. You could feel things simmering and sizzling inside him, and his silence was very loud."

Still, Dean had seemed so gentle that she was startled to hear otherwise from Jim Backus, who played his father. In the spring of 1955, Lee and Backus shared a goofy respite from the intensity of their film roles. Together they recorded a Decca single of two funny songs based on

Backus's alter ego Mr. Magoo, the bumbling, myopic codger of numerous cartoons. Lee and Gene DiNovi had cowritten both tunes. "Mr. Magoo Does the Cha-Cha-Cha" finds the character muttering and chuckling nervously while temptress Lee tries to teach him the dance. "Where are you going? Can't you hear me calling?" she sings in mock terror as the nearsighted Magoo falls down an elevator shaft. In "Three Cheers for Mr. Magoo," Lee heads the chorus that welcomes Magoo back to his alma mater to give a speech; an oom-pah circus band, with glockenspiel and tuba, pounds away comically.

At the session, Backus told her and DiNovi about the shooting of one of *Rebel*'s key scenes: the one in which Dean's character, Jim Stark, explodes at his weak-willed father while his frightened mother looks on. Backus was stunned at the rage that erupted from Dean. "He really started slugging me," said Backus. "He really hurt me. Look at this bruise!"

On April 29, Lee had her own trial to endure—her scene at the insane asylum where her character now resides. Rose sits in a cold, concrete-and-brick room, vacant except for the tiny stool she occupies and a toy piano beside her. Kelly has gone there in hopes of obtaining clues about Joey's assassin. Slamming a heavy steel door behind him—a sound that signals no way out—he finds her wearing a hospital-type nightgown and clutching a doll. Rose pokes out a melody on the piano, then says in an anesthetized, little-girl voice, "This is my baby. Would you like to say hello?"

When Kelly prods her gently for the information he needs, she answers by murmuring a song: "Red and yellow and pink and green, purple and orange and blue . . . I can sing a rainbow . . ." It was the work of Arthur Hamilton. It had grown out of a congratulatory wire he sent her hours before a Ciro's opening. The message read simply, "Sing a rainbow. Arthur." At around five in the morning, his phone rang. It was Lee, asking: "Which of us is gonna write that song first?"

Webb needed a song for the asylum scene, and Hamilton remembered the wire. He wrote "Sing a Rainbow" in minutes. "Jack loved it," said Hamilton. "He called me the next day and said, 'I played the song for Peggy yesterday and she cried.'"

"Sing a Rainbow" jogs Rose's memory; woozily, she mentions a place called Coffeyville in Kansas. "Bad people" are there, she says. Kelly has his clue. Before he leaves, she turns to him and asks, "Were we good friends?"

That line had come from Lee. Back in North Dakota, she had heard it from a mentally ill girl, the memory of whom had inspired her portrayal. But life itself had taught Lee about the disillusion that had ruined Rose. Lee had seen key loved ones drift away—the mother who had vanished; the father whose alcoholism had made him as ephemeral as the trains that passed through his depots; the "dream" husband whose exit she refused to comprehend. On that asylum set, Webb had drawn from Lee a direct and harrowing connection with her bleakest fears. He called for only two takes, and used the first. "I got so emotionally involved in it, it really made me feel ill," she said later. "It was so real to all of us that when I walked out that door I could just barely walk."

Technically speaking, she hadn't "acted" at all. "She was playing herself," said Hamilton. Richard Breen had acknowledged Lee's true name, and nature, in Rose's introduction of her "baby": "Sometimes she wakes up sad, and then her name is Deloris." The poet and psychologist Paul Pines saw other connections. "Peggy Lee has always resonated for me as the most lyrical, elegiac voice of utter abandonment. You can see it when she's hugging the doll. That's the very image of an abandoned child hugging herself."

In the summer of 1955, Lee luxuriated in two major film premieres. *Lady and the Tramp* opened at New York's Roxy Theater on June 23. Shortly beforehand, a segment of the TV series *Disneyland* explored the creation of the songs. Lee and Sonny Burke are shown at staged production meetings and at Burke's piano, where they reenact their songwriting process. In another scene, Lee stands at a microphone and records "He's a Tramp" while a vocal quartet, the Mellomen, bark, howl, and ham it up for the camera. Lee purrs the song's catchphrase—"What a *dog!*"—like Mae West.

The film's animals have the charisma of movie stars. Columnist Henry McLemore deemed Tramp "as manly as Gable or Brando, as roguish as Gleason, as reliable as Cooper and, when he loses his heart, as romantic as Power or Boyer. And as for Lady, well, she's just the sauciest, most seductive little bit that ever got her ears in her dinner or wore a license for a lavaliere." McLemore, who wrote for the powerful Hearst syndicate, called *Lady and the Tramp* the year's best film to date; "Bella

Notte," he said, was "the top song in any 1955 picture." The comically schmaltzy ballad appeared in one of the most memorable scenes in any Disney cartoon: Lady's candlelit date with Tramp in an Italian restaurant, where two waiters—one strumming a mandolin, the other playing accordion—serenade the dogs as they share a plate of spaghetti and meatballs. They slurp at one strand from opposite ends, and when their lips meet, Lady flinches and turns away shyly.

Yet other critics were unmoved. Bosley Crowther of the *New York Times* called the animation "below par," the story "sugary" and sentimental. "The Siamese Cat Song," with its mischievous felines who cavort slyly in unison, then vandalize Lady's home, amused him. Of Lee's contribution, Crowther wrote begrudgingly, "The musical score has tinkle, and it is rather nicely sung by Peggy Lee."

The movie failed to land even a single Oscar nomination. Still, audiences were touched by this story about two social classes united by love,

On TV's *Disneyland,* Lee and Sonny Burke recreate
their recording of "The Siamese Cat Song."

and *Lady and the Tramp* went on to become the seventh highest grossing movie of the year. In 2011, it made *Time*'s list of the twenty-five greatest cartoon features in history.

The film also proved that Lee was much more than a singer. John Tynan extolled her in *Down Beat*: "Few contemporary figures in show business possess her many applied talents and fewer still can match her consistent record of distinguished artistic achievement." A future favorite of Lee's, the Oscar-winning composer Randy Newman, called her lyrics "remarkable assignment songwriting."

But as Lee said at the time, "I'm still not content." Indeed, Tynan detected an "implied sadness" in all her striving. Few of her recordings pleased her, and her hunger for approval seemed insatiable. Friends feared she was working herself to death. During a return engagement at Ciro's, the singer was rushed to St. John's Hospital for treatment of "severe abdominal pains"; later the *Washington Post* reported that "Peggy Lee's losing weight so fast she has the doctors nervous."

It jolted her deeply when her similarly driven friend Victor Young, whom she called one of her "biggest influences," died of a heart attack at fifty-six. "So much work probably hastened his untimely death," she admitted.

Now here she was, facing the launch of another major movie just a month after *Lady and the Tramp*. On Sunday, July 24, *The Colgate Variety Hour* devoted a whole program to *Pete Kelly's Blues*. It shows Jack Webb demonstrating his diligent directorial style, which included noting every move he made on index cards, pinned to a wall. A morose Peggy Lee sings "He Needs Me," Rose's "audition" song for Pete Kelly. Lee stands nearly motionless and stares into space as she sang of a willfully blind love, shorn of self-respect: "No matter where he goes, though he doesn't care / He knows I'm there . . ."

Prior to the film's release, Lee was asked to sing at one of the most glamorous events in Hollywood, Warner Bros.' annual studio party, a lavishly catered bash on the lot. The hundreds of guests included almost every Warner star past and present, from James Cagney on down; and the company's entire top brass, notably the president, Jack Warner.

Some time into the party, Lee, dressed in a plunging black cocktail dress, stepped onto a platform, where a trio awaited her, and began her show. It thrilled Jack Larson, a Warner contract actor who played photographer and cub reporter Jimmy Olsen on TV's *The Adventures of Superman.* "You could tell Peggy was a bit zonked," recalled Larson, but he wasn't prepared for what lay in store. "She was beside the piano and had her right hand on the piano top. When she finished she made a low bow—and all but passed out. She didn't get up; she was just down there with her head by her knees. The pianist came around and helped her get up, and he got her offstage."

Uncomfortable murmurs spread through the crowd. "It couldn't have been more noticeable," said Larson. "This was not a triumphant thing to do in front of all the executives of Warner Brothers, after she'd just done a big film for them."

The repercussions of that mishap were still ahead. For now, all looked promising as Webb embarked on a thirty-city promotional tour. Massive crowds cheered the arrival of America's most beloved detective, who greeted fans with the firm handshake and laser stare they knew from *Dragnet.* In New Orleans, thousands jammed Canal Street as Webb inched along in a convertible, confetti and streamers raining down on him.

On July 27, 1955, *Pete Kelly's Blues* premiered in San Antonio, Texas. It went on to gross five million dollars, impressive for the time, and tied with *East of Eden* and *The Seven-Year Itch* as the year's thirteenth biggest box-office success. Lee's performance helped it transcend a host of mixed reviews. Edwin Schallert in the *Los Angeles Times* called the film a formulaic gangster yarn, but praised the period detail and the music; like most critics he singled out Lee as "outstanding."

Even so, *Pete Kelly's Blues* was overshadowed in a year of outstandingly lifelike dramas—among them *East of Eden, Blackboard Jungle, Marty, Picnic,* and *Rebel Without a Cause*—that scratched the wholesome patina of American life to expose something raw and seething underneath. Lush romantic dramas (*Love Is a Many-Splendored Thing, Summertime, The Rose Tattoo*), splashy comedies (*Mr. Roberts, The Seven-Year Itch*), and the musical drama that stole all the attention, *A Star Is Born,* also dominated 1955.

Despite its vivid characters and eye-filling recreation of the Roaring Twenties, *Pete Kelly's Blues* may have come off as a minor film, directed by and starring a man of the small screen. As with *Lady and the Tramp*, years would have to pass for it to get its due. Webb scored no award nominations; it was Lee who got the recognition. On December 3, the Council of Motion Picture Organizations announced the nominees in its First Annual Audience Awards, a poll voted on by a reported fifteen million viewers. In the category of Most Promising New Female Screen Personality, the candidates were Kim Novak, Joan Collins, Dorothy Malone, Terry Moore, and Peggy Lee.

More than ever, dreams of a film career filled Lee's head. They soared higher on December 6 when, at a gala dinner at the Beverly Hilton Hotel, British actor Alec Guinness presented the beaming singer with the award. Backstage, photographers snapped group photos of Lee and fellow winners Jennifer Jones, Natalie Wood, and Tab Hunter. Clutching an angel-winged figure holding a star aloft, Lee looked happily dazed.

Good news kept coming. That December in a film critics' poll, Lee was voted best female supporting actress. As for the Oscars, Webb told Lee she would probably land a nomination, but wasn't likely to win because she had no studio contract, and might strike industry voters as a lightweight contender.

On February 18, 1956, the nominees for Best Supporting Actress were announced: Natalie Wood (*Rebel Without a Cause*), Marisa Pavan (*The Rose Tattoo*), Betsy Blair (*Marty*), Jo Van Fleet (*East of Eden*), and Peggy Lee. The singer was ecstatic. For the next month, congratulatory telegrams and phone messages flooded in. Lee continued reading Ernest Holmes, hoping that maybe, through positive thinking, she could will the award to be hers.

On March 21, she attended the Academy Awards ceremony at the Pantages Theatre in Hollywood. Edmond O'Brien, her *Pete Kelly's Blues* costar, read the nominees in her category. When O'Brien tore open the envelope and announced the name of Jo Van Fleet, Lee's heart sank.

Still, it seemed like she would gain other chances to act. The *Los Angeles Times* reported that Webb had signed her to a multifilm deal with Mark VII Productions. In the same newspaper, Edwin Schallert reported that Lee had received "no fewer than thirty movie scripts" since the release of *Pete Kelly's Blues*.

The Mark VII signing, if it ever happened, went nowhere, and Lee never worked with Webb again. As for the rush of scripts, few, if any, came from major studios. Lee never made another film. Gossip about the Warner Bros. party had somehow eluded the press; and the question of why her film career ended so abruptly would occupy a central place in Lee's mythology. In years to come, Lee alleged a campaign by some mysterious group of moral watchdogs who were leaving notes in nightclubs, outing her as the same sad figure of *Pete Kelly's Blues.* "I was an alcoholic, passing out at parties, waking up all over town. Then, wherever I sang I used to find these little pamphlets on my dressing table. They were called *The Twelve Steps to Alcoholism.*" For the rest of her life, Lee swore that such accusations were nonsense. Drinking, she said, "was never a problem with me. They had me confused with David."

Her daughter disagreed. "She *did* have a problem with alcohol," said Nicki in 1999. Just after the film's release, newspaper reports had suggested a woman slipping out of control; at times it had seemed as though Lee were channeling the unreliability of Rose. Dorothy Kilgallen reported that "Peggy Lee has the Ciro's bosses irked for showing up late for her performances." The star, added Kilgallen, had "begun to display a bit of dat ol' debbil temperament . . .[she] walks off the floor if the waiters rattle a dish." George Schlatter recalled a night when Ciro's owner Herman Hover had asked Lee to shorten her early show to leave time to seat an unusually large late-show crowd, who would be arriving from a premiere. Lee did as asked. As she left the stage, said Schlatter, "she saw me and just drew a blank and went back on the stage and started to do the same show over again."

Even if she had behaved impeccably, there seemed little chance of a Hollywood future for Peggy Lee. The golden age of movie musicals had died, and, of all her singing contemporaries who had broken into film, only Doris Day and Frank Sinatra would maintain lasting careers onscreen. Lee, it seemed, had only one great acting performance in her. Later on she would act in two TV dramas, playing variations of Rose.

Memories of her stellar onscreen moment brought her as much regret as pride. "I would have liked to have another opportunity to know for sure whether I could act well enough to deserve those awards, but it never happened," she told the BBC's Alan Dell in 1992. After *Pete Kelly's*

Blues, Lee claimed she had longed for more scripts—"but I've never been offered one since."

Meanwhile, the film kept haunting her. Lee owned a 16-millimeter print, and loved screening it for guests. Her secretary Betty Jungheim watched it repeatedly. In the part of Rose, Jungheim, too, saw only Peggy Lee.

"Peggy is not the girl you'd run into at a high school prom,"
said a deejay. (COURTESY OF RICHARD MORRISON)

Chapter Eight

*T*HE LOSS OF that gold statuette helped keep Lee overachieving in other areas. After *Pete Kelly's Blues*, she did such landslide business at the Sands in Las Vegas that the hotel brought her back, doubling her fee. The singer spent countless hours in her home studio rehearsing, writing songs, and recording demos. There she wore a special hat—"It's orange and it's very happy"—to channel the muses. Lee took occasional jaunts in her car, but preferred to leave the driving to others. "I can't seem to keep my mind on the road," she said. "I keep writing poetry or songs." Tied in with her distractedness was a phobia about making left turns; to avoid them Lee circled blocks endlessly, or just made a U-turn and went home.

She continued recording copiously for Decca. A slew of new singles teamed her with Sy Oliver, a revered black arranger from the swing era. Oliver had heated up the Cotton Club in the 1930s with his low-down, bluesy charts for the Jimmie Lunceford orchestra; his writing had defined the budding sound of swing as surely as anything by Count Basie or Benny Goodman. Oliver had helped make the Tommy Dorsey orchestra a swing sensation in the forties. Now his style was back in, as R&B invaded the pop charts. In the hands of white musicians his sons' age, it exploded under the name of rock and roll.

With Oliver conducting, Lee slurred and growled her way through "The Comeback," a twelve-bar blues number by the raunchy-voiced king of jump blues, Memphis Slim. Singing a century-old spiritual, "Swing Low, Sweet Chariot," Lee belted about eternal salvation as though in the pulpit. She and an all-male choir swapped phrases in the call-and-response fashion of a gospel church.

Soon those discs were spinning in the jukeboxes of black clubs from Harlem to Chicago's South Side. But white America preferred to hear her sing "Mr. Wonderful," the schmaltzy title tune of a hit Broadway musical with Sammy Davis, Jr. Lee's version climbed to number fourteen. Its success bolstered her free rein at Decca to do whatever she wanted. Her song choices roamed far from the sanitized fluff that pre-rock singers like her were often assigned. In "Where Flamingos Fly," she sings of an illegal immigrant from a far-off island who is plucked from his lover's arms and shipped home. She and Oliver bring a stripper's bump-and-grind beat to a Sophie Tucker hit of the speakeasy age, "You've Got to See Mamma Ev'ry Night (Or You Can't See Mamma at All)." Willard Robison had written "Guess I'll Go Back Home (This Summer)," a wistful travelogue about revisiting a town much like Jamestown, North Dakota, where old friends and lost innocence reside. In the happiest of goodbye songs, George and Ira Gershwin's "They Can't Take That Away from Me," Lee swings joyously while barely raising her voice above bedroom level.

But it was in the long-playing format that Lee could let her imagination run the freest. *Black Coffee* and *Sea Shells* had helped pioneer the "concept album," which turned the LP from a space-saving compilation into a unified work of musical art. Now, in *Dream Street*, Lee turned a dozen torch songs into an arty reverie about faded loves and hopes. The arranger, Shorty Rogers, was known for his cool, brainy West Coast jazz; but on *Dream Street*, Lee drew him into her ethereal world. The mood is set by "Street of Dreams," a Depression-era classic that tells of a distant nirvana where "dreams broken in two can be made like new." A strain of that Victor Young song weaves in and out like a benevolent angel; it haunts such ballads as "Last Night When We Were Young" and "My Old Flame," whose protagonists live in mourning of their lost happiness. Dainty sounds—Stella Castellucci's harp, Larry Bunker's bell-playing, Bud Shank's flute, Bob Cooper's oboe—elevate the celestial mood; two new additions to Lee's band, pianist Lou Levy and bassist Max Bennett, tiptoe through their parts.

For most of the album, Lee sings with lips nearly pressed to the microphone; still she seems as uncapturable as a smoke ring. In the songs, as in life, her mood swung dramatically. Slashing through the gauzy ambiance of *Dream Street* is a tough, driving jazz-trio version of "It's All Right With Me" from Cole Porter's 1953 musical, *Can-Can*. Porter had conceived it as the pained lament of a man who tries to ease his broken heart with a one-night stand. "You should cry when you sing it," insisted the composer. But Lee gave that song the same predatory stamp she'd branded onto Porter's "My Heart Belongs to Daddy." Meeting Mr. Right Now, she blusters her way past every doubt—"It's the wrong time and the wrong place / Though your face is charming, it's the wrong face"—and moves in for the kill.

To many of the men she met, it came as a surprise that a woman who seemed so timid could stalk them like a tigress in heat. Mark Murphy once overheard Lee vamping an admirer: "Are you a fan or a man?" Professional boundaries didn't concern her; she seduced many of her musicians. And if her prey had wives, so much the better. In 1955, columnists reported on her romance with her handsome doctor, Lewis V. Morrill, who was married, though separated, from actress Rhonda Fleming. More eyebrow-raising was her gossiped-about affair with a pastor of the First Church of Religious Science, which dispensed Ernest Holmes's teachings. One of the practitioners brought her young daughter, Nancene Cohen, to services. "My mom told me she was dating our pastor at the time," said Cohen. "Next thing you know, our pastor and all the church funds disappeared. My mom said he ran off with Peggy Lee. We never saw him again."

Often Lee seemed resentful of happy couples, and tried to barge in between them. In 1955 she hired drummer Stan Levey, a six-foot, two-inch ex-boxer who played with surprising finesse for Charlie Parker, Dizzy Gillespie, Stan Kenton, and Benny Goodman. To Jack Costanzo, Lee's percussionist at the time, Levey "was like the bouncer of the band. If anybody came up and bothered us, Stan was watching over."

After his first rehearsal with Lee, the drummer leveled with his wife, Angela Neylan: "She's after me. If you want me to quit I will." Angela laughed it off: "She's got good taste. I have nothing to worry about."

Lee had gotten what she wanted from Levey's predecessor, Larry Bunker. Currently she was engaged horizontally with her handsome pianist, Lou Levy, one of the most laid-back of beboppers. Born in Chicago, Levy had worked in the late forties with Woody Herman, one of the few swing bandleaders who embraced the far-out, experimental sounds of bop. After that, Levy recorded several solo albums. But it was as an accompanist to top-flight singers—Anita O'Day, Ella Fitzgerald, Sarah Vaughan, Peggy Lee—that he made his greatest mark. In his chorus on "It's All Right With Me," his fingers fly across the keys, but Levy, like Lee, knew how to burn without breaking a sweat.

For a woman who loved to be seen with manly men, there couldn't have been a more fetching sight at the piano. His prematurely graying hair and ruggedly handsome face recalled the 1950s movie star Jeff Chandler; Lee introduced Levy to audiences as her "Good Gray Fox." Onstage and off, he was Mr. Cool, laid-back and witty—largely because he stayed continually stoned on pot. "When the night was over," said Max Bennett, "Lou disappeared, and we knew where he went."

Her dallying with her musicians helped Lee to spawn her famously sexual vibe onstage. But at rehearsal time she got down to more serious business. Even Victor Young had bowed to her as a woman in charge: "She can't write a note of music but she knows exactly what she wants to hear." The singer voiced her ideas gently but firmly. "There was no, 'Shall we do this?' or 'Shall we do that?'" said Jack Costanzo. "It was, 'Do this' or 'Do that.' I couldn't fault her on anything, musically." Lee's lack of a technical vocabulary forced her to express her visions poetically. "'Give me a clitter-de-bong,' she'll say, or she'll ask for 'feathers,'" reported John Tynan in *Down Beat*. Levy recalled other examples: "She'd say, 'I'd like it to be like a cloud.' And she always talked about Respighi's *The Pines of Rome*. It sounds funny, but we knew what she meant."

By the last rehearsal, she had added nuances to songs that their composers and arrangers had never imagined. Every musical detail, vocal and physical gesture, and snippet of patter had been planned. "I played the same thing night after night, and it never got boring," said Levy, who stayed with her, on and off, for the next twenty years. "The music was always great. The band didn't have to push her; she would generate the energy to us."

Frank Capp was fresh out of the Stan Kenton band, and just past twenty, when he became another of Lee's drummers. Rehearsing at her home, he recalled seeing the adolescent Nicki peering into a machine intended to strengthen her vision, which required her to wear thick glasses. Insecurity seemed to haunt her. Lee had enrolled her daughter in the Hollywood Professional School, attended through the years by Judy Garland, Mickey Rooney, Natalie Wood, and countless other showbiz youths. To mix with the entitled offspring of stars could be intimidating. Sometimes Lee multitasked Nicki into her professional life by taking her along to movie sets or nightclubs. At best, Lee's attention was divided.

She recalled the situation defensively. "I didn't get to spend a lot of time with Nicki, which was unfortunate, but I was making a living. She always had one parent with her, because I used to have David stay at the house when I was gone. So she knew that she was loved." But Nicki wanted more: "There were tremendous amounts of time when Mom just wasn't available. And I was being cared for by someone else. So it was very difficult." In their complicated relationship, love and resentment, envy and awe ran together. "She was way up there on a pedestal for me," remembered Nicki. "*Way* up." Seldom did they see eye to eye.

All her life, she had to live in the shadow of a glamorous and superachieving mother. Mark Murphy could see that Nicki had an "artistic gift" of her own: "I always saw her with pencil and paper, drawing something." But she longed for a sibling to keep her company. Instead she played with the three dogs of the house: a collie, Banjo; Viking, a Norwegian elkhound; and cocker spaniel Lady, a gift from Sonny Burke.

As for human friends, Nicki recalled being thrown in with "this group of show-business children, and we all went to the same parties, even if we didn't know each other very well. I look at pictures and I see my face looking up at the puppet show or something else that's going on, and I'm like this little lost child surrounded by a sea of faces that I couldn't recognize, except for a couple."

Nicki begged her mother to stay home more often. "She makes a long face whenever I leave," Lee confessed to a reporter. "And a mother can stand just so many long faces." The singer told of opening her suitcase in a hotel room and finding Nicki's favorite doll inside—the girl's apparent reminder to her mother that she existed. "I almost cried," said Lee. As the 1955 holiday season approached, she announced her decision to quit touring and devote more time to motherhood. But a reporter for *Red-*

book was skeptical. "If it becomes a choice between one or the other, no one who knows Peggy Lee doubts which road she will take."

————

IN THOSE SAME WEEKS of 1955, Lee returned to Ciro's. One night a short but handsome young man eyed her from the bar. Dewey Martin was a rising Hollywood hunk whom Howard Hawks—the director who had helped cement the fame of James Cagney, Humphrey Bogart, and Cary Grant—had taken under his wing. Martin had played several he-man roles for Hawks: an Air Force sergeant in *The Thing from Another World*; a frontiersman in *The Big Sky*; and, most marketably, a half-naked hero in the Egyptian epic *Land of the Pharaohs*. To gay filmgoers, the Texas-born actor possessed "the thighs that drew a million sighs." Jack Larson, who knew him, agreed: "He was spectacular looking. It wasn't a Hollywood pretty-boy face. His ears stuck out a bit. But he had this extraordinarily beautiful body, before people went to gyms." Another friend recalled him as "a huge flirt and a tease," especially with men, whom he hugged freely.

Martin asked Dick Stabile, the club's resident bandleader, to take him backstage. Lee drank in the sight of the hunky thirty-two-year-old actor, an ex–World War II fighter pilot who scuba-dived in the ocean near his Malibu home. Bare-chested beefcake photos of him adorned many a magazine.

According to *Modern Screen*, he greeted Lee by exclaiming, "I've been in love with you for ten long years!" In his Navy days, Martin had seen her at San Francisco's Golden Gate Theatre and "flipped." Lee offered him a drink; he asked her out to dinner. They wasted no time in embarking on a whirlwind courtship. Both were traveling for work, but they shared nightly phone calls. In one of them, he proposed. "There were two gentlemen that wanted to marry her at that time," explained Nicki. She urged her mother to choose Martin. "I thought Dewey was cooler than the other guy," she said. But Dona Harsh detected signs of a temperamental young man. "He was kind of sharp, definitely moody," she said.

Lee's parade of beaus had failed to fill the gap left in her life by Dave Barbour and Robert Preston. "She was one of those people who are in

Dewey Martin in *Land of the Pharaohs,*
1955. (COURTESY OF TOM TOTH)

love with love, and always searching for that," observed Stella Castellucci. The singer left little time to get to know Dewey Martin. She and her trophy fiancé set a wedding date of Saturday, April 28, 1956. Martin was busy filming a TV pilot in Utah; Lee was in Los Angeles, suffering anxiety attacks over her rash decision.

At home in bed, Lee stayed awake until deep in the night, accompanied, as ever, by her Science of Mind literature and praying for the best. All too soon, the big weekend arrived. According to a perhaps apocryphal fan-magazine report, Martin, who was still in Utah, chartered a small private jet to take him home. A sudden storm broke out, and the pilot refused to fly through it. Brashly, the actor arranged to borrow a two-seat plane. All alone, he zoomed through the rainclouds and descended onto a Burbank landing field on the afternoon of the appointed day. "There, praying him in, was Peggy," alleged *Modern Screen*. "They just had time to race to a Beverly Hills jewelry store, choose double rings, and make the license bureau five minutes before it closed." From there they drove to Palm Springs, where Lee had bought a house. They were wed at the local Church of Religious Science.

The singer vowed this time to put marriage before career. Meanwhile, her husband seemed sure that the words "I do" would transform Miss Peggy Lee into Mrs. Dewey Martin. He was three-and-a-half years younger than she, but in the pictures snapped on their wedding night he looked at least a decade her junior. Nonetheless, he expressed a typical 1950s male attitude about who would wear the pants. "She knows she doesn't have to work another day if she doesn't want to," declared Martin to a reporter. The actor bought Lee's Los Angeles home from her so that he would own it, then they redecorated it to both their tastes. Martin made it clear that he did not encourage the parade of visitors that made the house feel like "Grand Central Station," as Lee called it. "All that's changed," announced Martin. "Our home is for us, our family and friends."

Lee informed her musicians that she was taking a year off from the road. She canceled her June and July engagements and joined her new husband in Utah, where he finished his TV pilot. Back in California, the newlyweds had a quick honeymoon close to home, seeing giraffes and elephants at the San Diego Zoo and driving across the border to Tijuana to attend the bullfights Martin loved.

The singer's nephews, Lee and Lynn Ringuette and Glen Egstrom, were impressed by their new he-man, movie-star uncle. Glen, who had launched a lifelong passion for scuba diving, was thrilled to inherit a set of Martin's old gear; the actor gave the two brothers an Italian bike and some of his screen memorabilia. "He seemed utterly sincere," said Lee Ringuette. "He and my dad were quite good friends, and my mother liked him a great deal. He seemed to genuinely love Peg." And she loved him, or wanted to believe she did. But by the summer, a familiar sense of emptiness had set in, and the lost soul in Peggy Lee returned. "Sometimes I feel as if I'm on a treadmill, not knowing where I'm headed, who I am, or what it's all about," she confided to a reporter.

Her Decca contract was set to expire after the New Year. Lee adored recording, and the label had treated her royally. Still she felt nostalgic for Capitol, whose top brass had nurtured her like fathers. As Thanksgiving approached, Glenn Wallichs, the company's president, asked her to give them a second chance. She didn't hesitate.

The Capitol of 1956 was far statelier than the company that had let her go four years before. It now resided in the Capitol Records Tower, a gleaming white, cylindrical building that soared thirteen stories above Hollywood Boulevard and Vine Street. (Until 1964, earthquake zoning restrictions forbade anything taller.) The Tower was shaped like a stack of discs; a spike protruding from the roof evoked the spindle of a record-changer.

All this opulence had been bankrolled by Electric and Musical Industries, Ltd. (EMI), the British electronics firm to whom Wallichs, Johnny Mercer, and the estate of the now-dead Buddy DeSylva had sold a controlling interest. Some of the old Capitol guard feared that EMI would turn the company into a crass commercial enterprise. Rock and roll was officially two years old, and clearly more than a fad; the biggest hits of 1956 included Elvis Presley's "Don't Be Cruel" and "Hound Dog," Bill Haley & His Comets' "See You Later Alligator," and Frankie Lymon & the Teenagers' "Why Do Fools Fall in Love?" Parents recoiled in disgust, and they prayed their children would escape the plague of youth running wild.

Capitol's roster now included Gene Vincent, a twenty-one-year-old Virginian whose top-ten hit, "Be-Bop-a-Lula," helped launch rockabilly, another new sound that grown-ups hated. But Capitol still prided itself as a house of sophistication, and adult tastes continued to reign, at least for now. To all who entered the building and walked the shiny lobby floor to the elevator, the framed photos on the walls served as reminders of who had made Capitol soar. There was Nat King Cole, whose sixty-nine top-forty hits—four of them number-one—had given the company its nickname, "The House That Nat Built." Judy Garland, Dean Martin, Tennessee Ernie Ford, Les Paul, Margaret Whiting, and George Shearing—Capitol pillars all—smiled out from their eight-by-ten glossies.

But the label's emperor was Frank Sinatra. After capsizing in popularity around 1950, Sinatra had bounced back with his Oscar-winning performance in *From Here to Eternity*. Now, after a series of smash albums on Capitol, he defined winner.

Sinatra had told Capitol to "get Peggy back," but Glenn Wallichs already wanted her. That February, with the ink barely dry on her new contract, Sinatra—who lived up the street from Lee—dropped by the house and said offhandedly, "Let's do an album." He didn't mean duets. She would sing and he would conduct, a role he had rarely played. Sinatra prepared a long list of moonstruck ballads and asked Lee to choose twelve. As for who would arrange them, he enlisted his main maestro, Nelson Riddle, whose sumptuous orchestral writing had made him the Rolls-Royce of his profession. During the swing era, Riddle had apprenticed with Sinatra's former boss Tommy Dorsey. Then he joined Capitol, where he struck gold in 1950 as the arranger of Nat King Cole's "Mona Lisa."

Standing before the luxuriant orchestra on that recording was a twenty-nine-year-old whose thinning, wavy hair, double chin, and blank expression gave him the nondescript look of a small-town bank clerk. Yet out of Riddle's pen came some of the most luscious orchestrations in pop history. He draped singers in plush, impeccably woven carpets of lyricism, with motifs and countermelodies that were often as beautiful as what the composer wrote. Short saxophone or trumpet solos popped up, but Riddle kept a safe distance from jazz; every edge was buffed shiny-smooth and played with the cinematic sweep of Hollywood soundtrack music.

That sound was ideal for the *The Man I Love*, his project with Peggy Lee. Despite the toughness in their façades, she and Sinatra were two of the dreamiest romantics in pop. But in the spring of 1957, when they taped that album in the standard time frame of the day—three four-hour sessions—Sinatra the conductor had to make good in front of three-dozen top-rank session players who knew a faker from a pro.

He couldn't read music, but he knew how the best conductors breathed with singers, how split-second pauses or swells could make key phrases come to life. Riddle had coached him exhaustively, and Sinatra had brought him to the studio to watch over things. Band members Lou Levy and Stella Castellucci were surprised at how well Sinatra did. "He conducted as though he really knew what he was doing, I swear," said the harpist. Lee sang from her glass-walled isolation booth, but she kept an eye on Sinatra, who wore his trademark fedora, cocked over one brow, and a tie pulled loose. "He was following the score as if he knew every note in there," Castellucci said.

On *Black Coffee*, Lee had sung from a dead end of despair; now she floated on a cloud of euphoria. *The Man I Love* bespeaks a postwar fantasy of eternal love. Throughout the album, Lee sings of forever—"However he wants me, I'm his until I die"; "When I am tired of dreaming, then I'll be tired of you"—while Riddle casts her in an enchanted fairyland. A trilling flute evokes a bird of paradise; a distant tenor sax adds sexual intrigue. On the 1938 hit "Please Be Kind," a virginal plea to a first beau, the strings ripple like lilacs in the breeze.

Lee sang in her airiest, most intimate tone. Jess Rand, a Hollywood manager and press agent, recalled watching her from the control room. "A lot of times she would have the lights turned down to do a ballad. I'm telling you, it was magic. She would lose herself in the music."

The Man I Love included Lee's favorite song. She had heard Maxine Sullivan sing "The Folks Who Live on the Hill" in 1944, when, as Mrs. Dave Barbour, she basked in the glow of newlywed life and young motherhood. Written by Jerome Kern and Oscar Hammerstein II, it tells of a young couple's goal to find a heavenly love nest "on a hilltop high"—a Shangri-La "with meadows green" outside the verandah.

Riddle bookended the song with a theme so melodic and lushly orchestrated that Gary Schocker, a classical flutist and composer, likened it to "Debussy meets Copland." Above a shimmering bed of strings, harp, trumpet, and oboe play with a clean precision that Schocker called "so American"—evocative of Copland's *Appalachian Spring*. The effect is that of a wide-open prairie lit up as the sun rises: an idyllic setting for a house on a hill.

Lee never really "acted" in song; nearly everything she sang was somehow autobiographical, and "The Folks Who Live on the Hill" captured her ultimate dream—one that her career had made impossible. Any illusions about growing old with Dewey Martin had crumbled, as Sinatra learned while directing the album-cover photography. Martin embraces Lee with his back to the camera; the singer stares into it with moist eyes, induced by a few dabs of menthol. "Frank wanted me to look romantic, with a far-off, misty stare," Lee recalled. "But I told him that the man he had on the cover was not my true love."

The marriage had misguidedly joined a career-obsessed star and a hotheaded he-man who thought he could tame his wife's ambitions. "I don't remember them ever spending a lot of time talking," said Dona Harsh. "She was always in the bedroom getting made up or dressed, or going somewhere."

George Schlatter, by then a Las Vegas producer, recalled a fight that erupted between the Martins late one night at the Sands. "Dewey ran out of their hotel room and down the hallway, and there was Peggy behind him in a nightgown, yelling, '*Come back here, you son of a bitch!*'"

Asked years later if Martin had been a good stepfather, Nicki replied tersely, "No. Let's just leave it at that, OK?" But Stella Castellucci recalled "one instance where he was very abusive" to Nicki. "And I saw him scream and holler at Peg in front of me. He didn't care who was around." Max Bennett recalled him as "insanely jealous" of Lee; yet according to Dona Harsh, now Mrs. Fred Benson, the actor made a pass at her—and she was pregnant at the time. Lee claimed that Martin's temper scared off many of her friends, who would no longer come to the house. According to Fred Apollo, one of her agents at William Morris, that was fine with Martin. "He tried to isolate her from all the people close to her," said Apollo.

Meanwhile Apollo watched the singer's liquor intake rise. Lee began to tell various people, including Castellucci, that Martin was beating her. None of them witnessed the violence, or recalled seeing her with bruises, but they believed her anyway. Lee's most hair-raising story harked back to their wedding night in Palm Springs. According to Lee, the evening had begun cozily: as she cooked dinner in the kitchen, he sat in the living room watching TV. Then Robert Preston showed up on the screen. Martin knew about their affair, she said, and Lee alleged he flew into a rage. When she emerged from the kitchen, he hit her so hard that she fell to the floor, nearly blinded. "She had a joke about that— 'Instead of a wedding veil, maybe I should've worn a crash helmet,'" said the playwright William Luce. "It seems that each hurtful thing she claimed to have undergone, she also made light of, possibly as a martyr enhancement."

Considering her almost certain exaggeration of Min's brutality, it was hard to know which of her charges against Martin were true. But Lee Ringuette doubted the violence. "I never heard a word about that," he said, "and I would have, through the gossip in the family." He did overhear his parents talking about how the actor, like Brad Dexter, had wound up with the subservient job of holding her glass of cognac offstage. "She put him in the position that Brad had been put in. He might have had the prideful anger of a man from that era."

Given the emotional chaos going on at home, Lee's ability to adopt a cool, commanding, bright-spirited public face was all the more remarkable. But if her work gave her a place to vent her grief, it was also her safest and happiest refuge. And an ever-growing public paid close attention. Capitol released *The Man I Love* on July 22, 1957; that summer it became the twentieth biggest-selling LP in the country.

Rhythm-and-blues and rock and roll were now waging such a fierce war against mainstream pop that the old guard felt as if it were standing unarmed in the front line of battle. For the prerock idols—Doris Day, Joni James, Guy Mitchell, Rosemary Clooney, the McGuire Sisters, Jo Stafford—the hits were drying up. They took uneasy stabs at singing "the kids' music," but few of them, if any, sounded so at home with rhythm and blues as Peggy Lee.

Capitol remembered this as they tried to find her a new hit. Right after she had left the refined maturity of *The Man I Love*, Lee joined a doo-wop choir, a twanging electric guitarist, and a backbeat-pounding drummer to bounce her way through "Every Night": "I'm gonna please you, hug and squeeze you / Hold your hand, make you understand. . . ." The arranger was, of all people, Nelson Riddle, who had whipped up a fair facsimile of rock and roll. According to Stella Castellucci, Lee still "detested" that music, but she seemed just as comfortable singing on the beat, in R&B fashion, as she did singing off it, which jazz required. Otherwise, she altered nothing in her style. "Every Night" and similar followup singles didn't sell too well, but they proved, for future reference, that Lee could sing in a rocking manner and not sound silly.

At the end of that year, Riddle joined her for the first of several albums that countered her somber side. *Jump for Joy* was a party album of lighthearted swingers; the titles—"When My Sugar Walks Down the Street," "The Glory of Love," "Ain't We Got Fun"—announced a toe-tapping good time. It charted even higher than *The Man I Love*, and its success came just when Lee needed it the most. Like many Americans in that decade of deceptive financial bounty, she had recklessly overspent and mismanaged her money. As 1958 began, the IRS embarked on a witchhunt of top-earning celebrities who had "erred" in their taxes. As a nationwide scare tactic, the names of the starry culprits were leaked to the press. The offenders included Charlie Chaplin, Mickey Rooney, Otto Preminger, Judy Garland and husband Sid Luft, Vic Damone, and Peggy Lee. On February 4, the *Chicago Tribune* reported an IRS lien against Mr. and Mrs. Dewey Martin for unpaid back taxes. Lee shuddered at the amount owed: $22,348, a fortune at the time. Martin's earnings had dwindled; now she would have to work harder than ever to pay off their debt.

But nothing could make her downsize. In May 1958, Lee premiered an exorbitantly costly act, designed to bump up her star power. It opened at the Mocambo, the Sunset Strip emporium that had long rivaled the now-shuttered Ciro's. Lee had gathered an imposing creative team. Sammy Cahn and Jimmy Van Heusen, who had just scored an Oscar for "All the Way" (sung by Frank Sinatra in *The Joker Is Wild*), wrote special material; so did Sid Kuller, a former Duke Ellington collaborator who would become an important one of Lee's. Hollywood costumer Don Loper designed her glittering, forty-pound beaded gown, for which she paid a then-staggering five thousand dollars. A choir backed her on "Swing Low, Sweet Chariot" and "When the Saints Go Marchin' In." Nick Castle, who choreographed for Gene Kelly, Fred Astaire, Ann Miller, and Shirley Temple, did the staging. Castle, whom Lee would employ for years, gave her a vampish new move: she dipped a shoulder then spun her pearls around her neck while batting her eyes.

For Lee, the show was uncharacteristically cheerful. There were no tunes from *Black Coffee* and certainly none from *Sea Shells*; instead, "St. Louis Blues," "Lover," and songs from *Jump for Joy* kept the energy high. *Variety* singled out one new song. By 1950s standards, it was boldly suggestive. The words, set to an R&B beat, were an ode to coital bliss: "You give me fever / When you kiss me, fever when you hold me tight. . . ." Lee punctuated the beat by stomping her foot.

"Fever" had come to Lee through Max Bennett. The bassist was playing in a band at a seedy joint in downtown Los Angeles, and a young male singer asked if he could sit in. He handed Bennett the sheet music to "Fever." Like so much rock and roll, the song had only two chords, but its insinuating throb and smolderingly come-hither message made Bennett think: *perfect for Peggy.*

He called to tell her about it, and she responded excitedly. "Fever" was written by Eddie Cooley and Otis Blackwell, a black R&B songwriter from Brooklyn whose songs had attracted millions of white record-buying youths. Blackwell had penned "Don't Be Cruel" and "All Shook Up" for Elvis Presley; "Great Balls of Fire" and "Breathless" had sealed the stardom of Jerry Lee Lewis. While feuding with his publisher over contract terms, Blackwell had begun writing songs independently under the sardonically Waspish name of John Davenport; he used that pseudonym for "Fever."

Lee found a 1957 recording by Ray Peterson, a white, Texas-born teenager whose Elvis-inspired voice soared eerily into the stratosphere. She played his 45 until it turned gray. In the introduction, Peterson wails wordlessly over bongos; finger snaps usher in a sultry R&B orchestra led by Shorty Rogers. The youngster's voice quavers with pent-up lust; his yowled-out *"fever!"* is a cry for release.

The record—Peterson's first—was a flop; not until 1960 would he reach the top ten with the chaste teenage ballad, "Tell Laura I Love Her." After hearing his "Fever," Lee sought out the 1956 original, a top-forty hit that had somehow escaped her ears. It was sung by an eighteen-year-old black singer from Arkansas, William Edward John, a pint-sized R&B star billed as Little Willie John. His "Fever" was even more aggressively sexual than Peterson's, with a darker, nastier edge. Willie's record has finger snaps, too; they punctuate a horn line that prowls like a stalking panther.

"Fever" augured well for his future. But within a few years he had torpedoed his career through drinking, gambling, and unreliability. In 1966, John was convicted of manslaughter; two years later he died in prison at the age of thirty.

After his and Peterson's indelible versions, Lee wondered how she could possibly make "Fever" her own. Although she seldom acknowledged it, she got quite a bit of help. In a 1970 interview, Lee spoke of how the song's existing lyrics "didn't all sit," so she wrote some new ones "with a gentleman I was working with at the time." That was Sid Kuller, who had penned material for her splashy Mocambo act. A socially conscious New York Jew, Kuller had teamed with Duke Ellington in 1941 to create *Jump for Joy*, an all-black, pro-integration show. His name appeared in the credits of leftist revues, TV variety shows, and MGM musicals.

Kuller wrote with far more polish than Lee, whose lyrics, charming as they could be, often had a disjointed, first-draft quality. When she approached him about "Fever," he suggested adding some substitute verses based on hot-and-bothered historical figures. Lee began writing—and with Kuller's aid, she came up with several additional stanzas. One concerned Pocahontas, the daughter of a seventeenth-century American Indian colonial lord, and her "very mad affair" with John Smith, a British invading captain. Another was about Romeo and Juliet. Additional ones revealed her own case of "fever."

As for the arrangement, how to avoid copying her predecessors? Lee had heard about all the black artists whose singles had been shamelessly mimicked by white stars. Georgia Gibbs had scored a number-two smash by aping LaVern Baker's "Tweedlee Dee"; Pat Boone had covered tunes recorded by Ivory Joe Hunter, Fats Domino, and Little Richard and turned them into sanitized hits for white America.

Lee didn't wish to rip off her forerunners, white or black. The singer thought of paring down the denseness of Little Willie's and Ray Peterson's versions of "Fever" and giving the song some cool. She had plenty of ideas, but couldn't write them out. To that end, Dave Cavanaugh, the head of Artists & Repertoire at Capitol's pop division, brought in staff arranger Jack Marshall. Lee explained what she wanted. The finger snaps from the previous recordings would stay. Peterson's stark bongo sound appealed to her, as did his lasciviously barked "*fever!*" and rising keys. The horn line that had backed Little Willie John had also stuck in her mind. She hummed it for bassist Joe Mondragon, whom Cavanaugh had hired for Lee's session. (Max Bennett was on tour with Ella Fitzgerald.) Just two other musicians would join him, drummer Shelly Manne and guitarist Howard Roberts.

According to Lee, she and Marshall had argued over the concept. He wanted to beef up the chart with added instrumentation; she refused. Her philosophy, she declared, could be summed up in a quote by Earl Warren, chief justice of the United States: "The eternal struggle of art is to leave out all but the essentials."

She got her way. On May 19, 1958, all parties convened at Capitol's Studio A in Hollywood. Lee didn't want guitar, so Roberts and Cavanaugh were commanded to snap. Manne provided an array of subtle sounds: he used his foot on the kick drum, whose low *boom-boom* throbbed like a pounding heart; with his fingers he thumped on the tom-tom and the large, round snare drum.

In the hour or so that it took to produce a finished take, the chart took on a life of its own: sparse, shadowy, and dominated by the calm but lashing voice of a woman in heat. "Fever" filtered the sizzle of R&B through the sparseness of West Coast jazz. With each key change, Lee cranked up the temperature just a bit—a tantalizing hint of sparks about to ignite.

At a time when the pop charts were full of schmaltzy, string-laden love songs and rock and roll bombast, the minimalism of "Fever" was disarming. Vocal critic Henry Pleasants used it as an example of how Lee could give the "effect of belting" while using a "level of sound which, in a Merman or a Streisand, would suggest a stage whisper."

Eight times a week on Broadway, the same deliberate snapping that backed Lee on "Fever" formed the ominous pulse of "Cool," the prelude to a gang war in the musical *West Side Story*. Both songs dealt with a ticking time-bomb of emotions. And if Lee's concluding statement—"Chicks were born to give you fever"—befit a *Playboy* bunny, her steely tone made it clear that she, not any man, was in charge.

At the dawn of a broiling summer, "Fever"—with "those provocatively snapping fingers," as a reporter called them—hit the stores. By August, it had climbed to number eight. In England it went three notches higher. For the first time since 1952, Lee was back in heavy rotation in jukeboxes and on the radio.

"Fever" would define her permanently. Various singers, including Elvis Presley, made imitative covers, but no one could upstage Lee. Asked to explain the song's success, she offered: "The young people and anyone else, for that matter, will respond to good songs if they have a good basic rhythm." It was a coy explanation of the disc's appeal. As sexually free as she was, Lee operated in a decade of such stifling repression that, when the title character of *I Love Lucy* was expecting a child, CBS forbade use of the word "pregnant." Media and religious censors argued that they were protecting America from things it didn't want to know, but a series of hot-button events had proven otherwise. In 1953, a former *Esquire* copywriter, Hugh Hefner, published the first issue of *Playboy*. His purpose, said broadcast journalist Mike Wallace, was to "free the sexual slaves"—to drag sex out into the open and to make it part of a new, emancipated lifestyle. Hefner's nude cover girl, Marilyn Monroe, was the stick of dynamite that enabled him to bust down those walls. *Playboy* became an instant smash.

Presley had done even more to ignite American libidos. His pelvic gyrations on TV confirmed parents' worst fears about what rockers intended to teach their children. A Catholic newspaper editor wrote to FBI director J. Edgar Hoover, calling the budding superstar "a definite danger to the security of the United States," with a menacing power "to rouse the sexual passions of teenaged youth." When Presley appeared on Ed Sullivan, cameramen shot him only above the waist.

Censorship efforts had helped turn various films and books into box-office gold. Producer Otto Preminger, screenwriter F. Hugh Herbert, and United Artists Corporation defied the Motion Picture Production Code by refusing to expurgate *The Moon Is Blue*, a saucy comedy that starred William Holden and David Niven. The Hollywood censor objected to the film's "unacceptably light attitude towards seduction, illicit sex, chastity, and virginity"; United Artists released the film anyway, and the controversy helped make it the year's fifteenth biggest box-office hit.

For tearing the mask off a supposedly virtuous country, few could surpass Grace Metalious and Alfred Kinsey. Metalious, a tough New Hampshire housewife, inflamed America with her 1956 novel, *Peyton Place*, about the salacious goings-on in a fictional New England town—"truly a composite," she said, "of all small towns . . . where the people try to hide all the skeletons in their closets." The book unleashed a hailstorm of controversy, and several cities banned it. Yet by the time Peggy Lee was singing "Fever," Metalious's sexposé had outsold *Gone with the Wind*.

Comparable furor and titillation greeted the phenomenally scandalous "Kinsey Reports," which analyzed the American people's previously uncharted sexual behavior. Released in two best-selling books, the Kinsey Reports shocked the nation. According to Paul Gebhard, who worked for the Kinsey Institute, "People were outraged when we showed that the great majority of people had premarital intercourse, and that the incidence of adultery was higher than anyone thought."

Out of that atmosphere came Peggy Lee's "Fever." From then on, many parents thought her quite improper. Sidney Myer, a New York cabaret manager starting in the 1980s, had grown up in Philadelphia after the release of "Fever." Even at twelve he was mad for female singers, and when he read that Lee would be performing at the Latin Casino right in his own town, he insisted his parents take him. "My mother was a very elegant, refined lady, and we always were taught manners, and how to be respectful in every way. The first thing she said was, 'Peggy Lee is *vulgar!*' I didn't know what she was referring to; maybe it was the plunging necklines or the hint of sex. That didn't stop them from taking me in a car on a Sunday afternoon to the matinee at the Latin Casino. There was a spell from the moment Peggy Lee set foot onstage. I suppose I was responding to her beauty, her glamour, this dreamlike presence. People were clapping if she raised her shoulder or cocked her eyebrow in a sexy way. It seemed like a spell had been cast over us all. When we left I asked my mother what she thought. She said, 'Well . . .' There was this pause. Finally she said, 'She creates a certain mood.'"

In the company of such renegades as Metalious and Presley, Lee deserves at least honorable mention for providing a soundtrack to the burgeoning sexual consciousness of a nation. Yet no hue and cry followed "Fever," for Lee knew how to package sex with class. She could segue easily from suggestive R&B to the writing of children's songs. The latter was her task when George Pal, the filmmaker who had used her voice in his 1946 short, *Jasper in a Jam*, invited Lee to write two tunes for his next cartoon feature, *tom thumb* [sic]. Lee's contributions, "Are You a Dream?" and "tom thumb's Tune," helped the film earn a Golden Globe nomination for best musical.

She basked in the acclaim. But for the third time, Lee's career had driven a difficult marriage to the breaking point. Professionally, Dewey Martin's ego had taken a beating. "A year ago," wrote a reporter, "Dewey was tipped as being a hot new male lead for TV and pictures but nothing has happened." Alongside his wife he seemed almost invisible. After shows, Lee would spend hours greeting fans and friends while Martin waited at home. Around two AM she would march through the door, band members in tow. "Peggy would wake Nicki up and Nicki would have to make food, drinks," said Joe Harnell, who had just joined her as pianist. "We'd drink, and Peggy wanted us to improvise Bach, Gregorian chants, contrapuntal things, just for fun. Dewey would make an appearance. He wanted us to get out of there so they could go to bed. The tension that was building was very clear. At four in the morning Dewey would storm into the living room and say, *'All right, you guys, get out of here!'* And she would say, *'Don't you tell my friends what to do!'* There'd be a scene, and we'd all get the hell out of there."

Lee seemed clueless as to why Martin should have gotten so upset. Still, the decaying marriage had left her an emotional wreck, and her flair for manifesting ill health through worry had reached its peak. Her friends, as well as the press, couldn't keep up with her reported illnesses. Fred Apollo wasn't alone in thinking that Lee "exaggerated at times for sympathy," but the ailments seemed real to her. A month after recording "Fever," she collapsed on a train. The cause, wrote a columnist, was "infectious mononucleosis as a result of overwork." As "Fever" rose on the charts, Lee was home in bed, nurses hovering nearby; the name of her illness had been amended to "glandular fever."

Typically, nothing could induce her to follow doctors' orders and rest. While sick, Lee completed a short story, a song, and two paintings, and received a parade of concerned friends. Frank Sinatra arrived from his house up the street, bearing flowers, books, and LPs. Lee recalled him arriving with "a truckload of things" for a barbecue, "like the torches that you stick into the ground and light up, and the food. And he barbecued it and then he served it to us. I mean, personally."

As of July 15, 1958, "us" no longer included Martin. That day, the actor moved out. He went to New York on business, and when he came back to California a few weeks later, he was served with divorce papers. Martin didn't show up in Santa Monica Superior Court in September, when his wife pleaded her case to a judge. Her husband, she said, had caused her "grievous mental suffering." Lee declared him "hostile and moody" and "extremely jealous" of her career; she charged him with using "vile language to me in front of my friends" and claimed that "he always tried to upset me just before my concerts." She made no mention of his alleged physical violence.

Lee got her interlocutory judgment. But under the still-existing California divorce laws, she would again have to wait a year for the break to become final. To Max Bennett, the love life of this queen of romance and sex seemed doomed. "Nobody wanted to be Mr. Peggy Lee," he said.

"Basin Street East," wrote *Billboard*, "belongs to Peggy
Lee." (COURTESY OF RICHARD MORRISON)

Chapter Nine

AS THOUGH TO offset her latest marital fiasco, Lee went back
to Capitol in October to record the album *I Like Men!*, twelve
songs about the can't-live-with-'em, can't live-without-'em opposite sex.
Amid such carefree ditties as "I'm Just Wild About Harry" and "It's So
Nice to Have a Man Around the House," Lee sang a few tunes whose
darker themes couldn't have escaped her. She had conceived the album's
one memorable chart—the raunchy burlesque-style horns and stripper
drumbeat that backed her on "My Man," the 1921 tearjerker. "He isn't
true, he beats me too, what can I do?" sang Lee in the take-charge tone
of a woman who embraced suffering. From Cole Porter's *Kiss Me, Kate*
came "So in Love," a song of determined sexual obsession: "So taunt me
and hurt me / Deceive me, desert me / I'm yours till I die." In an old Cotton Club tearjerker, "Good for Nothin' Joe," a streetwalker mourns the
abusiveness of her pimp. "Still, there's nothin' I can do / Because I love
him so," she coos in a lullaby tone.

Shared emotional cruelty was a motif in many of Lee's relationships,
and it seldom had a happy ending. The increasingly needy singer leaned
on her musicians for support. "They were her family," said Fred Apollo.
"She kept them from leaving her after each show, which caused some problems with those who had wives or a life and didn't want to hang out until
the early morning hours." Those who refused, like Jack Costanzo, faced
an angry Peggy Lee. Secretaries, too, had to plead with Lee to let them go
before nightfall, even before midnight. Max Bennett's sister, Mary, hadn't
lasted long in that job. "Mary told me she left because she was gonna have
a nervous breakdown," said Bennett. "Peggy ran her ragged."

As for boudoir companionship, Lee didn't go lacking. According to

Frank Sinatra's valet, George Jacobs, her relationship with Sinatra wasn't platonic. In his memoir, *Mr. S: My Life with Frank Sinatra*, Jacobs wrote of how Lee was the "occasional beneficiary of Mr. S's largesse." Like her, the macho-acting superstar "couldn't be alone," Jacobs wrote. "He always needed a girl, and she didn't have to be famous." He would thumb through his little black book, phoning everyone from Marilyn Monroe and Judy Garland to his favorite hookers. "If all else failed, he'd call Peggy Lee, who lived down the block."

Lee was usually the predator, but her liaisons with Sinatra suggested how pliable she could be in the presence of a powerful man. That was how she had envisioned Dave Barbour—as a fatherly savior in whose strong arms she could surrender. Ultimately, though, Lee was usually tougher and more dominant than any of the men in her life, and few of their egos could handle it.

As she waited out her divorce decree, Lee, as usual, crammed every possible moment with work—this despite a new string of reported illnesses, among them "an acute virus infection." Two weeks after that purported malady, Lee was at Capitol to record a song written by an embattled black survivor who had stirred her as deeply as Count Basie. In his three years as a star, Ray Charles had become synonymous with soul; many greats, including Sinatra, called him a genius. Born in rural Georgia, Charles had lived a hardscrabble life with which Lee could identify. He had grown up in poverty, gone blind at seven, lost his mother at fifteen, and become a drug addict a year later. His piano playing and raspy, aching voice were the heart of the blues; Charles added gospel, jazz, and boogie-woogie, weaving them all into an exultant, foot-stomping sound that had extolled the full breadth of black music. Lee recalled the first time she heard Charles's trademark, "Georgia on My Mind." When he sang, "Georgia, Georgia, no peace I find," she couldn't keep from crying.

At a singles session on March 28, 1959, Jimmy Rowles, Max Bennett, Larry Bunker, Howard Roberts, Shelly Manne, and several more of her pet musicians joined Lee and Jack Marshall to record "Hallelujah, I Love Him So," the first of several Charles songs that Lee would cover, with appropriate changes of gender. Her version was swinging big-band jazz—full of glee as she boasted of the man who made love to her all night then served her coffee at dawn. Charles loved her effort. It became a Lee showstopper, as did her cover of "Alright, Okay, You Win," borrowed from Joe Williams and the Count Basie orchestra. Williams had grown up in awe of Lee, and she thrilled him again in 1959 when they crossed paths at the Riviera Hotel in Las Vegas. He never forgot that moment: "She stopped and she looked at me and she said, 'Sing, baby . . . sing!' Now *that's* inspiring!"

On April 10, Lee was back in New York to appear on a CBS-TV jazz spectacular, *Swing into Spring*, in celebration of Benny Goodman's twenty-five years as a bandleader. Other guests included Ella Fitzgerald, the Berlin-born classical and jazz piano wizard André Previn, and the daredevil vocal foursome the Hi-Lo's. All of them worked in the vanguard of modern jazz except Goodman, who had remained stubbornly anchored in the swing sounds of the forties. He had aged into a vague-looking codger, but hadn't grown any warmer. "He wasn't a wicked man," said Previn. "He just had no tact. I remember on that show, Ella came out for a dress rehearsal in a rather ill-chosen dress, because it was full of beads, and they glittered, and there was a lot of Ella. She said, 'What do you think, honey?' I said, 'You look great.' We walked down the hall. Benny came out of his room and saw her, and said, 'Shit, you're not gonna *wear* that?'"

Previn bowed to Ella, and even more so to Peggy Lee. "I was crazy about her. Of that school of singing, she was my favorite. She had the best time I ever heard in my life. You couldn't shake her." As she sang "Why Don't You Do Right?" in front of a flashing starburst, Lee stared into the eyes of America with no sign of her former terror. And this was live TV. "She owned the camera," said the TV producer Bill Harbach. "It was her friend." Alongside Ella's bouncy swing and the "hot" jazz of Goodman's group, Lee was the essence of stillness. She acted out songs almost entirely with her face; director Dwight Hemion kept her in close-up as often as possible. Lee had brought several songs from her *I Like Men!* album, including "When a Woman Loves a Man," Johnny Mercer's account of a woman who lays herself at her lover's feet, blind to his flaws. Eyelids fluttering and head tilted back, she seemed in the flush of some private erotic reverie as she sang: "Tell her she's a fool and she'll say, 'Yes, I know . . . but I love him so.'"

Away from the cameras, said Previn, "*Oh*, she was eccentric." Clark

Burroughs, the tenor of the Hi-Lo's, recalled her as morose and "very reclusive." She perked up on May 4, 1959, a night she had dreamed about for months. At the Beverly Hilton Hotel in Beverly Hills, the National Academy of Recording Arts & Sciences (NARAS) held its first Grammy Awards ceremony to honor outstanding achievement in the recorded arts. Early on that balmy evening, 516 industry figures in tuxedoes and evening gowns had filed past the swaying palm trees at Wilshire and Santa Monica Boulevards, then headed toward the hotel's International Ballroom. The big, round tables filled up with stars: Frank Sinatra; Sammy Davis, Jr.; Milton Berle; Dean Martin; Henry Mancini; Johnny Mercer; Gene Autry; Jo Stafford.

The Grammys began as an untelevised insider event, with only twenty-eight categories. The nominees, including Peggy Lee, waited and squirmed. "Fever" had scored nominations for Record of the Year; Best Vocal Performance, Female; and Best Arrangement. The last category named Jack Marshall, which made Lee fume. The setting for "Fever" was *her* idea, she insisted to friends; all Marshall had done was notate the musicians' parts.

No matter, because *The Music of Peter Gunn*, the soundtrack album of a hit TV detective show, won its composer and conductor, Henry Mancini, the Best Arrangement award. As Record of the Year, NARAS voters chose "Nel Blu Dipinto di Blu" ("Volare"), a continental trifle by Italian crooner Domenico Modugno. Near the end of the night, Frank Sinatra announced the nominees for Best Vocal Performance, Female. A huge cheer greeted his announcement of the winner—Ella Fitzgerald, for her *Irving Berlin Song Book*.

After such upsets, Lee typically called Ernest Holmes for solace; lately their phone chats had swelled into a near-nightly ritual. He tried to convince her not to take each disappointment so personally. Patiently the spiritualist told her she was an instrument of God, and that everything she accomplished was more his doing than her own.

Lee was on such a self-induced treadmill that she couldn't make the distinction. Many projects that bore her trademark polish were in fact thrown together at the last minute. Capitol had booked Lee to join George Shearing, the London-born, blind jazz pianist turned mood-music star, to record a live album. Dave Cavanaugh had chosen a chaotic setting: a national disc-jockey convention at the Americana Hotel in Miami Beach, Florida. The two stars were too busy to coordinate advance meetings, so they agreed to whip up the repertoire and arrangements at the hotel.

Lee flew through a storm to get there, and arrived at the start of the most bacchanalian party she had ever attended. Its grandiose title, "The Second Annual International Radio Programming Seminar and Pop Music Disc Jockey Convention," suggested an event of high respectability. In panel discussions, authorities would pontificate on the state of music broadcasting; as dessert, a smorgasbord of disc-jockey sweethearts— Patti Page, Connie Francis, Vic Damone, Julie London, Pat Boone, Andy Williams—would put on a gala show. Mitch Miller, Columbia Records' dictatorial head of Artists & Repertoire and the host of TV's popular *Sing Along with Mitch*, was on hand, ready to valiantly declaim rock and roll as the "worship of mediocrity" and "one step from fascism."

But the presence of cohost Morris Levy—the mob-connected industry mogul—hinted at misconduct. The convention helped trigger the first revelations of payola, the rampant record-company practice of bribing DJs into pushing certain singles. Six months later, Alan Freed, the slick-talking New York deejay—a hero to many teenagers—would take the fall for many of his peers when he lost his job for accepting payoffs. Widespread federal investigations of the radio industry followed.

The payola scandal painted one more blemish on the country's "wholesome" landscape. TV and radio had not fully recovered from the scourge of the blacklist, which in 1950 had set out to eradicate the voices of anyone with progressive social or political ties—all of which were lumped conveniently under "Communism." Then, in 1958, came the quiz show scandals. It shook many Americans to the core to think that their trusted television sets could bring such hypocrisy into their living rooms.

For three days in Miami, payola reigned. Record companies had lured an estimated two thousand five hundred DJs and radio executives to the Americana, where paradise greeted them in the form of lavish hotel suites; gambling; endless alcohol and food; free TVs, phonographs, and clothes; and what author William Barlow called "one of the largest contingents of hookers ever assembled in a Miami Beach hotel." A week later, *Time* magazine would accuse RCA Victor of plying DJs with a million dollars to spend on the aforementioned perks.

The call girls and booze outshone the entertainment. It included a soft-spoken enchantress from North Dakota and a jazz pianist who had turned his aristocratic hands to the production of boudoir music for the modern bachelor pad. Shearing's quintet, with its pastel sound of unison vibraphone and piano, played on such best-selling albums as *Blue Chiffon*, *Satin Affair*, and *Soft and Silky*. *Playboy*-ready models adorned the LP covers, which seemed to promise that if you spun those discs, girls like that might soon adorn your bedsheets.

Immediately upon reaching the Americana, Lee stepped into strife. Shearing's band, which included his black Cuban percussionist, Armando Peraza, had arrived first. Racism and segregation ran rampant in 1950s Florida, as they did in much of America; and when the front-desk staff got a look at Peraza, he was turned down for a room. "There we were," recalled the musician, "standing in the hotel lobby being humiliated once again, but this time it was Miss Peggy Lee who took control. She threatened to sue the promoter and the hotel, and would in no uncertain terms tell this convention full of disc jockeys what Miami Beach really stood for. She went toe-to-toe with these guys until they relented."

From there, Shearing and Lee scrambled to cobble together an album. Each had a few songs in mind, but the pianist hadn't notated a single chord—"because George is blind and doesn't use written music," Lee explained. "We had to memorize everything. How we lived through it and stayed alive, I don't know, because it was seventy-two hours that we were up."

On Friday night, May 29, the drunken throngs were herded into a large conference room for a free show. Attention spans were wavery at best when the artists took their places on a center platform: Lee in a white, shiny, flaring satin dress, Shearing with his trademark tuxedo, dark glasses, and toothy grin. His group included Toots Thielemans, a jaunty Belgian guitarist who had played with many American greats, including bebop's acknowledged genius, saxophonist Charlie Parker.

Unfortunately, the session was sabotaged by technical troubles, the rambunctious crowd, and underrehearsal. On a surviving recording of Cole Porter's "Always True to You in My Fashion," Lee gets lost near the beginning—"Oh, wait a minute, I'm sorry, I goofed!"—and never settles into Shearing's draggy tempo. Years later, Lee could hardly recall the performance: "I was so exhausted. I just remember standing there."

Producer Dave Cavanaugh, who was present, cut the taping short after a few songs. The next night, Lee and Shearing performed the whole show, but for some reason it went unrecorded. Tension clouded the proceedings, as the pianist seethed at Lee for some perceived snub onstage. Its nature mystified Eleanor Fuerst, the wife of Ed Fuerst, Shearing's first American manager. "I never had the feeling it was anything that Peggy did," she said, adding, "George was not the easiest person with whom to get along."

Rather than abandon the project, Cavanaugh tried a practical solution. Before they left Miami, Lee and the group would record the show without an audience. In a common practice at the time, Capitol's engineers would add crowd noises and applause to create a bogus live album. Frictions notwithstanding, by the time the tape rolled, the music had fallen so impeccably into place that no one could have imagined the stars fumbling through it days before. Shearing's charts were spare, graceful pieces of architecture, with tuneful intros, motifs, and tags springing out of the songs as though they belonged there. With such a background, Lee's delivery seemed to float on air. As heard in the musical *Kiss Me, Kate*, "Always True to You in My Fashion" was the breathless admission of a philandering sexpot; Lee and Shearing turned it into cool, syncopated whimsy, Latinized by Armando Peraza. On "I Lost My Sugar in Salt Lake City," a lament for a two-timing man, Lee wailed the blues without ever raising her voice. She offered Duke Ellington and Carl Sigman's tender "All Too Soon" as a nod to one of her now-deceased forerunners, Mildred Bailey, a rotund jazz singer who had swung with a featherweight ease.

Capitol called the album *Beauty and the Beat!* Above the artists' names, the cover declared: RECORDED LIVE AT THE NATIONAL DISC JOCKEY CONVENTION IN MIAMI, FLORIDA. The label could just as easily have issued the disc as a studio session; one had to wonder about Capitol's relationship to the nefarious organizers.

Back home, Lee faced more drama. On June 16, she permanently shed the title of Mrs. Dewey Martin. The singer had asked no alimony, just reimbursement of attorney's fees and full ownership of the house that Martin had bought from her. By now the actor's film career had more or less ended, although he did occasional TV work through the 1970s. Along the way Martin became a bartender in Alaska, lived with monks in a Japanese monastery, and finally retired.

Lee went from divorce court to the Flamingo in Las Vegas, where according to columnists she fell into the arms of its wealthy owner, George Capri. "The whisper around Las Vegas is that this romance is serious," wrote a reporter. It went nowhere. On November 9, both the cool siren of "Fever" and her disheartened true-life self went on stark display before Steve Allen's Monday-night TV viewers. They and the rest of the country had started the countdown to a new decade, but on *The Steve Allen Show* only his sponsor, Plymouth cars, hinted at the winds of change. Unlike many oversize, ostentatious 1950s automobiles, the company's streamlined 1960 model was hawked as a gas saver for a belt-tightening future. The commercials signaled the end of a delusional postwar era—a time marked by reckless spending and a naïve assurance that the Lord would provide.

The Steve Allen Show's wry, bespectacled host didn't know that his party, too, was nearly over. Allen's smart sketch comedy and classy pop-jazz had aimed at a cultivated, adult sensibility; he loved lampooning America's youth, and took special glee in solemnly reading the words to teenage hits: "Be-Bop-a-Lula, she's my baby / Be-Bop-a-Lula, I don't mean maybe . . ." Even the stodgy Ed Sullivan, who had pulverized Allen in the same Sunday-night time slot, embraced rock on his show, however reluctantly. That June, NBC would drop the ax on Allen.

His November 9, 1959, lineup had looked to the past with the sixty-one-year-old ex-vaudevillian George Jessel and the suave but fading black crooner Billy Eckstine. Allen also featured the six-foot-five, rugged blond hunk Chuck Connors, who starred in the hit series *The Rifleman*. But the favored billing of his fourth guest—"Extra Added Attraction, Peggy Lee"—revealed who Allen deemed the most important. Five minutes into the show she glided out, smiling and radiant. A plunging, white beaded dress clung to her body, which was at its most curvaceously hourglass. Diamond earrings dangled from beneath a blond bun as large as a pillbox hat. In a brief exchange with Allen, Lee sounded like a slightly potted Mae West. "Well, uh, I have a, kind of a . . . *swinging* little . . . number, and I've been, uh, shopping around for just the . . . *right* program on which to perform it."

"Well, everybody around here swings pretty good, you know," said Allen.

Lee waited a beat, then, in the accent of a Vegas thug, answered: "Well, den, diss must be de place!" As she swept past him and took her spot, Allen turned bopster-groovy: "Here is the wild Miss Peggy Lee, who *wails!*"

Snapping out the brisk tempo for "It's All Right With Me," Lee turned into a slinky jazz angel, shimmying slightly, eyebrows flirtatiously cocked, hands tracing little rhythmic patterns in the air. All the while, she gazed smolderingly into the camera and locked eyes with the viewer. She followed with "Smack Dab in the Middle," an R&B swinger borrowed from Count Basie and Joe Williams. To see her riding a big-band beat with sheer abandon, head thrown back and arms oustretched, was to understand what made Peggy Lee the happiest.

But she was no less at home in the show's heartrending finale, a suite of songs about lost love, arranged orchestrally by Nelson Riddle. It began and ended with the saddest ballad that ever bore her name. Sid Kuller had gone uncredited on "Fever," but not on "How Do You Erase a Memory?," whose lyric has a finesse that Lee rarely achieved on her own. The song poses a set of questions about a problem Lee faced constantly: the crashing of one more illusion. "How can you explain a change of heart? How can you hang on to hope?"

Kuller wove together an extraordinary medley, in which songs of woe overlap like passing clouds, depicting a woman for whom dreams and reality are at constant odds. Allen's gifted director, Dwight Hemion, staged the segment on an almost bare set; stacked-up chairs simulated a bar after closing. The host plays saloon pianist and confidante. "Yes, it's bad when your loved one is gone," sings Lee; Allen answers: "But it's worse when you try to hang on."

From there, Lee turns a misty gaze to the camera and recalls her old lover in song after song. "He had kind of sandy hair, eyes so shiny blue . . . I get along without him very well, except when soft rains fall . . . I hear him call me baby, *baaaaby. . . .*" Conflicting emotions, from fear to girlish rapture to erotic yearning, pass across her face and through her voice. At times she slips into the raspy moan of Billie Holiday, who had died that summer of liver and heart disease. Finally, with a harp glissando and a cymbal crash, the truth grabs hold of her. Her body shudders, and she's back to where she started: "How do you erase a memory? How can you replace a dream?"

Fantasy couldn't ease her frequent loneliness, but for a while, Bill Harbach could. As Allen's producer and the man who had launched the *Tonight* show, the tall, lanky New Yorker, then forty, was a genuine man about town. He seemed to know every star in show business, in part because he had descended from musical-theater royalty. His father, the lyricist and librettist Otto Harbach, had helped evolve operetta into musical comedy; as Jerome Kern's collaborator he wrote "Smoke Gets in Your Eyes." Bill, in turn, played a part in taking live TV from its awkward, primitive roots to the graceful production of Peggy Lee's torchsong montage.

Lee had seduced him from afar in her Goodman days; finally he got to know her when she played Ciro's. "We had a crush on each other," Harbach confessed. By 1959 she was unattached, but he had a wife and two daughters. The producer's "unavailability" made him all the more enticing to Lee, and Harbach didn't resist. One night she invited him back to her house. As he stood in her kitchen, drinking milk out of a bottle, Lee stared at him. "When you talked to her," he recalled, "she was looking behind your eyes, into your thoughts."

They began a brief affair. Harbach and Lee had to be discreet, so they met secretly at her home. For all his eminence, Harbach had grown up amid too much greasepaint to be pretentious, and his playfulness brought out a side of Lee that many never saw. "She was *funny*," he said. "It was cozy and easy—when it was one-on-one." The two of them shared an endless stream of jokes. Lee had a favorite. "Hey, Bill," she said. "A mother comes into her son's room. She's outraged. She says to the kid, 'I found a condom on the patio!' The kid says, 'Mom, what's a patio?' She thought that was a riot."

Lee and Harbach enjoyed many of their tenderest moments while listening to records. Over and over she dropped the phonograph needle on their favorite song, "Just for a Thrill," a track from a new album, *The Genius of Ray Charles*. Strings swooped around Charles as he sang, in his crushed-velvet cry, of how it felt to be tossed aside without warning: "Just for a thrill, you changed the sunshine to rain . . ." Jazz pianist Lil Hardin

Armstrong, the second wife of Louis Armstrong, had composed the song in 1936, five years after their divorce. The words, by Don Raye, reminded Lee of what Dave Barbour and Robert Preston had (she felt) done to her.

Compared to the messiness of her personal life, an album or show brought Lee the comfort of absolute control. In February 1960, Capitol released one of her cleverest records. Dave Cavanaugh adored "Lover," and he wanted Lee to make a whole Latin-style LP. He didn't only have art on his mind; Capitol had recently made a mint with *Cole Español*, an album of Nat King Cole singing in phonetic Spanish to Nelson Riddle's commercially south-of-the-border background.

Lee had too much respect for Latin music to do something that sounded so artificial. With Cavanaugh, she decided to take a dozen showtunes and heat them up with authentic Afro-Cuban rhythms. If Jack Marshall's arranging sounds Hollywood-slick, the band's native Latino musicians bring out the spirit that Lee wanted. The four-man trumpet section plays together so precisely that each phrase lands like the crack of a whip. Five percussionists beat out a storm of Latin rhythms on conga, bongo, güiro, timbale, and cowbell. Eddie Cano, a Mexican nightclub pianist from Los Angeles, jabs at the keys in a fiery, syncopated style.

Together they wipe away any hint of Broadway from the songs. *My Fair Lady*'s "On the Street Where You Live" becomes a rumba, "The Party's Over" from *Bells Are Ringing*, a bolero. In the musical *Damn Yankees*, a baseball coach tries to boost his failing team's morale with "(You Gotta Have) Heart"; *Latin ala Lee!* reworks it as a cha-cha-cha, peppered by a male choir chanting "*corazón!*" Surrounded by all that frenzy, Lee doesn't have to do anything except sing straight and on the beat.

During the session, the control-room door opened, and in walked Desi Arnaz, the Cuban bandleader who had costarred with his wife, Lucille Ball, on TV's *I Love Lucy*. Arnaz had just left a studio down the hall. Dona Harsh, Lee's guest, watched in delight as Arnaz "went over and sang with the guys singing '*corazón.*'"

On the cover, Lee locks arms with two male models dressed as gold-jacketed matadors, their backs to the camera. Her short lemon-yellow hairdo is unbecomingly tousled and topped by a fake-looking bun. Kitschy as it looks, *Latin ala Lee!* zoomed to number eleven on *Billboard*'s pop album chart. Beyond the States, it won the hearts of two budding singer-songwriters. Although Lee had yet to sing in England, "Fever" had made her a star there, and "Till There Was You," a *Latin ala Lee!* track, was released as a British single. Lee's bolero version of that ballad from *The Music Man* caught the ear of future Beatle Paul McCartney. On the 1964 Capitol album, *Meet the Beatles*, McCartney awkwardly sings lead on "Till There Was You" in an arrangement copied from *Latin ala Lee!*

Elsewhere in Britain, the album found its way into the hands of Raymond Edward O'Sullivan, the singer-songwriter whose feel-bad confessional hit of 1972, "Alone Again (Naturally)," made him internationally famous under the name of Gilbert O'Sullivan. *Latin ala Lee!* so captivated him that he dreamed of recording an LP called *Latin ala G!*

In 1959, however, Lee was nearly forty and beloved not by O'Sullivan's age group but by their parents, which placed her on the enemy side of the generation gap. Her efforts at R&B had failed to win many young hearts. Disc jockey William B. Williams, who played Lee daily on WNEW in New York, knew her audience's demographic. "The kids consider Peggy Lee a nice elderly blonde," he said. Then, referencing a twenty-nine-year-old fashion plate of film, TV, and supper clubs, Williams added, "I watched Polly Bergen do one of these television rock and roll shows and the kids looked at her as if she were their aunt from Toledo."

"The kids'" music, and the stay-at-home pleasures of TV, had begun to eclipse the upscale club circuit that Lee worked. But during a rehearsal for *Swing into Spring*, Benny Goodman had told her about Basin Street East, a new nightspot in the heart of Manhattan's East Side. He had just played it, and it would be perfect for her. Later, as she vacationed in Palm Springs, one of her agents called to say that Basin Street East wanted her. The place sounded promising enough for Lee to fly to New York and check it out. She saw a long, rectangular room that held three hundred and forty—the right size for a singer who liked to see her audience's faces. The stage was at one end, and the sightlines on the other weren't great. Lee agreed to sing at Basin Street East, but only if certain changes were made. She wanted the stage torn up and moved to the middle of the lengthwise rear wall. She demanded a wing to enter from and an expensive new bank of lights. "She cost us a lot of money," said one of the club's owners, Lennie Green. They paid it. And for the next five years, Peggy Lee was theirs.

To pianist Mike Melvoin, who would conduct for Lee at Basin Street East, the place was a dream combination of hip and chic. "Back then you'd go out and say, 'Where are the fucking nightclubs we see in movies?' Then you'd go to Basin Street East, and here it was." Located in the former grand ballroom of the Shelton Towers Hotel, one of Manhattan's first skyscrapers, Basin Street East hosted the aristocrats of jazz: Ella Fitzgerald, Duke Ellington, Sarah Vaughan, Count Basie, Buddy Rich, Stan Kenton. Just as her career was exploding, Barbra Streisand opened there for Goodman. But Lee commanded more money than anyone—ten thousand dollars a week. She and Basin Street East became synonymous.

The club was the last hurrah of Ralph Watkins, a millionaire's son who had founded an empire of historic New York jazz rooms, including the Famous Door, Kelly's Stable, the Royal Roost, and the Embers. In a business run largely by thugs, Watkins was a tall, slim, impeccably dressed gentleman. "He was so knowledgeable, so intelligent, a really upstanding guy," said pianist Barbara Carroll, a regular at the Embers.

In 1958, Watkins had received a pitch from Leonard (Lennie) Green, a dapper ex-model and dancer who now booked dance bands. Green sold Watkins on the idea of opening a club for the mustachioed king of Latin maestros, Xavier Cugat. Watkins said yes, but he informed Green: "Moe will be with us." Moe was his silent partner, Moe Lewis, a mafia-connected pal of Frank Sinatra's and a front man who dealt with the inevitable mob infiltration of places that served liquor.

By the time "Casa Cugat" had opened inside the Shelton Towers Hotel, the bandleader was past his prime; after a year the club had lost two hundred thousand dollars. Watkins and Green decided on an emergency fix; they would shutter Casa Cugat and make it a headquarters for the cool cats of modern jazz. The partners renamed their club Basin Street East, a twist on Basin Street, a failed Greenwich Village club owned by Watkins.

From its opening night in September 1959, Basin Street East seemed headed for the same fate. Green and Watkins looked despairingly at a smattering of beatnik jazz fans "with earrings, tattoos, and sweaters," said Green. "They loved the music, but there weren't enough of them." For about a week, a bittersweet sight greeted them out front: the doorman was Stepin Fetchit, the black film comic of the 1930s who had become a millionaire by acting the part of a lazy, illiterate numskull. By 1959, he needed a job; the civil rights movement was raging, and Fetchit (born Lincoln Perry) had lost all his money and become a pariah to the cause.

Watkins and Green weren't exactly thriving. As their club sank deep into the red, Watkins suggested a last-ditch solution. Instead of relying on hipsters and their shallow pockets, what if he and Green reached for the older, more affluent demographic who felt alienated from their kids' musical tastes?

In October, Benny Goodman and a nine-piece band opened. "It was like someone had turned the lights on in a dark room," Green recalled. The King of Swing's fans streamed through the swinging doors at 137 East Forty-Eighth Street, continued past the checkroom and the cocktail lounge, and filled the Last Supper–sized tables in the main room. Goodman, now fifty and balding, took his place onstage with his familiar owlish smile, then tootled his old hits as deftly as ever. Spotlights cut across the long room, making jewels and eyeglasses sparkle. The "huge crowd," wrote Bob Rolontz in *Billboard*, "enthusiastically applaud[ed] every solo Benny took . . . In a few words, 'the king is back.'"

Ralph Watkins, Lennie Green, and Moe Lewis of Basin Street East. (COURTESY OF DEBBIE AND LENNIE GREEN)

On Monday, March 7, 1960, Basin Street East welcomed the singer whom Duke Ellington had reportedly named "the queen"—a royal proclamation indeed, and a bold one at a time when Ella Fitzgerald, Sarah Vaughan, and a singer who had already dubbed herself "The Queen," Dinah Washington, were at their peak. All of them just sang; Lee arrived with a production. She had hired Nick Castle's brother-in-law Hugo Granata, a veteran wizard at creating elaborate lighting schemes for supper-club favorites. Jess Rand, a Hollywood publicist and manager, recalled him as a "homely" man who "never smiled"; to journalist Larry L. King, Granata had "the rugged face of a dance-hall bouncer." Yet he knew how to bring out the radiance in such stars as Marlene Dietrich, Dinah Shore, and Debbie Reynolds, whose looks mattered as much as their voices. "I can take fifteen pounds off *each side* of a gal singer," Granata boasted.

Lee needed it. With her seesawing weight and her proclivity for wearing too-tight dresses that clung to her like a sausage skin, clever lighting helped. It also served as an extension of her voice, adding color and shadow. In rehearsal, Granata sketched out exactingly timed charts while Lee fed him ideas. A few were outlandish, such as her request that he flood her flashy beaded gown with white light upon her entrance. "Peggy, I can't do that, it'll blind everybody!" he said. But according to Lou Levy, "her ideas worked fabulously when they worked. And Hugo's lighting looked exquisite, even from the piano."

As for the more mundane help she needed in order to create the Peggy Lee that audiences saw, she leaned on Phoebe Ostrow, the club's secretary and all-around gofer. Then forty-one, Ostrow (who remarried and became Phoebe Jacobs) was a Bronx-born jazz groupie whose father had owned a speakeasy. "She looked like everyone's Jewish Aunt Phoebe," said Sheldon Roskin, one of Lee's later publicists. Ostrow lived for jazz and the people who made it, and worked any job that would place her near them. At Basin Street East, Ostrow worked primarily for Moe Lewis, but her greatest joy came in performing personal errands for the stars, such as taking Duke Ellington's suits to the cleaners. "She was loud; she was all over the place, like horseshit," said Green.

In Lee's presence, Ostrow felt as though heaven's gates had been flung open. Smitten by "Peggy's spiritual ability," as she put it, Ostrow took proprietary hold of the star and never let go; she was there at a moment's notice to heed her every whim. At the same time, Ostrow could be so bossy, interfering, and abrasive that theirs was a love-hate relationship. "If Peggy needed Phoebe she would call her," said Lee's friend Betty Jungheim. "If she didn't need her, she didn't call her."

On the wall of her suite at the nearby Sherry Netherland hotel, the singer had pinned an English translation of a quote attributed to Michelangelo: "Perfection is made up of trifles, but perfection itself is no trifle." Nothing less than that unattainable goal would suffice. Her shows had a balletic complexity; without the complete concentration of everyone involved, so much could go wrong.

Fear suffused Lee as she sat at her makeup table, cigarette burning in an ashtray, and created the face that audiences knew as hers. It wasn't easy. Although Ostrow saw Lee as a "ravishing beauty," Bruce Vanderhoff, who became her hairdresser and friend in the late sixties, found her unrecognizable without makeup. "No eyebrows, no eyelashes, and no lips," he said, and "that white, white skin that goes red with the change in temperature."

A rainbow of creams and powders spread out before her, Lee went to work. "She made up her face as if it were a canvas, and she was painting a portrait," said Ostrow. Lee layered on foundation in varying shades; used eyeliner and shadow, eyebrow pencil, and thick false lashes to give herself the eyes of a lioness. She highlighted her cheekbones with blusher and painted on extravagantly plump lips, often in peach, her favorite shade. By now, peroxide had so thinned out her hair that Lee had quit trying to fluff it up. Only the front strands of any hairdo were hers; the rest consisted of lemony falls and buns or sometimes complete wigs.

As showtime neared, Lee's tension almost reached the breaking point. "You didn't know whether she was gonna be shot out of a cannon, or jump out of a plane five thousand feet above the stage," recalled Ostrow. "I don't care how much reassurance she had forty times over. But Peggy enjoyed every bit of anxiety, every bit of pain. Nobody forced her to do this. If she wanted to get herself a little whacked out because she wanted to be more perfect than perfect, so be it. She loved what she was doing. She wouldn't have changed one drop of it."

Once Lee was ready, the final preshow ritual began: a mandatory gathering of her core musicians, and selected others, in her dressing room. "We got together and prayed that all would go well," Ostrow said. "It was silent and it was intense, and we would hold hands. This was a privilege of very special people that could stand and pray with Peggy before she went on that stage." As she kissed them one by one, Lee murmured the mantra she had devised for each. Stella Castellucci's was "lima beans," because the harpist liked the way she cooked them. To her daughter, Lee intoned, "Clouds raised, jets, beams, oceans, rays, waxtras." Nicki, of course, had no idea what "waxtras" meant. Other insiders were sent away with simpler code words: "Power." "Burn." As she spoke them, her eyes bore into each recipient, transmitting the message that important business was about to unfold.

On March 7, 1960—her first night of a month-long booking at Basin Street East—anticipation was high, both for Lee and for the buzzing crowd of fans outside. This was New York, the city with the richest nightlife and the most jaded audiences in America. They expected only great things from the singer who had given them "Why Don't You Do Right?," "Lover," "Fever," and *Pete Kelly's Blues*. "This was not just going to see a marvelous singer sing," said Bill Harbach. "She was more than that. She was Peggy."

A late-winter snowstorm raged, and still an overflow throng showed up. Onstage, a modern-jazz master, arranger Neal Hefti, stood in white tie and tails in front of thirteen musicians in tuxedos. As Lee trembled behind a curtain to the left of the stage, Hefti counted off a brief, high-voltage overture. Then came the announcement: "Ladies and gentlemen, Basin Street East takes great pleasure in presenting . . . *Miss PEGGY LEE!*" Lee grabbed a glass of cognac from Phoebe Ostrow's hand, downed it in one gulp, then ascended the three steps to the stage.

The ovation and the spotlight hit her, and a white-sequined Lee glowed like a heavenly creature. Fear had melted from her face, replaced by the cool, assured smile of a sphinx set to devour her prey. Each detail she had fretted over gelled into a seemingly effortless whole. Precisely on cue, a pinspot hit her snapping right hand—her idea, not Granata's—as the bassist and drummer began the familiar vamp to "Fever." As she sang of Juliet and Pocahontas in the throes of lust, Lee's twinkling eyes and arching eyebrows gave the song salacious punctuation. Her elbows stayed close to her sides, and when a hand suddenly flew out to wave a finger in the air, or coquettishly brush her own cheek, she evoked a smiling Buddha on a mountain.

"(You've Gotta Have) Heart" led off a selection of songs from *Latin ala Lee!*; her expensively dressed, predominantly white audience chimed in with the band: "*Corazón! Corazón!*" She unveiled a frantic jazz waltz, "I'm Gonna Go Fishin'," that she had yet to record. The words were hers, set to a theme from *Anatomy of a Murder*, a film that Duke Ellington had scored. Lee raced through a barrage of words about a two-timing man she was all set to replace: "He'll be the loser, yes, he'll find out / I'm gonna go fishin' and catch me a trout!"

Unlike her bluesy La Vie en Rose act—performed soon after her breakups with Preston and Barbour and during her hopeless marriage to Brad Dexter—this one was a spirit-lifter. Critics couldn't avoid hyperbole. In the *New York Journal-American*, Nick LaPole raved: "In all her yesterdays, Peggy was never better than last night. Only a superlative artist could sell out a club the size of Basin Street on such a raw, snowy night—and leave the stage after half-an-hour with the over-capacity audience applauding wildly for three solid minutes." Arthur Godfrey, one of the most powerful TV hosts of the 1950s, gave a gushing but lofty endorsement of Lee's show:

> Peggy Lee is one of the very few performers who could ever get me into a nightclub. Her Serene Highness reigns over her subjects with such supreme authority as to place us all under her hypnotic spell. One forgets completely the torture of the place: the smoke, the reek of alcoholic breaths, the redolence of the perfume mixed with the sweat due to the horrible humidity, not to mention the libidinous intertwining of one's lower limbs with those of complete strangers of either sex or both, under the table and on either side. Nevertheless I will go anywhere, anytime and pay any price to watch Miss Peggy Lee at work. Then I go home and play all twenty-one of her albums.

No one was happier than Ralph Watkins and Lennie Green. For two shows nightly and three on weekends, the club could barely squeeze in another customer. Green recalled walking into Lee's dressing room and finding her new pal, Cary Grant, sitting on the floor. During the same engagement, Lee tore open a note sent to her dressing room.

> *Dear Peggy,*
>
> *Tonight was one of the most memorable evenings of my life.*
> *Thank you.*
>
> *Love,*
> *Bette Davis*

Never had Lee known a success quite like this. The next run would be even better. "Basin Street East," wrote *Billboard*, "belongs to Peggy Lee."

————

LEE HAD NEVER SEEMED happier. Free of marital strife, she basked in the worship of her New York audience, the most faithful lover she had ever had. Great artists both in and out of her field embraced her. "People of intelligence and sophistication were drawn to Peggy," said Stella Castellucci. "She had the most fantastic library—books on every subject you could think of. Literature, philosophy, history, science."

In Los Angeles, the film composer David Raskin, a casual beau, took Lee to a concert of madrigals. The small audience included Igor Stravinsky. After the performance, recalled Lee, "he took me into the corner and he talked to me about the use of dynamics for almost an hour." Then he introduced her to Aldous Huxley, the British writer whose science-fiction classic *Brave New World* gave an eerie glimpse into the future. Huxley listened with interest as Lee described her elaborate theory about the healing waves emitted by music. "We had a conversation like two old friends," she said.

The guests at her frequent parties were no less impressive. En route to her house, expensive cars ascended the winding roads of Coldwater Canyon. They drove north on Bowmont Drive, past the home of Frank Sinatra, then made a sharp left onto Kimridge Road. Car doors opened, and out came the stars: Cary Grant, Jimmy Durante, Bobby Darin, Steve Allen and Jayne Meadows, Bing Crosby. Celebrities along with family members and musicians filed up her driveway and entered a home decked out with balloons, streamers, and flowers.

If planning a show brought Lee as much pain as pleasure, the creation of a party was sheer fun, though no less exacting. For days in advance, Lee sat in bed devising seating plans at the dinner table; floral arrangements; choices of china, silverware, table linens, and candles; and, of course, the most glamorous cuisine possible. Guests received menus such as the following:

> Mousse of Salmon
> Belgian Endive Salad
> Veal Piccata
> Fettucini
> Petits Pois with Pearl Onions
> Viennese Torte
> Bavarian Ice Cream

The parties weren't always chic; for one of them, people had to come dressed as clowns. "She did wonderful themes that really seemed to delight everyone," said her nephew Lee Ringuette, who once found himself sitting "knee-high to Frank Sinatra." Grown-up attendees carried champagne glasses into the Japanese garden out back and gathered around the goldfish pond, or stood on the bridge that crossed it. Some stayed inside, camping out in the music room or sitting squeezed together on the sofa.

The lady of the house drifted from room to room, a cognac in one hand, a cigarette in the other. Alcohol brought out her mellowest, and her soft low laugh cut through the chatter. Steve Allen recalled "that unique '*Hiiiiii*, baby,' like she just woke up." An invited journalist spotted the most memorable sign of success in that Beverly Hills cloud nine: the two Picassos, both from his blue period, that hung on the walls.

———

LEE HAD FINISHED A decade of extraordinary achievement. Reporters devoted columns of space to her accomplishments. At a time when women had begun to feel straitjacketed by the standard formula for feminine happiness—marriage, motherhood, domesticity—Lee broke rules. The singer was thrice divorced in an age when the vow "till death do us part" seemed ironclad; she was an overtly sexual presence long before the sexual revolution. Although the public didn't know it, Lee had conceived her daughter out of wedlock—an act that, to much of America, would have earned her a scarlet letter.

But close friends, as well as a few journalists, sensed an emptiness in her. "Singer Peggy Lee's Aim: To Succeed as a Person," announced a *Boston Globe* headline. To one interviewer, Lee blurted out a desire "to gain control of my life." The writer sensed her sadness: "All of the fame, glamour and success of her present life have not made up for the love and security she lost so early." Bill Harbach, too, saw grief inside the fun-loving playmate he knew. It pointed back to the loss of her angel mother and her unshakable sense of herself as an abused child. "I would far rather have been Norma Egstrom with a real mother than Peggy Lee without one," she said. Lee told Harbach her tales of Min's atrocities, and he believed every word.

On April 7, 1960, just after she had closed the happiest engagement of her life at Basin Street East, Lee lost "Papa" as well. Dr. Ernest Holmes died of emphysema at seventy-three, and the news devastated her. The positive-thinking guru had been more of a father to her than Marvin Egstrom; with Holmes in her life, she had felt safe.

More than ever, Lee sought refuge in the womb of her king-size bed. The woman who had sung "Don't Smoke in Bed" so persuasively kept a cigarette burning on the nightstand. She rarely slept more than four or five hours, and seldom before dawn. Work was the only activity that seemed to bring her solace, and as sunrise approached, the bedclothes became littered with papers containing song and poem fragments, drawings, and to-do lists. Throughout the night she reached for Holmes's *The Science of Mind*, and reread its teachings on how to achieve an orderly life. "We are living in an Intelligent Universe, which responds to our mental states," wrote Holmes. "To the extent that we learn to control these mental states, we shall automatically control our environment."

But Lee no longer stopped at Holmes; books about worldwide religions filled her shelves. "She always spoke about Jesus," said Stella Castellucci. The singer was also beguiled by the most Christlike of Roman Catholic deities, St. Francis of Assisi, the ultimate humanitarian. "She had a statue of him in the garden of every house she ever had," recalled Stella. But his influence on her didn't go far; while Francis had revered poverty, Lee lived beyond her means in homes that proclaimed the stardom and wealth of their occupant.

Her dependence on religion as a panacea was typical of the time, but Castellucci had trouble recalling much peace in Peggy Lee. "She was a great comic, and did a lot of wonderful clowning around her friends. But I think she was the kind of person who, even if she was unhappy, would go into some joking just for the sake of the other person."

Lee had an abiding will to survive, but it ran on a parallel track with self-destruction. She indulged in rich food as well as cigarettes and alcohol; according to Max Bennett, "the most exercise she ever got was walking into her rose garden." Lee kept several doctors, and leaned on them so heavily that she often had them over to dinner. On her own, she kept turning to crash diets to lose weight, vitamin C shots to boost her energy.

The clash between the public and private Peggy Lees startled Mark Murphy, who became friendly with her in that time. Capitol had signed the young jazz-singing hipster for whom *Black Coffee* had proven an epiphany. He longed to get to know her, and Lee—who liked the way he looked as well as sang—was all for it. Recently Murphy had joined another of her pets, the twenty-six-year-old pop sensation Bobby Darin, in the studio audience of *The Bing Crosby Show*, one of the crooner's ABC television specials. Taped in Hollywood, it starred the golden summit of Crosby, Sinatra, Louis Armstrong, and Peggy Lee. This was the pinnacle of Lee's dreams—to appear on TV alongside the country's three most eminent male entertainers, not as an ornamental blonde but as their equal.

Lee had seldom looked prettier or more confident. She sang with all the men, separately and together, but Murphy was most riveted by her sultry solo rendition of "Baubles, Bangles and Beads" from the musical *Kismet*. That operettalike trifle told of how a bejeweled woman could land even more jewels, including a wedding ring. In a soprano range the song sounded coy and virginal; slowed down and dropped into Lee's vocal cellar, it was as sexy as "Diamonds Are a Girl's Best Friend." Lee performed it in a tight beaded dress amid a shimmery set of glass sculptures and chandeliers. Her bedroom glance matched her postcoital delivery.

Murphy couldn't believe his luck when she invited him to her house. He had heard horror stories about Lee, who seemed plagued by illness and depression and who could rail defensively at well-meaning friends.

But to him she seemed shy, funny, and dear. It was a hot California day. Wearing a one-piece bathing suit, Lee invited him out to the pool. Suddenly she grabbed his hands and put them on her waist. "Like the pretty view?" she said, fixing him with the same hot glance he'd seen her flash on *The Bing Crosby Show*. Unbeknownst to Lee, Murphy was gay. He fled out the door.

Lee had agreed to write the liner notes for his new LP, *Hip Parade*. He had used several of her favorite musicians, including Pete Candoli and Jimmy Rowles. She kept her word. But when Murphy saw the album, he was devastated. Lee had enthused over the band, but given him only the most backhanded praise. At the end came a line that made him shudder: "You might say, 'He blows' . . . and he's attractive, single." In the self-consciously macho and often homophobic field of jazz, Murphy lived discreetly, and her seemingly coded words left him depressed for days. Soon after he'd read her essay, Lee received a ribbon-tied box. Inside were a bunch of long-stemmed roses with the buds cut off. Murphy had enclosed a note: "Dear Peggy, I think you know what to do with these."

He never stopped revering her singing, but his glimpse behind the curtain, along with others he gained through the years, haunted him. "There was a hostility in Peggy that really upset me, an anger. I couldn't figure out how someone who looked so beautiful, who had terrific success at selling records, lots of money, could be this tortured." He recalled her poignant last scene in *Pete Kelly's Blues*, where she had reverted to a childhood state and clutched a rag doll. "I got to believe that Peggy Lee was actually a big doll that this woman had invented to escape from being so miserable."

Peggy Lee and husband number four, Jack Del Rio, on their
wedding day. "We were a little hasty," she said later.

Chapter Ten

AS THE 1960s progressed, Lee stayed lost in a whirlwind of projects: two or three new albums a year; countless TV appearances; nightclub acts of such intricacy and cost that, according to Lou Levy, "putting together a new show was like invading France." But for Lee, maintaining a relationship was even harder. Like other female singers who sang so knowingly of true love, Lee was usually without it. As much as she wished she could step inside the picture-perfect bliss of "The Folks Who Live on the Hill," her stature and ambitions intimidated almost every man she dated.

Afraid to be alone, she implored anyone she could to keep her company. A parade of visitors moved in and out of her home, where commotion reigned. People stepped (or tripped) over her scampering Pekingese dogs, Little One and Little Two. Lee's dresser, Virginia Bernard, and her Swedish housekeeper, Grethe, rushed around, following the star's commands. Every few weeks, Bernard helped her throw another lavish soiree. More than once, the lovely young film actress Stefanie Powers made the guest list. "They were the kind of Hollywood parties where behind every potted palm you saw a recognizable face," said Powers. "And some of the best musicians in town. People got up and sang, like Danny Kaye and Sammy Cahn. It was stellar. I was in such awe of her."

The rest of the time, reporters, secretaries, siblings, and band members found themselves greeting the dawn with Peggy Lee. She plied them with drinks and regaled them with hours of rambling reflections. In the absence of guests, there was always the phone. "It is not uncommon for journalists or disc jockeys to receive calls from Miss Lee when neither has all that much to say," wrote the journalist Larry L. King. "One has the notion she feels the compulsion to communicate, as she does with an audience, but prefers to keep her relationships at a distance."

Onstage or on record, though, Lee conjured up pink, frilly cocoons of fairytale love. In 1960, she gave her fans *Pretty Eyes*, another boudoir-ready LP. Unlike Nelson Riddle's luscious but unrhythmic charts on *The Man I Love*, several of those on *Pretty Eyes* had a toe-tapping bounce, thanks to Billy May, Capitol's rotund, jolly staff arranger. May liked to make things whimsical and bright, as he had on Frank Sinatra's smash album, *Come Fly with Me*. But he also had a romantic streak, and in *Pretty Eyes* he swathed Lee in pixie-dusted strings, buoyed by a swinging rhythm section. Both of them devoured the sly sexual innuendo of "You Fascinate Me So," a come-hither tune by one of her pet songwriters, Cy Coleman, who played jazz piano in New York clubs. His lyricist, Carolyn Leigh, was a Manhattan sophisticate whose barbed verse had a built-in bounce. Lee sang her words with a wink: "I feel like Christopher Columbus when I'm near enough to contemplate/ The sweet geography descending from your eyebrow to your toe."

Pretty Eyes included "In Other Words," a ballad sung in the chicest of New York cabarets, notably the Blue Angel. There the song's debonair author, Bart Howard, emceed and tinkled the piano between shows. "In Other Words" spoofed the lofty pronouncements of his idol, Cole Porter, and other highbrow lyricists who—as the verse of Howard's song went—"often use many words to say a simple thing." Howard waxed poetic about the moon and the stars, while giving a running translation: "In other words, hold my hand / In other words, darling, kiss me."

Obscure recordings of his songs by the likes of Mabel Mercer, cabaret's ladylike British doyenne, weren't going to rescue Howard from his nightly grind. But Peggy Lee did. Gently she suggested that no one would remember a title as bland as "In Other Words." Instead he should use the catchy first phrase of the chorus, "Fly Me to the Moon."

Howard obeyed. The song's fate was sealed when Lee performed it on *The Ed Sullivan Show*. Gowned in billowy chiffon, she strolled along a seashore—actually a filmed projection of one—and, like a cool Aphrodite, sang of a love too great for one planet to contain. That performance changed Howard's life. "All the big artists were watching what Peggy did, because she was so successful," he recalled. "And I had a hundred big records of my song after that."

Her flair for creating such detailed minidramas had grown with every year. But no one, including Lee herself, knew if her acting coup in *Pete Kelly's Blues* had been anything more than a fluke. She burned to prove that it wasn't. Finally she got her chance—not in a film but on an episode of *General Electric Theater*, a CBS series hosted by and featuring Ronald Reagan. In "So Deadly, So Evil," Lee played Natalia Cory, a department-store copywriter plagued by spooky calls from a stranger. He claims to know dark secrets about her, and ultimately breaks into her apartment in an ape mask and accuses her of murder.

Lee's menacing foe was played by Gavin MacLeod, the shiny-headed comic actor known later as newsman Murray Slaughter on *The Mary Tyler Moore Show* and as the captain of *The Love Boat*. "So Deadly, So Evil" was his first big television break. "When I realized I was gonna play opposite Peggy Lee, I almost lost it!" MacLeod recalled. Her "very sexy sound" had long made him swoon. "She was just a wonderful communicator," he said. "She turned you on." Now, in the apartment scene, he found himself pressed against her. "I was slightly aroused, shall we say," the actor confessed. Apparently Lee noticed. During the shoot, she invited him back to her house. The fact that he was married, of course, didn't faze Lee in the slightest. "I wouldn't dare go!" affirmed MacLeod. "But I was quite enamored of her."

Acting the sex kitten came easy to Lee, but there was only discomfort in this portrayal. Natalia, like Lee, was a woman of mystery; she had fled a far-off place, but it still haunted her. The character emerged as a watered-down Rose Hopkins with the slightly stammering speech of Peggy Lee. MacLeod sensed that the singer, once more, "was playing herself." And the fear that had haunted both her and Rose flared up. On the first day of filming, MacLeod arrived to find Lee on the set. He asked the crew how things were going. "They said, 'We had the hardest time. She didn't want to come out of her trailer.' Stuff was going on that they wouldn't tell me about." Someone had phoned Lee's agent, who managed to talk her onto the soundstage.

Songs, not scripts, were her haven; stripped of those, she could seem awkward and lost. In 1960, the singer appeared on *Person to Person*, the prestigious TV interview series. The host, Charles Collingwood, talked to celebrities in their homes via remote hookup. His cameramen found Lee in her garden. She was svelte, attired elegantly in a Chinese silk pantsuit, and smartly coiffed. But she couldn't hide her self-consciousness as she led Collingwood and the viewing audience from room to room, at one point bumping into a plant. As Lee sat on her bed and wrung her hands, the host asked about her childhood dreams. Her response revealed one of the great conflicts of her life. "Well, Charles, I had two goals, really," she said haltingly. "One was to be a successful singer. And the other was to have a family . . . I think it's good to have a goal, don't you, Charles?"

She proceeded to the parlor, where her "wonderful daughter," Nicki, sat on the sofa in a plain dress. Little One and Little Two sat in her lap. The sixteen-year-old was her "secretary," Lee said, when she wasn't in school. "She does many things. She types and shops for me . . . what else do you do?"

"Well, I answer the phone," explained a tense Nicki. "I sort of chauffeur my mother around." They must have a lot in common, said the host. Nicki's face went blank. She turned to her mother. "Yes, we do, uh . . . Charles," stammered Lee. "I think we have one of the nicest kinds of relationships. We're really very good friends, and we have the same kind of sense of humor, and, um, we like the same kind of music, and um, the same kind of dogs."

Lee entered the music room, where she opened two cabinet doors and turned on a reel-to-reel tape deck. Out came the lilting title song of *Christmas Carousel*, Lee's forthcoming collection of swingingly arranged holiday tunes, many with her own words. She mentioned having looked St. Nicholas up in the encyclopedia; in thanks, said Lee, he gifted her with the ideas for three songs.

A children's chorus joined Lee on the album. Even amidst a gang of kids, she forgot to shift from seductress to mommy. In "The Christmas List," tots line up with their gift requests as Lee plays a saucy Mrs. Claus. "Do you have candy?" asks a boy soprano. "*Mm-hmm*," purrs Lee.

"And cookies, too?"

"*Mm-hmmmmm*."

"You got gum to chew?"

"*Yessss*."

"And something for Santa Claus, too?"

"Oh, *yes!*"

Most fans preferred to see her in the adult atmosphere of Basin Street East. On Thursday, January 12, 1961, Lee returned there for a month to launch *Olé ala Lee!*, the campily titled sequel to *Latin ala Lee!* Just after the New Year, she waited with a sea of suitcases and trunks at Union Station in downtown Los Angeles. Then she boarded the Super Chief, the pricey streamliner whose wealth of celebrity passengers made it known as the "Train of the Stars."

In the jam-packed club car at the far end were the Oscar-nominated starlet Natalie Wood; her husband, actor Robert Wagner (R.J. to his friends); and the Mississippi-born Mart Crowley, who went on to write the groundbreaking gay play, *The Boys in the Band*. Crowley worked as assistant to filmmaker Elia Kazan, who had directed Wood's forthcoming star vehicle, *Splendor in the Grass*. Crowley and the Wagners were headed to New York to watch a rough cut. The club car teemed with a fashionably dressed, chattering crowd. Much buzz surrounded the Wood party, who sat crammed in a booth for two.

The door flew open, and in walked Peggy Lee, fully decked out for public view. "I was just in heaven," recalled Crowley. "She was looking great. Lots of makeup." Lee rushed over to Wagner. "Oh, R.J.!" "*Peggy!*" Wood was thrilled to be joined by her favorite singer. Crowley leapt up and gave Lee his seat. "She was as wide as Natalie and me side by side," he recalled. "She kind of dripped over the edge a little bit." Suddenly Lee grabbed Crowley's hand and pulled him onto her lap. "Come on, honey," she said. "I could change your whole life!"

"This woman knew I was gay from the get-go," said Crowley. "We all just screamed with laughter."

Lee reserved a table for them at Basin Street East. As ever, the jazz-loving smart set packed the room. Few of them seemed to imagine that this urbane chic would ever go away. The most tumultuous decade in American history was underway, but for that older, well-to-do crowd, the impending quakes amounted mainly to a bunch of headlines they read over breakfast. Most of them preferred to ignore the fact that their worldly values were coming under fire by their children's generation. Surely few Peggy Lee fans set foot inside the folk clubs of Greenwich Village, where raw, untrained voices rang out in praise of freedom and equality—a statement, in many ways, against the superficial lives of their elders. For all but the most progressive of Lee's contemporaries, "protest" was a dirty word. Lee herself paid scant attention to current events. Brand-new president John F. Kennedy's immediate concerns—the founding of the

Peace Corps, the attempt to send astronauts to the moon, the overthrow of Cuban dictator Fidel Castro—were not a part of Lee's conversations in the winter of 1961.

But she did keep up with news items pertaining to herself. One of her favorites of that period came in response to her playful treatment of "Mack the Knife," the murderous tale by Kurt Weill and Bertolt Brecht that Bobby Darin had swung to the top of the charts. Lee was thrilled to read in the syndicated column of Alex Freeman that First Lady Jacqueline Kennedy was "breaking up White House parties with a convulsing impersonation of Peggy Lee singing 'Mack the Knife.'"

Happily, Lee's favorite kind of soiree occurred nightly at Basin Street East. Behind its front door, rock and folk music didn't exist, Brooks Brothers suits and cocktail dresses remained de rigueur, swing was king, and Peggy Lee was queen. "This is the house that Benny built and Peggy made," exclaimed Ralph Watkins to a reporter. "She is the best draw we have."

January 1961 was a month of nearly zero-degree coldness and snow. But Basin Street East, wrote Arthur Gelb in the *New York Times*, was "sizzling." All month long, fabled celebrities—Sophia Loren, Joan Crawford, Ava Gardner, Cary Grant, Lena Horne, Frank Sinatra, Tallulah Bankhead, Judy Garland, Marlene Dietrich—filed past the bar and cocktail lounge and into the back room to see Peggy Lee. With her came the orchestra of a jazz singer's dreams. "When Peggy went to New York, or Chicago, or Las Vegas, every musician in town wanted that gig," said Lou Levy. "She got whoever she wanted, because she was so good."

The oversold audiences waited, and waited. "Miss Lee is late," observed reporter Jim Bishop. "She is always late. She has a chronic fear of failure and, when the time arrives to perform, she stalls." As the band played an overture of her hits, Bishop observed Lee in the wing. Just as she was announced, the star downed a cognac in one gulp. "She forces herself onstage," observed Bishop. Once there, of course, Lee was in shrewd command. Author Richard Lamparski observed the transformation a number of times. "As one would expect of a queen, she took complete charge from the instant the spotlight hit her. The audience were her subjects and the boys in the band, her court. She played off them and played them off each other. Nodding to one. Smiling at another. Making certain every one of them got sufficient stroking."

The phalanx of manly men onstage maximized her femininity. Ex-boxer Stan Levey cast a rugged presence at the drums; bodybuilder Dennis Budimir held his guitar with muscular arms. Oftentimes Lee turned to the piano and locked glances with her "*terribly* good-looking conductor," Lou Levy. She called him the Good Gray Fox, because of his leonine head of prematurely gray hair. It wasn't always ardor that burned in their eyes. "His relationship with Peggy was funny," said Steve Blum, one of her later guitarists. "They loved each other but they fought like cats and dogs. He wouldn't take any stuff from her, which is probably why he kept the gig."

By now Lee had a true saloon voice, rough around the edges—the sound of cigarettes, liquor, late nights, a frequently broken heart, and a never-say-die party spirit. With every song, she changed faces. Lee clowned her way through "Heart" with a Spanish peasant accent. For "I've Never Left Your Arms," harp, flute, and wind chimes conjured up far-off lands. "I know the purple plains of Burma / The crystal waters of the Coral Sea," she sang, and no one doubted it. At the end of her fifteen-minute salute to Ray Charles, she had the middle-aged crowd clapping and swaying in time to a swinging beat.

A reporter visited her dressing room between shows. There he saw a doleful sight. While a hairdresser primped Lee's hair, "she sagged in a leopard-skin dressing gown, and seemed to flinch from the harsh light of the bare bulbs along the edge of the mirror." The writer offered praise; she shook her head sadly. Lee, he wrote, "is never convinced by the ovations she earns."

Everyone else was, though, and that February Dave Cavanaugh recorded her at the club. Lee sounded hoarser than usual due to a cold, so various performances were taped, along with a studio session of songs from the show. From all those sources came the thirty-one-minute *Basin Street East Proudly Presents Miss Peggy Lee*, one of the defining albums of Lee's career.

The party, of course, didn't end with the late show. Around three AM, the unmarked door of her dressing room would swing open. "Miss Lee comes out in a luxurious silver fur, preceded by a lackey carrying two bags," wrote a reporter. She trekked back to her new Manhattan abode, the Park Lane Hotel, where celebrities who had come to the show partied with Lee until breakfast time.

Among the more striking regulars was a handsome, tawny-skinned black man, clearly much younger than Lee, with a mustache and a burst of take-charge energy. At twenty-eight, he had played trumpet with Lionel Hampton and Dizzy Gillespie, conducted albums for Dinah Washington and Sarah Vaughan, and toured internationally with his own big band. In a musical field built on black talent yet controlled by white businessmen, Quincy Jones was hell-bent on success.

Long before Jones had earned world renown as a producer and amassed nearly thirty Grammy Awards, Peggy Lee discovered him in a big way. The orchestral albums he made with her in 1961, *Blues Cross Country* and *If You Go*, helped inch him closer to the spotlight. Their working relationship, effused Lee, was "absolutely perfect." After hours, she partook of his other charms. "She was mad about him physically," said Betty Jungheim.

Professionally, Jones was so overextended that, in a common practice of the time, he employed ghostwriters (notably the Count Basie arranger Billy Byers) to complete his skeletal charts. How much he actually arranged for Lee was unclear, but any Jones band had his trademark tightness and precision and swung hard. "His skills at organization, motivation, and direction were tremendous," said Bob Freedman, who sometimes ghostwrote for him. "Much like Duke Ellington, he knew just how to cheerlead and get the best performance possible from the guys."

Jones dropped by Lee's house to work on their albums. "She wouldn't let him go," said Jungheim. "He was there for a month." They wrote seven songs together for *Blues Cross Country*. Their affair was conducted discreetly, for Jones was married; moreover, interracial couplings were still so vilified that mixed marriage remained illegal in twenty-one U.S. states. On his dates with Lee, Dona Harsh came along as beard. "Quincy and I danced together more times than you'll ever know," said Harsh, "because Peggy couldn't dance with him in public."

Their musical relationship, however, was a breeze, and she took the lead. Lee, explained Jones, "prerecords the tunes in her home studio and knows just what sound she wants." *Blues Cross Country* is a swinging romp across America, set to the brassy sound of a Basie-style band. Jones stocked it with Lee's favorite sidemen, including Lou Levy, Jimmy Rowles, trumpeter Jack Sheldon, and saxophonist Benny Carter, who helped Jones with the arranging. The album has a few standards, such as "St. Louis Blues," which races along like a speeding freight train. But the Lee-Jones originals make *Blues Cross Country* much more than a retrospective of the past. "New York City Blues" opens as a sultry valentine to Manhattan, with Lee confiding, "I've *got* to get back to you, if I have to walk, or crawl, or fly!" Then the brass explodes, the tempo zooms, and the blazing velocity of the city comes alive as Lee exclaims, "New York, New York is my town!" In "Boston Beans," Lee swings her way through that historic town, home to Captain John Smith, Paul Revere, and the Tea Party, but unfortunately not the asset she hoped to find: "They've got no beans in Boston / Plenty of fish!"

Down Beat's John A. Tynan called Lee's words "uniformly good; they make sense; they contain humor and little lyrical twists and turns." A month later, she and Jones got sentimental in *If You Go*, an album of coital ballads arranged with a Nelson Riddle–style plushness. Pizzicato strings quiver; bongos throb; a solo saxophone wails suggestively in the distance; a Spanish guitar adds Latin heat.

Seldom would Lee feel so appreciated as she did that year. She sang her way through the poshest nightspots in the country, leaving a trail of delirious critical praise: "one of the most compelling experiences of your life"; "provocative, regal, and insouciant"; "the hub of the universe." In the summer of 1961 she made her long-awaited British debut: a month at Pigalle, the London supper club that hosted the likes of Shirley Bassey, Sammy Davis, Jr., and (later) the pre-superstardom Beatles.

Lee never traveled light. She brought four musicians (Lou Levy, Max Bennett, Dennis Budimir, and vibraphonist Victor Feldman), Marianne as assistant, Nicki as secretary, and trunks galore, packed with more gowns than she would ever need. That July Lee boarded the S.S. *United States*, the swiftest ocean liner, at Pier 86 in New York. Four days later the boat docked at the U.K.'s bustling Port of Southampton. Pigalle staff greeted Lee and her entourage and swept them off to London by limo.

The next night, Lee was escorted to a restaurant for a press reception. So many reporters and photographers came that only a fraction could get near her. A writer from the British jazz magazine *Melody Maker* attended her first rehearsal. He saw Lee stalking the floor, chain-smoking and intensely focused on the music. "I've never known a singer who worked so hard at rehearsal," marveled her British conductor, Jack Nathan. "And she never really gets upset." Lee stayed aware of every detail: "That was dragging." "Were the drums too loud?" "Can you hear me?"

On opening night, July 16, Lee performed for a "diamond-studded gathering," as the *Evening News* called it, of British VIPs, including Bassey and the British Elvis, Cliff Richard. From the moment she stepped on-stage in a white, Grecian-style, sleveless dress, Lee could do no wrong. Fans shrieked as a pinspot lit her snapping hand at the start of "Fever"; they gazed raptly as she sang "Fly Me to the Moon" in front of a harp. "Big hunks of manhood stood up from time to time offering 'You're wonder-ful!' and other congratulatory expressions," reported *The Stage*. Lee had to do six encores. Intoxicating as the night was, a writer for the *Evening Standard* sensed a darker subtext; Peggy Lee, he wrote, was "a singer with a gift for the tragic interpretation of the happiest songs."

Lee may have become the toast of London, but Marianne wasn't hav-ing much fun. Paula Ringuette, her sister-in-law, queried her later. "Oh, it must have been wonderful, what did you see over there?" asked Paula. "The inside of the hotel," said Marianne. Nicki could be spied in the corner of the dressing room—a stocky teenager with glasses and a "painfully self-con-scious" expression, as one observer noted. By day she stayed at the hotel, typing thank-you notes and doing other clerical chores. Nicki fantasized about a singing or acting career, but her tenuous hopes sank even further as she watched this tidal wave of acclaim for her superachieving mother. The *Daily Mirror* surprised Nicki by interviewing her for a feature about herself. It had a revealing title: "How I Wish I Were Like My Mum—Says Nicki."

The young woman's attempts at singing bore that headline out. "Nicki could do Peggy," recalled Phoebe Ostrow. "She memorized every finger snap, every gesture." One night at Basin Street East, said Ostrow, Nicki donned one of her mother's gowns and stood behind her onstage, aping her moves. That was as much of the spotlight as Nicki would ever claim. "I shall never make the grade as a singer like my mother," she told the *Mirror*, adding: "I do wish I had a figure like my mum."

In mid-August, Lee sailed to Monte Carlo to sing at another opulent nightspot, the Sporting Club. Her jet-setting took her to France, then back to New York for her third Basin Street East engagement. That fall Ralph Watkins upped her salary to twelve thousand five hundred dol-lars a week. She spent more than the amount of her raise to squeeze nine string players and a French horn player onto the bandstand, along with a full horn section, a conga player, and her quartet. So many fans crowded the street outside that the club had to cordon them off with velvet ropes.

The "majesty" that the *New York Mirror*'s Frank Quinn had seen in Lee hid the ravaging effects of too little sleep, too much smoking and drinking, and a never-ending crush of anxiety. The singer had felt ill since her return from France, but was too busy to pay attention. One night in her Basin Street East dressing room, she told Ostrow that her bra felt tight. Ostrow touched Lee's forehead. It was hot. She announced that she was phoning the singer's doctor. Lee barked at her not to do it, but Ostrow called anyway. The physician arrived just before the late show and quickly examined the now-woozy star. Her temperature had reached 103. He called for an ambulance, but Lee stubbornly insisted on performing.

An hour or so later she stumbled back to her dressing room. The doctor and a pair of orderlies ushered her toward the waiting ambulance, which would rush her to the intensive care unit of Polyclinic Hospital. "*Why can't they X-ray me in the hotel room?*" snapped Lee.

For all of her hypochondria, this time she was in real danger. Doctors diagnosed her with pneumonia and pleurisy in both lungs, one of which seemed likely to collapse. Ostrow turned hysterical when the doctor told her to call Lee's family. She served as spokeswoman to the press. "Peggy's more than an entertainer to us here," she gasped tearfully to a reporter. "She's like one of the family. And she's very, very ill." As Lee put it later, "I came so close I saw through the veil."

Doctors pondered removing the failing lung. Instead, one of them suggested a technique called Intermittent Positive Pressure Breathing—a process by which a respirator inflates the lungs over and over with a stream of medicated oxygen, in hopes of restoring their normal function. To everyone's astonishment, it worked. After several days, Lee left intensive care. But her lungs were severely scarred, and she remained in shaky condition. As she lay beneath the white sheets of her hospital bed, Phoebe and Nicki sat by her bedside, reading her telegrams, fielding concerned calls, and showing her the lavish bouquets that Cary Grant, Frank Sinatra, and other celebrity friends had sent. According to Max Bennett, Sinatra picked up the hospital bill. On Thanksgiving, Lee remained in the hospital. A restaurant sent over a huge turkey dinner, but Lee felt too weak to eat it.

Each day she improved, but she was still panting for breath. From now on she would have to use a respirator daily. A doctor stunned her by announcing coldly that she might as well buy an inexpensive one. "Most people with your condition don't live very long," he said. Lee was instructed to give up performing or die in six months.

His remarks stirred up her defiance. Lee ordered a top-of-the-line model. Initially she would need to hold the mask against her nose and mouth two to four times a day for twenty minutes at a time, breathing in a mixture of oxygen, normal air, steam, and medicine. In order to "take the scare out of it," she christened the tank Charlie. For the next ten years Charlie would trail her on the road, pumping up her lungs in dressing rooms so she could get through a show.

By February, Lee was home. Doctors had warned her to stay in bed. She didn't listen. Once, she recalled, "I wanted desperately to brush my teeth. I dragged myself to the bathroom very slowly and weakly. I took a portion of tooth powder and, in the midst of gasping for air at the exertion, pulled the tooth powder into my windpipe. My chest and throat made a terrible, explosive noise, and I thought, 'Now I've killed myself.' I lay on the bathroom floor, feeling no pain, and I decided that I'd gone to heaven. About a minute later, when I realized that I had not done myself in but was still alive, it struck me as an hysterically funny experience. I learned long ago that life is a comedy or tragedy, depending on how we choose to take it. I choose comedy."

Lee had also opted to ignore her doctors' demands that she never smoke again. Within weeks she was locking herself in the bathroom and lighting up. Soon she stopped trying to hide it. Meanwhile, Ralph Watkins had given her another raise she couldn't refuse, so in the spring of 1962 Lee was back at Basin Street East to promote her new big-band album with Benny Carter, *Sugar 'n' Spice*. An appearance on Ed Sullivan guaranteed more sellout crowds; and Watkins, in turn, poured ever-increasing sums into keeping Lee happy. He closed the club for several days before her opening so she could rehearse until deep in the night. Watkins also had the stage rebuilt to accommodate her ever-growing orchestra.

Neither of them seemed to think the party would ever end. But increasingly they were caught on the far side of a gaping generational divide. Teenagers were dancing their hearts out to Chubby Checker's "The Twist," Little Eva's "The Loco-Motion," and Joey Dee & the Starliters'

"Peppermint Twist—Part I"—tunes that made parents cringe. Lee had a more open mind than most of her peers, but for all her love of R&B, she loathed its offshoot, rock. Capitol, she said, had begged her to record some. "I did only one number that might be called rock 'n' roll and I fought against it. They kept arguing. So I gave in. But I told them nobody would listen to it. Nobody did."

Billboard gave artists her age a safe shelter from rock in the Easy Listening chart, soon to be renamed Adult Contemporary. Its main-stays—Perry Como, Andy Williams, Henry Mancini, the Lettermen, Al Martino—offered soft, nonthreatening comfort food for aging fans. Easy Listening hits gave time-worn careers a sense of chart action. But the sales represented just a sliver of the market; a top-ten Easy Listening hit could still rank low on the almighty Hot 100.

Lee had barely made a dent on that chart since "Fever." Still, Capitol kept issuing singles of her club material, hoping for a hit. Broadway remained a rich mine of material, and Lee and her arrangers knew how to turn a stiffly sung, on-the-beat showtune into jazz. Cy Coleman and Carolyn Leigh's score for *Wildcat* had included "Hey, Look Me Over," a heavy-footed rallying march sung by Lucille Ball. Quincy Jones revamped it for Lee as a syncopated swing tune; she sang it as a passive-aggressive come-on. Lee's own "I Love Being Here with You," with music by Dave Cavanaugh (writing under the pseudonym Bill Schluger), had wowed her audiences at Basin Street East. It was the swinging confession of a woman who would rather be onstage than anyplace else. The words—"I love the east / I love the west / And north or south, they're both the best . . ."—were silly but endearing, and Lee sang them live for decades.

All those singles sank without a trace. Lee feared that, at forty-two, she might be too old to have another hit. Still, she kept hoping. Consumed by preparations for her fall 1962 engagement at Basin Street East, she thrust a stack of demo recordings into the hands of Mike Melvoin, her new pianist and maestro, age twenty-five. "I have to go fix my hair," she said. "Go through these and see if there's anything you like."

Melvoin, who had stepped in for the unavailable Lou Levy, was at the start of a career that found him crossing the generation gap with ease; over the years he accompanied or arranged for Frank Sinatra, Barbra Streisand, the Beach Boys, the Jackson 5, and John Lennon. Melvoin played all the shiny black metal acetates that Lee had given him. One of them, a feminist anthem with a stripper beat, caught his ear. The protagonist was a housewife unlike any on *Father Knows Best* or *Leave It to Beaver*—a sexy Supermom who ruled her roost with a firmer hand than the breadwinner. "I can make a dress out of a feedbag and I can make a man out of you!" she declared, after reeling off all the domestic chores she could ace like a champ. Why? "'Cause I'm a woman—*w-o-m-a-n!*"

Lyricist Jerry Leiber came from Baltimore, composer Mike Stoller from Long Island. Jewish and in their thirties, they looked like bank executives, but they had written some of the blackest-sounding hits on the charts. Starting with "Hound Dog," which Elvis Presley took to number one, Leiber and Stoller had cracked the code on how to make the black urban sound irresistible to middle-class white kids. Their songs were full of kooky characters, naughty scenarios, and catchy hooks. "Love Potion No. 9" (a hit for the Clovers) told of "that gypsy with the gold-capped tooth" who sold a brew that made libidos go berserk. In another chart-topping hit for Presley, mayhem sweeps through a cell block as a prison band gets everybody "dancing to the Jailhouse Rock." Two heated ballads, "There Goes My Baby" (for the Drifters) and "Stand by Me" (Ben E. King), tugged at youthful heartstrings on their way to the top ten. It wasn't just the songs or the performances that had sent them there; Leiber and Stoller were also producers, and their ingenious way in the studio helped launch an age when hit songs were inseparable from their production.

Leiber considered Peggy Lee "the funkiest white woman alive"; and it was no surprise that a woman whose style had sprung out of the blues would connect with his and Stoller's work. Lee had included their very first collaboration, "Kansas City," on *Blues Cross Country*. The partners had sent her their songs ever since, to no response. In the autumn of 1962, they were startled to read in the paper that "I'm a Woman" had found its way into Lee's act at Basin Street East. They made a reservation. There at the club, their song, arranged by Benny Carter, stopped the show. Lee growled and purred it like a tough mama who ruled the bedroom and the kitchen.

Lee didn't know that "I'm a Woman" was Leiber and Stoller's response to Bo Diddley's aggressively macho number-one R&B hit, "I'm a Man." The low-down vamp that ran through "I'm a Woman" had been lifted straight from Diddley's record. Still, the songwriters had broken ground. "I'm a Woman" said much about the 1960s woman, a precareer housewife who had just begun to know her strength. The term "women's lib" had yet to be coined, but the notion was percolating. In the suburbs of Rockland County, New York, housewife and freelance journalist Betty Friedan had begun to pen the movement's manifesto, *The Feminine Mystique*. Her book urged women to break out of their domestic cages and claim their identities.

Peggy Lee had seized hers in her teens, but she, like most of her female fans, had grown up with a traditional view of the female role. Lee had no greater idol than her mother, who had sewed superbly and who lived to make her children happy. Fifty years later, the protagonist of "I'm a Woman" was doing all the same things—but she wanted it known that it was she who wore the pants in the family.

Lee and her band recorded the song at a New York studio on a chilly November afternoon, prior to a night's work at Basin Street East. Stoller had already given Dave Cavanaugh some tips on how to heat up "I'm a Woman"; thereafter, Cavanaugh let the writers take over the production. Now the bumping, grinding vamp had a funky saxophone on top— Stoller's idea. The frantic tempo of Benny Carter's chart was slowed; this gave guitarist John Pisano the space for some bluesy strumming and let Stan Levey shake a tambourine as though he were in a Harlem church.

Released in the holiday season of 1962, "I'm a Woman" reached number fifty-four on the Hot 100—no huge splash. But deejays loved it, as did Lee's fans. The title was true. Peggy Lee *was* a woman, not a girl; and at a time when a female over forty was regarded as over the hill, "I'm a Woman" made a lot of her contemporaries feel sexy.

That record launched her rocky relationship with the most important songwriting team of her career. As star producers, they liked things their way. But Lee wanted it known that *she* was in charge. She got wind of the fact that Leiber didn't like her "too correct" singing of "I'm a Woman"; he had hoped for a blacker sound. From then on she stayed wary of him, as he and his partner did of her. To Stoller, Lee was "an impatient gal, a controlling gal, a volatile gal, and a gal shrouded in deep and impenetrable mystery."

She put all those qualities on ample display in a medley that jarred the Basin Street East crowd. During her time in London, Lee had sat in the Queen's Theatre, riveted by the biggest smash on the British musical stage. *Stop the World—I Want to Get Off* starred Anthony Newley as Littlechap, a circus mime whose loveless personal life clashes poignantly with his slap-happy stage persona. In his showstopping lament, "What Kind of Fool Am I?," he looks at himself and sees "an empty shell / A lonely cell in which an empty heart must dwell."

The image of the sad clown haunted Lee. Littlechap wasn't far from the vision that jazz singer Mark Murphy had of her—the garishly painted doll that a frightened Norma hid behind. Lee might not have disagreed. Her rebuke to Arthur Hamilton after he'd gushed over the goddess he saw at Ciro's—"I don't want to talk about *her* anymore"—revealed a woman who seemed to sense just how much fantasy she lived in.

That was clearly on her mind as she spun "What Kind of Fool Am I?" into one of the bravest set-pieces of her career. She prefaced it with two new Hamilton songs. In "Things," a relationship lies in tatters, reduced to lifeless keepsakes—old love notes, a music box, a singing doll—that had once seemed so meaningful. "All that is left of us—how did it happen?—All that is left is things," sang Lee as though to herself. In "Funny Man," she pleaded with a weeping clown to keep up his guard and "say something funny," lest she cry, too.

Choreographer Nick Castle called upon his young protégé Dick Foster, a boyish hoofer of stage and TV. During "Funny Man," Foster sprang into view—a replica of circus performer Emmett Kelly, who appeared famously as a hobo clown, his chalk-white mouth downturned and eyes brimming with tears. As Lee stood frozen, singing of lost illusions, Foster twirled behind her, dabbing at his eyes and dancing with a Peggy Lee–like doll. By the time Lee had reached Newley's song, she seethed over living a lie—one built on "empty words of love that left me alone like this."

Out went her Scandinavian reserve; Lee sang with such bug-eyed ferocity that audiences were stunned. But she didn't have to "act" these songs; their words—especially the key one, "empty"—spoke to her on a gut level. No matter how many men passed in and out of her bed, she always wound up alone. And now her daughter, who had barely dated, had surprised Lee and everyone else by landing herself a cute fiancé. Nicki's future mate was Dick Foster. Dona Harsh considered Dick "a sweetheart, such a charming kid"; but he was also a showbiz baby on the climb, and other friends of Lee's questioned his motives. The star herself wasn't pleased. Friends listened to her rail about Foster: she didn't trust him; she thought his family low-class. Some of her confidantes suspected deeper conflicts. Lee had missed so much of Nicki's childhood; now the young woman was fleeing the nest, perhaps eagerly, before she had even turned twenty. Friends like Betty Jungheim suspected how guilty Lee felt.

Nicki and Dick set a date in September 1963. A week before it arrived, Lee—who could easily think herself sick—canceled a tour due to illness. She had no choice, of course, but to accept the marriage. The couple were wed at a Catholic church in West Hollywood. Dave Barbour marched his daughter down the aisle. Lee held a glamorous second ceremony in her garden on Kimridge. Her guests included the man she still pined for, Robert Preston; seeing him made her all the more wistful.

But she didn't let on. To most of those around her, Lee remained a woman in power, especially sexually. "That was just her nature—she was a temptress," said Jack Sheldon, the West Coast trumpeter who worked with her often. "I don't know if she even meant to do it." But business came first, as Sheldon saw when he backed Lee on *Mink Jazz*, an album whose sleek sophistication matched its title. She and a handful of her favorite musicians—among them Lou Levy, Benny Carter, Max Bennett, and guitarist Al Hendrickson—had gathered in the studio with a bunch of standards and the barest lead sheets. Each tune, from her brisk nightclub opener, "It's a Big Wide Wonderful World," to the ethereal "Cloudy Morning," was a neat package of laid-back elegance. Sheldon remembered her having a ball: "She was over there by her little stand, dancing to the rhythm."

As always, her band members seemed like family, and she loved having them around. "She would always give everybody rubdowns at the house," said Sheldon. Certain male guests, and not just musical ones, were singled out for more. The trumpeter was friendly with actor Burt Reynolds, a hunky ex–football player who had begun his climb to stardom via TV dramas. Lee had met him and swooned at his linebacker build and swarthy handsomeness. Reynolds was sixteen years younger than Lee; Sheldon—a boyishly attractive ex-swimmer—eleven. Lee invited them over separately. Later they compared notes. "She went into the other room to change clothes," recalled Sheldon. "She was a great chick, but she was intimidating. We were both too afraid to fuck her. He left and I left."

Anyone who looked beyond the "temptress" found unfathomable

complexity. In the early 1960s, Lee kindled a friendship with Jack Jones, the young singer who led a new generation of post-Sinatra swinging balladeers. Lee declared that Jones had the best time sense of any male vocalist she knew; she also liked his clean-cut, Ken-doll handsomeness. He had seen her onstage for the first time at the Latin Casino in Cherry Hill, New Jersey. For Jack, whose father, Allan Jones, was a booming tenor of 1930s Broadway and Hollywood, Lee's show was a revelation in less-is-more. "Peggy hardly ever moved her body, but she danced with her eyes," he observed. That glance held intrigue, and Jones spent hours looking into it as they talked heart-to-heart. She even read him some of her poems. "Peggy," he explained, "was a delightful cuckoo clock. She was just out there, wistful, idealistic, had a great sense of humor. I used to make her laugh with dumb stuff."

Others had a darker view of Lee. Gossip columnist Alex Freeman compared her with the first lady of unhinged pathos when he called her "just as volatile and hard to figure out as Judy Garland." The difference, he wrote, was that Lee seemed "quieter about her unhappiness."

On December 1, 1963, she joined the parade of luminaries who appeared on *The Judy Garland Show*, Garland's short-lived but ultimately historic black-and-white variety series. Two years after her fabled concerts at Carnegie Hall, Garland—who was two years Lee's junior—had reached the end of her prime. The public saw her unravel before their eyes, as alcohol and barbiturates broke down what little control she had left. Both she and Lee had risen through tough ranks—one in the roller-coaster, sleep-deprived road life of the big bands; the other as the golden girl of MGM's so-called "Dream Factory," the movie-musical division whose relentless pressures had left her permanently hooked on pills. Unlike Lee, the pathologically needy Garland exposed all, tearing out her heart onstage and lapping up every drop of sympathy and applause. Lee had her own chemical dependencies, but the public wouldn't see signs of them for years; alongside Garland, she seemed all the more like the soul of composure.

In a black gown with a scooped neckline, Lee evoked a voluptuous mermaid; by her side in white, Garland was a tiny bird. Yet they meshed like sisters. Garland launched the show in bubbling high spirits with "It's a Good Day," then joined her guest on "I Love Being Here with You." An autumn chill banished the sunniness as Lee gave a tour de force rendition of

"When the World Was Young," sung against a backdrop of simulated stars. Lee shifted between the jaded sophisticate and the wide-eyed child who could still marvel at an apple tree. Panic filled her eyes as she beheld the brittle emptiness of her current life; fame and luxury were hers, but not joy.

Between songs, the stars bantered wittily. Garland was all slurred effusion—"Gee, Peggy, you were *mahhr*velous!"—while Lee stayed halting and shy. Their dialogue spoofed her vagueness. "I saw you at Carnegie Hall," murmured Lee, "and I want to tell you, that was one of the most exciting evenings of my life."

"Oh, that's nice," answered Garland with faux grandeur. "What night were you there?"

"The night Leonard Bernstein had his concert," continued Lee. "You were sitting three seats away from me." Garland blanched hilariously. "Well," she added, "I saw you at Basin Street East and you were just *mahhrvelous*, you really were."

"Oh, where was I sitting?"

"You were sitting on the *stage*, that's where you were sitting!"

Then they donned ratty feather boas and traded off a breezy string of songs about the men they loved. But it was all for show. Garland was now bitterly separated from her third husband, her former manager Sid Luft, whom she had accused of various abuses. Meanwhile, Lee's recent romances—with Moe Lewis, Basin Street East's hulking "protection" man; and Marvin Chanin, a wealthy Hollywood retail executive—had gone to seed. So had her once hot-and-heavy affair with Quincy Jones. "Quincy made a wonderful remark," said Dona Harsh. "He said, 'Dating Peggy is like dating General Motors.' In other words, it was like dating a huge corporation. Too many complications." In his 2001 autobiography, Jones barely mentions her. For decades, Lee's musicians laughed over a tale in which she waited late at night for Jones to return to her hotel suite. As hours passed, she drank and seethed. Lou Levy filled in the rest. Around three AM, Jones finally appeared—not alone but with Billy Byers, his main ghostwriter. "The door was open, and there was Peggy, passed out on the floor in blackface. Who else would have thought of that?"

To whatever degree it was true, the scene revealed a desperate woman, quick to feel rejected, looking to hurt back. The "loneliness, emptiness" her daughter saw in her seemed incurable, but Lee kept yearning for the man who could fill it. In January 1964 she found him, or so she thought. While singing at the Riviera in Las Vegas, Lee caught a show by trumpeter Dizzy Gillespie. His bongo player was a dark-haired, blue-eyed facsimile of Ricky Ricardo, Desi Arnaz's character on *I Love Lucy*. That night Lee cornered Gillespie's pianist, Lalo Schifrin, an Argentine soundtrack composer with whom she had written songs. "Who is *that*?" she asked.

"That" was Jack Del Rio, who like Schifrin hailed from Buenos Aires. A former percussionist with Xavier Cugat, Del Rio had played with Ella Fitzgerald as well as Gillespie. But at thirty-nine he was still scuffling. Schifrin introduced him to Lee. The fact that he could barely speak English only made him more alluring to the singer. Del Rio told two pals that same night that he was going to "marry this chick." Their first date took place quickly. Conversation was labored, but Del Rio made her so starry-eyed that she lost all reason. A few days later, Lee gathered her musicians in her dressing room to make an announcement: she and Del Rio were getting married—fast. According to columnist Herb Lyon, the lovebirds were "quietly hitched" before they left Vegas. "But they'll be restitched," he wrote, "at her Beverly Hills diggins in a religious ceremony."

Lee ordered her publicist to rush out an announcement. Soon a large array of surprised friends went scrambling to buy wedding gifts. Pals of hers who had time to meet him were scratching their heads. Yes, he was reasonably attractive, but they suspected hidden intentions, and said so. Del Rio needed a green card, not to mention a career. As ever in times of emotional stress, she took ill. Home in L.A., she nursed a "chronic respiratory ailment." Lee orchestrated the marriage from bed, planning the menu, the decorations, the dress.

On the evening of February 22, 1964, guests filed uneasily through her front door and assembled in the backyard. Swans circled gracefully in the fish pond and candles lit the twilight. A priest stood by to join the betrothed, who barely knew each other, in eternal wedded bliss. Lee's friends and family stood by, discreetly rolling their eyes. "I think she knew as she was doing it that it was a silly thing to do," said Nicki.

Soon after the couple were pronounced man and wife, the yard emptied out. Later on Lee would claim that, on their wedding night, Del Rio had stepped inside her house, glanced around, and declared, "All this is mine now!" A few days later, the Ringuette family dropped by. The

Del Rios greeted him in their bathrobes. "Peggy introduced him," said nephew Lynn, "and she did it almost sheepishly, like, 'What have I done?' Jack had big hugs for everyone—'My new family, *ahhhhh!*'" Dona Harsh, who had moved to Seattle, spoke with Del Rio on the phone. "He told me they were happy like 'tin-agers.' That was the only thing I understood." Betty Jungheim also paid a visit. With Del Rio out of earshot, Lee said of her Vegas Romeo, "I think the sand got in my eyes."

Still, she gamely vowed to make this marriage work. Lee repeated a sentiment she had voiced before by pledging to put aside her career and live only for "the man I love. I know it will work." It didn't. "A strange force kept pushing me on with my singing," she explained.

Lee had delayed her honeymoon until spring, to coincide with her monthlong debut at the Royal Box of the Americana, a commercial hotel in midtown Manhattan. The Americana had lured her from Basin Street East with a $4,000 raise (to $16,500 a week) and a reduced schedule (two shows nightly, not three on weekends). As always, she poured her pay hike into the production, which would boast a twenty-four-piece orchestra and a new maestro: Jack Del Rio, who had never conducted before. The marriage had earned him his U.S. citizenship. But when he told Lee he wanted to fly his whole family in from Argentina on her dime, the couple had their first blowout fight. Tension built as she put him on display at dinner parties. Del Rio struggled to converse in English with her important friends; Lee glared at him, furious and embarrassed.

At least he delivered in bed, and she hoped he would excel onstage, too. A week before her April opening, the star and her entourage—five musicians, a hairdresser, a secretary, a wardrobe mistress, and her hubby-turned-maestro—checked into the hotel. The Americana was a generic tourist trap, and when Lee entered the Royal Box she saw a sprawling, nondescript convention room done up as a nightclub. "It was a barn," said Vince Mauro, a young recording artist whom Lee had befriended. "You thought, maybe it would work for a mafia wedding—the Jewish mafia." The acts were hardly hip; they included Borscht Belt comic Myron Cohen; the slick Las Vegas lounge king Buddy Greco; and "The Singing Rage," Patti Page, who couldn't walk off without singing her number-one request song, "(How Much Is) That Doggie in the Window?"

Author-journalist Richard Lamparski went repeatedly to see Lee, so tickled was he by the halo of strangeness that surrounded her. Lamparski gained access to the dressing room, where he saw the star engaged in her preshow prayer ritual. She clutched Dick Foster's wrist, stared into his eyes, and demanded: "Say it with me. Straight up! Straight ahead! And *strong*! Straight up! Straight ahead! And STRONG!" Clearly Lee needed all the bolstering she could get, and it worked. "If both she and the young man had gone straight up in the air like Peter Pan," said Lamparski, "I wouldn't really have been astonished."

After the familiar introduction—"*Miss* Peggy Lee!"—Lamparski watched her cruise from the wings, smiling radiantly beneath her yellow bouffant wig. A long jacket hung over her beaded dress to hide excess pounds. "It was as if a custom-made, soft-pink Chrysler Imperial, with all its lights on low and blinking, was pushed into a slow glide out onto that stage," wrote Lamparski. There waving his arms awkwardly in front of the orchestra was her visibly younger husband. "Isn't he cute?" announced Lee. Del Rio looked merely uneasy. His wife had taken a good bongo player and put him in an unfitting role. The musicians mostly ignored him.

Onstage, Lee seemed as cool and graceful as ever. But she knew she had made a terrible mistake, and Lou Levy sensed a woman on the verge of snapping. When she glanced over and saw him focused on the keys and not on her, she fumed; after the show she tore into him for abandoning her. "I want you looking at *me*!" Lee saw a musician shift his wallet from one pocket to another during the show and exploded at him in tears after the show. Emilio Palame, one of Levy's successors, would have similar experiences with Lee. "She really needed to know that you were right there with her. She needed that almost spiritual connection."

Between tunes, she silently invoked a prayer that had comforted her ever since her first terrified singing appearances in North Dakota: "Father, if you let me sing this song, I'll stew your pears, I'll can your pears." But there was no soothing Lee. She was annoyed at the sound system, the layout of the room, and most of all at her husband. When Lee turned to him onstage during the thank-yous, she saw his back, not his face, which made her even more furious. Weeks into the marriage, she had but one concern—"figuring how to get out of it." There were fights in her suite before many shows, which began habitually late. Lee vented her frustration to her new manager, Barney Ward, who didn't last out the year.

On June 15, eleven weeks after their wedding day, Del Rio moved out. Lalo Schifrin sheltered him while he looked for a place of his own. "We were a little hasty," said an embarrassed Lee to reporters.

Divorce laws had changed in Los Angeles; the interlocutory one-year waiting period had gone. Lee's divorce was granted in full on November 4. In her brief time before the judge, she placed the blame, as she had with Brad Dexter, on her soon-to-be ex-husband's laziness. Del Rio had worked just once during their marriage, under her employ; therefore, said Lee, she was "forced to go to work to pay the bills." Del Rio demanded a twenty-thousand-dollar settlement. They settled on four thousand.

In years to come, Lee entertained friends by spoofing his accent and claiming that her Latin lover was really a Jew named Isaac Erslitz. Neither the jokes nor the vitriol could ease her sense that once more she was alone. Lee was forty-four, and both her bedmates and romantic prospects had thinned. She doubted that another man would ever marry her.

The husband who haunted Lee the most was thriving without her. One night in Las Vegas, her ex-pianist Hal Schaefer ran into his old drinking buddy Dave Barbour at a casino bar, sipping a Coke. Schaefer was in the throes of alcoholism himself, and Barbour knew it. The guitarist had joined Alcoholics Anonymous a dozen years earlier; now he worked devotedly as a sponsor. Schaefer took the next stool and ordered a drink. "You have the same problem I have," said Barbour. "Would you consider going to AA and seeing what they have to offer?" Schaefer was insulted. "I said some idiot thing like, 'Good for you, if you want to be a Boy Scout.'" But soon he hit bottom and followed Barbour's advice. Schaefer never touched another drop.

As much as Barbour's addiction had tortured her, Lee had tipped many a drink with him and Schaefer. For old time's sake, the pianist went to see her in her return to Basin Street East. Schaefer marveled at her authority onstage. Later he went to her dressing room. He was shocked to find Lee "so drunk that she didn't even recognize me." She stared at him blankly. "I . . . I . . . I know you," she slurred. "I know you."

"Yes, of course, Peggy!" He moved his hands back and forth as though playing the piano. "I'm Hal Schaefer. Hal Schaefer, Peggy." She stared some more, then finally said, "*Yessss* . . . I knew I knew you."

"Plump and unbecomingly coiffed but still glamorous":
Lee on *The Andy Williams Show*, May 31, 1965.

Chapter Eleven

ALCOHOL, FOR NOW, wasn't interfering with her work; if anything, it enhanced the boozy, crepuscular quality that had haunted her persona ever since *Black Coffee*. But it wouldn't mesh well with the new title she had just acquired: that of grandmother. In 1964 Nicki delivered her first of three children, David Allen Foster, named after Dave Barbour. For Lee, grandchildren were a chilling sign of growing old, and she bristled when journalists called her a "grandma."

Now she lived alone, and no amount of friends and staff could fill the void. In August, Lee put her Kimridge Road house on sale. "The place is too big," she told Louella Parsons. "I just want to get free of responsibilities for the moment." She leased a penthouse on the thirteenth floor of the Shoreham Towers, a brand-new luxury apartment building at 8787 Shoreham Drive, a block above the Sunset Strip in West Hollywood. The décor included her preferred over-plush white carpeting, floor-to-ceiling mirrors, and a bedroom designed in pink velvet. "Pink makes me happy and docile," explained Lee to a columnist.

But wherever tranquility appeared, Lee wreaked chaos. In the *Los Angeles Times*, columnist and TV interviewer Paul Coates wrote of having moved into the Shoreham with his wife. After bedtime on their first night there, a "piercing scream" from the next apartment made their heads fly off the pillows. Coates lurched out into the hallway in his underwear. Coming from behind the next door he heard "another high-pitched screech, and then hysterical laughter." He ran back inside and told his wife that some woman was in distress. She told him to mind his own business, and the din finally ceased.

The next day Coates asked the superintendent who lived beside him.

Peggy Lee, he was told. That night, the blood-curdling noises resumed. The next morning, he read a note pushed under his door.

Dear Neighbors . . .

I do hope you haven't been disturbed by strange noises from our kitchen. It is not a neurotic cook or what have you. It's my parrot, Gorgeous, who cries like a baby, barks like a dog and laughs like a maniac. If he projects too much, give us a ring and we'll cover him. Also, if you need a cup of sugar, please let us know.

Peggy Lee

But the racket was just beginning. Lee found that she hated apartment living, and she raised as much din as she could, hoping to break the lease. Celebrities traipsed through the lobby and filled the elevator en route to her parties. At one star-packed gathering, the guests included the raucous singer-comedienne and movie star Martha Raye; comedian Bob Newhart; the singing TV host Andy Williams and his sex-kitten wife, French singer Claudine Longet; and Cary Grant. Lee enjoyed making people think that something was going on between her and Grant; she was secretly annoyed when he brought his fiancée, actress Dyan Cannon, who was thirty-four years his junior. Lee's dog Sungyi-La—a shaggy Lhasa Apso from Tibet—scampered around, sniffing at guests' feet. Lee proudly noted that His Holiness the Dalai Lama had given her the pet in honor of her work as chairman of the Thomas A. Dooley Foundation, named after the great American humanitarian who had established hospitals throughout the Far East.

As Sungyi-La rolled around on the floor, looking like a fur muff, a quartet played cool jazz. Once the revelers were in their cups, they got up to perform, amplified by Lee's state-of-the-art sound system. Raye, a sometime jazz singer, joined Lee in improvising a madcap duet, "Scrub It Blues," while guests shrieked with laughter. "Did you know that she's a scrub nurse at Mount Sinai two days a week?" sang Lee of Raye. Turning to her friend, Lee asked in song, "Martha, did you ever give a man a bedpan and go out to lunch? Well, knowing you I just had a hunch!" Later, an intoxicated Lee quieted the room with her spot-on impersonation of a drunk and creaky Billie Holiday.

When the performing had ended, Lee played her new single, "Pass

Me By," a march that Cy Coleman and Carolyn Leigh had written for Grant's new film, *Father Goose*. It was arranged playfully with piccolos and a parade drum. Lee cranked up the volume full blast, and her voice boomed into the night: "I got me ten fine toes to wiggle in the sand . . ." She tied strings of Indian chimes around her ankles, and Grant led a sing-along parade around the apartment. Everyone filed out into the hallway and stomped to the end and back, singing *"PASS ME BY-Y, PASS ME BY-Y-Y. . . ."* No one gave a thought to the sleeping neighbors.

One day Thomas C. Wheeler, a writer for the *Saturday Evening Post*, dropped by to interview the woman who had made so many men's pulses race. When Lee opened the door, Wheeler wondered how the woman before him could possibly be the same Peggy Lee he'd seen onstage. "She looks like a librarian or a schoolteacher," he wrote. "Her face, with a nose a trifle too short, a chin too round, lacks any clear definition." Questions about her art yielded New Age bromides. "I like to make my music change and grow," Lee explained. "It is like a fruit tree becoming more fruitful." She went on to tell him that she had "learned courage from Buddha, Jesus, Lincoln, Einstein, and Cary Grant."

Thanks in part to friends like Phoebe Ostrow, who marveled aloud at how "spiritual" she was, Lee had come to regard herself as a vessel of the paranormal. Johnny Mandel wondered if she might be right. Mandel held a high spot in her stable of favorite arrangers; he had also composed the music for several top films, one of which, *The Sandpiper*, yielded a future standard, "The Shadow of Your Smile." At her home, Mandel played Lee the haunting theme from his score for *The Russians Are Coming the Russians Are Coming*, a forthcoming Cold War farce. "Without explaining anything about it," said Lee, "he asked me to listen to it and paint a word picture of what I heard."

When he read Lee's lyric, "The Shining Sea," he was floored. Her portrait of a sensual encounter by the sea—"We'd sit there on the sand / He'd kiss the hollow of my hand"—closely mirrored the scene the music would underscore: that of two young lovers, a Russian submariner and a Cape Cod girl, together on the beach. Mandel took Lee to a screening to show her. "When this scene came on," he recalled, "her mouth just fell open."

Friends of Lee's laughed over the line, "His hands, his strong brown hands"—a moonstruck reference, they believed, to Quincy Jones. But Lee credited that magical songwriting feat not to Jones but to extrasensory perception. She had tested hers by playing fortune-teller to her guitarist, John Pisano. "I see you in the future not being just a guitar player but doing other things," she informed him. Sure enough, he soon went on to join trumpeter Herb Alpert's Tijuana Brass, whose hit albums included several Pisano originals. He earned a bundle in royalties.

An incident in the Christmas season of 1964 yanked Lee down to earth. A thief broke into her car, parked in the Shoreham Towers garage, and stole an expensive tape recorder. In turn, Lee had no trouble breaking her lease. She began shopping for a real house. Before she could find one, however, she headed back to New York for her seventh engagement at Basin Street East.

By now young people ruled the Manhattan night. They danced the Twist near Times Square at the Peppermint Lounge, the hottest disco in town; at Gerdes Folk City in Greenwich Village, they listened raptly as Judy Collins mourned a slain civil rights leader with "Medgar Evers Lullaby." The long-beloved Blue Angel, the chicest of East Side cabarets, had closed after twenty-one years; Birdland, the "Jazz Corner of the World," was on the verge of filing for bankruptcy. Veteran showbiz columnist Hy Gardner looked at the changing city with fear and disgust. To him, New York had become a cesspool of "panhandlers, pimps, prostitutes, dope peddlers, con merchants, teenaged hoods, beatniks and short-changers."

Basin Street East was struggling to survive. Its roster of stylish pop-jazz artists had thinned; many of them were now earning far more money in Las Vegas or on concert stages. Lennie Green convinced a reluctant Ralph Watkins to let him add rising comics to the mix. Green's choices— which included Bill Cosby, Woody Allen, and Richard Pryor—gave the room a boost, but not enough to restore its past luster; all those comedians would defect to the much cooler Village Gate downtown. Next, *Billboard* reported that Basin Street East would "aim for the youth market via the allure of hot recording artists." Watkins found himself presenting Lesley Gore, Bo Diddley, the Righteous Brothers, and Dusty Springfield—all substantial talents, but not the kind he had ever wanted to host, nor the company Peggy Lee preferred to keep. "They started to lower their standards," complained Lee to two producer friends, Ken Bloom and Bill Rudman. "I kept telling them, 'Please don't do that, or I'll just have to leave.' And that's what happened."

Basin Street East had less than two years to go. On March 1, 1965, Lee launched her last hurrah at the most simpatico nightclub of her career. The old-fashioned opening was "crowded to the very limit," wrote a critic, with "socialites, columnists, some of 'the boys,' and plain ordinary Manhattanites who had the wherewithal." Her show now incorporated such middle-of-the-road hits of the day as "Hello, Dolly!" She still loathed rock and refused to surrender to it, with one exception. Lee bought mop-top, Beatles-like wigs for the band to wear as she sang "A Hard Day's Night," one of the group's seven number-one hits since they had joined her label, Capitol, about a year before. Lee's graying fans rejoiced when Benny Goodman showed up to join her on that song; it made the bitter pill of "today's music" easier to swallow. A spring-summer reunion tour with her old boss made Lee seem all the more like a nostalgia act.

AS OF THE MID-1960s, most Americans her age were spending their nights watching television, not gallivanting on the town. This was the golden age of the TV variety show, which brought a vaudeville-style bounty of talent into one's living room. Three of the genre's fatherly hosts treated Lee like visiting royalty. "Whenever she's on the show it's not an appearance, it's an event!" enthused Dean Martin, the unflappable, tipsy-acting crooner-comic. "Here is one of the greatest of all time," declared star-maker Ed Sullivan, whose woodenness won him a comparison in *Time* to "a cigar-store Indian." Andy Williams, a sweater-clad, singing TV star in the Perry Como tradition, raved to Lee on camera: "I think I'm your biggest fan. I have every record you ever made."

Color TV had swept America, and Lee's Jello-hued gowns gave home viewers their money's worth. They saw her in skintight magenta, blood orange, and lime green, trimmed with fur and feathers. Another dress, said Lou Levy, "looked like it was made out of Reynolds Wrap. It could have been an experimental uniform for astronauts to test in."

Illustrator Robert Richards found most of Lee's 1960s wardrobe dismaying. "Peggy wasn't a fashionable woman," he said. "She wore those heavy beaded dresses, which were expensive and too tight. She liked that sausage look that was prevalent at the time, but that made you seem thirty pounds heavier than you were. She wasn't toned, and those dresses had a vulgarity about them." Lee wore different wigs each year; and even though it was common then for female singers to don conspicuously fake and oversize coiffures, most of Lee's looked as though she'd plucked them off store mannequins.

But the classiness of her music transcended all. And in the mid-1960s, Lee displayed it at its best on two hour-long TV shows. Both were part of a syndicated series called *Something Special*, a showcase for pop stars—Julie London, Tony Martin, Kay Starr, Patti Page—who had passed their commercial primes. On one show, Lee wittily traced the history of the instruments in her orchestra while spotlighting the men who played them. On a multilevel soundstage bedecked with pedestals and statues, she brought forth Levy, Max Bennett, percussionist Francisco Aguabella, guitarist Mundell Lowe, and the Belgian harmonica wizard Toots Thielemans, who toured with her for two years. Thielemans played with whimsy and a feel for the blues, and Lee spotlighted him nightly in "Makin' Whoopee!," the 1920s comedy song about the dangers of said diversion. As they stood shoulder to shoulder, Lee sang in mock distress of how sex disrupts lives; Thielemans let out wittily hot-and-bothered outbursts on harmonica.

Lee's other *Something Special* closed with "The Folks Who Live on the Hill." The sight of her in her fur-trimmed gown, seated in a simulated gazebo on a TV set, hinted at why the bucolic wedded bliss in the song would never be hers.

She did get the home, however. Her ex-manager Ed Kelly had turned to real estate, and in 1965 he sold her a sprawling ranch house at 1195 Tower Grove Drive, Beverly Hills. It stood in the canyon called Beverly Glen, one of the city's most expensive neighborhoods, soon to bear the high-prestige zip code of 90210. From the moment she stepped inside that five-bedroom, five-bathroom abode, Lee just had to have it. Much of the house was taken up by what a friend called "this huge, gymnasium-sized living room," sixty feet long, with a high ceiling, a dining area, a white tile floor, and an all-glass back wall. "You see the garden and that becomes part of the house," she raved. The place was ideal for the grand parties she loved to throw. In preparation, she added a bar and a U-shaped, white modular sofa—"about twice as long as Broadway," she bragged to a reporter.

The rest of the house was designed in colors meant to soothe its anxious owner. Lee would rehearse in the "Yellow Room," with its blond Steinway piano and white bookshelves packed with books and records. Her boudoir, said her future hairdresser Bruce Vanderhoff, "was everyone's idea of what Mae West's bedroom would be. It was like a pink Fabergé Easter egg." Chandeliers hung on either side of the bed, lending grandeur to the acts she anticipated performing there.

But those had dwindled mostly to sleeping. In August 1965, the *Hartford Courant* reported her torrid affair with former screenwriter Ali Ipar, the ex-husband of the 1940s B-movie actress Virginia Bruce. Lee pursued him with such a vengeance that, according to columnist Alex Freeman, the only way Ipar could escape was to claim he'd left town.

Only with her musicians, it seemed, could she find true intimacy. Lee considered them her soulmates, joined in a profound pact to lift songs off the page and turn them into flesh-and-blood slices of life. Before every tour or record date, her rhythm section spent weeks with her in the Yellow Room, analyzing tunes and arrangements. Although she couldn't read music, Lee would hum instrumental lines or phrases to guide her musicians. She wouldn't give up until everything shimmered or popped in just the right way. As crackerjack as her players were, she taught them that each note had to enhance her storytelling.

All this deliberation, said Lou Levy, felt "endless and sometimes excruciating." But Grady Tate, her longtime drummer, understood. "Guys who played with her said, 'Oh man, she's rough to work with.' And she *was* rough to work with. She demanded one-hundred-and-fifty percent every time you sat down with her, because she was giving it all she had."

Once she and her combo had settled on a rough chart, they recorded it in the Yellow Room. She sent the tape off to whichever arranger she thought appropriate. One of her favorites, Bill Holman, had written for the giants of big-band jazz, notably Stan Kenton. But the screaming brass and orchestral tumult that Kenton loved had no place in a Peggy Lee arrangement. "She explained to me that saxophones made her sing an interval off from where she should be," said Holman. "I never could figure that out, but she swore it was true." Even his most explosive charts for Lee, including a propulsive arrangement of "Come Back to Me" from the musical *On a Clear Day You Can See Forever*, followed her rule.

What she really liked, said Vince Mauro, were "airy sounds." As soon as she heard a song, specific instruments began playing in her head. Many of her ideas came from classical music. Respighi's *Pines of Rome* had made her fall in love with the oboe, whose bright, ethereal tone, in a soprano range, set off her low throatiness. She adored French horns, whose mournful richness added pathos to her sad songs. So did the dark, woodsy quality of the alto and bass flutes. Holman cradled her voice in sounds so shimmering and delicate that Lee could sing at the volume of a sigh. In the Michel Legrand–Norman Gimbel ballad, "Watch What Happens," she sang of love's awakening as though it were a flower in bloom: "Let someone start believing in you . . . let her hold out her hand . . ." A mellow alto flute curled around her voice, while guitar strings quivered underneath, as though coaxing that love to life. "She didn't have to get big vocally because her arrangements did everything for her," said her actor friend Walter Willison.

On records and TV, nuances like these were easy to catch. In the concert hall, many were lost, which is why supper clubs suited Lee best—especially the more sensitive ones like Basin Street East. But near the end of 1965, the raucous Copacabana made her a money offer she couldn't refuse. After twenty-five years, the cavernous, old-school showbiz emporium still epitomized "nightclub" to tourists worldwide. The Copa, said Mel Tormé, "was the pinnacle, the watering place for every jaded garment-district *macher*, mob guy, and talent evaluator in town."

It stood on Sixtieth Street, just east of Fifth Avenue and a block north of the majestic Plaza Hotel, but it was a world away from chic. The horseshoe-shaped, tiered seating area surrounded a dance floor where, at the start of the show, the club's famous chorus line, the Copa Girls, kicked in unison and smiled as though their lives depended on it. Mostly B-grade comedians warmed up the crowd. The main acts were proven comics and recording stars known for excitement but not for subtlety: Bobby Darin, Della Reese, Sophie Tucker, Jimmy Durante, Paul Anka. Greasing the maître d's palm ensured a good table.

Beyond the footlights, the Copa clung to a gangster's idea of class. Single ladies couldn't sit at the bar—a move against prostitution—while band members were forbidden from fraternizing with the showgirls. Supervising at the back of the club was Jules Podell, the short, pudgy, mob-appointed owner. "When something irritated him," said Mel Tormé, Podell "created early sonic booms by rapping on a table with a pinky ring the size of a grapefruit and venting his considerable wrath on almost anyone within earshot." As waiters dashed around delivering trays of drinks and the club's trademark Chinese food, Podell scowled and barked, *"Move your fuckin' ass!"*

He saw Lee as a fragile, ladylike flower, though, and he met her every demand. He even let her use the club for a full week of rehearsals before opening—a privilege he had never granted a Copa act before. For this engagement, Lee played it safe. In a show that the *New York Journal-American* called a "triumph," she leaned toward her hits and other songs that were sure to wow the tourists. In "Big Bad Bill (Is Sweet William Now)," Lee waved a white feather boa and sang with mock coyness about the domesticating effects of marriage: "He was stronger than Samson, I declare/Till a soft-skinned Delilah bobbed his hair!" Cy Coleman and Carolyn Leigh's score for the upcoming Broadway show *Sweet Charity* had given Lee her newest showstopper, "Big Spender," a dance-hall hostess-cum-hooker's salespitch, with a stripper beat. Audiences saw a speakeasy babe with a heart of gold, both vulgar and delicate.

Backstage, her vulnerability ruled. To Sheldon Roskin, her publicist, Lee seemed like little-girl-lost. "She needed people around her, touching her, holding her, just being there," he said. The agency where he worked, Solters, Sabinson & Roskin, also represented Frank Sinatra and Barbra Streisand, two closely protected stars. "But when you worked with Peggy Lee, no one was there," he said.

Lee did have caring friends, like Dave Cavanaugh. When he appeared backstage, she threw her arms around him and gave him a big kiss. Roskin remembered him as "tall and kind of heavy-set; he had a lovely Irish face and cinnamon-colored hair. He was so sweet. They would sit and talk about new albums and projects." Other dressing-room visitors found the sparkling performer weak and out of breath. After some cordial chit-chat, Lee excused herself, explaining, "I must do my breathing now." Her wigged head disappeared under an oxygen tent with Charlie, her respirator.

An hour later she was back onstage, reigning over a tightly controlled musical world. This "woman of endless contradictions," as the *Saturday Evening Post* had called Lee, "drives herself relentlessly to perfect her songs." Lee loved to quote Ralph Waldo Emerson: "God will not have his work done by cowards." She was quick to show journalists the bulky, black loose-leaf binder that served as her traveling Bible. Her secretaries labored over it, typing pages that listed each detail of every show, from song lists and orchestra personnel to hand gestures, stage diagrams, makeup charts, and lighting cues:

> "I'm a Woman":
> DIM TO LOW, WARM STAGE
> SPOT 1: ON FACE IN PINK
> SPOT 2: READY IN RED TO BUMP
> ON [Cause I'm a] "WOMAN":
> SPOT 2: BUMP UP IN RED ON FULL BODY AND "RED SPE-CIAL" BUMPS ON DRESS AT SAME TIME (B28 DOWN LIGHTS MAY ALSO BE BUMPED WITH RED FRONTS HERE.)

The book also contained notes on new diets she planned to follow, and a numbered, coded inventory of what was inside the twenty or more trunks that she took on tour—"down almost to the last lipstick," a reporter wrote.

In the 1960s, Lou Levy estimated that Lee spent upward of $25,000 on a new show—a massive amount in its time. She employed a retinue of people to carry out her whims. Lee's new hair stylist, Kathy Mahana, was a perky California blonde who had apprenticed with George Masters, the Beverly Hills hairdresser who had designed Marilyn Monroe's curly platinum bob. But for Lee's staffers, job descriptions became meaningless; anyone around her might be asked to do anything. Bruce Vanderhoff, the boyishly handsome hairstylist who joined her in 1968, found himself driving Lee to the doctor and injecting her with vitamin B_{12}. Kathy wound up packing her bags. "She'd hire a cook and a gardener, then she'd switch their jobs just to watch them struggle. I ended up doing everything but her hair." But Kathy saw the bright side: "She exposed me to things I would never have had the opportunity to do, that were extremely helpful to me."

It was Lee, of course, who needed the most aid. Each day she awoke so slowly and listlessly that, during an engagement, her assistants wondered how she would ever make the show. One of them would ease her into consciousness by serving her breakfast in bed; somebody else would prepare a warm mineral bath—another protective womb. Lee could hardly bear to leave it, and kept reaching for a bottle of perfumed oil. "She poured so much of it in the tub, I thought one day she'd go right down the drain," said Kathy.

Then began the hours-long transformation of Norma Egstrom into Peggy Lee. Frequently she sat up all night in bed, making sketches of hairdos; the next day she would ask her designers to turn her convoluted creations into reality. "Most of the time my answer was no," recalled Bruce Vanderhoff. Throughout their long friendship, he never hesitated to tell her what he thought—a stance that, surprisingly, gained him her permanent respect.

Attired in floral or leopard lounging pajamas, she sat before a mirror to do her makeup. Her friend Doak Roberts, a decorative painter and furniture refinisher who would manage Lee briefly, watched the process many times. "She had a conglomeration of things on her makeup table that went back to the forties. She would shade under her chin with this dark brown stuff. Then she would start working on her face with all these undercoatings and layers. She ended up looking like porcelain. She was a master of makeup, let me tell you."

But Vanderhoff considered the whole process—which included two sets of false eyelashes—a typical exercise in Peggy Lee excess. "If she'd worn less makeup she would have been prettier," he said. "She exaggerated everything like a drag queen." But without all the camouflage, observed Roberts, "she was just a matronly, Nordic grandmother."

At the venue, Kathy would prepare Lee's dressing room by spraying it with Arpège, the singer's favorite scent. A half hour before showtime, Lee would gather the musicians in her dressing room for the nightly joining of hands and prayer ritual. Jack Sheldon, like her other band members, found it "pretty goofy," but Lee, of course, was boss.

An essential step remained. Nothing gave the star as much energy or comfort before a show as anger, and her staff devised various ways of pushing her buttons. The stage manager, they would claim, had left her dressing room unlocked the night before; the lighting man had lit her in unflattering green. Lee herself joined in. One night a friend watched her place a drinking glass perilously near the edge of her makeup table. Then she asked another bystander to reach across and hand her an object. Inevitably the glass shattered on the floor. The resulting rage would turn Lee's hazel eyes black. "She would just glow and be so beautiful," Kathy recalled. Just before her entrance, Lee liked to stamp her foot and yell.

Like everyone else, Kathy saw the lunacy in Lee's process. "You had to buy into it," she said. "Some people thought she was completely insane and couldn't deal with any of the nonreality of it."

Rarely did Lee go on without a swig of cognac. Midway through the act, when Lee walked off briefly while the band vamped, Kathy or some other assistant waited in the wings with more of that grape-flavored liquor her boss loved. Lee gulped it down, then floated back onstage, where she grew mellower with each song. For now, at least, critics didn't deduce why. Instead they swooned at her come-hither drawl in such ballads as "(I'm) In Love Again," a ballad she had written with Cy Coleman. The redundancy in the first two lines—"I'm in love again / And the feeling's not new"—distracted no one. "She seems almost to be singing to herself and yet never loses her mesmeric grip on the audience," raved a reviewer.

Once the show ended, Lee could truly relax. Friends like Dr. Jonas Salk, the jazz-loving megaheiress Doris Duke, and Cary Grant, along with her musicians, crowded Lee's dressing room. "Each time she reaches for one of the innumerable cigarettes she is surrounded by helpful flames from all sides," noted a reporter. A photographer snapped pictures of her and Tony Bennett sharing a joint. Invariably the party moved to her hotel suite, where after several more drinks Lee would ask Toots Thielemans to whip out his harmonica and play a sentimental Swedish song that she loved. Tears rolled down her cheeks.

———

THE STUDIED QUALITY OF Lee's recent shows seemed worlds away from the breezy fun of her music with Dave Barbour. Now, said her sometime publicist Peter Levinson, "everything she did was calculated. Ella Fitzgerald had no glamour but she had enormous jazz talent. She said, 'Here's the song.' For Peggy, the dress had to be right, the makeup, the hair, and then came the song. There was a different priority."

Norman J. O'Connor, a jazz-loving priest and critic, was distressed by the change he saw in Lee. His article for the *Boston Globe*, "Peggy Lee Manufactures Smooth Night Club Performance," didn't mince words. Her sex-symbol pose, he felt, was wearing thin. "Age has done the usual mean things to Peggy Lee that it does to all of us," wrote O'Connor. The "girlish appearance" was gone; the voice had "thinned out." Her act, he wrote, had become "contrived and automatic"; it could "fill a host of rooms across the country with people who are attracted to bogus emotions."

Even in 1950, Barbour had sensed something shallow and desperate in his wife's hunger for the approval of strangers. Leaving her world, then conquering his alcoholism, had freed him. Now, in his home near the beach in Malibu, California, Barbour played the guitar almost nightly for pleasure, but he performed and recorded little; the royalties from the songs he wrote with Lee helped keep him afloat. His new calling lay in attending AA meetings and sponsoring others who fought to stay sober. Otherwise he fished, walked on the beach, read, and spoke almost daily with Nicki.

Lee had stayed amicably in his life, more by her choice than his. In 1960, Barbour had married Marian Collier, a beautiful ex-model turned actress. Collier performed on a score of top TV shows, including *Bachelor Father* and *Leave It to Beaver;* in the film *Some Like It Hot* she made a memorable cameo as a clarinetist in an all-girl band. "When Marian married David," said Angela (Mrs. Stan) Levey, "Peggy treated her like some little person off the street that had wandered in and was staying at David's house or something, but David was still hers. It infuriated Marian."

As much as Collier loved Barbour, they divorced after three years. Later on he formed a relationship with an easygoing Latin woman named Chileta. "After being with Peggy Lee, it must have been like getting out of a Turkish prison," said Kathy Mahana. "Peggy was so intense and incredibly engulfing. Chileta was as unlike her as you could imagine." Once again, Lee blocked out the existence of her ex-husband's new mate. "David and I will get back together someday," she told Dona Harsh.

Lee had no beau with her on Saturday night, December 11, 1965, when she attended a holiday party at the Beverly Hills home of Alan Livingston, the president of Capitol Records. The hostess was his wife, actress Nancy Olson, whose supporting role as a movie-studio script girl in *Sunset Boulevard* had earned her an Oscar nomination. An elegantly dressed crowd of Hollywood achievers milled about in clusters, clinking glasses and toasting in the holidays.

Olson excused herself to answer the ringing phone. It was Nicki, asking to speak to her mother. Olson plucked Lee out of a conversation and led her toward the phone in the library. The actress closed the door and left her alone.

A few minutes later Lee emerged, pale and dazed. "She just fled," said Olson.

Nicki had broken the news: Dave Barbour was dead.

Barbour had been feeling achy and feverish; he assumed it was the flu. Saturday night had found him at home in Malibu with Chileta. He rose from the sofa and headed for the bathroom. After several minutes he still hadn't emerged, and Chileta couldn't hear a sound. She knocked on the door and called his name. No answer. She opened it up—and there was Barbour, slumped over. Hysterical with panic, Chileta called Malibu Hospital. Several agonized minutes later, paramedics arrived and loaded the guitarist's unconscious body onto a stretcher. The ambulance sped off to the hospital, but it was too late: Barbour had died of internal bleeding caused by an ulcer. He was fifty-three.

Three days later, as lawns and windows in Los Angeles twinkled with Christmas lights, a few dozen people gathered at a funeral home in Van Nuys to bid farewell to David Barbour. The mourners included his closest family members, many AA pals, and some musicians. From her seat in the back of the chapel, Marian Collier had a view of the family section ahead. It included a tearful, hunched-over Peggy Lee. "She's sitting in the front row with a black veil," recalled Collier, "and I'm his last wife!" But to Lee, neither Marian nor Chileta mattered; *she* was the widow. She held a reception afterward at her house. Collier refused to go.

Predictably, every obituary identified Barbour as "former husband of the singer, Peggy Lee." The surprise appeared farther down: "Recent reports from friends indicated the two were near a reconciliation." Those "friends" went unnamed, but the only conceivable source was Lee, whom numerous writers had phoned for information. Everyone close to her and Barbour knew it wasn't true. "My father was involved with somebody else," said Nicki, "and I don't think he would *ever* have gotten married again." Collier put it more bluntly: "There's no way in hell he was ever going back to Peggy!"

Yet the reconciliation became part of Lee's homemade myth, and she recounted it in growing detail for the rest of her life. Later she told friends that she and Barbour had walked hand-in-hand through her rose garden, and that he had turned to her and said, "Peg, what do you say we try it again?" The theme was always the same, a fairy-tale love torn apart by fate, not once but twice. From her early childhood, Lee's fantasy life had helped protect her from the truth. But that shield had grown more brittle and transparent by the year, and her "daydreams" no longer brought her joy; reality was becoming harder to deny.

Having lost her guitar-playing prince, Lee tried to smother the pain with excess, and not just the alcoholic type. Previously she had employed one or two guitarists in her band; now she used four—a gang of imaginary Daves who might help her feel as though he were still there. The following summer, Lee recorded *Guitars a là Lee*, an album with seven guitar players on every track. Bob Bain arranged but didn't play; those who did included her standbys Dennis Budimir and Laurindo Almeida.

Given the emotional nature of the project, the songs leaned surprisingly toward fluff hits of the day, such as "Strangers in the Night" and "Call Me." But among them were two songs that became prominent in her act; they heralded her emerging persona—that of a spurned, disillusioned older woman whose hope had run dry. Given her liquor intake, one of the songs was ironically titled "An Empty Glass," written for Lee by a pioneer of the bossa nova, guitarist-composer Luiz Bonfá, and lyricist Dick Manning. It set a chilling scene: the last toast between a woman and the man who had spurned her as soon as she fell in love. In what critic Peter Reilly called her "three A.M. pitch-dark-side-of-the-morning voice," Lee lashed out bitterly. "Here's to you now, for the last time . . . Here's to love, an empty glass."

Hugo Peretti, Luigi Creatore, and George David Weiss, who had penned "Can't Help Falling in Love" for Elvis Presley, had given Lee "Good Times," the confession of an aging thrill-seeker whose fun was ending. "Be careful of the good times / They can fool you, make you cry," warned Lee. Audiences didn't realize how much of herself she had exposed.

But Steve Blum, her new eighteen-year-old guitarist, sensed her pain. At the time, he was a freshman and jazz student at the University of Miami. Just before a show in Miami Beach, Lee had needed a sub fast for an indisposed member of her guitar quartet. Someone recommended Blum. "A couple of days later we were rehearsing," he said. Blum stayed with her on and off for two years. "She told me I reminded her of Dave Barbour," he recalled.

The young man didn't comprehend the weight of that compliment; he barely knew who Barbour was. But soon he found himself in the bedroom of her hotel suite, listening to her favorite classical music and having deep discussions about life. Nothing sexual occurred, said Blum—"Not too many eighteen-year-olds are thinking of making it with a forty-six-year-old woman"—but for Lee, at least, the relationship took on romantic overtones. Young as he was, Blum felt an emptiness in Lee that seemed beyond filling, no matter how loud the applause or how many doting friends hovered near. "She had to have people around her," Blum observed, "and when the party was over, really early in the morning, I think she was afraid to be alone."

———

AS THE LATE SIXTIES began, everything in her career went on as before, or so it seemed. The successful runs at the Copa and elsewhere continued, as did the TV appearances and record dates. But Peggy Lee was receding into the past. In 1967, she costarred on *The Girl from U.N.C.L.E.*, a campy and short-lived knockoff of *The Man from U.N.C.L.E.*, the popular espionage sitcom. The "girl," an undercover spy, was played by twenty-four-year-old Stefanie Powers; guests were mostly faded names from the Golden Age of Hollywood. In "The Furnace Flats Affair," Lee plays a purring, Mae West–like millionairess involved in an elaborate (and largely incomprehensible) espionage scheme in a western ghost town. Her stammering line readings, punctuated frequently by "uh," reflected her real-life speech; but on TV it sounded as though Lee were struggling to remember the script or, worse, that she had been drinking.

At film premieres, Lee looked up from her seat at the hottest young leading men of the day: Paul Newman, Steve McQueen, Sean Connery, Warren Beatty. But one actor above all others still made her heart flutter, and he was now a gray-haired sixty-three. "How could you be a woman and not love Cary Grant?" she insisted. For some time, an executive at Columbia Records had been asking Grant to make a holiday single—perhaps a recitation of some time-honored holiday verse. The latter struck him as trite. Instead, he proposed having a friend write him a lullaby. "I'm quite nutty about Peggy Lee," he said, "and I think many of her lyrics are quite profound—strangely profound. She has a unique choice of words." When Cy Coleman agreed to write the music, Grant was sold.

"Christmas Lullaby," as Lee called it, wasn't anything too special: "Angels bless you, little one . . . my little one, sleep well." But as Lee sat alongside Grant at a Hollywood studio and gazed at him while he talk-sang her words, he could have been intoning Emily Dickinson.

The record sold nicely, but it hardly helped update Lee's image. Many reviews of her current shows depicted the singer as an enduring throwback in an age of youth. Her first facelift was behind her, and she would make many more trips to the plastic surgeon. Yet critics kept pointing out her age as well as her girth. "Plump and unbecomingly coiffed but still glamorous," wrote Doug McClelland of Lee at the Copa. A critic for *Time* echoed Father Norman J. O'Connor when he wrote that her voice had grown "thin at the top and breathy at the bottom. So she spends her notes in the same way that dispossessed nobility lives on a dwindling income: with frugal selectivity but stylish aplomb."

Lee Wiley, a singer she had grown up admiring, would have none of it. In the 1930s, Wiley, an Oklahoma-born pop-jazz favorite, had perfected a languid, husky style, tinged with honeysuckle and Southern Comfort. Now retired, she reminisced, none too kindly, about colleagues of hers who had stayed too long at the fair. She named no names, but one of them wasn't hard to guess. "For one thing they've gotta take oxygen or dope themselves up, and I don't think that's right. What they should be doing is being at home with their children. . . . Or they should be doing some volunteer work at a hospital or something—in my opinion."

But Lee had no intention of stopping. Capitol had kept churning out around two Lee albums per year—"so many it is difficult to keep track of them all," wrote Rex Reed in *Stereo Review*. Often they were random compilations of singles and stray tracks, with skimpy running times and generic headshots on the covers. *Extra Special!*, *Pass Me By*, *Big Spender*, and *In Love Again!* contained some first-rate tracks; a few of her singles, notably "Big Spender," had scored respectably on the Adult Contemporary chart. But Lee hadn't gotten near *Billboard's* Hot 100 since "Fever." And at Capitol, changes were afoot that frightened her. Most of the veterans had left the roster. Nat King Cole had died; Frank Sinatra had defected to his own label, Reprise. Country star Tennessee Ernie Ford, comic actor Jackie Gleason (in his sideline as a mood-music conductor), and the sleek pop-jazz songstress Nancy Wilson had hung on since the 1950s. But Peggy Lee had spent more years there than anyone, and she knew she was getting edged aside.

Money, youth, and changing tastes had taken over. For years, the mega-labels—Columbia, RCA Victor, Decca, Capitol—had mostly fought rock, while the independent ones who nurtured it were reaping fortunes. The elder companies had to get with it or die—but their old-school executives were stubborn. In 1963, Dave Dexter, Jr., the pioneer Capitol executive, had opened up a carton of eighteen singles issued in England through EMI, the British conglomerate that owned nearly all of Capitol's stock. EMI and Capitol shared right of first refusal on the release of each other's product; each company, of course, was anxious to expose its artists overseas. Among the records in that box was "Love Me Do" backed by "P.S. I Love You," the debut single of the Beatles, newly signed to EMI's subsidiary Parlophone.

The disc had made the British top twenty, but Dexter was "not impressed." To him, the Beatles were "just a bunch of long-haired kids," and his boss, Alan Livingston, took his word for it. Capitol passed on the Beatles. By February, the group's followup single, "Please Please Me," had topped the UK charts. By that summer the Beatles had become "the hottest thing that England had ever encountered," as Dexter contritely admitted. Livingston had a change of heart.

After he died in 2009, nearly all of his obituaries led with a variation of the same headline: "Music Executive Signed the Beatles to Capitol Records." The group's first Capitol release, "I Want to Hold Your Hand," overwhelmed the label; pressing plants could barely handle the demand for product. For the rest of the decade, if there were ever a question over whose record would get pressed first, or in the highest quantity, the Beatles won. Even Capitol's previous cash cows, the Beach Boys, felt snubbed.

The face of Capitol kept changing. In 1967, country singer Glen Campbell, a modest seller there for years, broke through with two top-forty hits, "Gentle on My Mind" and "By the Time I Get to Phoenix," and won four Grammys in the same night. Now both rock and country were Capitol's priorities. In 1968 and 1969, the label touted its new discoveries: the Steve Miller Band, Bob Seger, The Band, and Grand Funk Railroad.

Peggy Lee had become commercial deadweight. By now she sang mainly to her contemporaries and to a coterie of younger gay men who cherished the female icons of the past. They saw her in old-fashioned supper clubs that could accommodate an orchestra—"exclusionary" places, as Vince Mauro called them. Lee and her peers, he said, "were playing venues that cost an arm and a leg to get into, and who could go? Older, affluent people."

Her R&B phase behind her, Lee clung mainly to what her fans wanted: romantic ballads and big-band swingers. Singers her age were pouncing on any contemporary song they could credibly sing that might make them look current in the eyes of the young. Lee had made a mildly rockish single of "Lonesome Road," a gospel-style hit from 1927. Orchestra and strings gave it her traditional sound, and even though she sounded right at home with rock rhythms, the record died. Lee feared that her time had passed. Whenever a rock song came on the radio, she rushed to change the station. "When you feel left out of something, you don't like it at all," she confessed.

The Beatles' success had dizzyingly raised the bar on what EMI expected to earn. Lately, Capitol had begun feeling pressure from its controlling stockholder to jack up profits. The label now stood as a single branch of one more umbrella conglomerate, Capitol Industries. Lee watched in dismay as her dwindling core of allies got shifted around, demoted, or let go entirely. Following his fabled rejection of the Beatles, Dave Dexter, Jr., had been downgraded to "a job with no title," as he called it. Lee Gillette, a producer there since the 1940s, found the changes at Capitol so disheartening that he took early retirement. In March 1968, Alan Livingston was ousted as president of Capitol Records and appointed head of Capitol Industries. Now big business, not music, was his career. Four months later he was fired.

His replacement at Capitol Records chilled Dexter's blood. Stanley M. Gortikov, age forty-nine, had worked as the company's head of distribution; his hard-nosed, bottom-line attitude pleased EMI. "To Gortikov a record was like a cake of soap, a pair of shoes, or a loaf of bread," said Dexter. "He gave the impression, in his dealings with performers, that they functioned like bookkeepers or plumbers." Gray heads were rolling fast, as Capitol's executive offices filled up with cocky newcomers who sported mod suits and long sideburns. To them, Peggy Lee was their parents' music.

By December 1968, Capitol had seventeen staff producers, most of them under forty. "We have to broaden the number of people we depend on for hits," explained Karl Engemann, who headed the pop division. The handsome young vice president had one foot on each side of the generational war. He had discovered the Beach Boys, one of whom was his brother, Bob; but he also liked Peggy Lee, and he wanted to save her. That meant somehow modernizing her image. Engemann looked outside the company and recruited a hotshot producing and publishing team, Charles Koppelman and Don Rubin. The pair were millionaires in their twenties, thanks to the seventeen gold records they had masterminded for Gary Lewis & the Playboys, the Lovin' Spoonful, the Turtles, and other sensations.

But Engemann was more interested in the makeover that Koppelman and Rubin had performed on Bobby Darin. For much of the 1960s, Darin had been a finger-snapping Sinatra clone, singing "Mack the Knife" for an audience of his seniors. His bosses at Atlantic Records, president Ahmet Ertegun and producer Jerry Moss, seemed content to let him stay that way. At thirty-two, Darin felt like a cliché. His earliest hits, like "Splish Splash," had sold to millions of teenagers; now those fans were grown, and many were protesting the Vietnam War and social injustice. Darin, who had grown quite political, wanted them back. In 1966, he approached Koppelman and Rubin for help. They produced his next single, "If I Were a Carpenter," a folk-rock ballad by one of their clients, singer-songwriter Tim Hardin. Atlantic was stunned when the record made the top ten—and his own generation fell back in love with Bobby Darin.

Engemann hoped for a similar magic act with Lee. It wouldn't be easy. She was sixteen years older than Darin, and few in his age group cared about her. Why would they buy a record of Peggy Lee singing their music? Furthermore, Koppelman and Rubin were known for picking the songs, hiring the arranger, and dictating the sound. Lee had always kept tight control over what she sang, and how; everyone concurred that she knew best. She might not like being told what to do—especially by two upstarts who weren't much older than her daughter. But this was the new system, and she knew she had to comply; her future was at stake. "I want to move along, to go wherever music is going," she declared bravely.

The producers met her at her home. They found themselves seated opposite a "tough broad," as Koppelman recalled her—a woman shrewd enough to size them up fast and, if need be, to flatten them. Throughout the visit, she downed Black Russians and stared at the partners with probing eyes.

Rubin was surprised at how open she was to their ideas. Lee liked the folk and soft-rock tunes they had picked out for her, written by Hardin and the Lovin' Spoonful. It comforted her somewhat to learn that her arranger would be Shorty Rogers, the 1950s cool-jazz bandleader who had written for her before. Rogers now wrote for one of the hottest groups in the country, the Monkees.

So far, so good. But Lee bristled when she learned that she wouldn't get to sing in the studio with Rogers's band; instead she would overdub her vocals onto finished orchestral tracks—a burgeoning custom that she hated. Koppelman saw it as a practical choice: "Her voice wasn't that terrific at the time. It was difficult recording her."

In March 1968, Lee stood in an isolation booth in an otherwise empty Hollywood recording studio. Headphones around her blond hairpiece, she sang with a rock band for the first time in her life. The song was Hardin's "Reason to Believe." Lee heard Fender bass, twangy guitars, tambourines, horns, and strings, all piled into a monophonic "wall of sound"—the dense, echoey engineering technique heard in a long series of hit singles masterminded by producer Phil Spector.

Koppelman was right; Lee sounded hoarse and low on lung power. But she connected with the song's driving beat as well as its angry words: "Knowing that you lied straight-faced while I cried / Still I look to find a reason to believe." Stylistically, she didn't change a thing. In the past, she had bridged swing, modern jazz, blues, and R&B; rock was a branch of the same tree, and Lee fit right into it. The other tunes had only faint trappings of late-sixties pop. Hardin's "Misty Roses" was a folk ballad arranged with a tinge of bossa nova; the Spoonful's "Didn't Want to Have to Do It" a graceful waltz with strings.

Before releasing the singles, Capitol engaged Koppelman and Rubin to produce a safe and economical Peggy Lee album, an on-site recording of her act at the Copa, which had opened to raves on April 11. Off they went to see it.

Koppelman found the Copa an archaic land of "pinky rings and mobsters and fans of Peggy Lee," but on its stage, the singer had taken one more step across the border of change. There she stood, stationary as a pillar, swathed in a pale-blue chiffon dress that looked like a night-gown. A rhinestone headband held her bobbed pageboy wig in place. As she sang "Reason to Believe" and "Didn't Want to Have to Do It," a slowly revolving psychedelic wheel was projected behind her—an incongruous backdrop for the now-matronly singer.

Lee had made two wise selections from the recent charts. In "By the Time I Get to Phoenix," a hit for Glen Campbell, Jimmy Webb details a lover's escape, by car, from a blasé partner who "just didn't know/I would really go." Both partners were left alone—a bittersweet victory for the one who had fled. Lee sang Webb's song with a quiet ache; Toots Thielemans's bluesiness echoed her heavy heart. Lee was just as moved by "Until It's Time for You to Go," a hit for the Canadian-Cree singer-songwriter Buffy Sainte-Marie. Images of lovers torn apart by the Vietnam War haunted its lines: "Although I'll never in my life see you again / Here I'll stay until it's time for you to go."

Songs of farewell had become prominent in the shows of a woman for whom lovelessness remained a fact of life. "For some years now," wrote Peter Reilly, "her best material has been that which allows her to project the ripe autumnal womanliness of someone who has been glad, been sad, and often been had, but who has extracted a wry wisdom from it all." The latter, though, brought cold comfort.

She unveiled one of her saddest new songs at the Copa. Lee had gone to the 46th Street Theatre on Broadway to see *I Do! I Do!*, a hit musical about the ups and downs of a fifty-year marriage. It starred Mary Martin and Lee's second greatest love, Robert Preston. Lee watched in a funk. Tom Jones and Harvey Schmidt's score included one song that riveted Lee. In "What Is a Woman?," Martin voiced sentiments that tore at Lee's heart: "Why is a woman afraid of not being in love? . . . To be a woman means being lonely."

Before the Copa opening, Lee had sung "What Is a Woman?" on TV's *The Hollywood Palace*. In her baby-doll blue gown, she looked like an older woman who had never quite grown up. Lee had taken to leaning on pedestals and chairs in her television appearances, and on *The Hollywood*

Palace she clung to an aluminum block for support. The feisty prefeminism of "I'm a Woman" had crumbled away; with Women's Liberation in full swing, Lee peered deep into her viewers' eyes and declared that minus a man, a woman was as good as dead.

The rest of her Copa show was a polished but predictable outing of recent showtunes, reprises of her hits, and originals, including "Here's to You," a salute to citizens of every nation. In a slightly woozy voice, she dedicated it to "all of you who have ever smiled."

None of this excited Koppelman. The show, as he recalled it, "was vintage Peggy Lee. Dated. Look, Bobby Darin was a performer. She was more a sultry singer." When he heard the Copa tapes, the hoarseness in her voice concerned him. He and Rubin did all they could to create an acceptable album. That included having Lee rerecord songs and patter in the studio, then asking the engineer, Brooks Arthur, to patch them into the live tapes, surrounding them with bursts of actual Copa applause.

During this process, Capitol released the Koppelman-Rubin singles. Lee's tireless cheerleader, Leonard Feather, heralded them with a feature in the *Los Angeles Times*: "Peggy Lee Turns to the Now Sound." It didn't help. Seldom had any of her recordings flopped so badly. DJs shunned them, as did her fans. Youngsters, too, were not about to seek out Peggy Lee—nor Steve Lawrence and Eydie Gormé, Ella Fitzgerald, Mel Tormé, or Andy Williams—to hear rock. For Lee to slip "Reason to Believe" into her nightclub act was fine, but her followers, conceded Rubin, "weren't gonna buy the kind of records that we made with her."

The response depressed her. Yet she became all the more determined to prove to them and to herself that she *wasn't* just an aging chanteuse chained to the past. "Working with Koppelman and Rubin changed my whole approach," she insisted.

Her Copa album awaited shipment. Promotional copies had been mailed, and Douglas Watt of the *New York Daily News* had written a favorable review.

But decades would pass before the public heard *2 Shows Nightly*. To Lee, the orchestra sounded out of balance. On a few of her overdubbed phrases, the "ghost" of the original live performance peeped through. Applause faded up and down with conspicuous fakeness. Lee had grown neurotic about Capitol; she was sure they were eager to dump her. And to Lee, *2 Shows Nightly* was nothing less than sabotage. The cover even sported the same nondescript headshot that had appeared on another album, *Somethin' Groovy!*

When Lee felt spurned, she banished common sense and grew vengeful. Without giving a thought to how it might affect her shaky footing at Capitol, she halted the release of *2 Shows Nightly*. Until it eventually appeared on CD, the album remained extremely rare. Lee diehards touted the "perfectionism" that had led her to yank it from the market. But those who found promo copies wondered what all the fuss was about. *2 Shows Nightly* was one of her best albums in years, and its technical shortcomings were forgivable.

Her young producers moved on. "At that time, I was involved with a million projects," said Koppelman. "I can't tell you I was heavily invested in her emotionally." Capitol hadn't recorded her since the Copa dates, and after the *2 Shows Nightly* debacle, months passed with no new sessions. Lee feared the worst.

Somehow, Dave Cavanaugh had survived the company's upheavals. True to his father-bear demeanor, he feared for his remaining friends there, notably Lee. Cavanaugh sensed that the label was on the verge of dropping her. From his office in the Capitol Tower, he placed a call to Brian Panella, Capitol's New York executive in charge of artist relations and promotion. The producer asked Panella if there were anything he could due to pump up Lee's visibility and boost her sales.

A Boston University graduate, Panella was Italian, handsome, a mod dresser, and in his twenties. Lee was pushing fifty. But to him, she was a goddess. "From the time I was a kid I was a fan," Panella said. "When she sang, it was very stirring to me. Also, I thought that she was absolutely beautiful. I've always been a sucker for blonds."

After one meeting, Lee became his pet project. Knowing she had his attention, she leaned on him more and more heavily. Soon she convinced him to quit Capitol and become her manager. Naïvely, he took on a job that Larry L. King, in a *Cosmopolitan* profile of Lee, would term "about as relaxing as refereeing the United Nations while wrestling alligators on the side." Panella didn't know that yet, but Betty Jungheim saw trouble ahead. "The minute I saw him I thought, 'She's gonna be too much for you.' Because he was so nice."

He flew to Los Angeles to talk business with Lee on Tower Grove. "I had come out thinking that she was a big star," he said, "and I find this horror show. She owed the IRS a fortune, and they put a lien on her house, which was in foreclosure." Living in the guest cottage were Nicki, Dick Foster, and the three children born to them in quick succession, David, Holly, and Michael.

Panella realized that "managing" Lee would mean tending not just to her career but her life, and devising magical fixes for both. "There was a lot of pain inside Peggy and a lot of unresolved things," he observed. At the house he watched a parade of friends, hangers-on, and musicians; Lee plied them with drinks and held them captive as long as she could. More than ever, her bed was her womb. Once home from the road, she hurried under the covers and left only when necessary. "She'd have breakfast, lunch, and dinner in bed. The grandkids would come in and pile on. She'd hit the buzzer, and the household help would come running."

Lee couldn't perform or otherwise make a move without hearing the grandmotherly voice of her faultlessly loyal friend, Adela Rogers St. Johns, then in her seventies. When a preshow panic attack seized her, Lee would send anyone at hand—Panella, Jungheim, Kathy Mahana, Bruce Vanderhoff—to the phone. "I can't breathe," she would gasp. "Get me Adela." During a rehearsal at the Palmer House in Chicago, the air conditioning went out, and Lee dispatched Jungheim to dial up St. Johns. The Science of Mind minister responded with patient exasperation. "You know, Betty, I say a prayer for her every morning, and I say a prayer for her every night. She doesn't have to call me about the air conditioning."

St. Johns would recite Ernest Holmes's edicts as Lee held the receiver to her ear. "Trust the divine self that you possess, the higher self," St. Johns would advise. "Go there in your mind."

But finally, Lee seemed beyond comforting. It troubled St. Johns to see her friend, an artist known for cool control, spiraling toward an emotional collapse. Having long ago conquered what she called "the curse of my life"—severe alcoholism—St. Johns saw into the heart of Lee's addictiveness; no one else in the singer's life was brave enough to confront her about it. "And she would take it," said Panella.

And yet the drinking went on, as did her heavy smoking. All the while, Panella had to prepare the oxygen treatments that expanded Lee's damaged lungs enough for her to sing for an hour. She asked whoever was nearby to jab her with injections of vitamin B_{12}, Lee's preferred energy booster. After the show, she tore into fried-chicken box dinners. Hours later, the singer who had just seduced hundreds of strangers with her love songs retired to a usually empty bed.

It seemed odd that Lee, who could make people feel she knew all their secrets, could so easily be fooled when "romance" stepped in—especially if it came in the person of a fatherly protector-figure, like a doctor. The pattern fascinated Grady Tate, a drummer who entered her band, and her bed, in 1968, and played for her until the late 1980s. A former English teacher, Tate was black, attractive, and a precise, swinging timekeeper. Lee was smitten. In college, Tate had minored in psychology, and she gave him a lot to ponder. "She was the biggest hypochondriac I've ever known. When we weren't performing she was always under a physician's care. It was as though when she wasn't receiving the total admiration and involvement of the people, she had to get it from someone else."

But more and more, she saw herself as a woman alone. In a *Life* profile, "A Queen on a Lonely Peak," Albert Goldman marveled at how Lee had "sustained herself for an astonishing total of thirty years in a business that takes its toll swiftly and often fatally." Lee and her music, he observed, "now represent one of the peaks to which popular art has climbed in America." She was a survivor, but recent experiments aside, her attitudes were not of the present. For all she had achieved as a woman in the music business, she had no time for the feminist movement. Women's Lib upset her, reported Ernest Leogrande in the *New York Daily News*. "Aggressive females," he wrote of the frequently contentious singer, "put her on guard." At a press conference in Dallas prior to Lee's run at the Fairmont Hotel, a female reporter raised a hand. What, she asked, was the star's opinion of Women's Lib? "I've always been fortunate," said Lee, "and have never regretted being a woman at all."

As fifty approached, Lee feared love would never find her again. For most of her life she had put career before everything; now that her star was falling, she had little else to fall back on. "I'd like to have a happy marriage now, but, um, I don't think that's in my future," she said wistfully to a reporter. All she could hope for was a "nameless something" that might bring her happiness.

There were always new songs. In September 1968, Jerry Leiber and Mike Stoller gave her a demo of two of their latest. Playing the tape at home, Lee was incensed. "Some Cats Know" was a slow, sinuous look at the art of sexual prowess. "Some cats know how to make the honey flow," it declared, "but if a cat don't know, a cat don't know." The song seemed like classic Peggy Lee. But the woman who had injected more sex into 1950s pop than almost any other female singer could be unaccountably prudish, and when she heard the bridge—"Don't you know how the birds and the bumble bees buzz each other? Didn't your papa ever tell you how he buzzed your mother?"—she felt insulted that the partners would send her such filth.

Temper still flaring, she played the second song. It consisted mainly of talk—four monologues with a sung refrain, delivered by Leiber in his pitch-deprived but enthusiastic song-plugger's voice and backed by Stoller playing barroom piano. The first line caught Lee's attention: "I remember when I was a very little boy, our house caught on fire." From there, the narrator recounted the milestones of his life, all of them oddly anticlimactic; he wondered what, if anything, ultimately mattered. Lee listened over and over, riveted. She *had* to sing this song.

Like her, Leiber and Stoller were weathering their own midlife crisis. Their familiar skill—the creation of black music that entranced white youngsters—no longer seemed to matter; now *Billboard*'s Hot 100 was a shrine to soul, the sound of late-1960s rebellion and the search for truth. The partners had scored one last commercial coup in 1964, when they founded Red Bird, an independent record label. Out of it came several girl-group hits, including "Chapel of Love" for the Dixie Cups. Now, in their late thirties, they were burned out on jukebox pop and searching for something deeper. They hoped to write ambitious theater music—but who would want that from the authors of "Hound Dog"?

In fact, Leiber was immersed in intellectual literature. He had discovered Thomas Mann's "Disillusionment," a short story published in 1896, when Mann was an old soul of twenty-four. The future Nobel Prize-winning German writer was struggling with his homosexual feelings; illness, death, and the passage of time obsessed him. "Disillusionment" describes a chance meeting in a Venice café. An elder man startles a young stranger by venting his most intimate regrets. "Do you know, my dear sir, what disillusionment is? Not a miscarriage in small, unimportant matters, but the great and general disappointment which everything, all of life, has in store? . . . From my youth up I have carried it about with me; it has made me lonely, unhappy, and a bit queer."

A lifetime of traumas—even the loss of his greatest love—seem meaningless. "Is this all there is to it?" he asks. "So I dream and wait for death . . . that last disappointment! At my last moment I shall be saying to myself: 'So this is the great experience—well, and what of it?'"

Leiber borrowed heavily from Mann's story to create "Is That All There Is?" Lee was stunned by the song's dreamlike recollections. They seemed torn from her life: the blaze that levels her entire world but leaves her oddly unfazed; a trip to the circus—"the greatest show on earth"— that doesn't thrill her as hoped. Then down falls the love that seemed destined for eternity. "I thought I'd die," says the narrator. "But I didn't."

Those words shook Lee the hardest. They made a lie of the love songs she had sung all her life, and they echoed the aftermath of Dave Barbour's exit. She hadn't died, although she had thought—perhaps wished—that she would. Now there was nowhere else to go, nothing left to long for. "Let's break out the booze and have a ball / If that's all there is," went the refrain. It summed up a song about an emotional vacancy that seemed unfillable, combined with a dogged drive to press on. Stoller had set the words to a loping, "oom-pah" circus rhythm. The harmonies derived from Kurt Weill and Bertolt Brecht's Weimar-era theater music, and their woozy dissonance fit right in with Lee's semi-intoxicated, floating delivery. But Leiber and Stoller didn't think so at first. Off they went to find some other artist of note who might take the authors of "Jailhouse Rock" seriously as writers of art songs. It would have incensed Lee to learn she was far from their first choice, but by the late 1960s, Leiber and Stoller felt sourly toward her. They had given Lee her last significant hit with "I'm a Woman"; since then, she had ignored every song they sent. To Leiber, Peggy Lee would have been all wrong for "Is That All There Is?"; he fantasized instead about Marlene Dietrich, the German movie and cabaret goddess whose cool glamour held infinite mystery. Burt Bacharach, her conductor, scheduled a lunch for him and Leiber at Dietrich's apartment on Park Avenue in New York.

At sixty-six, the star who greeted them looked eerily frozen in time, with eyes that had seen it all, yet could still bore through people like an

X-ray. "Well, gentlemen, I hear you've brought me a hit song," she said in her deadpan, accented murmur. As Bacharach played piano, Leiber nervously performed "Is That All There Is?" Dietrich listened raptly. At the end, she broke into demure applause. "Gentlemen," she said, "that is a lovely piece of material." Then she turned to Leiber and asked if he had ever seen her perform. He hadn't, he confessed, except onscreen. "I'm glad you told me the truth," she said, "because I would have known the truth anyway." Then she gave Leiber what he recalled as "the most consummate response" he had ever gotten from an artist. "That song is about who I am, and not what I do." She declined to sing it. Leiber walked away disappointed yet dazzled. Marlene, he exclaimed later, was "a fucking genius!"

He and Stoller pressed on, determined to find a singer willing to give life to their oblique little creation. The first to consent was Georgia Brown, a lusty-voiced British theater star who had recorded an album of Weill. Brown performed "Is That All There Is?" on her BBC special, *Georgia's Back*. It made little impression. Meanwhile, the writers were startled to find that Dan Daniel, an amiable New York DJ and sometime crooner, had gotten hold of their demo and cut a soon-to-be-issued single of the song. He sounded as dramatic as a friendly postman, and Leiber and Stoller—who had far loftier hopes for the song—blocked the release.

In the summer of 1968, they produced an LP for Leslie Uggams, the ebullient African-American songbird and actress. Uggams had graduated from teenage stardom on TV's *Sing Along with Mitch* to a Tony-winning Broadway performance in *Hallelujah, Baby!*, a civil-rights-themed musical. On her new album, *What's an Uggams?*, Leiber and Stoller tried to recast her as a pop-soul belter. Uggams sang the brooding "Is That All There Is?" to the rafters, a smile in her sunny voice. Leiber knew it wasn't a match.

Almost as a last resort, he and Stoller sent Peggy Lee the demo, which also contained "Some Cats Know"—a much more likely choice for her, they thought. Within days, she phoned Leiber about "Is That All There Is?"

"If anybody else gets their hands on this song, you can forget it."

"Forget what?"

"*Everything.*"

Lee's last great love: WNET producer and host David S. Prowitt.

Chapter Twelve

*L*EE DECIDED THAT Jerry Leiber had written "Is That All There Is?" for her, or at least about her. "I've lived that whole thing," she asserted. Still, the notion that her life was a giant anticlimax troubled her. She had to find the positive spin. Finally she came up with one. "There are two words in there that are quite important: *if* that's all there is, and *is* that all there is. It's *not* all there is! 'Is that all there is?' is simply a question. And if it makes you think, one might find their own answer."

The song, she resolved, had to be her next single. No matter that even the authors didn't think it had a chance of selling, or that her youth-obsessed label was on the verge of dropping her. Lee viewed "Is That All There Is?" as her salvation, and wouldn't be deterred. Sidney Myer, the New York cabaret manager, compared Lee's courage to that of Gloria Swanson in making *Sunset Boulevard*. "That movie was offered to so many actresses who didn't wish to be seen in an unflattering light, in a context that was against the image they had worked so long to create. 'Is That All There Is?' wasn't full of the romance and the glamour and the eye-batting of Peggy's other hits. It was risky."

She began planning the session. Leiber and Stoller opted to produce. But as usual, Lee took control. "As hard as they would try to tell her, you should cut it at this tempo, you should use this pianist, and don't let anyone arrange it except this guy, they were talking to a wall," said Brian Panella. "Nobody knew the best arrangers, the best players, like Peggy Lee."

And for her, only one musician was up to the task of arranging "Is That All There Is?" Johnny Mandel had played her one of Reprise Records' costlier flops of 1968; it had captivated her ever since. *Randy Newman* was the debut album of a twenty-four-year-old, brainy smart-aleck who played piano and sang original dark-humored social parodies, steeped in irony. Lee had bravely sung Newman's "Love Story" at the Copa. It portrayed the Great American Dream of marrying young and growing old together as a form of slow death; by the end, the couple in the song has been shipped off to a "little home in Florida," where the only movement happens on a checkerboard. Another song on the album, "Davy the Fat Boy," concerned an orphan who knew only the most condescending kindness. "Isn't he round?" exclaimed Newman in his gravel voice—"a put-on of old and crotchety," as Ben Ratliff called it years later in the *New York Times*.

Newman's songs spoke to the side of Lee that feared a storm cloud behind every rainbow, but that also saw the humor of it all. With America's youth questioning every value they'd been force-fed by family, church, and media, Newman's intellectual cynicism had come at the right time. But still he seemed headed for commercial doom. As rock grew harder and blunter, Newman's music leaned toward "ragtime or blues or Kurt Weill art-song dissonance," as Ratliff wrote. Over the course of several albums, though, his public grew, and in 1977 his number-two hit, "Short People," sealed his stardom.

Lee had "gotten" his "happy-sad" songs before almost anyone. "I really consider him one of the brightest of the new young writers," she said. "It's kind of interesting to think that such a young man could know so much about way back then, and way ahead, and right here. His music is full of a poignant satire."

She commanded Leiber and Stoller to hire him to arrange "Is That All There Is?" He was stunned by the request to work with this icon, twice his age, who had her pick of the best jazz musicians in America. "I'd seen her all my life; I'd heard her since I was a little boy," said Newman, a Hollywood kid whose three uncles, Lionel, Alfred, and Emil Newman, formed a triumvirate of esteemed film composers. Leiber and Stoller, to Newman, were also aristocrats. He called Leiber "about the best lyricist that pop music—the incarnation of it that begins with rock and roll—ever produced."

Having heard Newman's album, the duo gave him carte blanche to revamp their song however he chose. All involved were thrilled—except for Capitol's executives, who rolled their eyes. To them, the plan promised another expensive bomb—one that would unite a faded singer, two has-been rock-and-roll tunesmiths, an obscure young maestro who wrote mostly unsalable tunes, and a chatty art song that was slow, depressing, and way too long.

Clutching at straws, Lee took the Leiber-Stoller demo to Glenn Wallichs, Capitol's original cofounder, who had helped launch her there. EMI had bought out his shares, and even as chairman of the board in the 1960s, he had seen his clout declining. But now he was in a position to help her. Following the dismissal of Alan Livingston, Wallichs had been appointed interim president of Capitol Industries. He succeeded in green-lighting "Is That All There Is?"

Randy Newman went to work. He thought the song "needed something in the front" besides the rote and undramatic chords Stoller had written. He threw them out, along with the barroom jauntiness of the demo. As Lee spoke about watching "the whole world go up in flames," an eerily childlike waltz would play behind her. And when she told of the circus visit that had left her cold, the horn section would play a sinister countermelody in the background.

Before they recorded, Newman went to her house to talk things through. Finally he met Peggy Lee—a singer tarnished by life, faltering commercially, and hoping against hope that his work would help save her. Lee's white outfit matched the nearly all-white décor. As they spoke, her vulnerability struck him. So did her lack of self-confidence—a surprising thing, he thought, "for someone of that attainment." But her future, Lee felt, rested on this song, which her label didn't like; they didn't even want her.

———

ON JANUARY 24, 1969, the participants convened at United Studios in Hollywood for a nighttime recording session. As the thirty or so musicians set up, Newman walked in with Stoller, who was exhausted from having spent eight hours producing a record by "some pseudo-rock group," as he called it. Then Leiber showed up, as did Lee. After saying her hellos, she quickly took her place inside a glass-walled isolation booth. She sat in near-darkness—her choice. The fewer distractions, the better, for a song that was all about her and her memories. Tension was high. The key parties all needed a hit, and no one was sure if this strange, experimental song had a chance.

Newman counted off the first take. Pianist Maury Dell played the timid introduction and Lee began to speak. "I remember when I was a little girl, our house caught on fire . . ." She could hear the musicians through her headphones, but they couldn't hear her. "We're playing this thing," recalled trombonist Mike Barone, "and I thought, this is a piece of shit! All I heard behind me was, oom-PEE, oom-PEE—trumpets behind me playing afterbeats." At the end of the first take he stepped into the control room to hear the playback. He couldn't believe his ears. "I thought it sounded fantastic!"

But the writers weren't pleased. What they had heard from Lee was an exaggeration of her familiar bedroom delivery—not the "something a little new, something different" they had hoped for. What they wanted, they couldn't quite explain. "Is That All There Is?" was an acting job, and while Lee communicated superbly in song, spoken lines were another matter. They called for another take, then another, then another. Even these, said Leiber, "weren't great." Lee was getting angry, and taking frequent gulps from a bottle of cognac. After her sixth effort, she snapped: "Listen, I never do this many takes!"

Yet Leiber and Stoller were determined to nail the perfect one, and they kept pressing for more. Stoller chain-smoked nervously—that day he finished five packs—and tinkered with the arrangement, while giving pointers to a quiet Randy Newman. Tony Terran, one of the trumpeters, had played on Newman's dates before. "I was always impressed with him. He was easy to work with. He took care of business and didn't bullshit."

Lee's cognac kicked in, and as she neared the twentieth take, Leiber and Stoller began to relax. Her strained attempts to "act" had given way to a Zenlike calm. A critic later wrote that she uttered her "hallucinatory recollections in a hauntingly low, flat, emotionless voice." Finally came a take that startled the writers. "I almost fainted," said Leiber. "It was perfect." Every layer of the song—the cynicism, the resignation, the humor, the perseverance—had come together. And when she uttered the line about the ultimate disappointment of lost love—"I thought I'd die, but I didn't"—she gave Leiber goose bumps.

Flush with success, all of them filed into the control room. As Lee sat down in an available chair at the console, Leiber asked the engineer for a playback.

At twenty-six, Sandy Lehmann-Haupt—a pageboy-wearing, good-looking hippie—had as colorful a history as anyone there. The brother of *New York Times* book critic Christopher Lehmann-Haupt, Sandy had begun using hallucinogens well before they became the rage. He met the countercultural, drug-crazed novelist Ken Kesey, later famous for *One Flew Over the Cuckoo's Nest*, and joined his Shakespearean-named Merry Pranksters, a gang of hippies who rode cross-country on a psychedelically painted school bus, getting high and raising hell. Their hijinks became the subject of Tom Wolfe's bestselling book, *The Electric Kool-Aid Acid Test*.

No one knew whether Sandy was under the influence on January 24, 1969, but when he pushed "play," nothing came out. "What's wrong?" asked Lee. Sandy didn't know.

"Either he didn't record it or he erased it," recalled Leiber. "The kid was mortified and contrite, but there was nothing that could be done." Leiber and Stoller were sure that Lee would explode. But she surprised them. "Guess I'll have to sing it again," she said with a sigh. She walked back into her booth, the orchestra reassembled, and she delivered a performance that Leiber called "nothing short of marvelous." Still he mourned the "perfect" phantom take. In years to come, Leiber—who seldom let the truth stand in the way of a good story—recalled it as the thirty-sixth. Yet the box that held the final version said "take 20"; Mike Barone couldn't recall anywhere near thirty-six takes.

It was almost eleven o'clock; the session had ended. The planned B-side, "Me and My Shadow," would have to wait. Lee felt good; so did the writers, and everyone headed out to dinner.

The next day, he and Leiber got their hands on all of Lee's takes and went to work in an editing room. They used the last performance as a template. The sung refrains were fine, but Leiber grew obsessed with creating flawless versions of the monologues. He and Stoller listened to every previous take and isolated line readings that sounded dead-on; then they strung them together. Lee had made a few changes in the text; one of them so galled the lyricist that he never forgave her for it, even though he had let it pass. In the final spoken chorus, the singer had altered a reference to death. Commenting on why she didn't just do herself in, she explained, "I'm not ready for that final disappointment"—not "I'm in no hurry for that final disappointment," as Leiber had written. The distinction would have escaped most people, but not Leiber. Lee's rewording was "somber," he felt; what he had written was wry and ironic. "She really didn't understand the song on the deepest level," he groused.

Neither did Capitol's executives, as Lee and the songwriters would soon learn. But thanks to Dave Cavanaugh, Lee had earned a surprise reprieve at the company. Cavanaugh had maneuvered a deal for one more Peggy Lee album, but not another recital of standards. This disc would recast her as a soul-singing mama—a shift she was eager to embrace. Cavanaugh placed her in the hands of Phil Wright, one of the young producers whom Capitol had hired to shake up its A&R department. Then thirty, Wright had come from Chess, the Chicago R&B label. There he had arranged and produced a wealth of hits, including "Rescue Me" (Fontella Bass) and "We're Gonna Make It" (Little Milton).

By the time Wright joined Capitol, Aretha Franklin was the reigning queen of soul, with a gospel-bred, melismatic wail that reached for the heavens. Lee was a white pop-jazz songstress who purred into the listener's ear. But to Wright, soul was soul, and he heard it in Lee. "She had a feeling for the blues," he said. "Things like 'Fever' were not that far away from soul music." Lee, he believed, was up to the task of covering Franklin's exultant 1968 hit, "(You Make Me Feel Like) A Natural Woman"—a song coauthored by a white woman, Carole King.

At her dining-room table, Wright sat with Lee for hours, "deciding what we were gonna do, how we were gonna do it, the musicians she wanted." Lee kept a pack of cigarettes and a never-ending flow of booze at hand. "Her butler made drinks in very large glasses," said Wright; Lee made it clear that she expected him to drink with her. He wondered how he would ever drive home.

They jotted down some rock and soul hits of the day, including "Everyday People" (Sly and the Family Stone), "Spinning Wheel" (Blood, Sweat and Tears), "(Sittin' On) The Dock of the Bay" (Otis Redding), and "Can I Change My Mind?" (Tyrone Davis). Lee added Randy Newman's desolate "I Think It's Going to Rain Today" and one of the most wounded songs she'd ever heard Billie Holiday sing, "Don't Explain." From Percy Mayfield, a West Coast bluesman of Lee's generation, came an R&B prayer to God, "Please Send Me Someone to Love."

Virtually no pop singer of her era could have tackled such a program without sounding silly. But Mike Melvoin, who arranged and played keyboards on several tracks, knew that Lee could do it. "She was not a rock-and-roll singer by any stretch of the imagination, but she had internalized the blues melisma. She got it musically and she got it emotionally."

The funky orchestra included Lee's sometime flame, Grady Tate, and Bobby Bryant, a fierce trumpeter who had played with the Charles Mingus band. There were tambourines, gospel-style piano, and Melvoin on organ, along with backup vocals by Sisters Love, a wailing black trio who toured with the Jackson 5. "I could hardly wait to get to the studio," Lee exclaimed. Vermettya Royster, one of the Sisters, made Lee feel right at home. "I fell in love with her and that voice of hers," said Royster. "And when I opened my mouth to sing she just stood there." Lee thrilled Royster by exclaiming, "Oh, you've got such a wonderful voice!"

Capitol employees drifted into the control room. John Hallowell of the *Los Angeles Times* came, too. "It is cold, stark, butts on the floor, big shiny black mikes, a clock on the wall, paper cups with coffee and more, but no one notices. For as the lady sings she turns that recording stage into the Mississippi Delta; a strobe-light show; two lovers in bed after love."

Lee was in a playful mood. When a sung phrase emerged as a croak, she announced, "There's a frog for ya!" and started croaking, "Ribbit! Ribbit!" Everyone laughed.

But the singer ruled with force. "She knew what she wanted and that was it," said Wright. "If you tried to force her into something it wouldn't work." After the Koppelman-Rubin sessions, she had vowed to never again sing to prerecorded tracks. "There's no overdubbing on the album, no sweetening," Lee enthused to a reporter. "The emotions are full and strong." She still relied on her respirator, and in between takes she vanished into a side room and put the mask on her face. Wright noticed her breathing troubles, but they seemed to vanish when the tape rolled.

As usual, she didn't have to raise her voice to sing the blues; they were there in her every train-whistle bend and slur. In "(Sittin' On) The Dock of the Bay," Lee mourned a dead-end life spent "watchin' the ships roll in / And I watch 'em roll away again." The horns blared and Sisters Love piped in—"*ships roll in, oh yeah!*"—but nothing disturbed Lee's brooding introspection. Aretha Franklin had turned "A Natural Woman" into an ecstatic gospel cry; Lee delivered it in confidence to the man who had saved her life. To Melvoin, her version had all the passion of the original. "I think she sang the shit out of it," he said.

She let loose on "Don't Explain." That torch song, coauthored by Holiday, depicted a woman as willing victim, helpless without a man and willing to endure anything rather than be alone. Desperation, weakness, rage, and denial collided in Lee's voice as a forlorn oboe snaked around it. "Cry to hear folks chatter, and I know you *cheat!*" she snapped in anger; then she crumbled. "Right or wrong don't matter / when you're with me, sweet." At the end, she exploded with the rawest yells she had ever recorded—"*Don't explain! Don't explain!*"

When one of the planned songs didn't work out, Lee proposed the first tune she had ever sung with Benny Goodman, "My Old Flame." Singing in 1941 about a vaguely remembered lost love, Lee had sounded dulcet and virginal; the flame could have been a prom date who never phoned again. Now, after decades of smoking, drinking, and saloon life, combined with serious lung damage, she sang it four tones lower, in a husky, weary voice. "My Old Flame" became a slow-motion bar song, blurred with drunkenness and disorientation. Near the end, Lee let out an off-key wail; she didn't try to fix it.

That track was saved for a later LP, but her soul album came out that spring. Many of Lee's old fans seemed to feel she had crossed over into the enemy camp. Yet in *Cosmopolitan*, jazz critic Nat Hentoff called her disc "a stunning illumination of her capacity for self-renewal." To Cliff Smith, the "new" Peggy Lee was "a bundle of seething but controlled emotion" with "a style no other white woman I know of could get away with." Jerry Shnay of the *Chicago Tribune* compared Lee's singing to "a long fingernail running down your spine."

One essential contradiction jumped off the cover. Lee appeared in a photo by John Engstead, who specialized in glamorously artificial portraits of stars from the golden age of Hollywood. She stood amid what looked like a wheat field, but was actually a patch of shrubs at the end of her street. Long, straight hair fell past her shoulders—the folksy look of

Joni Mitchell and Mary Travers—but in Lee's case, most of it was pinned on and colored her preferred lemon-yellow. The hair framed a flawlessly unlined face, which owed much to surgery and a mask of makeup. Huge pasted-on lashes highlighted expressionless eyes. The look suggested a Beverly Hills Mona Lisa. Above her head, in greeting-card script, was the album's title: *A Natural Woman.*

Sales were slim, but a single of "Spinning Wheel" hit number twenty-four on the Adult Contemporary chart—the same demographic Capitol had hoped to transcend. To Melvoin, it was a "fool's assumption" that a middle-aged artist like Lee could sing rock and soul and attract the young. "Peggy managed to preserve the black identity better than most," he said, "but she did not sell records to young white people. She sold records to adults."

The gap was obvious when she sang "Spinning Wheel" on *The Andy Williams Show.* As good as she sounded, her segment was a symphony of misjudgment. Lee had squeezed her girth into a fussy, old-fashioned yellow beaded dress. Dangling earrings swung beneath a campily ornate headful of blond sausage curls, so coated in hairspray that they didn't move. She stood in the center of a mechanical wheel; protruding rods of light bulbs revolved awkwardly around her as she sang. Afterward, as she and Williams shared a duet of the Mamas and the Papas hit "California Dreamin'," a fly buzzed persistently around her lacquered head. Even Lee had to laugh.

———

IN LAS VEGAS, NO amount of excess was too much. The town had remained a pot of gold for singers like Lee, whose past hits could lure gamblers into its web of showrooms and slot machines. But Lee's engagements there were thinning out. Her temperament and demands—not to mention her fading name—had exceeded her drawing power, and Lee's agency, William Morris, was finding her harder to book.

On March 9, 1969, some surprising news hit the press. That summer, Peggy Lee would inaugurate the Casino Theater of the International Hotel, the most hyped and bankrolled new resort in Vegas history. For sixty million dollars, megamogul Kirk Kerkorian—later named the richest man in Los Angeles—had ordered up the world's biggest hotel: thirty stories containing 1,519 rooms or suites. The International would become the Las Vegas performing headquarters of Elvis Presley. For now, however, it was a mess of plaster dust, exposed planks, and swinging electrical cords, as workmen scrambled to get it ready for a July opening.

Peggy Lee could hardly wait. The monthlong run would launch a two-year contract for the heftiest fee she had ever received. She owed the invitation to the hotel's entertainment director, Bill Miller. A grand old man of the nightclub business, Miller had presented Lee in the late 1940s and early fifties at his star-filled Bill Miller's Riviera in Fort Lee, New Jersey. The white-haired, permanently tanned impresario had gone on to book various showrooms in Vegas. Now he was in a position to give Lee a much-needed break. Word of it brought a snicker out of Joyce Haber, an acid-penned gossip columnist in her thirties. "Remember Peggy?" she asked in print. "Shades of Jack Webb and G.I. Joe."

But nothing could quell Lee's excitement—until she learned about her competing act at the International. For every night of Lee's run in the five-hundred-seat Casino Theater, Barbra Streisand, age twenty-six, would headline at the hotel's seventeen-hundred-seat Show Room International. Lee would provide the late-night "dessert" after Streisand's prime-time main course. Four weeks of singing would earn the young superstar a million in cash and hotel stock—four times the salary Lee was getting. All over Vegas, it was Streisand who had set the town abuzz. This was her first nightclub appearance in years; behind her were a smash star turn on Broadway in *Funny Girl*, a dozen hit albums, a *Time* magazine cover, four TV specials, and one Emmy; soon she would score a Best Actress Oscar for the screen adaptation of *Funny Girl*. Currently Streisand was filming another grand-scale movie musical, *On a Clear Day You Can See Forever*.

All this was more than Lee's pride could take. She froze when the *New York Times* asked her to comment on how she had felt upon hearing the news of this twin billing. "Naturally I was thrilled," she said tersely. "Barbra's got talent."

But Bruce Vanderhoff knew her real feelings. "If the truth be told," he said, "Peggy hated the ground Streisand walked on." In 1964, Lee had sat in the Beverly Hilton Hotel's Grand Ballroom as Streisand's first LP, *The Barbra Streisand Album*, blew away its competitors—including Lee's *I'm a Woman* album—in three categories of the Grammys. Streisand had gone on to snag the film career that Lee had always wanted. Now the unhumble young superstar was poised to render Lee invisible in an engagement she sorely needed. Betty Jungheim heard Lee haranguing one of her agents on the phone. "She screamed and yelled—'it was the lounge, the lounge!'"

Her insecurity belied the fact that she was simultaneously set to make the New York supper-club debut of her dreams. On April 7, she would launch a long-term association with the Empire Room of Manhattan's Waldorf-Astoria Hotel—the luxury Art Deco dwelling that had played host to the likes of Cole Porter, Frank Sinatra, and Herbert Hoover.

The extravagantly sized Empire Room was its "crown jewel," as the hotel called it. Lena Horne had tigerishly reigned over the club's habitués for years; Édith Piaf's epic self-destruction had triggered a famous collapse onstage there during a show. Lately the Empire Room had added some safely "mod" acts—Diana Ross, Sonny and Cher, Petula Clark—to its roster of middle-aged idols, such as Sammy Davis, Jr. and Liberace. But no matter what, tradition had to be honored, for the Empire Room reached for the majesty of an imperial palace. Huge crystal chandeliers hung from a high ceiling; candelabrum sconces and faux windows with tassled draperies lined the walls. Against the rear wall, a riser held a tuxedo-clad orchestra; in front of it was a small dance floor. The headliners performed there, surrounded by a sea of tables. Majordomos in black tie circulated, taking drink and dinner orders with old-world courtliness.

The Empire Room had opened in 1931, and it was showing its age; besides that, many of the sightlines were poor. Soon it would be moved to a similar space across the foyer and given an even more dated design. But to Peggy Lee, the Empire Room was the last word in glamour. This was just the sort of place she had fantasized about as a teenager, when she sat in the Fargo Theatre and watched Fred Astaire twirl Ginger Rogers in some tony nightspot.

At the time of Lee's Waldorf debut, Sidney Myer was a college boy in Philadelphia. Pricey though the Empire Room was, he made his way there again and again. "It *was* intimidating—the formality of it, this opulent grandeur," he recalled. "But I thought it was beautiful. It had the whole mystique for me of Park Avenue. There was this huge orchestra. Everyone was dressed up. In those years the whole world was in chaos; it was all hippies and marches. In the Empire Room, none of that existed."

Still, Lee wasn't about to play it safe. For this engagement, she decided to spotlight the soul music from *A Natural Woman*. "Is That All There Is?" would form the centerpiece of the show. The master tape of her recording still sat untouched at Capitol, and Lee was desperate. She hounded Brian Panella and her publicist, Peter Levinson, to pressure Capitol; she begged Glenn Wallichs to intervene. She played an acetate of the record for journalists, hoping to win them as allies. Levinson—an exceedingly persuasive promoter of the biggest stars in jazz—didn't have the heart to tell her that her campaign seemed hopeless.

Lee still didn't know that Jerry Leiber had really wanted Marlene Dietrich to sing the song. There were few female performers whom Lee envied, but she worshipped Dietrich and had borrowed from her heavily. The clinging, bugle-beaded gowns that Lee favored had long been a Dietrich staple. So had a minimalism that surpassed Lee's. Dietrich stood onstage with only a standup mike; the orchestra stayed hidden behind a curtain or in the pit. Dietrich's phrasing was clipped and plain, but her acting was transcendent; all alone, she summoned up dramatic scenes with Technicolor vividness. Some of her concert posters bore a line drawing of her famous face; Lee commissioned one of her own.

Dietrich wasn't offended. In *Marlene Dietrich's ABC*, her book of alphabetized opinions on anything that had entered her head, the star had written under "Lee, Peggy": "Honey-dripping singing, timing, phrasing; awakening no memories of other voices but awakening all senses to a unique feast." Dietrich could afford to be generous, for the sight of her in concert still made audiences gasp. At sixty-eight, she looked not a day older nor a pound heavier than she had in her old films—a feat enhanced by makeup, adhesive strips that gave her an instant facelift, a punishing rubber foundation garment that she wore beneath her "nude" beige beaded dress, and the lighting alchemy of Lee's own Hugo Granata.

Lee pumped him for backstage tidbits. When he told her that Dietrich employed a rare "chocolate gel"—a filter that subdued the harsh white spotlight in the manner of tinted glasses—Lee had to have it, too. Bruce Vanderhoff saw the results. At rehearsals, he said, "Hugo would be up in the booth. She'd say into the microphone so all the world could hear, 'Hugo, it doesn't feel like the chocolate gel is on my face!' That was just to make the rest of us see that Peggy Lee was the ultimate perfectionist. Then she'd say, 'Well, I think we need a double.'"

Lighting, of course, was a mere adornment to Dietrich's larger-than-life presence, which in the 1960s had filled two of Broadway's biggest theaters, the Mark Hellinger and the Lunt-Fontanne. Lee's subtlety worked best in spaces no larger than the Empire Room, which seated four hundred. The management treated her like a queen. One of the most sumptuous suites in the Waldorf Towers, 37F—the one favored by Baron Hilton, the son of Waldorf owner Conrad Hilton—would be hers throughout each run. At Lee's insistence, the Empire Room even halted food and drink service during the show.

On the night of Monday, April 7, a black-tie crowd waited for Peggy Lee to take the stage there for the first time. Just before the overture, Lee rode the freight elevator downstairs, which became her nightly ritual. Her friend Doak Roberts often accompanied her. "I helped hold up her gown as she got into elevator, which had about three inches of rotting food on the floor. The elevator starts going down, and she looks at me and says, 'This is glamour!'"

Yet Lee strolled across the lobby like a queen, then slipped inside a hidden cubicle to the left of the Empire Room stage. From the piano, Lou Levy raised his arm, and the orchestra began a pulsing Afro-Cuban overture. As it burst into a drum fanfare, he voiced the magic words: "*Ladies and gentlemen, Miss Peggy Lee!*"

Levy struck the downbeat, and out she bounded, smiling broadly with hands held wide in an earth-mother embrace. The hourglass figure of her Basin Street East days had swelled to Zaftig proportions; Lee had poured it into a voluminous white beaded dress with balloon sleeves. Blond ringlets dangled from a hairdo as high and swirled as a wedding cake. "What a day this has been, what a rare mood I'm in / Why, it's almost like being in love!" caroled Lee—a mother angel in whose arms everyone felt safe. For the next hour she showed them a mature, glowing, but melancholy woman who had spent a lifetime in the romantic trenches, and seemed to know everything about love, sex, and the agony of watching them flee. Now here she was, still ready to "break out the booze and have a ball."

Stereo Review's Peter Reilly saw the stagecraft behind the enchantment. "She wings into view all of a piece, rather like a fully dressed set on a turntable stage, and remains all but stationary throughout. The lighting complexities alone would do credit to the Hayden Planetarium, and all the rest runs with the chill, glittering efficiency of a sequined computer. . . . She operates out of a self-created world, and to get the dramatic effects she wants she must control it absolutely."

Yet at the core was a humanity that touched Sidney Myer's heart. "So many things at the time were loud and assaulting, but there was something soothing about her voice and her sensitivity. A lot of the other lady singers then, Barbra Streisand, Ethel Merman, Eydie Gormé—watch out! They sang the house down. It was fabulous. But Peggy Lee had this quality that compelled you to focus. You didn't want to miss a thing."

Lee kept finding new ways to manipulate reality. Hidden inside the piano were battery-operated fans. Flicked on before the show, they made the wisps of hair around her face flutter. If she looked as big as a gospel singer, she would use it to sexy effect. During the rousing refrain of "A Natural Woman"—"*You make me feel . . . you make me feel . . .*"—Lee hiked up her gown at the thighs and whipped it back and forth.

The Waldorf audience may have cringed when their children played the hit version of "Spinning Wheel" by Blood, Sweat and Tears. When Peggy Lee sang it, however, she swept the crowd along in the promise that life goes on, whatever the cost. "Let it ride! Let it ride!" she exclaimed, and the funky organ and rock drumming didn't seem to offend them in the slightest. But failed romance was still the main theme of her show. In Jimmy Webb's "Didn't We," Lee murmured dejectedly about one more love that had "almost" worked out. Each time she reached that word, she took a pained pause—"This time we *almost* . . . made the pieces fit . . . This time we *almost* . . . made some sense of it."

Her fans had not heard "Is That All There Is?" until that night. Lee gave it one of her vague, breathy intros: "So many things today are . . . wonderful little stories, and little dramas. And here is one by Leiber and Stoller." The song mesmerized journalist Albert Goldman. She performed it "with open yet unseeing eyes," he wrote, "staring out into the glare of an arc lamp like a somnambulist and then suddenly awakening from each spectral memory to ask naïvely, 'Is that all there is?' She followed it by answering her own question with the alcoholic bravado of a Reno divorcée—'Let's break out the booze and have a ball!'"

At the end, following several encores, the show-me clientele rose to its feet. Days later, the new issue of *Variety* arrived in Lee's suite. A critic had extolled her for her open-minded acceptance of "today's trends" and young composers. He added: "In virtually all departments, Miss Lee is the consummate singer."

Her stock was rising. Lee's singular art in creating a show—specifically her approaching turn in Las Vegas—would soon be immortalized in a documentary for WNET. The idea had come from David S. Prowitt, a young staff producer who hosted science shows. Prowitt had assembled a weighty team. Producer Robert Foshko was the Emmy-nominated head of cultural programming at KCET, the network's West Coast chapter. Nick Cominos had directed a string of historical and nature specials. Cameraman John Alonzo would later earn Oscar nominations for *Chinatown* and *Scarface*.

Mindful of the privacy of the high-rollers and mobster types who occupied prime tables, the International Hotel would only allow cameras backstage and at rehearsal. Foshko opted to mount and film a preview performance of the show at the Mark Taper Forum in downtown Los Angeles.

The first half of *Miss Peggy Lee* shows the star and her retinue at work on Tower Grove Drive. Foshko and crew captured a bustling swirl of activity, all orchestrated by Lee. She had asked Betty Jungheim to scurry around and play the role of secretary; one more had just quit. On camera, Virginia Bernard, in servant's white garb, pulls dresses and shoes for Lee to consider. A butler lugs out suitcase after suitcase in preparation for the Vegas trip. In the living room, goateed Johnny Mandel pores over a score. Mundell Lowe, Lee's newly appointed "music coordinator," makes comments in his calm southern drawl. Arranger Dick Hazard is there too, wearing a 1950s hipster getup of dark glasses, buzzed crewcut, and a pirate's pointy mustache. The perpetually cool Lou Levy plays piano.

Cast and crew move into the Yellow Room for a rehearsal. There sits Lee, a fiftyish woman in the guise of a Raggedy Ann doll. A long yellow fall hangs down on either side of her face, tied with thick pink yarn; her lavender, yellow, and white print pajamas look like a child's bedroom wallpaper. Lee had painted on her big trademark lips with peach lipstick; giant false eyelashes wave like fans as she blinks.

Cecil Smith, a veteran writer for the *Los Angeles Times*, is shown in deep discussion with the singer. "Peggy," he says, glancing at his pad, "you've gone through era after era and change after change in music and have always emerged at the tops of the waves . . . How do you do it?"

Lee mumbles a disjointed response. "I think it's keeping a constant interest in what's going on . . . But even now with the new trends of music . . . the component parts of it are really not new . . . well, they are different to the extent that they're put together in, uh . . . a new way . . . It's as though they've taken some of the old and then embellished that . . ."

But when it comes time to rehearse, her concentration sharpens as she and her rhythm section patiently work out dramatic and musical nuances. "Is That All There Is?," explains Lee, "has a very Kurt Weill-ish kind of feeling. It's really just the bass, drum, and the sock cymbal. Very strict. It's what we might have thought of before as funny, but it isn't . . . now. You know what I mean? This is a very . . . *serious* song."

Then comes a rehearsal with orchestra. After running through a new Johnny Mandel ballad, "I Never Told You," Lee glances at Levy. The arrangement isn't pleasing her. "I think we should take five and discuss it," she says with a steely calm. "Since there is such a difference in the way *I* feel about the interpretation and what is written there . . . then, we have a problem." This arrangement, Lee says, lacks the "tender, sweet quality" she wants. "It's lovely but it's . . . spooky. As an instrumental it's beautiful, but it doesn't allow me to say what *I* feel the lyric is saying."

Cut to Las Vegas in the forty-eight hours before opening night. A cameraman sweeps down the strip in a moving car, driving past the International's huge sign. It reads:

CASINO THEATRE

MISS PEGGY LEE

As the vehicle passes, the camera catches a glimpse of what's on the other side: the single name "Barbra," in fancier type.

Inside the Casino Theatre, all is chaos. Stagehands and carpenters bolt around, carrying hammers and dragging wood; technicians precariously climb tall, skinny ladders. The second-floor pool is leaking into the gambling area, causing further mayhem. Hugo Granata barks out commands in his tough-guy voice: "Get the houseman in and get him to have that stage cleared! She will never, *never* open!"

Granata had underestimated Lee. As she and the orchestra rehearse

"Brother Love's Traveling Salvation Show," Neil Diamond's new gospel-style hit about a traveling evangelist, the singer maintains an unearthly cool. "Peggy was the eye of the hurricane wherever we were," recalled Robert Foshko. "She had a way of controlling things quietly without being unpleasant about it, even off-camera."

Executive producer David Prowitt had left most of the creative choices to Foshko. But from the start of the project he had held private meetings with Lee at her home. At thirty-five, Prowitt looked like a clean-cut college professor; he had short, wavy hair and, like Lee, an air of unshakable calm. But he was a superachiever. By the age of twenty he had worked for the *Chicago Sun-Times* and ABC News; then he developed *Spectrum*, a WNET science series in which he played the onscreen role of a story investigator. According to the *Los Angeles Times*, Prowitt had "planned for five years to do a definitive study of Peggy Lee."

Behind his half-smile was a man of secrets. He told Peter Levinson that, apart from his hectic TV career, he also did "government work." Prowitt offered no details, but later he moved to Washington, D.C., ostensibly to become Bureau Chief for the station's local program division. Lee "got it in her head," said Lou Levy, that Prowitt worked for the CIA; no one knew if he had really told her that or if she had imagined it. She shared the provocative news flash with Betty Jungheim. "You're not to tell a soul!" said Lee in an excited schoolgirl tone.

Jungheim knew, as did Lee's other close friends, that she and Prowitt had begun an affair. The singer couldn't contain her joy. Just when she had given up hope of ever finding another man to love her, along came Prowitt—young, handsome, intellectual, and successful. She boasted about him to all her friends, while letting it "slip" to a reporter that she and a certain TV producer were an item. "She was just nuts about him," said Jungheim. "Oh God, this was the romance of the century."

But her excitement gave way to frustration, as Prowitt disappeared frequently to parts unknown. Lee left scores of messages for him at his office; sometimes he called back, often not. His elusiveness kept her on the brink of despair. But onstage or off, Lee craved drama, and Prowitt supplied it. He was a conquest, and Lee vowed to win.

A comparable challenge awaited her in Las Vegas. Many in her circle, not to mention Lee herself, feared that the extravagantly hyped Streisand engagement—"the toughest ticket in town," as one newspaper called it—would thrust Lee into the shadows. No one had foreseen the wave of anti-Streisand sentiment that stirred up before opening. The young diva was notoriously uncooperative with the press, and that summer they wreaked revenge. "For lack of anything better to do," wrote columnist Norma Lee Browning, "La Streisand hiked up to Vegas a week early and has been tooting around town in 95-degree heat with her mink hat and bubble gum. My Gamblersville spy tells me she was popping her gum so noisily at Dean Martin's Riviera show that nobody within chomping distance could hear a note."

Much of her fabled arrogance bespoke the insecurity of a superstar who seemed terrified about living up to her own myth. And on her opening night of July 2, Streisand misfired. In an attempted joke about the much-publicized million dollars she would earn for a month's work,

From the WNET documentary *Miss Peggy Lee*, 1969.

Streisand opened with "I Got Plenty o' Nuttin'" from *Porgy and Bess*. The crowd wasn't amused. From then on, Streisand felt a mounting wave of impatience; she responded by growing more and more aloof.

The critics, especially Charles Champlin of the *Los Angeles Times*, came down on her hard. Champlin deemed her "curious, cold and intensely disappointing"; her show, he wrote, was "too long," her patter "self-conscious and unmoving." Streisand struck him as a "dazzlingly efficient and invaluable but chillingly impersonal machine . . . who still, it turns out, has some lessons to learn."

When the concert ended, many of her viewers headed to the Casino Theatre. Streisand's missteps had predisposed the critics to love Lee, who exuded humility and warmth. *Cue's* reviewer wrote a love letter. "The acclaim a glossy first-night audience withheld from [Streisand] it lavished extravagantly on Peggy Lee, giving her a moist-eyed, table-pounding, triple-standing-ovation send-off she could never forget." Champlin chimed in. Lee, he wrote, had "suffused the room with love and good cheer. We gave her the roaring, whooping, standing ovation which we had hoped, I think, to be able to give Miss Streisand." For John Hallowell of the *New York Times*, "the old pro clobbered the new. Miss Lee walked off with the night. . . . Streisand is a novice beside her."

The next day, Streisand rushed to revamp her act. It worked: she won over the critics, and packed the Show Room International for the rest of her run. Lee, however, wound up sabotaging herself. Still wracked by competitiveness and jealousy, she began making demands. In one of them, she ordered the hotel to print tent cards advertising her show and to place them in every room—*and* in the space where Streisand performed. Told that this wasn't in her contract, Lee demanded it anyway. Streisand ordered the removal of the cards. The hotel complied, and Lee began a war. "But if you were the management, of course you were going to go with Streisand," said Brian Panella. "Peggy—screw her. Let's get rid of her."

They did. That engagement, which had begun in triumph, was Peggy Lee's last at the International.

The recording she saw as her lifeline stayed captive in a box. Lee kept badgering Capitol's executives to release "Is That All There Is?"; Peter Levinson, too, stayed on the case, but he got nowhere. "Is That All There

Is?" was unreleasable, they said, because it was "too long." Moreover, the record was mostly talk, set to odd music and sure to depress listeners. Who would buy it?

Levinson didn't accept their excuses. Commercial pop had never seemed more experimental, nor steeped in doom, as it was in the late sixties, and a young public's ears were wide open. In 1967, Capitol had issued "Ode to Billie Joe," country singer Bobbie Gentry's Southern Gothic tale of suicide in Mississippi. Just seven seconds shorter than "Is That All There Is?," the record had reached number one. Soon after that, actor Richard Harris had filled two sides of a single with "MacArthur Park," Jimmy Webb's lushly romantic elegy for lost love. That disc had hit number two. In 1969, the Rolling Stones released their milestone album *Let It Bleed*, a violent portrait of what Mick Jagger termed the "apocalypse" of late-sixties life. Elvis Presley's single "In the Ghetto" dealt with the endless circle of American poverty and crime; it stunned RCA by making the top ten.

The nihilism in Lee's record sounded far gentler and prettier. Still, Capitol wouldn't budge. As Mike Stoller told writer Franklin Bruno, the label deemed it "some kind of weird, uncommercial shit." Randy Newman doubted it would ever come out. "It was unlike anything, ever," he said, "and things like that are not the common hits."

In August, a new change at Capitol Records indicated an almost certain end to Lee's dream. Stanley Gortikov had been fired as president and moved over to Capitol Industries. His replacement was Sal Iannucci, the former vice president of business affairs at CBS. Even more than Gortikov, Iannucci flaunted a philosophy of out-with-the-old, in-with-the-new. "The principal thrust of this company," he announced, "must be the idea of new artist development."

That "sullen, cold-steel attitude," as Dave Dexter perceived it, seemed like a death knell for the company's few long-term survivors, including Peggy Lee. But as the last summer of the 1960s wound down, Lee figured out how to get her way. An invitation had come from *The Joey Bishop Show*, a much-pitied television flop. ABC had thought that Bishop—the Rat Pack's nasal, testy jokester—could compete with *Tonight* show host Johnny Carson, the king of late-night TV. Carson pummeled him in the ratings, and *The Joey Bishop Show* didn't last out the decade.

Back in 1955, Bishop had made his Las Vegas debut as the warmup act for Peggy Lee. He had loved her ever since. Capitol was courting him to book some of its new young acts. He agreed to feature them—*if* he could have Peggy Lee. When his request reached her, Lee saw possibilities. She said yes to Bishop—but only if he would let her perform "Is That All There Is?" Of course, she could.

Lee told Peter Levinson to inform Capitol that on August 21, 1969, she would introduce the song on network television. They *had* to release it first. Weak as Bishop's ratings were, Capitol caved in. A meager fifteen hundred copies of "Is That All There Is?" were pressed—barely enough to take it to the bottom of *Billboard*'s Adult Contemporary chart. The B-side was "Me and My Shadow," a song everyone knew. But people had never heard that hammy 1920s tearjerker performed like this. Lee breathed its sad-sack lines—"me and my shadow, strolling down the avenue"—over a wry one-finger piano line, a nearly silent bass, and the gentle rubbing of sandblocks, which shuffled like footsteps in the dark. Mundell Lowe had arranged it for her, and this track, too, seemed destined to bomb.

That month, Peggy Lee could not have seemed less relevant. All attention turned to two galvanizing social events that defined the polar extremes of the 1960s. From August 15–18, a small town in upstate New York hosted the Woodstock Music & Art Fair, an outdoor festival. It united dozens of rock and folk's most searing voices—and three- to four-hundred-thousand music fans—in what Jon Pareles of the *New York Times* called "a moment of muddy, disheveled, incredulous grace," all of it about "making love, not war." Not even that grand oasis, however, could banish the sting of the bloodbath that had occurred days earlier, when Charles Manson's cult "family" had savagely murdered seven people in two Los Angeles homes. The nation was left reeling.

On the night of Lee's Bishop appearance, the normally acidic host introduced her as "one of the greatest performers of the era." He read a series of critical raves that extolled her as one of the business's great long-distance runners, and one who still mattered. "Ladies and gentlemen, Miss Peggy Lee!" he announced. The camera cut to the overweight, fussily gowned and coiffed, forty-nine-year-old singer. First she plugged her album *A Natural Woman* by singing the title tune. The song was considered Aretha Franklin's property; Lee's version surely struck many listeners as an aging songstress trying to "get with it."

After the applause, a pianist played the childlike introduction to "Is That All There Is?" Lee sounded nervous. Then anger crept into her voice. It might have come from her resentment of Capitol's new guard, who had treated her as worthless, then forced her to connive in order to get a puny release of the best song she had found in years. Singing "Let's break out the booze and have a ball," she spat out the last word sarcastically. "I'm not ready for that final disappointment!" emerged as a battle cry. No matter what, Peggy Lee would not be cast aside.

When she sat on the panel, neither Lee nor Bishop said a word about the song. Instead, he segued into safe nostalgia when a film projector rolled "The Siamese Cat Song" from *Lady and the Tramp*. He and Lee followed it with benign small talk about Disney and the old days at the Sands.

The next morning, viewers woke up to more headlines about the spectacularly violent end of the 1960s. The Vietnam War's American casualties had passed thirty-five thousand; and for all the strides made by the civil rights movement, its key leaders had gotten snuffed out, one after another.

Peggy Lee's "weird" little song, which questioned the meaning of life and the future, struck a chord. After the show, said Mike Stoller, "the phones at ABC rang off the wall." Enough viewers rushed to their record stores to wipe out the single's first pressing and force another. Few DJs had received advance copies, but over the next two weeks, "Is That All There Is?"—all four minutes and twenty-two seconds of it—began to appear on the radio. On September 27, the disc debuted on the *Billboard* charts and began a slow climb. By October 18, it was number one on *Billboard*'s Adult Contemporary chart. On November 8, it peaked at number eleven in the Hot 100. The artists in the top ten included the 5th Dimension ("Wedding Bell Blues"), the Beatles ("Come Together"), Elvis Presley ("Suspicious Minds"), and the Temptations ("I Can't Get Next to You"). Beyond her wildest dreams, Lee had won.

Some youngsters, like the future *New York Times* writer Rob Hoerburger, hadn't a clue what this "old woman" was doing on AM radio with this "gin-and-irony-soaked midlife crisis set to an oompah beat. Our parents loved it but to us it was aural castor oil." But Sidney Myer understood.

"I think most people my age had thought that she was just this middle-aged pop singer from the same conveyor belt that had brought them Patti Page, Connie Francis—singers who had nothing to say to them. Then suddenly came this song that was so odd and offputting, sung by a woman who was not Joni Mitchell or Judy Collins. There was nothing Easy Listening about this song! It hit people in so many ways. People were writing editorials about it, and having these fierce debates about what it meant. This wasn't just a song on the pop charts. It was a headline."

The success of "Is That All There Is?" struck its authors as miraculous. "Maybe the world needed some kind of thoughtful piece of material to ponder through all that noise," reflected Jerry Leiber. Their "extremely pessimistic idea for a pop song" transfixed the playwright Neil Simon. "No matter what she finds in life, it's not good enough," he said. "Which at times I think we all think about, in our disappointment."

Brian Panella felt sure the single could have done even better, had Capitol not fallen short on the job. "They still refused to believe in it while it was happening. They were a day late and a dollar short in getting the product into the field."

Even so, Lee was gaining attention that her label had never anticipated. In another unlikely coup, she wound up alongside Stevie Wonder on Dick Clark's *American Bandstand*, the weekly cavalcade of jukebox hits, whose teenage fans, assembled on a dance floor, judged a new tune by whether it had a "good beat" and you could "dance to it." Now a woman older than most of their mothers was standing before them and singing one of the strangest songs they had ever heard.

If "Is That All There Is?" spoke to them in some abstruse way, the song's themes of disillusionment and death gave her older fans a jolt. It startled Lee to read tabloid allegations of suicides it had inspired. On the NBC radio series *Monitor*, Jack Eigen confronted her about her record's true intentions. "Some people think that it's a big putdown of life, that it reflects a feeling of utter futility," he stated. "Many people are a little concerned, because you say, 'Is that all there is? Well, let's have some booze and have a ball.' In other words you are trying to say, the only way to have fun is to escape with booze."

"No!" maintained Lee. "If it were really that negative, I couldn't sing it. . . . It's more like saying that life is a comedy—or a tragedy. I was singing about—you show me all these things, and if love finds me worthy, there's more. It's *not* all there is!"

But the poet and psychologist Paul Pines saw little hope in the song, or in Peggy Lee. "When you've reached a certain age, images, fantasies, things that were protective, that were your survival strategy, just crumble. You look out at the landscape naked. 'I thought I would die but I didn't'—I think that explains the whole story. Children who suffer deep trauma, like Peggy did, remain in fearsome, unconscious pursuit of that same feeling of total emptiness. 'Is That All There Is?' to me can be read as the recognition of being trapped in a pattern to which there is no exit."

Mike Stoller disagreed. To him, Leiber's sentiments were "very liberating. Hey—if that's it, then let's have a good time." Panella, too, chose to accept Lee's philosophy. "When she went to the chorus she had a smile on her face that said, 'Let's go get 'em baby. Let's keep dancing.'"

———

WITH "IS THAT ALL There Is?" scaling the charts, *Miss Peggy Lee* premiered on public TV to raves. It won her newfound respect for her painstaking craftsmanship. Professionally, Lee had gotten everything she wanted. She *wasn't* a has-been.

But one crucial thing was missing. "In the life of Peggy Lee there always has to be a man," wrote John Hallowell in the *New York Times*. "Past love or present, good or bad, flirtation or for real, a man is there and she sings to him." In the preceding months, Lee had convinced herself that David Prowitt truly loved her. She had last seen him at a screening of the documentary. The next day she phoned him. He wasn't there. She left a message. He didn't respond. "She kept calling him and calling him," said Betty Jungheim. A week passed, then another. Still nothing. "He was gone," recalled Kathy Mahana. "He disappeared off the face of the map."

Soon thereafter, she dropped by the house and walked into Lee's bedroom. She found her friend in bed staring at the ceiling, "paralyzed with emotional pain." Mahana had never seen her in such anguish. Sometime later, Lee saw Prowitt's picture in one of the tabloids. "He was escorting Beverly Sills," said Mahana.

To Brian Panella, the Prowitt affair "may have been her last shot at opening herself up to a real solid relationship. I don't think she ever got over him." Nearly twenty-five years later, she mythologized Prowitt namelessly in a song, "Flowers and Flowers," that she wrote with composer Paul Horner for her one-woman Broadway show, *Peg*. "His eyes were gray / Oh, how he thrilled me / He belonged to the CIA / It nearly killed me."

For Lee, "Is That All There Is?" was growing ever truer. Her latest white knight had gone, and she wanted to die, but she didn't. And her renewed fame seemed hollow.

Having begun the decade as the sparkling, energetic First Lady of Basin Street East, Lee was ending it in a sea of depression. Songs about desertion increasingly defined her shows. Onstage, much of the life seemed drained out of her, and heartache wasn't the only cause. In the wake of Prowitt's exit, Lee found solace in Valium, the prescription tranquilizer that had become the American housewife's best friend. It made its debut in 1963, and by 1969 it topped the list of favorite pharmaceutical drugs. Valium's effect of slowing the neurological system made it a popular treatment for nervousness and insomnia, both of which Lee suffered from. It was also useful for easing the symptoms of alcohol withdrawal, which came in handy as she tried to phase out drinking. Valium was highly addictive—but for Lee, excess was a way of life, and she began taking far too much. "Peggy Lee, I used to say to people, is like this," explained Bruce Vanderhoff. "If one aspirin will fix your headache, take ten. It'll go away ten times faster."

The drug's effects are obvious in a 1970 appearance on *The Dean Martin Show*. In both a surging arrangement of "Almost Like Being in Love" and a snail's-pace "Watch What Happens," Lee behaves the same. Her eyes blink in half time; otherwise her face doesn't move. Her head swivels in slow-motion, and her once briskly animated hands hang down lifelessly. The long blond fall, curled at the ends, and the near-frozen face and body begged unwanted comparisons to the septuagenarian Mae West. Vocally, Lee's rhythm was still secure, and always would be; but to some of her musicians, a spark was flickering out.

Recently Lee had shared a whole installment of the NBC series *Kraft Music Hall* with Johnny Cash, country music's fabled "Man in Black." America loved Cash, a tall, rugged outlaw from Arkansas with huge shoulders, thick dark hair, and weary eyes that had seen too much. His brother had died at fifteen after a saw at the mill where he worked nearly sliced him in two. Amphetamine and barbiturate addiction plagued the singer, who was jailed seven times, mostly on drug-related charges. He went temporarily clean in 1968, when he was thirty-six. Then he attempted suicide.

Cash poured it all into his songs, which spoke empathetically of the lost and downtrodden. His craggy bass-baritone had a permanent ache; it was an utterly human sound, strong but with a vulnerable quaver. It made him the perfect counterpart for Peggy Lee.

She concealed her now-shapeless figure with a free-hanging, black coat-style dress, brought somewhat to life by sparkly trim down the front and on the cuffs. On the show, a trio of Peggy Lees perform "Is That All There Is?"—first the real Lee, then two projected ones, who appear on-screen like ghosts to sing the subsequent choruses. It was an eerie depiction of a woman known for her multiple personalities.

Later on, Lee and her fellow lonesome traveler present a medley of somber story-songs, staged on a set that evokes a bare, snow-covered forest. As they lock eyes, powerful chemistry bonds the stars—one an icon of embattled masculinity, the other a wounded woman who could easily melt in his arms. Lee and Cash trade folksy ballads—the lazy waltz, "Down in the Valley"; a farm couple's epic love story, "Kisses Sweeter Than Wine." Leiber and Stoller had written Lee a new song, "Whistle for Happiness," one of several attempted follow-ups to "Is That All There Is?" It opens with the slow beating of a marching drum, then expresses a tear-stained resolve to soldier on: "Whistle for happiness, and it will come / Crowned with a gaily-colored plume." Cash followed with the young poet and song-writer Rod McKuen's "Love's Been Good to Me": "I have been a rover, I have walked alone / Hiked a hundred highways, never found a home."

In her most arresting moment, Lee sings the lament of a Civil War–era maiden whose young man has been called to war. Inanimate as a statue, she intones soberly: "I must not doubt and I must not cry / My Johnny will come marching home." Hope falters and her eyes flash with terror; then she hears "the familiar sounds of familiar feet," and Johnny is hers once more.

Lee still dreamed that Prowitt might march back into her life, but he never did. Johnny Cash, however, had found what proved to be enduring love in his second marriage, to the singer June Carter. The couple invited Lee and Brian Panella to dinner at their lakefront home outside of Nashville. To Panella, the Cashes were "the most gracious, kind, supportive human beings you could ever ask for." Their baby, John, was an infant in his crib; Lee gazed at him, spellbound. Throughout dinner, Cash and Carter regaled them with stories about their lives and their courtship. "They talked about their love for each other, and you could feel it," said Panella. Lee nodded wistfully. Such a relationship seemed far beyond her now; all she could do was to "keep dancing," alone.

"She had two sides. There was the little girl you wanted to protect, and the tough-as-nails lady who could destroy you with a few words." (HEATHROW AIRPORT, LONDON, JUNE 15, 1970; COURTESY OF RICHARD MORRISON)

Chapter Thirteen

$\mathcal{F}$OR PEGGY LEE, the 1970s began with staggering news. "Is That All There Is?" had been nominated for three Grammy Awards: Record of the Year, Best Performance by a Female Vocalist on a Contemporary Record, and Best Arrangement Accompanying Vocalist(s). Lee's choice of Randy Newman had resulted in the young underdog's first nomination. Lee had earned eight, but never won—and now the industry had stamped the forty-nine-year-old singer "contemporary."

Journalists applauded her endurance. Benny Goodman had launched her nearly three decades ago; since then, most of her peers had descended into obscurity or camp. But John Hallowell compared Lee to "an obstinate volcano that won't be declared obsolete." His all-night interview at her home led him to a shrewd conclusion. "Those who can survive and go the distance in this most precarious, destructive business are usually like Katharine Hepburn or Angela Lansbury: strong, disciplined, healthy, temperate. Not Peggy Lee. I have never met a survivor who lives so close to the wire."

Lee's frail lungs sucked in oxygen from a tank along with a noxious fog of cigarette smoke. She ate rich food, didn't exercise, and was now addicted to tranquilizers. Hallowell could only guess at how much pain she was carrying. Lee confided in more than one friend her certainty that no man would ever love her again; it was too late.

Still, new doors kept opening. In February 1970, she accepted a request to perform at a White House state dinner in a mere six days. Richard M. Nixon was welcoming Georges Pompidou, president of the French Republic, and his wife on their first visit to the U.S. Traditionally those dinners closed with a dinner show by some beloved all-American entertainer; recent ones had featured Bob Hope and Pearl Bailey. According to a press release, Peggy Lee was chosen for the Pompidou night "because she is rather like the French entertainers."

In truth, the White House was desperate. Several artists had turned the offer down in protest of France's anti-Semitic responses to the Arab-Israeli conflict in the Middle East. France had supplied Arab countries with its new Mirage jet fighters while neglecting to send any to Israel, which had bought and paid for a fleet of them. Demonstrations against France were breaking out in American cities.

None of that concerned Peggy Lee. "One of the reasons I was asked to sing was because I'm a non-political, non-prejudiced person," she explained, and she meant it; close friends didn't even know if she voted. For Lee, the prestige of the invitation trumped all. She would perform for about forty minutes in the East Room, whose high ceiling, gold silk draperies, and teardrop chandeliers recalled the supper clubs where she performed. The one hundred and ten guests at that white-tie function would include Nixon administration officials (among them Henry Kissinger, the National Security Advisor), the president's family, and French and local journalists.

Allowed only a minimal entourage, Lee hurriedly phoned a few of her core musicians—Lou Levy, Mundell Lowe, Grady Tate—and Peter Levinson. On February 24, 1970, all of them passed through the White House's stringent security check, then strode down the red-and-gold carpet of the Entrance Hall. The Nixons greeted Lee, but there wasn't time for socializing.

After a rehearsal, Lee retired to her private quarters. She studied the French words to "La Vie en Rose," her salute to the Pompidous, and sipped cognac to ease her flaring nerves. Hours later, it was showtime. Guests had moved into the East Room and taken their seats; the band was assembling on a riser. Levinson stood in the back, waiting for Lee. He hadn't seen her since that afternoon, and he shuddered when a musician told him: "You're not gonna believe how much cognac she drank."

In walked the Nixons and the Pompidous to a standing ovation. They sat in the front row. Nixon stepped onstage for the introduction. Peggy Lee, he explained, had come from the heartlands of the U.S. and gone on to reach the "pinnacle of success," just like President Pompidou. For that reason, he noted, she was the "most interesting and, shall we say, relaxing" choice possible to entertain such distinguished visitors.

With that, Nixon introduced "*Miss* Peggy Lee." To a grand orchestral fanfare, she swept onstage in her most tasteful outfit, a high-necked, long-sleeved, black silk chiffon gown and a strand of pearls. During the first few songs, Lee sounded a bit breathless and frail, and she clung to the piano. Almost any observer would have chalked it up to nerves.

But at the seventeen-minute mark, the alcohol suddenly hit her, and the bewildered guests found themselves facing an obviously drunken star. In a slurred, dragging voice, Lee halted the show and began reciting snippets of favorite poems, including one by Princess Grace. Then she turned inappropriately risqué. "I'm very fond of poetry . . . among *other* things," Lee groaned in her best Mae West voice. After a wobbly effort at "Is That All There Is?," Lee switched to another non sequitur. "You've all been to Disneyland, I presume," she slurred. Lee had forgotten that the Pompidous were French and in the States for the first time. The room went silent. "No? Well—you *must* go. *I'm* going to be *Tinkerbell* one day! Don't you know what Tinkerbell does? She *hits* that peanut-butter jar and she flies over the Matterhorn. I think she's about seventy-five . . . Now, she does something magic, because she turns the lights on. Now you will see, I do *somethinnnng different*! I turn them all *off*!"

That was the cue for a blackout, and a pinspot on her snapping fingers as she began "Fever." During the song, she slipped into a Brooklyn accent that surely left the Pompidous clueless. "Yay, I *boin*! I boin? I burn? What's with that, doth burn, doth boin? Ooh, look out for the Indians!"

All this was typical Peggy Lee humor, the kind that amused tipsy friends at her parties. Tonight, however, Levinson watched in horror as embarrassed glances and whispers were exchanged. The Nixons maintained frozen smiles; the Pompidous looked confused. Lou Levy noodled at the piano, powerless to get Lee on track. Mundell Lowe stared down at his guitar, cringing. "I was thinking, you shouldn't do that, Peg. You shouldn't do it."

But Lee was just beginning. Now she addressed Nixon. "I had a pet chicken, Mr. President. I thought it was an Irish setter. But it was a Rhode Island Red. I fed that chicken gravel, promised it wheat, did everything. It went the way of all chickens. Don't blame me, I was only four years old. I was a terrible cook!" She lapsed into doggerel Shakespeare, switched to baby talk, then began to wheeze out the words to "Yes Sir, That's My Baby." By now, few people were even clapping politely.

She turned to Pompidou. "Do I have your permission, Mr. President, in my very bad French?" He just stared. "Do I? I'm gonna try." She managed a few muddled phrases of "La Vie en Rose," then gave up. "She knew she was bombing," recalled Levinson. And still Lee wouldn't give up. "Well, I've written a very short number for just such an occasion, to break a mood like this. Will you *pleeease* sing along with me?" She murmured an original couplet she thought was hilarious:

I don't know just what it was
But as long as it's gone it's all right!

From the back, a White House representative tried to signal her to stop. Finally Lee introduced her closing ode to worldwide brotherhood, "Here's to You." Her greetings in multiple languages—"*Ciao! Viva! Pace! Salute!*"—emerged in a near-catatonic drone. The band played her exit music, and Lee stepped off the platform to strained applause. She walked over to the Nixons and Pompidous. Lee had been instructed that presidents should not be touched unless they extended their hands. Lee bent forward and kissed Nixon on the cheek. Pompidou graciously kissed her hand.

Levinson had seen reporters scribbling in their notebooks, and he braced himself for the worst. It came. A French journalist called the show "a disaster." To *Washington Star* columnist Betty Beale, Lee's performance "was in such bad taste that it should convince the Nixons never to have a nightclub performer [sing] for a visiting chief of state." No one called Lee drunk, but Vera Glaser, one of the city's toughest reporters, scolded the star for her "sexy routines," adding: "The buxom, blond Miss Lee went over like a lead balloon."

White House spokesperson Connie Stewart tried to smooth things over in a statement: "We made a special effort to give the Pompidous a warm reception and Peggy was part of that warm reception. Everybody enjoyed her." Lee attempted her own repair work. Speaking to Judy Klemesrud of the *New York Times*, she declared the stories about her debacle to be "totally inaccurate." Defensively she added: "If I'm sexy, I can't help it. Mrs. Nixon gave me a warm embrace and I returned it. I would *never* kiss the President. I just leaned forward as he spoke to me, and it may have looked like it, but I didn't kiss him."

No amount of denial, however, could alter the truth. In front of world leaders and dignitaries, Lee had sabotaged herself, just as she had at the 1955 Warner Bros. party that had probably sealed the end of her film career. Many years would pass before the White House invited her back.

Lee stayed in a funk for weeks. Depression clouded her excitement over the impending Grammy Awards; in any case, Lee felt sure she would lose. Nevertheless, on the evening of March 11, 1970, she took her seat in the grand ballroom of the Century Plaza Hotel in Los Angeles, and she braced herself for more bad news.

Her heart sank when Blood, Sweat and Tears' "Spinning Wheel" won in the Best Arrangement category, beating out Randy Newman. Much later in the ceremony, singer Della Reese read the nominees for Best Performance by a Female Vocalist on a Contemporary Record. There were five other nominees, none of them older than thirty: Brenda Lee ("Johnny One Time"), Jackie DeShannon ("Put a Little Love in Your Heart"), Dusty Springfield ("Son of a Preacher Man"), Dionne Warwick ("This Girl's in Love with You"), and Vikki Carr ("With Pen in Hand"). Reese tore open the envelope and announced the winner.

"Miss Peggy Lee!"

A roaring ovation rose up as the shocked singer walked toward the podium. Capitol's executives—including some who had wanted to kill "Is That All There Is?"—looked on as Lee took her place between Reese and copresenter Glen Campbell, one of the label's biggest moneymakers. Holding the award as though it might crumble through her fingers, Lee spoke in the calm but candid tone heard on the record.

"I've been so busy thinking about . . ."—she paused—"anything that I could think about, so that I wouldn't think about this night. But I would like to thank Leiber and Stoller for writing the song, I'd like to thank Randy Newman for the arrangement, and I'd like to thank all the musicians who played in it. And I'd like to thank God, and I'd like to thank Capitol for putting it out. I wish I wouldn't get so humbled like this— you'd think I would get over being shy—but it means a great deal to me, and I thank you *very* much."

Record of the Year wasn't announced until May 7, on a televised Grammy special. Lee would lose to the 5th Dimension's version of "Aquarius / Let the Sunshine In," the psychedelic hippie anthem from the musical *Hair*. But it didn't matter. The Grammys had crowned a golden rebirth of her career, and the White House incident seemed forgotten. To Nicki Lee Foster, her mother had once more risen "like the phoenix out of the ashes."

Usually these were the cinders of self-annihilation, though; and even though Lee had once again triumphed, she was so accustomed to turmoil that she seemed lost without it. On March 27, she had returned to Washington, D.C., now a city of depressing memories for her, to play the Blue Room of the Shoreham Hotel. During her run, Lee reported severe laryngitis. She made sure the press knew about her latest affliction and her valiant resolve to press on, as she headed straight to an engagement at the Waldorf. "What a remarkable trouper she is!" marveled columnist Marilyn Beck. She reported that Lee had gone on with the opening despite "stern warnings from doctors."

Both stints drew raves. But as in "Is That All There Is?," everything had begun to seem anticlimactic. A year after their breakup, Lee still pined for David Prowitt. During the Waldorf engagement, Capitol had released her latest album, *Bridge Over Troubled Water*, produced by Phil Wright. The songs cut a wide swath through the best current pop, notably the inspirational title song, a number-one hit for Simon & Garfunkel. But most of the album was a diary of her emotional distress. The titles said it all: "The Thrill Is Gone," "He Used Me," "(There's) Always Something There to Remind Me," "Have You Seen My Baby?" Lee threw in a tearjerker from 1937, "I See Your Face Before Me." Wearily she sang, "I close my eyes and there you are, always."

Bridge Over Troubled Water included a bitter rebuke, "You'll Remember Me," by Stan Worth and Arthur Hamilton. It copied the marching-band rhythm of "Is That All There Is?," but not even Lee could call it a song of hope. "You can tear my heart in half if it makes you laugh," she sang, "but I guarantee, you'll remember me." The number stopped her live shows, but as a single it failed to break *Billboard*'s Hot 100. No record of hers ever would again, even though she milked that circusy sound in such tunes as "Where Did They Go?," a eulogy for "the sweet years, filled with laughter every day"; and "One More Ride on the Merry-Go-Round," Neil Sedaka and Howard Greenfield's whirling French-style waltz about innocence lost.

None of this pseudo-European despair held interest for the youth of the day. America had survived a harrowing decade, and the sun had come out on the pop charts; many hits of the early 1970s—the Carpenters' "We've Only Just Begun," Cass Elliot's "New World Coming," the Beatles' "Let It Be," Ray Stevens's "Everything Is Beautiful," B. J. Thomas's "Raindrops Keep Fallin' on My Head"—spoke of peace and acceptance and new beginnings. "Is That All There Is?," popular as it was, had marked more of an end. And Peggy Lee's record sales returned to their former slump.

On May 26, 1970, Lee celebrated an uneasy milestone—her fiftieth birthday—with one of her last grand house parties. Everyone had to come dressed as a clown. Lee had erected a tent in the garden and filled the swimming pool with balloons. Peanut vendors roamed the crowd while the hostess greeted guests in a pink-and-white, polka-dot suit with dead-white makeup and a white ostrich plume wrapped around her head. "It was so interesting to watch people, because they were not on guard," she said later. "They were hiding behind some façade. They could be anyone they wanted to."

To her British fans, Peggy Lee was still the laid-back sex kitten who had entranced so many of them at Pigalle in 1961. Finally, in the late spring of 1970, they got her back. On June 22, Lee played a concert at the venerable Royal Albert Hall. The space's capacity—5,272—was far too large for a singer of her restraint, but most seats were full, and critics loved her.

During the same trip, Lee thrilled one of her most beloved disciples when she agreed to appear on Petula Clark's ATV special, *Petula*. Its thirty-one-year-old star was a homegrown, wholesome pop sensation who had conquered the charts worldwide. In America, her 1964 number-one single "Downtown" had set off a winning streak of fifteen consecutive hits. Clark's tangy-sweet voice was easy to recognize and utterly likable, though neither sultry nor mysterious; no wonder she named two of pop's great temptresses, Lena Horne and Peggy Lee, as her favorite singers. But it was Lee's "delicate touch" that attracted her the most. "She had that jazz in her life, but she never pushed it," recalled Clark. "There was always something she was holding back, and I found that fascinating—extremely sexy, too. It was never, 'Look what I can do'; it was, 'Yes, I can do that, but I've decided I'm not going to.'"

Clark had never met her idol; now at a TV studio outside London, she reached "that scary moment when you come face-to-face with someone you've adored so long. But she seemed to be just as excited as I was." Near the start of the show, the young star introduced Lee for a duet of "I'm a Woman," rewritten to establish a mutual admiration society. "She was born in North Dakota but you'd never know it from the way she sings!" caroled a euphoric Clark, dressed in white. Then Lee appeared in the distance in her plain black gown and her long blond wig, and stole the show. Seated back-to-back, the women segued into a 5th Dimension hit, "Wedding Bell Blues." Clark was the girl next door; Lee, with her saucy, gleaming eyes, seemed like her deliciously wicked older stepsister. "It was a great moment for both of us," said Clark, "and we *loved* the way we sounded together."

Smiles vanished in Lee's solo. "What Are You Doing the Rest of Your Life?" was Michel Legrand and Alan and Marilyn Bergman's Oscar-nominated ballad from the previous year's *The Happy Ending*. Nearly every singer of Lee's ilk had pounced upon the song, but her presentation was daringly unlike any other. The scene could have come from her affair with Prowitt. Lee sang while sitting up in a brass bed; next to her lay a bare-chested younger man, asleep. Outside the half-lit room, rain poured down the window. Staring wistfully at her motionless swain, she cut through the song's sentimentality—"When you stand before the candle on a cake/Oh, let me be the one to hear the silent wish you make"—as she pleaded with him to never leave her.

Home in Los Angeles, Lee had managed to fill the empty space in her bed. Her new flame was Brian Panella, two decades her junior. Why their business relationship had suddenly blossomed into an affair was hard to fathom. But her manager was in a failing marriage to the mother of his two children, and Lee was feeling especially needy. She convinced him to move in. "I can't say that I fought it so well," he admitted. It was an awkward situation, for Lee's daughter and son-in-law and their three young children lived in the guesthouse.

He stayed only a few months, but the relationship gave Lee a temporary glow, and she continued her golden summer. July 27 found her back in Manhattan, where she and the post–hippie generation had a happy encounter. For the first of three consecutive years, Lee brought her touring show, orchestra and all, to Central Park for the highly popular Schaefer Music Festival. Founded in 1966 by promoters Ron Delsener and Hilly Kristal, it brought a bounty of pop, rock, and jazz stars into the park's outdoor Wollman Skating Rink. For ticket prices of one to three dollars,

New Yorkers could see the likes of Bruce Springsteen, Led Zeppelin, Miles Davis, the Beach Boys, Neil Young, Sly and the Family Stone, Billy Joel, Buddy Rich, and Carmen McRae. Judy Collins performed there twice in the wake of her 1968 top-ten hit, "Both Sides Now." The ethereal folk star loved the festival. "It was so accessible," she said. "It was always packed with people. And it was *very* young. Sometimes it was pouring rain, and everybody had umbrellas, and they didn't leave. You could see people in the other parts of the park listening from the trees, or trying to climb the fence. You could always smell a little grass in the air. It was so sixties."

Lee was one of the oldest stars to play there, and she got a queen's treatment. Most of the shows had double bills, but Delsener gave Lee the whole night. Behind her was a celebrated big band, the Thad Jones–Mel Lewis Orchestra, with a string section added. They sat neatly arranged on a huge, high platform surrounded by scaffolding, and backed by a panorama of trees and apartment buildings. It was a sweltering night, but the musicians wore tuxedoes.

After a rousing Afro-Cuban overture, Lee sailed onstage and kept the energy high with "Come Back to Me." This was her rock-star moment; spread out before her, almost as far as she could see, were about six thousand people in folding chairs or on the grass. Long-haired young men and girls in halter tops were seeing the first Peggy Lee show they could afford. As a tape of the show proves, they screamed for her. Somehow, Lee's nuances traversed the huge space; that alluring setting, combined with near-perfect acoustics, helped create a magical night. The band sounded hot; Lee's voice floated over it. Roaring ovations followed songs as old as "Why Don't You Do Right?" or as current as "Raindrops Keep Fallin' on My Head," as limpid as her Debussy-like arrangement of "Watch What Happens" or as raucous as "Spinning Wheel." Fans yelled out requests and shouted, *WE LOVE YOU!* Lee did encore after encore. She was clearly touched. "I must say I will remember this night always," she said dreamily.

———

IN INTERVIEWS AND PUBLIC appearances and on first meetings, Lee seemed gracious, bashful, and sweet. "She led with that," said playwright William Luce, her future collaborator. Those who knew her better saw what hid behind the mask: a volcanic brew of restlessness, anger, touchiness, fear, and growing eccentricity. "I think a big part of Peggy's makeup was that she was a Gemini," said Robert Strom, her assistant in the 1990s. "She had two sides. There was the little girl you wanted to protect, and the tough-as-nails lady who could destroy you with a few words."

The woman who had grown up feeling so dwarfed by Min sat propped up under a blanket in her bed, ruling her kingdom as imperiously as if she were on a throne. All employees had to address her as Miss Lee. Robert Richards, who would later move in with her to collaborate on a design project, saw her in action. "If Peggy had had a staff of a hundred and fifty people," he said, "she could have kept every one of them on the edge of a nervous breakdown. The thirst for ordering people around, for having people do her bidding, was frightening. She would consume you and have no respect for who you were, what your previous life had been, for your accomplishments. You were just in the service of."

He also saw her flipside. More afraid than ever of being alone, Lee did whatever she could to hold employees after hours. She asked them to meditate with her, to join her for dinner; she told countless jokes and stories. So many secretaries had quit that employment agencies refused to send anyone else. In the past she had transformed family members like Nicki and Marianne into personal assistants; now she had begun asking friends such as Angela Levey, the wife of her former drummer Stan Levey, to work for her. Stan warned Angela that she'd be sorry if she did. But she said yes, with the proviso that she would work from eleven to five and not a minute later. Perhaps resenting Angela's happy home life, Lee ignored that rule from the first day, while drawing her into a web of domestic intrigue. "She played everybody in the house against each other," said Angela. There was no telling what innocent remark might set Lee off, but to bring up age was risky. "*Don't* mention her grandchildren," her publicists warned journalists. Lee insisted that David, Holly, and Michael call her Mama Peggy. "I don't think that was a happy thing for her daughter to hear, because she was their mom," said Brian Panella. "But Nicki would say, 'I'm your mama and she's Mama Peggy.'"

One day Angela asked Lee how old her dog was. The singer turned to steel. "How old are *you*, Angela?" she snapped. "When are *you* gonna die?" Levey just stared at her. "I thought, 'I gotta get out of here.'"

Next Lee called upon Betty Jungheim, her friend for twenty years. Jungheim had grown up in Hollywood and knew showbiz intimately; now a divorced mother of two, she accepted Lee's persistent pleas to work for her. With her blond bouffant hairdo, she could have passed for the singer's prettier, more petite younger sister. She proved as patient and caring as anyone Lee had employed since Dona Harsh.

Now, as a paid assistant, Jungheim witnessed a Lee she had never quite known. "We used to have a lot of laughs together, but there was always tension, because you never knew who was gonna get it that day." The bedroom TV stayed on around the clock. "I don't think she ever really slept," said Jungheim. Nor did the "perfectionist" seem to do much actual work. Sitting amid her bedsheets and pillows, Lee pondered what she wanted for breakfast, lunch, and dinner; maintained her peach-painted, talonlike nails; flipped through her address book and phoned friends to tell them jokes. Often the sheer oddity of her sense of humor was funny in itself. One year Lee spent months telling whoever would listen that male penguins held a female's eggs between their feet for the whole gestation period. She thought this hilarious, and most guests couldn't resist laughing with her.

Over time, Jungheim grew less amused. All day long, Lee kept pressing the buzzer wired to Betty's desk on the other side of the house. Back and forth the secretary walked; often she had just barely left Lee's bedroom when that impatient *BZZZZ-BZZZZ* sounded again. The employee who fared the best was Virginia Bernard, whom Bruce Vanderhoff had nicknamed Ginger. Before a show, Bernard—a small, thin black woman who smoked even more than Lee—trailed behind the star, holding up the hem of her floor-length gowns as she walked to the stage. Like all of Lee's staff, she wound up doing far more than she'd been hired for. But she took none of the star's guff. Bernard stormed out of the house if she didn't like Lee's attitude; the singer had to grovel in order to get her back. One day Lee decided to rest her voice by summoning Bernard with a bell. "Oh, no, honey," came the response. "Don't you be ringin' no bell. That's from back in the slave days!" When Lee tried to keep her past quitting time, Bernard turned on her heel and left. "My kids need me, and they come first!" she said over her shoulder.

Nicki had seldom come first in Lee's life, and as much as they loved each other, there were constant tensions. Just as the singer could never stop pining for her lost mother, so was she an elusive presence in her daughter's life. "I think Nicki always yearned for her mom, because she never really had her," said Dona Harsh. "Peggy always had to be Miss Peggy Lee, which of course kept everyone in money. You had to consider that." The fact that Nicki and her whole family lived in her mother's home didn't seem to have bridged the emotional distance.

By now Dick had switched from performing to TV producing. Motherhood occupied Nicki, but still she yearned for a creative outlet that would make her more than just the daughter of Peggy Lee. She loved to paint, as did her mother, but Nicki was clearly the more talented at it. She specialized in watercolors, and produced a series that depicted heavy-set women. But because Lee was a star, she got the offers. Sylvania, the consumer electronics line, commissioned her to create four oils that they would reproduce in a portfolio as a gift to buyers of their new TVs. Lee's "love" pictures, as she called them, depicted lemons, oranges, and wildflowers. The work was amateur, revealing little grasp of shadow or perspective.

But Nicki forged ahead with her art, as she did with her mother-daughter relationship. Years later she confided in William Luce that while Lee hadn't abused her physically, she had certainly done so emotionally. Such behavior was Lee's legacy from her stepmother. Min had long since retired from her job as depot agent of the tiny Millarton stop on the Midland Continental. She returned to Jamestown, where she occupied her time with church and civic work. On January 14, 1971, Marianne phoned Lee with the news that Min had died. She was seventy-eight. Her son Edwin, his wife, and other Egstrom relatives attended the funeral. Lee did not.

Now that Min had died, Lee railed openly about her to journalists. But venting didn't comfort her. Longing for peace of mind, she plunged into Transcendental Meditation (TM), an international fad thanks to such celebrity followers as the Beatles. Harried American housewives learned about it from afternoon TV talk shows and bought instructional paperbacks from spinning supermarket racks. TM promised "a direct input of ease and order"; all it took was a twice-daily twenty-minute session of repeating a mantra (a symbolic word or phrase) in one's mind. "At some point you transcend," explained Lee to a reporter.

Certain pains in her life, though, were unconquerable. When her guru, Margaret, gave her a mantra, she insisted on another, because the first one reminded her of Min. Lee hoped to draw "ease and order" directly from TM's creator, the Maharishi Mahesh Yogi, to whom stars could gain access. On one occasion, the Maharishi held a ceremony at Lee's house for her and her friends; at another time, she, Nicki, and Betty Jungheim piled into the car to attend his appearance in Santa Barbara. The women stopped for lunch in Malibu, and there Nicki brought up the name of Alice Larsen. Jungheim asked who that was. "Oh, that's the woman who raised me," said Nicki.

With that, said Jungheim, "Peggy pitched a fit. She said, 'I was on the road working!'" She insisted they leave the restaurant; the trip was off. "We didn't talk all the way home. She was furious."

As a child, Lee had deduced Min's weak spots and learned how to twist the knife. Now Nicki, it seemed, had mastered the same skill. One Sunday night at home, she sat her mother in front of the TV to watch Ed Sullivan. His guests included Jim Bailey, the hottest young gender illusionist in the business. Bailey was famed for his evocations of Barbra Streisand, Judy Garland, and Phyllis Diller. Not for him the slapdash impersonations seen in drag bars; Bailey sketched his subjects in such probing detail that he made it to Carnegie Hall. Lee's exaggerated makeup, hair, and dresses certainly had a camp factor, but Bailey was interested in realism, not satire. Sullivan announced him, and out he came as Peggy Lee, singing a medley of her hits. Lee stared in frozen shock. "I was watching," she recalled, "so I thought, surely it wasn't me." After several silent moments, she finally spoke. "I think I've died," she said. She left the room.

Lee told writer Shaun Considine that her phone kept ringing during the show. "Friends were calling to say, 'You're on Ed Sullivan and you look awful. What happened to you? You look embalmed.'" Bailey's appearance, it seemed, had served as a deeply unsettling look in the mirror.

Nicki had helped him. Months before, she had heard that Bailey intended to "do" her mother. She and Dick Foster went to see him perform. Backstage, she invited him to the house for pointers and a screening of Lee footage. "What was I gonna say, no?" recalled Bailey. "As a kid I'd seen Peggy on television. She fascinated me. She was the hardest to sing of all the ladies I'd done. There was no belting. It was all about the eyes.

Lips. A few hand gestures. I could see the pain. She wasn't obvious about it, but I could tell she'd had a lot of unhappiness."

A nervous Bailey showed up at Peggy Lee's home. He feared that Lee might be there, but she wasn't; Nicki had waited for her mother to go on the road before having him over. She took him into Lee's bedroom and into her closets. His eyes scanned everything. "I was filing it away mentally. I was asking about eyebrow pencils, and what color lipstick. I felt guilty in a way. I felt that if Peggy Lee knew about this, she'd have me arrested."

Grateful as he was, Bailey had to ponder Nicki's motives. "Was this a way of getting back at her mother for some slight? I felt that Nicki doing this wasn't in the best taste. It's exposing somebody, in a way." Nicki didn't tell her mother about the visit, but she found out through Grethe, her Swedish dresser and alternate housekeeper. Predictably, Lee was enraged. Soon Bailey would be at the Empire Room of the Waldorf Astoria as Peggy Lee, which made the star even angrier.

Lee still had a circuit, if a dwindling one, of supper clubs to work. In Las Vegas, however, the fallout from her recent misconduct wasn't forgotten; word had spread that Lee was demanding and difficult. By 1970, Panella couldn't get her a job there. That fall he sought help from his mentor Sam Weisbord, a top executive at the William Morris Agency. "She's burned a lot of bridges," Weisbord told him. Panella offered a proposal. If, in the future, another Morris client were to bow out of a Vegas run, Lee could be brought in to sub. Panella vowed that she would cause no trouble.

She got her chance. On December 27, Lee opened at the Desert Inn on a bill with comedian Charlie Callas. Panella pleaded with her to behave. "And she did," he said. The audience adored her: "Standing o's every night."

One Vegas kingpin had never left her thrall. After a show, Panella led Lee into the freight elevator that took her to her suite. Two brutish men followed, pushing a laundry basket, piled high with towels. As the elevator rose, all were silent. "I'm thinking, something's not right," said Panella. At that moment, his and Lee's eyes fell upon a gnarly hand, with untrimmed, clawlike nails, that had reached out of the basket. Instantly they knew it belonged to Howard Hughes, who owned much of Las Vegas, including the Desert Inn. The madly eccentric and reclusive tycoon had lived in the penthouse until recently; why he was there now wasn't clear. Hughes wouldn't have dared enter the showroom, but for years he had made it known that he "was crazy about Peggy," said Panella. "He wanted to sleep with her and never got to." Apparently he wanted a peek at her. "We got off the elevator and I said, 'Do you realize what just happened?' She said, 'Yes! Howard was in that basket!'"

Lee herself was turning ever more eccentric, but she still impressed most reporters as the apex of professionalism. "It's no wonder that we love Peggy Lee, whose performances are so glittering and polished," wrote a *New Yorker* reporter. Asked whose music she liked hearing, she reeled off a list of current names: Carly Simon, Leon Russell, Credence Clearwater Revival, Bread, Chicago. The writer attended a rehearsal for her new Waldorf show, in which poetry by Carl Sandburg and Lois Wyse, who wrote bestselling, greeting card–style verse, bridged pop tunes of several eras. "She stopped 'Fire and Rain' several times because a guitar figure didn't sound right, and she hummed what she wanted until she got it. In a new tune called 'It Changes' she heard a wrong note from the cellist. Though the cellist was playing what was written, Lou Levy agreed with Miss Lee that it sounded wrong, so it was changed." Lee explained afterward: "Now, you don't have an audience of musicians, but the music still has to be just right . . . I think the audience enjoys it more if it comes off well, simply because *I* enjoy it more, which gives me a sense of well-being and relaxes me, and enables me to do a better job."

But when Mary Daniels of the *Chicago Tribune* sat in on a rehearsal at Chicago's Palmer House hotel, she saw much that seemed out of whack. Daniels noticed the singer's dramatic weight gain and the cigarette that burned constantly in her hand, despite her well-known lung damage. "The way she smokes seems to indicate that she has never seen a TV public health message," wrote Daniels. "From a foot away her face is still very pretty and presentable, but magazines photograph her through heavy, gauzy screens."

Lee changed her look with almost every show, searching in vain for a happy sight in the mirror. In her bedroom, Jim Bailey had gazed upon a huge expanse of shimmery fabric. "It was a dress, but I thought it was a bedspread. When Peggy gained all the weight, she made her own trap. It was tent city. Muumuu time."

The star had entered her next fashion phase, swathing herself in flowing, high-necked chiffon caftans with jeweled collars and cuffs. The designer was Bob Mardesich. An apprentice of Marilyn Monroe's famed costumer, William Travilla, Mardesich had fitted a near-emaciated Judy Garland for *Valley of the Dolls* before her drinking lost her the job. With Lee, Mardesich had other challenges. "There are different tricks of camouflaging weight," he said. "We tried them all." When Lee appeared on *The Carol Burnett Show* to sing Carole King's "I Feel the Earth Move," she wore a pale orange caftan with huge ruffled sleeves that hung to the floor. To vocal critic Henry Pleasants, the Lee of that period looked like Aimee Semple MacPherson, the flamboyant celebrity evangelist and faith healer of the 1920s.

Atop those voluminous gowns were hairdos to match: "vanilla-Whip-'N-Chill pudding tresses," as Mary Daniels called them. Lee had a home hairdressing appointment almost daily. "We touched it up every fourth day," said Bruce Vanderhoff. "Ridiculous. Sometimes I'd say, this is too much."

But too much is what Lee usually wanted, and she got it from her new hairstylist, Bruce Richard. An ex-model, he had come to Lee via

Hairdresser Bruce Richard at Lee's fifty-third birthday
party, May 26, 1973. (PHOTO BY BOB MARDESICH)

Vanderhoff, his former boyfriend, who wasn't always available. Alongside Lee, Richard got most of the attention. Over six feet tall, blue-eyed, and sporting a mane of brown hair that anticipated the Bee Gees in their *Saturday Night Fever* phase, Richard was a stunner, and he knew it. "He looked like Hercules," said singer Leata Galloway, who worked later in Lee's backup vocal trio. Richard alternated between head-to-toe leather and mod suits, with shirts always opened to reveal his hairy chest. Aggressively charming, he cruised to appointments in a Rolls-Royce, while indulging after hours in recreational drugs and S&M. In his off time he had rock-star-like headshots taken.

Richard aspired to an aristocracy of flashy hairdressers-to-the-stars such as Jon Peters (Barbra Streisand's future boyfriend and producer) and Gene Shacove (who inspired Warren Beatty's lead character in the film *Shampoo*). But Robert Richards recalled him mainly as a "demented queen" who sniffed amyl nitrate poppers and wore chaps while doing Lee's hair. Often he drove by Streisand's house, hoping to catch a glimpse of her. "Oh, you want to do Barbra Streisand's hair?" asked Mardesich. "No," said Richard, "I want to be her friend!"

For now he had Peggy Lee. "She's the best thing that has ever happened to me," he told writer Joan Rattman Heilman. "And the most phenomenal woman I've ever met. We're very dear friends. I get five hundred dollars a week and all my expenses. And I go first-class." If he coveted her fame, she loved to be seen with such a head-turner. Predictably, he assumed other responsibilities besides hairdressing. "Bruce is always out front during Peggy's shows, and reports on how she looks and how she's going over," wrote Heilman. "Between shows, or when she comes off on bows, he hands her a glass of water, powders her face, touches up her hair."

He did more than that. During her false exits, Richard waited with a Valium clenched in his left hand. Lee swept by, scooped it up with one of her long nails, and downed it with the glass of cognac he held in his other hand. This was the decade of proud chemical overindulgence, and to Richard it was all a lark. But Brian Panella saw calamity in the making, as all this anesthesia began taking a toll on her work.

In April 1971, near the end of an exhausting five-week tour, she began a weeklong booking at the fifteen-hundred-seat Latin Casino in

Cherry Hill, New Jersey. Lee seldom drank before rehearsing, but this time she did, and it left her in no condition to guide the band. She blamed the sound, the lights, the wait staff, the orchestra; Panella had to fight with everyone on her behalf. Hugo Granata walked around scowling, his arm in a sling after a fall off a ladder during a previous engagement. He had lost patience with Lee, who kept complaining about his light scheme. "This is the way it was last year," he insisted. "Same room, same lights."

"No, Hugo, it wasn't."

"Yes, it was."

"No, I remember it differently."

"Then you remember it *wrong.*"

For the first show, Lee would have to entertain a convention of car dealers. By showtime many were drunk, and as she sang they rose from their tables and milled around, joking and laughing. From the stage, Lee gestured in their direction. "I'm gettin' a lot of conversation from over here," she said testily. Panella rushed over and tried to silence them. It didn't work. He too lost his temper. "I went to the obvious ringleader, the loudest, most boisterous buffoon with a cigar. I leaned over his chair and I said, 'Look, you fucking asshole. I'm gonna pull you out of this fucking chair and I'm gonna break it over your fucking head. Do you wanna shut the fuck up? Or what do you want?'"

Instead of quieting down, they refused to pay their check. Shouts came from another table: "Sing 'Fever.'"

"Oh, but that's for dessert," said Lee gamely.

"Come on, sis, sing 'Fever.'"

"*Sir,*" she hissed, "*I've . . . had . . . just . . . about . . . enough!*" She cut the show short and fled in tears to her dressing room.

Moments later, Panella entered. He found Lee rummaging through her purse on the makeup table. "Are you all right?" he asked gently.

"Yes, I'm fine!" she snapped.

"Do you want something to eat before the next show?"

"*No, I don't!*"

Lee took her purse into the bathroom. Quickly she emerged, slammed the purse down on the makeup table, and stormed out.

"She came back, looked under the purse, went back in the toilet," said Panella. "Now she's a wreck. I looked under the table and saw a little manila envelope. I opened it. Quaaludes." For Lee to down them on top of the Valium and alcohol in her system would be "a cocktail for total disaster. I knew I'd have a freakin' zombie on my hands. And it might kill her." He stashed the envelope in his pocket. But he couldn't stop Lee from ordering a double vodka. He believed she took a Valium with it. She did the late show "partially blitzed," Panella said. "They loved her, but she was screwing up her lyrics."

Back in the dressing room, he shored up his courage and showed her the packet of Quaaludes. "Are these yours?"

"*What are you accusing me of?*"

"I'm not accusing you of anything. Is this what you lost?"

"*No, it is not,*" shouted Lee, "*and I resent you accusing me!*"

"You're absolutely right. I apologize." Panella walked into the bathroom, dumped the pills in the toilet, and flushed it. "She went nuts."

Panella's job had shifted from management to damage control. The rest of her innermost circle had caught on. Bruce Vanderhoff called Lee "the queen of self-medication"; Phoebe Ostrow (by now Phoebe Jacobs) agreed. "She was a sneak pill-popper. She used to hide them under the bed, under the pillow, in pocketbooks, in the coat pockets." Lee had acquired doctors in various cities; she had researched symptoms of various ailments and used them to obtain "all kinds of prescriptions for everything," said Jacobs. Her housekeeper Grethe couldn't clean without finding pills. While Lee was still on tour, Nicki pleaded with Betty Jungheim to intervene. Jungheim urged her to call Lee's most trusted doctor.

He agreed to admit her to the hospital for tests, while keeping the reason vague.

Jungheim accompanied her. "I don't understand why I'm here," said Lee. Then she glimpsed the word "detox" on a report. Lee exploded at Jungheim, who once more found herself caught in the middle. "I was trying to save your life," countered Jungheim.

It seemed that no one could. Increasingly, audiences saw a stoned Peggy Lee. In July, talk-show host Merv Griffin featured a full program of Lee and Tony Bennett performing at Caesars Palace in Las Vegas. Lee appeared in flowing power-blue chiffon, with a Bruce Richard hairdo that consisted of two voluminously teased sacks of curls that hung like kittens from either side of her head. She and Bennett sang selections from their current acts. But when the two friends stood shoulder to shoulder for "Sing," songwriter Joe Raposo's childlike hit from *Sesame Street*, it looked as though creatures from different planets had collided. The eager-to-please Bennett had no mystique; a grin was never far from his lips, and he flung a hand toward the sky at the end of most songs. Sometimes he spun around in glee.

Lee stayed immobile and half smiling. Her face had the unlined perfection of a doll; she sang in a low-voltage drone. During "Is That All There Is?," a strange disconnect overcame the singer; her eyebrows kept arching in a slow-motion vamp, as though she thought the song were "Fever."

Within days of that taping, some bad news shook her temporarily out of her fog. Louis Armstrong, who for years had sent her an orchid and a good-luck wire on her opening nights, had died. His widow, Lucille, asked her to sing "The Lord's Prayer" at the funeral, which took place at a small, sweltering church in his hometown of Corona, Queens. Armstrong was sixty-nine. He had suffered a heart attack, the result of a lifetime of fatty soul food and cigarettes as well as laxative abuse to control his weight.

Lee refused to face the truth about her own self-destruction. "Oh, I take very good care of myself," she told a writer. But in November 1971, near the end of a tour, she began feeling ill. She canceled the last engagement and flew home to California, and from there went straight to St. John's. Diagnosis: a return of pneumonia. Just as she had a decade before, Lee spent Thanksgiving in her hospital bed.

X-rays of her lungs revealed a high degree of scarring and the inflammation and tar buildup of a thirty-seven-year smoking habit. The doctor gave Lee a choice: quit or die. "I want to live," she said. She had gotten the same warning in 1961, but this time she took the ultimatum to heart. With the help of a mentholated plastic cigarette, Lee gathered her deepest determination. This time it worked.

Far too soon, she went back to work. She could never have resisted two of the offers that came her way in 1972. In both cases, she was asked to act on TV—an opportunity she had thought she would never have again. On *The Carol Burnett Show*, Lee gave a bittersweet reprise of her asylum scene from *Pete Kelly's Blues*. Seventeen years after that film, Lee's inner Rose had risen much closer to the surface. The tinkling of a child's music box again underscored "Sing a Rainbow"—this time to even more sinister effect, for Lee was over fifty, yet seemed more a lost child than ever.

The duality was spelled out further when Lee played a close facsimile of herself on *Owen Marshall, Counselor at Law*. The ABC series starred Tony-winning actor Arthur Hill as a defense attorney with a heart. Lee's episode, "Smiles from Yesterday," centers around Jenny Rush, a washed-up singer and songwriter who faces a plagiarism suit from an obscure tunesmith. John McGreevey, an Emmy-winning veteran of TV screenwriting, penned the script. McGreevey specialized in historical drama, etched with diligent research; he dug deep into Lee's past—including the "Mañana" lawsuits—and filled in the gaps with intuition.

Consequently, Lee didn't have to act. In most regards, she *was* Jenny Rush—a forlorn, faded woman who could still turn on her wiles when a man walked in. McGreevey had done his homework. Jenny had sung with bands as a teenager, money troubles plagued her, she had a troubled relationship with her grown child. Much of the dialogue touched upon Lee's darkest fears; the fact that she had agreed to speak it suggested some degree of brave self-awareness. Songwriter Hoagy Carmichael, whom Lee had known since her twenties, played Jenny's live-in "uncle" and protector. "Now he's broke and old," says Jenny. "That gives us something in common." In her first meeting with Marshall, she describes herself as a "has-been" and a "loser." Admits Jenny: "You know, the story got out that I was drunk." After Marshall agrees to defend her in her plagiarism case, her ex-husband shows up at his office to swear that Jenny *did* steal the song. "She's a camouflage expert," he says, adding, "Jenny does a great job of forgetting what it's inconvenient to remember."

In the show, Lee wears her own colorful caftans and her Mae West fall. She also lets loose with an authentic Peggy Lee outburst. When Marshall asks her point-blank if the song is really hers, she shouts: "*Of course it's mine!*" In the end, she learns that her ex-husband has been conspiring against her. She *did* write the song in question, "Smiles from Yesterday."

After the taping, Lee resumed a growingly shaky singing career. The woman who had tapped into a nationwide sense of disillusion with "Is That All There Is?" once more seemed commercially irrelevant. She still spent about half the year playing clubs, but at Capitol, her time was winding down. Lee's recent albums, including *Make It with You* and *Where*

Did They Go, languished in a market now dubbed "middle of the road"—
a commercial graveyard-in-waiting for singers of her vintage. The repertoire combined mostly forgettable new songs with current hits—"My
Sweet Lord" (George Harrison), "Make It with You" (Bread), "I Don't
Know How to Love Him" (Helen Reddy)—that buyers preferred to hear
in the famous versions. Lee had always sung the tunes of the day, but
now, when singer-songwriters ruled, to cover other artists' hits—even as
distinctively as she did—seemed lazy and square.

She couldn't help noticing that her label's top moneymakers—Grand
Funk Railroad, the Steve Miller Band, Bob Seger, Linda Ronstadt, Helen
Reddy—were young enough to be her children. Hot as they were, the
label bled an estimated sixteen million dollars in 1971. That year, Sal Iannucci was fired as president of Capitol Records. EMI had appointed an
aggressive young replacement, Bhaskar Menon, to turn the losses around.
He did—but the lingering deadweight at Capitol would have to go. One
final Lee album was scheduled for the spring of 1972.

Capitol had been Lee's foundation for the better part of twenty-eight
years. Their rejection of her was almost too hurtful to bear. "I helped
start that company!" she railed to Jungheim. Futile as it seemed, Panella
thought that somehow, if the new record were perceived as something
fresh, and if sales picked up, even a little, Capitol might give her another
chance. They'd done it before. He hoped that at the very least he could
help create a record that would make Lee attractive to another label.

Panella reached out to Tom Catalano, a canny young producer who
had groomed Neil Diamond and Helen Reddy into pop sensations who
sold to all ages. Panella sensed that Catalano was arrogant, bossy, and
flush with his own success. "His ego was as big, if not bigger than Peggy's.
But I knew he would give her the best production, the best engineer, the
best studio environment—a lot of things she didn't always have."

As pianist and musical director, Catalano hired Artie Butler, one
of his regulars. At twenty-nine, Butler had worked on hundreds of sessions with everyone from Louis Armstrong to the Dixie Cups; it was he
who played the bells on that group's milestone smash of 1964, "Chapel
of Love." But Lee was his true idol—so much so that he used to bribe
the Copacabana's doorman into letting him eavesdrop on her rehearsals. Now, he couldn't believe that "a little pisher from Ocean Parkway in

Brooklyn," as he called himself, would have the chance to make an album with the great Peggy Lee.

Catalano picked most of the songs. Without even knowing her, he formed a mosaic of Lee's emotional state in 1972. Running through his choices were themes of pain that wouldn't heal, of last chances swept away, of time running out on hard-earned joy. Even in the happier tunes, like Motown songwriter Mike Randall's "When I Found You," Lee pinpointed a sadness that would make this album the most melancholy one of her career.

Prior to the four recording dates, which took place in Los Angeles, Lee never bothered to meet with Butler. That puzzled him; Lee was known for taking firm control of every aspect of an album. Now, it seemed, she simply hadn't the heart. Lou Levy dealt with Butler, who rehearsed the orchestra without her.

April 24, 1972, the day of the first session, arrived. Perhaps as a parting slap against Capitol, or a reluctance to face the end, Lee arrived an hour late. Once there, however, she got briskly down to business. First up was the British songwriter Lesley Duncan's "Love Song," a slight piece with an early-seventies theme of releasing the past and starting anew. The words had a post-flower-child dippiness: "Love is the key we must turn, truth is the flame we must burn." Yet the arrangement was anything but treacly; it surged ahead, with the horn section exploded into a high-flying storm of brass. A soft acoustic guitar added a sense of wistfulness. Lee connected with Duncan's plea to move ahead, and she sang the refrain with a desperate urgency: "*Do you know what I mean? Have your eyes really seen?*"

"Everything just fit," said Butler. "After the first take, the entire orchestra applauded." The response softened Lee; she hugged Butler and asked him where he'd been all her life.

Other songs threw her into a funk, for they dredged up her grief over David Prowitt. Leon Russell and Bonnie Bramlett's "Superstar," the Carpenters' number-two hit, particularly depressed her. It tells of a groupie who pines for the guitar-playing pop star who stole her heart—maybe in one night, maybe more—then left town without a trace, except for the record of his that played on the radio. "Don't you remember you told me you loved me, baby?" she asks over and over. "Superstar" became the lament of an older woman whose last chance at love had walked out the door, never to return. "*Loooone*liness is such a sad affair," sang Lee in a moan as pained as any by Billie Holiday.

Leon Carr and Robert Allen, two writers of 1950s novelty hits, did an about-face with "It Takes Too Long to Learn to Live Alone." Its protagonist is a woman whose man left her a year before; still she sees emptiness and desolation in every corner: "Habits are so hard to break; I think of you, and I still ache."

Panella sat with Catalano at the control board; Lee stood behind the glass window of her isolation booth. "I'm watching her break down at the microphone," he recalled. "Tom said, 'Let it go. We want it on tape.'"

The most devastating song came from *Snoopy Come Home*, an uncommonly sad entry in the animated film series based on Charles M. Schulz's "Peanuts" comic strip. "It Changes" was sung by a crying Charlie Brown after his dog has left him to rejoin his original owner. The songwriters, brothers Richard and Robert Sherman, had scored such juvenile confections as *Mary Poppins* and *Chitty Chitty Bang Bang*. Now, in *Snoopy Come Home*, a little boy sang: "All at once you're all alone and scared / All the happy hellos that you've shared / Change to goodbyes."

The song made many of Charlie Brown's child fans burst into sobs. But Peggy Lee seized upon "It Changes" from the moment she heard it, and added it to her show. Charlie Brown's desolate spoken monologue from the song made its way onto her record, complete with its most piercing line: "I *hate* goodbyes."

Lee's probably last album for Capitol ended, fittingly, with a song of farewell: "I'll Be Seeing You," a number-one hit in the depths of World War II. As she sang of "all the old familiar places" that now seemed bare— "that small café / The park across the way"—panic entered her voice.

Butler finished the album even more captivated with Lee than when he began. "Whatever the craziness was, it manifested itself in the magnificence of her artistry. We all know people who have the craziness but not the artistry. With Peggy, they went hand in hand."

Catalano jarred Panella by announcing his intended title for this soul-baring album: *Superbitch.* Clearly the producer saw it as a last-ditch attention-getter, but Panella knew that Lee would never allow it. Catalano wouldn't budge. Reluctantly, Panella shared the news with Lee. Her response was no surprise: "*Has he lost his mind?*"

Panella went back to Catalano, who threatened not to release the album unless *Superbitch* remained. But finally he relented. Catalano devised an alternate title: *Norma Deloris Egstrom from Jamestown, North Dakota*. It was a curious name for an album that aimed to show the world a revitalized Peggy Lee. The back cover bore a map of Lee's home state; it included Wimbledon and Valley City, the towns that had launched her professionally. Now here she was, at the end of the line.

That summer Capitol released the album, minus the saddest track, "It Changes." Lee stared out from a front-cover close-up that had been airbrushed almost beyond recognition. Only the title, not her name, appeared there—an overly confident artistic choice for a faded artist. But the album didn't go unpromoted. On July 8, Capitol placed a full-page ad in *Billboard*; beneath the cover photo a caption read, "Norma Deloris Egstrom From Jamestown, North Dakota Has Recorded Her Greatest Album." Once more, no other name was used.

In the end, it may not have mattered. A new Peggy Lee album was hardly news. A critic from the *Chicago Daily Herald* described this one as "sort of after-dinner cocktail music"; Patrick Scott of the *Toronto Star* seemed to think that Lee had changed her name back to Norma Deloris Egstrom. One review that might have mattered—a page-long critique by her loyal cheerleader, Peter Reilly, in the influential *Stereo Review*—didn't appear until a year later. And Reilly wasn't enthusiastic. Despite "three or four stunning bands," the LP fell short, he thought. What's more, he added, no amount of top-forty covers by Lee would attract the youth market. "Who sees her in Vegas, New York, or Miami?" asked Reilly. "All the over-the-hill gang that still thinks Tony Bennett or Robert Goulet or Steve and Eydie is where it's at, that's who."

By this time, Capitol had truly wiped its hands of Peggy Lee. Woolworth's and other discount chains that stocked "cut-outs"—out-of-print or overstock LPs—had begun selling bulk copies of Lee's Capitol swan song, priced at $1.99.

Panella vowed to somehow keep her afloat. For singers of Lee's vintage, double bills with another vocalist or star comic had become a practical way of filling houses. Tony Bennett, for instance, had teamed with Lena Horne for a touring concert that went to Broadway. And in November of 1972, the neon billboard outside of Caesars Palace in Las Vegas advertised *A Man and a Woman*, starring Peggy Lee and comic Alan King, a TV star and Caesars favorite.

Panella worked out the details. Lee would open for King—a touchy prospect for a woman used to headlining. Conscious of her pride, Panella arranged for King to lead off with a short routine, then to bring on Lee. After her set, King would come back to deliver his comically beleaguered rants about the woes of the common man: air travel, hospital food, insurance firms. Afterward, Lee would join him for a long medley of songs about life's foibles.

For three weeks, the pairing filled the hotel's eight-hundred-seat Circus Maximus showroom. Lee adored King; he returned the sentiment, with reservations. Years later he told a young jazz singer, Spider Saloff: "Peggy was great, but she was cuckoo. Everything had to be blue, or everything had to be green. Dealing with her before and after the show—ooh, I avoided that."

Despite the format, Lee knew she was the supporting act. Illness had always helped her tilt the attention, and when Leonard Feather profiled her for the *Los Angeles Times*, Lee complained of a crushed vertebra and arthritis of the spine. "Last night I felt that an incision, from an operation I had a while back to remove a benign cyst, had come open. This was just before show time. I was in such excruciating pain, I thought Bruce [Richard] was going to faint."

On another night, she nearly did—but out of ire, not pain. At two AM, just before the late show ended, TV host Ralph Edwards walked out onto the huge stage of the Circus Maximus. He held what looked like a scrapbook. When Edwards uttered his famous phrase—"Peggy Lee, *this is your life!*"—Lee let out an audible groan. She was trapped.

So were all the subjects of *This Is Your Life*, a long-running show in which Edwards and his cameramen interrupted stars on the job and took them on a tour down memory lane, replete with friends, family members, and long-lost figures from their past. Surreptitiously, Nicki had helped Edwards's staff to plot the tribute. She had flown to Las Vegas with her three children, allegedly to see the show. As she maneuvered on Edwards's behalf, the crew laid TV cables backstage, hiding them under carpeting.

Now, as Lee stood, glowering, on the Circus Maximus stage, a table, sofa, and chair were dragged out to accommodate the parade of those who had known her when. Lee didn't like losing control, and there were many in her past whom she did *not* wish to see again. But she softened when Edwards brought out Ken Kennedy. Snuggling her head to his chest, she declared: "He *made* me sing. I was very shy." Out came her brother, Clair, and Rose Savage, an old friend from Nortonville. Chuck Barclay, who had booked her into the Jade in 1938, emerged next, followed by the guest she seemed happiest to greet, Duke Ellington. "You knew all about this," she told him with an undisguised edge. Then came Nicki, whose long, straight brown hair and flowing multicolored dress evoked the similarly proportioned singer, "Mama" Cass Elliot. When Edwards mentioned the missing guest, Dave Barbour, Lee looked off wistfully. By the close of the show, she seemed genuinely touched.

That look back certainly seemed sweeter than the look ahead, which held no record deal and fewer venues that could afford her lushly orchestrated glamour. At least the Waldorf still enabled her to live like Cinderella. Entering the hotel before her engagements, the singer passed through a lobby festooned with placards that announced Miss Peggy Lee's return. Throwing open the door of suite 37F, she found her requisite crystal glassware at the ready. As opening night approached, dozens of extravagant bouquets arrived, accompanied by signed cards that made Lee's guests swoon.

She had planned it that way. Part of Betty Jungheim's job was to phone Lee's florist and order an array of floral arrangements. She would add ersatz messages from Lee's celebrity friends. Doak Roberts helped. "Betty and I would sit at her desk and make up all these things like, 'You're mine forever, and who could forget those wonderful days—love, Cary Grant.'" By the time an engagement ended, said Roberts, "she thought that maybe Cary Grant *had* sent her flowers."

Grant didn't drop by as much, but the privileged guests who did were summoned up to 37F for the nightly meet-and-greet. They accumulated in the living room, and were called into the bedroom in ones or twos. Her friend Robert Richards was a regular. Then around thirty, the Manhattan-based illustrator had become known for his meticulously detailed, glamorized images of figures from fashion, music, and gay porn. Richards was the kind of New York character Lee loved. He wore eccentrically flashy suits and a pair of round, oversize glasses; and while his taste in music leaned toward older pop-jazz singers like Lee and Sarah Vaughan, he was always up on the latest gossip from Manhattan's fast lane.

Once admitted to the inner sanctum, he found the star in bed, "completely made up, with the hairdo from the show, and the big long nails. She was in very frilly and feathery stuff, with a blanket pulled up to her breasts. A little dessert plate rested somewhere between her chest and her stomach, with a chicken sandwich. She would gingerly nibble on it, and tell you that the crusts had been removed. And she drank tea, very properly. You'd have to be from a place like North Dakota to have this totally Hollywood vision of yourself."

Her entourage tended to her as though she were a dowager queen. Panella kept asking how she felt, and if she needed anything. Virginia Bernard carried glasses of water and whatever pill "Miss Lee" had requested. Bruce Richard massaged her feet. Everyone present was discouraged from leaving. One night Lee summoned Shaun Considine of *After Dark* magazine to her suite to apologize for having canceled an interview. She kept him there all night. Lee volunteered news of her recent mishap: "I slipped on the bathroom rug and fell into the tub, hitting my head." This had caused a "bruised brain." Further details followed. "But please," she concluded, "let's not talk anymore about my health."

Hearts raced at the occasional presence of Lee's longtime fan and chum, Doris Duke. Dubbed "the richest girl in the world," the heiress shared much in common with Lee, from their love of jazz to their striving for happiness via TM and plastic surgery. Both women used the same surgeon, who outfitted them with nearly identical protruding chins. Lee had introduced Duke to the two men who would trigger the greatest scandals of her life. Eddie Tirella—gardener, decorator, movie set designer, and gay confidant—had helped Lee to design her home on Kimridge Road. Duke, in turn, hired him to create decorative gardens for her estates in Newport, Rhode Island, and Hillsborough Township, New Jersey. She was used to getting what she wanted, but when she fell in love with Tirella, the results were bound to disappoint. In 1967, he announced he was leaving her employ. Within days he was dead—mangled under the wheels of Duke's car as he opened her gate to let her drive out. A court ruled it an accident, but Tirella's friends were sure she had done it on purpose. Lee took Duke's side.

Friends of the singer noted the bizarre irony that unfolded next when Duke hired Lee's former butler Bernard Lafferty, a portly, gay Irishman with reddish-blond hair and a drinking problem. Bruce Vanderhoff and other friends of Lee's had laughed for years at his sheepish doting, voiced in an Irish brogue: "Is everything OK, Miss Lee?"

Both she and Nicki found him hilarious and lovable, but Lee fired him at least three times for drunken inefficiency. Why she had recommended him to a close friend—no less a woman as demanding and neurotic as Duke—is a mystery. But the heiress grew heavily dependent on Lafferty,

and appointed him executor and cobeneficiary of her 5.3-billion-dollar estate. When she died of cardiac arrest in 1993, Lafferty was charged with foul play; some accused him of having coerced a drugged, mentally unstable old woman into letting him take control. Neither claim was proven, and Lee vehemently defended his innocence, as did Nicki.

While the less-than-pretty Duke couldn't help but attract gold-digging men, Lee still had her feminine wiles. But according to an unnamed friend quoted in a 1971 *Cosmopolitan* profile, the "sexy act" was just for show: "Actually, she's pretty much a prude. She's offended by the skin-flick movies that are so popular now, and she likes cussing held down." Lee's notions of romance remained as starry-eyed, and often as deluded, as a high school girl's. One day she announced to a stunned Betty Jungheim that she and Bruce Vanderhoff were deeply in love and planning to marry. They had spent the evening together, explained Lee, and had cried tears of joy. Vanderhoff groaned loudly when he heard the story.

But nothing could shake Lee of her self-image as a grand seducer of all. In late 1972 she lay in bed, poring over the story of a woman she considered her soulmate. French author Pierre La Mure had written the fanciful *Clair de Lune: A Novel About Claude Debussy* in 1962. It contained the fictional character of Alix Vasnier, a mature but glamorous singer for whom the composer played piano in his twenties. In La Mure's telling, Debussy fell madly in love with her, and she with him; but Alix vanished from his life, just as David Prowitt had from Lee's. Obsessed with the story, she decided to produce it as a film, starring herself as Alix. She bought the film rights from La Mure, then announced that she would write the screenplay and start filming in France the next spring. "It was going to be a very sweeping romantic epic," recalled Robert Richards. "Madness. Without moonlight!" Lee knew even less about screenwriting than she did about producing, though, and she ended up mostly plagiarizing La Mure's dialogue.

No film ever resulted, but Lee's fixation with the novel went on for at least a year. Another of La Mure's characters, Gabrielle Dupont, leaves a life of riches and success to share a garret with the great composer. Eventually she dies in a poorhouse—one of Lee's darkest fears for herself. Out of bed, Lee did a painting of herself as a gaunt-cheeked Gaby.

Such dark forebodings sent her running for escape. One day in the living room of Lee's suite in the Waldorf Towers, her actor friend Walter Willison spotted some little red pills on the floor. He had never seen Seconal, a popular alternative—or in Lee's case, an addition—to Valium. Seconal calms the nerves, but can also induce nightmares, somnolence, impaired motor functions, irritability, and confusion, all of which Lee was experiencing. Willison asked her New York assistant, Gail Bixby, about the pills. "Gail said, 'Oh my God, my pockets are full of them. She drops them all over the apartment, and before anyone comes over I have to run around picking them up.'" The young man had always thought Lee's mellowness was "spiritual."

So had her audience, but they were learning otherwise. Lou Levy recalled a show in which Lee had worn her White House attire—an elegant black gown and a long string of fake pearls. During a song, the strand broke. Rather than making light of it and moving on, the glazed singer looked down at the floor for several long moments, then got down on her hands and knees and tried to pick the pearls up. Eerie silence fell over the room. Eventually Lee straightened up and ended the show. At the end, fans filed out slowly, looking as though they were leaving a funeral.

Panella knew he had to "try to protect Peggy from herself." The task encompassed making excuses to promoters for spectacles like the pearl incident; it also involved, on one occasion, sweet-talking a drunken Lee into handing over the carving knife she was recklessly using to slice up a sausage from room service. Panella's duties extended to her outer family. The Fosters had finally acquired their own house in nearby Cheviot Hills. One day their Hispanic housekeeper phoned Lee in a panic. She struggled, in her broken English, to report an emergency; it involved little David and a gun. His parents were out. A terrified Lee begged Panella to jump in his car and race over. Minutes later he reached the house. The housekeeper pointed him to the backyard. There was David, scampering about with a double-barrel shotgun, perhaps loaded. He had already pushed the hammers back.

Panella spoke to him calmly, from a distance. "Gee, David, I need to ask you a couple of questions. Can you come over here?" David approached him, shotgun in hand. "Wow," said Panella, "that's a beautiful gun. Do you mind if I hold it for a minute?" David handed it to him—"but I want it back! It's mine!" Panella snapped the hammers into safety position. Then he opened the breech. It contained two shells. As David whined for "his" gun, Panella left the house with it. Back at Tower Grove, he had to tell Lee what had happened. She went "berserk," and immediately phoned Nicki and Dick. "I became persona non grata with them," said Panella. "Nicki believed I blew the whistle on her and could have covered it up. She didn't realize that her mother already knew."

Increasingly, his fiercest opponent was Lee herself. When he tried to gently caution her about her misbehavior, to tell her that her demands were alienating promoters and pushing budgets over the edge, she exploded. Only later did he realize that anyone who posed a threat to Lee's fantasy-fueled life would soon be expelled from it.

Panella had helped maneuver a pairing of Lee with America's hottest funnyman, Don Rickles, the king of insult comedy. Rickles jumped at the offer; he had adored Lee ever since his days as a sailor in World War II. The bill would guarantee sellout crowds at the chosen venue, Westbury Music Fair, a three-thousand-seat theater-in-the-round in Westbury, Long Island. Once more, Lee would open the show. But Rickles agreed to accept equal billing and to introduce Lee with a short opening routine. Her publicist, John Springer, convinced the local press to review the stars separately, so that Lee would seem like a headliner.

All of this—as well as the handsome paycheck—should have appeased her. But Lee was hostile, and Panella wondered why. He didn't know she was shopping for an excuse to fire him, and that Bruce Richard was egging her on, telling her how "beneath her" it was to play second fiddle to an insult comic.

In February 1973, Lee and Panella arrived at Westbury for opening-day rehearsal. Rickles had filled her dressing room with flowers; Lee made a snide remark about his excess. Bruce Richard was there to do her hair. Each time Panella entered the dressing room, he found them whispering together and glaring at him as though he had intruded. Panella told the singer that Rickles wanted to drop in and thank her for agreeing to perform with him. "Why would I want to talk to that . . . *second-rate comedian*?" hissed Lee. "I will never forgive you, and I will *not* speak to that man, no matter what!"

Showtime came. During the overture, Panella stood in the wings alongside a seething Peggy Lee. On her other side was Bruce Richard. Lee turned to the hairdresser and said imperiously, "Tell Mr. Panella that this is the *worst night of my life!*" Grinning, he obeyed. The overture ended, and Panella announced into Lee's hand-held microphone: "Ladies and gentlemen, *Miss Peggy Lee!*"

Lee turned to Panella and said, "You're fired!" She grabbed the mike and floated onstage, arms spread, beaming.

In the audience were several William Morris executives, including the agency's wheelchair-bound former president, Abe Lastfogel. After the show, Lee kept them waiting backstage for an hour. Panella made every excuse he could think of. Finally he entered her dressing room. "Miss Lee, whatever your problem is with me, these people are important to you. They have been waiting for one hour. They are about to leave. I suggest for your own good that you go out to see them."

"No! Bring them in."

He ushered in the now-testy group, while acting as though all were well. In front of them, Lee turned to Panella and repeated her preshow edict: "You're fired!"

Panella nodded. "Thank you all very much," he said. "Have a good night." And he left.

He was understandably devastated. "I had worked so hard to build things back for her. Then to have this happen, to be undermined by people on the periphery . . ." But in the end, no one could control Peggy Lee. "Peggy didn't fall out with people," explained Bruce Vanderhoff. "She used them up till they had nothing more to give." The musicians threw a little party for Panella. "They did not want me to leave," he said. Thereafter Lee wouldn't take his calls, nor pay him his final commissions. At two AM on the night of the blowup, Lee phoned Betty Jungheim from her hotel suite. "I want you on the next plane!" she declared.

Decades later, after he had successfully managed a string of other artists, notably the singer-actress Diahann Carroll, Panella looked back wistfully on his five years with Lee. "I learned so much about music, staging, ambiance from her—I could go on and on. It was a million-dollar education that no university could teach."

David McMacken's cover illustration for *Mirrors*, the most
courageous and reviled album of Lee's career.

Chapter Fourteen

*N*ICKI LEE FOSTER'S life was in its own upheaval. In her father's final years, Nicki had accompanied him to Alcoholics Anonymous meetings. Dave Barbour wasn't the only member of her family to have struggled with a drinking problem, of course; so had Peggy Lee and Marvin Egstrom. "It was very nice for me to realize that I had the predisposition for alcoholism," explained Nicki. "'Course, a little later I forgot about that, and went out and became an alcoholic."

By 1973, her marriage had fallen apart. She decided she had to escape Los Angeles and her mother's world. "I was really unhappy with the value system I saw," she said. "I had said a lot of times that I would never do for my children what was done for me." Nicki thought of Sun Valley, Idaho, where Dick Foster had once taken her on business. Sun Valley embodied the drastic change she wanted, and she moved there with the children. Searching for creative fulfillment, she became lead singer of Nicki Knight and the Hoops, a band that covered the hits of Gladys Knight and the Pips. She also opened a framing shop, Nicki's Hangup, in nearby Ketcham; it became a casual art gallery.

Her daughter's move depressed Peggy Lee greatly. But she refused to fly to Idaho, claiming the altitude would hinder her breathing. Her relationship with Nicki shifted mainly to the phone, which struck Robert Richards as the place where mother and daughter got along best. "The conversations always seemed to center around money," he recalled. "I think Peggy usually helped her if she could, with a generous spirit."

Lee herself was rudderless; now she lacked not only a record deal but a manager. Just before her spring 1973 engagement at the Waldorf, Lee sought interim management from Doak Roberts. Never mind that Roberts, who did decorative painting and design tasks in private homes, including Peggy Lee's, knew little about running a singer's career. Almost instantly, he learned what Brian Panella had been up against. "There was the fragile part of Peggy, then there was the ball-busting part. She always insulted the wrong people. She was like the little girl with the little curl. At times she was sincerely wonderful, but that person didn't appear too much."

The more she felt her career slipping, the more Lee tried to compensate by pulling rank. As soon as they had checked in to the Waldorf Towers, she ordered Roberts to go downstairs and inform the management that she expected nothing less than star treatment. Timidly he entered the executive office to state his case. Roberts was cut off in midsentence: "We know why you're here. Yes, yes, we will certainly give Miss Lee all of

Fairmont Hotel, San Francisco. (PHOTO BY TAD HERSHORN)

"He was spectacular-looking," but "kind of sharp, definitely moody," said acquaintances of actor Dewey Martin, the third Mr. Peggy Lee. The stormy marriage began in Palm Springs in 1956 (*left*) and ended in Santa Monica divorce court in 1959 (*right*).

Jimmy Durante appears at Lee's 1:00 AM "supper show" at Basin Street East, February 1961. (AUTHOR'S COLLECTION)

"Well, I answer the phone. I sort of chauffeur my mother around." Nicki Lee Barbour and Lee's complicated relationship goes public on CBS-TV's "Person to Person," October 20, 1960. (COURTESY OF ROBERT STROM)

In the golden age of TV variety shows, Lee was a first-call guest.

On *The Frank Sinatra Show* with the conductor of her album *The Man I Love*, November 8, 1957.

Singing of hopeless love with Steve Allen at the piano. *The Steve Allen Show*, November 9, 1959.

Lee and Judy Garland's *I Like Men!* medley. *The Judy Garland Show*, November 8, 1963. (ALL PHOTOS FROM AUTHOR'S COLLECTION)

On *The Merv Griffin Show*, March 13, 1963, with (*left to right*) announcer Frank Simms, Vince Mauro, Carl Reiner, Merv Griffin, and Lee's spiritual mother, journalist Adela Rogers St. Johns. (COURTESY OF VINCE MAURO)

Lee joins Tony Bennett on *The Andy Williams Show*, March 7, 1966. (AUTHOR'S COLLECTION)

With Bing Crosby on *The Hollywood Palace*, January 13, 1968. (COURTESY OF RICHARD MORRISON)

Lee's drunken performance at a White House state dinner "went over like a lead balloon," wrote a journalist. (*Left to right*) Georges Pompidou (president of the French Republic) and wife, Claude; Richard M. Nixon; Lee; Mrs. Pat Nixon. February 24, 1970. (COURTESY OF NIXON PRESIDENTIAL LIBRARY & MUSEUM)

Less than three weeks later, disaster turned to triumph when Lee won a Grammy for "Is That All There Is?," the hit single that Capitol had planned to kill. Glen Campbell and Della Reese presented the award. Century Plaza Hotel, Los Angeles, March 11, 1970. (COURTESY OF ROBERT STROM)

A new beginning: Paul McCartney produces the title track for Lee's Atlantic album, *Let's Love*. The Record Plant, Los Angeles, June 1974. (COURTESY OF JAMES FORTUNE)

Lee with Boston Pops maestro Arthur Fiedler on *Evening at Pops*, summer 1974. (AUTHOR'S COLLECTION)

Lee, Vic Damone, and Lena Horne: three commercially faded but still-mighty pop titans united on the 1976 CBS special *America Salutes Richard Rodgers: The Sound of His Music*. (COURTESY OF RICHARD MORRISON)

"Together we will make *Peg* Broadway's most incredible hit," promised producer Zev Bufman to Peggy Lee. But a writer called this one-woman show "the heaviest magic carpet ride on Broadway." Three days after it opened, *Peg* closed.

Bufman and Lee, New York, September 10, 1982.

Backstage with stylist Vincent Roppatte and the show's composer, Paul Horner. (PHOTO BY MARIANNE BARCELLONA)

The final dress rehearsal, December 1, 1983, Lunt-Fontanne Theatre.

"They didn't have to do any retouching!" marveled Lee about a publicity photo (*above*) by Hans Albers, ca. 1982. By the late 1980s (*right*), she had recast herself as an angel ascending.

Though riddled with illness and barely able to walk, Lee sold out a two-week engagement at the short-lived Club 53 of the New York Hilton. Backstage with Liza Minnelli, August 1992. (AUTHOR'S COLLECTION)

The tribute of a lifetime: Lee is fêted by the Society of Singers at the Beverly Hilton Hotel, Beverly Hills. (*Left to right*) Assistant Robert Paul, Lee, secretary Jane David, and S.O.S. cofounder Ginny Mancini. May 11, 1994. (COURTESY OF JANE DAVID)

Lee's last big night on the town: the twentieth wedding anniversary of Frank and Barbara Sinatra. Malibu, July 11, 1996. (COURTESY OF JANE DAVID)

At home in Bel Air. (COURTESY OF JANE DAVID)

the attention that she deserves." Later, at the Fairmont in San Francisco, Roberts stood by as Lee "raised holy hell" in her suite over some perceived snub by an employee. "One of the hotel managers was up there," said Roberts, "and a bellboy who was getting ready to leave. Peggy said, 'I am a star, and don't you forget it!' As the bellboy passed, he muttered, 'If you gotta tell 'em, you ain't!'"

If commercially Lee had seemed obsolete, few doubted her eminence as the premier white, female survivor of a classy age of pop-jazz. On February 11, 1973, Lee, now fifty-two, appeared as senior songstress on an all-star TV spectacular, *Duke Ellington . . . We Love You Madly*. Quincy Jones had convinced CBS to televise his latest production, a tribute to one of his idols at the New Shubert Theatre in Los Angeles. Jones liked to modernize his jazz elders by teaming them with current pop stars; for this show he mingled Sarah Vaughan, Ray Charles, Billy Eckstine, Joe Williams, Count Basie, and Sammy Davis, Jr., with Roberta Flack, Aretha Franklin, and the jazz-rock fusion band Chicago.

At the time, Lee wasn't too happy with Jones. She didn't like it when her bandmembers, past or present, married other women; if the musicians had once been her bedmates she got even angrier. When her hairdresser Kathy Mahana married Lou Levy, both landed temporarily on the outs with Lee. Jones had never proposed to her; then he had the temerity to wed another blonde with the same initials—Peggy Lipton, the former model and costar of TV's *The Mod Squad*.

But Lee couldn't quibble with the showcase he gave her on primetime TV. Jones presented her in a setting copied from the 1943 MGM musical *Thousands Cheer*, which featured his ultimate goddess, Lena Horne. In one scene, the brass players of the Benny Carter orchestra stand in a circle and play a chorus of "Honeysuckle Rose" filmed from above, their gleaming gold instruments set against an all-black background. Jones's special finds Lee gowned in black and standing in the center of a group of trombonists. She sings the song she had written with Ellington, "I'm Gonna Go Fishin'." Later in the show, Lee shares a blues medley with Vaughan, Franklin, and Flack: three reigning black divas teamed with the woman who may have been their only white peer. Former schoolteacher Flack wore a huge Afro and sang with a pensive soulfulness; Franklin turned every stage into the most euphoric of revival meetings; Vaughan had a sprawling bebop instrument with an operatic grandeur.

Alongside them stood the Lee of 1973: diminished of voice, though larger than ever inside her Bob Mardesich gospel-singer gown. The star who had so long identified with black singers seemed inexplicably shy amid these three. On camera with them, she almost disappeared.

Another performer she loved was experiencing his own slow fade. Onstage, Bobby Darin had lost little of his charisma, but at thirty-six he was dying of a failing heart, the consequence of childhood rheumatic fever. That April, Lee sang on the last episode of his short-lived NBC variety series. Before the shooting he paid his last of many visits to her home. Betty Jungheim welcomed him in. "He sat down on the couch and he was white as a sheet," she said. While waiting for Lee to appear, he asked Jungheim for a cup of tea. He barely finished it. By the time Lee greeted him, he felt so ill he had to leave.

Backstage at *The Bobby Darin Show* he was ashen, and breathing from an oxygen tank. Yet once the camera rolled the trouper in him took over, and he became a close semblance of his old vivacious self. It was Lee who seemed feeble and overmedicated. Still trying to promote her failed final album for Capitol, she performed one of its most poignant songs, "Someone Who Cares." She sounded pinched and wavering; illness, combined with smoking, had robbed her of her husky chest resonance. Her weakness enhanced the pathos as she pleaded quietly for "someone who cares, someone who dares to love you." A duet of sad standards underlined the low ebb that both stars had reached.

Lee's spirits perked up briefly when Blackglama, the manufacturer of shiny mink coats, added her to its array of legendary poster girls, including Bette Davis, Lena Horne, Maria Callas, and Marlene Dietrich. The yen to appear as young in real life as she did in that heavily retouched advertising photo obsessed her. "If she looked in the mirror and saw that even a slight sag was forming," said Doak Roberts, "she'd go have surgery, to the point where the hairline got higher and higher." Roberts joked to friends: "If she gets one more facelift she'll have a beard."

Lee had always used binge eating to soothe her troubled mind, yet she couldn't understand why she kept ballooning up "for no reason."

Some cursory research on eating disorders led her to a bizarre conclusion: Lee told friends she had contracted a rare disease that only astronauts got, whereby standing up caused pounds to accumulate. The fact that she spent most of her life in bed didn't strike her as a contradiction. On the eve of her tours, when self-consciousness seized her, Lee went on alarming crash diets. She discovered a new brand of appetite-control candies and "started eating them by the handful," said Roberts. Later she tried a meal-substitute shake mix whose recipe called for the bizarre addition of half a cup of cooking oil. Believing that the powder contained some magical weight-burning component, Lee drank six or seven shakes a day. At the end of the week she rose from bed and weighed herself. The number on her scale sent the depressed singer back under her blanket.

Toward the end of 1973, she withdrew from public view for several weeks. After that, a "new" Peggy Lee appeared, thinner by about forty pounds. Lee shared details with the *National Enquirer*. A thyroid specialist, she explained, had attributed her weight gain to goiter. Rather than undergo surgery, she "turned to God for help." By focusing intently on her neck and massaging it with her fingers, she managed to channel His healing force. A few months later, the goiter was gone. "It was a miracle," she declared. "I knew then that God had done this for me. He had saved my career."

Friends had their own theories. Bruce Vanderhoff suspected that Bruce Richard had scored her "some fantastic diet pills." Bob Mardesich met a nurse who had just tended to Lee at the hospital; she told him that the singer had undergone liposuction. Whatever the cause, Lee hadn't looked so good in over a decade. "It's so marvelous to be thin!" she exclaimed. No longer did she need Mardesich's caftans—or Mardesich.

Lee felt as regal as a queen that November, when she flew to London to appear on *Julie's Christmas Special*, an hour of English cheer with her dulcet-voiced admirer, Julie Andrews. Doak Roberts was there to help Lee check into the Dorchester, another of her preferred five-star hotels. Lee required the Oliver Messel Suite, an exorbitantly priced two-bedroom, two-bathroom paradise designed by the acclaimed British stage designer. The toilet seats were gold leaf, the walls yellow silk; a private terrace offered a stunning view of the city. The Messel Suite was also the preferred London dwelling of Elizabeth Taylor and Marlene Dietrich, the two women whose glamour and notoriety she most coveted.

Accompanied by Roberts, Lee went to the TV studio to rehearse. The script had a slim premise. Andrews has been diligently taping scenes for her Christmas special, and slips into her dressing room for a brief nap. Drifting into a dream of Christmas past, she finds herself at the portals of the sexy Sugar Plum Fairy: Peggy Lee, lounging on a chaise in clouds of white chiffon. Lee beckons Andrews in and they "improvise" a medley of standards.

Despite her drastic weight loss, Lee remained highly self-conscious about the width of her hips, and she complained to Roberts that the blocking emphasized her rear end. It was then that he observed her backhanded approach to confronting problems. Lee retired to her dressing room, where she had a mysterious collapse that halted rehearsal—"simply because she did not like the blocking," said Roberts. When the ambulance came, Roberts discreetly conveyed to the medics that they should use caution in medicating her, lest she overdose. "I was trying to say, she's zonked."

Lee was rushed to Intensive Care. The next day Roberts visited her. "*Where have you been?*" yelled Lee. "*How dare you leave me here? You're fired!*"

"Fine," he thought. "I'm out of here."

But he stayed in London. And on Monday, Lee was back on the set. In her gentlest tones, she explained that her scene would have to be reblocked to give her maximum comfort. She got her way. The shoot caught her in glowing command. "She was fluttering her false eyelashes, loving every minute of it," said Roberts. The women playfully swap old tunes—Andrews with her operetta-style light soprano, sincere and demure as a singer could be; Lee with the smoldering purr that flung open the bedroom door. On "Just in Time," she vamps the camera with the glance that had seduced countless men.

For her solo segment, Lee had chosen a song by a young man who enchanted her: David Gates, the former lead singer and songwriter of the soft-rock group Bread. "I think he's really a poet," she said. Bundled in a fur coat, Lee stares out an airplane window and sings her favorite

Gates song, "Clouds," the lament of a traveler who never settles down long enough to stay close to anyone. To fly above a bed of white, she sings, "makes me wonder why I'm up so high, when really I am down so low." She segues into "Have Yourself a Merry Little Christmas," sung with the heavy heart of a woman who didn't foresee one for herself.

———

IT WAS HARD NOT to respond to such open-hearted vulnerability, and for years that quality had helped Lee to seduce the press. Interviewers walked away convinced that she had opened herself up to them as she never had before. As with most stars, however, Lee's stories and sound bites came from a tried-and-true repertoire. "Success is the reward for loving your work," she told countless journalists, "and my work is the one thing that has never let me down." Over and over she repeated a quip she thought hilarious: "My favorite color is plaid."

Back in Los Angeles, Colin Dangaard of the *Washington Star* visited Lee at home. She dazzled him. "An English butler has carried in a bottle of fine Chablis for me," he wrote. "Peg pours hot tea from a silver pot in whose polished side is reflected the fire of a California sunset. She nods to the butler, calms her poodle and says very quietly: 'The journey is so incredible, I often wonder how I made it. From starvation to . . . to all this.'"

The occasional writer was skeptical. Before leaving the Dorchester, Lee had received Scarth Flett of the *London Sunday Express*. He sensed a woman as fantastical as the Sugar Plum Fairy. Lee, wrote Flett, wore "a flowing gown of candy-pink silk" and "an inordinate amount of beige makeup; false eyelashes; thick pink lipstick outlined in dark pink pencil and above her mouth a large beauty spot." Her sense of unreality bewildered him. "I once played classical music to the trees in my garden," she remarked, "and they began to dance and sway. Honestly, and there wasn't a breath of wind." Flett's profile was divided into subheadings— "Damaged," "Deficiency," "Weird."

Bruce Vanderhoff wouldn't have argued. One night he drove Lee home after a concert at the Music Center in downtown Los Angeles. "By the way," asked Lee, "did you turn Charlie off?" Charlie was her respirator.

"No, Peggy. I've never turned Charlie off."

"Well, I don't think Ginger did. We've got to turn around and go back."

"If the valve isn't off, it doesn't know, it's perfectly OK."

"Oh, no! It could turn into a missile!"

"A missile?"

"Yes, it could turn into a missile. It could blow up the Music Center."

"Then I surely don't want to go back."

They didn't. Vanderhoff deposited a miffed Lee at her front door.

Truman Capote was one of the few who could look past the oddness and see the wounded soul inside. The great Southern-born writer also lived on an emotional tightrope. Like her, he had yearned for his absentee mother, who divorced his father then moved to New York. In the story *One Christmas*, he wrote of a "crushing pain that hurt everywhere" and wouldn't leave. Like Lee, he leaned on alcohol, drugs, and delusion. Capote would die of liver cancer at fifty-nine.

Eccentric, emotionally scarred characters fascinated him. Knowing and loving her singing, he had to meet Peggy Lee. His author friend Dotson Rader arranged a dinner for the three of them. It started with drinks at her home, where Lee greeted them in white chiffon. "Oh, my God!" exclaimed Capote in his childlike Louisiana drawl. "I'm in the presence of an angel!" They ate in Beverly Hills at Le Restaurant, a trendy and expensive eatery opened by Vanderhoff. Through the cacophony of mealtime chatter, Lee brought up the subject of past lives. According to Rader, she explained: "I've been reincarnated many times. I've been a prostitute, a princess, an Abyssinian queen."

"Oh, really?" asked Capote. "What else do you remember?"

"I remember being a prostitute in Jerusalem when Jesus was alive. I remember the crucifixion very well . . . I'll never forget picking up the *Jerusalem Times* and seeing the headline 'Jesus Christ Crucified.'"

Lee excused herself to use the ladies' room. "She's totally bonkers," said Capote to Rader. After she returned, however, "something happened that I noticed a lot with Truman," Rader said. "He would meet someone, make fun of them, although they weren't aware of it, and then they would say something that revealed a vulnerability, some heartache or pain, and suddenly Truman's attitude would change." Lee volunteered grisly stories about Min's violence; Capote sensed the sincere hurt within them. She talked about her early struggles to make herself heard as a singer in noisy rooms. "Suddenly he became very protective of her," said Rader. Capote asked Lee to sing for him; she obliged, and they merrily traded songs for the rest of dinner and on the drive home.

The public eye could be harsher than his, however. On April 2, 1974, Lee appeared in compromised form before a worldwide audience—the viewers of the Academy Awards. As at the White House, Lee was a last-minute substitute. In an unexplained fit of diva pique, Barbra Streisand had declined to sing the nominated title song of *The Way We Were*, the film for which she had scored a Best Actress nomination. No amount of pleading from the tune's lyricists, her dear friends Marilyn and Alan Bergman, or from the show's producer, Jack Haley, Jr., could sway her. Whether by coincidence or as revenge, Haley chose as her substitute the singer who, five years before, had made mincemeat of her in Las Vegas.

Streisand wasn't pleased. According to one of her biographers, Christopher Andersen, she declared to Haley: "I wanna do the song now. Get rid of Peggy Lee." But Haley refused; Lee had canceled a show in Toronto to sub for her. In turn, Streisand refused to sit in the audience along with the other nominees; she would wait backstage and emerge only if named Best Actress. (The award went to Glenda Jackson.)

The crowd at the Dorothy Chandler Pavilion in Los Angeles included many stars who loved Lee: Best Song nominee Paul McCartney and his wife Linda, Burt Bacharach, Burt Reynolds, Sammy Cahn, Natalie Wood, Shirley MacLaine. Elizabeth Taylor would cohost.

At the end of the night, much bemused chitchat concerned the night's two mishaps: the surprise appearance of a "streaker" behind actor David Niven as he introduced Taylor; and Peggy Lee's performance.

When director John Huston brought out Lee to sing "The Way We Were," many wondered why Streisand wasn't performing it—especially when they saw a disoriented and confused Peggy Lee. Blanking out on the first line—"Memories light the corners of my mind"—she sang, "Memories . . . of the days . . . light the corners of my mind . . ." Panic flashed on her face. Until the middle of the song, Lee remained so thrown that the conductor, Henry Mancini, wondered if she would ever find her way.

Finally she did, and "The Way We Were" won the Oscar as Best Song. Yet the Bergmans were mortified, and a *New York Times* critic called Lee's appearance "disastrous."

The humiliation proved unbearable. Hours after the performance, she entered St. John's Hospital in Santa Monica. She sent out word through a spokesman that she had undergone "minor surgery"—a possible smokescreen for her condition at the Oscars.

As always, Lee bounced back. In London, she had invited the McCartneys to dine with her at the Dorchester. This was Paul's first meeting with the singer whose "Till There Was You" had inspired him to sing it with the Beatles. Initially the group's deadlock on the pop music world had made her fear for her career, but in time she learned to love them. Now McCartney's post-Beatles band, Wings, had released its second number-one hit, "Band on the Run." His presence at Lee's dinner table amounted to a royal appearance.

McCartney remembered thinking: "I'm either gonna take a bottle of champagne or a song." Choosing the latter, he grabbed an incomplete effort of his and Linda's called "Let's Love." It wasn't much: "Lover, let's be in love with each other / Tonight is the flight of the butterfly." But Lee was overjoyed to receive a song from a Beatle, and when McCartney offered to produce a Peggy Lee recording of it, she felt another renaissance in store.

McCartney's vow helped interest Atlantic Records in signing her to what the *Los Angeles Times* reported as a "long-term contract." It would begin with an album named after the McCartneys' song. For Lee to share a label with Led Zeppelin, King Crimson, Canned Heat, and Aretha Franklin—and to go there hand-in-hand with Paul McCartney—was a stamp of relevance that none of her contemporaries could claim. "I am so thrilled about the whole thing," she told a journalist. "The material is strong and I love the one Paul wrote." Although some of her friends doubted he had actually penned it for her, Lee chose to believe he had: "To think that he would go to all that trouble. He said that it was his way of returning an inspiration."

The McCartneys joined Lee for a second dinner, this time on Tower Grove. Lee did her best to impress them; household staff milled around, including a waiter in a white jacket who served champagne in long-stem crystal. After dinner, Lee sat gleefully at the piano with McCartney, who played and sang the final version of "Let's Love."

The new album, produced by the arranger and soundtrack composer Dave Grusin, would plunge Lee into the commercialized realm of mid-1970s soul—a world of burbling synthesizers, twangy electric guitars, slick black session singers, and swirling strings. The songs included a cover of the Stylistics' hit "You Make Me Feel Brand New"; new tunes by James Taylor and Melissa Manchester; and a funk version of Irving Berlin's "Always."

On April 23, 1974, McCartney arrived at a Hollywood recording studio. He had brought along Linda and a finished backup track for "Let's Love" on which he played piano. Lee still didn't like singing to a prerecorded band, and Betty Jungheim saw the singer's stifled annoyance when McCartney directed her within full earshot of everyone. "He said, 'Peggy, do that again, you didn't do this right, I think it would be better this way.' She didn't like that." But she sang his and Linda's song with a broad smile in her voice; and at the end of the date Lee was in her glory as she and McCartney stood by the piano and led a teeming press conference. The reporters were clearly there to see McCartney, and they pelted him with questions about a hoped-for Beatles reunion. He graciously tried to keep the spotlight on Lee. When Lee told him that she was his fan before he had ever heard of her, McCartney answered, "No, that's not right. . . . I was a fan of yours before you knew about *me*, Peggy."

The younger journalists seemed impressed to find that a star of her day had tackled the sounds her contemporaries loathed and feared. "Rock music tore everything apart," explained Lee, "but it also opened the path for new freedom in songwriting, both in the lyrical content and the musical form. It's no longer necessary for everything to rhyme, as long as it makes sense."

Once more, Lee's ear for the blues helped her connect with the pop-soul that comprised her Atlantic album. She had the sound of a worldly older mama—bruised but smiling, and still flirtatious. The new sexual candor in pop suited her just fine. Singing a ballad by James Taylor, Lee spelled out her needs in a lazy wail: "Save your goodbyes for the morning light / But don't let me be lonely tonight." The Stylistics' hit of that year, "You Make Me Feel Brand New," took on the postcoital dreaminess that

Lee had been exuding since her twenties. Synthesizer, electric guitar, and horns turned Irving Berlin's 1925 love song, "Always," into 1970s funk.

In one original song—a departure from the album's sound—she evoked the far-off innocence of her teens. Lee had penned words to the theme of *The Nickel Ride*, a new crime movie that Grusin had scored. The tune was a slow, bittersweet waltz, and since the film's name reminded her of her girlhood stint as an amusement-park barker, she conjured up those days in verse. Seldom, if ever, had Lee written a more touching or self-knowing lyric. As Grusin played piano, she sang and spoke about a beloved old ride that broke down—a metaphor for the joy in her life that had gone awry. "Things were fun then, and I still had my pride . . . What went wrong then? Something went wrong inside."

"The Nickel Ride" didn't fit the album, and it stayed unreleased for decades. But in the summer of 1974, *Let's Love* hit stores. In the magazine *High Fidelity*, Morgan Ames, an L.A. studio singer and lyricist who doubled as a record critic, marveled at how Lee "keeps on happening . . . To this day, Peggy Lee can sound comfortable in any style she wants to. She's not a judger, but a doer."

The title song, issued as a single, made a modest showing on the Adult Contemporary chart. But few young people were buying it. In his *New York Times* piece, "Not All Pop Legends Are Indestructible," Shaun Considine scorned Frank Sinatra's now-labored singing on his new album, *Some Nice Things I've Missed*, which included such AM-radio trifles as "Tie a Yellow Ribbon Round the Ole Oak Tree" and "Sweet Caroline." As for *Let's Love*, Considine called the production "first-rate . . . but the lead star vocal is completely lost in the surroundings." Such attempts at going modern were in vain, he felt; for both Sinatra and Lee, wrote Considine, "it seems the dance is just about over."

Lee, of course, disagreed. That September, she launched *Let's Love* in her new show at the Waldorf. More determined than ever to sound "with it," she gave Betty Jungheim the woeful task of firing Lou Levy, who couldn't stand her forays into pop-rock. "He's not contemporary," the singer stated. Following a tip from a friend, Lee hired Frank Fiore, a budding twenty-year-old pianist and conductor, to lead her group of seasoned pros. Born in Queens, New York, Fiore had amassed an impressive résumé, but the stars for whom he had conducted—including Ann-Margret and the 1960s TV actor and singer George Maharis—didn't exactly place him on the cutting edge of pop. Now he would be conducting for the great Peggy Lee—a job he was brash enough to accept. "I was way too young for any of this," he reflected years later.

Still, Fiore was hungry to learn, and his half a year with Lee proved the greatest education of his life. Above all else, he learned the meaning of restraint. "She taught me how to play a lot less notes—how dramatic and effective it can be to leave holes."

Lee imparted the same lesson to Leata Galloway. The magnetic pop-soul songstress toured with Lee for months as part of a black female backup trio. Galloway had appeared in the original Broadway production of *Hair*; in her future were a return to Broadway in *Sophisticated Ladies* and her own album on Columbia. For now she, like Fiore, faced a new challenge with Peggy Lee. "Back then I was a soloist, but when I got offered the job I thought, 'I'm gonna learn a lot from this woman.' One day we were in a big concert hall rehearsing, and she never opened her mouth. And the place just filled up with her voice. I thought, how the hell is that happening? At that point I learned, you don't have to scream your lungs out—just sing where you are, and it's the sound man's responsibility to create that ambiance and volume that you need in a giant hall."

Onstage, said Galloway, "I was in heaven. I was doing what I wanted to do, singing with an orchestra, with Peggy Lee." But the star's minimalism had its stranger aspects. "There was never any real expression to her face, and I used to stare at it and wonder, why isn't her face moving when she talks or sings?" It took Galloway a while to deduce the reason: "Plastic surgery had tightened it so much that there was nothing to move." She never witnessed Lee's Valium use, but she certainly saw its effects. Between songs, Lee spoke at the breathy crawl of a woman detached from real time. Audiences leaned forward, waiting through long silences for Lee to complete her thoughts. "When I was in *Lonnnnndon* . . . I had such pleasure in meeting . . . Paul McCartney after *alllll* these years of being friends across the ocean . . . and . . . when he came to dinner . . . he didn't bring a bottle of champagne or . . . a bouquet of flowers . . . but he said he would write me a song . . . and he did. And so I'd say . . . that if you have a good friend . . . you have something *verrrry* . . . precious."

Until now Lee had managed to spoon-feed modern pop, in modest portions, to audiences of her contemporaries. But the *Let's Love* show, with its synthesizer sounds and funk grooves, took her out of her old fans' comfort zone. Sitting amid them at the Empire Room, David Tipmore, the *Village Voice*'s young cabaret critic, felt mostly discomfort. In all her attempts to stay current, Lee had caught herself in a catch-22. The patrons at her beloved Waldorf-Astoria greeted her new repertoire with pale applause, and only perked up when she sang her hits. Rock-loving youngsters had no desire to come to the starchy Waldorf to hear Peggy Lee sing their music.

Tipmore wasn't having much fun. There in that ornate shrine to the past, he watched a fussily coiffed, cosmetically altered chanteuse who, for all her teasing glances, seemed as remote and stonelike as a sacred relic. "To criticize her is to deface the Statue of Liberty," wrote Tipmore. "Rarely does anyone address how disinterested and selfish a performer she can be, how scantily she uses her rather meager voice." In "You Make Me Feel Brand New," he observed, "the soul of the song was supplied not by warm singing or acting, but by the red gels and the bleached black back-up trio and Mr. Fiore's electronics." The dutiful standing ovation at the end struck him as equally mechanical. "The audience wants the old Peggy Lee back," he declared. "So do I."

As she and her touring caravan traveled their circuit of traditional nightspots, Lee replaced many of the pop-soul titles with safer, older tunes—"because we were dying, buddy," said Fiore. To him, the venues were mostly "clip joints—overpriced, with padded bills." Lee's beloved Empire Room struck him as "scary and cold. It certainly wasn't acoustically or architecturally designed to be a performance space. The audience was too far away, the stage and the ceiling were too high."

Between shows, Lee stayed in bed. "She lived as a kind of recluse," he said, "doing her business on the phone, doctors coming, food being delivered, oxygen tanks." The star had ordered her young road manager, Robbie McAlley, to build ramps on either side of the bed so that her two matching shih tzus could run up and down. Hovering nearby was a flame of Lee's from her Benny Goodman days: Peter "Snake Hips" Dean, an artists' manager and the uncle of singer-songwriter Carly Simon. The white-haired sexagenarian had reinvented himself as a ukelele-strumming crooner of ditties from the 1930s. "But at that moment," said Fiore, "he was Peggy's best-friend-advisor-sort-of-manager, because she didn't really have a manager per se." While Bruce Richard took his boss's backup singer Leata Galloway on late-night sprees to gay bars, Lee had no particular life beyond the stage. "When I first began with her, the musicians used to hang out in her suite, but after awhile she stopped that," said her guitarist John Whitfield. "She would just go to her room and keep to herself with Virginia, who had a room right next door to Peggy."

Galloway was too much in awe of Lee to pursue a friendship, much as both of them might have liked it. "Once she called me into the bathroom when she was taking a bubble bath. I was a nervous wreck. She was covered in bubbles, but I thought, god, where do I look? She wanted somebody to talk to. So I thanked her for having me in the group, and I started crying. She was sweet. But I don't think she was happy at all. She had all these people around her, this money, beautiful clothes, but she didn't really have a soul mate. She was just performing. It was sad."

Lee tried in various ways to forge bonds with the people who worked for her. After each show, she summoned her band and singers to her suite, where they would listen to a tape of the show they had just performed. "We would get notes," said Fiore. "She was extremely moody and obviously medicated, so we were at the mercy of whatever body chemistry kicked in at that moment." On happier nights, she followed those listening sessions with The Laughing Game, one of her favorite postshow pastimes. "She got out of bed for this one," explained Fiore. "Everybody had to lie down on the floor in the living room. One person would put his or her head on the stomach of the next person and we would form human dominoes. Miss Lee would always be in the front. And she would start laughing. And before you knew it everyone would start laughing. This would just tickle her silly."

Whatever the intimacies, she remained "Miss Lee." Perceived slights would bring chastisement—some of it hair-raising, some hilarious. "I remember a time when we got to the hotel and her room wasn't ready," said Galloway, "so she got a pillow and lay right on the floor in the hallway. I said, 'Peggy, my room is ready; why don't you come and crash in here?' But no. She was trying to make a point." So it continued, night after night—*Sunset Boulevard* as seen through a funhouse mirror. "It was the Hollywood I had read about," recalled Fiore. "I thought, this is as weird as it gets—they really *are* like this!"

———

CONFRONTED WITH UNWELCOME TRUTHS, Lee reacted like an angry tiger. Her extravagance was decimating her income, and repeatedly Betty Jungheim warned her that her money was running out. *"I don't want to know!"* snapped Lee, while insisting that countless people were ripping her off. Each week Jungheim wrote checks for the star to sign; then she sat by Lee's bedside as the star challenged each expense, including her own long-distance phone charges. *"What is this for?"* she asked accusingly. She refused to authorize certain payments, and Jungheim had to field angry calls from creditors. In turn, Lee blamed her for letting the bills go unpaid.

Soon she cut one more voice of reason out of her life. In February 1975, a friend accused Jungheim of having spoken critically of Lee. The singer flew into a rage. After Jungheim had left for the day, Lee rose out of bed and stormed into the office. The next morning she summoned Jungheim to her bedside. Lee declared the files disorganized, and pelted her with accusations. She told Jungheim to pack up her things and leave—"and you'd better not talk!" So ended five years of employment and twenty-five of friendship.

For a woman who, as Mike Stoller said, "seemed to run on anger," there was nothing like the memory of Min to provide a jolt of survival fuel. Friends had wearied of the singer's tirades about her stepmother. "Everybody's sick to death of that Min!" said Robert Richards. For all of Lee's fond reminiscing about North Dakota, she had no wish to return. Even in death, Min seemed like an ever-lurking demon there, and the place contained other ghosts. On her last visit there in 1950, Lee had seen her father in his deathbed; Dave Barbour had accompanied her on that trip when their marriage, too, was expiring.

In 1963, the state's then governor, William L. Guy, had picked Lee—"North Dakota's best-known and best-loved woman," as he called her—to receive the Rough Rider Award, given to distinguished natives. Recipients included Lawrence Welk, newscaster Eric Sevareid, and novelist Louis L'Amour. Lee made excuses and declined.

The current governor, Arthur A. Link, tried again. North Dakota State University in Fargo sweetened the invitation by awarding her an honorary doctorate of music. This time, Lee could not refuse.

On Wednesday, May 21, 1975, she arrived at the small Fargo airport with an entourage of seven. They included John Pisano and his recently wedded wife, Kathy Mahana Levy. "Lou divorced her and I married her," said Pisano. A car took them all to the hotel, and Lee gazed out for the first time in twenty-five years at the flat, monotonous landscape that had defined her childhood. Kathy asked the driver, "What do you guys do when you get out of school here?" He said, "We leave!"

Fargo welcomed her back like a queen. At WDAY and elsewhere, signs were hung that proclaimed PEGGY LEE SANG HERE. For the next two days, the city kept her on grand display. She gave a press conference, then attended an alumni dinner. On a scorching Friday afternoon, Lee donned a black robe and joined the graduating class to receive her doctorate.

That night at a campus sports arena, four thousand North Dakotans saw Lee and an orchestra perform an expanded version of her latest show. Many old friends, including Ken Kennedy, had come. The woman they saw was heavier and slower than the teenage dynamo they remembered, and the obvious melancholy in her voice made the reunion heartrending. After the last strains of her closer, "I'll be Seeing You," Guy and Link walked onstage to pay lavish tribute to the singer. Link thanked her for her "tremendous contribution to the enrichment of millions of lives all over this great land." Then he gave her the Rough Rider plaque, along with a leather scroll emblazoned with the words, "Strength from the Soil," which she certainly possessed.

Lee seemed on the verge of tears. "I really am overcome," she said. "I can't tell you what beautiful memories I will take home with me, and I hope it won't be so long until I'll come back again."

She never did. And the afterglow from that idyllic homecoming didn't last. Composer Alec Wilder, a father figure to Lee since her Goodman days, looked with dismay at the scared and desperate woman she had become—one who was all too quick to hurt others the way she had been hurt. Wilder detested change, and clung to his vision of a past where "taste" and "manners" had reigned. But he was also a shrewd judge of character, and in his 1975 book, *Letters I Never Mailed*, he told loved ones the things he hadn't the nerve to say to their faces. His remarks to Lee held a sad resignation.

> Just where, can you tell me, has the belief and sweet sadness, the genuine love and the genuine touch gone? Into the bitterness or loneliness of age? . . . So you aren't young? So a great deal has happened to make a person crouch in the shadows? So an age of innocence, of joy and wonderment is at an end? So we must survive and somehow come to grips with today's goblin society?
>
> All granted. But must we allow the best of ourselves, still breathing and living a lonely life in the secure world of our memory, die because the face in the mirror has changed or because little brown spots begin to sprinkle the backs of our hands?

If Lee read his words, she didn't let on. She continued to sink into a twilight zone where she stayed numbed from the truth, or tried to. A chill was in the air, literally, at the supper clubs in which she sang, which had begun to feel like morgues. "She loved cold, cold air-conditioning," explained Lou Levy, "and everybody would be freezing to death. The guys in the band could hardly play, the instruments were so cold." All the while, audiences beheld an embalmed-looking figure whose slow-burning delivery had turned distant and numb.

Let's Love had not sold as hoped, and Atlantic had declined a follow-up. Once more, her recording career seemed finished. Then she remembered an offer made to her by Leiber and Stoller when "Is That All There Is?" was hot. The partners had longed to produce a whole Peggy Lee album of their more esoteric songs. "She kept putting us off," said Leiber. "She was on the road, always on the road."

The duo had never approved of Lee's attempts to be "current," as Stoller put it, "by singing covers of the Beatles and Aretha Franklin that, to my mind, had nothing to do with her style. I mean, they're great songs, but we thought we could make her into a real cabaret singer in the European sense." According to Phil Wright, however, Leiber and Stoller had "wanted a lot of money" in return. "That's why I ended up producing her," he said.

In the winter of 1975, Lee phoned Leiber to remind him of his offer. "Peggy," he said, "we've lost a little momentum." Nonetheless, he and Leiber jumped at the chance to fulfill their "long-languished dream"—an LP that would show the world how much depth they really had.

Their currency in the pop world had faded. In 1972, Leiber and Stoller had produced the acclaimed debut album of Stealers Wheel, a Scottish folk-rock band; it had yielded a top-ten single, "Stuck in the Middle with You." Otherwise, the hits had dried up, but money flooded in anyhow. Years earlier, the team had bought up lucrative publishing rights to such musicals as *Cabaret* and *Fiddler on the Roof*, along with a wealth of standards, including "Body and Soul," "The Very Thought of You," and "Fever"—the song whose composer royalties Lee felt she should share. "Those purchases relieved the pressure of being forced to write hits to make a living," said Stoller.

Now he and Leiber could devote their time to a project as commercially dubious as an album of Peggy Lee singing their undiscovered songs. They gathered some and presented them to her on Tower Grove Drive. Stoller found her conversation more disjointed and confusing than ever, but when they convened at the piano she snapped to attention. The songs revealed the broad range of Leiber and Stoller's gifts. "Saved" was a witty spoof of a revival meeting. Other titles delved into such topics as insanity and murder, with atonal and bitonal touches. "Ready to Begin Again," from an unproduced musical version of Jean Giraudoux's fantasy play *The Madwoman of Chaillot*, detailed a bald, toothless matron's rise from the ashes. "A Little White Ship" came from another unrealized project, a musical version of Tennessee Williams's *Camino Real*. The song could have been a lullaby or a descent into drug-induced euphoria. "Tango" was an imagined peek into the scene of a crime: the 1968 murder of silent-film heartthrob Ramón Novarro in his Los Angeles home by two male prostitutes. Such songs were at least as daring for Lee as "Is That All There Is?" But bravery had always marked her choices, and she unhesitatingly opted to move forward.

Leiber and Stoller took the project to A&M Records, a company known for taking risks. The label could afford to; it was earning untold millions from hits by the Carpenters, Cat Stevens, Joe Cocker, the Captain and Tennille, Peter Frampton, and other young sensations. A&M's founders, trumpeter Herb Alpert (who had led the chart-topping Tijuana Brass) and Jerry Moss, were known for following their hearts as well as their bankbooks. In 1971, Alpert had produced *Wings*, an epic cantata by the French film composer Michel Colombier; the album employed 158 musicians and 29 singers, and barely sold. Other high-flown concept albums came out of A&M's jazz division, Horizon. "They just wanted to do these things," said illustrator David McMacken, who worked in the art department. "They didn't care if they made money or not."

But Peggy Lee was known as difficult and demanding, and Moss scoffed at the idea of signing her. It took a heavy push by Gil Friesen, one of his trusted staff producers, to change his mind. Still, Moss insisted that Leiber and Stoller produce the album themselves—a job that would involve keeping Lee under control. They promised they would.

Bygone as "Is That All There Is?" now seemed, the songwriters harbored a vague hope that lightning might strike again. Moss cooperated. He signed Lee for one album, with an option for another if he chose. Cost was no object. "To have an album from Peggy Lee was a big deal for us," he explained. "We wanted to do it right." Once the contract was ready, Lee met him for the first time. She encountered a thirty-nine-year-old whose thick mustache, dark wavy hair, and sideburns reminded her of Burt Reynolds. Although she never let him know it, Lee was instantly smitten with Moss, who had a wife and children. He had given her his home numbers—a gesture he lived to regret. "She had *lots* of questions," Moss said.

But most of them concerned business. He had just reached his weekend home when the phone began to ring. It was Lee, reading him passages of her contract, which was full of legalese. "She said, 'I have had contracts with Capitol for years, and I've *never* seen language like this.' I said, 'Peggy, please don't worry about the language. I guarantee you it's not a problem. We'll settle all this on Monday.' This wasn't her lawyer calling me, it was her. She was a girl who didn't want to be taken advantage of."

The first recording sessions rambled along with no seeming focus. In late May, at A&M's high-tech Studio B in Hollywood, Lee and the songwriters felt their way in a series of demos. Not all the tunes were Leiber and Stoller's. According to the composer's son, recording engineer Peter Stoller, the partners feared that a too-arty album might scare off the top brass—so they cut some pop tracks "as a backup plan." A torch song from 1929, "Love Me or Leave Me," took on a generic disco feel. "Crazy Life" came from Gino Vannelli, a curly-haired, hairy-chested Canadian pop star on whom Lee had a crush. Singing over bland electric keyboards and Latin percussion, she sounded so sluggish that a sexy groove was impossible.

But Leiber and Stoller's witty "Don Juan," the tale of a fallen Lothario, awakened her funky swing, while her languid sexiness shone through on "Some Cats Know," the tune of theirs that Lee had rejected in 1968. Leiber had replaced the risqué bridge that had offended her, but the song

Recording with Mike Stoller and Jerry Leiber.
(COURTESY OF THE LEIBER & STOLLER ARCHIVES)

remained a single-entendre reflection on those rare men who know "how to make the honey flow."

Overall, though, the results of those initial dates were pale enough to incite worry that the partners had lost their golden touch. Then came the fourth session, and everything changed. A&M's extraordinary largesse had enabled the duo to contract a symphony—eighty-six pieces. Stoller had enlisted one of Lee's favorite arrangers, Johnny Mandel. The two orchestral pieces recorded that day were downright chilling. In "The Case of M.J." a spookily dissonant, Kurt Weill–inspired waltz, a "good" little girl named Mary Jane drifts, verse by verse, toward madness. An eerie spoken refrain—"How old were you when your father went away?"—hints at patricide, as does the news that Mary Jane has "made a mess of her pretty white dress." High, icy violins enhanced a horror-movie soundtrack. Lee maintained a sinister smile in a voice that had grown thin and girlish enough to resemble Mary Jane's. Echoes of little Norma's spiraling anger toward Min weren't far away.

"I Remember" began and ended with Lee humming; in between, her thoughts drifted in what could have been a Valium-induced haze: "I remember when you loved me . . . I lie in my bed, hand under my head . . ." A bed of strings rocked as woozily beneath her as a ship at sea; harp and bells added a dreamlike twinkle.

Leiber and Stoller hadn't written these songs for her. But as with "Is That All There Is?," they had managed to capture, in words and in music, the psyche of Peggy Lee. Her lost-in-space sound of 1975 suited the material ideally.

The songwriters met with Alpert, Moss, and Friesen to play the recordings. Most of them left Moss cold. But Friesen perked up when he heard "The Case of M.J." and "I Remember."

"That's really interesting and beautiful stuff," he said. "You should do a whole album like that."

A theme was emerging—one of surreal story-songs that grimly reflected the truth. All the lighter tunes recorded thus far, other than "Some Cats Know," were shelved. The strange meters and tonalities of the others kept her off-balance; the stories tore off her masks one by one. "She was completely involved emotionally," said Kathy Levy, who attended the sessions. "She disclosed a lot."

Except for "Ready to Begin Again," which Perry Botkin Jr. arranged, the album would be orchestrated and conducted by Mandel. For added comfort, Lee rested between songs in a chaise brought in at her command. She kept her trusty cognac nearby. But none of this could calm her down; on the contrary, she stirred up as much drama as she could to fuel herself for the challenges at hand. When she emerged from her state-of-the-art isolation booth, Moss proudly asked her what she thought of it. "I couldn't breathe in there!" she gasped. "I was dying!" The old friction with Leiber flared up, and Lee banned him from the studio. "I won't record if he comes to the session!" she told Stoller. Later, said the composer, "she got closer to Jerry and hated me, and told Jerry pretty much the same thing. I had a little ulcer problem. Jerry told her that and she said, 'I hope he dies!'" When a slipup by his copyist made Mandel late, Lee stormed out of the studio to meditate. She returned a half hour later, even madder.

Up next was the song about Ramón Novarro. It begins with a slithering, minor-key tango, played in 1920s style. The volume dropped, and Lee delivered a Brechtian spoken monologue that details a dance with death. One false move, it warns, and "the frail body breaks with a slap and a twist." Then, over a spooky baroque harpsichord, Lee sang about the setting of Novarro's murder, a fussily appointed home in the Hollywood Hills. There lay the former heartthrob "in his silk dressing gown . . . one arm flung out for the peacocks to peck."

Lee had initially loved "Tango." Now, explained Robert Richards, "she suddenly got it into her head that she had been forced to sing this obscene homosexual song. Why it should have bothered her so profoundly was very strange for a woman whose house was buzzing with queens." But it was Lee's custom to manufacture anger as a defense in trying moments. Before the session, recalled Stoller, Lee had "some bitter argument with a hairdresser"—probably Bruce Richard. In response, Lee demanded that in a key line of "Tango"—"He was a collector of beautiful strangers"—the "he" be changed to "she."

Leiber refused. Enraged, she sang it her way—"and gave an absolutely beautiful performance," said Stoller. Later, at the editing block, the writers snipped the "s" from "she"—which, of course, made Lee fume.

At least she could smile her way through a sardonic ragtime tune,

"I've Got Them Feelin' Too Good Today Blues," which tickled her sense of humor: "When I'm unhappy I'm tippy-toe-tappy in my shoes!" Other songs pushed her voice to its limit. "Professor Hauptmann's Performing Dogs" required Lee to relive her carnival-barker roots by shouting, over a raucous circus band, the praises of a weird menagerie of dog acts: "One rides a pony and carries a purse / One is on roller skates dressed like a nurse." Lee struggled just as hard with the floating polytonality of "A Little White Ship." Here, at an etherized tempo, she beckoned the listener to "come aboard, come aboard / I guarantee you a pleasant journey"; its nature is sinister but vague. Stoller's tune sails as aimlessly as a boat lost at sea; the harmonies—thick as those of Richard Strauss—provide the fog.

Two remaining songs tore down her smokescreen of self-delusion. "Longings for a Simpler Time" looks back upon an age when "kids behaved and fathers shaved"; when "hearts were true, red white and blue, and skies were sunny." Lee sang this listless waltz with the vacuity of a dementia patient. Beneath the meandering tune, an "unstable tonality gives the lie to the lyric's nostalgia," as composer William Bolcom observed. Finally the song admits it: "We're longing for a simpler time that never was."

In the album's crowning performance, Lee came face-to-face with the most crushing reality of all. "Say It" was another tune from Leiber and Stoller's effort to musicalize *The Madwoman of Chaillot*. The song brought a fantasy ballroom to life, and cast Lee as an aging Cinderella. To the lush, swirling strains of music that echoed Ravel and Fauré, she begged a "bright and shining youth" to tell her he loves her—"for I love a lovely lie." This was one reality she couldn't face; instead she chose to view the song through a rosy lens. "It brings back an era that's very pleasant in my mind," she noted. "I have a whole make-believe concept of what 'Say It' says . . . I feel, oh, almost like Jean Harlow, kind of, and dancing."

Ultimately, there was no telling if Lee grasped the deeper implications of anything on the album. To Johnny Mandel, "the recordings worked out beautifully. She seemed anxious and insecure, but I was used to that. She knew when she was getting it and when she wasn't." In the mixing, the songwriters and engineer Hank Cicalo went heavy on the reverb; it added an aural vapor that made Lee sound even more as though she were a ghost in her own dreams.

But what to call the album? A line in "Say It"—"Waltz me far beyond these walls, and mirrors of the truth"—gave Lee the answer. In an interview with writer Freeman Gunter, she strained to describe her murky and conflicted feelings about the material: "Like a mirror, you look at it different ways at different times and each time you feel differently about what you see."

A&M treated *Mirrors* as an event. Like many of the company's releases, this one would have a gatefold (fold-out) jacket. Photographer Hans Albers, who produced hazy glamour shots in an old Hollywood style, had taken a blurred cover portrait of Lee in a white gown. A&M art director Roland Young relegated it to the inside. He wanted something different, and asked David McMacken to create an illustration of Lee's face.

McMacken was young, and barely knew Lee's work; to him she was "just a sultry singer" from the past. But as he listened over and over to the *Mirrors* tapes, another vision formed in his mind: "She was just so kind of . . . odd. I loved her." McMacken had never met Lee; instead he perused recent publicity stills and album covers. With each year, the images had grown fuzzier. The cover of her 1970 album *Bridge Over Troubled Water* had literally been shot through her screen door. "She didn't want to be old," McMacken realized. "She had a plastic idea of how she should look."

With that in mind, he went to work. Young had gone so far as to obtain samples of Lee's makeup for him. McMacken created an image of a frozen doll with a touch of madness in the eyes. He caught Lee's eerily waxen skin; the painted-on peach lips; the Barbie-like lashes. It was the perfect image for *Mirrors*. Lee saw no subtext in his work; to her it was just a pretty drawing. It appeared on the cover in a shiny silver border.

Tour dates in support of the album were slated quickly. The first one would take Lee to an unlikely place for a *Mirrors* show: the Flamingo Hilton in Las Vegas. Lee had hired a new young pianist, Byron Olson, the former accompanist of her old Capitol colleague, June Christy. Anxiety had already set in. Olson had conducting experience, but in a move designed to create tension, Lee decided that her tried-and-true guitarist, John Pisano—who had never conducted—should do the job instead, while doubling on guitar. She had Olson coach him.

During a rehearsal, said Pisano, "Peggy made some derogatory remark, the way she would always needle her conductors. I kept working. But as soon as we were in the dressing room, I said, 'Peggy, I don't need to do this. I didn't want to do it, and I don't appreciate—' She looked at me and she actually started crying."

Lee had programmed an awkward mix of *Mirrors* songs, contemporary pop-soul, and her old hits—not what the Flamingo was expecting. The real surprise came just before the opening. The Flamingo shared the same management as the Las Vegas Hilton, formerly the International. While Lee rehearsed, word came that the Hilton's cash cow, Elvis Presley, was sick and couldn't perform. Lee was asked to move *Mirrors* for that night to the same huge space that Barbra Streisand had packed for a month in 1969. It was a risky prospect, but she agreed.

Kathy Levy watched the early show from the wings. After a few songs, the walkouts began. "I saw she was in huge trouble," said Levy. So did the manager. "We have to get her out of here," he said. "She'll never sell the second show."

Soon after Lee had left the stage and returned to her dressing room, the manager knocked on her door. Moments later came a cry: *"KATHY!"* Levy hurried inside. "She looked at me. And she looked at him. And she said, 'Dick doesn't feel we can fill this room. What do you think?' I said, 'Here's your purse.' I gave her my arm. I walked her down the stairs and to the limo, and we went back to the other hotel."

Lee spoke not a word about the incident. But she was crushed; never before had she been asked to leave a venue. The Flamingo engagement went on, but *Mirrors* wasn't a hit there, either. She began lopping out the Leiber-Stoller songs and replacing them with crowd-pleasers.

The singer moved on to one of her regular stops, Chicago's Palmer House Hotel, which had its own Empire Room. To Ron Powers of the *Chicago Sun-Times*, the nightspot was "frozen in time a half-century ago, a pocket of aristocratic make-believe with its plumes and mirrors and soft-peach lights flung on the vaulted ceiling." Such a setting might have lent an ironic backdrop to the *Mirrors* material, but Lee's audience wasn't there for irony. For years she had brought them playful current songs they could accept—"Maxwell's Silver Hammer," "Sing," "Oh, Babe, What Would You Say?," "My Sweet Lord," "Brother Love's Traveling Salvation

Show." Now, as she sang the opening lines of "Ready to Begin Again"—"When my teeth are at rest in a glass by my bed, and my hair lies somewhere in a drawer"—the crowd tensed up visibly. The *Chicago Tribune*'s Will Leonard, who had been raving about Lee since her Buttery days, wasn't charmed by *Mirrors*; he called "Ready to Begin Again" "corny comedy." Later in the show, the audience jarred her by giggling during her recitation in "Tango."

Doubts about the project seized her. Already, she looked for people to blame. A week before the October 17 release of *Mirrors*, Lee joined guest host Joey Bishop on the *Tonight* show. She sang the album's two "little lightening procedures," as she called them, "I've Got Them Feelin' Too Good Today Blues" and "Some Cats Know." When Bishop asked about her "controversial" new release, Lee brought up "Tango," with its homosexualizing pronoun. "There's a verse in there that I don't approve of. I thought it was out, and I heard the final mix and it was in . . . Well, I tried reciting the poem, it is a poem at the beginning, and I got laughs when I wasn't supposed to—you know what that feels like?" She delivered the whole monologue. "That's funny, eh?" said Lee testily. Bishop changed the subject: "So why do you bite your nails?"

A&M forged ahead in its efforts to make *Mirrors* a success. Posters with the McMacken drawing were glued all over New York. To advertise Lee's upcoming run at the Waldorf, the label ran ads with a Robert Richards sketch—a glamorous but ghostly black-and-white image of the singer glancing over her shoulder in a backless dress.

Just before the opening, the label threw her a sumptuous party at the Waldorf's Starlight Roof. Four hundred guests were invited, along with a battery of press. Waiters circulated, bearing trays of champagne and oysters. The Waldorf was treating the show like a theater piece, selling advance tickets and printing a program. All this attention made Lee even more nervous, and with good reason. Opening night came—and almost from the first minute of the show, she smelled trouble. Her deceptively jaunty welcoming song, "I've Got Them Feelin' Too Good Today Blues," earned only strained applause. The macabre humor of "Professor Hauptmann's Performing Dogs" caused palpable discomfort; the audience seemed to feel it had missed the joke. "Say It" and "A Little White Ship" unsettled them further. Lee alternated the *Mirrors* selections with a half dozen of her hits. But they couldn't lessen the sting of songs about a toothless old lady and a gay murder.

In her suite after the performance, dismayed friends asked her why she was doing this. More resistance came from the *New York Times*, where John S. Wilson called the show "disappointingly superficial." The songs, he wrote, "suggest an emotional depth that is not conveyed by her bland delivery. . . . Nothing cracks the perfection of her carefully arranged image. Nothing is ever out of place. Nothing shows."

The record reviews followed. Seldom in A&M's history—and never in Lee's—had a release been panned so savagely as *Mirrors*. Because it was a Leiber and Stoller project, the album made it into *Rolling Stone*, one of whose critics, Stephen Holden, dismissed most of it as "dreck." The duo's songs, he wrote, were "tuneless and wordy, implying less in twenty-five couplets than one verse from any of their countless hits for the Coasters or Elvis Presley."

His opinions broke Stoller's heart. The composer read a subtext in them: "These guys know rock and roll and rhythm and blues, what are they trying to do? What is this pretentious shit?" In *Down Beat*, America's top jazz magazine, twenty-five-year-old Mikal Gilmore was hardly kinder. He deemed the record a "failure," and blamed Leiber and Stoller: "*Mirrors*, a cabaret album without any noticeable urgency, provides Peggy with about as much support as clouds would a faltering airplane." He compared the album to "a joke that everyone laughs and titters at, but where nobody really catches the punch line." To the usually sympathetic Peter Reilly of *Stereo Review*, *Mirrors* was "at times pretentious, gimmicky, and rather overdecorated even for her."

Even Jerry Leiber joined the naysayers. "I was embarrassed by the criticisms," he said in 1999, "and I think that some of it was supportable. I thought some of the stuff *was* pretentious." He held Lee partly accountable, pronouncing her past her peak and not up to the music's demands.

If *Mirrors* had come to her at an ideal moment emotionally, its commercial timing couldn't have been worse. This was the peak of the disco era, one of the most frivolous, escapist times in pop history. No wonder so many critics found *Mirrors* leaden. Morgan Ames, who had helped contract the orchestra, was shocked by the responses. *Mirrors*, she said, was "more than disliked; it was actually resented. It was so different from anything going on at the time, and nobody understood it. It was a brutal punishment for Peggy, because she had had such a huge hit with 'Is That All There Is?,' which was art music too."

The castigation cut deeper than that, for Lee had never exposed herself so nakedly on an album. Her *Mirrors* show "didn't last too long," said Byron Olson. Lee began dropping the Leiber-Stoller songs and replacing them with more of "the old warhorses" her fans wanted.

Typically, she accused others of sabotage. The songwriters had forced her into doing the album, she claimed, then into darkening her interpretations, which spoiled their humor. None of that was true, but Lee had blown the "Tango" incident into the realm of fantasy. She placed a series of angry, accusatory calls to Jerry Moss, thus ensuring that A&M would never record her again.

Once the smoke had cleared, rage gave way to hurt. "I'm not going to get that sad again," she vowed to Max Jones of the British magazine *Melody Maker*. "I didn't really think it was right to depress people that much." She cited "Longings for a Simpler Time," one of the tracks that had fallen most heavily on fans' ears. "People believed the song in a basic, sentimental way, and then at the end they felt I had tricked them." The cover drawing that she had initially loved now embodied the death of one more dream. "It looks like a corpse," she told a friend.

A few people saw *Mirrors* differently. "It's all of a piece, it's a work of art," said Robert Richards. "It's still deeper than anyone has gone in the pop field." Johnny Mandel was disgusted by "these new rock-and-roll writers who took it apart, as if they knew. Most of them were idiots. It's a wonderful work. I think it's classic and it's timeless."

Many years passed before *Mirrors* developed a cult of fans who hailed it as a masterpiece. In 1988, William Bolcom, the Pulitzer Prize–winning composer, compared it to a "fine wine" that had been opened too soon.

Once more Lee felt stranded, unwanted. She was also nearly broke. At a vulnerable moment she confided in Richards: "I've never had a day when I didn't have to worry about money." A lot of that problem, of course, was of her own making, but Lee preferred to blame fate. Having released one of the most rarefied albums of the year, Lee agreed to record a set of radio spots for McDonald's. She saw poverty ahead, and her paranoia over finances increased. Lee had refused to give Betty Jungheim her final paycheck or to reimburse her for expenses owed; she had also badmouthed her former secretary widely and sent defamatory letters about her. Bruce Vanderhoff was so disgusted by Lee's behavior that he encouraged Jungheim to sue. He introduced her to a pair of lawyer friends, who took the case.

According to *Variety*, Jungheim filed a $300,000 suit against Lee and her lawyer, Ludwig H. Gerber, on July 23. It charged libel, slander, and nonpayment. Lee's response was volcanic. On August 27, the *Los Angeles Times* reported that Lee was countersuing Jungheim for "slander, fraud, embezzlement, and mishandling of business affairs." The initial amount was six million dollars; it pole-vaulted to fifteen, then twenty-two. Jungheim learned why. Recently a court had awarded Doris Day a twenty-three-million-dollar settlement against the business partners of her late husband and manager, Marty Melcher, for mishandling her funds and nearly wiping her out. Lee had decided that if Day could win twenty-three, she would try for twenty-two. She had also consulted her psychic, who informed her that Jungheim had hidden the allegedly embezzled funds in her garage. "I want to put her behind bars!" railed Lee to Virginia Bernard.

Lee's friends were appalled. "It's the dumbest thing I ever heard in my life!" said Dona Harsh. Brian Panella agreed: "If there were anyone I ever met who I thought was honest to a fault, it was Betty." Lee's favorite ex-hair stylist never forgave her. "If Betty Jungheim embezzled one dollar, I'm not Bruce Vanderhoff!" he said. "I was so upset about Betty getting fired for Peggy's lies. Peggy was in financial ruin due to her spending. She would have had to declare bankruptcy. Peggy was infamous for taking too many of her own musicians on the road, which ate up all the profits. For paying hairdressers too much money. Because she was the star. The sky's the limit. Betty took the fall. It was all for show."

Her legal actions were costing Lee money she didn't have, but she wasn't through. Citing "gross negligence," she managed to block Jungheim's unemployment payments. "That's when I sat down and cried," Jungheim said. Lee continued her smear campaign. Newspapers printed her charges against Jungheim, which nearly destroyed the younger woman's chances of finding another job in the industry. Meanwhile, her legal expenses were mounting. Vanderhoff came to her rescue by putting her to work in the office of Le Restaurant. When Lee heard about it, she called him and insisted he ban Jungheim from the premises. He refused. She slammed down the phone.

Jungheim, who had two teenagers, wound up nearly penniless. It took her years of hard work to recover financially. All the while, she recalled some advice she'd received from a sympathetic member of the district attorney's office, where Jungheim had gone for her deposition. Putting his hand on her shoulder, he told her: "Don't ever go to work for a friend."

"The magic was gone," said Mel Tormé of the Waldorf's fading
Empire Room. In her last days there, Lee kept company
with Mike Russo, her hulking protector.

Chapter Fifteen

ON TOWER GROVE Drive, new secretaries came and went rapidly. Lee had always hired short-term help for the Waldorf, and for her next engagement, her confidante and personal shopper Helen Glickstein recommended Magda Katz, a friend of her daughter Wendy. A budding show-business writer, Katz jumped at the opportunity. At one PM on a frigid day, she stood at the door of 37F and rang the buzzer. A housekeeper let her in. "Miss Lee is in the bedroom," she said, pointing to a partly open door.

Katz saw that the room inside was dark. "Come right in," murmured a weak voice. The curtains were drawn and the air-conditioning turned on. From either side of the room, humidifiers sprayed plumes of mist that surrounded the bed with a ghostly vapor. Lee lay under a blanket, a scarf around her neck. "Sit down," she whispered, nodding toward a chair by the bed. Katz kept her coat on. "Do you know how to take dictation?" the singer asked. Katz said yes, although she didn't. Lee wanted to send a letter to Johnny Mercer, who had an inoperable brain tumor. "Dear Johnny . . ." said Lee, followed by some unintelligible mumbling.

"I thought, oh my God, I don't understand what she's saying," recalled Katz. "How was I gonna do this? Meanwhile my coat's getting sopped because of all these sprays, and I'm freezing. I could barely see." She asked Lee what she was trying to say. "He's very sick," came the response. Katz managed to extract a few more details, then moved to a typewriter in the living room. Though it took her several tries on Lee's pricey stationery, she created a convincing note of sympathy. Lee liked it, but a bigger concern snapped her out of her fog: "Be very careful with my stationery. It's very expensive!"

Katz got the job, and kept it for the balance of Lee's Waldorf engagements. On the surface, the runs went well, and loyal fans continued to crowd the shows. But Lee's expenses had shrunk the profit margin. The Waldorf paid her twenty thousand dollars a week, more than she earned elsewhere. Accommodations for her musicians, said her guitarist John Whitfield, were "always first-class." After Lee had written checks to them and to her employees and covered the costs of travel, gowns, publicity, and incidentals, only a fraction remained. After Katz gave birth to a daughter, she asked Lee for a thirty-dollar raise to pay the babysitter. "She went crazy on me," said Katz. The singer lunged out of bed, reached inside a cabinet, and pulled out a wad of bills. She threw them on the floor in Katz's direction. "Here! Take it! You're just like everybody else. Everybody wants money!" The young woman calmly picked thirty dollars off the floor and handed Lee the rest.

Soon she met the dazzled admirers who made up her employer's inner circle—notably Phoebe Jacobs, Robert Richards, and Lee's longtime fan and pal Frank Ralston, who despite having a prosthetic leg ran any errand she asked of him. But Katz looked at the star's New York retinue and saw mostly "a lot of hangers-on." Two hairdresser friends waited until Lee was sleeping or busy, then raided the cupboard of 37F for groceries and took them home. Another regular on the scene was Mike Russo, a hulking, fussily groomed pursuer of Lee's. No one knew for sure what he did for a living, but her friends had their theories. Russo, who claimed a friendship with Frank Sinatra, began monitoring Lee's incoming calls and otherwise assuming a take-charge attitude, throwing muscle around on her behalf as though he were her manager. He wooed Lee with expensive gifts, which she accepted, while apparently never repaying him in the way he wanted. "He gave me the creeps," said Katz.

Another regular was Freeman Gunter, a bearded young writer who covered cabaret for gay publications. In a profile of Lee for *Mandate*, a magazine of male nudes and erotic fiction, Gunter proclaimed the singer "a living legend and a woman who lives her legend twenty-four hours a day." But beyond the Empire Room and her suite, Lee was hardly seen. Katz and others tried, in vain, to pry her out of her suite for lunch or coffee. "She seemed to have no curiosity, no interest in the outside world," said Wendy Glickstein.

Friends had to come to her. One of the singer's favorites was Walter Willison, a boyish young singer-actor whose costarring role in the Richard Rodgers–Martin Charnin Broadway musical, *Two by Two*, had earned him a Tony nomination. Willison was a mad fan, and his golly-gee enthusiasm so charmed her that she let him hang out in her suite after shows. One night he showed up with his friend Lee Horwin, a young cabaret singer who would eventually make it to the *Tonight* show. She idolized Peggy Lee, and after she and Willison had seen Lee at the Empire Room, the star thrilled Horwin by receiving them upstairs. Lee even rose from bed and greeted them in the living room. She motioned for Horwin to sit next to her on the couch. "She was in a muumuu, munching on a bologna sandwich, and she started picking my brain about different aspects of her show," Horwin recalled. "I thought, this can't be happening. I was just starting out, really." Youthful opinions about her work mattered to Peggy Lee; but Horwin sensed that the singer was also "giving me time, giving me my moment. She was very generous."

One night she showed her tougher side to a delighted Willison. As he sat near her bedside, she answered a call. "Yes," said Lee into the receiver. "Mm-hmm . . . mm-hmm . . . mm-hmm." Finally she said in a steely tone: "Eliminate him!" She hung up.

"I guess she had fired somebody," recalled Willison. "I thought, ooh, that's so mafia!"

Having regained her lost pounds, Lee reverted to her strange techniques for weight control. Katz's daily tasks included drawing a scalding-hot bath for Lee and pouring in rosewater and alum, a double-sulfate salt used as an astringent and blood coagulant. Lee shed her robe, whereupon Katz draped her in Saran Wrap and helped lower her into the tub for twenty minutes. "It shrinks you before you go onstage," Lee explained. One day Katz waited a little too long; she ran inside the bathroom and found her boss in the water, reddened and dazed. She panicked. "All I could think of was the *New York Post* headline: 'Magda Katz Kills Peggy Lee.'" She struggled to hoist Lee out of the tub, and the singer kept going limp. The doorbell rang, and it was Helen Glickstein. Katz blurted out the problem, and the two women somehow managed to hoist Lee up and onto her feet.

As always, nothing made her snap to attention like anger. Lee could find cause for it in the most innocent of statements and gestures. When

Katz relayed a message from Frank Sinatra's right-hand man, Jilly Rizzo, that Sinatra had invited her to a party he was throwing at the Waldorf, Lee turned as red as she had in the bathtub. "I'm not going!" she growled. "I can't stand the man!" Katz could only assume that Lee had resented him for not calling her personally.

One night she was unusually late for her show, and the nervous Empire Room manager kept phoning upstairs. Lee was still in her bathrobe, raging to Katz about the brutalities of Min. "You don't know the trauma!" she insisted. Yes, said Katz, she did; her parents were holocaust survivors. The remark made Lee even angrier. *"Those people didn't go through half of what I went through!"* The singer yanked open her robe. She was stark naked underneath. *"Look what my stepmother did to me!"* she sputtered. Katz saw some light marks that may have been scars, but she didn't believe Lee's story; like others who were close to Lee she doubted that the beatings had happened at all. Finally Katz calmed her down enough to get her dressed and into the elevator.

The singer's spirits rose when an offer came to tour Japan, where she had sung only once before. On this return trip, Lee would play four lucrative concerts and serve as the guest of honor at two post-Bicentennial galas: a fireworks festival to be attended by forty thousand, and a dinner to be thrown in her honor by the U.S. ambassador. Shigeru Okada, president of Japan's Mitsukoshi department-store chain, was sponsoring the trip. He had chosen Lee, he explained, "because her great warmth and lovely personality are representative of the American people." But once she had reached the Far East, no amount of enthusiastic applause or tributes from officials could break through her New York malaise. Lee showed no interest in sightseeing, beyond what appeared outside the windows of limousines; she did what was required of her, then retired to her room.

One last glamorous TV showcase awaited her. In the summer of 1976, the singer taped an appearance on *America Salutes Richard Rodgers: The Sound of His Music*, a two-hour CBS homage to the seriously ill composer. The semidramatized special starred Gene Kelly as Rodgers and Henry Winkler (Fonzie on the smash sitcom *Happy Days*) as Lorenz Hart. Diahann Carroll, Sammy Davis, Jr., Sandy Duncan, Cloris Leachman, and John Wayne saluted Rodgers in imaginatively conceived set-pieces. They were staged and directed by Dwight Hemion, whose masterful presentation of music on TV had helped earn him eighteen Emmys. Broadway composer Larry Grossman, music arranger for TV's newly launched *The Muppet Show*, did the same for the Rodgers tribute.

Its centerpiece, an intricate medley of twenty-four songs, gave a Tiffany setting to three pop aristocrats. Legendary beauty Lena Horne was a haughty tigress who had broken historic ground as a black entertainer. Vic Damone crooned with an agelessly creamy, unprobing delivery. Peggy Lee was the ethereal minimalist, smaller than ever of voice but still strong of mystique. All of them, in 1976, were stars of high prestige but waning box office. The special was a big deal for them, and they seemed thrilled to be invited.

Rodgers, however, was not too pleased at the inclusion of Lee. Through an artificial voice box—the result of throat cancer—he expressed his hope that she would not sing her version of "Lover." "He hated it," said Grossman. It went in anyway.

The arranger went to her home to discuss songs and keys. "It was surreal," he said. "She came wafting in wearing this white diaphanous gown, fully made up, with candles going." Of the songs on his list, Lee refused to sing only one, "This Can't Be Love." She had heard Benny Goodman play it countless times, she explained, and she did *not* wish to be reminded of the King of Swing. Otherwise, said Grossman, Lee seemed "pretty warm, but shaky," as though she were "slipping away a little bit."

That didn't apply to her professionalism. The singers came to the first rehearsal with Grossman's wealth of tricky cues and counterpoint almost fully memorized. The two women maintained a cordial distance; drama came only at the start of the shooting, an all-day affair on a multilevel soundstage in Los Angeles. In Horne's presence, all other females tended to vanish, and Lee found a way to grab the attention. "Peggy was wearing a big diamond ring," said Grossman, "and it suddenly disappeared. There was this whole psychodrama—someone had stolen her ring, she said, because they didn't want her to do well."

Batteries thus charged, Lee rose to her current peak, as did Damone and Horne. The medley was the most talked-about segment of *America Salutes Richard Rodgers*; it helped the show win eight Emmy nominations and five awards. Primetime network audiences got to see Lee at her most elegant, with a tasteful, streamlined hairdo and a plain white gown with pearls.

But after fifteen years of tawdrier getups, many viewers, especially young ones, had come to think of her as camp. In a new low-budget Canadian film comedy *Outrageous!* and in nightclubs across the country, female impersonator Craig Russell gave a drag-queen's impression of Lee—blond curls spilling out of a headband, a mask of makeup on a ghoulishly smiling face, arms that waved around as though she were a mad spider. *The Muppet Show* also had a go at Peggy Lee. Muppet designer Bonnie Erickson, whose mother had lived in the North Dakota of Lee's day, had invented the program's leading lady: Miss Piggy Lee, a blowsy, self-obsessed, zaftig blond singer with a supreme confidence in her own allure. Frank Oz, who provided her voice, gave the *New York Times* a bio of the character. It sounded like a thinly disguised précis on Peggy Lee: "She grew up in a small town in Iowa; her father died when she was young, and her mother wasn't that nice to her. . . . She has a lot of vulnerability which she has to hide, because of her need to be a superstar."

Miss Piggy Lee was an instant hit, and plans arose to give her a manager, Irving Bizarre, named after Irving Lazar, the hard-nosed Hollywood agent. But Peggy Lee was not amused. She threatened to sue, and Miss Piggy Lee became Miss Piggy. That didn't stop the show from having one more chuckle at Lee's expense when Piggy teamed with a Muppet based on screen sexpot Raquel Welch to sing "I'm a Woman."

Lee's complaint might have seemed sour. But for some time she had feared professional doom, and she did not wish to go down in history as the inspiration for Miss Piggy Lee. "I often wonder whether my work *will* live on," she told a reporter. "Movies seem to live on, and movie stars. They seem to remain so . . . *alive*. They walk, they talk, they're almost human. I'm not sure the same thing happens to records or to singers." Lee began voicing a plea to friends: "Please don't let people forget me."

Her original songs brought her a modest income; otherwise she relied on the road. All around her, however, the supper-club circuit was dying. Disco fever still held sway over the country; young people wanted to be part of the fun, not to watch it at a safe remove. Dallas, New Orleans, and San Francisco's Fairmont hotels all had their Venetian Room cabarets, which showcased such nostalgic legends as Patti Page, Carol Channing, and Ginger Rogers, but similar venues had grown few. The decades-old Maisonette of New York's St. Regis Hotel had recently closed; the Plaza

Hotel's Persian Room had become a boutique. The Empire Room of the Waldorf-Astoria survived, a hermetically sealed time capsule of bygone Manhattan. But to Mel Tormé, who played it in May 1976, "the magic was gone."

Even in its prime, the atmosphere could be off-putting. "It was an expensive room," said Robert Richards, "and run in a very old-fashioned style. You'd have to grease the maître-d's palm, and then they would say, well, what about the captain, what-about-the, what-about-the. You were embarrassed at every turn. And people weren't buying that anymore." Columnist Jack O'Brian certainly wasn't. "The cost of attending Peggy Lee's opening night at the Waldorf Empire Room: $64.80 a couple—if that couple neither drinks nor eats; after that the nightly dinner zap is $65 per couple including tax, tip, dinner, and one cocktail!"

Most of Lee's finest peers, notably Ella Fitzgerald, Sarah Vaughan, and Frank Sinatra, had graduated to concert halls, which they filled with the grand scope of their deliveries and charisma. But Lee was a true nightclub singer, known for intimacy. She had clung to the supper-club stage, and now, it seemed, she was sinking with the ship.

Still, there was the Empire Room. It felt like home to her, and the rehearsal tapes for her two-week, October 1976 engagement caught her at her jolliest. John S. Wilson had written skeptically of Lee for years, and even he was seduced; he called the new show "one of her very best . . . Everything—sound, orchestrations, programming, her voice—are under control and in balance." She wore the minimalist fashions of her new find, Zoran, a Croatian-born designer with a select, upscale clientele. Lee favored his solid-colored tunics with roomy slacks, made from expensive materials like cashmere and as comfortable as pajamas. They disguised everything, while giving women her size the illusion of a figure. Lee had seldom looked so chic.

Her repertoire was just as elegant. The show opened with the heavenly sound of wind chimes over strings; then Lee drifted onstage, singing Vernon Duke's "Autumn in New York" so slowly that it lured people into her floating realm of altered time. In her favored new greeting, Lee drawled breathlessly: "Are you en*joyyyy*ing yourselves? That's the *whooooooole* idea!" Then she jolted them with a discofied version of Cole Porter's "Love for Sale." For the rest of the show, that roller-coaster pacing kept fans on the edge of their seats. A twelve-minute Rodgers and Hart medley traced a relationship from first meeting ("Who Are You?") to instant heartbreak ("Glad to Be Unhappy") to disillusion ("It Never Entered My Mind") to rebirth ("Bewitched"). For the first three of those tunes, Lee sounded as winded as though she were singing with her last breaths. Then in "Bewitched," the tired, spent delivery vanished; Lee let out the song's victory cry—"I'm *wild* again!"—with the force of an ocean wave, and the crowd burst into applause. She repeated that feat throughout the show. Lee struggled to keep up with Édith Piaf's raucous "Milord," then pulled out a grand, rollicking ending.

That constant alternation between weakness and strength ensured unending sympathy, but it also drove the Waldorf management to distraction, for they never knew in what state of chemically induced unravelment they would find her. Guitarist John Whitfield recalled one of her most memorable entrances. Lee had just begun her first song. When he looked up from his bass: "No Peggy." She had slid under the piano.

But alcohol was no longer the culprit. Now she relied solely on prescription downers, which Lee knew she could not combine with liquor. During her midshow false exits, her Irish wardrobe assistant waited offstage with two Valiums, crushed between spoons. As the orchestra vamped, Lee quickly downed the powder with a cup of hot water. Then she scooped out the contents of a tiny jar of Dior lip gloss and stuck it in her mouth. The Vaseline-like paste alleviated the dry mouth that Valium caused. After two or three songs, the drug would hit her noticeably.

From there, disturbing things could happen. At one out-of-town appearance, a light bulb exploded above her head, raining down shards of glass. Lee didn't react at all; she simply kept singing. The audience wondered if she had even noticed. Robert Richards witnessed a private fiasco in 37F. Just before she was due downstairs for the late show, a reminder call came from the Empire Room, as it always did. A heavily drugged Lee wandered into a shower stall that she never used. Fully dressed and made up, she turned on the water. It poured through her hair and down her face, soaking her gown. "She was just standing there, completely baffled at what she had done," said Richards. "Of course this required a big repair."

During the second week of the run, a member of the management gave Lee some sad but inevitable news: this would be her final engagement. The Empire Room was closing that December; soon New York's last grand hotel supper club would be stripped down and turned into a conference and event room.

For Lee, the latter part of the announcement didn't register. The remnants of her fairy-tale life as a nocturnal New York goddess had been snatched away. So had a substantial chunk of her earnings. Within days she received another crushing blow. The William Morris Agency notified her that they were letting her go after the Waldorf run. Lee's temper and demands had made her impossible to work with.

This dismissal, like that of the Waldorf, struck her as a thunderbolt from out of the blue. She fired off a witheringly sarcastic telegram, addressed to company president Nat Lefkowitz and all the agents with whom she had worked. She was "delighted," she wrote, that Morris planned to cut her loose after all the money she'd made for them. "After twenty-some years you might feel some gratitude," she wrote. "I would like to find some gratitude for you but I can't quite find a reason."

The rest of the run found her at her most agitated, and her most drugged. Valium can affect one's sense of balance, and that might have contributed to another mishap that occurred one night between shows. With Robert Richards at her side, Lee rode downstairs to perform her late show. Walking ahead of them was Freeman Gunter, Lee's frequent guest. The singer wore a multilayered, floor-length gown. As she stepped off the elevator, her heel got caught in the hem. Lee stumbled and fell into Richards—"but she didn't hit the ground," he said. "I, of course, fell on my fucking head. She weighed about 398 pounds!" Lee was concerned about her makeup and hair. They went upstairs. "In two minutes everything was fine," said Richards. The late show proceeded perfectly.

Soon came October 23, 1976—Lee's last night at the Waldorf-Astoria after seven and a half years. Her New York followers had packed the Empire Room, as they always had for her closings; few of them knew that this was the end. "Let's break out the booze and have a ball" became the theme of the late show, as Lee let fly with a mixture of anger-fueled excitement, touching affection for the fans who had stuck by her, and score-settling. Recently she had begun singing "Is That All There Is?" for laughs. She turned the payoff line of each chorus into comedy: "I said to myself: "Where's the fire department?" . . . "Where are the peanuts?" . . .

"And then one day he died on me." While singing the refrain, she interjected the obvious: "I'm getting tired of this song. And that goes for Leiber and Stoller, too. I said that?"

Near the end, she gave a poignant farewell speech in a quavering voice. "Well, it's time. And . . . I don't know quite how to thank you. I thought I knew how . . . And then . . . I found I didn't know just that you mean a lot to me. And I'm very grateful for everything you've done. And of course I'm awfully glad you came here tonight, because I don't plan to come back here." Cheers of sympathy drowned her out. "Some of us will find you!" yelled a fan. She responded with a chilling announcement: "Look for me in St. John's Hospital. 'Cause that's where I'm playing next week."

Before checking out of 37F for the last time, Lee had ordered Magda Katz to take some dictation. She reeled off a list of ailments suffered in her "fall" in the lobby. "Especially painful: Upper left arm and shoulder to the elbow. Bottom of the rib cage going to the back. The pain from these is relayed down to the center between the breasts. I hit the hip joint which created a pain in the inner pelvic bone and made it very sore. Also, bruised inside hand and large toe. Grazed left side of my head . . . Two other people fell in the same spot." Katz was alarmed. "She walked around perfectly fine. There was nothing wrong with her."

The true casualties of her Waldorf years were the relationships she'd severed—with Lou Levy, Brian Panella, Betty Jungheim, Bob Mardesich, Doak Roberts. Now Bruce Richard, on whom Lee had harbored a crush, had gone, too. Resentment had built on both sides. "He got so he hated Peggy," said Doak Roberts. "At the Waldorf, every time Peggy would get a basket of flowers or something, she would say, 'Bruce, give that to Virginia and have her pack it away and I'll take it home.' Bruce would go into Virginia's bedroom and throw it out the thirty-seventh-floor window." According to Mardesich, the end came when Richard asked Lee for a raise. She refused. He never returned.

Richard's years with Lee had formed the peak of his professional life. Soon he sank more deeply into drugs. In the mid-1980s he died of AIDS.

———

LEE'S BOOKINGS KEPT THINNING, as did the crowds. She was relieved to find a new venue, the Drury Lane, a midsize theater in the

Chicago suburb of Oakbrook Terrace. Rick Kogan reviewed her for the *Chicago Daily News*. "What she has left," wrote Kogan, "she gave sparingly Tuesday night in front of a half-empty house." Her "Autumn in New York" opener left some listeners giggling; had Lee gotten off at the wrong stop? Her greeting to the audience—"Let's fill the theater with love!"—sounded more like camouflaged fury. "Peggy Lee," Kogan concluded, "is no longer an object for sexual fantasy."

She kept returning to the Drury Lane, but Kogan's critique devastated Lee, who until lately had earned almost consistent raves. Lee began considering other creative avenues that might provide a payoff. Maybe she could design a line of children's clothes, or publish an illustrated children's book about Little Joe, a character she had created. Neither idea panned out.

But once home in Beverly Hills, she launched a more promising endeavor. Lee had acquired a bedazzled fan in Shigeru Okada, the Tokyo-based department-store magnate who had sponsored her Japanese tour. Okada employed Robert Richards for illustration work, and during her last Waldorf engagement, Richards had helped Lee to craft a proposal for a line of beddings and towels that would bear her flower drawings. Okada loved the idea, and expressed interest in licensing it as an exclusive for his Mitsukoshi Limited Department Stores. In a letter to Lee, he raved: "They are, indeed, the most delicate and elegant arrangements, which, as you have explained in your note, will create an atmosphere to make a person happy and be contented."

According to their agreement, Richards would complete the artwork based on her ideas, and they would split the proceeds. Lee saw riches ahead, and suggested adding a line of greeting cards.

Nearly overnight, her mood changed from flat-out despair to childlike excitement. She loved collaborating with "Ro-bair," as she called him, and he was just as enthralled to be around her. Aside from revering her music, he found her a poignant figure. "I guess to me she represented what she did to a lot of people—kind of the last of the blondes." At the same time, he decided, "she was Norma Desmond without Max"—the butler-protector to an aging, forgotten star in *Sunset Boulevard*. "There wasn't that faithful retainer, that person who believed in her, who gave her that strength. And I think she suffered from that."

Richards flew from New York to Beverly Hills to spend a couple of days at Lee's home and talk business. Near the start of his visit came an omen of dark times to come. One night they returned to the house after an outing. It was pitch-black inside, and the main door wouldn't open. Lee was frightened. They went in through another entrance. Checking the blocked door, they saw that a chest had been pushed in front of the door. On top was a typewriter with a letter in the roller:

> *Dear Miss Lee,*
> *Fuck you.*
>   *The staff.*

In the kitchen, a turkey turned slowly on a rotisserie.

"She was *very* upset by this," said Richards. "The employment agencies weren't too enthused about sending more people up. By not too enthused, I mean adamant." Lee asked him to extend his stay. She didn't have to plead.

But emptiness still hung in the air. "The party was over by the time I got there," he said. The living room, once a bustling center of traffic and festivities, had turned into "a big frozen space, like a picture." Lee's lifestyle struck him as bizarre, starting with her proclivity for keeping the house ice-cold: "There you were in sunny California freezing your nuts off." The chill didn't encourage Lee to leave her bedroom. "I think I saw her out of bed three times," he said. "It made the house very haunted." Lee sat up in bed all night, doodling on sheets of white paper. On one of them, Lee sketched her own face; alongside it she wrote two long columns of the word "happy"—a seeming attempt at creative visualization.

She and Richards had a presentation to finish for Okada, and the illustrator tried to move it along. "I began to see that it was only possible to work one day out of every three or four. The mornings would be fine—the morning being from one in the afternoon until around three o'clock. Then this monster would appear and take over. The bed was full of shoeboxes and things with pills—very mad. The day was lost. We would have a two-hour discussion over something for dinner. She kept saying to me, 'Don't you think California is as intellectual as New York?' I would just remain silent. We were doing nothing, we were talking about Fettuccine Alfredo!"

Other obsessions consumed her. Lee had heard that Clare Boothe Luce, the famed American writer and Republican Congresswoman, had suffered asbestos poisoning in her Roman villa. As ever, Lee hadn't been feeling well, and she decided she had the same ailment. Without having the house tested, she called a contractor and made arrangements for the ceilings to be lowered.

For now, the atmosphere was still kooky enough to tickle Richards. One day he boasted of his new living arrangements to Bruce Vilanch, the comedy writer for Bette Midler and a future regular on TV's *The Hollywood Squares*. "Oh my God, I'd love to meet her, she's so nuts!" said Vilanch. Richards asked Lee if he could invite Vilanch and his friend Henry Post, a journalist from New York, to the house for lunch. Fine, said Lee—but she didn't care to join them. Richards couldn't persuade her.

"They came," said Richards, "and they were like, '*Where's Peg?*'" He broke the news that she wouldn't be joining them. The guests were disappointed, but soon they were installed with Richards in the Yellow Room, eating and roaring with laughter. At a certain point, all of them became aware of someone standing outside the door, listening. They sat in frozen silence. Finally the illustrator said, "Peggy? Come in!" The silence continued. Then the door cracked open—and they watched the familiar hand of Peggy Lee reach inside, a big diamond ring on it. Lee started snapping out the rhythm to "Fever." Then she left. Vilanch, said Richards, "lived off this story for months."

More and more, Lee was inclined to wallow in self-imposed isolation rather than join the party. So it was when another of Richards's friends, singer-songwriter Peter Allen, came to town. The flamboyant Australian showman was on an upswing that would take him from cabarets to small concert venues to Radio City Music Hall. In 1977 he played the Roxy, a Sunset Strip hotspot. Richards was invited, and he asked Lee to join him. The singer had long performed Allen's "I Honestly Love You," a number-one hit for Olivia Newton-John; other early songs of his, such as "Don't Cry Out Loud," had made her bond with him emotionally. "He has a quality in his singing that, although he is not crying at all, I hear a sadness, a little sorrow inside of his voice," she said. "I feel that somehow he's been hurt."

Lee stunned Richards by flat-out refusing his offer. He asked her why she didn't want to go. "I just don't, that's all. Why would I go?"

"Because it'll be fun. All Hollywood is gonna be there."

Still she refused. This time he wouldn't give up. Finally Lee said wistfully, "You know, it might be fun, wouldn't it."

"What do you mean, it *might* be fun?" said Richards. "It *would* be fun."

"She said, 'But there'll be a commotion if I go.' Commotion, what commotion was there going to be? Warren Beatty, Jack Nicholson, Raquel Welch were going. Anyway, the hairdresser was at the house at nine in the morning. We went through thirty pairs of lashes."

They were among the first to arrive. Lee wore a red Zoran outfit and "looked fabulous," said Richards. Still fearful of a stampede of attention, she insisted on entering through the back. They took their place at a prime table. Larry, Allen's assistant, stopped by to welcome them, and asked Lee if Allen could introduce her during the show.

She froze. "*Introduce* me? I didn't come here to be used!" Larry was aghast. He apologized profusely and hurried off. Lee stood up. "*We're going!*" she announced to Richards, adding loudly, "I can't *believe* that he would invite me here and then try to use me like this!"

Suddenly, there stood Peter Allen at the table. "Peggy, I apologize to you a thousand times," he said. Allen explained that he would be announcing the VIP guests, and wanted to pay her the courtesy of asking her permission. "I absolutely don't want you to," insisted Lee. Allen locked eyes with Richards, then left. "Don't forget," said Richards later, "he'd been married to Liza Minnelli, so he knew a few things about crazy women."

Once onstage, Allen shook maracas, did Rockette kicks, and sang at the piano of big-city life, love, and heartbreak. The show was a riotous success. Near the end, he acknowledged his stellar attendees. Then he introduced his song "Quiet Please, There's a Lady on Stage," a defense of a struggling older chanteuse: "She may not be the latest rage / But she's singing, and she means it / Doesn't that deserve a little silence?" Allen had written it for one of his favorite cabaret singers, Julie Wilson. But most people assumed that his former mother-in-law had inspired it, and Allen didn't argue.

"I'm gonna sing a song that people associate with Judy Garland," he said. "But I don't want to sing it for Judy, I want to sing it for somebody else. And I love her very, very much." Allen began the song, and Lee soon realized she was that someone. "She was trembling so hard that the table started to shake," said Richards. "People were looking. I could see that she was completely confused." Suddenly Lee stood up. Allen saw her and nodded in her direction. A spotlight sought her out, and the entire audience rose and burst into applause.

Well-wishers crowded her afterward. "She was devastated," said Richards. "She was like a child. All the way home she kept saying, 'Robert, I have to go out more. It's so much fun to go out!' And I was just staring at her like, 'You work in nightclubs, you're staring at five hundred people, what do you think they're there for, as punishment?' The next day the phone rang all day long with people saying how thrilled they were to see her, how beautiful she looked. She was in seventh heaven. But three days later she was back in her depression, Valiuming herself into a coma."

———

A TRIP TO LONDON always boosted her spirits, and in March of 1977 Lee embarked on a whirlwind two-week visit. It would include two concerts at the London Palladium, a live album drawn from them, and an additional studio recording. Soon her schedule burgeoned to include a TV special and a performance in Amsterdam.

Lee owed most of this to Ken Barnes, a British record producer who adored her. Barnes cherished the Great American Songbook, and had masterminded albums with a series of legends—Fred Astaire, Johnny Mercer, Bing Crosby—whose recording careers had dwindled. He had proposed a new LP to Lee a couple of years before, but at the time she still hoped for a future with A&M. When that and other prospects dried up, she remembered Barnes's interest. She called him. Excitedly he contacted Polydor, the British label for whom he worked. Barnes persuaded the executives to let him produce two Peggy Lee albums—one at the Palladium show, the other in the studio.

"People had said to me, don't work with her because she drinks; she's an alcoholic," recalled Barnes. But he and his conductor of choice, Pete Moore, flew to Los Angeles to meet her, and found Lee on her best behavior. "I liked her right away," he said. "I never had any real clashes with Peggy. She was wonderful to converse with. You could talk with her about almost anything. She had a belly laugh that was infectious. I found that she was innately friendly. But she was a taskmaster when it came to working."

He also knew that Lee could be "a demon to negotiate with," and he urged Polydor to let him finesse her contractual needs. They insisted on handling the matter themselves. Polydor wound up covering first-class roundtrip airfare for Lee and two assistants, along with an extended stay at her preferred Oliver Messel Suite at the Dorchester—perhaps the priciest lodging in London. Before Lee had recorded a note, the project was costing a fortune.

Her schedule in London was intense, but Barnes saw not a hint of disability. "Nothing was too much trouble for her," he said. "She was certainly okay on her feet." Shortly after her arrival, she was in an isolation booth at CBS Studios for the first of three morning sessions. Her studio album, *Peggy*, aimed to present a vintage singer—then nearly fifty-seven—who knew how to "keep up with trends and not bury herself in the past," as Barnes put it. Amid the gossamer clouds of Pete Moore's orchestrations, Lee floated all over the musical map. *Peggy* included Peter Allen's Carnival party song, "I Go to Rio"; "I'm Not in Love," a number-one hit for the British electronic art-rock band 10cc; "Every Little Movement," a coy showtune from 1910; the 1950s make-out classic "Misty"; and a disco-tinged reworking of "Lover."

Her valiance remained, but *Peggy* found Lee in sluggish voice, clearly past her peak. When she sang of loss and regret, however, she still delivered. In "The Hungry Years," Neil Sedaka and Howard Greenfield, the 1960s jukebox hit makers, explored one of their mature themes—a sinking feeling that success hadn't spelled happiness. Lee sounded appropriately heavy of heart as she sang: "How could I be so blind not to see the door / Closing on the world I now hunger for?"

Her rawest autobiography came in "Courage, Madame," a Lee lyric that Pete Moore had set. It was a stoic vow to forget the "scars and tears" and "walk with quiet dignity, and time will heal." She pronounced the title in French, adding a hint of a brave smile.

At least a record company cared enough about her at this late date to pamper her. Polydor threw a party for Lee at the Dorchester, and voiced plans to release "Lover" as a single. "I'm very, very happy about the record," she exclaimed to Max Jones of *Melody Maker*.

Peggy turned out to be her last studio LP with a full orchestra. But thanks to Barnes, she had the chance to make her first authentically live album. On March 13, 1977, Polydor's technicians recorded her early and late shows at the Palladium. *Live in London* reprised her final Waldorf act, with a few alterations. The Brits had requested "Sing a Rainbow" and a song from *Sea Shells*, "I Don't Want to Play in Your Yard," which had somehow caught on in the U.K. These two children's songs grew more moving as Lee sang them in a frail but plaintive voice.

Barnes heard no reticence when he asked her to sing "Is That All There Is?" Declared the star: "That's out of my act." When he argued that she couldn't possibly omit it, Lee explained that she was "mad at Leiber and Stoller," and wouldn't be singing any of their songs. Finally she relented.

Her recent vow not to "depress people" was likewise discarded in London. Four years earlier, Bruce Richard had urged her to sing "Touch Me in the Morning," Diana Ross's number-one hit. The song had mesmerized her ever since, and she sang it at the Palladium. Written by Ronald Miller and Michael Masser, it tells a harrowing story of desertion: a woman lies in bed in the middle of the night, knowing that the man by her side will vanish after dawn, never to return. Ross had sung it with her customary AM-radio lightness. "I've revived it by doing it dramatically," said Lee. "I get all torn up in that song." At the Waldorf, her version had reduced the veteran Broadway star Mary Martin to tears. "I've never seen her before," said Martin afterward, "and now I don't want her to ever leave that stage."

"Touch Me in the Morning" is one of Lee's most masterful and exposed performances—the plea of a spent woman, too tired to fight but not to feel. In a tearful, parched murmur, Lee asks for one last crumb of affection before love flees her life forever. "Must've been hard to tell me/ That you've given all you had to give," she sings, anger turning her voice to steel. It softens again with her sad plea: "Leave me as you found me/Empty like before." Words like "empty," "yesterday," "gone," and "dies" were lightning rods for Lee; she often sang them with a gasp or a slight moan.

The London Palladium audience responded. According to Ray Coleman of *Melody Maker*, "the impersonal Palladium was transformed into a hall of nightclub intimacy as the singer caressed her songs of lost love and forlorn hopes, unique and brilliantly sung."

Lee quickly plunged into the taping of a special for Thames TV. Her guest was Charles Aznavour, the worldly French-Armenian chansonnier. A protégé of Piaf, Aznavour was the suavest of showmen, and the most calculating. Alongside him, Lee, for all her premeditation, seemed even more heartfelt. The two singers shared a duet of "Yesterday, When I Was Young," Aznavour's lament for a frivolously squandered youth. Fear showed on her face as she sang of time slipped away and the "pain and emptiness beyond."

The release of *Peggy* and *Live in London* offered her hope for the future. "The albums were quite well received," recalled Barnes, "and they didn't perform too badly at all." Even so, he said, Polydor "closed the book on Peggy, because everything had cost so much. She was not expensive to record but she was expensive to accommodate." Decades later, though, he remained immensely pleased with their collaboration. "I think I got the last of the best of her," said Barnes. Certainly he had caught the vulnerabilities of a woman whom "you always wanted to protect—that you never wanted anything bad to happen to."

But as Brian Panella had seen, Lee needed safekeeping not from the world, but from herself. Back in Los Angeles, she complained to Robert Richards that she had lost money in England. Once more her finances had her in mortal fear, and wounded pride made it worse. Months after Richards had moved in with her, they finished their design presentation for Shigeru Okada. Richards mailed it to Tokyo. Not a week had passed when Lee began complaining angrily: "Why hasn't he called?" Richards explained that such decisions took time, and perhaps the package hadn't even arrived. Lee wouldn't listen. She threatened to cancel the whole deal. A couple of nights later she snapped, "I have had *enough* of this waiting!" She placed a harsh call to Okada, demanding the return of her presentation. "And indeed, he did ship it back," said Richards. "This entire six months of work was negated completely. We had nowhere else to put this."

After a heated confrontation, Richards moved out. The friendship never recovered. Some months later came an odd postscript. Lee had hired a young gay secretary. When the singer went on tour, he phoned Richards and invited him to a party at her house. All his friends were coming, he explained, and they were planning to dress up in her gowns and wigs.

"I said, 'You can't have strangers there, it's her home!' But he hated her guts. He went ahead and had his party. A few days later I got a call from a lawyer, accusing *me* of having had the party."

AS THE SPRING OF 1977 ended, Lee's prime emotion was rage, aimed at everyone she felt had wronged her: Okada, various employees, William Morris, the now-shuttered Empire Room for having "fired" her. Lee felt robbed. And she felt abandoned—her most explosive hot button. "She had to be the one to do the leaving," said Dona Harsh. "Nobody else could leave her."

The singer phoned columnist Earl Wilson, who printed any news she gave him. Wilson reported that Lee was at St. John's Hospital in Santa Monica, trying to recover from a "cracked rib" and "fractured pelvis" suffered in a fall at the Waldorf. A lawsuit was likely.

Shortly thereafter, a representative of Lee's informed the wire services that the star was suing the Hilton Hotel corporation (which owned the Waldorf) and the Johnson Wax company for a near-fatal fall on an overwaxed lobby floor. The suit claimed that sand had fallen from a "toppled spittoon" (actually a tall, cylindrical ashtray) near the elevator, causing her to skid.

From there, her allegations snowballed. Columnist Marilyn Beck wrote that the tumble had "left her with a permanent hearing loss and temporary blindness, plus injuries to her head and rib cage, broken back teeth and sciatic nerve and foot disorders." To that list, Lee added a "cracked skeleton." She wasn't through. "I literally could not walk across the room," she informed Kathy Larkin of the *New York Daily News*. Lee told the *Chicago Tribune* that she had "nearly died . . . My ribs were torn from my spine, and I developed a heart condition because of the injuries." The singer claimed a loss of ten million dollars in performing income, then fifteen. In truth, there wasn't much performing to do. What appearances she had made, including her European ones, revealed no afflictions.

After their unfailingly gracious treatment of her, the management of the Waldorf was stunned. Their lawyers looked in bewilderment at Lee's proposed evidence: Polaroids, taken by a friend, that showed sand on the floor and a raised carpet edge into which her foot had allegedly gotten caught—another claim that didn't quite jibe with a slide on a sandy floor.

The case would drag on for six years. She refused to withdraw or to consider a settlement agreement; for Lee, being angry meant feeling alive. But with far fewer chances to sing, her days seemed empty. A star who had barely touched a domestic task in decades now had the time to crochet an afghan for Nicki. She listened to classical music, notably Satie's "Gymnopédie No. 3," which she loved for its "calming effect." And she kept writing lyrics, most of which went unsung. Her romantic life seemed over in reality, but not in her imagination. Lee sent out a press release that declared her engagement to "Count" Philip Ashley, an Englishman who had allegedly flown to Toronto to propose to her during a tour. Years later, close friends of Lee's recalled nothing of him or the engagement, which yielded no marriage.

One interview tactfully described her as "very selective in accepting bookings," when in fact she was starved for them. Before a February 1978 concert at the Dorothy Chandler Pavilion in Los Angeles, the always-sympathetic Leonard Feather allowed Lee to speak out at length in the *Times*. She sounded heartsick as she surveyed the current recording scene—in particular the "great power wielded by producers," whose extravagant spending "all comes out of the artist's royalties." She cited one team "who spent a great deal of what was supposed to be our working time just lying around in the sun in the South of France . . . It wound up being nothing but a very costly demo, which in effect I paid for." Already she felt nostalgic for the albums she had made in London: "The musicians were very well prepared and they didn't waste time fooling around."

If rock and roll had scared Lee in the 1960s, heavy metal revolted her. "Grotesque" was the word she used to describe Kiss, the leather-clad band who painted their faces in black and white, spat artificial blood, set off flames, and hinted at Nazism and Satanism. Lee was equally appalled by the tongue-in-cheek horror imagery of "shock rock" metal hero Alice Cooper—specifically by the urban legend that he had bitten the head off a live chicken onstage. She likened Cooper to the "mentally ill" sideshow freaks at carnivals. Lee was "shocked" by the fact that A&M had dismissed her but signed the Sex Pistols, the superstar British punk band. In London, she had heard about "God Save the Queen," the group's proletarian anthem, which compared the royal family to a "fascist regime." To Lee, the hit tune was merely some "dreadfully offensive song." Heavy metal was called a "subculture of alienation" and "outsider music for outsiders," sentiments to which Lee could relate. But there was no way she could appreciate a form so violently nonmusical; to her, it symbolized the end of all she valued as a singer. She wondered if she should just retire.

But as so often happened, an offer came along just in time to buoy her hopes. That summer she was booked as the premiere act at Scandals, a Hollywood nightclub hyped as a Ciro's for the disco era. Scandals had a projected budget of over two million dollars and lofty intentions to match. Owner Leonard Grant, the former agent for Ann-Margret and Liberace, had conceived a mini-Vegas-style emporium that would encompass a dance floor and a tiered, 315-seat showroom. Amid French brasserie décor, crystal chandeliers, and red-leather booths, Broadway and pop veterans of largely gay appeal, including Rita Moreno, Chita Rivera, and Peggy Lee, would entertain, backed by an orchestra.

Grant admitted that he and his investors were "sticking their necks out on a limb." Yet Lee was sure that Scandals would revive the "all-out elegance and glamour" of Ciro's and the Mocambo. On August 3, 1978, just before the opening, Johnny Carson featured Lee on the *Tonight* show. She hadn't seemed so vibrant in years. Dressed in black and white Zoran, she sang three songs, including "Goin' to Chicago Blues" from her *Blues Cross Country* album, and chatted at length with Carson. She was going to an acupuncturist, Lee noted; this and her excitement over Scandals had made her feel like a "new person." Forgetting her Waldorf suit, she enthused: "I've never had so much energy. All those bones that ached from falling on them are all fine now."

Lee was at her most charmingly scattered. She described the grounds around her home as a veritable Wild Kingdom, replete with "bunny rabbits," coyotes, "enormous" robins, a squirrel "that throws acorns at you," raccoons that "come and wash their faces in the pool," quail, and a herd of deer that roamed the hill. The singer told an involved story about a six-foot snake that had appeared at her back door just before she hosted a press party for Scandals. She phoned the animal regulations office and an exterminator, and learned that it was unlawful to kill a snake. "My daughter said, 'Is it against the law if the snake kills you?'" quipped Lee. "I knew it wouldn't do any good to put Raid on a six-foot snake."

On August 15—three weeks late—Scandals opened, but the place was a mess. Six out of the eight bathrooms didn't work; paint cans, ladders, and drop cloths were in view. Laser light effects shot through the sky above Hollywood Boulevard and North La Brea Avenue, but Della Reese, not Peggy Lee, sang that night. At the last minute, Lee had been hospitalized at St. John's for what *Variety* described as an "acute viral infection" with "hepatitis-like complications." Reese finished out Lee's engagement. Before she could be rebooked, Scandals had sunk.

Cancellations aside, certain critics were disheartened by the diminished Lee they saw, and found themselves straining to offer praise. "Peggy Lee Still Has Some of the Ol' Magic Left," read the title of one review. On June 28, 1979, Lee returned to New York for the first time since her Waldorf farewell. She would share a bill at Radio City Music Hall with the Buddy Rich orchestra. It thrilled her to sing at this cavernous landmark, and Lee sounded fairly spirited onstage, with some of her old swing restored. John S. Wilson, however, called the current Lee tired and rambling.

On she soldiered. Lee's fans reacted with joy to the news that she would be making her first American album since *Mirrors*. The label was DRG, an independent company that specialized in show music and reissues of classic pop. An orchestra was out of the question; *Close Enough for Love*, as the record was called, would feature seven musicians, including her veteran band members Max Bennett, Dennis Budimir, John Pisano, and conductor Dick Hazard.

The album was another attempt to mingle Lee's style with the sounds of the 1970s, including electric bass, guitar, and keyboards. On one original song, "Easy Does It," Lee sighed and moaned in the style of the 1973 hit "Pillow Talk," a drugged-sounding, orgasmic reverie by soul singer Sylvia. Two songs she had recorded years before, "Just One of Those Things" and "I Can't Resist You," reappeared in disco arrangements— this at the time of a disco boycott, expressed on T-shirts that read DISCO SUCKS and DEATH TO DISCO.

On slow, dreamy ballads, notably a new Arthur Hamilton song, "Rain Sometimes," her magic crept through. But Bennett found the sessions dismaying. "She wasn't at her best vocally," he said, "and the approach by her producer"—Hugh Fordin, DRG's owner—"wasn't working. It just didn't jell." *Close Enough for Love* got Lee on a few talk shows, but the three-album deal that Fordin had announced went no further.

As 1980 and her sixtieth birthday approached, Lee was so identified with accidents, injuries, and hospitalizations that one reporter called her a "walking calamity." Recently she had begun fainting; in addition, one of her eyelids now sagged. Lee blamed Bell's palsy, a form of facial paralysis with a variety of possible causes, including stroke. But friends suspected plastic surgery gone wrong. Later, in working with playwright William Luce on a one-woman show, Lee prepared a dramatic third-person account of her mishap: "What was the twisting sensation in her face? Why wouldn't her eyes close when she blinked? My God! Paralyzed. No. Yes." She could sing but not speak, she claimed. Lee wrote of "leaning on the arm of a friend" during an outing. That friend was Bruce Vanderhoff, who recalled nothing of Lee's paralysis or blindness. The story alternated with her Waldorf fall as an excuse for why she wasn't working much.

Lee bragged of having ESP, but increasingly she relied on her psychic to illuminate a scary future. She hung on his every encouraging word. "Something is correcting or something is straightening itself out," he told her. "The vitality's coming back, and you're going to find out how really strong you are."

"Somebody's got to really fuck up for this not to work," said Lee's daughter, Nicki, of *Peg*, the singer's one-woman Broadway show of 1983. At the theater, Lee rehearsed with drummer Grady Tate.

Chapter Sixteen

*L*EE'S BIG HOME felt too lonely for one, and she had long thought of selling it. Certainly she could use the cash flow, and when she got an offer she couldn't refuse, Lee embarked on her new beginning. Around the end of 1979, Vanderhoff helped her go househunting in Bel Air, the exclusive community of gated homes in the fussily groomed hills of West Los Angeles. Bel Air had a long history of star dwellers, including Burt Lancaster, Kim Novak, Ronald and Nancy Reagan, Tony Curtis, Alfred Hitchcock, Howard Hughes, and Gregory Peck. Lee was particularly conscious of the fact that the woman she most envied—Elizabeth Taylor, who got every man, diamond, and luxury she desired—lived there, too.

The house at 11404 Bellagio Road called out to her. "It would shimmer at me every time we drove slowly by," explained Lee, and it blinded her to any intention of downsizing. Unlike many Bel Air homes, this one wasn't hidden behind trees and manicured shrubbery; passersby beheld a white, nondescript two-story box. But the five-bedroom, white French Regency villa was even larger than her home on Tower Grove, and the interior dazzled her. Upon entering, guests passed through a two-story foyer with a grand circular staircase. Farther back was a spacious sunken living room, with French doors that opened out onto a patio and pool; beyond them lay a panoramic view of West Los Angeles. "I've found my dream house!" she exclaimed to Maggie Daly of the *Chicago Tribune*. "It's so chic!"

Lee was busy touring, so she let Nicki organize the move. Once she had moved in, the singer, aided heavily by Bruce Vanderhoff, began designing her palace. Sixteen crystal chandeliers were hung throughout the house, one of them over her bathtub. Behind the white living-room sofa, Nicki's watercolors covered an expansive wall. Peach, beige, and white dominated the house. "The colors sort of soothe the senses," Lee noted. "You get that feeling of well-being." She tried to create the same sensation underfoot. In the living room, the white carpet "was so thick," said the record producer Ken Bloom, "that you left footprints on it as if you were walking through snow." At rehearsal time, a chaise was wheeled into the foyer—"which we call Le Petit Music Salon"—while the musicians gathered close by at the living-room piano, made of blond wood.

Lee had an elevator installed, but rarely would she venture upstairs; the center of activity remained her bedroom, just off the living room. As always, she would spend most of her time in the queen-size bed, which faced a TV and an alabaster fireplace. To her left, French doors offered a view of her precious rosebushes, tended by her new full-time gardener and houseman, José Prado. The plants bore the pale pink "Peggy Lee" rose, named after her by the American Rose Society. A long-stemmed, oversize cabbage blossom, it had all the shapely voluptuousness of Lee in the 1960s. What's more, it bloomed almost year round—a perennial that, like the singer herself, could seemingly withstand anything.

Its magical properties didn't end there. Lee told a visiting journalist about the "Peggy Lee" rosebush that she could see from her bed: "When I watch it the roses turn toward me and bend, like a bow."

Nothing could stop Lee from living like a star—not even the fact that she was hurting for work. She had entered an eight-year gap in her album career, and it agonized her to think that maybe the industry was through with her. "Some people still like good music," she argued to Dennis Hunt of the *Los Angeles Times*. "You have no idea how much I miss recording. It's like part of me is gone."

Lee was taken aback at an offer from Norman Twain, a stage director. Early in 1980, he invited the singer to star in a regional production of *Side by Side by Sondheim*, the celebrated revue of songs by composer Stephen Sondheim, the darling of the theatrical elite. Throughout the decade, Sondheim's brainy virtuosity had yielded a string of prestige musicals, including *Company, Follies, Sweeney Todd*, and *Pacific Overtures*. For another show, *A Little Night Music*, Sondheim wrote his most famous song, "Send in the Clowns," the elegy of an aging actress who had placed career before love. Lee could relate to its theme, but she refused to sing it: "I've already done too many clown and circus songs." Overall, she and Sondheim hardly seemed an ideal match; most of his songs came more from the head than the heart, and their airtight construction resisted swing.

But they certainly had drama, and even though the prospect of a scripted musical intimidated her, she rarely shirked a challenge. The production—a monthlong summer run at the Birmingham Theatre outside of Detroit, Michigan—wasn't auspicious. But Lee's name would go above the title, and the work was easy enough; she would narrate the action from a chair on the side and occasionally rise to sing, either alone or amid four fresh-faced young actors: George Lee Andrews, Marti Morris, Eric Michael Gillett, and Teri Ralston, an original cast member of *Company*. In keeping with the show's small-scale coziness, the "orchestra" consisted of two pianists, Eileen LaGrange and Paul Horner.

Although Twain was the nominal director, he left that job—along with almost every other responsibility—in the hands of Teri Ralston. She was puzzled when their headliner showed up with her adolescent granddaughter, Holly Foster, but without a manager to protect her. Kathy Levy knew why. "She couldn't keep one long enough to work out a trusting relationship. She was tough to handle. And a lot of the time she was wrong."

Ralston tried to keep Lee happy, a trial at times. "She was very neurotic. She had a lot of illnesses and she worried about them. She could be very difficult. She could also be very loving." Lee proved it by inviting the young actress over more than once and cooking dinner for her. With Ralston's help, Lee chose her own songs. They ranged from "Anyone Can Whistle," the poignant admission of an emotional cripple; to "The Boy from . . . ," a gay comedic spin on "The Girl from Ipanema"; to "I'm Still Here," the survival anthem of an indomitable has-been. "Send in the Clowns" was unavoidable, and it went to her as well.

All this was a lot for her to learn. Lee couldn't memorize her narration, so she read it from the script. "She was a little disconnected at the runthrough," said Ralston's friend Greg MacKellan. "The other performers were seasoned stage vets and she wasn't, but she was still Peggy Lee, and it was great to see her."

Regardless of that, Lawrence DeVine of the *Detroit Free Press* found her "ill at ease" as well as miscast. "As the hostess of this get-together, she distracts attention from the other crew by her very considerable presence, sitting down in a homely office chair over at stage left, biding her (and our) time until it's time for Miss Peggy Lee to get up and sing 'Send in the Clowns.'" For the finale, she and the cast used top hats as props and sang "Side by Side by Side" from *Company*. One night, Lee accidentally whacked Ralston in the face with hers.

She hoped the production would move to Broadway. It didn't, but a separate dream took root in her mind. The source was Paul Horner, the shy, bearded young Englishman at one of the pianos. Horner worshipped Lee as a singer; he proudly told friends that on her *Live in London* album his was the voice shouting *"MORE!"* from the balcony. Horner had studied at the city's prestigious Royal College of Music; after that he had scraped together a living by accompanying singers, writing special material for the BBC-TV specials of the campy singing comic Stanley Baxter, and playing in restaurants and bars. Now he lived in Los Angeles, where he cleaned apartments for extra cash. Ralston knew him, and when she called him in to audition for Peggy Lee, he thought a lucky star had shined upon him at last. Lee, in turn, was struck by his pianistic sensitivity, notably in his Debussy-like accompaniment for one of her *Side by Side* solos, "Small World" from the musical *Gypsy*.

During a rehearsal break, she heard him playing a slow, stately tune at the piano. Entranced, she walked to the piano. "What's that, Paul?"

"Oh, I wrote it, Miss Lee."

"You wrote that? Can I write a lyric to it?" The music, she said, suggested a title to her: "I Gave It Everything I Had."

The next day she came back with a finished set of words. They were the bittersweet backward glance of a woman whose life was just about over: "I gave it everything I had, my heart, my soul / But then, it wasn't all that bad; I found my goal."

Lee brought him another autobiographical lyric, "Mirrors and Marble," inspired by the master bathroom in her home. The words told of a girl who grew up to find all the luxury she had ever craved. Now here she stood, "all alone in my mirrors and marble, holding out my hand, touching empty air."

Seldom had she penned such candid songs. Before they left Detroit, she and Horner wrote others: "Mama," a valentine to Selma Egstrom; the swaggering "That's How I Learned to Sing the Blues." Lee had found her new soul mate. For Horner, life had become "a Hollywood movie." One day, as she rode her chairlift down from the second-story dressing room, Lee declared to him mysteriously: "We're writing something that's gonna keep us for the rest of our lives."

LEE REVEALED HER PLAN to the *New York Daily News*. "I was down to nothing in my career because of a near-fatal disease," she explained, "but I've now regained my full strength." The reason: She was hard at work on an autobiographical musical. "It's all true, based on a number of incidents and times in my life. I've written fifteen songs for the show and the lyrics. Now I'm working on the book and hope to have it finished in two months."

And who would star? "I hope I'll play me the first time around," Lee said.

She envisioned a lavish spectacle with a giant cast, including younger actresses to play her in bygone years. It hadn't occurred to her to try a one-woman format. But she took note of *Lena Horne: The Lady and Her Music*, the 1981 solo show that had made its sixty-three-year-old star the toast of Broadway. Horne was Hollywood's first black goddess and a ferociously seductive cabaret star, but racism and crushing loss had marred her seemingly charmed life. Horne's tale of struggle and ultimate triumph exhilarated audiences; it won her two Grammys and a Tony award along with living-legend stature. Lee wanted all that, too. After all, she told a friend, "my life would be *much* more interesting to an audience than Lena's."

What mattered to her the most, apart from an end to financial woe, was control. Lee's show would enable her to do what Horne had done: to revise history, settle scores, and craft the persona she wanted the public to see—the one she yearned to believe was real.

In the meantime, Lee had piles of bills to pay and ever-shrinking funds. She had quietly sold some of her jewelry; in the meantime she looked ahead to a fifteen-million-dollar payoff for her purported near-death experience at the Waldorf. After five years of legal wrangling, a court date was finally close. Her lawyer, Jim Moser, pronounced the case a "life or death situation"; because of Lee's alleged semi-paralysis, he had managed to move the proceedings to Los Angeles. "The trial will start any moment," he informed Marilyn Beck. "We're on beeper alert. The minute a courtroom becomes available, our case gets underway." Deliberations, he explained, would last for four to six weeks and involve fifty to one hundred witnesses—including, Beck reported, "an economist and accountants who will estimate the singer's loss of income at ten million dollars."

Her physical disabilities were news to Horner. At the Birmingham Theatre, he recalled, Lee—momentarily forgetting her chairlift—had "run up the six steps" to his piano upon hearing him play the music for one of their eventual songs, "I Gave It Everything I Had." Robert Richards had received a series of "very nasty" letters from Lee's lawyer, pressuring him to testify about her injuries. He declined. "I really felt that I could only tell the truth. I knew I was supposed to say there was sand on the floor. There wasn't any sand." Lee, he maintained, had not fallen at all. But the singer's friend and diehard fan Freeman Gunter did testify on her behalf—not about having seen her fall, but about the alleged sand. Asked how Lee could have possibly gone on to perform in such dire condition, he fired off a carefully prepared statement, saying that an artist of such supreme professionalism could hide any malady.

The trial ended, and the parties awaited a judgment. Meanwhile, Lee forged ahead with her Broadway plans. The singer placed a call to her friends Marge and Irving Cowan, two tycoons whom she had known since the 1960s. The Cowans ran the Diplomat Resort and Country Clubs, a phenomenally lucrative beachside complex in Hollywood, Florida. At its heart was a lavish showroom, the Café Cristal. Irv, the Diplomat's president, hadn't skimped on the entertainment: Frank Sinatra, Judy Garland, Bob Hope, Diana Ross, Peggy Lee.

For Marge, whose father, the grocery-store magnate Samuel Friedlander, had built the Diplomat, luxury was a way of life. She and Irv reigned over South Florida society; their party-throwing, art collecting, racehorses, and VIP friends had made them frequent boldface names in the columns. But no one meant quite so much to Marge as her girlfriend Peggy Lee. The couple had attended Nicki Barbour's wedding to Dick Foster; the next year Marge served as maid of honor for Lee's marriage to Jack Del Rio. She raved about a party Lee had thrown for her and Irv in 1966, attended by Garland and Rock Hudson. Lee and the Cowans were so close, said Irv, that "our kids used to bathe with her in the tub." But while

Marge found her unreservedly dazzling, Irv was more skeptical. "Peggy had the ability to be as gracious as she wanted to be," he said. "Or not."

Now it was the spring of 1982, and Marge listened excitedly as Lee effused about her Broadway-bound musical. Marge couldn't wait to hear the songs. The singer complied by unveiling them at a birthday party she threw for Irv at her home. Lee had invited a host of celebrities, among them Peter Allen, singing couple Steve Lawrence and Eydie Gormé, and Doris Duke. Also present was producer Allan Carr, who had spearheaded the number-one hit film of 1978, *Grease*. Lee hoped to lure him aboard.

She had everything planned. About halfway through the party, her friend Frank Ralston asked her to sing some songs from *Peg*. Horner took his place at the piano, and they began their minirecital. Guests responded with breathless effusions. Marge was particularly entranced. This show *had* to get to Broadway, and she convinced Irv that the two of them ought to pay for it. What's more, they knew just the man to lead the way.

———

MARGE HAD ALREADY PLACED a call to another close friend, Zev Bufman, an Israeli-born theater owner and producing mogul. Columnist Liz Smith proclaimed him "the now-famous Zev Bufman of Broadway," and indeed, Bufman was in the news a lot lately. He had just imported a smash British musical, *Joseph and the Amazing Technicolor Dreamcoat*; it was his twenty-second Broadway show, and it ran for nineteen months. In South Florida, Bufman was a theatrical titan; he had acquired nearly every important house and used them to mount Broadway-caliber productions. His empire spread to New Orleans when he bought the city's most important theater, the Saenger.

In the tabloids, Bufman's main appeal centered around his alliance with the star to whom he was "connected at the hip," as he himself put it. The year before, Bufman had convinced Elizabeth Taylor to make her Broadway debut in a revival of Lillian Hellman's *The Little Foxes*. Taylor had nothing to lose; her screen career had dwindled mostly to TV movies, even to a few appearances on the soap opera *General Hospital*. Bufman's casting coup scored a million dollars in advance sales. In return, he had to shoulder the calamities of a star whose history of life-threatening illnesses, mishaps, and major operations dwarfed even Peggy Lee's.

But Bufman loved playing in the big leagues, whether through co-founding the Miami Heat basketball team or by getting even more deeply involved with Taylor, his oft-rumored flame. (Both were married—she to the Republican senator John Warner, he to his longtime wife Vilma.) They went on to form the short-lived Elizabeth Theatre Group, which aimed to bring classic dramas and big-name Hollywood stars to Broadway. Taylor costarred with ex-husband Richard Burton in Noël Coward's *Private Lives*, but her frequent absences sank the show. Later, Bufman would help her check into the Betty Ford Center for drug and alcohol abuse.

Throughout the chaos, he remained poised, suave, and charming. An old-school impresario in the grand manner, Bufman looked like a man who meant business. Short, with graying curly hair, he wore impeccably tailored suits and traveled by limo. In his briefcase he carried one of the first mobile phones; he used it to wheel and deal in his lightly accented, refined speech. But Bufman was as calculating as any hard-boiled Broadway titan. Jon Wilner, whose Broadway ad agency handled many Bufman shows, recalled him as "one of the great producers I ever worked for. He was very dedicated. He made all the decisions, and he was very clever about raising the money. Unfortunately he had flop after flop, but that's the luck of the draw."

Bufman had grown up idolizing Peggy Lee. "She was a dream to me," he said. "I thought, one of these days I'm gonna meet this lady." It finally happened in 1981, when Irv and Marge invited him to hear her at the Diplomat. That night, Lee had sung two *Peg* songs. He loved them. Later, when the Cowans urged him to produce her on Broadway, Bufman didn't hesitate.

From the first business meeting, they charmed each other completely. Lee saw him as her new savior, and in the early months of their relationship, both felt like they were walking on air. "Everyone told me Peggy would be difficult to deal with," said the producer to Bob Thomas of the Associated Press. "In fact, she has been an absolute dream."

Bufman, of course, knew how to romance his leading ladies, and he understood Lee's need to feel her seductive sway over men. He dispensed lingering glances, hugs, and flirtatious notes. Lee wanted more, and one of his telegrams convinced her he would provide it: "I KISS YOUR LIPS KISS YOUR EYES AND KISS THAT FABULOUS MIND OF YOURS. TOGETHER WE WILL MAKE PEG BROADWAY'S MOST INCREDIBLE HIT."

With him and the Cowans on board, a more formal backers' audition was planned, again at Lee's home, for a few potential investors. Lee opted to turn the event into a dinner party. "If you had dinner you couldn't say anything bad," explained Horner. "It would be ungracious!"

With his wife, Vilma, out of town, Bufman called Lee and asked if he might "bring a friend" who also lived in Bel Air. Lee asked who. "Elizabeth Taylor," he said. He thought this might add to the night's glamour, which in turn might loosen purse strings. Lee hesitated. She knew that Taylor overshadowed almost any woman. She agreed only reluctantly.

The pressure to shine had grown that much heavier. Lee hired Bruce Vanderhoff to provide his poshest catering, courtesy of his fashionable *Le Restaurant*. He seldom did hair anymore, but Lee asked him to give her a special coiffure—one that would help her eclipse even Movieland's foremost beauty. Vanderhoff suspected hidden motives. "Do you know what was really behind that whole evening? Peggy had her talons out to snatch Zev."

As the doorbell started ringing, Lee stood in the foyer alongside the grand staircase, wearing "something long and diaphanous," as Horner recalled. The dozen or so guests included Danny Thomas, her costar in *The Jazz Singer*, who had made a mint as a TV star and producer; Michael Smuin, codirector of the San Francisco Ballet; and playwright William Luce, Bufman's choice of collaborator for Lee's show.

But from the moment she swept through the front door, all eyes turned to Taylor. She arrived on Bufman's arm, dressed in flowing violet to match her famous eyes. Waiters hovered nearby to answer her every whim; awestruck guests hung on her words. Lee kept glancing over in annoyance, realizing she was no longer the star of her own show.

She had planned to hold court at the dinner table with ebullient talk of *Peg*, but Taylor casually took over. The actress delighted everyone with stories about the filming of *Cleopatra*, during which she had begun her extramarital affair with the also-married Richard Burton. As Taylor spoke, she waved a hand adorned with the famous 33.19-carat, square-cut diamond ring that Burton had given her. Somebody asked about it. "It was off her finger in a flash," said Luce. Taylor giggled and said, "Let's pass it around!" The hefty ring moved from guest to guest. When it reached Lee, said Luce, "she grimly passed it on without looking at it." Taylor noticed.

"Here, Peggy," she said, "why don't you wear this for luck?" Answered Lee with faux concern: "Oh, no, I might break it!"

After dessert, everyone adjourned to the peach-painted living room and its sea of matching chairs. Lee settled onto a chaise in between two speakers; Horner sat at the baby grand. After a spoken introduction, Lee began her first number. Previously the songs had invoked gushing praise from friends and fans; now she looked uneasily into a roomful of stern, critical faces. "These were business people," said Horner. "They were thinking in terms of putting money into this." One song led to the next, earning only polite applause. All the while, Lee noticed people's eyes darting over to Taylor to monitor her reactions.

As Lee and Horner began a ballad, Taylor reached into her purse for a cigarette. Bufman grabbed his lighter and held it out for her. Lee glared their way, and coughed lightly to get their attention. She didn't. At that point, said Luce, "Peggy went ballistic. She slammed down the mike, with a resulting blast from the speakers. We all jumped." Lee lurched to her feet, hissing: *I can't sing when someone is blowing smoke in my face!*" She stormed off. Bufman leapt up and chased after her. All eyes returned to an incredulous Taylor, as tense murmurs filled the room. Finally Lee returned. Clearly rattled, she began her next song. But her confidence had crashed, and even through the microphone she was barely audible.

The program closed to a mild ovation. Danny Thomas piped through the silence with an offer to invest in the show. He named a painfully low amount. "At the door," recalled Luce, "people thanked Peggy with encouraging comments, plus insincere praise spoken out of pity. I could see she was trying to hold back the tears. For a backers' audition, it was a disaster."

Neither the Cowans nor Zev Bufman were discouraged. "I knew there was a show there," Bufman said. "I sensed some things that worried me, but I figured, we can fix those. I've worked with leading ladies all my life. She'll listen to reason. It's Peggy Lee."

But Lee was incensed at Bufman for bringing Taylor, and she never forgave him. She still needed him, of course, even if both Smuin and Taylor wanted nothing more to do with her. "I'm not gonna be involved with that woman!" said Taylor to Bufman. Later, when the Elizabeth Theatre Group's planned production of *Inherit the Wind*, set to star Burt Lancaster and Kirk Douglas, fell through, Bufman announced that *Peg* would take its place. Taylor had her publicist fire off a curt rebuttal, saying that neither she nor her company were in any way connected with Lee.

The Cowans remained committed to the show—she a bit more than he, said Irv. "Marge and Zev sucked me into it," he recalled with a laugh. "At the time, it seemed like not a very bad idea. She was Peggy Lee." They handed Bufman seven figures to bring her to Broadway. From there, the couple brought in two more deep-pocketed sources: Georgia Frontiere, who owned the Los Angeles Rams; and Hugh Culverhouse, owner of the Tampa Bay Buccaneers. Irv and Marge were delighted. "This was their fun," said Jon Wilner. "They didn't get their money by investing in things like this. This was playtime. They could tell their friends, their dentist, 'Oh, we're producing a Broadway show with Peggy Lee! It's gonna be a big hit!'"

Everyone's point of comparison was *Lena Horne: The Lady and Her Music*. But whereas Horne's show told the epic tale of a woman who had mirrored and influenced decades of social history, Lee's story was essentially all about her. Its theme was the hardscrabble rise and hard times of a splendid and uniquely American singer and songwriter—a pre-feminist achiever who had weathered the shifting tides of popular fancy.

Lee had one thing Horne lacked: hit records, if bygone ones. And the score for *Peg* held promise. Furthermore, the timing seemed right: Horne's renaissance, along with that of the fifty-six-year-old Lauren Bacall in the recent hit musical *Woman of the Year*, had made Lee's endeavor seem a good gamble. "Faded stars are big hits on Broadway," explained Wilner.

In August of 1982, Bufman threw a press conference and luncheon at the Beverly Hills Hotel's Polo Lounge, a fabled celebrity hangout. While reporters and photographers gathered to await Lee, Bufman pumped them up. The score of *Peg*, he told them, revealed "a side of Peggy no one has seen before—so private, so womanly, so intimate, so open."

He brought on Lee, who sailed into view in a black chiffon pajama suit and wide-brimmed hat. The ovation that greeted her, and the lightning storm of flashbulbs, boded a bright future for *Peg*. "This is one of the happiest days of my life!" she exclaimed. "It'll be my Broadway debut, and I'm training for it like an athlete." She sang three songs, accompanied by Horner. Afterward, she flitted through the crowd, posing for pictures and luxuriating in the attention. To Bufman, the supposedly injured star seemed "like a rock."

Word of her impending Broadway turn surprised Earl F. Riley, the judge in her Waldorf case. He had yet to render a decision on the suit of a woman who, in the words of her lawyer Jim Moser, had "needed support" at a recent public event to get through one song. Asked about the announcement of *Peg*, Moser said: "We hoped to have a verdict before then."

Later that month, Riley awarded Lee $325,000—a handsome settlement for the time, awarded to a sympathetic and famous plaintiff. Yet it was a fraction of the fifteen million Lee had wanted. "Peggy deserved nothing," insisted Bruce Vanderhoff, "because her story was totally fabricated." But Lee was miserable. She had talked of her "fall" so many times that she truly seemed to believe it had happened. More dismayingly, legal bills would erase much of the award.

At least she still had *Peg*. To almost everyone concerned, most of all Peggy Lee, the show had the makings of a hit. She shared her vision with reporter Kathy Larkin: "I've been around for a while, and I figured it would be *War and Peace* and *Gone with the Wind* and *Forever Amber*—all combined."

Early announcements mentioned a cast of twenty-two. The right actor had to play Dave Barbour. Lee wanted Dustin Hoffman, with his "quiet intensity"; the suitably Italian but age-inappropriate Tony Bennett has offered his services. Lee decided that either Maureen Stapleton or Colleen Dewhurst, two Tony-winning Broadway veterans, should portray hatchet-faced Min. Plans were announced for a nationwide talent search to cast three women as the younger Peggy Lees. If she had ever seriously intended to stay out of her own show, the notion was shot down by the Cowans, Bufman, and by her own ego. Perhaps, as in *Side by Side by Sondheim*, Lee could serve as onstage narrator, she thought. A chaise on the side of the stage would be perfect.

Every choice hinged upon the advice of her psychic, Don Torres. At one of their sessions, he sat by Lee's bed and predicted wondrous things. "You have some tremendous public acclaim coming as a legend, as a truly great individual . . . Physically things are beginning to improve . . . I have never seen your aura as clear . . . There's a healing going on here." He urged her to tend to her health and rid her body of toxins; she would need to shore up her strength.

Lee took him at his word. She replaced her fattening meals with yogurt, granola, and vitamin drinks. Soon she decided she wanted to dance onstage, something she had never done in her life. The costumes, she vowed, would show off a streamlined Peggy Lee—svelte as the one in *Pete Kelly's Blues*.

One thing was certain: Lee knew nothing about writing a script; all she had was a bunch of songs and anecdotes. William Luce stepped in to try and save the day. Luce specialized in biographical portraits of stellar artistic women; his 1976 Broadway hit, *The Belle of Amherst*, had starred the venerated Julie Harris as Emily Dickinson. Who better than Luce, reasoned Bufman, to write *Peg*? "He was gentle; he was sensitive; he was not a fighter," said the producer. "He was just a sweet person with uncanny instincts as to how to write about women."

The playwright's agent had urged him to decline. "He reeled off tales of her explosive outbursts of temper and sudden paranoid distrust of friends and colleagues," said Luce. But Bufman won him over. "She's really very sweet," he argued. And the money was tempting. Luce agreed to meet her.

He arrived at her home. Lee saw his curly hair, beard, and soulful eyes, and felt his warm and shy demeanor. She turned on her charm full force, and he melted. "It was like an old friend had walked into my life," he said.

Eager to stoke their rapport, Bufman paid for Luce to accompany her to New Jersey in September for a weekend of reunion shows in honor of Capitol Records' fortieth anniversary. Called "Forties in the Eighties," the concerts would take place in Hackensack at the run-down Orrie de Nooyer Auditorium. For old-record fans, the series was a feast: On one stage they would see a parade of the label's old stars, reprising songs they had sung on heavy shellac 78s and long out-of-print LPs. Besides Lee, the cast included emcee Margaret Whiting, Betty Hutton, Keely Smith, Ella Mae Morse, Johnny Johnston, Gordon MacRae, the Pied Pipers, Andy Russell, Nelson Riddle, the Four Freshmen, and Nancy Wilson.

Before the plane they were taking from L.A. had even left the ground, Lee turned into a fire-spitting diva. As soon as the passengers were told to fasten their seat belts, she called down the aisle, demanding a plate of fresh fruit. A flight attendant promised to bring it as soon as the jet was in the air. "I'm diabetic and I need it *now!*" sputtered Lee. Passengers turned in alarm. Lee yanked at Luce's arm. *"Get that girl's name!"* she ordered. "I tried to calm her down," recalled the playwright. "When she finally stopped fuming, she said with sarcasm, 'So this is what Zev calls *first-class*?'"

The first performance of "Forties in the Eighties" ran a stultifying seven hours; singers who were starved for applause far exceeded their allotted handful of songs. By one-thirty AM, when the biggest star of the group was called from her trailer to go onstage, more than half the twelve hundred seats were empty. Lee began what Stephen Holden, by then a *New York Times* critic, called an "eerie, somnambulistic set," heavy on ballads. "Despite a tiny, faltering voice," wrote Holden, Lee wove a "dreamy spell."

Luce was spellbound, especially by her traditional closer, "I'll Be Seeing You." As so often happened with Lee, her singing salved the sting of her ill behavior. "I felt that I had met another Peggy Lee," he said. "She conveyed allure and intimacy, a place deep inside where romance still existed as a young girl's most vulnerable emotion. She took her listeners there. This is when I came to believe that Peggy's show might really be a winner."

She certainly felt that way about Luce—so much so that she asked him to leave the hotel Bufman had put him in and move in with her, which would place him on twenty-four-hour call. Luce declined, but he put in long, daily hours at the house in an effort to drag a script out of Lee. A ritual of frustration and minimal productivity ensued. Luce arrived at noon. He waited in the living room for up to an hour while Lee worked on her makeup and outfit. The living-room phone would ring, and ring. It was Peggy Lee calling, from her bedroom, with dictation for Luce.

Finally she called him into the inner sanctum. Lee lay in bed, propped up with pillows. She was fully made up, with a turban, diamonds, and feathers. Luce sat at a wobbly card table near the bed.

He tried to elicit reflections from her to formulate a rough script. Each day she handed him written lines, many of them rhymed. "Sometimes it was a litany of woes," he said, "but other times it was a bit amusing. At her best, Peggy had a droll sense of humor." But for all her insight as a singer, Lee, he found, "didn't seem disposed to mentally work out her own problems, or to analyze her possible responsibility for causing them." For years she had leaned on Ernest Holmes, then Adela Rogers St. Johns, to hold her hand through every crisis, real or imagined. Now, said Luce, "she depended on astrologers, metaphysical practitioners, and clairvoyants to talk her out of emotional upsets and depression. I made sure not to be drawn into this ongoing dependence she demanded of others, so I used my work on the *Peg* script as an excuse to move to another room when Peg got on the phone for up to an hour or more."

A videotape of *Pete Kelly's Blues* ran over and over in the background. She played with her Lhasa Apso dog, Genghis—her second canine gift from the Dalai Lama, she informed Luce, to replace the departed Sungyi-La. José Prado brought lunch into the bedroom, then dinner. Mealtimes took hours. As evening neared, with little achieved, Lee tried to make Luce stay and watch TV with her. When interviewers came, she enjoyed showing him off as the playwright of her forthcoming Broadway show. One writer asked her opinion of the female singers of the day. "Peg paused as if deep in thought," remembered Luce. "'Let me see,' she said, as if unable to come up with a name." The journalist mentioned Barbra Streisand, who was then in the process of coproducing, cowriting, directing, and starring in the movie *Yentl*. "Peg said thoughtfully, 'Yes . . . she's coming along nicely.'"

Lee had never forgiven Bufman for (as she saw it) sabotaging her dinner party/backer's audition by bringing Elizabeth Taylor. She ordered Luce to keep count of every sheet of paper he used at the upstairs copy machine; all possible costs, she stressed, would be charged to Zev. Try as the playwright did to resist, Lee kept him in her web of melodrama. One day, with him at her bedside, Lee flew into a rage over some matter concerning the producer. She yanked the phone from its cradle and announced that she was calling Vilma, Bufman's wife, to inform her that her husband was having an affair with Taylor. Luce pleaded with her not to: "How could you do such a mean thing?"

"*Because he lied to me!*" snapped Lee. Exactly how was unclear, but Luce couldn't stop her from dialing Vilma. "I don't even want to hear this," said Luce. He left the room. Knowing of Lee's old affair with the married Robert Preston, he couldn't help but think her a hypocrite.

And a needy one. To tear himself away from the lonely and needy star was a nightly challenge. Then, often as not, the phone in his hotel room would ring after midnight. "If you dared to say, 'I'm getting sleepy, I've got to sign off,' she would slam down the receiver. She wanted to be the one to terminate." Lee would call back in tears, begging forgiveness. "So much pressure," she sniffled, "and everyone is against me."

Lee compensated by pulling rank—even over her daughter, who visited occasionally; and Marianne, who was living there as her sister's employee. "She was like a little ghost moving through the house every now and then," said Luce of Marianne. Lee treated both Nicki and Marianne "like servants," he observed, and didn't hesitate to fling withering sarcasm at them in front of others. Having heard Lee vent so much about Min's slave driving, Marianne watched with dismay as her sister morphed into the woman she hated.

But Lee was at her most gracious when Martin Charnin, the Tony-winning director and lyricist of Broadway's *Annie*, came over at Bufman's request to explore the possibility of directing *Peg*. Lee arranged a fancy catered lunch. Then she directed José to create one of her favorite house-keeping effects, which entailed vacuuming the living-room carpet in rows, one up and one down, giving it a vaguely Art Deco look. "Five minutes before Martin arrived," remembered Luce, "Marianne walked across the center of the carpet in her bedroom slippers, from the kitchen to Peg's bedroom. She walked back in another direction. When Peg saw the footprints, which had totally damaged the *House Beautiful* feature, her reaction to poor Marianne was scathing. And there was no time to correct the silly little detail."

The doorbell rang, and in walked Charnin. "Martin was affable and pleased to meet Peg," said Luce. But after a few pleasantries, he got down to business. Lee mentioned lunch. "No thanks," he said. "I just ate break-fast." The disgruntled star joined Luce on the living-room sofa, where he read a scene for Charnin. The director thanked them and left. He declined Bufman's offer. "Peg said it was because I read too fast," said Luce.

Lee didn't like it when a man turned her down. More than ever, she leaned on her imagination to keep her feeling desirable. That included casting Luce as her would-be swain. Late at night in his hotel room, the playwright answered his phone. He heard Peggy Lee breathily cooing a hit from *Show Boat*: "I love him because he's wonderful / Because he's just my Bill."

"Do you like me singing to you, darling?" cooed Lee.

He paused. She had made such remarks before. "Peggy," said Luce, "you know I'm gay, don't you?"

Silence. "I guess I never thought about it. I guess I'm too feminine to care."

"But you know I've had a partner for years. You've talked with him on the phone."

"And I like Ray very much, and I'm glad you have him in your life—and he has you in his."

The flirting ended. But still she clung to her fantasies, as Luce saw when she proudly handed him her new headshot. The photographer, Hans Albers, had reduced Lee to a ghostly blur of an old-time glamour queen, with everything but her platinum-swirled head and part of a hand shrouded in a white fur coat. As Luce stared at the murky image, Lee exclaimed: "They didn't have to do any retouching!"

No one quite knew what she saw when she looked in the mirror. But a photo taken later in the *Peg* dressing room by Marianne Barcellona for *People* magazine gave a clue. It showed Lee gazing at herself in the mirror while Vincent Roppatte, her hairdresser and makeup artist on *Peg*, fussed with what little hair the singer had left, and Paul Horner smiled broadly in the background. Lee's hairline had receded almost to the top of her head; a silver headband covered it. Roppatte fingered the wisps of hair that hung from the back. Lee's face looked as stonelike and featureless as that of an Egyptian sphinx. Through eyes hooded by giant false lashes, Lee beheld her reflection with a cool smile and a look of complete satisfaction. Marilyn Monroe or Sophia Loren could have been staring back at her.

One day at the house, she allowed Luce to witness her daily transformation into Peggy Lee. As he waited to be summoned to her bedroom, Lee startled him by padding into the living room in her robe. Sans makeup, with her hair an unruly mess, she was almost unrecognizable as the Lee he knew. "I got a late start," she said with a smile.

Once in the bedroom, she began her transformation. As they chatted, Lee brushed back her hair and pinned on her artificial chignon. Luce noticed the facelift scars on the back of her neck and behind her ears. "Over a reddish, mottled face she applied a makeup base with a sponge. Then powder with a small brush, and blush. Lashes were attached, eyebrows penciled perfectly, and finally glossy lipstick. 'Voilà,' she said, looking at me in the mirror and laughing." She awaited his reaction.

"Wow," he said. "Here you are."

Luce was impressed. "It was the most honest moment we'd had," he recalled. "I felt there was a new bond." Lee, he decided, had wanted him to see how masterfully she controlled the world's vision of her.

Now, with *Peg*, she could welcome everyone into her carefully crafted view of the truth. It began with the autobiographical lyrics that Paul Horner was setting. Lee couldn't make music with a man without stirring in some romantic spice; not surprisingly, she harbored a crush on Horner. It went nowhere, for he too was gay. But he "dearly loved her," and didn't discourage her illusions. Lee knew what pains he took to get to Bellagio Road; lacking a car, he had to ride three buses and take a steep uphill walk through streets where pedestrians were liable to be questioned by police. All exertion was forgotten as they dined together in her bedroom, laughing and trading stories. Their intimacy unleashed some of Lee's most inspired lyric writing. "Daddy Was a Railroad Man" looked back at her rural North Dakota life. The words swung—"Boxcar connected to the old caboose / Take 'em to the yard and then he'd turn 'em loose"—and Horner set them to trainlike rhythms. "Angels on Your Pillow" was a tender lullaby in memory of baby Nicki; it harked back to that brief time when her daughter's future meant more to Lee than her own: "I wish for you the dearest things . . . A happy heart that always sings . . ."

Domestic bliss, of course, had never been Lee's for long, and Horner saw the latest threat to it as he stood amid the soft peach environs of her living room. While Lee readied herself in the bedroom, he noticed a letter on the piano. He couldn't resist glancing at it. A bank had denied her application for a loan. Horner later learned that Lee had been in danger of losing the house. It helped explain her desperation for a hit show.

At the start of 1983, prospects looked bright. Lee was back in London, reveling in a welcome as loving as ever. This was a quite different Peggy Lee, of course, than the one they had encountered at Pigalle in 1961 or at the Royal Albert Hall in 1970. At sixty-two, the star was a stout figure, camouflaged by white feathers. Lately she had tried foregoing wigs; her thin hair was parted and pulled back tightly, accentuating her high forehead and the mascara-lined slits that were her eyes. In a rehearsal studio, Lee met Boy George, the flamboyantly androgynous star of the white glam-soul group, Culture Club. He wore long braids tied with ribbon, lipstick, and wing-tipped eye shadow. To Lee, who still considered Cary Grant the pinnacle of manhood, George was a strange sight indeed. He loved her look, but not for the reasons men always had. "You look outrageous!" he said, adding, "You win the biscuit of the day."

If her appearance had edged into the bizarre, Lee's newfound health regimen had taken years off her voice, which sounded rounder and less nasal. She showed it off on *London Night Out*, a TV variety show. For Billie Holiday's swinging trademark "Them There Eyes," Lee teamed with the French-born Stéphane Grappelli, who at seventy-five was widely acclaimed as the world's foremost jazz violinist. Masterful though he was, Grappelli let her take the lead; when they traded phrases he played off of her just as saxophonist Lester Young had done in his 1930s recordings with Billie Holiday.

Then the singer announced "something wonderful" that had just come her way. "My producers, Zev Bufman and Irving Cowan, are taking me to Broadway in my own play. And I'm so thrilled I can't stand it!" She leaned into the curve of the piano and, with clouds of violins swirling around her, sang "Angels on Your Pillow." Her British fans roared their approval.

No one doubted that *Peg* would be a musical feast. Instead of hiring one arranger, as most Broadway shows did, Lee reached out to many of the greats she had known: Gordon Jenkins, Bill Holman, Johnny Mandel, Artie Butler, Don Sebesky, Billy May, Torrie Zito, Benny Carter. Her choices ensured that *Peg* would sound like a Peggy Lee show, not like a Broadway musical. Just as important to her, though, was the freedom to tell her story her way—especially with regard to Min and her *Paradise Lost* tragedy with Dave Barbour. "We're going to treat this all with a light hand," she promised a reporter. "But it's really about survival."

Ostensibly it was also about healing, and dismissing lifelong demons. "I know the value of forgiveness," explained Lee of Min, "and I've long since forgiven her." But with each new interview the "compassion" wore thinner. "If hers had been my lot in life, to feel that way and to inflict physical and mental violence on someone, I wouldn't want to be alive. I feel sorry for her, really sorry." Kathy Larkin of the *New York Daily News* caught Lee on a particularly livid day. "Look," said the star, pointing to her cheek. "My stepmother hit me here, in the face, with a metal-edged razor strap. And here"—Lee touched her head—"that's where she hit me with a heavy cast-iron skillet." She told Paul Horner that she identified with the slaves, because of having had to rise before dawn and do chores.

"I took it with a pinch of salt," he said. "I'm sure her stepmother was a for-midable woman, but I don't think that being a stepmother is an easy task. And being the stepmother of Peggy Lee—well, Peggy was a very willful child when she was sixty. But Peggy's truth, in her mind, was the truth."

And as Horner learned, challenging her was forbidden. Production meetings were typically held around her bed, and one day he and Luce sat alongside it as Lee told them of her eleventh-hour reconciliation with Barbour. Nicki was visiting from Idaho and attending patiently to her mother. Hearing that tale yet again, she silently fumed. Later, when the two men were in the kitchen, Nicki walked in. "This is bullshit!" she said. "My father was very happy with somebody when he passed away!" From inside the bedroom came Lee's voice: "Be quiet, Nicki!"

———

IN THE HEAT OF a scorching New York summer, *Peg*'s creative team, including its star, convened in town in preparation for the show's work-shop. At the Minskoff Rehearsal Studio near Times Square, the still-rough script and profusion of new songs would (with luck) coalesce into a musical. Confidence was high. "We seemed to be floating in a kind of euphoria," said William Luce. Despite her reservations about the claims her mother planned to make, Nicki told Paul Horner, "Somebody's got to really fuck up for this not to work."

Yet there was cause for worry. "Our star was a famous performer," explained Luce, "but she had never acted on Broadway with other ac-tors. Stage directions would be new to her. The interaction of dialogue between players, memorization, blocking—all these required training and experience that she had never had." Then there was the issue of her physical condition. Although still quite ambulatory, she had begun using a wheelchair offstage. How would she manage to give eight two-hour shows a week? Horner met Mel Tormé at a party, and filled him in about *Peg*. "Peggy Lee," said Tormé, "will *never* last in a Broadway show." Zev Bufman secretly feared the same. "I chose not to worry about it," he said.

The producer had found a challenging home for *Peg*: the Lunt-Fontanne Theatre, home of Broadway blockbusters ranging from *No, No, Nanette* (1925) to *The Sound of Music* (1959) to *Beatlemania* (1979). Bufman had taken a three-year lease on the theater to house his productions. At 1,505 seats, it seemed perilously large for the soft voice of Peggy Lee. But there was still talk of a sizable cast to shoulder most of the burden. In any case, Lee approved of the theater. She had gone there in 1967 to see the Broadway debut of Marlene Dietrich in her one-woman show; if Dietrich had conquered the Lunt-Fontanne, so would she.

Now was Lee's chance to feel as important as another goddess, too. She knew that Bufman had pampered Elizabeth Taylor with the most extravagant star treatment on Broadway, including a rented Rolls-Royce and three gold-and-diamond bracelets. Lee would not be outdone. When time came to choose her New York lodging for the duration of *Peg*, no mere hotel suite would do. She settled on a penthouse in River Tower, a luxury high-rise on one of the ritziest blocks in Manhattan, East Fifty-Fourth off Sutton Place. Staggering though the cost, Bufman complied; after all, he was spending his investors' money, not his own. He had the apartment outfitted with a white baby grand and a plush matching carpet. Her teenage granddaughter would live with her as hand-holder and amanuensis. Holly Foster didn't mind at first, for she adored her grandmother. "I was like a little Peggy Lee," she said. "I loved to dress up in her clothes. I thought she was the most glamorous thing."

Lee's demands continued. While starring in *The Little Foxes* at the Martin Beck Theatre, Taylor had occupied a giant second-floor dressing room, painted lavender (her favorite color) and decked out with a jumbo fish tank and bathtub. Lee wanted the same space—and both it and the bathtub would be painted peach. Getting upstairs, of course, meant she would need an elevator. "I think that she wanted the one thing Elizabeth hadn't thought of," said Bufman. According to an arcane union rule, no elevator could be built. But Bufman pulled strings, and Lee got her way, at a reported cost of fifty thousand dollars.

She had dismissed the first two personal assistants assigned to her, but the third passed muster. Andrew Sarewitz was an aspiring actor-singer who had worked in Bufman's office. When introduced to Lee, the twenty-four-year-old brashly called her Peg, not the mandatory Miss Lee. Surprisingly, she liked his audacity, and surely didn't mind the fact that he was tall and good-looking. To Sarewitz, however, Lee was a strange sight indeed. "She fit a little bit of a stereotype of how I thought she'd be—talking out of one side of her mouth, having a tremendous presence but not great energy, dressing a little like a drag queen. Her hair had broken off, so she was wearing a wig and giant glasses. Whiter skin than you can imagine, pencil-thin lips. Always wore high heels even though she was in a wheelchair. I think she felt—not necessarily incorrectly—that everyone knew who she was and that she deserved respect." She won his. "At the beginning," he said, "it was very much a lovefest."

His job was simple: to make sure she had her health foods and whatever else she wanted. Sarewitz held her hand throughout the demanding next phase, to begin on July 18: the workshop, during which a still-amorphous show is beaten into working shape. Bufman had allotted three weeks—a longer time than usual, and a costly one, for the twenty-six-piece orchestra would be present.

But so far, *Peg* was a shambles. William Luce had fashioned a draft script with Lee as narrator; she would comment on the action and converse with key actors, notably the women who would play her junior selves. But not a single actor had been hired, nor a director.

Instead, Lee had enlisted her composer friend Cy Coleman as *Peg*'s heftily paid "creative consultant." With several Broadway hits to his name—*Sweet Charity, Seesaw, I Love My Wife, Barnum*—Coleman gave everyone hope that he could set the show on track. He decided that the only salvation for *Peg* was to turn it into a concert with autobiographical patter. Both the Cowans and Lee concurred. If it had worked for Lena Horne, how could Peggy lose?

From there, he called in Robert (Bobby) Drivas, who had directed the recent Broadway revival of another Coleman musical, *Little Me*. Greek-American and a longtime actor as well as director, Drivas was a pet favorite of Coleman's—a handsome, hypercharged bundle of energy with a bitchy-funny sense of humor.

But there wasn't much he could do for Peggy Lee. As though on principle, she fought Drivas on everything, and he rapidly grew to loathe her. At the Minskoff Rehearsal Studio, Lee sat in her wheelchair in the shadow of a wide-brimmed hat, and likewise in the dark about almost everything needed to make a Broadway show work. To yield to the experts meant giving up control, and this she could not allow.

What Lee did do was exude waves of intimidation to keep everyone in place. Choreography was out of the question: she had stipulated that she did not want to move onstage, except for walking on and off, sitting, and standing. This confused Luce, for he had heard her say repeatedly that the show should be more "like Lena," a physical dynamo onstage.

Presumably Lee was referring to Horne's inspirational fervor. To that end, she showed up every day with newly written passages of verse for Luce to cobble into the script. Lee proudly read them aloud. They provoked discreet giggles; Luce thought of Helen Steiner Rice, whose poems of faith appeared on millions of 1960s greeting cards and on TV's *The Lawrence Welk Show*. Lee insisted that, after every long day of the workshop, Luce should go home with her to make more poetic revisions. He refused. "You're here for one thing," she announced, "and that is to take care of *me!*"

Luce wouldn't budge, and Lee ordered Coleman to go over his head and make the changes for her. Later, without her permission, the playwright crossed out some of the more mawkish lines. Once more, Lee was enraged. She insisted that Coleman scold him the next day in front of the company. Coleman obeyed. Afterward he pulled Luce aside. "I'm sorry," he said, embarrassed. "She has to have her way." And if anyone challenged it, she gave them her stock warning: "You are upsetting me. My doctor has told me not to get upset because I could have a heart attack. And if I die it will be your fault."

Surely, thought Bufman, Lee would appreciate the wardrobe design. He had hired the most prestigious costumer on Broadway, Florence "Flossie" Klotz, whose work on dozens of shows, including *Follies* and *A Little Night Music*, had earned her several Tonys. When Klotz was ready, most of the *Peg* team—Bufman, the Cowans, Bobby Drivas, stage manager Larry Forde, Sarewitz, and Lee—sat around a table in Bufman's office and waited eagerly to see her drawings. The designer unveiled drawings of long, glittery, voluminous gowns with shoulders padded to aid the illusion of a slimmer silhouette. Jackets would add further concealment, as would turbans, which Lee sometimes wore to hide her thin hair.

The singer was incensed. "I look like a football player!" she barked. After so many weeks on her new diet regimen, she considered herself svelte. And at that meeting, everyone got a glimpse of Lee's fanciful self-image. She rose from her chair and, forgetting her wheelchair dependency, strutted from one end of the office to the other and back again, swaying like a model on a catwalk and bumping and grinding à la Mae West. Sarewitz watched every head in the room drop in embarrassment. Drivas scrawled a note and handed it to him:

SHE LOOKS LIKE TRUMAN CAPOTE IN DRAG

When he saw the young man fighting not to laugh, he tortured him with another note:

SHE LOOKS LIKE AN ALBINO GORILLA

As Klotz rushed to make changes, the singer once more blamed Zev Bufman. Her resentment of him "came out like acid when he walked by," said Luce. She gave him the silent treatment, while not hesitating to bad-mouth him in front of others. "In a close-knit theater company," observed the playwright, anyone who indulges in that sort of character assassination "forfeits respect."

That didn't apply to her talent, of course. "We were all in wonderment of her ear, what she demanded musically, how the orchestrations sounded," said Bufman. "She was a perfectionist with the musicians. This was a commitment that other stars rarely have." Still, Coleman doubted that an all-original Peggy Lee would sell many tickets. Some of the more somber songs, including Horner's favorite, "Mirrors and Marble," got the ax. Understandably, Coleman felt she had to please the tourists with some of her hits. Now *Peg* would open safely with "Fever."

But she huffily denied his plea to trim the many pages of script she had written about Min. Instead she expounded upon them even further in a song she wrote without Horner, "One Beating a Day." Coleman cringed when he heard it; so did many of the musicians. The words were a dossier of her stepmother's abuses: "She hit me in the head with a frying pan / She shoved my face in the garbage can." Lee had a vengeful laugh at the fall that had broken Min's leg, while portraying herself as an angel of forgiveness.

Coleman begged her in vain to shelve the song. But she did heed his advice about lightening it up. Lee decided a calypso-and-reggae rhythm would do the trick. The composer still hated "One Beating a Day." In response, she defiantly published it in sheet-music form—believing, apparently, that lots of people would want to sing it.

Lee had succeeded in emasculating one of her dearest friends and collaborators. One day, after a particularly heated scuffle, he stormed out of the building and didn't return for a couple of days. After one of their uglier clashes, he ran up to the third-floor men's room, where he hid. Rising from her wheelchair, Lee took the elevator upstairs "and boldly charged in," said Luce. "Cy was trapped. He was terrified of her. I felt he was a weakling, the way he behaved."

Paul Horner was feeling similarly helpless. No one had invited him to participate in the workshops; still, he had refused to believe that Lee could ever cross him. Now he feared otherwise. Whenever she heard anyone praise his music for *Peg*, the star bristled. "It's *my* life!" she intoned. Lee's psychic had urged her to make sure she controlled the copyrights to her songs; in this case, it would be at Horner's expense. Lee had pressured him to let her publish their *Peg* collaborations through her company, Denslow Music. That would place them under her command, and earn her publishing royalties he wouldn't share. Horner's attorney, Abraham Marcus, advised him to found his own publishing company, and to send Lee a letter confirming their fifty-fifty split on all rights. In May, she received his cordial handwritten note.

Her written response stunned him. "How dare you question my honesty?" she demanded. Lee reminded him of what a "pretty lucky fellow" he was to be writing with her, and she dropped veiled threats of replacing him. "You have certainly put a dent in our relationship," she declared.

Mortified, Horner dashed off an apology. He envisioned their partnership crumbling if he stepped out of line. Still, he didn't cave in. When a Japanese composing partner of Lee's wrote out new copies of all the *Peg* songs for her, she directed him to note at the bottom of each: © Denslow Music. Thereafter, Horner read an enthusiastic plug for *Peg* in the column of Liz Smith, one of the kindest of gossip scribes. "The music for the incoming Broadway musical 'Peg,' by the lady herself, is said to be simply fabulous," wrote Smith. Horner couldn't believe his eyes. But Luce wasn't surprised. He had heard the gossip on the company grapevine: Lee had allegedly told Drivas and Coleman that she wanted credit for the show's book, lyrics, *and* music. Apparently she then decided to capitalize on Coleman's name. Smith ran another advance rave: "Already they are saying Peggy's song, 'Soul,' written with Cy Coleman, will stop the show." The true composer, of course, was Horner.

Decades later, Smith recalled her source for these tidbits: Lee's adoring hairstylist and makeup man, Vincent Roppatte, who also worked for Smith. Horner's name had thus far been so minimized that Smith barely knew about him. "I guess Vincent kept telling me bullshit," confessed Smith, "and I would just go and write it as if I had ferreted it out."

Abraham Marcus sent a letter to Bufman's production company, Theatre Now, Inc., and cc'd it to Lee's lawyer. Diplomatically he noted that there was "somewhere an effort to divert Mr. Horner's credit"; he asked that "care be taken in the future" and that "improper attribution be prevented." For now, the composer persisted in hoping that all would turn well. But William Luce deemed *Peg* a hopeless case. Not much of his writing remained in the script. Through his lawyer, he wrote to Bufman that Lee had "revised the libretto in a manner with which I disagree." Luce resigned, and asked that his name be stricken from the production.

The backstage pressure mounted. Lee began a manic process of rewrites—anywhere from five to thirty pages' worth per day. The more she changed, the less "like Lena" her show became. Horne had employed a tart, sassy tone of self-deprecation; Lee depicted herself as a tragic martyr-angel, saintly and defenseless as fate singled her out for its cruelest punishments.

Andrew Sarewitz sat at a typewriter in the producer's office until deep in the night. His occasional typos enraged Lee. She went to Larry Forde, *Peg*'s stage manager, and accused her young assistant of trying to "sabotage" her. "Why would he do that?" said Forde.

In Horner's view, Lee had sabotaged herself. He flew in from Los Angeles to watch the first full rehearsal of *Peg*, and his heart sank. "It was just a mess," he said. Lee stumbled through the narration, sometimes jumping whole pages. An alarmed Bufman asked Horner if Lee had remembered her lines in *Side by Side by Sondheim*. "Well, no," he said; she had kept her script onstage with her.

Lee was clearly in over her head; all she could do to save face was shift the blame. When someone commented gently on her memory issues, she gestured toward Larry Fallon, the conductor. "He's got his script in front of *him*!" she snarled. During a rehearsal break, the show's pianist,

Mike Renzi, demonstrated a song mentioned by another member of the company. "What is this, a piano recital?" said Lee. "You're not being paid to do that!"

Renzi had invited singer Jane Harvey, one of Lee's successors with the Benny Goodman band, to watch the rehearsal from a distant seat. Harvey had performed with Renzi and the rest of Lee's trio, Grady Tate and bassist Jay Leonhart. "I kept looking at Grady and Jay, who were rolling their eyes," she said. Horner burned to make suggestions about his music, but hadn't the nerve: "Everybody was saying to me, 'Keep quiet, Paul. It's your first Broadway show.' Cy Coleman came up and said, 'Don't say *anything*.'"

At one point Lee skipped two songs, and nobody wanted to tell her. D. Michael Heath, one of Lee's six young backup singers, took on the task. Heath regarded her with awe; he also sensed a frightened woman. He walked up to Lee and told her of her mistake. She thanked him. Heath became her friend and one of her few allies; almost everyone else wondered how the producers could ever have thought that *Peg* might work. Lee even balked at doing the required eight shows a week. One day she didn't show up for a rehearsal; she had gone to have her hair done. Heath sang her part.

Peg's advertising director Jon Wilner dreaded the worst. Unlike many Broadway shows, *Peg* hadn't opened out of town, where it might have improved or been canceled altogether, avoiding the shame of a Broadway flop. The star struck him as "sweet" but "totally wacko. If she was someone else, you would have put her in a home. But this was Peggy Lee. You wanted her to succeed."

———

AROUND HALLOWEEN, THE SHOW'S poster began appearing around New York and in ads. It promised an elegant outing. Against shimmery silver, the name *Peg* appeared in lavish script; the curve of the "g" outlined a Dietrich-style line drawing of Lee's eyes, nose, lips, and beauty mark. Along the bottom lay a Peggy Lee rose in white and pink, drawn by Nicki.

Beyond that classy image, *Peg* was in ominous disarray. The show played its first preview on Thursday, December 1, 1983. Her performance, and most of the ones she gave thereafter, bore the familiar signs of

Valium use, Lee's longtime weapon against fear. Once again, it backfired. Both her narration and her singing sounded drugged. She stumbled over words and forgot lines or even long passages. Lee went blank during "Mañana," and Andrew Sarewitz typed out the words, to be placed on a music stand nearby her at the next show. But there was no predicting what would go wrong next. Blanking out at another preview, Lee began singing, a cappella, a song from later in the show, sending Larry Fallon into a panic as he scrambled to alert the orchestra. The preview audiences, largely her fans, seemed to accept the flaws as growing pains, and they cheered for everything, even "One Beating a Day."

"But in my opinion," said Sarewitz, "everyone backstage knew we were in big, big trouble. The entire time, she was in denial. She was also not being told the truth."

Bobby Drivas was still listed as director, and his reputation, he felt, was on the line. He ordered Sarewitz to sit, script in hand, beneath the soundboard, which was located inside the wing at stage left. Whenever Lee flubbed, Sarewitz would feed her the line.

"Bobby, she's gonna kill me!" he said.

"I don't give a fuck what she thinks. This is *my* show, it's my name, and you're gonna do what I tell you to do."

After the show had ended, Lee called Sarewitz into her dressing room. Patiently, she explained that his cues were distracting her. "OK, Peg," he said. The next night, he nervously resumed the job. Finally Lee told Sarewitz he was fired. But she hadn't the authority—he worked for Bufman, not her. Back went the young man to the soundboard. "I became her absolute enemy," he said.

At a subsequent preview, Lee made the brief exit that preceded a segment of songs she had sung at Basin Street East. She encountered Sarewitz in the wing. Lee glared at him with hate in her eyes. *"You're through!"* she declared. The star sailed back onstage with a radiant smile to sing "I Love Being Here with You." After the tension of the last few days, he cracked. "I started crying like an eight-year-old girl," he said.

That moment typified the atmosphere of *Peg*, in which Lee dispensed a message of peace and healing while wreaking havoc behind the scenes. After a performance, Otis Blackwell came to the stage door to see her. His song "Fever" opened the show. But Lee refused to see him. She still seethed over the fact that her lyrics had been added to the sheet music and were recorded by many singers, with no songwriter royalties for her. She had a point. But Lee had almost never acknowledged Sid Kuller for helping her write them—and now she spoke as though Blackwell hadn't penned "Fever" at all. "The world knows that I wrote it," she said. "The people who are taking the credit for it should be ashamed of themselves." Someone had asked her what she would like printed on her tombstone. "I thought, well, I could say: SHE WROTE FEVER."

The advance press for *Peg* suggested a woman who, despite all the tumult, refused to believe her show could fail. Lee talked with the *New York Post*'s Martin Burden about the searing honesty of her script. "What we see could be unsettling," she warned. "There is violence, but there's humor in it, too." Yet with the show a week from opening, Drivas and Coleman felt hopeless. To Bufman, *Peg* was "beyond salvation." Lee took his skepticism as a personal insult. "I was accused of losing confidence in the show, which means I lost confidence in her. I was the enemy; I was the guy who said no, no, no. Nobody else would say no. Even Cy stopped saying no because it was useless."

According to Bufman, he pleaded with Lee and the Cowans to close for two weeks and do emergency fixes. "Cy was in my corner," he said. But the Cowans and Georgia Frontiere were not. "They thought it was the greatest show on earth," recalled Bufman. "And they did not want the embarrassment of postponement."

Years later, Irv recalled nothing of Bufman's suggestion—which in any event was "ridiculous," he thought. "The best people in the business were already aboard. And he would have had to come up with a great deal of additional money. We had spent a fortune in targeting an opening night and renting the theater. Him offering to be the White Knight and coming in as a rescuer—it's kind of insulting."

Lee stopped speaking to Bufman. She told the Cowans that he was herewith barred from her dressing room. At that point, he said, "I had no more role to play."

In fact, Bufman pulled off a dramatic last act, one that Lee never foresaw. It happened on Wednesday, December 14, *Peg*'s opening day. By that afternoon, Frank Rich, lead drama critic of the *New York Times*, had filed his review of *Peg*, which he had seen in previews. The show's team—if not its leading lady—waited in fear. In the crowded landscape of print and TV coverage that Broadway then faced, no review meant more than that of the so-called "Butcher of Broadway." Since 1980, Rich's barbed, intellectual pans as well as his raves had determined the fate of countless major shows.

According to members of the *Peg* company, David Powers, the show's press agent, had somehow learned that Rich hated *Peg*. Around three PM, said Jon Wilner, "David leaked it to Zev." Bufman denied it; Rich, he said, "was so guarded, cracking him was like cracking Fort Knox." But although he knew nothing of the *Peg* backstory, Rich acknowledged later on that such slips could happen, "through typesetters or office gossips or whatever."

With the opening-night curtain set to rise at six-thirty, Bufman sold almost his entire share of *Peg* to Irv and Marge Cowan and Georgia Frontiere. The investors had chosen to stay optimistic. "During previews," said Irv, "everyone stayed in their seats. The songs were more than good. And they were played by some of the best musicians in the country. Sometimes when you're in the middle of these things you don't necessarily use the best judgment."

Bufman claimed that the purchase was their idea. "They said, 'If you're that uncomfortable, then we'll take over, is that okay?' I said, 'Whatever you want to do. This is not gonna make it.'" But in the 1986 book, *New York Confidential: The Lowdown on the Big Town,* by Sharon Churcher, Marge remembered it differently. "He never said that," she declared. Before the deal was sealed, claimed Marge, the Cowans had asked Bufman if he had a sense of what the critics thought. "He told us he went out of his way not to have any knowledge of what was in the reviews." According to Churcher, Bufman claimed that Cy Coleman had already told them about the *Times.* Irv's response: "Maybe one of us had a lapse in memory, and it wasn't me."

In the end, the argument didn't matter. The Cowans had seen the previews; they knew the problems. Nothing discouraged their loyalty to *Peg* and its star. "They wanted to be Peggy's heroes until the end," said Bufman. Shortly before showtime, they and Georgia Frontiere handed Lee an opening-night gift: a Blackglama mink coat and fur hat. It was Marge's idea, not Irv's. But the gifts were nothing less than she felt she deserved. "I'd say it was part of my salary," remarked Lee afterward. "I worked very hard." That night at the Lunt-Fontanne, the producers sat behind Paul Horner and his mother, who had flown in from England. Horner saw them "laughing and shaking hands," although he didn't know why. But Bufman did. "I was done," he said later. "And happily so."

———

PEG'S OPENING NIGHT DREW a fair number of celebrities: Anthony Quinn, Gina Lollobrigida, Joan Fontaine, Carol Channing, Stockard Channing, Judy Collins, Lorna Luft. Lee's fans filled the Lunt-Fontanne, thrilled to see their idol on one of Broadway's grandest stages with a big orchestra and fourteen new songs to sing, plus ten old favorites. Backstage, the *Peg* team prayed for a miracle.

The show began excitingly. In place of a traditional overture, Grady Tate beat out a pulsating drum solo; the name PEG appeared in king-size, lavish lettering on a scrim. At her insistence, the orchestra was onstage, not in the pit. Out walked the star—a self-anointed saint in blinding white and silver, from her glass-beaded headdress to her sparkly, robelike gown. With no hair visible, Lee's unlined face looked oddly like a new-born baby's. Out of this sexless figure came "Fever."

The *Peg* set, by Tom H. Johns, consisted of two beige easy chairs with potted plants behind them. For the rest of the show, Lee's movement consisted of switching from one seat to the other and occasionally standing.

As soon as the crackle of "Fever" stopped, an etherized fog seemed to roll in, as Lee slipped into a tone of sluggish self-pity. In "Soul," she held a sepulchral inner dialogue with herself: "Soul / I'm sorry for the time I've let you down . . ." Then Lee began to speak in slow, solemn tones:

> It was the dawn of the Roaring Twenty
> When flappers were dressed in diamonds and plenty . . .
> In the time of the crocus
> Came a child who could sing
> To be troubled for sure, and beaten and all
> But one who would rise each time she would fall . . .

Heaviness reigned as Lee unveiled her revisionist history. Norma was a Dickensian waif, robbed of her mother and her childhood home, abused daily by her stepmother, yearning for her traveling father. Their voices spoke from beyond—sometimes to the audience, sometimes to her, but always giving the sense of Norma as a lonely, abandoned little girl. "Where did she go . . . Mama . . . I need to know . . . Mama, Mama, Mama . . ." sang Lee at a snail's pace.

Certain songs—"Daddy Was a Railroad Man," with its chug-chugging percussion; the jaunty ragtime of "That Old Piano"—woke things up. And an occasional ray of self-insight crept through. Lee's story about singing to an imaginary flock of chickens, with its tagline—"I was a *strange child*"—scored the heartiest laugh of the night. But when Lee began her intended comedy song about Min, "One Beating a Day," discomfort swept through the house. Nervous titters greeted her roll call of Min's atrocities, sung in Caribbean dialect. "This was supposed to be funny," said Mike Renzi, "but it wasn't." And when Lee sang of the day Min broke her leg on the ice—"That was nice!"—her theme of compassion fell just as flat.

The stories behind her hits went untold; insights into her singing style were few. Instead, Lee filled the narration with greeting-card sentiments: "The night falling—falling like black velvet"; "And the years went by, full of comedy and tragedy." The latter kept winning out. About to board her first train to California, Norma waved goodbye to her Dakota friends: "Good-bye, Ebbie Jordan. Remember how we used to drink Raleigh's Mouth Wash and pretend it was liquor? Oh, Ebbie. I'm sorry you fell off that horse and got killed."

Cut to the Jade club in Hollywood, then to Chicago and her dreamlike emergence as Benny Goodman's "canary." For Lee, that break of a lifetime mattered for only one reason—it placed Prince Charming at her feet. "One day he appeared—the handsome Italian . . . No shining white charger but a soulful guitar . . ." Lee, wrote Sharon Churcher, "cast her gaze upward, her lips embalmed in a motionless beatific smile." And Act I ended.

After intermission, the star, now in a Druid-like hooded white gown, shifted to a fairytale account of her relationship with Barbour. Moony recollections of their early married life gave way to tearful tales of his alcoholism and near-death in surgery. "They gave him up nine times," she said, inflating the number by at least seven. In "I Never Knew Why," Lee denied any responsibility for his decline: "I used to blame myself and my career / But all the doctors said no, my dear / It isn't you . . ." She and

Dave were "still so much in love" when he asked for a divorce—solely to protect Nicki, Lee explained.

The act had its bright spots—"What Did Dey Do to My Goil?," a fanciful account of Jimmy Durante's appearance at the "Mañana" trial; "Flowers and Flowers," a wry recollection of her many "Mister X's," arranged in "Fever" style; the Basin Street East medley, with a spoken preface by Grady Tate. But Lee anxiously segued back to Dave and the tragic denouement of their story. Now sober, he proposed that they remarry the next day. "How about next week?" said an ecstatic Lee. Then fate struck him dead. The dream of a lifetime—over. "Well, of course life had to go on," said Lee with a sigh.

In a closing monologue, she attempted an inspirational speech. "Some of you have wondered where I've been for the last few years. And some of you who've seen me have wondered—why doesn't Peggy Lee smile anymore? Why doesn't she move the way she used to? Well, the answer is simple. I was paralyzed. My eyes wouldn't close. My speech was slurred. And I went blind for a while. And I've even had that experience of going through that door you've heard about. And that's why I have the right and I believe it's a great privilege to tell you that I believe—in fact, I know—that there is more."

Again staring toward heaven, Lee lifted her arms up from her sides, and her giant balloon sleeves made her look like a human chalice. Violins washed in, and Lee intoned "There Is More," a dirgelike hymn to eternal life and salvation: "The sun will shine on all of us no matter who we are / We are only on a journey to a star." Her diehard fans stood and cheered, and *Peg* ended.

Crew members saw Lee walk to her dressing room as though floating on air. She was sure she had a hit. Out in the theater, however, crowds moved to the exit "feeling mildly sedated," wrote critic Jacques le Sourd. Many of the same patrons had left *Lena Horne: The Lady and Her Music* in a state of giddy exhilaration. Horne's finale, "If You Believe," had found her wailing like Aretha Franklin, shaking a fist in the air and exhorting people to "believe in your*SELF* . . . as I believe in *YOU!*" *Peg*'s ostensibly happy ending had come as too little, too late, and didn't ring true. The famously cool-but-vulnerable star had lifted the veil on a Peggy Lee no one wanted to see: maudlin, self-obsessed, devoid of irony, and not much fun.

Her friends were stunned. "I was really distressed," said Vince Mauro. "I thought it was awful." Bruce Vanderhoff had squirmed in his seat. "I was so embarrassed," he said. So was Artie Butler: "My heart sank. I saw it as a great artist, a hero of mine, making a big mistake. You can't say anything to certain people, and Peggy was certainly one of them." Mary Young, who had seen Lee at the Powers Coffee Shop in Fargo, raised an eyebrow at her childhood horror stories. "Somehow, Peggy just couldn't *walk away*. People don't want to go hear about wicked old stepmothers! Come on—it was hard to be a stepmother in the Depression."

No one felt such crashing disappointment as Paul Horner, who saw *Peg* as "revenge on a stick." For its star, the show meant reinforcement of her commercial validity. For Horner, it was the pipe dream on which his whole future rested. And he had just watched it crash.

He and his mother made their way to Top of the Sixes, a penthouse restaurant on Fifth Avenue, for the opening-night sit-down dinner. Three hundred guests were invited. Bufman came early and stayed only long enough to tell his investors and staff that he had quit; surely he didn't want to chance running into Lee. But the star made a fashionably late entrance, observed by Arthur Bell of the *Village Voice*: "Peggy Lee swept in, a vision in vagary, and made the rounds, offering her cheek to everybody and everything in sight, including a waiter whom she mistook for a guest."

Horner had arrived to find that he and his mother would be seated in a smaller second room, far from Lee. When photographers tried to take their picture together, she resisted. Cy Coleman had hardly been his ally, but nevertheless Horner brought the composer a gift. "Oh, aren't you sweet," said Coleman. Just then, a woman approached them. "Mr. Coleman," she exclaimed, "I think your music for the show is just fabulous!" Coleman thanked her and walked away, stepping on Horner's foot.

Bell approached several celebrity guests and asked what they had thought of *Peg*. "Yes, indeed," grumbled Joan Fontaine, before "raising her eyebrow and walking away in a snit." Gina Lollobrigida showed sympathy. "She has a beautiful voice," said the Italian film goddess, "but she lived a very sad life. This would have been more entertaining as a concert."

The party was still in progress around ten-thirty, when the *New York Times* went on sale. Mike Renzi and some of the other musicians took an elevator down the forty-one floors to Fifth Avenue, where they bought a copy at a newsstand. They took it to a local bar and thumbed their way to the arts section. There was Frank Rich's review. It was even worse than expected.

The star, wrote Rich, "takes to the stage of the Lunt-Fontanne like a high priestess ascending an altar . . . There is some entertainment in 'Peg,' not to mention some striking musicianship, but the show is most likely to excite those who are evangelistically devoted to both Peggy Lee and God—ideally in that order."

Rich had only begun. "In addition to sacrificing introspection for inspirational homilies ('God has never let me down'), the star regards her personal history from an omniscient and self-deifying perspective . . . Many of the anecdotes sound as if they were long ago homogenized by press agents for mass dissemination through talk shows." Rich termed the score merely "professional," save for "Daddy Was a Railroad Man." *Peg*, he felt, was swallowed up by the cavernous Lunt-Fontanne, which needed a larger-than-life persona to fill it. "Lacking so sizable a presence," concluded Rich, "Miss Lee has let her ego inflate to fill the gap."

Word of the review reached the party. Then a TV was tuned in to the eleven-o'clock news. Joel Siegel, film and drama critic for ABC, began to speak about *Peg*. "If this had been a concert, this would have been a good review," said Siegel, for Lee, he said, was in "very good" voice and the orchestra was superb. But *Peg*, he announced, "pretends to be a Broadway show . . . pretends is the verb of choice because *Peg* isn't fooling anybody. On a set that looks like they got it on the cheap from a canceled TV talk show, Peggy Lee tells us odd stories about her childhood. Shameless . . . The songs are good. She is a fine lyricist with one exception, a song about child abuse done in calypso." Lee, he noted, had never identified the mysterious, paralyzing illness discussed at the end—"this after a first act where we learn the street address of her first apartment and what her father's favorite lunch was."

Marge Cowan walked around in shock. "They didn't like it!" she moaned to a friend. Irv was less surprised. "What went on in that period of her life that made Peggy so hellbent on becoming Goody Two-Shoes, I have no idea. Everybody knew that was b.s. If you're not willing to admit mistakes and faults then you have no business calling it an autobiography."

Lee watched as people filed out quickly without saying good-bye. She knew why. Horner approached her. After having ignored him all night, she reached out and clutched his hand.

One by one, the other reviews came in. "The heaviest magic carpet ride on Broadway," wrote Arthur Bell. Saber-penned John Simon led off his *New York* magazine critique by asking: "Have you paid a visit lately to a singing mortician?" Lee, he wrote, was "rather like a bleached sarcophagus placed upright on the stage and jerked about by a puppeteer who is himself close to mummification." To Linda Winer of the *Chicago Tribune*, *Peg* fell "somewhere between a concert, *This Is Your Life*, and a songbird Christ story." *Variety*'s Richard Humm deemed the music "virtually flawless," and called Lee's voice "one of the glories of popular music." But *Peg*, he wrote, drowned in "self-glorification" and "sympathy-begging." Bobby Drivas got panned for the stagnant direction. Nearly everyone agreed that *Peg* should have been a simple concert.

To open in the holiday season could not have helped. Advance sales were dismal—but according to Jon Wilner, bad word of mouth had spread fast after the first preview. Irv and Marge held a quick meeting with Georgia Frontiere and other *Peg* principals to see if there were anything that might save the show. "The unanimous opinion was that there was not," said Irv. With heavy hearts, he, Marge, and Frontiere knocked on Lee's dressing-room door the next afternoon. They broke the news: Given the poor box office and reviews, they saw no choice but to close *Peg*. Saturday night's show would be the last.

Lee was thunderstruck. Whatever the critics had thought, audiences seemingly loved her. The Cowans, especially Marge, had enthused for so long about the surefire success of *Peg*. So had Zev Bufman, until recently. Lee felt massively betrayed.

Stepping into her dressing room later, D. Michael Heath found Lee on the phone, frantically trying to find new investors to keep *Peg* open. "She kept saying over and over, 'I've put all this time and work into this, now we can't even give it a chance to fly.'" Once the news got out, some of Lee's fans rushed to see *Peg* while they still could. But there weren't enough of them. Lee looked out from the stage at what she thought were sold-out houses. She didn't seem to notice the near-empty balcony and back rows. Nor did she know that the main floor was heavily "papered" with comped or discounted ticket holders.

Even on Saturday, Lee wouldn't give up the fight. She called Wilner that morning to tell him she was organizing a picketing of the *New York Times*. Would he join in? Of course, he couldn't; he worked for the producers. But he understood her panic. "People feel helpless when there's a flop. This gave her strength to go onstage for the final performance. She was hoping they'd come onstage and say, 'We're not closing!'"

But the Cowans were gone. They had flown home to Florida. Lee was furious; once more, she felt abandoned. "You get to a point," she said, "where so many things have happened, you think, 'Is this it, God? Is this the final disappointment?'"

Speeding on rage, she came alive that night. The sluggishness of her prior performances vanished; *Peg* became, at least in spirit, the show it might have been. She mustered up a fair degree of smiling-through-your-tears good humor, but sentiment was thick. Grady Tate began his monologue about Basin Street East by referring to "this particular night of anguish." In a long speech of farewell, Lee reflected: "This is one of those happy-sad moments. Happy because you're here, because you're so wonderful to me. But it *is* our closing night. I can't even believe it. We just opened. We had a party. And got a good night's sleep. And they posted the notice." Cries of "No! No!" echoed through the hall. Lee saluted the orchestra, the singers, even Horner, then went on to villainize the press for shutting *Peg* down. She implied sabotage—a full-page *New York Times* ad, she announced, had contained "a disconnected number." People gasped. Years later, in her memoir, Lee noted the alleged misprint: 586-5555. It was, in fact, the correct number of the Lunt-Fontanne, the one that had appeared in all the ads.

But the sympathy she had sought in her script came rushing toward her. "It's just beyond my ken to understand why I have to go back to California," said Lee, eliciting more cheers. "I love it here. I wanted to stay." Fans clapped and cheered: "*WE LOVE YOU, PEGGY!*"

Peg's fifth and final performance, not counting thirteen previews, ended with another standing ovation. "I began to feel some tears coming," she recalled, "so I had to leave and go back to my dressing room."

In the days to come, denial helped see her through the pain. Speaking to George Christy of *Interview*, Lee magnified the show's final two-minute standing ovation to forty-five. "People were in tears," she declared, "calling out, 'Don't close this play!' It would have been nice if the producers had been there to witness that."

Privately, Lee blamed Bufman for deserting her. She cited poor promotion, ignoring the stacks of articles, column mentions, and ads, as well as an appearance on the *Today* show to sing "Daddy Was a Railroad Man." Lee even decided that the Cowans had only done *Peg* as a tax writeoff. The claim ignored Marge's complete belief in the show, right up to the opening-night party. Lee was stung by complaints about what a downer she had given the public. "If my life was depressing, that's too bad," she said. "I tried to make it funny. But it wasn't funny when I lived it."

Horner had seen almost every performance. To him, Lee was the main culprit in *Peg*'s demise: "She stamped her foot and got her way on everything, and that was the price she had to pay." Jon Wilner didn't disagree. "She was a nice woman who knew nothing about Broadway. She was one of those people whom everybody yeses and nobody tells the truth to. A lot of stars do these one-person shows. They talk about their husbands and their successes and their failures and they think everybody wants to hear that. They're forgetting that what people want is to be entertained. I felt sorry for her because I liked her. I felt that she didn't have much of a life anymore. She was needy. Everyone was treating her as a star. And she liked that." Supper clubs, said Zef Bufman, were "the minor league. She wanted the big-league ego boost because she felt she deserved it. And she wanted people to say, 'Poor Peg. What a life.'"

Of the *Peg* team, only D. Michael Heath retained his affection for the project: "The orchestra was incredible. The stories were fun. Fictional or true, we learned a lot about someone we loved very much. I didn't find it depressing; I found it heartfelt, and I found a survivor in it."

On Bufman's extended lease, Lee decided to stay in her pricey East Side penthouse for a while. She had some espionage in mind: Lee wanted the arrangements, which she considered her property. They weren't, in fact; they belonged to the producers, who had paid for them. Nonetheless, an accomplice at Cy Coleman's office smuggled them out of the theater, copied them for Lee, then returned them. The move incited yet more bad blood between her and the producers. Ultimately it didn't matter; the charts were never played again.

But the ill will remained. Seemingly it had spread to Vincent Roppatte and, in turn, found its way to Liz Smith, who printed one of the sternest rebukes she ever gave a misbehaving star. "The Peggy Lee flop, 'Peg,' has left the bitterest feelings up and down the Rialto that I've observed in many a turkey trot. Peggy did not cover herself with glory onstage for the critics, many of whom privately dubbed the show 'The Lady and Her Misery.' And she sure didn't win any prizes backstage where she ended up almost universally disliked by the minions who toiled for the star. I think she was scared out of her wits, but it's no excuse for mistreating people."

Lee phoned Horner for solace. He didn't turn away, nor would he for years; the composer still seemed to hope that somehow the rift between him and his favorite singer would mend. But their battle over the songs' ownership raged on. In 1990, Lee made a whole CD of originals, *There'll Be Another Spring: The Peggy Lee Songbook*. She invited Horner to her home to hear it. He hurried over. They listened together to the album—which contained not one song from *Peg*.

Only after her death, when Horner went into litigation with her estate, were the proper fifty-fifty rights established. Still, the misbegotten score remained largely unknown.

After *Peg*, the Cowans faced their own hard times; a fire at the Diplomat had helped hasten the demise of the faltering resort, which eventually closed. Real estate dealings and a stable of prize racehorses kept them on top of Florida's social loop, but never again did they invest in a Broadway show. Zev Bufman's career as a theater owner continued to thrive; soon, though, he would wind down his glamorous but money-losing run as a Broadway producer. But not quite yet. "Zev never mentioned *Peg* again," said Jon Wilner. "He wiped his hands clean and went on to the next show."

"I'm not quite sure what God had in mind when he kept me around, but I know I'm still here for a purpose." (MARINES MEMORIAL THEATRE, SAN FRANCISCO, JAN. 9, 1987; PHOTO BY STEVE GRUBER)

Chapter Seventeen

∾

*L*EE STILL HADN'T a clue as to why *Peg* had exploded in her face, so she turned to her *Science of Mind* books for answers. Few came, but still she pressed onward. The singer told Michael Kearns of *Drama-Logue*: "This has probably been one of the most difficult years of my life but I have no real regrets. I expect something really wonderful is coming up."

Quickly after *Peg*, Lee returned to what most people felt she should have stuck with all along: just singing, in clubs and intimate theaters. Lee toured Canada and the United Kingdom, then in the summer of 1984 she played a three-week, sold-out run in Los Angeles at the Westwood Playhouse (later renamed the Geffen Playhouse). There in that four-hundred-and-fifty-seat, state-of-the-art venue, audiences welcomed back the Peggy Lee they loved. *Peg* had encouraged her to talk more onstage; Leonard Feather, her diehard champion, scolded her in the *Los Angeles Times* for "reminiscences that sometimes rambled a little too long, about everything from London to Japan to her potassium intake." But Lee's nephew Lee Ringuette was glad to see that she could still mesmerize: "The audience sat quietly, absolutely transfixed throughout. They didn't want to miss anything."

In the 1980s, Lee adopted the last new set of musicians who would enter her life. All were Italian, like her first husband. All were young enough to be her sons. And all provided a steadying arm to a woman whom age and ill health were wearing down. They, in turn, gained an education they still raved about decades later—even if it came from one of the most exasperating, mercurial artists they had ever known.

Guitarist John Chiodini had worked with the Boston Pops before moving to Los Angeles. He had played on Lee's *Close Enough for Love* album, then joined her band at the Westwood Playhouse. When she heard his graceful, spare guitar lines, tinged by the blues, she felt she had found one more heir apparent to Dave Barbour. Just past forty, Chiodini vowed to make the most of this opportunity. He placed himself at Lee's beck and call, spending untold hours at her bedside, where they lovingly wrote songs together and laughed away the hours. Around him, the sixty-four-year-old singer wove her last romantic fantasy. "Look at those beautiful eyes!" she told one audience. Lee showered the musician with superlatives—"sensitive," "talented," "beautiful"—and dropped broad hints about their relationship. Discussing "Boudoir Productions," as she called her bedroom, on *CBS This Morning*, Lee volunteered: "John Chiodini and I write in there, and that's all we do! . . . I'm saying that for his wife's benefit."

After Lee fired three pianists in her first three nights at the Westwood Playhouse, Chiodini placed a post-midnight panic call to his friend Emilio Palame, a promising but unknown thirty-year-old pianist. Might he step in? Palame couldn't believe his ears. Since moving to L.A. from his native Buffalo, he had eked out a living playing weddings, parties, and small clubs. Chiodini came over and coached him until dawn. The next night, Lee approved of his funky minimalism, in the Jimmy Rowles and Lou Levy tradition. He stayed for eleven years. "Being associated with her set my career on fire," said Palame, "because everyone knew that Peggy Lee only hired the best."

Until the end, he shared the job with Mike Renzi, who had played in *Peg*. For pop-jazz vocalists, Renzi was the gold ring of accompanists. Sylvia Syms, Frank Sinatra's favorite saloon singer, had discovered him while he was a student at Boston Conservatory. Renzi went on to play for Mel Tormé, Lena Horne, Cleo Laine, and other greats. Seated at the piano, he had an eye-catching look—jet-black beard, Afro-style hair, gold wire-frame glasses—and a lush, impressionistic style, the opposite of Palame's. If Lee rarely sang with strings anymore, she now had a pianist whom Stephen Holden of the *New York Times* would praise for his "extraordinary grace as a pianistic arranger" and "panoramic orchestral sweep."

No matter how strong or gifted the men onstage, Lee still had to rule, both as musician and siren. Even though Palame was less than half her age, and married with children, his job, like Chiodini's, involved maintaining an amorous spark. After a show, his parents wanted to meet her, but Grady Tate discouraged it. "It's gonna blow the whole vibe," Tate warned. "To be her pianist you've got to be like her husband."

At the same time, if anyone forgot that she was *Miss* Peggy Lee, there would be hell to pay. Before a show at the Cape Cod Melody Tent in Hyannis, Massachusetts, Renzi called her Peggy in front of a reporter. Later, Lee summoned him to a chair by her bedside, where she scolded him as though it were the principal's office. He argued that he hadn't known her rules, but Lee wouldn't relent. Finally he did what few of her musicians ever had the nerve to do: "I just stood up and I said, 'Get yourself another fucking piano player. I'm outta here.' I walked toward the door. Off came the covers, and she jumped out of bed. 'Where are you going?' I said, 'I quit!'"

Lee turned to Tate, who was seated nearby, and clutched her chest. "Baby, you OK?" he asked. No, said Lee—she needed her doctor. "Oh, my heart is racing!" She turned to Renzi. "You can't leave! I can't find a replacement! Please, I have to be alone now."

Renzi didn't quit. The next day at soundcheck, Lee acted as though nothing had happened. "Hi, my darling," she cooed with a smile. "After that," he said, "she never bugged me again."

Still, her word remained law. Chiodini knew what happened if you challenged Peggy Lee. "There were three strikes. The first was, 'When was the last time *you* had a hit?' If it went to strike two it was, 'Oh, really? Are *you* a legend?' The third one was, 'When was the last time *you* died and came back to life?' She definitely got me on that one."

The more she declined physically, the more she relied upon anger as an essential drug to pump herself up. She kept pouring it from creative new bottles. Chiodini saw the latest of them in Atlantic City, New Jersey, where Lee and the group taped a TV special with the New Jersey Symphony. While they rehearsed, the lighting man experimented with settings. Lights kept flashing at the stage—and when he dropped something with a bang, Lee turned on him with a savagery that scared everyone. That day her band learned about the "vortex"—a swirling black hole, like purgatory, into which Lee claimed she could be sucked by forces of rage. "She said to him that she was now officially in a vortex," said Chiodini, "and she had all of us as witnesses, and if she died, it was his fault, and she would make sure he was charged with murder after the fact."

Sometimes she found serenity in the company of Palame, who, like her, considered himself on a spiritual path. Late at night he lingered in her suite, talking heart-to-heart. "Most of our conversations revolved around spirituality, going toward what was positive, going toward the white light. She wanted to heal the wounds of her past. She wanted to get into a sense of true forgiveness." Lee's Bible was *Letters of the Scattered Brotherhood*, a collection of anonymous letters written by Catholics and published in an old religious weekly. The theme was a quest to free oneself from the chains of sadness and fright.

> Let us consider then this outer you, distraught, melancholy, lonely, hypnotized by his own states, without judgment, sound asleep in inertia—mental inertia. . . . The overcoming will be instant when you eliminate from your mind all thoughts and emotions which benumb, frustrate and leave cobwebs.

But it was hard for Lee to let go of fear when illness kept cutting her down, potentially for good. On January 22, 1985, she checked into St. John's Hospital in Santa Monica, complaining once more of chest pains. This time they were real. Doctors discovered dangerous arterial blockages leading to the heart. The next day Lee underwent angioplasty—the insertion of inflatable catheters to let the blood flow through.

The more her body failed her, the harder she fought back. The operation had worked, but sooner than the doctors wished, she flew to Dallas and did eight shows. Once home, she had to have another angioplasty.

Part of her determination was practical: she needed the money—hence an action that shocked her friends. Long before, Lee had given her sister Marianne and brother-in-law Leo the downpayment on a house in the San Fernando Valley. But Lee demanded it be put in her name. "For years they tried to get it changed," said Betty Jungheim. "Marianne and Leo paid on this property all their lives, but Peggy wouldn't budge. What could Marianne do?"

Liver disease took Marianne's life in 1986. The family had a farewell gathering at the house. According to Virginia Bernard, who attended, Lee remarked, then and there, that the house was now hers.

TO HER, MANHATTAN WAS still the ultimate, its audiences the acid test of how good she was. "She had that old-school thing about New York—'If I can make it there I'll make it anywhere,'" said Emilio Palame.

The failure of *Peg* had left her burning for one more chance to prove herself in the Big Apple. But the deluxe supper clubs that had pampered her for years had packed away their linen tablecloths and dismantled their orchestra-size stages. What remained was a handful of cabarets. Some were fancy, like the Carlyle hotel's ninety-five-seat Café Carlyle, which hosted a high-flown sophisticate, the pianist-singer Bobby Short. At the slightly larger Oak Room of the Algonquin Hotel, veteran saloon singers such as the sequin-clad Julie Wilson relived the long-lost heyday of Cole Porter, Rodgers and Hart, and their peers. Newcomers broke in their acts at Don't Tell Mama, a raucous sing-along piano bar with a no-frills backroom cabaret. And at Michael's Pub, a stucco-walled restaurant-cabaret with Irish-bar décor, pop-jazz luminaries of the Basin Street East brand—Mel Tormé, George Shearing, Sylvia Syms, Anita O'Day—performed with a cool authority born of decades on the road.

None of these places had the budget or the grandeur to accommodate Peggy Lee. If she wished to play New York, she would have to relax her expectations. In 1985, Irvin Arthur, a cabaret owner turned booking agent, pitched Lee to Greg Dawson, who owned The Ballroom, a black-box cabaret-theater. The Ballroom was bigger than the competition; it held two hundred at cramped tables spread throughout a long, rectangular, tiered space. At the far front was an elevated stage. It could comfortably hold the sextet that Arthur proposed, and had the wings that Lee required. The club took lighting and sound seriously. What's more, Dawson, a Yale graduate and former press agent, was known for eclectic taste. His past bookings had included Jane Olivor, the hyperemotional Brooklyn chanteuse whom Columbia Records had signed as its new Streisand; Joseph Papp, the founder of New York's Public Theater, in his short-lived caprice as a song-and-dance man; and cult jazzbird Blossom Dearie, whose childlike vocals and featherweight swing as a pianist had enchanted Miles Davis.

There were minuses, though. The Ballroom stood on Twenty-Eighth Street near Eighth Avenue—a dark, forbidding stretch at night, with little or no foot traffic. Would Lee's aging audience want to venture there? The cabaret was plain gray and black, closer to Weimar Berlin than to East Side chic; the dressing room, wrote a reporter, was "more of an alcove with a door." Alongside the showroom, in The Ballroom's popular Spanish restaurant, salamis, peppers, and ears of corn hung over the bar—a far cry from the towering chandeliers of the Waldorf.

Arthur demanded twenty-five thousand a week. Dawson had never paid more than twelve. Other demands piled up, including an around-the-clock limo and driver and a pricey apartment rental. But Dawson was intrigued. He and his partner, Tim Johnson, decided that *maybe* they could make this work—but only if Lee did nine shows a week for a twenty-five to forty-five-dollar cover, the highest they had ever charged.

They signed the deal. For four weeks, starting on July 10, 1985, Peggy Lee would play her first New York club engagement since 1976. If all went well, her presence at The Ballroom would catapult it to a level Dawson had never dreamed possible.

He met Lee at the airport. When he caught his first glimpse of her, Dawson couldn't hide his shock. There was Lee in a wheelchair, rolled his way by her blond, pretty granddaughter Holly, now a teenager. The singer sat immobile inside a big fur coat; she wore tinted, rhinestone-trimmed glasses that looked like twin headlights. "I thought she might very well be dead," said Dawson. "She wasn't, but all the way into the city I kept wondering, how the hell was she going to perform? And could she still sing? I was very depressed."

Lee didn't like the roomy East Side apartment he had rented for her, and insisted on moving into a hotel at more than twice the cost. "I had visions of going broke with this whole thing," he said. "Except that, from the moment we announced her engagement, the phone started to ring and reservations kept piling in."

That helped Dawson survive the bumpy road to opening night. The day after she had checked in to her hotel, a limo deposited Lee in front of the picture window and French door that formed The Ballroom's exterior. Dawson ran outside to greet her. She startled him by stepping out of the limo unassisted. Lee sat back down in her wheelchair, and Holly pushed her inside The Ballroom and down a short corridor that led to the showroom. When Lee saw it, her eyes turned to stone. Clearly no one had told her how unlike the Empire Room the place was.

As Dawson showed her around, Lee was in a foul mood. She didn't like anything. Soon the demands started. The stage made "sounds," she said, and had to be carpeted. She wanted a ramp built from her dressing room to the stage a few yards away. She tested the sound, and hated it. As a favor to her, Phil Ramone, a Grammy-winning recording engineer, spent a day pushing levers and twisting knobs. Little needed changing—"but the fact that he was there made her feel better," said Dawson. "Peggy claimed she had the ears of a bat and was even the subject of a special sound study at UCLA. Bad sound, she claimed, could cause her to vomit or faint—possibly in the middle of a show. *That* was how she initially dealt with me— the subtle, never-exactly-stated threat that she couldn't perform or might have to cancel—unless such-and-such happened. Since we had so much resting on this show, the terror was always lurking, producing constant anxiety." Then the rehearsals began. "I nearly died," he said. "She sounded terrible! I thought, she's lost it. This is going to be a disaster."

The engagement began on a sweltering summer night. All seats was full, and dozens more had been jammed in for the most talked-about cabaret opening in years. Retirement-age Peggy Lee fans in suits and dresses comprised about half the crowd; the rest consisted of younger, nostalgia-loving gay men and straight couples who looked barely old enough to remember "Fever." Amid them all sat an elderly man with tortoise-shell glasses and a vacant smile. It was Benny Goodman, back to scrutinize Lee as he first had in 1941. The air seemed to buzz.

At eight PM, an employee passed through the curtain to the left of the stage and knocked on the dressing-room door.

"Half-hour, Miss Lee."

A cool response came from inside: "We'll see."

The lights dimmed at 8:47. Grady Tate launched into a drum roll. Dawson feared the worst as he spoke into the microphone in the sound and light booth: "Ladies and gentlemen, Miss *PEGGY LEE!*"

Out she sailed, unassisted. The cheer that met her was so loud and long that Lee reared back in satisfied delight. "Oh, hel-*LO!*" she caroled. The spotlight made her pink satin gown and beaded cape glitter; diamond earrings dangled from her ears. Behind a silver headband, Lee's own hair—without a fall—was tied in a chignon; the dark glasses hid her drooping eye.

Sitting on a stool center stage, she began her familiar welcoming song, "I Love Being Here with You," with such vitality that she sounded reborn. Dawson could scarcely believe his eyes and ears. "It all came together. She was magic. A kind of force that sucks in all the energy in the room instead of projecting it out, like most performers."

Having heard so much about how depressing *Peg* was, Lee had promised an "upbeat show" at The Ballroom. "She was tired of feeling down," said Emilio Palame, who divided the engagement with Mike Renzi. "She was tired of singing about unrequited love." Lee clung to crowd-pleasing chestnuts ("As Time Goes By," "I Want to Be Happy," "Fly Me to the Moon"); much-requested tracks from her albums ("Heart," "Love Me or Leave Me"); and her hits. The band followed "I'm a Woman" with striptease music, and Lee did a few strutting bumps and grinds. Rarely had she seemed so joyful. "Can you imagine I wait all day long, a grown woman, to come down here and make a fool of myself?" she asked. "I love it, I love it, I love it!" She flirted with her young vibraphonist, Mark Sherman ("Don't get any more handsome! You're looking better every night!"), and introduced Palame with the warmth of a proud mother: "I've come to love this gentleman very much, and you will see, more than you have already, what a fantastic talent he is."

Lee was contracted to sing for an hour per show, but seldom did she do less than an hour and forty-five. The eleven-o'clock show couldn't begin until one-thirty in the morning; fans lined up all the way down the block, just as they had at Basin Street East. "It got to be a mess," said Dawson, "but no matter how much I begged, she wouldn't cut the show. Think of it—here was this woman, seemingly at death's door, performing for three and a half hours each night! And loving it. She seemed strong as an ox."

New York Times writer Charlotte Curtis rejoiced at the return of Lee's "hip cool" and her "elegant, self-deprecating wit. . . . Her timing is infallible. The power of her low, sultry voice invests the pieces with the grandeur and good fun of times past." If her once-lush tone now seemed dry and nasal, no one seemed to notice. The sound suited an encore that Lee had done ever since Basin Street East, when the mood struck her. She strung together four Billie Holiday trademarks—"Good Morning Heartache," "Some Other Spring," "Don't Explain," and "God Bless the

Child"—and shifted back and forth between her own voice and an imitation of Holiday's. The effect was chilling; it sounded like an otherworldly dialogue between Lee and the ghost of her idol.

Dawson had to admire her. "She was a very smart, funny lady. Oh, she could be a bitch, all right. She could scare the crap out of anyone. But she was tough in a way I came to appreciate—the result, no doubt, of having to take a lot of shit from a lot of people on her way up stardom's ladder. And tough in order to get things done, or effectuate conditions that ultimately made her more valuable, to everyone's benefit."

Lee's run was the greatest success The Ballroom had ever had. To her relief, Manhattan still loved her.

———

MANY JOURNALISTS ASKED LEE how it felt to be a legend. The question thrilled her, and she showed no false modesty. She had triumphed in a hard, male-run business and won near-unanimous respect, while surviving close brushes with death, the loss of key people in her life, the embarrassing failure of *Peg*, and numerous other disasters.

But most of the time she didn't feel too well. Just as her career was coming back together, her health fell apart again. On October 6, 1985, while singing at the Fairmont in New Orleans, her chest pains returned. Lee checked into the city's Touro Infirmary. The angioplasties had failed: Lee needed double bypass surgery fast. Holly had come to New Orleans as her assistant, and she was by Lee's side as nurses prepared her for the operation. One of them reached to remove her false eyelashes—which she had worn even in her hospital bed—and her nail polish. "She was having a fit!" said Holly. "They ended up only taking the nail polish off one hand. They did take her eyelashes off, but I put her big movie-star glasses on while they wheeled her in. She wanted to be a star even in open-heart surgery."

The delicate procedure took five hours. After she came to, Lee mourned her canceled shows, most of all a performance at a White House state dinner—a chance to wipe away whatever bitter aftertaste remained from her 1970 debacle. During her recuperation, pneumonia and pleurisy set in. "She almost died," said Holly. Word of Lee's health hit the news, and Frank Sinatra called to check on her. Once she was strong enough, he had her flown home on a private jet. From there, she checked into St. John's for a month. Sinatra "called all the time to see how things were," said Lee later to the BBC's Alan Dell. "And then he came out to St. John's. And I'll always remember that he walked in carrying a bunch of flowers in his hand, not in his arm but in his hand, lovely white flowers, and he brought them in as if he was a teenager."

Bouquets filled her room and get-well messages flooded in from all over the world, one from President Reagan. Her doctor released a statement to the Associated Press: "Miss Lee's spirits have remained indomitable throughout this lengthy and tedious hospital confinement." Finally she returned to Bel Air. Lee hadn't needed an oxygen tank in ten years; now a new one stood beside her bed.

With her health on the downslide, the time seemed right to honor her for lifetime achievement. On March 31, 1986, in Los Angeles, the Songwriters Guild of America gave Lee its Aggie Award, granted in the past to Johnny Mercer, Henry Mancini, and Sammy Cahn. The enfeebled singer watched from her chair as figures from her past paraded out in *This Is Your Life* fashion: Danny Thomas, Arthur Hamilton, Johnny Mandel, Leiber and Stoller, Benny Carter, Lou Levy, Billy May, Stella Castellucci, Dick Hazard, John Pisano, Joe Harnell. Rarely had Lee felt so grateful to be anywhere. "I came very close to checking out," she told Don Heckman of the *Los Angeles Times*. "I think when you survive what I went through, you realize that you're not finished yet for a reason. I'm not quite sure what God had in mind when he kept me around, but I know I'm still here for a purpose."

In *Peg*, Lee had seen herself in angelic terms. Now she really seemed to believe she *was* an angel. Perhaps the illusion helped her to rise, emotionally, above the pains of a body that had become a burden. But for Lee, this was no joke; she began to tell friends that she thought she would live forever. "I'm in tune with the infinite," she explained to her band. Lee read aloud to John Chiodini from a treasured five-volume set on her shelf, *Life and Teaching of the Masters of the Far East*. The author, Baird T. Spalding, explained that physical immortality was attainable by those with a divine mission and a dogged love of life. All illness could be surmounted, as it had by Jesus and Buddha, who, Spalding asserted, still walked among us.

For Peggy Lee, that mission seemed clear: to transform and enlighten through song. Downtrodden tunes like "Black Coffee" or "It Takes Too Long to Learn to Live Alone" had no place in her new philosophy; she sang "Is That All There Is?" only reluctantly, and played it for laughs. In return engagements at the Westwood Playhouse in April and at The Ballroom in June, focus stayed on the miracle of her survival. "For any of you who thought a thought, said a prayer, I want to thank you from the bottom of my heart, because I know that's why I'm here," announced Lee from her onstage chair.

Many fans were moved, even to tears, by her resilience. Others snickered at her conversion into an icon of saintliness. Ted Ono, a Japanese producer of jazz recordings, brought his artist Maxine Sullivan, Lee's original inspiration, to see her at The Ballroom. "Maxine just laughed and said, 'Oh, God, she takes herself so seriously now!' " Her audiences, said Vince Mauro, were "too filled with sycophants, I thought. If you belch and they start applauding, then it's all over. When she was forty-two she said to me, 'A lot of times I don't believe people when they say how great I am.' Well, by now she believed anybody who said that anything she did was great."

But Lee was clearly having fun as she talked with the audience for minutes at a time and wandered through her safe selection of standards and hits. Fans who had come to hear her classics, like "Fever," "I'm a Woman," and "Johnny Guitar," got the same thrills of old, and the six-week run sold out. "As freaky as she looked, she was bringing a long-lost glamour to the stage," said Robert Richards. "And she still had that haunting quality. But it got a little pathetic at The Ballroom. She was a diminished talent. The shows were weak, and they were careless. And that was the last thing you wanted to see from her."

A practical joke played on her by a friend made Lee feel like a laughingstock. Mario Buatta was a high-end interior designer known in New York and the Hamptons as "The Prince of Chintz." Lee obsessed him, and he barely missed a night of a Ballroom engagement; there he sat at a prime table, often with a large party of friends in tow. His sense of humor was epitomized by a stunt that made the columns. Cheered on by Bernard Lafferty, the drunken but lovable Irish valet whom Lee had fired and rehired for years, Buatta brought a chimpanzee to the show. The animal sat next to Buatta wearing a vest that bore his name, Zip. Throughout part one of Lee's two-act show, all eyes were on Zip, who prattled away in his chair.

Lee had been upstaged by Elizabeth Taylor, but never by a monkey. She voiced a few tart remarks. Everyone laughed, but the edge in her voice made it clear that she was not amused. She cut Act I short, then stormed into her dressing room. In Act II, the animal was gone. Later, on the phone, she raged to her friend Jean Bach about what Buatta had done.

His friendship with Lee survived. But at The Ballroom, the anger she hoped to dispel kept flaring up. One night when she lost her place during "Fever," her vibraphonist, Mark Sherman, wound up taking the fall. *"What was that rhythm you played?"* she said midsong, shooting him a cold glare. Other cutting remarks followed.

Robert Richards was there. "There was a cord on the floor of the stage, and she said, 'What, is the management now trying to kill me?'" Lee finished the performance and left the stage. Customers were paying their checks. "All of a sudden," said Richards, "she burst out of the dressing room wearing turquoise pajamas and a black mink coat." Having entered The Ballroom in a wheelchair, she now stood, clutching the handles of a walker. Face frozen in rage, Lee dragged her way along the still-full showroom as though it were on fire; then she fled through the front door.

———

INJURY AND ILLNESS AS much as music now defined Peggy Lee. In the 1980s and '90s, Lee regaled nearly every interviewer with a litany of her physical woes, from her bypass surgery to her foot troubles, a byproduct of diabetes. When columnist Michael Musto of the *Village Voice* arrived at her hotel room with a photographer, Lee blurted out: "Please don't shoot my feet. They got squeezed tapping my toes, which caused an ingrown toenail and an operation." Moments later, she added: "Please don't shoot this hand. It's swollen because I'm writing my memoirs longhand. Suddenly my ring doesn't fit." To Patrick Pacheco of the *New York Daily News*, Lee's suite looked "a little like a hospital," complete with steaming humidifiers, a wheelchair, and boxes of bandages. In his article, "Like a Statue Rising Above the Ruins," Lee explained that she couldn't walk well, and her eyesight was failing. To another reporter, Sheryl Connolly, Lee mentioned the view from her deck in Bel Air. "I can see the boats out there with my field glasses. That is, I don't see the boats terribly well, but I know they are there."

Phoebe Jacobs lost patience. "I used to call her Camille. I'd call her up and say, 'How do you feel?' She'd start telling me about her coughing and her legs and her veins, and she couldn't get out of bed. I'd say, 'You've gotta force yourself, Peggy.' I'd put the phone down, walk away. I'd come back—still complaining. I'd say, 'I'm gonna call you up when I want to get depressed.' I used to tell her, 'You're like an old Jew.' That's what Jewish people do—they kvetch."

Lee had grown willfully accident-prone, and in February 1987, the mishap she had faked at the Waldorf happened for real. Caesars Palace in Las Vegas had booked her to open for the ninety-one-year-old comedy legend George Burns in a two-week engagement. One night as the band vamped, Lee strolled out in trademark fashion: walking in semiprofile, smiling broadly at the audience, arms outstretched. As she glided to center stage, her high heel got caught in a steel plate with a hole. Lee tripped and hit the floor hard. The audience let out a collective gasp. A stagehand quickly dropped the curtain, and everyone rushed over to Lee. She had fractured her pelvis. "Frankly, I prayed," she said later. "I was in excruciating pain."

Someone ran to call an ambulance, but Lee was adamant. The show had to go on. "I wanted them to know I wasn't dead," Lee explained.

A thronelike chair was brought out—and minutes later she was singing and trying to joke about the disaster. She finished her thirty-minute set; then orderlies carried her by stretcher to a waiting ambulance.

Caesars Palace, said Emilio Palame, shifted its concern. "Some people came up to me and said, 'So she tripped on her dress, huh?'

"No," he answered. "She didn't trip on her dress." Her heel, he explained, had gotten stuck in their floor. "They said, 'No, she tripped on her dress, right?' Almost as if they were telling me, 'That's what you're gonna say.' I said, 'No! She didn't.' They were kind of giving me this strongarm vibe. I was like, 'No, that's my girl. No way.'"

Astonishingly, with a legitimate case to fight, Lee declined to sue. "I think she just didn't want to deal with it," said Palame. "It sort of fit into where she was spiritually—'OK. I'm gonna let that go. I don't need to do this.'"

Following the surgery, Lee lay restless in bed for weeks. She was so eager to recover and return to work that she ventured into her pool, where she had seldom gone, and did laps. Lee told Mary Campbell of the Associated Press that she even rented an exercise bicycle—"and overdid it. That put me back in bed for a little bit."

From now on, she would sit for her shows. "She never really wanted to sit, but finally she had to," said Nicki Lee Foster. Lee made the best of it. In March 1987, she was rolled onto the stage of the Pasadena Play-house in a wheelchair. Balloons covered the stage and the chair—her way of making a strained atmosphere seem like a circus. Humor saw her through. As entrance music, the band played Jerome Kern and Dorothy Fields's "Pick Yourself Up"; Lee opened with another Kern song, "I Won't Dance." By the time she played the Ritz-Carlton Hotel in Washington, D.C., Lee could walk onstage with a cane in her right hand, with her left arm supported by Mark Sherman. She lowered herself gingerly into a chair. "Your part is to applaud until I'm thoroughly seated," she told the audience. "My part is to get there." Pathos ran high. "Everywhere we played," said Palame, "people loved her so much. She touched people's hearts so deeply."

More than ever, Lee had become a mash-up of contradictions. There was the needy star who, like Judy Garland, had a bottomless craving for sympathy. There was the sex kitten who had to feel that men still crumbled at her feet. And there was the Lee who now dominated the mix—the celestial figure who, having been "through that door you've heard about," now saw herself as a divine messenger. White had always been her favorite color; now it obsessed her. The centerpiece of her new look was her stark white pageboy wig, made of Dynel, a synthetic fiber favored by low-end wigmakers. It had the texture of horsehair. Lee ordered the wigs in quantity from the Beverly Hills division of René of Paris, an international wig manufacturer that prided itself on its "natural" designs. Ten to twelve of her chosen style came with her on every tour.

She took that look to the extreme. Suddenly everything went white: the beaded jackets with fur collars, the satin gowns with feather trim, the nail polish. For years Lee had employed a rainbow of lighting tints; now she wanted technical directors to engulf her in white. "She was into the spiritual concepts of white light and how it was purifying and strengthening," said Palame. The key to a great show, she told him, was to "cover ourselves in white light."

For some viewers, the sight of her was not only otherworldly but macabre. At sixty-eight, she hadn't a wrinkle. Her eyes remained hidden behind her tinted rhinestone glasses; onstage, one could hardly see any of her. "She was completely immobile," said Robert Richards, "and suddenly a hand would come out of nowhere, and she looked like a singing laundry bag."

Lee was hardly the guest to enliven a 1988 reunion of Frank Sinatra and Sammy Davis, Jr., two now-fading survivors of the "Rat Pack." Sinatra's and Davis's hell-raising was far behind them; after decades of overindulgence, their bodies were collapsing. A month earlier, their "Together Again" tour had lost its third Rat Pack titan, Dean Martin, whom illness had forced off the road. Davis now had throat cancer, and would die in 1990. Sinatra's memory, along with his health, had begun to fail him.

Their star quality shone on, of course, and on April 6, the show made a sold-out, five-night stop at Radio City Music Hall. The last night brought a sentimental guest appearance by Sinatra's onetime neighbor Peggy Lee, who hobbled out with a sequined cane. Davis and Sinatra tried their best to recapture their carefree brashness of old; Lee's low energy didn't help. Rumors that she would join them on tour never came to pass.

———

IN THE 1960s, WHENEVER Lee had wanted to show off her performance in *Pete Kelly's Blues* to guests, out came a projector and a can of sixteen-millimeter film. Now it was the late eighties, and forty-eight million American homes—nearly half the country—were popping VHS tapes into the videocassette decks beneath their TV sets. Home video had become one of the fattest of cash cows, especially for Walt Disney Productions. In 1980, Disney had begun issuing its major cartoon features— *Cinderella, Snow White and the Seven Dwarfs, Pinocchio, Bambi, Sleeping Beauty*, and many more—in Beta and VHS editions. Family staples all, they sold in landslide numbers. Disney's 1987 releases included *Lady and the Tramp*. In 1955, the film had opened to mixed reviews; after one year on home video, Disney reported 3.5 million units sold and a $90 million profit; others estimated a much higher take.

To boost home-video sales, Disney liked to send its original voice actors out on the publicity trail. Most were retired, and happy to relive their pasts for the honorarium—or less—that Disney offered. Of all those performers, none was more famous than Peggy Lee. The singer was immensely proud of *Lady and the Tramp*, and she recalled it in a slew of TV and print interviews. Lee heaped respect upon Walt Disney, who had died in 1966; she introduced clips of herself as the mangy canine showgirl Peg and the other three characters to whom she had given voice. Reporters raved about her broad contribution to the film, including the songs she had written with Sonny Burke. "He's a Tramp," "The Siamese Cat Song," and "Bella Notte" were as beloved as almost any Disney tunes.

Over and over, Lee heard about the huge success of the video. Disney had reportedly spent $20 million to market it—"five times what it cost to bring the film to the screen back in the 1950s," said a reporter. And she thought about how little *Lady and the Tramp* had earned her. Lee would later tell reporters that she and Burke had agreed to split a one-thousand-dollar songwriters' fee for sheet music and recording rights. Disney published the songs through ASCAP; from that point on, both she and Burke received a standard royalty for record and sheet-music sales along with other uses. Besides that, Lee had agreed to a flat fee of $3,500 for her performances on the soundtrack. The deal had seemed reasonable in 1952 when Lee had signed her contracts. Since then she had tried to buy back the publishing rights for her songs; naturally, Disney wouldn't budge.

Now, as she heard reports that *Lady and the Tramp* had become the best-selling home-video title of all time, she tried to take it lightly. When Stephen M. Silverman of the *New York Post* asked her if she was sharing in Disney's financial bonanza, Lee called her original deal "a little joke I played on myself. I signed on as an artist for hire. . . . Still, it's a thrill today to watch something go like that, and that's the way one likes to be paid."

Her mind began to change as she fretted over her ever-shrinking funds. Lee told Paul Horner that Roy Acuff, the Grand Ole Opry star and music publisher, wanted to buy her Denslow Music catalog. Though tempted, she couldn't bring herself to accept. Meanwhile she kept promoting *Lady and the Tramp*. Lee agreed to travel by car to Disneyland

Park in Anaheim, California, to do a television interview in front of the Disney Castle. But when the company offered her what she deemed an "insulting" fee—$500—Lee was "outraged," said John Saulle, the balding, bearded young Italian who worked then as her assistant.

Lee gave a halfhearted interview on her living-room sofa. Later, she summoned Saulle. "Pull my contract!" she said, referring to the agreement she had signed with Disney twenty-five years before. Off he went to the garage, where Lee's lifetime of paperwork resided in a series of filing cabinets. There he found not one but two contracts. The earlier one involved her songwriting. The other, signed on October 20, 1952, governed her soundtrack performances. Nearly every Disney contract offered a flat buyout fee and no royalties or rights. But Lee's was different. It stated: "Nothing in this agreement shall be construed as granting to us the right to make phonograph records and/or transcriptions for sale to the public, wherein the results or proceeds of your services hereunder are used."

Disney had used that clause when signing musical artists who, like Lee, had outside record contracts. It promised that the company would not sell commercial recordings or sheet music of the artists' Disney performances. The wording seemed sloppy, though. At the time, "transcription" meant a sixteen-inch disc of material distributed to radio stations for broadcast only. Transcriptions weren't sold to the public—and the term didn't apply to sheet music.

But according to modern dictionaries, transcription now held the broad meaning of "copy," including one in a medium besides the original. By selling *Lady and the Tramp* on video without her consent, Disney seemed to have breached its contract with Peggy Lee. Never mind the fact that in 1952, the company could not possibly have foreseen the advent of home video.

The singer searched for a Los Angeles litigator who would take the next step. Every firm she called turned her down; none would dare cross swords with one of the toughest corporations in show business. Finally Lee phoned Alvin Deutsch, the Manhattan lawyer who handled her music publishing. She asked if he would consider pleading her case. Lee sent him the old Disney contract. He showed it to his partner, David Blasband, who specialized in copyright law. Spotting the transcriptions phrase, Blasband sensed potential. He and Deutsch said yes to Lee.

On June 17, 1988, Deutsch wrote to Michael Eisner, CEO of the Walt Disney Company. Deutsch called the clause to Eisner's attention, then politely requested to hear from him "within a week regarding the appropriate compensation for our client." A member of Eisner's legal staff called and promised a response by July 1. It didn't come. On July 11, Deutsch wrote again. This time, John J. Reagan, VP of Legal and Business Affairs for Disney, answered swiftly. Reagan insisted that Lee had "granted Disney all rights to the results and proceeds of Ms. Lee's services, including the right to distribute 'Lady and the Tramp' in the home video market, without the payment of additional compensation. The sole reservation was not to the grant of rights for video cassettes, but to phonograph records and sheet music. . . . While no one questions the value of Ms. Lee's contribution to 'Lady and the Tramp,' we cannot agree that Disney owes Ms. Lee any additional consideration for her services over and above what she has already been paid pursuant to the agreement."

Disney had an arguable case, but so did Lee. The company, she told the *Hollywood Reporter*, "just acted as if that clause didn't exist. . . . All I received was a condescending little pat on the head."

Anyone who brushed off Peggy Lee did so at his own peril. On November 17, 1988, the *New York Times*, *Variety*, and other papers announced the news: Lee was suing Disney for twenty-five million dollars. Later she expanded the suit to include Buena Vista Home Video, Disney's subsidiary company. War was on.

DESPITE THE RENOWN OF its heartwarming family tales, in which animals have a human sensitivity and good conquers all, Walt Disney Productions was viewed by many insiders as a steely monolith, as merciless as the evil queen in *Snow White*. Lee Ringuette, Peggy Lee's nephew, had become a music producer for several film studios, including Disney. He and some of his colleagues called the company "Mouse-schwitz." Disney's lawyers, he said, were "ruthless business people," its artist contracts "absolutely ironclad." Nancy Olson, the costar of Disney's *Pollyanna* and *The Absent-Minded Professor*, had liked Walt—but his company, she said, had "*no* respect for artists. They were frightened of spending a lot of money."

According to a report in *Video Age International*, Disney kept a huge legal staff on hand and filed approximately eight hundred lawsuits and regulatory cases a year, a quarter of them related to copyright and trademark. "When it comes to intellectual property, you can't be too litigious," declared Eisner. The article explained: "Such a large legal staff allows Disney not only to 'terrorize' potential bootleggers, antagonists, competitors and business associates, but also to creatively leverage the fine points of the law to its advantage."

As examples, the magazine cited Disney's attempt "to sue three private children's centers in Florida, for decorating their walls with Disney's characters"; and a suit against the Academy of Motion Picture Arts and Sciences "over the unauthorized use of Snow White during the Oscar telecast." The company seemed determined to avoid issuing royalties whenever possible; the Motion Picture Industry Pension Plan filed suit against Disney for nonpayment of residuals.

But Disney was a hallowed name, and many artists jumped at the chance to place it on their résumés, no matter how stingy the terms. Many years would pass before Disney agreed to pay eye-popping sums to such stars as Tom Hanks, who earned fifteen million dollars for his lead voiceover in *Toy Story* 3. For now, though, a deal was a deal—and Peggy Lee had signed hers with the likely knowledge that Disney would profit nicely from *Lady and the Tramp*, and that she was earning mostly prestige. Later she admitted having had full knowledge of the industry definition of transcription. "Sure, I thought it was kind of a coup to have a Disney credit," said Lee in 1988. "But you can't eat pride. When something makes that much money and everyone else is making money, why shouldn't I?"

In her suits against Betty Jungheim and the Waldorf, Lee had built flimsy cases wielded out of rage. With Disney, she was on somewhat sturdier ground. Earlier in 1988, Paramount Pictures had been shot down in a case involving the scope of "sync" (synchronization) rights—the license to use music in conjunction with visual media, in this case film. Paramount argued that sync rights bought for the TV distribution of their films applied also to home video. The court decreed otherwise. "Numerous licenses have been renegotiated since that ruling," reported *Variety*. Now here came Peggy Lee with a case that had equal potential to rock the industry. It involved a gray area: What did studios owe veteran performers and their estates, if anything, of their profits from the titanic new medium of home video?

Variety's Tom Bierbaum consulted several entertainment lawyers. They thought Lee's claim a "stretch." How could she make a case that Disney owed her money for a format that hadn't existed? Disney chairman Jeffrey Katzenberg discussed Lee's suit with his friend and skiing partner Cheech Marin, the comic actor who provided voices for many Disney characters, including Banzai the Hyena in *The Lion King*. "He explained to me that she wanted to get remunerated for all the work she did. I said, 'Why don't you remunerate her? I don't know if what you're gonna get out of the case is worth the publicity.' But he was adamant about making a stand." A victory by Lee might open a floodgate of similar lawsuits. "They'd be forever in litigation," said Marin.

Press and fans rallied to her side. Lee's was a storybook case of a lone artist—in this instance, a sick old woman—fighting a corporate gargoyle. And she made sure they knew how frail she was, of body if not of spirit. On November 16, 1988, twelve days before she filed her suit, she held a press conference in a suite at New York's Helmsley Palace Hotel. Reporters and photographers found her "seated on several pillows because of a back injury," wrote Matthew Flamm of the *New York Post*. They were instantly sympathetic. "I'm not being a saint, saying I don't want the money—I want it," said Lee. "I think it's shameful that artists can't share financially from the success of their work. That's the only way we can make our living."

Disney's lawyers declined comment. But they had to respond to Lee. Buena Vista pulled the *Lady and the Tramp* video off the market, and a deposition with Lee—the pretrial exchange of information by the litigants—was scheduled. Claiming illness, she succeeded in having it held in her living room. Typically, she turned it into a lunch—one more ploy to soften her opponents. The participants, including both sides' attorneys and a stenographer—filed one by one into her foyer, wearing suits and toting briefcases. An early arrival from the Disney camp was startled when Lee beckoned him warmly to the piano and played and sang one of her songs.

It was a cunning reminder that she wasn't just any plaintiff; she was Miss Peggy Lee. And some of her opponents loved her work. During the visit, a Disney lawyer took Saulle aside and asked: "Do you think that Miss Lee would autograph a photo for my wife?"

Saulle stared at him. After a pause, he answered: "I'm sure she would love to."

Once the deposition had begun, Lee's poise impressed Saulle. "The attorneys asked questions and she answered them. Never raised her voice. From the moment we started she knew she was right and was gonna win."

The case kept growing. David Blasband saw the need to bring in a lawyer based in Los Angeles, where the trial would occur. His choice couldn't have made Lee happier. Blasband engaged Elizabeth Taylor's lawyer, Neil Papiano, a Beverly Hills litigator who was known for fighting seven- and eight-figure lawsuits for his clients. Bald and portly, with a hint of a sneer, Papiano would win a whopping suit against the *National Enquirer* for libeling Taylor. He also represented David Levy, who devised the TV series *The Addams Family*, in a fifty-million-dollar suit against Paramount Pictures, whose hit film based on the show allegedly posed "unfair competition, trade libel, and title slander." But to him, all those fights apparently paled in comparison to Lee's. "This is the case of a lifetime!" he told Blasband.

Papiano's firm, which included his tirelessly efficient associate, Deborah Nesset—"She did *all* the grunt work," said Blasband—charged a reported two hundred dollars an hour; Deutsch's averaged $228. Lee could ill afford such out-of-pocket costs. But as she knew, attorneys could choose the option of working on contingency (a fee drawn based on a percentage of a winning settlement) if they felt confident of success, or liked a case's prestige. Lee lucked out.

Now she wanted her day in court. And she didn't wish to wait. The singer asked one of her doctors to spell out her failing health in writing. Soon John Chiodini understood, as never before, her ability to manifest psychosomatic ills. "I saw her get sick after she read that letter," he said. At a rehearsal, she waved it around as a weapon against her musicians, lest they challenge her on anything. "I remember her yelling at Mark Sherman," recalled the guitarist. "She was quoting the letter that I think she helped dictate and paid for." Its theme, said Chiodini, was clear: "Everybody says I'm faking, but now I have proof!"

Where the Disney case was concerned, however, Lee's ploy didn't help. By depicting herself so aggressively as a woman on the brink of death, she gave the company unforeseen rope. As the suit proceeded, she grew convinced that Disney intended to drag things out until she died. Not even Blasband could support that theory. But whatever it cost her, Lee was prepared to do battle. She raised the damage amount from twenty-five to fifty million. If Disney didn't know it, Peggy Lee did: the longer anyone fought her, the angrier she would get—and that anger only fueled her to keep going.

———

MUSICALLY, TOO, LEE BARRELED forth, breathlessly busy. "I can't stop," she told a reporter. "I mean, sit there and wait for what? My last breath? What do I have to lose?"

As ever, her king-size bed doubled as her office. One side of it was covered with paperwork, boxes, and a small white towel; placed upon it were a bowl of food and a brush for Baby, her tiny, prowling silver chinchilla cat. On the other lay the star, false eyelashes in place whether guests were coming or not. "She didn't get out of bed," said John Saulle, "but the gardener came every day, the cook came every day, the housekeeper came every day, I came every day." The French doors in her room stayed closed. "She never saw the light of day," explained Saulle. "She *hated* going outside. She was the whitest person ever." Occasionally her friend Helen Glickstein flew in from New York to visit. Once there, she found herself chained to Lee's bedside. "I didn't come out here to sit in this bedroom!" groused Glickstein.

Two invitations did get Lee out of bed and on planes to New York. Not since 1979 had she made an album, but to her joy, some serious independent record producers wanted to capture her autumnal work before it was too late. Now she would have two new albums. Both of them nodded to the blues, which many critics felt she understood better than any other white singer.

MusicMasters, an independent label devoted to classical works and historic jazz, signed her to record *Miss Peggy Lee Sings the Blues*. It gathered the embattled, low-down plaints of several pioneers, notably Ma Rainey ("See See Rider"), Bessie Smith ("Tain't Nobody's Bizness If I Do"), Lead Belly ("Birmingham Jail"), Lil Green ("Love Me"), and Billie

Holiday ("Fine and Mellow"). The other CD, *Love Held Lightly—Rare Songs by Harold Arlen*, saluted a Jewish songwriter who loved the blues, and who referenced them in songs of such refined urbanity that they worked perfectly on Broadway and in Hollywood. Arlen had written dozens of standards, among them "Blues in the Night," "That Old Black Magic," "The Man That Got Away," and "Over the Rainbow."

But the producers, Ken Bloom and Bill Rudman, wanted to shine a light upon obscure Arlen, notably "Happy with the Blues," a song he had written with Lee in 1961. Bloom was a much-published authority on the American Popular Song, Rudman a theater director; as record producers, they loved to place singers of Lee's class in jewel-like settings. Maxine Sullivan had made far too many sloppy discs; Bloom and Rudman showcased her in choicely programmed tributes to the composers Jule Styne and Burton Lane and to the Cotton Club.

Lee found the two producers "thoughtful and supportive and enthusiastic," and when they proposed their Arlen project, she said, "Yes, I *would* be interested in talking with you!" At steep expense, they flew her and her nurse into New York and, per her demands, housed them in Cole Porter's former suite at the Waldorf. Once in the studio, Lee sat in a wheelchair and turned out impeccable performances. Pianist Keith Ingham led a nine-piece band that included her anchors, Grady Tate and John Chiodini.

But Lee had meant it when she vowed, after *Peg*, never to drag people again onto gloomy ground. The smoldering fire of her old *Black Coffee* performances had cooled to the faintest flicker; the tumult of love seemed a distant memory. Lee was trying her best to replace hurt with humor. Just to leave her bed was painful; she looked to music for comfort. "When I sing, I seem to go into another dimension," she explained. "Things just don't hurt so much there."

On the MusicMasters CD, she held her desperate survival tales at a safe emotional distance; a quintet of New York jazzmen played them with clean conservatory precision. Lee's sound was now pinched and dry, but her time and pitch remained flawless, her phrasing as wise as ever. In *Stereo Review*, Chris Albertson, Bessie Smith's biographer, raved: "Jennifer Holliday, Diane Schuur, Patti LaBelle, and all the other screamers who mistake volume for soul ought to be locked up with this album until they get it right."

Love Held Lightly had a rockier birth. As an act of respect, Bloom and Rudman had granted Lee approval of the master. They sent her a cassette. Word came back that she was appalled at how they had recorded her, and wanted the disc shelved. The producers were floored. To everyone but Lee, it sounded first-rate. Lee explained her issue to a reporter. Her voice, she said, was "a center core with rings of overtones. If they don't record it properly, it just picks up the center core, and it shaves off the layers of overtones." She heeded the advice of her psychic. Mercury was in retrograde, which tended to make things go wrong. This was no time to release an album.

Only later did Rudman and Bloom get to the heart of the problem. The audio system in Lee's bedroom was a boombox with one dead channel. Long after her initial refusal, she left Rudman a voicemail: "You know dear, I don't know why we shouldn't release this if you still want to." *Love Held Lightly* at last came out on Angel, a high-toned classical label.

Miss Peggy Lee Sings the Blues appeared in time for Lee's fourth run at The Ballroom, which opened on January 31, 1989. Each year her New York fans had watched her grow frailer. Determined to stand onstage for at least a few moments, Lee hobbled out with a sequined cane. In honor of the blues, she wore a black velvet gown, not her usual white. Neal Karlen of the New York weekly *7 Days* detailed her entrance. "Miss Peggy Lee peeks out from behind the curtains, her upper body glowing in a heart-shaped spotlight, her cartoony eyelashes flapping . . . The crowd claps encouragingly and tries not to notice as she haltingly walks the few steps to her center-stage armchair." Once settled in, she purred her stock greeting: "Are you enjoying yourselves? . . . That's the *whooooole* idea!" Out among the tables, customers traded uneasy glances.

They relaxed, particularly when Lee announced she was about to tell "the story of the blues." The room went dark. Wind chimes tinkled, chains jangled, then came a sound akin to a hammer pounding nails into train tracks. With only her white wig visible in ghostly silhouette, Lee sang: "Been working hard on the chain gang/Still got so terrible long to go . . ." The stage turned bright, and she began to narrate a blues suite:

> *I love the blues . . .*
> *They're happy, sad; they're lighthearted,*
> *downhearted.*

They came out of the jails . . . in from the
fields . . . little snatches of life.
And sometimes it helped to sing. It was a
release . . . an expression of the soul.

Immobile in her chair except for a slow swaying of the head, Lee was a living monument to suffering and survival. According to Stuart Troup of *Newsday*, the singer "left more than a few in the full house emotionally overcome."

But most of them were diehard Peggy Lee fans, and one had to wonder how the odd sight of her struck the uninitiated. An answer came when Rob Hoerburger, a young music writer and future editor for the *New York Times*, showed up at The Ballroom with a group of friends. "To us she had *always* been an old woman," he wrote, starting from the time when she "crashed our Top 40" with "Is That All There Is?" Now, wrote Hoerburger, "she was beyond old, seemingly held together by laminate and scarabs, and we laughed because we couldn't decide which was more ludicrous: that she looked like a retired bordello matron, that she was still trying to perform when she could barely stand or that we were paying money, money that we didn't really have, to watch."

They kept returning, however, lured by her peculiar charisma. Hoerburger learned more about her along the way, and gained respect for her as a vocal and sexual trailblazer—a "purrer" throughout ages of shouters. Lee's voice, he wrote, "had grown heavy and slow"; still it "navigated the fissures of time like a luxury liner."

Reporters of all ages came to interview at her hotel suite. She held them rapt with tales from a life more colorful than any of them had lived. Most of them believed every word—and if someone looked askance at her in print, she fired off a huffy response. Comparisons between Lee and Norma Desmond weren't new, but when Lee read one of them, she fired off an inflamed letter to the editor: "I believe the fictitious character of Norma Desmond was insane. Are you saying I am insane?"

Even though the public had rejected *Peg*, Lee was still intent on telling her story her way. In 1985, while bedridden after open-heart surgery, she had started her memoirs. The book found an independent publisher, Donald Fine, who had issued the life story of New York's notorious "Mayflower Madam," Sydney Biddle Barrows, and *Eye of the Needle*, Ken Follett's bloody espionage thriller.

Lee's story had no end of violence and mayhem, but Fine wasn't keen on the book's sanctified tone or the singer's curious primness about her love life. He tried to argue his points, but Lee resisted so adamantly that he ultimately gave in and hoped for the best.

Like *Peg*, however, *Miss Peggy Lee* revealed how little perspective she had on her life, times, or on anyone who had passed through them. Her endearing wit was again in short supply. "Sometimes life is sadder than death," she wrote, establishing that even her survival skills were a burden. Critics who viewed her as eternally sexy and indomitable were baffled by the saintly martyrdom of her self-image. Rex Reed, in the *New York Observer*, called the book a "morass of morbidity." Aside from the expected pages on Min's abuse, Lee, wrote Reed, "was almost sold into white slavery, nearly drowned, suffered from sore throats, fainting spells and malnutrition. After surgery and a lump in her throat, she was dropped on a tile floor, breaking her front teeth and slicing her tongue after hemorrhaging from blood transfusions . . . Plagued by raging fevers, she also developed diabetes, the inner-ear affliction called Meniere's disease and a heart condition. Packed in ice, she went blind."

Once stardom came, the portrait turned from black to rose. Recalling her triumphs at Basin Street East, the singer observed: "I sang and sang and sang. They loved it all, and so did I." As for social context, Lee offered: "Clothes and the fifties . . . It was a big time for both." God had blessed her with so many celebrity friends. Frank Sinatra, she wrote, "has always been somewhere near . . . just touching the elbow . . . holding the hand." The tough-guy actor Robert Mitchum was as misunderstood as she; they drank lemonade together at parties, and he loved to sing "America the Beautiful." Predictably, she devoted a hefty chunk of the book to her misbegotten love of Dave Barbour, but brushed over Brad Dexter, Dewey Martin, and Jack Del Rio.

Michael Musto, one of the dishiest of gossip hounds, gave Lee begrudging points for discretion, while noting the "gloppy unrealness" of her accounts. "If we don't want her to wallow, we would at least like to know how suffering has transformed her, onstage and off, and how she's different from all the other dark ladies who turned dejection into art." The book, he said, contained "nothing about how she digs into her soul and comes up with a singing style that's sexy and chilling at the same time." But the bubble she lived in had no room for frank self-reflection; she saved that for her music. "Singing is both Peggy's expression of angst and her escape from it," he wrote.

Miss Peggy Lee exasperated even Phoebe Jacobs. "I told her, 'Maybe you think you're gonna grow into that person you created for the book. She hasn't got flesh and blood, it's just like a paper doll.' But it was important for Peggy to keep up an image. She wasn't gonna let her hair down in the book, in an interview, or anywhere else."

After the book's release, some of the friends who were in it confronted Lee about her fanciful, edited, or sometimes imagined accounts. She gave a standard reply: "No one would ever believe the truth."

———

WHEN SHE SANG, AT least, Lee never uttered a false word. And in January of 1990, plans were made for her to lift her voice throughout the U.K. in a nearly monthlong tour. Getting there was an ordeal. "She was tired," said Emilio Palame. "She was weak. It was difficult for her to get around. She was always in a wheelchair." Yet she wouldn't give up. A TV interviewer asked Lee if she ever thought of retiring. "No!" she said. "I think it would frighten me to death. I shouldn't say that!"

Lee was set to play London, Manchester, Brighton, Cardiff, and Edinburgh. But her ego took a blow when most of the tour was canceled; for the first time, her British ticket sales were too low to justify continuing. Understandably, she sank into a funk. Later bookings in Australia went off as planned, but Lee was in a foul mood there, and complained about almost everything.

At least she could look forward to her fifth run at The Ballroom, in the town whose acceptance she cared about the most. This engagement would last three weeks, down from the six of 1985 and 1986. It marked the release of her second MusicMasters CD, *The Peggy Lee Songbook: There'll Be Another Spring*, coproduced by John Chiodini and Mike Renzi. The repertoire spanned decades of Lee's songwriting from the 1950s ("Where Can I Go Without You?," "Things Are Swingin'," "Sans

Souci") to her newest songs with Chiodini and Palame. For the occasion, Lee tossed out almost all of Otis Blackwell's words to "Fever" and replaced them with new ones of her own. The disc offered a reminder of what clever, catchy, and endearingly spacy lyrics Lee could write at her best. On "He's a Tramp," Lee even regained her old bouncy swing. The addition of strings made *The Peggy Lee Songbook* seem that much closer to one of her 1960s albums.

Inside her cubicle of a dressing room, the singer placed a silver-framed photo of her cat, Baby, on the makeup table. Lee did her own makeup, but now, as she approached seventy, it wasn't so easy to look in the mirror. Injections of prednisone, a synthetic steroid commonly prescribed for heart-failure patients, had made her face as round as Raggedy Ann's. Her Dynel pageboy and the huge rose she inserted into it added to the doll-like effect. This time Lee had bravely foregone wearing glasses, which necessitated a ritual: With a doctor's rubber reflex hammer, she tapped the area around her sagging eye to wake it up.

Night after night, on the arm of Mike Renzi, she struggled onto a small stage crowded with her rhythm section—Chiodini, bassist Sean Smith, drummer Peter Grant, and Renzi—and a string quartet. "I really hate falling into that chair," she said wearily. But once there, she became charming, relaxed, and full of loopy Peggy Lee humor: "I always wonder, when I wear these gowns, how do those ostriches sit on their feathers?"

At other times, audiences saw a woman who seemed to live on the threshold of some otherworldly abyss. In "Circle in the Sky," written with Palame, Lee gazed toward space, spotting the eternal love that had eluded her on earth. The song was as slow and somber as a baroque adagio, and Lee sang it as though in a trance. Dave Barbour seemed to rise again as she sang the first lines—"I drew a circle in the sky / Inside I wrote 'You and I'"—and traced a finger in a clockwork motion through the air. "Forever," sang Lee, "our love is stronger than a star."

"Circle in the Sky" was her eeriest latter-day performance—a trip into the twilight zone with a singer who seemed about to evanesce before one's eyes. But a Peggy Lee appearance at The Ballroom was no longer news. Many of the shows didn't sell out, and as Lee's salary demands increased, Greg Dawson could no longer afford her. At the end of this engagement, Lee would once more bid goodbye to New York for a while.

The enigma that was Peggy Lee kept growing murkier. She devoted hours each day to seeking spiritual enlightenment while numbing her senses with Valium. Reading and rereading *Letters of the Scattered Brotherhood*, she memorized lines about achieving a Christlike inner tranquility: "This power held in stillness will go far toward stopping wars . . . Come closer to the center of all light; come freed from the ignorant emotional habits." Then she demanded majority ownershop of "Circle in the Sky," all of whose music Palame had composed. For Lee, it seemed, there could be no peace.

At home in Bel Air with Baby, 1997. (PHOTO BY JANE DAVID)

Chapter Eighteen

A YEAR AND A half had passed since Lee had called battle upon the "evil empire," as she called the Walt Disney Company. Progress had been slow, and the singer was desperate. Her performance income had crashed, and the specter of financial ruin once more hung over her. She even came close to selling her home.

The long wait for her trial was hardly uncommon in L.A., with its jammed court calendars. Sometimes it took twice that long for litigants to have their day. Lee kept pushing her lawyers to speed things up. As determined as she was to fight to the end—and to exact an eight-figure payoff—Lee wanted it known that, yes, she might die at any moment. And if she did, it was Disney's fault.

But the company's lawyers had plenty of confidence. In February 1990, they motioned for a "summary judgment"—a judge's predetermination of guilt or innocence. The 1952 definition of "transcription" would surely prevail.

Unbeknownst to Disney, David Blasband had made a useful discovery in *Nimmer on Copyright*, the definitive textbook on copyright law. He read that in 1968, Disney had sued the Alaska Television Network for unlawfully airing videotapes of its films. To prove its case, Disney had invoked the 1909 Copyright Act, which defined transcription in just the sense the company was now trying to deny: as a copy.

On March 30, Blasband and Disney's chosen litigator, Roy Reardon, convened before a judge for the summary judgment hearing. Blasband brought up the 1968 case. "I thought I'd have to argue for hours," he recalled. "The judge cut me off after a minute. He grilled Roy and Disney's inside counsel for thirty minutes about that case. They couldn't really get around it."

With that, Judge William Huss of the Los Angeles County Superior Court made "what could be a landmark decision," as the *Hollywood Reporter* suggested. Huss ruled that Lee's original contract *did* entitle her to payment for all commercially sold versions of *Lady and the Tramp*, notably home video. Now a jury would decide the amount of damages owed to Lee. And it might happen soon, for her legal team had successfully invoked an obscure California law that guaranteed priority scheduling to people older than seventy.

Disney tried to shoot the judgment down, but failed. A company spokesman maintained the position that a transcription did *not* mean a copy of a film. Disney had to hold its ground. *Entertainment Weekly* warned: "Stars are dusting off decades-old contracts, hoping to find clauses that will allow them to share video's $10-billion-a-year revenues."

Mary Costa, the voice of *Sleeping Beauty*, had already filed suit against Disney for a multimillion-dollar share in the movie's ten-figure video profits. Costa's attorney, Lise Hudson, had incited more fear in Disney by announcing that she had uncovered sixteen other contracts with the "transcription" clause.

Disney could not allow Lee to set a potentially costly precedent. Despite the speedy trial she had been promised, the company lawyers erected every roadblock they could. Lee would wait almost another year to go to court. For now she sat in bed, writing in longhand a book about her experiences with Walt Disney—"a dear, sweet man"—and the monsters who had succeeded him.

———

ONCE UBIQUITOUS ON TV, Lee now went on it rarely. Gone were the variety shows that had brought her on to promote her latest Capitol LP or single; Johnny Carson, her longtime champion, was soon to wind down thirty years as host of *Tonight*. When a show did invite her on, Lee's entrance backstage in a wheelchair, with an attendant and oxygen tank at hand, alarmed the staff; and her current appearance jarred many viewers. Her daughter cringed at the unkind things she heard audience members say about her mother's looks. "Maybe that's my codependence," Nicki admitted.

In May of 1990, Lee flew to New York for a very special occasion: *Night of 100 Stars III*, televised from Radio City Music Hall. The three-hour galaxy of celebrity cameos included a sentimental tribute to the American Popular Song. On a two-level set, a series of risers held white pianos; at all of them, songwriters teamed with their hit-making muses. With composer Jule Styne at the keys, Carol Channing performed "Diamonds Are a Girl's Best Friend," her showstopper from the 1949 Broadway hit *Gentlemen Prefer Blondes*. Singer B. J. Thomas and lyricist Hal David reprised "Raindrops Keep Fallin' on My Head," their shoulder-shrugging 1970 ode to optimism. In a flashback to the 1974 Oscars, Barbra Streisand had once more declined to perform "The Way We Were"; Gladys Knight, who had recorded a competing version, sang it in the company of the lyricists, Alan and Marilyn Bergman.

With Leiber and Stoller at one of the upper-tier pianos, Peggy Lee, seated in the instrument's curve, offered a minute-long fragment of "Is That All There Is?" Millions of viewers saw the onetime vixen looking as wide as an easy chair—an explosion of black beaded fabric and ostrich feathers, with a foot-high black plume rising out of her wig. But twenty-one years after she had recorded that nihilistic hit, there she was, still "not ready for that final disappointment." She smiled her way through the oft-told tale about the burning-down of her house, and sounded much as people remembered.

Still, the woman who had recently sworn that she would keep singing "as long as I have a breath" didn't do it much anymore. That month, ASCAP had given Lee its Pied Piper Award for lifetime achievement, but such sweeping honors usually signaled careers that were almost over. Her near-inactivity baffled Robert Strom, the young president of her fan club. Strom, who had moved to L.A. from Northern California, had stepped in as personal assistant after one more of Lee's secretaries left. He idolized her "more than any living human being," he said. "I expected her to be employed, going out on the road, into the studio. I didn't expect her to be in the house all day, every day. She was in bed twenty-four-seven."

But for Lee, performing had become an agonizingly drawn-out, painful process; and with her disabilities widely known, few bookers were eager to gamble on her. Ahead of her in 1991 were two shows at Pasadena's Raymond Theatre and at the Sundome in Sun City, Arizona, and not much else.

And so she stayed in bed. But her mind raced constantly, and even from a horizontal position she stirred up a whirl of activity. A parade of business appointments, social dinners, and interviews took place at her bedside; she dictated letters, signed photos for fans, had her hair and nails done, and made to-do lists for her staff. John Chiodini and Emilio Palame pitched in by helping her organize a shrine to her musical past. Along a living-room wall were a series of cabinet doors; behind them, in cubbyholes, rested her lifetime of musical arrangements. Each had been placed in a coded Ziplock bag and filed alphabetically. A three-ring-binder held the master log, which Lee kept within reach of her bed.

By now, of course, she didn't have much need for it. Lee made greater use of the fax machine, also at her bedside. It rang and hummed throughout the day as friends sent her jokes to keep her spirits high. When she read one she liked, she repeated it for days. Forgetting the three-hour time difference between Los Angeles and New York, Lee would frequently call Rex Reed to regale him with some surprisingly filthy humor. She adopted a French accent to tell friends about a grade-school English teacher in France.

"Today, class, we're going to learn to use the word 'probably.' Who wants to use the word 'probably' in a sentence? Oh yes, Jacques?"

"Well, my mother is cutting up some potatoes and some onions and some lamb and some turnips, and she has some water boiling on the stove, and I think she is probably making a stew."

"Very good, Jacques! Michelle?"

"Well, my mother is cutting up some fabric, and she has some knitting needles and some thread, and I think she is probably going to make a quilt."

"Very good, Michelle. Maurice?"

"Well, the other day I saw my sister and her boyfriend in the music room. And he was pulling down his pants and she was pulling up her dress. And I think they were probably going to shit on the piano."

Lee's low, hearty laugh would boom into the hallway outside her door. The staff knew it was a good day.

The scene on Bellagio, said Strom, had its "sitcom moments," with a cast of characters to match. It included Lee's live-in cook Erica—"the stone-faced German," Strom said, "who in Peggy Lee's opinion was 'dressed like a clown!' Her son was there all the time. He was constantly in the garage using the Xerox machine." José Prado had brought in his wife, Yolanda, to do laundry and cleaning. Never had Yolanda met the likes of Miss Peggy Lee. More than once she came crying to Strom: "Oh, Rrrrobbie—Mees Lee ees loca!"

No one disagreed. One day she told Strom she had just seen her long-ago flame, Quincy Jones. "He was on me like a blanket!" she declared. Looking out of the French doors in her bedroom, Lee noticed that the Peggy Lee rosebushes seemed thin. She decided that José was making extra bucks by selling the flowers to fans who showed up on celebrity tour buses, hoping for a glimpse of her. Bruce Vanderhoff found the notion hysterical. "That story is *so* fabricated Peggy Lee," he said. "No tour bus went there!" Lee lived in an obscure corner of Bel Air; even some friends had trouble finding the house. What's more, her staff knew that deer roamed the grounds and loved to eat roses. But Dona Harsh knew how neurotic Lee had grown. "Someone was always ripping her off," she said.

Lee had hired an accountant, Pam MacGregor, to work at the house. Pam belonged to the Science of Mind Spiritual Center in Los Angeles; later she became Pastor Director. She did her best to safeguard the strained finances of a star who lived as though she were rich, and who employed too many people. Comic relief was helpful, and Pam provided that, too. "She had a wild, off-the-wall sense of humor," said Strom. "She always made Peggy laugh, and she could quickly change things from bad to good. Remember, they 'worked' for each other in the Science of Mind fashion, which was all about positive thinking." But even MacGregor had her limits. Two times, when the day had dragged on much too long and she couldn't bear one more of Lee's demands, the accountant conspired with Strom. He turned off the alarm system, and Pam escaped out a back window.

Many people phoned, but apart from her granddaughter Holly and a handful of other regulars, few came to visit. Lee's best friend was now Baby. As the tiny animal nuzzled her face, the seventy-year-old's eyes lit up. "Hi, little darling!" she said in the same maternal tone she had once directed at Nicki. Covered by a blanket, Lee began writing a children's book about her pet, who attended every boudoir business meeting. When Ken Bloom and Bill Rudman (who had produced her *Love Held Lightly* album) dropped by, Lee offered hours of stories about Frank Sinatra and *Pete Kelly's Blues* and her glory days as a Capitol goddess. "Now here she was, in bed with the cat," said Bloom.

When the occasional journalist arrived, Lee offered a carefully staged look at a Hollywood legend. After a suspense-building wait in the living room, the reporter would be ushered into the master bedroom by some member of the staff. Lee sat in bed, eyelashes and turban in place, a queen in her court. After pleasantries were exchanged, Lee rang a bell and José appeared, bearing a sterling-silver tray of watercress sandwiches, chocolate mousse cake, and tea. "That bell belonged to Commodore Vanderbilt," Lee would explain; she also pointed to her "prize-winning" Peggy Lee roses outside. A masseuse was sometimes there in a white uniform, massaging the star's feet.

As always, Lee charmed each writer with her warm, lulling voice and seeming candor. Her revelations about her ill health ensured a kind article. In the 1990s, she channeled most of her ailments into a condition she named "polymyelitis rheumatosis." It was "a distant relative to polio," she noted, "and it boils down to being paralyzed due to inflammation of the nerves, muscles, and joints—everything from the neck down. Horrifying pain." No disease by that name existed in the medical textbooks; the nearest namesake, poliomyelitis, bore little resemblance to the ailment Lee described. But everyone, it seemed, took Lee at her word.

Reporters invariably asked her to name her favorite current singers. Lee mentioned Whitney Houston, Sade, Linda Ronstadt, Anita Baker, and Tina Turner, none of whose records she played. She preferred to recount the past. Hers seemed as rococo as *Oliver Twist*, and no less fraught with danger and death. When the BBC's Alan Dell flew in from England to record a long interview for broadcast, Lee rewarded him with some of her most fantastical tales. To the story of her train ride from Fargo to Hollywood in 1937, she added a rainstorm of such torrential force that it kept washing out the tracks behind them. "I almost drowned," said Lee. "And I was an excellent swimmer." The account bore a close resemblance to her father's story of a 1918 storm that had swept away the Midland Continental tracks; a railroad car had overturned, killing several people.

She rewrote history further by calling her early vocal resemblance to Billie Holiday "only a coincidence," and explaining that Richard Rodgers had grown "very much in favor" of her version of "Lover." In fact, said Lee, "he told me he used it as the subject of lectures on songwriting and how different interpretations could give the song more life or longer life, and he gave me permission, carte blanche, to do anything with his music that I wanted to." His daughter, Mary Rodgers Guettel, couldn't recall any of it.

The credit-stealing that had caused Paul Horner such anguish had spread to other collaborations. Lee now claimed that she, not Duke Ellington, had written the music for "I'm Gonna Go Fishin'," when in fact she had set her words to a theme from his already-finished score for the movie *Anatomy of a Murder*. For years Lee had sworn that she and Barbour, not Willard Robison, had penned nearly all of "Don't Smoke in Bed." Now she said that Dave's music for that and other songs were, in fact, "my melodies"; Barbour, she said, had only added harmonies. "I've never told that much until lately," she allowed.

Bruce Vanderhoff had no doubt that Lee believed these claims: "After she'd said them ten times, they were cemented in her mind." But for Lee, the emotional and physical costs of so much illusion had long been steep. Valium still helped her escape, but now that she had reached her seventies, she was less able to withstand the amounts she took. One day Robert Strom couldn't wake her up. He panicked. After a while Lee regained consciousness, but he phoned Nicki in Idaho to tell her that her mother seemed in serious danger. She was concerned, but didn't feel she could change anything; this was a two-decades-old issue. Nicki, said Strom, "knew that Peggy would not go to any kind of treatment program, like Betty Ford."

No amount of pills or attention from doctors and nurses could ease Lee's regrets. One of them involved her failings as a mother. Lee had read *Mommie Dearest*, Christina Crawford's exposé about her allegedly abusive mother, Joan Crawford; and *Going My Own Way*, in which Gary Crosby detailed the brutal maltreatment he had suffered at the hands of his superstar father. Lee defended both Bing and Joan. Celebrity children, she insisted, "don't realize how spoiled they are, because they're given a lot of things that other children don't get."

Lee had long ago absolved herself of any responsibility for Barbour's decline. "David's problem had nothing to do with my career," she insisted. "He was proud of my success." She recalled him romantically to audiences: "I loved him then and I love him now." But once in a while, residual anger welled up. "There were days when Dave was on her shit list," said Strom, mostly due to the fact that he had left her. "The abandonment thing," as Strom put it, remained her ultimate sore spot.

LEE KEPT WAITING FOR the giant Disney settlement that would solve all her problems. The case was costing her dearly. "It's a drain financially, it's a drain physically, emotionally," she told a reporter. "I've been insulted. It's a strange way to try to begin winding down your career."

She planned to leave the money to Nicki and her grandchildren, she said, "and to a program that helps children who are visually and hearing-impaired." In the meantime, Pam MacGregor helped her cover expenses by placing calls to record companies in search of royalty checks. In 1990 EMI sent two, each for $15,000. But given Lee's expenses, such sums vanished in weeks.

At last came the news she'd been pining for. On March 11, 1991, *Peggy Lee v. Walt Disney Company* would commence at the Superior Court Building in the mid-Wilshire district of Los Angeles. First she trekked to court to join all involved lawyers, and Judge Stephen M. Lachs, for a pair of pretrial meetings.

It was then that the opposition truly saw the challenge they faced. Reporters from *Variety*, the *Hollywood Reporter*, the *Los Angeles Times*, and CNN had shown up to cover what promised to be a Hollywood fight to the death. Flashbulbs and TV cameras greeted the heart-tugging sight of an attendant wheeling Peggy Lee into the courtroom, white wig, black dress, glasses, and oxygen tank in place. Her face looked bloated and weary. "She suffers from a heart condition and severe diabetes," reported the Associated Press, "and is unable to walk after fracturing her pelvis in a fall."

Sharon Bernstein of the *Los Angeles Times* made no attempt to hide her sympathy. "Sitting up in her wheelchair, frail and with failing eyesight, singer Peggy Lee hardly fits the image of a Hollywood giant killer." Lee sounded winded as she pleaded for justice. "I put my whole heart and soul into this thirty years ago," she told Bernstein, "and I deserve to have my contract honored."

But underneath the illness and age resided an iron will. "I'm still doing sold-out performances and getting standing ovations all over the place," she declared. "They're trying to wish me gone, but I'm not. I'm still here."

In the press, anti-Disney sentiments mounted; *Barron's*, the weekly financial Bible, called the company's executives "control freaks." In an ill-timed juxtaposition of cases, Disney had crossed swords not only with a seventy-year-old icon in a wheelchair, but with the world's most beloved set of talking animals, the Muppets. Henson Associates, Inc. had sued Disney for the unauthorized sale of Muppet-themed merchandise and unlawful use of Muppet characters in its films. Disney had filed a counterclaim of fraud.

All this proved catnip to the readers of the daily trades. The court had chosen twelve middle- to lower-income jurors. They may well have known and liked Peggy Lee; but her opponent held its own weight; it wasn't a faceless corporate monster like Exxon, but Walt Disney, a name that evoked images of cute dwarves and cuddly deer; of handsome princes, Snow White, and Cinderella.

Now the controlling figures had gathered in the cold, clinical space of a courtroom for two weeks to fight over eight-figure sums. TV cameras were there—a rarity in court—to publicize a case that was shot through with drama. Up front were the stars. Stephen M. Lachs—who would later mediate divorce hearings for Janet Jackson and Tony Bennett as well as two child custody cases for Michael Jackson—sat on the bench. He wore a black robe, a mustache, wire-frame glasses, and a stern look. There to represent Disney was Roy L. Reardon, a "confident, button-down-shirt-kind of New York lawyer," as one observer saw him. His foes, David Blasband and Neil Papiano, would take turns arguing Lee's case. Their client sat in her wheelchair, her mournful black dress in stark contrast with her white scarf and wig, which framed a haggard face. "Almost in front of the jury," recalled Lachs, "they stacked, like, four, six oxygen tanks, which they said were absolutely necessary for her to have right there, at the jury box, just in case. That kind of little game was obviously going on."

Reardon knew how hard it would be to convince a jury that Lee deserved little. As the trial wore on he came to feel that Lachs, too, was squarely in Lee's corner—yet even Reardon didn't doubt the importance of her role in the film.

The summary judgment had established Disney's guilt; it was the jurors' job to determine the amount of damages, based on their assessment of what Lee had contributed to *Lady and the Tramp*. Lachs had approved a request from Lee's team to screen the entire film in court, along with *Walt Disney's Cavalcade of Stars*, the 1955 TV program that showed staged scenes of Lee writing songs with Sonny Burke, working with the Disney team, and recording "He's a Tramp."

Once more, *Lady and the Tramp* was a hit. Jurors and the public grinned as the dogs slurped spaghetti in an Italian restaurant to a soundtrack of Lee and Burke's song: "This is a night, it's a beautiful night, and they call it bella notte . . ." They laughed at the stripper moves of showgirl-mutt Peg, who in Lee's voice sang "He's a Tramp" while a canine chorus howled. Looking back on the trial in 2014, Lachs called it "the only case I've had where we sat through a full movie in court. It's a film that to this day will bring tears to my eyes. The jury was watching the film, which has wonderful music, and yeah—you became very sympathetic."

In the testimony that followed, Lee gave a performance as shrewd and winning as any from her musical heyday. Speaking directly to the jury, she talked of all she had done to influence *Lady and the Tramp*—including her successful plea to Walt Disney to not let Lady's friend Old Trusty, the aged bloodhound, die in the film. Lee wove in amusing stories about her career, while making much of the fact that "dear Walt" would never have wanted her to be treated like this.

Blasband kept an eye on the jurors. "They were rapt," he said. "They couldn't help but like Peggy Lee, and they couldn't help but want to do something good for her." Reardon's job was getting much tougher. Blasband had nothing but admiration for his opponent. "What a lovely guy," he recalled, adding: "Roy, in my opinion, is the best trial lawyer I've ever seen, and a class act."

The plaintiffs hadn't brought him many witnesses to cross-examine. William Zulager, Disney's director of financial reporting, testified as to how much the company had earned from the tape. The figures were impressive: a $72,236,000 worldwide gross, with net profits of $36,875,000.

Then came the appearance of Lee's "expert witness," entertainment lawyer Marc Bailin. Lee's counsel had hired him to perform a nebulous task: to scrape up whatever facts, figures, and precedents he could in order to substantiate the maximum damages possible.

Using the reported gross for the video, Bailin stated that according to "industry norms," Lee deserved 12.5% of the gross—$9,027,000. The figure, he claimed, incorporated all that Lee had contributed, including four character voices and big-name clout.

Reardon lost patience. This man, he countered, knew nothing about the animated film industry or how much its voice actors deserved to make. Bailin's main credential was his negotiating for *Callanetics*, a blockbuster series of exercise videos; otherwise, as he acknowledged, he had cobbled together his figures by reading about similar deals in the showbiz dailies. In a private huddle with the lawyers, the judge addressed Papiano. "I honestly am amazed," he said, "that you couldn't find anybody with more experience than this gentleman." The attorney had to admit that it was all but impossible to find anyone willing to testify against Disney. Reardon tried to have the testimony thrown out, but Lachs let it stand.

Throughout the case, Reardon had heard Lee and her counsel throw a lot of big numbers around. First she wanted twenty-five million, then fifty, then twelve and a half. Now they had settled on Bailin's nine. "Where do these numbers originate, and on what basis?" asked Reardon.

On Wednesday, March 13, Reardon began calling his own witnesses. Anne Daly, the Disney marketing executive who had handled the *Lady* tape, testified that its buyers were primarily mothers of small children— hardly Peggy Lee's audience. The singer's voice, she believed, hadn't affected sales in the slightest.

Next up was Katie O'Connell, Disney's vice president of business and legal affairs. O'Connell declared that no Disney voice actor had ever received a piece of video sales. And if Lee had negotiated such rights, she would only have received—according to Screen Actors Guild guidelines—$397,000.

In his cross-examination, Papiano tried vehemently to shoot down that claim. Peggy Lee, he argued, was not just another of Disney's anonymous voiceover actor. She was a star—the reason Walt gave her special privileges. No proof of that claim had surfaced, but it didn't matter; it gave the jury food for thought. So did the surprise move Papiano made while cross-examining O'Connell. He pulled out a multipage document and asked her if she had ever heard of Mary Costa, the voice of Sleeping Beauty. In his hand was Costa's contract with Disney. "Did Mr. Reardon tell you that Mary Costa has also filed a lawsuit?" he asked.

Reardon leapt out of his chair. "Oh, your honor, this is so improper!" he shouted. Accusing Papiano of "bizarre conduct," he asked that the question be stricken from the record. Lachs declined, but he turned to the jurors and instructed them to disregard it; the fact was irrelevant to the case at hand. Even so, they had heard it, and it may well have swayed them even more in Lee's favor.

Disney's witnesses surely did. In Blasband's view, Disney had made a "big mistake" by recruiting pretty Jodi Benson, the voice of Princess Ariel in *The Little Mermaid*, to testify in their defense. Benson was there to help convince the jury that actors worked with Disney for the honor more than the money—and that voiceovers were but small cogs in the epic splendor of a Disney vehicle.

Blasband cross-examined her. "She was so dazzled by Peggy," he recalled, "that I remember her testifying to the effect that whatever the jury wanted to give her, she deserved that and more. She greatly weakened Disney's position. She was probably the best witness we had except for Peggy herself."

Cheech Marin came close. Millions knew the Mexican-American comic actor as half of Cheech & Chong, the bong-smoking hippie hellions of motion picture and recording fame. Marin had made an unlikely leap to the Disney family of voiceover actors. Jeffrey Katzenberg had asked him to testify. But Marin happened to be a "big Peggy Lee fan," as he said later. "I knew all her songs; I loved *Lady and the Tramp* and *Pete Kelly's Blues*."

Now here he was, "a character reference for the defense," as he laughingly recalled in 2013. What Katzenberg wanted him to do, he explained, "was testify that actors in general and me in particular had done animated film because we wanted to do it for our children, and we didn't expect a lot of remuneration; that it was just a fun thing to do." In his brief appearance in the box he felt the probing gaze of Peggy Lee and the halo of compassion that surrounded her. "I mean, she was in a wheelchair in the courtroom," Marin recalled. The only way her team could have done better, he added, was "if they'd brought her in on a stretcher."

Under Reardon's examination, he stated that he, too, had only earned minimal rates for his Disney work. It was the prestige that mattered—and besides that, he wanted to make a movie that was clean enough for his kids to watch before they turned eighteen. Everybody laughed—even Peggy Lee. "I wanted to kind of make light of the situation," remembered Marin, "because I didn't have anything of evidential value to give." He slipped in a joke about his booking agency, International Creative Management (ICM), whose contracts, apparently, were just as ruthless as Disney's; ICM, he said, stood for "I Cover Myself." Once more, he saw Lee chuckling. "I thought, 'I'm cool with Peggy! That's cool!'"

The fun stopped when Reardon called his prime witness: company executive Roy Disney, Walt's nephew. Roy contradicted all Lee had said about Walt's generous nature. In matter-of-fact tones, he testified that his uncle knowingly paid flat fees so that his company could keep the profits. Voiceover artists in Disney films, he said, *never* got royalties. "Any inference that the Disney organization was skulking around looking to do her out of video rights is unfair," he announced. "You could pick up the contract and never think of videocassettes."

Furthermore, said Roy, the true stars of a cartoon film were the characters and the animators, not the voice actors. Lee was heard in the film for just a fraction of its running time, and her name didn't appear on the video box; even in the credits of the film, hers was one of twelve names acknowledged under the heading, "With the talents of"—nothing more. In no way could it be proven that her name had influenced sales.

Papiano glared at him and whispered to a colleague. Lee watched with hands folded and a look of contempt. Of all the slights she'd suffered, this was the worst: to have her work minimized as though it meant nothing. But in truth, her side could offer no proof that people had bought the tape because she was on it.

The trial had worn down a woman who already felt terrible. But according to her granddaughter Holly, who sometimes accompanied her, her visits to court were "in a way also a show for her, because fans were there; they would meet her, cheer her on. She loved seeing the people."

Time had come for the jurors to determine damages. Lee's counsel had named four issues for them to consider:

- that Buena Vista Home Video had breached Lee's contract by issuing the video without her consent;
- that they profited unlawfully from doing so;
- that Disney may have used the singer's name and voice without permission in its domestic promotion of the tape;
- and that Buena Vista *and* Disney—here regarded as separate entities—had done the same in its overseas marketing.

Lawyers for both sides had agreed that the jury should treat each category as distinct, and calculate separate amounts. But because the points were "alternative theories"—recovery on different theories for the same damage, which was breach of contract—Lee would receive only the largest award, *not* the sum of all four.

Concerned that the jurors might not understand, Blasband asked that their instructions be worded as clearly as possible. After some debate, the two sides settled on an explanatory line: "The award of damages is not cumulative." Blasband was still worried, however, and he asked Papiano to elucidate the rule in his closing statement.

On Friday, March 15, Papiano and Reardon spoke to the jury for the last time. Reardon held that Walt Disney had probably not intended for Lee to get anymore than she did. She may have been a big recording star at the time, he said, but in terms of voiceover work, she was a neophyte. To Papiano, the truth was all there in forty-year-old print. Disney's lawyers, he contended, now "wanted to rewrite history and rewrite the terms of this contract. She retained rights, and that's what she should be paid for." The issue about the tallying of awards went unclarified.

Monday, March 18, was deliberation day. Lachs sent written instructions to the jury room. The guidelines cautioned that Lee's songwriting for the film and her helpful suggestions to Walt Disney were not to be considered. By Wednesday jurors were done. Court reconvened that afternoon. Until then, there had often been many empty seats in the courtroom, which held about a hundred spectators. But for the grand finale of Peggy Lee vs. Walt Disney Productions and Buena Vista Home Video, the place was as packed as Basin Street East.

Excited murmurs followed the announcement of each award. For breach of contract, the jury had settled on a sum of $2,305,000. For Buena Vista's unlawful profiting from the tape, $500,000. For foreign distribution without compensation to Lee, $200,000 against Disney and another $200,000 against Buena Vista. And for Disney's unsanctioned use of Lee's name and/or voice in its U.S. distribution, $625,000.

Soon afterward, Neil Papiano enthused about this "victory" to Sharon Bernstein of the *Los Angeles Times*. Everyone hopes for more, he allowed, but this "$3.8 million award," he told Bernstein, was "a very nice number and a nice judgment."

His comment ignored the fact that, according to the unanimously agreed-upon rules, Lee would take only the largest award: $2,305,000. Disney vice president Ed Nowak rushed to set things straight. Lee sat in her wheelchair, seething. This was far from the fifty or even nine million she had hoped to get; legal bills and taxes would erase much of the award. Papiano, a big-time celebrity litigator, now had an unhappy client who wasn't known for keeping her feelings hidden. And reporters were outside, waiting to talk with her.

Back in court, he insisted to Lachs that the jury had misunderstood the rules, and had clearly intended to give Lee the full $3.8 million. "To take that away would be a complete distortion of the justice system!" he thundered. Lee, of course, agreed. "I believe I'm entitled to a new hearing," she said. "We had a very fine jury and the instructions they were given were very confusing. I didn't understand them."

Her counsel quickly prepared an affadavit for the jurors to sign, where they would confirm that, indeed, they had intended to give Lee the full $3.8 million. Everyone complied.

Just how effectively Lee had seduced the jurors became clear as they filed out of the courtroom and spoke to the press. "The message of the case is that a big company should treat Peggy Lee, or anybody, as a person," said Albert Fong. M'elena M. Kaplan saw Lee as the savior that had rescued Disney from a potentially fatal slump in the 1950s. "I think she turned Disney's business around," Kaplan told a reporter. "*Lady and the Tramp* is the movie that made Disney what it is today."

At a follow-up hearing on April 13, Lachs rejected the affidavits. He took a hard but defensible line: All had been explained to the jurors. If they hadn't understood, they were free to ask questions. Furthermore, he noted later, "Lawyers are supposed to use part of their final argument to explain things that they feel are important to the jury. It was Papiano's burden. He should have gone over that very, very carefully."

A weary Peggy Lee issued an "official" statement. "I accept the verdict for what it is," she said. "It will at least show other artists that they should never be afraid, no matter how big the organization is." Roy Reardon deemed her win "a compromise effort to reward an extremely sympathetic plaintiff."

Grasping at straws, Lee convinced her counsel to file a motion against Disney to recover an additional $473,313, the purported sum of every legal expense she had incurred since 1988—including xeroxing, the costs of her press conference, and whatever future expenses the case might require. The motion was denied.

Meanwhile, Disney announced plans to appeal the Lee judgment. As expected, the company now faced a feeding frenzy of similar lawsuits. "People are coming out of the woodwork," said Deborah Nesset, who had researched old Disney contracts meticulously. "A lot of these people are quite elderly. When the estate brings a lawsuit, it's not going to be as effective as the actual performer." Disney settled out of court with the Philadelphia Orchestra, which had played on the soundtrack of *Fantasia*, a huge seller on video. But suits by the heirs of the orchestra's conductor, Leopold Stokowski, and by the publisher of Stravinsky's "The Rite of Spring" (used in the film as background music), didn't fly. Nor did a 1991 action by the production company that owned the rights to Winnie the Pooh, a Disney staple.

The Mary Costa trial was set for May 28, 1991. Rather than invite more bad publicity, Disney made an out-of-court settlement. The previous December, singer Ilene Woods had filed a twenty-million–dollar suit against Disney over the video of *Cinderella*, whose title character featured her voice. Woods's contract lacked the wording that had spelled success for Peggy Lee. But the company paid her one hundred thousand dollars anyway. "If they didn't want my wife for something, we wouldn't have gotten any money," said Wood's husband, drummer Ed Shaughnessy, who had played on *Black Coffee*. "One way we got revenge was, if they wanted her to do an event, like an autograph show, we'd say we don't go anywhere for less than ten grand. That's what they had to pay."

It was a humbling time for the company, which according to the *Los Angeles Times* had suffered its "worst quarter in six years." Even Roy Disney softened his stance, at least verbally: "As the company gets bigger, it's easy for it to lose what we stand for." The *Times* quoted a nameless Disney executive: "When it comes to the hardball issue, we are guilty and we know it. We also know that we better change it. It's been win-win for us for a long time. But it's time we introduced some compassion and sensitivity into the process."

Disney kept *Lady and the Tramp* off the home-video market for years. In 1997, the company negotiated a small per-unit royalty for Lee and the estate of Sonny Burke, who had died in 1980. It wasn't retroactive; the deal began from the date of signing. As for the broader effects of Lee's victory, the case had merely made Disney and other studios much more careful in their wording of contracts. From now on, they retained rights to disseminate their films—as Cheech Marin said—in every form "that can possibly be invented on this planet or in any universe."

Where Peggy Lee was concerned, Disney refused to give up. The company filed with the California Court of Appeals. In October of 1992, they lost. "Then they tried to get to the California Supreme Court," recalled Blasband. The effort failed. Disney could plead the case no higher. Lee's check, Blasband said, "came very promptly after that." It contained approximately $1 million above the $2.3 million. Lee's counsel had managed to recover attorney's fees and interest, covering the time Disney had spent appealing. Out of Lee's money came attorneys' fees. Since a breach of contract award qualified as taxable income, the IRS would take out a sizable chunk.

Disappointed as she remained, Lee sorely needed the funds. "That battle depleted her," said Jane David, her new secretary. "She was mad that she had to work. She didn't want to anymore, really. But she had a household staff to pay. She had a home, a mortgage." Other expenses included the live-in cook who monitored Lee's diet, and the private nurse who came twice a day to check the diabetic singer's insulin level. No matter what, Lee still kept up appearances. David's duties included buying peroxide to maintain the star's platinum blondness. "But don't tell any-body," Lee cautioned her. "Everybody thinks it's real."

Through it all, David proved herself invaluable. A vivacious blonde with glasses, she was the girlfriend of publicist and record promoter Dick LaPalm, Lee's friend of forty years. David developed a genuine fondness for Lee. She persevered even when the star made her redo stacks of sealed letters because a few stamps weren't perfectly straight; or pack seventeen bags for one out-of-town show. "She was abusive, but I took it. I used to say, 'Miss Lee, because you sing so well, I'll let that one slide.' There were times when I'd say, 'I'm going home,' and I wouldn't come back for months. Then she'd send me a little peace offering, a gift."

Lee needed David's help, for work was coming in. It included shows in Melbourne, Florida; Palm Desert and San Carlos, California; and, first up, a concert with strings at the Pasadena Playhouse. This was her wel-come-back, and the sellout audience cheered their conquering hero. The "depleted" singer sang with a vigor and lung power that she hadn't shown since the 1960s. Lee never mentioned Disney by name; instead she sang "He's a Tramp," then added a remark that got the biggest laugh of the night: "I'm kinda glad I never was afraid of mice."

On the contrary, Lee could still "make a grown man cry," according to David. "I'd be sitting in the office, and there'd be men that had come for meetings—agents, musicians, lawyers. I'd see them walking out sniveling."

Gone from her band was John Chiodini, her guitar-playing muse, with whom she had written over a dozen songs. Like Paul Horner, Chio-dini had made an oral agreement with Lee to divide ownership of their collaborations equally. He saw her taking steps to edge him out, and he filed a lawsuit. The even split was restored, but not their friendship. He left Lee to join Natalie Cole, the singing daughter of Capitol Records' onetime favored son, Nat King Cole.

NOTHING THAT LEE DID—not even her war with Disney—could dis-suade the general public that she was above all else a tender, vulnerable creature. Softness remained her most powerful tool, a nightclub her most seductive setting. Lee would never find another Empire Room, but in 1992 she took the next best available option in Manhattan. Jerry Kravat, a

New York manager of cabaret artists, was the latest in a long line of aspiring impresarios who wanted to revive a long-lost supper-club glamour. That summer Kravat took over a function room in the New York Hilton at Sixth Avenue and Fifty-Third Street. Club 53, as he planned to call his new boîte, was still unbuilt when he heeded a tip from David Rothenberg, Lee's trusted Manhattan press agent, to present her.

Everyone knew she was intimidatingly costly and demanding. But to have her there would make Club 53 a true happening. Kravat signed her for five weeks, from July 28 through August 29. The forty-dollar cover charge, plus a ten-dollar minimum, made this the priciest cabaret outing in town.

But when Rothenberg's office released word of the engagement, the reservations book filled up. Opening night sold out the quickest—and still the club continued to book tables. Old-school celebrities would occupy some of them: the 1940s MGM star Gloria DeHaven; Eartha Kitt; lyricist Sammy Cahn, who had scored his first Oscar nomination in 1942.

On July 29, they and a well-heeled crowd of mature Peggy Lee fans were herded into a multilevel but nondescript club. Guests were squashed together elbow-to-elbow; waiters and waitresses forced their way through too many tables and tried to take orders. At 9:30—forty-five minutes after the show should have begun—dinners kept emerging from the kitchen, and "they were still stuffing tables onto the already-oversold floor," wrote Bob Harrington in *Back Stage*. Patrons started banging silverware on plates and glasses to try and get Lee onstage.

It worked. The room darkened and a quartet began the fanfare. A blinding flash of light hit a narrow entranceway to the left of the stage—and there she was, standing, though on the arm of Mike Renzi. She wore no glasses. Many of the fans present had seen her sail onstage with her mermaid figure at Basin Street East; now, as the band vamped and people cheered, Lee—a blizzard of shiny white from head to toe—labored her way to the swivel chair that awaited her, too many steps away, on a small corner platform. Would she make it? And if she did, what kind of sound would emerge from a face that was still puffy from prednisone?

After a painfully long entrance, Lee settled gingerly into her chair. She began "I Love Being Here with You" in a voice that had almost the same shimmer of old. Relief spread through the room, replaced by wonderment. "It was like a resurrection for her," said Rothenberg. The next day, a critic exclaimed: "When she sang, all those medical disasters evaporated and she was Miss Peggy Lee—cool, warm, sexy, in full command of one of the legendary instruments of American popular song. . . . She touched us with her will to live and with her singing, which is her reason for living." Everyone laughed at her familiar introduction to "Fever." Explained Lee: "I used to have a magic act, but I lost the rabbits. I decided that I would change it." She held out a palm, blew on it as though extinguishing a candle, and the room went to dark, save for the pinspot on her snapping hand. Swelling caused by diabetes had made it hard for her to snap, but Renzi and her other musicians—bassist Steve LaSpina, drummer Peter Grant, guitarist Jay Berliner, and saxophonist Gerry Niewood—kept the rhythm moving.

Reviving a swinging showtune she had recorded in the 1960s, Sammy Cahn and Jimmy Van Heusen's "Walking Happy," Lee got lost in its thicket of rhymes. She joked about it: "The smoke detector went off in my room and knocked all the lyrics out of my head." Yelled Cahn from his table, "Even when you sing it bad it's good!" The ever-eerie "Circle in the Sky" led into her heart-tugging finale, "I'll Be Seeing You." Lee's audience stood as one. Holding out her arms, Lee rose shakily to her feet. She lost her balance, and fell back into her armchair.

In the *New York Times*, Stephen Holden took a less sentimental view of the show. Through a combination of "will power, musicality, and professionalism," he wrote, Lee had managed "to project a fair degree of the old magic." With so much mobility gone, her minimalism served her well: "Miss Lee hasn't lost the knack of making small rhythmic gestures and subtle changes of intonation imply volumes of information."

For five weeks, New York treated Lee like a homecoming queen. Al Pacino came to the show and raved to her afterward, while eagerly posing for a picture with her. Lee had Jane David frame it for her. "She just couldn't believe that Al Pacino was such a big fan," David said.

One night, Lee's audience included the world's biggest and most provocative pop star. At thirty-four, Madonna had pushed themes of sexual boldness and female empowerment to lengths undreamed of by the blond temptresses she had studied, including Mae West, Marilyn Monroe, Nancy Sinatra, and Peggy Lee. A former Catholic girl from Bay City, Michigan, Madonna combated her inbred guilt and shame by wearing dominatrix drag onstage, miming masturbation, and mixing sexual and religious imagery to the point where she inflamed the Vatican. She seemed colder and tougher than Lee could ever be, but in many of her songs, such as "Rain," she cried out for a heart-to-heart connection, a little peace: "Rain, wash away my sorrow, take away my pain."

Rob Hoerburger of the *New York Times* saw a resemblance between the two stars: "Like Madonna, Lee was a Middle Country misfit who loaded up a small voice with sex." Both singers had lost their mothers at an early age; Madonna, likewise, deemed herself a "lonely girl who was searching for something." Lee had blossomed in a time of traditional femininity; no matter how tough show business had forced her to be, she was still "a woman, *w-o-m-a-n*," and yearned for a man's love. Madonna did, too, but her playing field was a steely wilderness of electronic beats and eight- and nine-figure financial stakes. Her singing emerged as soulless and cold, while Lee's was never less than sheer humanity.

She couldn't relate at all to Madonna's art; the couple of videos she'd seen appalled her. Lee conveyed sex by implication, not bludgeoning explicitness. As coquettish as she was onstage, and as sexually aggressive in private, blunt sex talk or displays made her very uncomfortable. Lee sensed the same sort of disconnect in Madonna. "I can't figure it out," she said. "Is it just a role she's playing, or what?"

Madonna's interest in Lee took wing in August 1992. The pop superstar was completing her dance album *Erotica*. Only one track, "Goodbye to Innocence," remained unfinished. According to her producer, Shep Pettibone, it "just wasn't working." He whipped up a new bass line. Apparently it reminded Madonna of "that lounge-lizard-act staple, 'Fever,'" said Pettibone, and Madonna sang snippets of Lee's hit instead. "It sounded so good that we decided to take it one step further and actually cover the tune," said the producer. "Too bad no one knew the words." According to Pettibone, Madonna called Seymour Stein, the cofounder and president of her label, Sire Records, a Warner Bros. subsidiary. Stein rushed over copies of Lee's and Little Willie John's versions. "I explained to her, you know, Peggy Lee was a great songwriter in the days when—forget about women—male singers weren't writing songs," said Stein. Madonna, he recalled, "was intrigued."

Word reached Lee that the "Material Girl" would be attending her show—an unimaginable coup at an engagement whose boldface names were mostly of the Hedda Hopper vintage. Sure enough, one night during the second week, the star and a sizable entourage made a conspicuous entrance into Club 53 just as the lights were dimming. They assembled themselves at a corner banquette. The group included her boyfriend and bodyguard Jimmy Albright, her publicist Liz Rosenberg, Stein, and Epic Records executive Eliot Hubbard.

They watched the show. Later, in an empty ballroom that Lee used as a greeting space, the blond vixens met and chatted. Madonna seemed "quite shy," recalled Lee, as she mentioned that she was a longtime fan. Lee was surprised at how "well-mannered" the superstar was—"a perfect little lady. She dressed impeccably." The next day, Lee called Phoebe Jacobs in delight. A bouquet of "beautiful cabbage roses" had arrived in her suite, courtesy of Madonna.

On August 15, Madonna recorded "Fever." Her techno dance treatment owed little to its forerunners. Whereas Lee's version sounded cool yet sultry, no degree of fever could warm Madonna, whose vocal had the robotic numbness of a drugged-out night on a disco floor. The record hit number one on *Billboard*'s Hot Dance Music/Club Play chart. She performed it on *Saturday Night Live* with body language appropriated from Peggy Lee—the outstretched arm and the snapping hand.

At 75 Rockefeller Plaza, the New York headquarters of Warner Bros. Records, Seymour Stein ran into writer David Munk, who worked in the building as an assistant to Gerald Levin, CEO of Time Warner. In an article on his blog, *Stargayzing*, Munk recalled Stein telling him proudly of having turned Madonna on to Peggy Lee. "Stein understood how cool Peggy Lee was," he wrote, "and I could see what a thrill he got from this music-publishing equivalent of a home run."

Madonna and Lee crossed paths again. On August 26, Sire artist and Peggy Lee fan k.d. lang made her Radio City Music Hall debut. Lang was riding high on the success of her album *Ingénue*, whose hit single, "Constant Craving," would earn the thirty-year-old singer-songwriter her third Grammy. Gerald Levin hosted a jam-packed afterparty for lang in the glass-roofed atrium of Remi, a midtown Manhattan restaurant. Munk stood among the VIPs, who were "corralled at the far end like penned-in animals." He spied a "commotion" across the room. It was Peggy Lee, enthroned in a wheelchair that a male attendant was pushing. "She was still every inch the great star: cloaked in a voluminous satin dress with fur trim and matching satin shoes; her white blunt cut wig shimmering in the light; her make-up just perfect; and, most perplexingly, a small bejeweled crown perched atop her wig."

Lee's helper struggled to roll her through a dense sea of partiers toward the velvet rope. "It was painful to watch, this terrific legend bumping into chair legs and roadblocks in her attempt to get to k.d. and Madonna. The whole time she smiled proudly; she handled what could easily have been considered an ignominious entrance with tremendous class."

Munk was standing next to the two young stars as they spotted Lee. He overheard Madonna's words: "Oh shit, where the fuck is *she* gonna go?"

"Moments later," said Munk, "when she finally rolled up at the feet of Madonna, the younger singer proved to be a far better actress than she had ever demonstrated on film, as she gushed over Miss Lee." Finally her attendant put Lee's wheelchair in reverse, and they began their long, labored exit. Having been consecrated by Madonna, the elder singer received bursts of applause as she rolled by. Lee was aglow. These world-renowned, chart-topping women loved her. At seventy-two, she was in.

———

LEE AND PHOEBE JACOBS boasted that Madonna wanted to star in a Peggy Lee biopic—"based, I'm sure, on that wonderful book," said Robert Richards. The film, of course, never happened. And while Madonna would eventually be named the greatest-selling female rock artist of the century, Peggy Lee made her final album on a tiny, Manhattan-based boutique label. Near the end of the Hilton run, Chesky Records invited her to turn the show's songs into a CD. Lee had never heard of Chesky; she only knew that it wasn't Capitol or A&M. But no other company had asked. And Chesky had a fine reputation, even if Lee didn't know it. The brothers who founded it, David and Norman Chesky, recorded quality jazz and classical music with state-of-the-art equipment, but they abhorred modern-day technical gimmickry. Chesky placed all singers and musicians together in one room and recorded complete takes, just as Lee had done in her Benny Goodman days.

She called the album *Moments Like This*. Chesky's audiophile miking captured an elderly voice, stripped of its beauty and most of its energy. But her weathered sound imparted interesting subtexts to songs she had introduced in her much younger days. On "Why Don't You Do Right?," the lass of twenty-two had become an old woman, her cry of defiance worn down to a vague mumble. In 1942, a whole big band had roared behind her; now just a drummer and a saxophonist remained. The man she was hounding to "get out of here and get me some money, too" might now have been an aged, doddering loser with a gin bottle. Given her vacant delivery, Lee could even have been singing to a dead man's ghost.

"Remind Me" had appeared on Lee's 1960 make-out album, *Pretty Eyes*. In that song, by Jerome Kern and Dorothy Fields, a starry-eyed woman plays hard-to-get, with a wink. Thirty-two years later, she sang each phrase haltingly, as though she truly needed reminding of how ardor felt. Mike Renzi, her sole accompanist, followed her gingerly, dropping a chord here and there to guide her way.

The track enchanted Diana Krall, a budding jazz singer-pianist who still lived in her native Canada. Krall loved Peggy Lee, and she adopted Lee's cool toughness, though not her vulnerability. Krall sought out Renzi and told him she loved his voicings; could she study accompaniment with him? They met several times, and Renzi gave Krall a push toward her career as the multiple-Grammy-winning, best-selling artist in jazz.

Not until 1992 had Lee begun to realize how many younger artists she had affected. Another was Gilbert O'Sullivan, the sweetly nerdish singer-songwriter from Ireland. O'Sullivan's number-one hit of 1972, "Alone Again (Naturally)," had spoken to the dejected lost soul in millions. They didn't know that, as a teenager, he had studied Peggy Lee's albums. "I was learning my craft," he explained, "and I couldn't have had a better teacher, in terms of interpretation."

In 1992, he sent her a new song, hoping his idol would consider a duet. "Can't Think Straight" tickled Lee's obtuse sense of humor. A phone rings; a boy has called his new girlfriend to beg forgiveness after their first fight. Her friend answers instead and becomes his mother-confessor. "My name is Peggy and I know how you feel / Same thing that happened to you did to me," she sings, while trying to talk sense into the sniveling lad.

Before she had left New York, O'Sullivan flew there with a finished backup track. The mundane lovers' quarrel in the song took on the camp majesty of a Bette Davis melodrama. An orchestra boomed with an over-the-top lushness; bells tinkled; a heavenly choir added mock gravity. In a recording studio, a crew and O'Sullivan waited for Lee. The Irishman didn't know her medical history, and his jaw dropped when an assistant wheeled her in with her oxygen tank. Once she was settled before a microphone, though, Lee sang with such sincerity that the silly scene became almost touching. Videographers captured a happy moment: Lee "counseling" O'Sullivan with a smile in her eyes as he watched her adoringly.

"Can't Think Straight" appeared on O'Sullivan's album *Sounds of the Loop*. When the track arrived at her home, Lee played it for some of her musicians. Its humor escaped them. O'Sullivan was dismayed when several British DJs declined to air the song—"because the Peggy Lee they remembered didn't sound like the Peggy that was on our record." Even so, it hit number fifteen on the British charts, and became a showstopper in his concerts, where he performed his part live while staring up at a projection of Lee singing in the studio.

Other famous fans of hers rushed to grab time with their ailing idol. The breathy-voiced smooth-jazz star Michael Franks enticed her to record a duet of his cotton-candy bossa-nova tune, "You Were Meant for Me." In 1992, k.d. lang managed to score a bedside lunch date. Lee had never seen the likes of lang, a gender-bending, lesbian successor to Patsy Cline. Like that pop-country legend, lang had a full-throated, golden sound, but sent up her tales of troubled love with a hint of a smirk. In the *New York Times*, critic Jon Pareles described her in terms that recalled Lee: "Her voice sounds at once sincere and utterly controlled; compared with the frantic display of most current singers, Ms. lang can seem to be singing in a surreal slow motion."

It was *Latin ala Lee!* that had gotten the teenage Kathryn Dawn Lang hooked—"profoundly," she said. At home in Edmonton, Canada, she and her roommate "just lived that record. We were, like, mental about her. I was a total country punker, but Peggy Lee was intravenous. She had a way of taking lyrics and putting them in bold metallic print right onto your heart." Amid the throbbing bongos and the congas, lang heard a lightning rod of truth. "It was astounding information that she gave me through her voice about phrasing. See, that's like being a good painter.

It's like knowing when the movement of the brush needs to stop or when it needs to go left. That's not an intellectual process. That is soul. That is direct contact with the muses."

Before lang had left Edmonton, Lee went there for an engagement. The young singer was "totally broke," but determined to meet her. Learning the name of Lee's hotel, she showed up, hoping to get *Latin ala Lee!* signed. "I just hung out all day like some sort of weird stalker, waiting for her to walk past. And she did." Lee didn't have much time for her; but lang, undaunted, went to the lobby of the theater where Lee was singing and waited night after night, hoping to get inside. "Finally the manager felt so sorry for me he let me in."

Less than a decade later, lang was seated in Lee's bedroom in Bel Air. "Miss Lee loved k.d. lang's singing," said Jane David, and the star gave her a royal welcome. "She whipped out all her special satin," David recalled. "The bed was all made." The young star was "not dressed for the occasion," David said, and Lee momentarily froze; with her old-Hollywood vision of femininity, she could never have appreciated a woman whose androgynous look sometimes got her mistaken for a man. But lang's sincere awe won her over. Lunch was rolled in on a cart by Robert Paul, the bearded, handsome youth who had come aboard as her right-hand man. There in bed, Lee tossed a salad for two, then morphed into the Peggy Lee that lang had always hoped to find. After lunch, lang kicked off her boots and crawled up on the bed with Lee, who took out a small electric keyboard. The women talked music and "far-out subjects," said Lee, like "philosophy and metaphysics, which I've studied for about forty years."

Lee had a far more prickly rapport with Mel Tormé, even after nearly a half-century of acquaintance. But with so few singers of their ilk left, they had agreed to their first of three autumnal pairings. On July 17 and 18, 1992, Tormé and Lee appeared at the Hollywood Bowl as fellow guests of the Los Angeles Philharmonic. As ever, they were oil and water. Lee's badges were small-scale nuance, interpretive mystery, and heart; Tormé was a vocal exhibitionist intent upon creamy perfection of tone and daredevil gymnastics.

Mike Renzi, who played for both, observed "a lot of phony friendliness" between them. But as fellow singer-songwriters and survivors of a fading genre, they were rivals. Their clash of egos didn't surprise Ellie Fuerst, who had known them for decades. "Mel Tormé was a very, *very* difficult person," said Ellie, the wife of George Shearing's early manager, Ed Fuerst. "Mel was so multitalented, but anger and spitefulness penetrated everything he did. He was a man who wanted and needed all the attention, and he did some very mean-spirited things to see that he got it."

Tormé made sure that in all their shared concerts, Peggy Lee would open for him. In his set at the Bowl he appropriated two of her trademarks, "Why Don't You Do Right?" and "When the World Was Young." At sixty-six he remained in peak vocal form, but Lee got a far more emotional response; and at the close of her set, the audience of eleven thousand stood up. Comic actor Jay Mohr was there. After Lee had left the stage, he recalled, "The Hollywood Bowl emptied to about half-full. Her crowd wanted no part of Mel." During his set, said Mohr, Tormé "really goofed off." At the end, he thanked the remaining viewers for "this wonderful *sitting* ovation."

Lee returned for three duets with Tormé. Her critic friend Leonard Feather stayed faithfully in her corner. In the *Los Angeles Times*, Feather wrote: "She was able to walk onstage and sit down to offer glowing evidence that the Lee timbre, the Lee phrasing and the Lee sensitivity are undiminished."

From then on, though, she had few chances to display them. Lee rang in 1993 with a show at the Beverly Hilton hotel; that year she played the Concord Pavilion in Concord, California, and Ruth Eckard Hall in Clearwater, Florida. Critics and loyal fans were never less than enthralled. But often during intermission, her granddaughter overheard "hurtful things" in the aisles or the ladies' room. "Women in particular were brutal about her appearance," Holly said.

It was safer for Lee to linger in bed and sing to Baby, her cat. "What she really needed was a girlfriend," said Jane David. "She had alienated so many people over the years." As before, the bedroom TV provided steady company. Whenever a violent show or news report came on, Lee joked to David: "As long as it stays in the TV set we'll be OK."

The women spent hours doting on Baby, the second queen of the household. David groomed the purring cat with a silver brush and comb, and she and Lee would polish Baby's jewelry. The cat lapped water from a silver-and-crystal bowl; in the morning, Lee would feed her bits of bagel and lox from the breakfast tray.

On rare occasions, David coaxed Lee out into the world. José Prado would drive the women into Beverly Hills, where Lee shopped or went to the dentist. Wheelchair-bound, with Baby in her lap, Lee ran into acquaintances and fans. Frequently, David's heart sank. "People would stop her and say, 'What *happened* to you?' People don't want to see an aging star. That's why she pretty much stayed in the house."

Holidays were still honored in the Lee home. Before her Easter dinner parties, she would send David out to buy rabbit ears and bonnets for the guests. In December, Lee dispatched David to Neiman Marcus with an extravagant holiday shopping list. One year, although she could ill afford it, each recipient got cashmere.

As Lee faded from the public eye, she grew more and more depressed. Requests for signed photos and fan letters poured in; Lee answered them all. But some of the mail, she confessed, "makes me want to weep, because they think I've retired already." David tried to cheer her by playing videos of her old TV appearances; she kept the conversation focused "on her successes, on the good things. When she got press, any kind of clipping, I'd lay it out." But Lee felt herself disappearing, and she continued to voice her longtime plea: "Don't let people forget me."

On May 11, 1994, she saw overwhelming proof that they hadn't. An organization called the Society of Singers had taken up the cause of vocalists in financial need. Cofounded by former singer Ginny Mancini, the wife of Henry Mancini, SOS raised much of its funding through gala tribute shows in honor of various singing legends. In 1989, the group's "Ella" award had gone to the star for whom it was named. The next year, Lee sang at a seventy-fifth-birthday salute to Frank Sinatra. Handsome Hollywood tenor Tony Martin had won the Ella in 1992. Now it was Lee's turn.

George Schlatter, former general manager of Ciro's who had graduated to TV producing—*The Judy Garland Show* and *Rowan and Martin's Laugh-In* ranked high on his résumé—set out to give this siren of his youth the celebration of a lifetime. All would gather at the sumptuous International Ballroom of the Beverly Hilton hotel in Beverly Hills. Lee set out to look as glamorous as she possibly could. With David's help, she slipped into a voluminous, robe-style white satin gown trimmed with mounds of fluffy white fur. On went her dark sunglasses, big dangling earrings, a glittery necklace, a bracelet of colorful stones, and several rings, which drew the eye to her talon-length, peach-painted nails. Lee painted on her biggest, reddest lips ever. She wore her own hair, parted in the middle and tied in a short chignon. Out of it stuck a Peggy Lee rose.

Lee was due at the Beverly Hilton in the late afternoon for the pre-show reception and photo shoot. A limousine waited in the driveway outside her door. Robert Paul helped Lee out of her wheelchair and into the backseat, where she sat with Baby and Jane David. The car took off.

No one anticipated the comic turn of bad luck that happened next. The limo stalled on Wilshire Boulevard in Westwood, which bordered Beverly Hills. Her driver quickly ordered a replacement, but Lee couldn't wait. She ordered Paul to push her in her wheelchair to the Beverly Hilton—two miles away. No one could dissuade her. While David waited in the limo, Paul rolled Lee for blocks. Finally they managed to hail a cab, and at last the guest of honor arrived at the hotel in her movable throne.

Paul moved her to a central spot in the jam-packed reception room. All over it were tuxedo-clad older men and surgically altered, senior Beverly Hills glamour girls, swathed in fussy sequined or beaded creations and fresh from the hairdresser's. The celebrity guest list was like an episode of *The Hollywood Palace* come to life: Tony Martin and his wife, dancer Cyd Charisse; 1960s TV stars Connie Stevens (*77 Sunset Strip*) and Hugh O'Brian (*The Life and Legend of Wyatt Earp*); comic Jack Carter, an Ed Sullivan regular; campy Latin bombshell Abbe Lane. But Lee was the snowy-white center of attention. As guests stood in line to congratulate her and flashbulbs popped, she basked in their loving praise. "This is incredible!" she exclaimed. "It's like a movie of my life."

Just before showtime, the star and her entourage were placed at a long center table strewn with pink roses. Lights dimmed, and the festivities began—a cavalcade of spoken tributes, archival footage, songs from a huge choir and a parade of pop and jazz luminaries. Ruth Brown, the R&B pioneer known as "Miss Rhythm," sang "Fever" in the Little Willie John style; Rosemary Clooney recalled *Latin ala Lee!* with "Heart," backed by a quartet of tuxedoed men chiming, "*corazón!*" Joe Williams, the singer whom Count Basie had called his "Number-One Son," spoke of his youthful thrill at hearing Lee's early Capitol single, "What More Can a Woman Do?," in a black record store in Chicago. Jack Jones reprised his 1966 cover of "The Shining Sea"; Natalie Cole upped the funkiness of "I'm a Woman." k.d. lang told of how she had tried, to no avail, to copy Lee's phrasing. Then she sang "Black Coffee" and one of her favorite tunes from *Latin ala Lee!,* Cole Porter's "I Am in Love," as no one but she could.

Lee had nixed an appearance by Jim Bailey, whose 1970s impersonation of her was too close for comfort. But Cleo Laine, Johnny Mathis, Beatrice Arthur, and the Manhattan Transfer all met her approval, as did the 1950s Hollywood beauty turned cosmetics mogul, singer-actress Polly Bergen. The crowd cheered when Bergen chided Disney for having tried to deny Lee "what she truly deserved for her contribution to one of their major hits." Lee's triumph, Bergen added, "opened the door for all artists whose work hasn't been properly acknowledged and compensated." She peered into the audience in mock search of Disney's top brass: "Are you here, Jeffrey? Michael? I live in Montana. To hell with them."

After ninety minutes of salutes, a spotlight sought out Peggy Lee. Everyone turned in her direction and joined in a standing ovation. Once the clamor died down, she spoke. The audience hung on her every slow, measured word. "It's been said by many great philosophers that love is the greatest force in the universe. And I think I've felt and heard more love here in this room tonight, and I . . . I know that *that* is the shining truth." Lee talked empathetically of how "really rough" a singer's life could be, then saluted SOS for stepping in to help—"quietly and with dignity. I don't think I'd better say much more, or I'll cry. I'll try singing."

A night of full-throttle vocalizing and effusive testimonials closed with the sparest, most leisurely, intimate, but heartfelt statement of them all: Lee's version of George and Ira Gershwin's " 'S Wonderful" (" 's marvelous, you should care for me . . .") set to a languid bossa nova beat by Mike Renzi. Lee hadn't lost the rhythm that had enchanted musicians for over fifty years. A recording found its way to São Paulo, Brazil, and into the hands of author and former bassist Zuza Homem de Mello, the country's most widely regarded expert on popular music. In Lee's singing he found the *leveza* (lilt) that had defined the bossa nova. He marveled at "the ease with which Peggy Lee floats above the beat, independent of it," with an "irresistible rhythmic movement" to guide her along.

Clearly, there was still life left in Peggy Lee. The day after the tribute, her phone rang almost nonstop with congratulations on how beautiful she had looked and sounded. But once the messages died down, Lee had little more to look forward to. Holiday time remained a special ritual. The singer lay in bed creating an elaborate Christmas Day menu, which Jane David had printed for guests as they arrived. The staff ordered a white pine tree for the living room; José Prado decorated it with balloons and strings of white bulbs. "Then we'd make a baby one for the bedroom," said David—a twinkly beacon of whiteness for Lee to stare at from her bed like a child on Christmas Eve.

The New Year brought her several milestones. On March 1, 1995, the National Academy of Recorded Arts and Sciences (NARAS) gave Lee a Grammy Award for Lifetime Achievement. Lee had earned twelve nominations, but won only once, for "Is That All There Is?" Now she sat in her wheelchair amid the audience at the Shrine Auditorium in L.A. as she received her trophy. Later she watched the singer whose name alone made her cringe—Barbra Streisand, twenty-two years her junior—accept her own Lifetime Achievement award onstage, presented by Stephen Sondheim.

June 23 reunited Lee with one more inescapable nemesis. For the first time in her career, jazz impresario George Wein had booked her to play his legendary summer series—first known as the Newport Jazz Festival, now called the JVC Jazz Festival. At seventy-five, Lee would sing at Carnegie Hall, the stage of her dreams since 1938, when she read about her then-hero Benny Goodman's spectacular debut there. The bad news: Lee would again open for Mel Tormé.

In an obvious gesture of one-upmanship, she decided to hold an "intimate press reception" on the day before the show to announce *her* Carnegie Hall concert. To organize it, she hired Chen Sam, Elizabeth Taylor's press agent. Lee would greet the media in a large conference room at Le Parker Meridien, the hotel where she was staying, down the block from Carnegie Hall.

Well before the three PM starting time, a table outside the conference room was arrayed with tall coffee urns, stacks of cups, and dozens of nametags for the invited journalists. At 2:55, the objects remained nearly untouched. Lee hadn't anticipated such intimacy: only five journalists were inside, waiting in the front row of folding chairs. A very nervous Sam and her assistants stood in the back; Phoebe Jacobs paced around, expecting a storm.

Sam held off as long as she could, but when no further press arrived, Lee was wheeled out by her longtime friend and former flame, producer William Harbach. She had dressed with ladylike care in a black satin dress and matching cap. Lee made light of the mortifying moment: "Do you think they all got stuck in the elevator?"

For the next half-hour, that handful of writers saw the many sides of Peggy Lee: charming, quick-witted, resilient, revisionist, and, between the lines, clearly angry. Lee told jokes, reminisced, and fielded questions. Several concerned her long-standing association with Tormé. Lee damned him with faint praise: "Mel has really come a long way in developing his voice," she said, smiling. Someone asked how she was doing. "I've been feeling fine," Lee answered cheerfully, "but my body's been quite broken. I spent about two and a half or three years in bed mending." Soon, she said, she would resume her unfinished book about her Disney experiences—a perfect response to Disney's new hit film, *Pocahontas*. "There he goes again, Mr. Eisner," said Lee. "They really got it from 'Fever.' But I wish him all the best with it. I was madly in love with Hiawatha, so I don't know how I feel about Pocahontas."

The conference ended, and Harbach rolled Lee to the elevator. Chen Sam and Phoebe Jacobs were quickly summoned to Lee's suite. Jacobs's prediction came true: "Peggy hit the ceiling."

The next day, as she prepared for the show, fear replaced her ire. "She was worried about how people would accept her," said Jacobs. "She was worried if she could make it vocally. She was afraid that she was a has-been." Her costar offered no comfort. Lee passed him in the Carnegie Hall stage entrance as Robert Paul wheeled her into the elevator. Tormé frowned and asked: "You're not gonna be in *that* when you're performing, are you?"

The New York audience didn't know what to expect, either. They hadn't seen her onstage since 1992, and Lee's health had been shaky then. Tension was high as Stan Martin, a DJ from the Manhattan-based nostalgia radio station WQEW stepped out to introduce her. Once he had spoken the line that made her fans' hair stand up—"Ladies and gentlemen,

Miss *PEGGY LEE!*"—Lee appeared from out of the left wing, on foot and holding tight onto Mike Renzi's arm. A roar erupted from the crowd of twenty-eight hundred, and it continued as Renzi led the star, tiny step by step, to a red swivel chair in front of her quintet. "One didn't know quite what to make of the lush, creamy pink apparition," wrote Gene Seymour of *Newsday*. "It seemed so fragile that one was almost afraid that the thunderous applause greeting its appearance would shatter it into a million crystalline pieces."

She purred the first words of "I Love Being Here with You," and relief swept through the house: Lee could still sing. "*WE LOVE YOU, PEGGY!*" shouted a fan. Lee called out: "I love you too! I missed you more than I thought I did!"

At times during the next hour, tempos grew so slow and the atmosphere so eerily still that the show felt like a séance. Attention stayed rapt, as though everyone, including the star, was trying to envision the Peggy Lees of the past. "That Old Feeling" reached back to 1944, when Lee was a gorgeous newlywed with an infant in a crib and a guitar-playing husband she thought was hers forever. "Mr. Wonderful," her 1956 hit, brought to mind the Lee of that time, with her gun-moll toughness and yearning eyes. She offered "Fly Me to the Moon" in memory of the first place she had sung it, Basin Street East, the mention of which set off a wave of applause. The woman whom Duke Ellington had deemed an authentic blues singer proved it in Lead Belly's "You Don't Know." Most of the audience had never heard her raise her voice; on this night she showed them she could, as she belted at the lover who had jilted her: "The flame that you left is still burnin' / Burnin' down deep in my soul!"

Lee had wished for years that she could leave out "Is That All There Is?"; tonight, at last, she did, along with "I'm a Woman." But Leiber and Stoller got their due in "Some Cats Know" from *Mirrors*, the album that now stood as a monument to Lee's courage.

She didn't omit "The Folks Who Live on the Hill." In 1957, when Lee had first recorded it, she still dreamed that she, too, might walk into eternity with the love of her life. She got the house, but she was there alone as she faced the end. For Sidney Myer, who had seen her shows for twenty-five years, the impact of this one hit him in a single riveting second. It followed the line, "And when the kids grow up and leave us"—

lyricist Oscar Hammerstein II's signal of freedom for the aging couple. "She stopped, and slumped back in the chair," said Myer. "And it looked like she was experiencing what she was singing about. It was like letting go. Desertion. Defeat."

Her allotted time was almost through. "I have to leave very quickly," Lee noted. "Mr. Tormé is coming out here." By way of farewell, she looked into the great beyond with "Circle in the Sky." It led into "I'll Be Seeing You," which had never seemed more final. As a standing ovation thundered, Renzi walked Lee off of the last New York stage she would ever inhabit.

Minutes later, an emotional Phoebe Jacobs spoke to a journalist in the lobby. "You will never know what it took to get her up there," she revealed.

Reviews treated her as the headliner. In the *Times*, Stephen Holden wrote that Lee remained "a master of the small gesture that has earth-shaking implications." Her ballads, he said, "had the sad and disturbing quality of someone trying to remember an elusive dream."

For weeks to come, Robert Richards, who had seen Lee's show, kept running into performers who were her grandchildren's age, and had experienced her for the first time on June 23. "They said, 'No wonder she's so legendary! Oh, she was so great!'"

August 2 found Lee at the Hollywood Bowl, this time on a triple bill with Tormé and the George Shearing Quintet. Shearing, who opened, had resented Lee ever since 1959, when the two had clashed while recording their album *Beauty and the Beat!* Backstage before the Bowl show, Lee sent a note to Shearing's dressing room, asking him if he and his group might consider joining her for a song. The pianist read it and fumed for all to hear at the mere suggestion that he would consider such a thing. At the rehearsal, said Stella Castellucci, Tormé and Shearing "completely ignored her. She was very hurt."

Prior to her entrance, Emilio Palame, her pianist that night, had never seen Lee more afraid. "She cared so much about what people thought of her. Every gig was, 'Do you love me?' She wanted that feeling all the time. She was an artist. And she took it really seriously. She wanted people to know how much it meant to her. She wanted to connect with them. To have them feel what she felt."

Seated and obviously infirm, she began her set with a wink by reviving "I've Got Them Feelin' Too Good Today Blues" from *Mirrors*. But nerves, and the cavernous Bowl, seemed to swallow her up. Warm but restrained applause followed every song. On came Tormé, primed to kill. He opened with "You Make Me Feel So Young"—"which no doubt he did in Lee's pink and teary wake," wrote Tony Gieske in the *Hollywood Reporter*. As with their other shows, however, swarms of people left after Lee's segment, and the receiving line backstage was "endless," Castellucci recalled. Lee stayed for nearly two hours, greeting everyone. She left in a somber mood. "Maybe she knew it was her last time," said Castellucci.

On August 26, the harpist accompanied her to Group IV Studios in Hollywood, where Lee made her last recording. It was a single track on *Benny Carter Songbook*, an anthology of tunes written by the great tenor saxophonist and arranger. Lee and Carter had been friends and collaborators since the 1940s. And although the song assigned to her, "I See You," was weak, she couldn't refuse him. With the eighty-eight-year-old playing behind her, and Lee in weary but controlled voice, one of her fondest musical teamings had its last hurrah.

Lee looked forward to appearing on Tony Bennett's *Concert of Hope*, an all-star CBS special to be taped on October 16 at the Pantages Theatre in Los Angeles. It would benefit the National Center on Addiction and Substance Abuse. As the day approached, Lee hadn't the strength to sing, but she did attend. On December 7, she went to the Society of Singers tribute to Steve Lawrence and Eydie Gormé. From her wheelchair, she feebly sang "I'm Glad There Is You." It was her last public performance.

Her friend Frank Sinatra had grown just as frail; for years he had needed teleprompters to get through his shows. But on July 11, 1996, Lee honored an invitation from Sinatra and went to Malibu, where he and his wife Barbara were celebrating their twentieth anniversary by renewing their vows. Getting Lee out of bed, dressed, made up, and in her wheelchair was an ordeal for Jane David; they arrived at the Our Lady of Malibu Catholic church well after the ceremony had begun. At the end, as he made his way down the aisle with his wife, Sinatra spotted Lee in the back. He rushed over to give her a hug. His concern meant more to her than almost anyone's, and Lee left the reception elated.

Sinatra had sung for the last time over a year earlier. But Lee still

had hope. "I intend to sing again, God willing," she told Ray Rogers of
Interview. "Once in a while I just try it out to see if it's still there—and it
is." She told David of her dream to do a farewell tour, including Europe.
"But first," Lee said, "I need to find out what's going on with my heart."
She mentioned her diabetes, too, as well as the mysterious polymyelitis,
"which is terrible, like having arthritis all over your body."

Medical scares occasionally sent Lee to the hospital, but she didn't
want any ambulances pulling up to the house in view of the neighbors.
She insisted that David drive her. "On the way, she's telling me, 'Take the
back roads!' I said, 'Miss Lee, no one would ever believe that it's you in
my Honda!' All she could think of was bad publicity. Just to make her feel
better I took the side roads."

Yet the next glimpse she gave of herself was a sad one. Jerry Leiber
and Mike Stoller were basking in the success of a Broadway jukebox
musical of their songs, *Smokey Joe's Café*. Gene Davis, a documentary
filmmaker, fêted them in *Baby, That's Rock and Roll: The Story of Leiber
and Stoller*, which aired on the Bravo cable channel. Lee agreed to an
on-camera interview. A crew arrived at her home on February 25, 1997.
It included a stylist who, at Davis's behest, gave Lee a more natural look.
She wore her own hair, which hung straight down, along with a peach
blouse and pearls. Remarkably, a glimmer of the young Peggy Lee shone
through. But she seemed in pain, and the few remarks Davis could glean
from her revealed a mind that had begun to drift. "In the case of 'I'm a
Woman,'" she said, "I didn't write that as a political . . ." Silence. "I didn't
write that, come to think of it. Uh . . . Leiber and Stoller did."

One last outing awaited her. On May 20, 1998, David took Lee to
the Good Shepherd Catholic Church in Beverly Hills for the funeral of
Frank Sinatra. The hard-living star had died of complications from heart
and kidney disease, bladder cancer, and dementia, but he had made it to
eighty-two. The seven hundred guests included various stars who had
worked with Lee in better days: Joey Bishop, Tony Bennett, Anthony
Quinn, Steve Lawrence, Don Rickles.

Sinatra's passing gave Lee one more reminder of her own mortality.
The time had come for some honest self-reflection, notably with regard
to her ill health. "I did it to myself," she admitted. In the fall of 1998, Lee
shocked her daughter by telling her that she didn't think she would ever

sing again. "I never thought I would hear those words," said Nicki. Lee had always attended lovingly to fan mail and requests for signed pictures, but arthritis had caught up with her; now her tiny penmanship and familiar inscription—"With love, Peggy Lee"—looked too shaky for public viewing.

Lee's most faithful confidante was Kathy Levy, her longtime hairdresser. Levy now worked as a Beverly Hills realtor, but made ample time to sit at her friend's bedside. The two women reminisced of a sweeter past. Lee reflected: "What is it that happens, that suddenly you just turn around and it's gone? Was that a time pocket, a time warp? It just went, *zoop*, and everything is different."

In late October, Levy noticed some alarming changes in her friend. The right side of Lee's face looked stiff; she wasn't speaking much, and what she did say sounded slurred. "I'm having problems with my words,"

The Peggy Lee puppets, together in Bel Air.
(PHOTO BY JANE DAVID)

said Lee. The next night, Levy noticed that her friend's mouth was drooping. A night later, her face looked purplish. A private nurse was on duty; Levy warned her—to no avail—that something seemed wrong.

On the morning of October 27, Holly Foster phoned Levy at her office. Peggy Lee was in the hospital. Sometime in the night, the seventy-eight-year-old had suffered a stroke. Levy rushed to St. John's. She found Holly, her husband Dan, and Jane David at Lee's bedside. The star lay unconscious. Levy took Lee's hand. Slowly, the singer's eyes opened. She stared at Levy, then murmured: "Did I take care of you?"

"It doesn't matter! Take care of *you!*"

Lee spent the next four weeks in intensive care. Nicki and Phoebe Jacobs had flown in, but Lee didn't seem to recognize either of them, nor could she articulate words or swallow. The singer had suffered severe left-brain damage; no one knew to what degree, if any, she would recover. But at least she had survived. By January 1999, Lee still couldn't speak coherently, but she was stable enough to go home.

From now on, the daughter who had felt so disempowered would be in charge. After the stroke, Nicki had left Idaho and moved into one of her mother's upstairs bedrooms. "Nicki changed her attitude about her mother a lot during that time," said Levy. As concerned calls, cards, and gifts flooded in, Nicki, said Levy, "was just so amazed by how many people loved her mother"; she even talked about "how sweet she'd been to her."

A rigorous and costly program was set in place to revive Lee. It included physical, speech, and occupational therapists and five rotating, round-the-clock nurses. There were encouraging signs. One day in January, Nicki walked into the master bedroom to find her mother singing. "Didn't necessarily make sense but it sounded great," she said. Lee could clutch a visitor's hand tightly and make eye contact; she seemed to understand what people were saying. Every now and then a clearly voiced, if hallucinatory, thought came out of her mouth. "Virginia would say, 'Oh, my God, she's on the bus with Benny Goodman,'" recalled Jane David. "Then she'd talk about eating, like, 'I'll have one egg and a muffin.'" Then Lee would revert to babbling. "She had different words, a different language," said Kathy Levy. "But she was in quite a good mood about it." In March came an unmistakable sign of the Lee that Levy knew. For days the singer had been almost comatose. Levy was there when her friend suddenly came to. Lee glared at the ceiling and asked imperiously: *"Who picked this color?"*

For the next year and a half, her condition seesawed dramatically. There were many hospitalizations. In July, an MRI indicated that her brain was healing, but a month later she could barely communicate. Soon thereafter, she got a pacemaker. By December, pneumonia had set in. Still she rallied.

However dire her health became, Lee's living will had made one thing clear: any and all "heroic methods" of resuscitation were to be used to keep her alive. Lee hadn't seemed to realize, or care, that such methods might leave her a vegetable, or in chronic, excruciating pain. Certainly she didn't care what it might cost her or her family. The promises of Christ-like immortality in her favorite book, *Letters of the Scattered Brotherhood, had* to come true for her.

Back and forth she went from home to St. John's. Pets were banned there, but Jane David was sure that Lee missed Baby terribly. David began smuggling in the cat, using a wicker carrier. One night Baby scampered out of Lee's room and ran into another, "and just sat there with her big eyes. The next thing you know I'm evicted, never to come back." Undeterred, David came back the next day, Baby in hidden tow. A sympathetic doctor was in Lee's room. David boldly sat the carrier on the bed and opened the door. Out walked Baby, who immediately nuzzled up to Lee. The singer, who hadn't spoken coherently in some time, suddenly exclaimed: *"That's my friend!"* From then on, Baby was an authorized guest.

Each time Lee returned home, a little less of her remained. Certainly she was in no shape to fly to New York, where on June 9, 1999, she—along with Bruce Springsteen, Broadway and movie lyricist Tim Rice, "Fly Me to the Moon" composer Bart Howard, and (posthumously) Bobby Darin—would be inducted into the Songwriters Hall of Fame. Nicki collected the award for her.

Lou Levy was in his own dire straits, but typically he found humor in them. The pianist had undergone surgery for a brain tumor and survived, although not for long. In 2001, he collapsed and died in the kitchen of Max Bennett, his and Lee's longtime bass player. In his final days, Levy wrote his former boss a letter: "Dear Peggy, at last we are on the same level. I want a raise." Kathy Levy brought him over for a visit; she was pleased to hear the singer laughing in response to his jokes—proof that she understood more than she seemed to.

Otherwise, silence and emptiness now filled 11404 Bellagio Road. "It's very strange, like being in a dream," said Kathy at the time.

Further changes were afoot. As so often happens with ailing stars of financial means—or with the promise of wealth to come—and no more ability to speak for themselves, a power struggle had erupted within Lee's inner circle. Certain longtime members found themselves removed. A few months after the stroke, Lee's attorney, Cy Godfrey, and Jon Hanson, the banker who served as her trustee and financial manager, fired Jane David. Given Lee's condition, Jane was ostensibly no longer needed. But the true reason for her release, she thought, was her outspokenness about Lee's care.

Kathy Levy looked with increasing dismay at the goings-on in the house. She detailed them in a letter to Godfrey. Levy mentioned the nurse who had ignored her warnings about the apparent danger signs prior to Lee's stroke. Another of Lee's nurses should have noticed them; now she denied responsibility. The emergency-room doctor, Levy claimed, had reported some disturbing news: Lee's stroke had begun at least eight hours before she reached the hospital.

After the stroke, continued Levy, she had complained to Hanson, but the nurses were still there. Nicki had been smoking with one of them in her bedroom—"which Peggy never has allowed in her home." Levy wrote of Nicki's barking dog and of visits by Chileta, Dave Barbour's final partner, whom Lee had never allowed there. The singer, semiconscious in a hospital bed, "gets nervous and keeps asking, who's that?" But Hanson saw no wrongdoing, Levy said, and insisted that Lee was at peace. That letter, and a follow-up a week later, got Levy temporarily banned from the house.

She wasn't welcome at St. John's, either. Her barely lucid friend lived there as grandly as she had at the Waldorf Towers. Lee occupied an executive suite with a bedroom, a waiting area, private nurses, and a full-time guard. The costs—approved by her representatives—were draining Lee's already parched resources. One day Levy barged in and sailed past the guard, who tried to eject her. "I'm not leaving," she said, while moving to the opposite side of the bed. "Peggy was starting to laugh," recalled Levy, "because she knew damned well I wasn't leaving." A nurse finally said, "She's okay," and waved the guard away.

"Where . . . where have you . . . been?" stammered Lee.

"I'm here now," Levy said.

But nothing could halt Lee's deterioration. By February she had begun having seizures. A month later, she seemed barely cognizant. "She seems peaceful, off somewhere," observed Levy.

Lee was home on May 26, 2000, her eightieth birthday. Nicki had organized a party, complete with cocktails and a buffet, and invited Lee's closest friends and family members. Stella Castellucci played harp, adding a celestial air to this celebration of a woman who was evanescing more each day. Lee had been brought out in her wheelchair; a line of people waited with pasted-on smiles, ready to offer strained congratulations. Lee could only mumble in response, except for one phrase that Nicki overheard and repeated to Castellucci: "I don't want this."

Months passed, and a woman who seemed on the brink of death hung on. So many times she had defied expectations and rebounded from doom; several friends insisted that Lee would outlive them all. "Oh, she's gonna get out of that bed," declared Virginia Bernard. Levy wishfully agreed: "She's gonna get well, and she'll come in here and kick our asses like she always does." Lee Ringuette came to visit, and marveled how healthy his aunt looked: "She had a little makeup on. The stroke and its attendant problems had caused her to lose weight. Her diabetes had gone away."

Much of the time Lee lay with her eyes closed, but she sometimes responded to visitors. "She hugged me," said Dona Harsh, who came to visit with their friend Jeanne Hazard, wife of Lee's arranger Dick Hazard. "She smiled, and seemed happy. Her hair, which had been bleached all those years, was now brown, and it didn't have one gray hair in it." Then Dick arrived. "The minute that a man walked in she came to life," said Harsh. "She absolutely loved men."

According to Ringuette, Lee finally lapsed into a coma. The singer missed hearing a piece of news she would have liked. In 1999, Cy Godfrey had filed a class-action suit against the Universal Music Group, which owned the Decca Records catalog. Godfrey had charged Universal with underpayment of CD-reissue royalties to Lee and 160 other artists of her era, or to their estates. He set the damages at $4.75 million. On January 14, 2002, a judge issued a preliminary ruling (later confirmed) against Universal. The win would bring some much-needed income to Lee's family; her long-term medical bills and spendthrift lifestyle had nearly crippled her financially. According to Bernard, the singer's Screen Actors Guild insurance coverage had finally run out, and she owed an enormous sum to St. John's.

As Godfrey later told a reporter, he preferred to believe that somehow Lee knew of this latest David and Goliath victory, and could at last let go. The doctors at St. John's sent Lee home; they could do nothing more to help her. On Monday, January 21, Lee was back in the bedroom where she had long felt safest. Nicki, her three children, Bernard, and José were there. Around ten in the evening, Holly called Kathy Levy and told her to get to the house as quickly as possible. Levy jumped in her car and raced through the Hollywood Hills. As she hurried through the front door of 11404 Bellagio Road, she passed Nicki, who said, "I have to warn—" Levy ignored her and raced into the bedroom. She'd arrived too late. Just moments before, Peggy Lee had died of a myocardial infarction—a heart attack.

"I touched her," said Levy. "She was still warm. I just stood there and said, 'Thank you, thank you, *thank you* for everything." Levy held her friend's hand until it turned cold.

Epilogue

*L*EE'S MEMORIAL TOOK place on Saturday afternoon, February 2, at the luxurious Riviera Country Club in Pacific Palisades. The scenic West Los Angeles neighborhood was known for its multimillion-dollar homes, movie-star residents, and views of the Santa Monica Mountains. Nicki, who arranged the event, had spared no expense; this was "Peggy Lee's last party," as the *Los Angeles Times* called it. A reported 450-plus guests filled several large rooms; they milled around tables of rich food and sweets. "There were roses on every flat surface," wrote the *Times*. "White-coated waiters passed hors d'oeuvres to guests who wore diamonds and furs."

All over the Riviera were luminaries from the golden age of supper clubs and TV variety shows—Kay Starr, Steve Lawrence, Andy Williams, Jack Jones, Nancy Sinatra, Buddy Greco, Dolores (Mrs. Bob) Hope—and a few contemporary figures, such as k.d. lang. Lee's hit songs filled the air, played by two bands stocked with her pet jazzmen: Frank Capp, Max Bennett, John Pisano, Emilio Palame, John Chiodini. Ninety-four-year-old Benny Carter braved the crowds; so did Billy May, then eighty-five. Scores of Lee's friends and employees, including Brian Panella, Robert Strom, Virginia Bernard, and José Prado, reunited for one last time.

The ceremony began. After some sugar-dusted sounds from harpist Corky Hale—who had played at Lee's 1953 wedding to Brad Dexter, and later married Mike Stoller—Reverend Mark Vierra of the North Hollywood Church of Religious Science took over. He recalled the Ernest Holmes philosophies by which Lee had tried to live—that God and the Kingdom of Heaven were within everyone, and that the power of the mind could control all.

There were tasteful reminiscences by Cy Coleman, Johnny Mandel, Leiber and Stoller, Nicki, and the grandchildren; and sassier ones by Phoebe Jacobs. Wearing a pair of Lee's tinted glasses and one of her hats, she drummed up knowing laughs when she said: "When she was good, she was very good, but when she was bad . . ." As a finale, Lorraine Feather, the jazz-singing daughter of Leonard Feather, sang the star's sentimental closers, "Circle in the Sky" and "I'll Be Seeing You."

The next day it was back to cold reality, as Lee's family and business associates faced the task of sorting out her messy finances. Jon Hanson had been appointed executor of the will. For all her sincere desire to leave a secure future for Nicki and the three grandchildren, Lee's insistence on living like a star had brought more headaches than riches.

Profits from the sale of her "home on a hilltop high" in pricey Bel Air had proven disappointing; an unchecked problem with mold had caused structural damage that sank the value. On August 29, 2003, Lee's house was sold for $1.8 million, and later demolished. Further downsizing occurred when Cy Godfrey and Jon Hanson were released from the family employ. Nicki Lee Foster returned to Idaho. Despite serious illness, she turned seventy in 2013. Holly Foster-Welles took on the job of running Peggy Lee Productions from her home in Los Angeles, and doing her best to maximize her grandmother's legacy.

DESPITE HER FEARS, THERE was no immediate danger of the world forgetting Peggy Lee. In *Pulse* magazine, Justin Green, a cartoonist known for his cheeky comic-strip recountings of famous lives, sketched out the panoramic journey of the star whose "Fever," he wrote, was "one of the greatest torch songs/mating calls ever recorded." He reached a conclusion that Lee would have liked: "While other singers might be emblematic of fads and brief epochs, the greater part of the twentieth century belongs to Miss Peggy Lee."

In the twenty-first century, when commercial pop is overrun by a fleet of Auto-tuned robots, lip-syncing onstage to prerecorded vocals and camouflaged by smoke and mirrors, the achievement of Lee—who sang unaided by anything except musicians, lighting, and a microphone, and who exposed her heart at every show—seems even grander in its humanity.

Jazz singers revere Lee unanimously. "I love everything about her; her elegance, her wit," said Diana Krall. "She is one of the greatest influences in what I do as an artist." But her impact has proven far more pervasive than that. Since her death, Lee's voice has turned up on the soundtracks of numerous TV shows (*Six Feet Under*, *Mad Men*, *Las Vegas*, *Cold Case*, *Bones*, *The O.C.*, *Chuck*, *Doctors*) and films (*The Curious Case of Benjamin Button*, the 2005 remake of *King Kong*, *Savages*, *Gangster Squad*). It adds film noir intrigue to any scene, even with a song as bright as "It's a Good Day."

"Fever" and "Is That All There Is?" have surpassed nostalgia to take on a deathless mystique. Covering either song is risky, but many singers have tried. In 1980, Cristina Monet, a French-American New Wave songstress, joined with Kid Creole and the Coconuts to belligerently deconstruct "Is That All There Is?" in punk style. To a soundtrack of breaking glass, a police whistle, and a cuckoo clock gone berserk, Cristina yowled: "I remember when I was a little girl, my mother set the house on fire. She was like that . . . And then I met the most wonderful boy in Manhattan. We'd take long walks down by the river, and he'd beat me black and blue and I *loved* it!"

Leiber and Stoller were not amused. They had this "atrocity" yanked from the market, which only enhanced its cult appeal. "It wasn't a parody; I was quite serious," Cristina told Jeff McLaughlin of the *Boston Globe*. "The lyrics per se I thought could legitimately be made a springboard for an expression of a 1980s sensibility." Her version, like another by the arty British singer-songwriter P. J. Harvey, pushed the song's nihilism to the darkest limits. Harvey's "Is That All There Is?," made in 1996, had a dragging, drugged-out beat and a funereal organ. If Lee had sounded shellshocked but still yearning, Harvey was the numbest of fatalists, without enough spark left to break out the booze and have a ball.

That certainly wasn't so for Bette Midler. In 2005, the star paid whimsical and heartfelt tribute to Lee on the CD *Bette Midler Sings the Peggy Lee Songbook*, produced by Barry Manilow, her accompanist in the early 1970s. Midler, too, tried her hand at "Is That All There Is?," as did Tony Bennett and Chaka Khan. But no one who sang it could match Lee's mystery. The same held true for "Fever," which a profusion of artists have covered. In the first of two versions, Beyoncé aped the barebones bass playing and finger-snapping, but larded her vocal with as much melisma as anything on *American Idol.* Later the statuesque diva remade "Fever" in a Lee-inspired husky whisper.

She used that track to promote her fragrance, Heat. A video showed Beyoncé in a steam-filled bathroom, writhing as she spilled out of a red satin dress. Stephen Holden took a dim view of such displays. "Lee," he wrote, "could conjure more erotic sparks by lightly snapping her fingers, rolling her eyes and flashing the hint of a smirk than a dozen gyrating scantily clad pop sirens strutting their curves."

In Wimbledon, North Dakota, the Midland Continental Railroad Depot Restoration committee and its treasurer, Mary Beth Orn, rescued a link to Lee's past. The depot where Norma had lived and her father had worked—the only surviving one from the long-defunct line—was painstakingly restored and turned into a Peggy Lee museum. On view are depot artifacts, displays of Lee album covers and photos, and one of her 1950s gowns in a glass case. The launch took place on May 26, 2012. Many months later, the depot had an honored guest: Nicki Lee Foster. Despite impaired mobility, Nicki had made the trip from Idaho to see this shrine to her mother.

Other salutes came from surprising places. The instrument-smashing, stage dives, and savage drug abuse of Iggy Pop, the slithering, shirtless godfather of punk, would probably have distressed Lee, who liked her rock as soft as a pillow. But as a "symbol of unrepentant endurance," as the *New York Times*'s Jon Pareles called him, Iggy and Peggy had something in common. In 2007, record producer Mark Vidler did a mashup of Lee's "Fever" with Pop's "The Passenger," a punkster's answer to Jack Kerouac's *On the Road.* Pop was proud to be joined at the hip, electronically speaking, with Peggy Lee. "Peggy was a super-sassy super-hottie," he said. "Her phrasing was unlike any other white woman's. She had incredible confidence onstage. You could see she was justifiably thrilled with herself. She also had beautiful eyes and a bomb ass. There's nobody like her now."

In 2010, Lee entered the age of sampling. Marko Milićević, a Serbian DJ known as Gramophonedzie, took a chunk of her 1947 version of "Why Don't You Do Right?" and remixed it into his song, "Why Don't You?" He wound up with a number-one U.K. dance hit. In the video, a film noir–type babe appears at his door in a short sequined cocktail dress and stiletto heels, and lip-synchs to Peggy Lee.

The star's camp appeal wasn't ignored. In an act he debuted at the Manhattan cabaret Don't Tell Mama, booked by Sidney Myer, female impressionist Chuck Sweeney channeled the 1980s Peggy Lee—replete with white wig, tinted Coke-bottle glasses, swarms of feathers, and spacy patter. Two of Lee's dearest friends, Phoebe Jacobs and Mario Buatta, were seen in the audience, nearly doubled over in laughter. Sweeney's performance of "Fever" included a hyperactive pinspot and a high kick Lee could never have managed. "I do Pilates," murmured Sweeney. In Bay Ridge, Brooklyn in 2011, the Scandinavian East Coast Museum hosted a Peggy Lee Impersonation Festival, with men and women performing her songs in Lee drag. Seventy-one-year-old Bob Carlson dressed as late-period Peggy to sing "Mañana." "She'll be turning over in her grave if she saw my replica of her," said Carlson to *The Brooklyn Paper*. He added: "I hope I don't get wrapped up in one of my boas."

On June 23, 2003, a more august salute took place at Carnegie Hall as part of the JVC Jazz Festival; it was repeated at the Hollywood Bowl. *There'll Be Another Spring: A Tribute to Miss Peggy Lee* was produced by Richard Barone, a downtown New York alternative rocker and music producer. Pop and jazz songbirds past and present, including Petula Clark, Chris Connor, Nancy Sinatra, Jane Monheit, and Dee Dee Bridgewater, dominated both shows. The moody jazz minimalist Shirley Horn evoked the oasis of Lee's "The Folks Who Live on the Hill"; the growling folk-blues belter Maria Muldaur brought a Cajun bite to "I'm a Woman." Actress-singer Rita Moreno recreated the stark, early-morning bedroom scene of "Don't Smoke in Bed." Other women on the bill tried to channel Lee through off-the-shoulder dresses, boas, and purrs. Deborah Harry, former leader of the New Wave band Blondie, reached for camp irony by copying Lee's white-blond, hard-boiled look of the 1950s. But when she tried to navigate the Latin rhythms of "Lover" she wound up in a train wreck—demonstrating, once more, how Peggy Lee had made the difficult seem easy.

Lee's inscrutable smile, her simmering sexuality, her skewed sense of humor, the whiff of anger—all of it added up to that hard-to-define but compelling sense of less-is-more known as cool. Nowadays, said Barone, popular singing is "all about how loud and histrionic you can sound. Peggy could do barely anything and make her point. Most artists are love-me, love-me. She didn't force you to like her. You had to come to her. There was a lot left to the imagination. She wasn't overly smiley. She will always be cool."

But cool only works if something hot is bubbling beneath. That Pandora's Box of emotions has spoken to the young ever since the heydays of James Dean and Chet Baker—stars who knew the power of withholding. Tragedy was an essential part of the mix. Yet for all her crises, illnesses, and addictions, Lee was no Billie Holiday to the public. Instead she seemed tough and victorious—qualities that harked back to the iconic image of her snapping her fingers and barking "*Fever!*" with the sting of a well-cracked whip.

Playing the smiling vixen came easy to her. But Paul Pines wasn't surprised that Lee had died of a heart attack. "She was a brokenhearted woman," said the psychologist. No amount of luxury or universal adoration, it seemed, could ease the ache in Norma Deloris Egstrom. As doggedly as she told herself that "there is more," "Is that all there is?" became the key question of her life. The song was a lost soul's anthem in 1969, and it spoke to the angst in every generation that followed.

For Emilio Palame, the trembling tot in the first chorus wasn't so different from the Peggy Lee he knew. "Through all of what she went through," he said, "she still saw the world through those child's eyes." He glimpsed them in the face of the old lady in bed, clinging to her cat.

On CNN's obituary segment, Lee's favorite myth was revived as fact: days before his death, an announcer stated, Dave Barbour had proposed to her anew. Lee appeared onscreen in an early 1990s interview. "I was in agreement, I was going to marry him," she said.

Now she, like Dave, had made her final resting place at the celebrity-filled Westwood Village Memorial Park cemetery in Los Angeles. A bench-style monument in The Garden of Serenity, a columbarium, held her ashes. It was poetically engraved:

"Music is my life's breath"
Miss Peggy Lee
1920–2002
Angels on your pillow, Mama Peggy

One day Marion Collier, the second and last Mrs. Dave Barbour, went to Westwood to visit his gravesite. She was stunned to find that Barbour's ashes had been moved from their original spot to a place below Lee's bench. Nicki had maneuvered the switch, and reserved spaces for herself and her children. Mother and daughter would join together peacefully in death as they seldom had in life. Meanwhile, Peggy Lee's fifty-year reverie had come true: she and Dave were reunited for all eternity.

Acknowledgments

This book might never have happened were it not for Wayne Lawson, former executive literary editor of *Vanity Fair*. In 1999, Wayne commissioned me to write a Peggy Lee profile; it burgeoned into the biography you now hold.

To everyone who submitted to my questioning, and whom I have quoted herein, thank you so much for your candor and insights. Others who offered memories, leads, or introductions include Morgan Ames, Ray Anthony, Allen Bardin, Perry Botkin, Lincoln Briney, Tom Burke, Steve Campbell, Francine Cherry, Marian Collier, Jim Czak, Dolores Hollingsworth DeMars, Gene DiNovi, David Allen Duke, Glen Egstrom, Connie Emerson, George Emerson, Carmen Fanzone, Danny Fields, Terese Genecco, Debbie Green, Denise Grimes, Freeman Gunter, Helen Hample, Robert Hicks, Megan Hogan, Charles Hsuen, Eliot Hubbard, Magda Katz, Cathy Kerr, Bill King, Hilary Knight, Dick LaPalm, Dana Marcoux, Vince Mauro, Helen Mawby, Bob Merlis, Audrey Morris, Barbara Morrison, Ted Ono, Kevin O'Sullivan, Stephen Paley, Patty and Linda Peterson, Bucky Pizzarelli, Mike Renzi, Christina Rosenthal, Shirley Hollingsworth Rott, Spider Saloff, Gary Schocker, Nan Schwartz, Yvette Shearer, Robert Sher, Donna Shore, Barbara Sinatra, Liz Smith, Corky Hale Stoller, Sorrell Trope, Veerle Van de Poel, Carson Vaughan, Lilian Wehler, John Williams, and Walter Willison.

This book owes a huge debt to Richard Morrison and his extraordinary research into the early life and career of Peggy Lee. Richard's staggering generosity and his eagle-eyed fact-checking and suggestions made it possible for me to tell the story I set out to write. Likewise, Robert

Strom, author of *Miss Peggy Lee: A Career Chronicle*, gave me no end of invaluable materials, insights, and encouragement.

I couldn't have explored Peggy Lee's childhood in such depth without access to the remarkable memory and perceptiveness of her best childhood friend, Artis Conitz Tranmer. Professor Kate Stevenson of Jamestown College and her fellow Jamestown resident George Spangler spent days showing me the North Dakota of Lee's youth and leading me to its still-living inhabitants. Wes Anderson, curator of the Barnes County Historical Society Museum in Valley City, ND, shared fascinating oral histories that recalled Norma Deloris Egstrom. Composer Paul Horner and playwright William Luce, Lee's collaborators on *Peg*, gave me countless hours of their time along with stacks of important documents and just as much encouragement. For my understanding of Lee's court case against Walt Disney Productions, I owe special thanks to judge Stephen M. Lachs, Lee's attorney David Blasband, and especially to Roy Reardon, Disney's trial counsel, who went to the trouble of sending me hundreds of pages of court papers. Three of Lee's secretaries, Dona Harsh Hutchinson, Betty Jungheim, and Jane David, contributed immeasurably to my understanding of the day-to-day life of Peggy Lee. So did Kathy Levy, Brian Panella, and Bruce Vanderhoff, who knew Peggy Lee as well as almost anyone.

To my collector friends Alan Eichler, Steve Gruber, Harry Locke, Michael Mascioli, Richard Norton, and Ken Williams, thank you for helping bring these pages to life with so many of your Peggy Lee–related treasures. Others who shared valuable materials from their archives include Peter Burke, Jack Allen, Arne Fogel, Robert Foshko, Will Friedwald, Lee Hale, D. Michael Heath, Tad Hershorn, Bob Mardesich, David McMacken, Bill Reed, Robert W. Richards, Joe Sardaro, Peter Stoller, Lea Sullivan, David Torresen, and Elga Woodell Weisgram. My late friend Jess Rand was a never-ending font of insider stories from the Golden Age of Hollywood, and an irreplaceable man who can't do enough to be helpful. Author Richard Lamparski's eloquence and pinpoint recall helped me to understand much about Lee and her world. Ken Bloom and Bill Rudman allowed me to hear their 1993 recorded interview with Lee— a gem of astute interviewing and in-depth knowledge.

I thank the public institutions that made this researcher's life much easier—notably the Institute of Jazz Studies at Rutgers University in Newark, New Jersey; the New York Public Library for the Performing Arts; the Warner Bros. Archives at the University of Southern California in Los Angeles; the Nixon Presidential Library & Museum in Yorba Linda, CA (Jon Fletcher, archivist); and the North Dakota State University Archives (John Hallberg, archives associate). Ivan Santiágo-Mercado's exhaustively researched peggyleediscography.com saved me an enormous amount of legwork.

A lot of this book was written in the homes of friends who were kind enough to host me in my travels. For generously giving me so much space and support, my heartfelt thanks to Joel Thurm (Los Angeles), Yvans Jourdan (Los Angeles), Clark Bason (Palm Springs), Geoffrey Mark (Palm Springs), James Jarrett (San Francisco), Jim Key and Jim Walb (Fire Island Pines), Spider Saloff (Chicago), Patrick Summers and Beau Miller (Houston), Candice Dempsey (Jamestown, ND), Robert Green and Dook Supraditaporn (Sydney), Waluya, Sue, and Benny Dimas (Melbourne), Fred Sill (Rio), André Tavares (Rio), Frank Sonnek (Rio), Zuza Homem de Mello and Ercília Lobo (São Paulo), Juan Weik and Fernanda Koprowski (São Paulo), Affonso Barros da Cunha (Salvador, Bahia), and Paulo Vilara (Belo Horizonte, Minas Gerais).

In 2009, my soul sister, author Sheila Weller, introduced me to literary agent Elisa Petrini (then of Inkwell Management in New York), who brought me to Atria Books for the second time. Thanks, Sheila and Elisa, for helping change my life. From there, David Forrer of Inkwell took over as my agent and has kept me truly happy ever since. I love working with you, David—as I do with my wonderful editor at Atria, Peter K. Borland, who has made me feel cared about, and has taken great pains to help make this the book I hoped it would be. I have been lucky to collaborate with Atria's dedicated team: assistant editor Daniel Loedel and his successor, Daniella Wexler; production editor Isolde Sauer; managing editor Kimberly Goldstein; assistant managing editor Kristen Lemire; associate publicist Tory Lowy; marketing specialist Jackie Jou; and interior designer Paul Dippolito. Collectively, they bring beautiful books into the world—a noble calling. Attorney Elisa Rivlin combed through the manuscript with utmost attentiveness and made the vetting process a pleasure. Senior counsel Felice Javit is an enormous comfort—the best at what she does. Jacket designer Anna Dorfman created a cover that gives me goose bumps. And Judith Curr, publisher of Atria, welcomed me back into her family of authors and has made me feel enormously proud. Thank you for having me, Judith.

My lawyer, Mark Sendroff, has been a true-blue friend and a port in many storms. Eternal thanks, dear Mark. The great Hollywood portrait photographer Michael Childers took a jacket photograph of which I am very proud, and has gone out of his way over and over to help me. So have my friends Darren Ramirez, the most debonair man in Los Angeles; Mart Crowley, whose way with words gives me something to aspire to; and film historian Tom Toth, a friend of limitless knowledge and generosity.

To my friends Cindy Bitterman, Lisa Bond, John Boswell, Tammy Faye, Adam Feldman, the late Jane Harvey and Bill King, Joe Kirkendall, Charles Michel, David Munk, Mark Murphy, Jacqueline Parker, Paul Pines, and the late Ann Ruckert, thank you for seeing me through various or all stages of this book and showing me in so many ways that you care. For Cindy Bitterman, a friend from whom so many of the best things in my life have sprung, there are no words to say thanks. Finally, to my parents, Viola and Jack: I would never have made it this far without you.

Notes

All information contained in this book has been drawn from interviews with the individuals, books, and articles referenced below, as well as the sources thanked in my acknowledgments.

INTRODUCTION

1 "If they're waiting": Howard Kissel, "A 'Fever'-Pitch Comeback," *New York Daily News*, July 31, 1992.
1 "an intergalactic": Rex Reed, *New York Observer*, Mar. 18, 2002.
1 "warm and sexy": Gerald Nachman, "Coping with the Over-the-Hill Gang," *San Francisco Chronicle*, Oct. 4, 1992.
1 "strange": Rex Reed, *New York Observer*, Mar. 18, 2002.
1 "there was no": Mike Melvoin to JG, Dec. 14, 2010.
2 "an aura": k.d. lang to JG, Feb. 22, 1999.
2 "When I get": Ray Rogers, "The Goddess of Pop," *Interview*, Sept. 1997.
2 "I knew I could": *Dusty Full Circle: The Life and Music of Dusty Springfield*, BBC, 1998.
2 "Are you sure": Phoebe Jacobs to JG, Feb. 11, 1999.
2 "Peggy had": Grady Tate to JG, Feb. 13, 1999.
2 "In singing": Rebecca Freligh, "Peggy Lee Still Rates 'Miss Standing Ovation,'" *Cleveland Plain Dealer*, Feb. 14, 1993.
2 "Barbra and Judy": Jim Bailey to JG, Aug. 19, 2011.
3 "She came up": Artis Conitz Tranmer to JG, Jan. 8, 2012.
3 "Whatever you": Xeroxed page from PL papers, date unknown.
4 "I can't take": Nicki Lee Foster to JG, Jan. 30, 1999.
4 "The greatest": Louis Armstrong to PL, signed photo, family collection.
4 "I didn't want": Nicki Lee Foster to JG, Jan. 30, 1999.
5 "I don't remember . . . for that?": PL to JG, Jan. 13, 1998.
5 "Peggy operates": Robert W. Richards to JG, Feb. 15, 1999.
5 "Peggy was": Phoebe Jacobs to JG, Feb. 11, 1999.
5 "like a jazzy": Mark Murphy to JG, Mar. 7, 1999.

CHAPTER ONE

7 "North Dakota was": John Hallowell, "Peggy Lee Is Very Different from You and Me," *Los Angeles Times*, Apr. 12, 1970.
7 "The Dakota": Frank Sonnek to JG, Feb. 21, 2012.
7 "a weird little": Larry Kart, "Like a Lily in the Mud," *Chicago Tribune*, Feb. 13, 1983.

7 "I had some very": Scarth Flett, "Meeting People: What Man Would Stand for His Wife Writing Songs in the Middle of the Night?," *Sunday Express* (London), Nov. 25, 1973.

7 "I used to daydream": "Like a Lily in the Mud."

7 "I knew where": Hal Boyle, "Menial Tasks Aided Career of Peggy Lee," *Washington Post*, Apr. 17, 1953.

8 "You will never": Artis Conitz Tranmer to JG, Nov. 12, 2011.

8 "There is a cruelty": Rhiannon, "Last Train Home / Love of the Land," from CD *Almost Home*, 1991.

8 "was like strong": Lois Phillips Hudson, *Reapers of the Dust: A Prairie Chronicle*, St. Paul: Minnesota Historical Society Press, p. 64.

9 "The work had": Russell Duncan, *I Remember*, Fargo, ND: self-published, 1978, p. 21.

10 "So did most": Glen Egstrom to JG, June 6, 2011.

10 "In that culture": Frank Sonnek to JG, Feb. 21, 2012.

11 "What else": Artis Conitz Tranmer to JG, Jan. 8, 2012.

11 "He was a sweet": Ibid.

11 "puny": Mary Young to JG, Nov. 3, 2010.

12 "You'd park": Ibid.

12 "the Nuthouse": Glen Egstrom to JG, June 6, 2011.

12 "almost impossible . . . malnutrition": "How Well Are We Treating the Mentally Ill in North Dakota?" *Bismarck North Star Dakotan*, Jan. 1915.

13 "We were satisfied": Connie Emerson to JG, May 31, 2011.

13 "so we'd be": Sidney Fields, "It's No Longer Cold Outside," *New York Daily Mirror*, July 25, 1949.

13 "Following her return": "Ill Many Months; Burial at Volga," *Jamestown Daily Alert*, Aug. 7, 1924.

14 "There they were": PL, notes to William Luce for musical *Peg*, 1982.

14 "Can I see . . . my Mama?": PL, *Miss Peggy Lee*, p. 28.

14 "I thought": Phyllis Battelle, "Peggy Lee and ESP," *Los Angeles Herald Examiner*, Oct. 20, 1976.

14 "I was so puzzled . . . ended": Glenn Plaskin, "Lee's Triumph of Spirit," *New York Daily News*, Aug. 17, 1992.

14 "I always thought": Phyllis Battelle, "Peggy Lee and ESP."

14 "grieved terribly": Lynn Ringuette to JG, June 29, 2011.

14 "really tore": Glen Egstrom to JG, June 6, 2011.

15 "Bulging thyroid eyes": PL, notes to William Luce for musical *Peg*, 1982.

15 "warm and loving": Janice Wiese Duffy to JG, Nov. 2, 2011.

15 "because of all": PL, notes to William Luce for musical *Peg*, 1982.

16 "I never saw": Artis Conitz Tranmer to JG, Nov. 12, 2011.

17 "absolutely took care": Janice Wiese Duffy to JG, Nov. 2, 2011.

17 "It was just": Jeanette Loy to JG, June 27, 2011.

17 "There was really": Lee Ringuette to JG, June 28, 2011.

17 "Norma had quite": Artis Conitz Tranmer to JG, Nov. 12, 2011.

17 "Where were": *Miss Peggy Lee*, p. 34.

17 "I said, just kidding": Dona Harsh Hutchinson to JG, Feb. 9, 2011.

18 "Peggy nearly": Betty Jungheim to JG, Feb. 9, 2011.

18 "If the water . . . bleeding": *Miss Peggy Lee*, p. 52.

18 "Peggy went on": Betty Jungheim to JG, Feb. 9, 2011.

18 "But Peggy": Dona Harsh Hutchinson to JG, Feb. 9, 2011.

19 "Min *never* . . . Invisible": Artis Conitz Tranmer to JG, Jan. 8, 2012.

19 "I think that one": Paul Pines to JG, Jan. 5, 2012.

19   "There are two": Robert Strom to JG, Jan. 8, 2012.

20   "He was a dear": Ibid.

20   "He had light-brown hair": Whitney Balliett, "Still There," *New Yorker*, Aug. 5, 1985.

20   "I could get": PL, notes to William Luce for musical *Peg*, 1982.

20   "Mama's gone": Ibid.

21   "There were only": Recorded interview, PL to Ken Bloom and Bill Rudman, June 1993.

22   "the sad whistle": "A Candid Talk with Peggy Lee," *New York Post*, Feb. 3, 1942.

22   "When she wanted": Steve Blum to JG, Sept. 6, 2011.

22   "You could see": "Portrait of a Lady, Part One," *Gene Lees Jazzletter*, 1996.

23   "Hank Schmidt": PL, notes to William Luce for musical *Peg*, 1982.

23   "I envied her": Pearl Hickey Anderson to JG, May 23, 2012.

23   "just a new": Mattie Foy Brandt to JG, May 23, 2012.

24   "When you're already": Katherine Stevenson to JG, Nov. 1, 2010.

24   "be as sweet": Artis Conitz Tranmer to JG, Nov. 12, 2011.

24   "delicious lunches": *Edgeley (ND) Mail*, June 29, 1933.

24   "Min was strict": Artis Conitz Tranmer to JG, Nov. 17, 2011.

24   "I think she was": William Luce to JG, Aug. 17, 2012.

24   "She knew": Artis Conitz Tranmer to JG, Nov. 12, 2011.

25   "She and Clair": Pearl Hickey Anderson to JG, May 23, 2012.

25   "She was gonna": Mattie Foy Brandt to JG, May 23, 2012.

25   "Her many friends": "Nortonville R.R. Station Burned," *Edgeley (ND) Mail*, Jan. 9, 1930.

25   "He could tap-dance": Artis Conitz Tranmer to JG, Nov. 12, 2011.

26   "That's a funny song": PL, notes to William Luce for musical *Peg*, 1982.

26   "I used to": *The Studs Terkel Program*, WFMT-FM, Chicago, 1988.

26   "*made* her walk": *This Is Your Life*, Mar. 11, 1973.

26   "She didn't sing": Artis Conitz Tranmer to JG, Nov. 12, 2011.

26   "She used to": Pearl Hickey Anderson to JG, May 23, 2012.

27   "This man came": Shaun Considine, "Miss Peggy Lee: '. . . quite simply the finest singer in the history of popular music,'" *After Dark*, June 1974.

27   "They yell at me": Lois Shirley, "Empty Hearted," *Photoplay*, Oct. 1929.

27   "there wasn't a shy": Artis Conitz Tranmer to JG, Nov. 12, 2011.

27   "She was a big": Russell Krueger to JG, Nov. 25, 2011.

28   "I remember standing": Larry L. King, "Rappin' with Peggy Lee," *Copolitan*, Sept. 1971.

28   "Mrs. M. O. Egstrom": *Edgeley (ND) Mail*, Oct. 13, 1932.

29   "I'm quite sure": *Miss Peggy Lee*, p. 43.

29   "Each day": Ibid., p. 44.

29   "You may well": Ibid., pp. 52–53.

29   "Clair never": Lee Ringuette to JG, June 28, 2011.

30   "I often thought": Paul Horner to JG, Apr. 28, 2013.

CHAPTER TWO

31   "just plain": Edith Lockett to JG, June 27, 2011.

31   "Daddy took": *Miss Peggy Lee*, p. 53.

32   "She wasn't": Connie Emerson to JG, May 31, 2011.

32   "there was something": Ginny Lulay to JG, Nov. 2, 2010.

32   "Oh, I can't sing": Edith Lockett to JG, June 27, 2011.

32   "back on the job": *Wimbledon News*, Sept. 20, 1934.

32 "sang two numbers": Ibid.

32 "She could write": Edith Lockett to JG, June 27, 2011.

32 "say bad words": Ella M. Fetcher notebook, 1923–1976.

32 "I know that": *Wimbledon News*, Dec. 19, 1935.

33 "Radio made me": Gerald Nachman, *Raised on Radio*, New York: Pantheon, 1998, p. 6.

34 "more than a form": H. Howard Taubman, *New York Times Book Review*, June 18, 1939.

34 "We kept": Count Basie with Arthur Murray, *Good Morning Blues: The Autobiography of Count Basie*, New York: Random House, 1985.

35 "nothin' but": Nathan W. Pearson, Jr.: *Goin' to Kansas City*, Urbana and Chicago: University of Illinois Press, 1994, p. 138.

35 "hot as hell": Ibid.

36 "When I'm asked": Bing Crosby with Pete Martin, *Call Me Lucky: Bing Crosby's Own Story*, New York: Simon & Schuster, 1953.

36 "I literally": PL, notes to William Luce for musical *Peg*, 1982.

36 "She just went": Artis Conitz Tranmer to JG, Nov. 12, 2011.

37 "lie on the floor": Lilian Wehler to JG, May 23, 2012.

37 "someday the torch": PL, "The Change of Subjects," *Wimbledon High School Ice Breaker*, Mar. 12, 1936.

37 "mystery comedy . . . girl servant": "One Act Play Contest," *Wimbledon News*, Nov. 28, 1935.

37 "musical contest": Pearl Hickey Anderson to JG, May 23, 2012.

37 "our comical": "Junior Class Play Thurs.," *Wimbledon News*, Dec. 5, 1935.

37 "was the only": Kirtley Baskette, "Peggy Lee: She Can't Stop Giving," *Redbook*, Apr. 1955.

38 "She got up": Jeanette Loy to JG, June 27, 2011.

38 "Mammy Jinnie": Program, *Eighth Annual Kiwanis Barnes County One-Act Play Contest*, Valley City, ND, Nov. 1936.

38 "I remember": Larry L. King, "Rappin' with Peggy Lee," *Cosmopolitan*, Sept. 1971.

39 "Miss Egstrom sang": *Wimbledon News*, Dec. 3, 1936.

39 "The truck drivers": Jeanette Loy to JG, June 27, 2011.

39 "All us kids": Ginny Lulay to JG, Nov. 2, 2010.

40 "we thought": Edith Lockett to JG, June 27, 2011.

40 "Some of the girls": "Cupid Said Busy," *Valley City Times-Record*, Feb. 27, 1942.

40 "To Doc": Alfred G. Aronowitz, "Miss Peggy Lee," *New York Post*, Mar. 20, 1972.

40 "dark and handsome": *Miss Peggy Lee*, p. 60.

41 "I was so busy": Alfred G. Aronowitz, "Miss Peggy Lee."

41 "little blues singer": *Miss Peggy Lee*, p. 61.

41 "I had to scrub": Ginny Lulay to JG, Nov. 2, 2010.

41 "*extremely* determined . . . sing a song": Connie Emerson to JG, May 31, 2011.

42 "it wouldn't": Recorded interview, PL to Ken Bloom and Bill Rudman, June 1993.

42 "Success Awaits . . . *labor's gate!*": "Class Poem," *Wimbledon News*, May 27, 1937.

43 "The Sunshine Girl": PL to Skitch Henderson, "The Music Makers" radio interview, 1982.

43 "excess poundage": Letter, PL to Red Homuth, July 20, 1937.

43 "I guess . . . you did": Letter, PL to Red Homuth, Mar. 14, 1994.

44 "beehive": WDAY station brochure, c. 1934.

44 "Bill literally": George Christy, "Peggy Lee: Still at Fever's Pitch," *Interview*, Oct. 1984.

45 "But I told": *This Is Your Life*, Mar. 11, 1973.

45 "It had . . . Peggy Lee": "Peggy Lee: Still at Fever's Pitch," George Christy, *Interview*, Oct. 1984.

45   "Guess she hasn't": WDAY folio, 1937.

46   "In the bakery": PL to Ken Bloom and Bill Rudman, recorded interview, June 1993.

46   "I think basically": *Good Morning America*, Jan. 27, 1988.

46   "almost like": Recorded interview, UK, source unknown, c. 1982.

46   "I liked . . . natural": Recorded interview, PL to Ken Bloom and Bill Rudman, June 1993.

47   "This must be": Connie Emerson to JG, May 31, 2011.

47   "practically": Sidney Fields, "It's No Longer Cold Outside," *New York Daily Mirror*, July 25, 1949.

47   "I may go": John Hallowell, "Peggy Lee Is Very Different from You and Me," *Los Angeles Times*, Apr. 12, 1970.

47   "I think": PL, notes to William Luce for musical *Peg*, 1982.

48   "Three for": Phoebe Jacobs to JG, Feb. 11, 1999.

48   "the softest": Shaun Considine, "Miss Peggy Lee: '. . . quite simply the finest singer in the history of popular music,'" *After Dark*, June 1974.

48   "poor old soul": *Miss Peggy Lee*, p. 75.

48   "He let": Shaun Considine, "Miss Peggy Lee."

49   "spent her last": *This Is Your Life*, transcript of unedited show, Mar. 11, 1973.

49   "Barclay, whose height": PL, notes to William Luce for musical *Peg*, 1982.

49   "corn-fed": Kirtley Baskette, "Peggy Lee: She Can't Stop Giving," *Redbook*, Apr. 1955.

49   "Larry said": *This Is Your Life*, transcript of unedited show.

49   "the smell of the gardenias": *Miss Peggy Lee*, p. 77.

50   "Sunburnt": "'Sophie Tucker,'" *Chicago Defender*, Mar. 16, 1940.

50   "midget entertainer": Read Kendall, "Around and About in Hollywood," *Los Angeles Times*, Oct. 24, 1938.

50   "head-balancing act": "The Jade, Dragon Room, Hollywood," *Billboard*, May 2, 1942.

50   "sang just": Lucia Perrigo, "Mañana Comes True for Peggy Lee," *Massillon (OH) Evening Independent*, Aug. 30, 1948.

50   "thought it was": *Miss Peggy Lee*, p. 78.

50   "Both girls": "The Jade, Hollywood," *Billboard*, June 4, 1938.

51   "Why don't": PL, notes to William Luce for musical *Peg*, 1982.

51   "I didn't want": Jack Smith, "Peggy Lee Tells How She Reached Heights," Jack Smith, *Los Angeles Times*.

51   "We'd all grown": *This Is Your Life*, transcript of unedited show.

52   "We sat": Artis Conitz Tranmer to JG, Jan. 8, 2012.

52   "a small town": *Miss Peggy Lee*, p. 83.

52   "I nearly died": PL, notes to William Luce for musical *Peg*, 1982.

52   "I watched": *Miss Peggy Lee*, p. 84.

52   "cancer of the blood": "Young Daughter of M. O. Claimed by Death," *Stutsman County Record*, Nov. 24, 1938.

53   "Us girls . . . added": Mary Young to JG, May 23, 2012.

54   "She always": Peggy Clark Schwartz to JG, Oct. 9, 2010.

54   "sang very . . . little-girl talk": Ann Clark to JG, Oct. 11, 2010.

54   "We thought": Peggy Clark Schwartz to JG, Oct. 9, 2010.

54   "popular, pretty": Newspaper ad, 1939; source unknown.

55   "A Revelation": *Fargo Forum*, Feb. 5, 1940.

56   "Sometimes": Letter, PL to friend Helen, Sept. 25, 1939.

56   "My mother": Lee Ringuette to JG, June 28, 2011.

56   "who was *really*": *Miss Peggy Lee*, p. 85.

57   "We would sit": Paula Ringuette to JG, Aug. 28, 2012.

CHAPTER THREE

59 "Minneapolis's": Don Lang, "Sev Olsen into Army Soon; Chirp to Lead," *Down Beat*, May 15, 1942.

59 "first big romance": PL, notes to William Luce for musical *Peg*, 1982.

59 "I just couldn't": *Miss Peggy Lee*, p. 87.

59 "It was a": Jeanne Arland Peterson to JG, Nov. 25, 2011.

60 "The gal trills": *Variety*, Jan. 1, 1941.

60 "amateurishness": "Water Follies," *Variety*, Dec. 4, 1940.

60 "badly infected throat": Adelaide Kerr, "New York Night Club Favorites Reached Top After Many Hurdles," *Niagara Falls Gazette*, Nov. 15, 1941.

60 "mentally ill . . . lip": PL, notes to William Luce for musical *Peg*, 1982.

61 "I cried": Adelaide Kerr, "New York Nightclub Favorites."

61 "I knew": Mary English, "Softly, with Feeling," *Record Whirl*, Oct. 1955.

61 "By that accident": Charles Mangel, "The Name Is Woman," *Look*, Oct. 19, 1971.

62 "I'm hiring": *Miss Peggy Lee*, p. 92.

62 "There I sat": Norma Lee Browning, "She Has a Love Affair with Chicago: Peggy Lee Returning to Where It All Began," *Chicago Tribune*, Mar. 16, 1969.

62 "We didn't": Dave Dexter, Jr., *Playback*, New York: Billboard Press, 1976, p. 94.

63 "those hilarious": *Chicago Tribune*, Oct. 12, 1941.

63 "Peggy's singing . . . was on": Jean Bach to JG, May 18, 2011.

64 "gaily puffing": Wambly Bald, "In the Groove," *New York Post Week-End Magazine*, Oct. 30, 1949.

64 "life sentence": Helen Forrest, *I Had the Craziest Dream: Helen Forrest and the Big Band Era*, New York: Coward, McCann & Geoghegan, 1982, p. 95.

64 "by far": Ibid., p. 94.

64 "noodling": Ibid., p. 105.

64 "This is it": Ibid., p. 108.

64 "went right": *Adventures in the Kingdom of Swing*, American Masters, WNET, 2000.

65 "I wish": Charles Champlin, "Peggy, Benny in the Swing of It," *Los Angeles Times*, Apr. 28, 1965.

65 "character": Thomas C. Wheeler, "The Timeless Charm of Peggy Lee," *Saturday Evening Post*, Oct. 10, 1964.

65 "I know": George Christy, "Peggy Lee: Still at Fever's Pitch," *Interview*, Oct. 1984.

65 "What can you lose . . . y-yes": Aida Pavletich, "Thrushing with PL," *Los Angeles Free Press*, May 10, 1974.

65 "I was in": Charles Champlin, "Peggy, Benny in the Swing of It," *Los Angeles Times*, Apr. 28, 1965.

65 "I guess": *Miss Peggy Lee*, p. 6.

66 "Negro's supremacy": John Hammond with Irving Townsend, *John Hammond on Record: An Autobiography*, New York: Ridge Press, 1977, p. 68.

66 "bedlam broke . . . helplessly": "Swing Addicts Storm and Take the Paramount," *New York Herald-Tribune*, Jan. 27, 1938.

67 "If something": Louise Tobin to JG, Apr. 27, 2011.

67 "this self-absorption": *Adventures in the Kingdom of Swing*, American Masters, WNET, 2000.

67 "The guys complained": Peggy Clark Schwartz to JG, Oct. 9, 2010.

67 "I think": Ed Shaughnessy to JG, Dec. 8, 2010.

67 "He'd break": Johnny Mandel to JG, Nov. 14, 2010.

68 "Benny made": Louise Tobin to JG, Apr. 27, 2011.

68 "I had the feeling": Alan Jackson, "That's Not All There Is, Says Miss Lee," *Times* (London), June 15, 1994.

69 "I had a psychosomatic": George Christy, "Peggy Lee: Still at Fever's Pitch," *Interview*, Oct. 1984.

69 "ice-cold": George Avakian to JG, Dec. 15, 2010.

69 "she stood . . . can't sing": Ross Firestone, *Swing, Swing, Swing: The Life & Times of Benny Goodman*, New York: W.W. Norton & Co., 1994, p. 303.

69 "Miss Lee is": Ibid.

70 "I'd like to stomp": PL, *Monitor*, NBC radio, Mar. 4, 1972.

70 "Miss Lee should": Dave Dexter, Jr., *Down Beat*, Oct. 1941.

70 "Never Been": *Down Beat*, c. May 1942.

70 "She couldn't sing": Frank Farrell, "Peggy Lee at Copa," *World Journal Tribune*, Oct. 28, 1966.

70 "never said": Helen Forrest, *I Had the Craziest Dream*, New York: Coward, McCann and Geoghegan, p. 95.

70 "He said, 'I've heard'": PL, press conference, The Ballroom, New York, June 13, 1986.

70 "She's one of": Helen Ward, *The Joe Franklin Show*, WOR-TV, 1978.

70 "All the way": Dona Harsh Hutchinson to JG, Apr. 20, 2011.

71 "was like boot camp": Bob Thomas, "Peggy Taking U.S. Flag to Land of Rising Sun," *Tennessean Showcase*, Aug. 8, 1976.

71 "If I'd known": Gerald Nachman, "There's Gold in Them Thar Hollywood Hills," *American Spectator*, July–Aug. 2011.

71 "a million miles away": Peggy Clark Schwartz to JG, Oct. 9, 2010.

71 "They were all": Helen Ward, *The Joe Franklin Show*, WOR-TV, 1978.

71 "I used to": PL, press conference about Benny Goodman's death, The Ballroom, June 13, 1986.

71 "We were like": PL, notes to William Luce for musical *Peg*, 1982.

72 "the biggest thrill": Ann Clark to JG, Oct. 11, 2010.

72 "I was strong": PL, notes to William Luce for musical *Peg*, 1982.

72 "My God": Hal Schaefer to JG, Feb. 7, 2011.

72 "New Yorker Hotel": PL, notes to William Luce for musical *Peg*, 1982.

72 "better to": *The Larry King Show*, 1988.

72 "He had it roaring": *The Studs Terkel Program*.

73 "Benny, that's not the way": *The Studs Terkel Program*, WFMT-FM, Chicago, 1988.

73 "It's with a": Dave Dexter, Jr., "Ray Paige's Kids Surprise with Album of Standards; Goodman Chirp Phenomenal," *Down Beat*, Dec. 1, 1941.

74 "hushed the house": George T. Simon, "Benny Absolutely Stupendous on Stage," *Metronome*, July 1942.

74 "He had": Brian Panella to JG, Oct. 17, 2010.

75 "You know": "A Candid Talk with Peggy Lee," *New York Post*, Feb. 3, 1942.

75 "Instead of buying": Whitney Balliett, "Still There," *New Yorker*, Aug. 5, 1985.

76 "Are wedding bells": "Cupid Said Busy," *Valley City Times-Record*, Feb. 27, 1942.

76 "the man . . . first sight": PL, notes to William Luce for musical *Peg*, 1982.

76 "He played like": Steve Blum to JG, Sept. 6, 2011.

76 "a very good": Hal Schaefer to JG, Apr. 2, 2012.

77 "There was a depth": PL to Ken Bloom and Bill Rudman, recorded interview, June 1993.

77 "He managed": "Barbara Lea Sings Willard Robison," *Alec Wilder's American Popular Song*, National Public Radio, Oct. 3, 1976.

77 "There was a": Gene DiNovi to JG, Dec. 19, 2010.

77   "watched his": *Miss Peggy Lee*, p. 97.

77   "You know, I": Lucia Perrigo, "Mañana Comes True for Peggy Lee," *Massillon (OH) Evening Independent*, Aug. 30, 1948.

79   "until he": *The Studs Terkel Program*, WFMT, Chicago, 1988.

79   "After a week": Amy Lee, "Peggy Lee—Lyricist, Composer, and Singer," *Christian Science Monitor*, July 17, 1969.

79   "but Benny": *The Studs Terkel Program*.

79   "Benny ran out": *The Grammy Treasure Chest* #76–144 (radio), 1975.

79   "I'm not really": Shaun Considine, "Miss Peggy Lee: '. . . quite simply the finest singer in the history of popular music,'" *After Dark*, June 1974.

80   "big surprise": *Metronome*, Dec. 1942.

80   "You can hear": "Peggy Lee," *Look*, Nov. 17, 1942.

81   "I didn't know": PL to Alan Dell, BBC Radio 2 interview, rec. 1992.

81   "She was elated": Margaret Whiting to JG, Mar. 13, 1999.

81   "Never before": George T. Simon, *The Big Bands*, p. 224.

82   "Miss Lee was forced": "Baptized E'Lane for Astor Date," *Billboard*, June 26, 1943.

82   "what a horror": Dona Harsh Hutchinson to JG, Feb. 9, 2011.

83   "Only yesterday": John Crosby, "Long-Haired Music, Short-Haired Disc Jockey," *New York Herald-Tribune*, May 2, 1951.

83   "You know": *This Is Your Life*, Mar. 11, 1973.

CHAPTER FOUR

85   "a little ole": Jean Burden, "A Flair for French," *Los Angeles Times*, Oct. 30, 1949.

85   "Those were": Phyllis Battelle, "Peggy Lee and ESP," *Los Angeles Herald-Examiner*, Oct. 20, 1976.

86   "It's the kind": Kirtley Baskette, "Peggy Lee: She Can't Stop Giving," *Redbook*, Apr. 1955.

86   "They were very": Margaret Whiting to JG, Mar. 13, 1999.

86   "She was just": Peggy Clark Schwartz to JG, Oct. 9, 2010.

86   "Pegalah": Dona Harsh Hutchinson to JG, May 17, 2011.

86   "It was strange": Kirtley Baskette, "Peggy Lee: She Can't Stop Giving."

87   "we forged ahead": Paul Grein, "Capitol Records: The Story So Far, from the Beginning," *Billboard*, June 13, 1992.

88   "no bargain": Dave Dexter, Jr., "Benny Goodman," *Down Beat*, Oct. 1941.

88   "I'm retired, Dave": Dave Dexter, Jr., liner notes for LP *The Capitol Jazzmen 1943–1947*, Swaggie Records, 1984.

88   "What does": Dave Dexter, Jr., *Playback*, New York: Billboard Publications, 1976, p. 92.

88   "If you can get": Dave Dexter, Jr., *The Capitol Jazzmen 1943–1947*.

89   "This chick": Dave Dexter, Jr., *Playback*, p. 93.

89   "standing at": Phyllis Battelle.

89   "You was": George Christy, "Peggy Lee: Still at Fever's Pitch," *Interview*, Oct. 1984.

89   "the best": *It Wasn't All Velvet: An Autobiography by Mel Tormé*, New York: Viking, 1988, p. 58.

90   "was on an": Anita O'Day with George Eells, *High Times Hard Times*, New York: Putnam, 1981, p. 130.

90   "heated pipes": M.H. Orodenker, "Record Reviews," *Billboard*.

90   "Most Outstanding": *New York Amsterdam News*, Oct. 27, 1945.

91   "I like those": Leonard Feather, "Sarah Doesn't Dig Bessie," *Metronome*, Mar. 1949.

91   "began to": PL, notes to William Luce for musical *Peg*, 1982.

91 "thinking about how": Gene Handsaker, "Trivial Events Inspire Writers," *Lubbock (TX) Avalanche-Journal*, May 25, 1947.

91 "He made me": John S. Wilson, "Peggy Lee Sings Tonight and Mañana," *New York Times*, July 31, 1981.

91 "He said, 'Put this'": PL, press conference, Le Parker Meridien, New York, June 22, 1995.

92 "was singing": Margaret Whiting to JG, Mar. 13, 1999.

92 "No. I don't": Ross MacDonald, "Peggy Lee," *New Liberty* (Canada), 1948.

92 "She always seemed": Dave Dexter, source unknown.

93 "I looked out": Jack Long, "Wild About Peggy," *American Magazine*, 1948.

93 "just tasting": Maurice Zolotow, "Is That All There Is, Peggy?" *Los Angeles*, July 1983.

94 "Nobody could . . . orchestration": Hal Schaefer to JG, Feb. 10, 2011.

94 "not really": Shaun Considine, "Miss Peggy Lee: '. . . quite simply the finest singer in the history of popular music,'" *After Dark*, June 1974.

94 "She felt she had": Leata Galloway to JG, Mar. 30, 2013.

95 "that certain": "Peggy Lee Heads Opening Program at State Theater," *Hartford Courant*, Sept. 11, 1948.

95 "He was not": Nicki Lee Foster to JG, Jan. 30, 1999.

95 "Peggy was a": Mundell Lowe to JG, Dec. 2, 2010.

96 "I love you . . . nagging me": Ibid.

96 "We believe": Founders Church of Religious Science website: founderlosangeles.org.

97 "for spiritual . . . in faith": Kirtley Baskette, "Peggy Lee: She Can't Stop Giving."

97 "She *loved* Papa": Dona Harsh Hutchinson to JG, Feb. 9, 2011.

97 "They're sort of": George T. Simon, "Hooray for Love," *Metronome*, Dec. 1948.

98 "the eternal loser": Desmond Stone, *Alec Wilder in Spite of Himself*, New York: Oxford University Press, 1996, p. 87.

98 "lovable eccentric": *Miss Peggy Lee*, p. 128.

98 "sweet sadness": Alec Wilder, *Letters I Never Mailed*, New York: Little, Brown & Co., 1975, p. 164.

98 "really gave her": William Engvick to JG, May 10, 2011.

99 "Dear Peggy": Hal Schaefer to JG, Feb. 10, 2011.

99 "How absolutely": Alec Wilder, *Letters I Never Mailed*, p. 164.

99 "He was extremely": Dona Harsh Hutchinson to JG, Feb. 9, 2011.

100 "She and Dave . . . own it": Hal Schaefer to JG, Feb. 7, 2011.

100 "You had to wonder": Mark Murphy to JG, Mar. 7, 1999.

101 "It was so": George Christy, "Peggy Lee: Still at Fever's Pitch," *Interview*, Oct. 1984.

101 "wrote special lyrics": "It's No Longer Cold Outside," *New York Daily Mirror*, July 25, 1949.

101 "It was never": George Christy, "Peggy Lee: Still at Fever's Pitch," *Interview*, Oct. 1984.

102 "these gorgeous . . . movie set": Hal Schaefer to JG, Feb. 7, 2011.

103 "She was *always*": Virginia Wicks to JG, Apr. 12, 2012.

103 "Most of the time": Dona Harsh Hutchinson to JG, Feb. 9, 2011.

104 "among the elite": Lee Ringuette to JG, June 28, 2011.

104 "I used to listen": Shaun Considine, "Miss Peggy Lee."

105 "with all kinds": "Peggy Lee Goes South of the Border, and Dave Barbour Takes a Shine to Crewcut," *Metronome*, Oct. 1950.

105 "singers like Peggy": Larry Douglas, "Theatrically Yours," *Atlanta Daily World*, Nov. 27, 1952.

105 "always loved Peggy": Leonard Feather, "Lady Day Has Her Say," *Metronome*, Feb. 1950.

105 "She stole": Donald Clarke, *Wishing on the Moon: The Life and Times of Billie Holiday*, New York: Penguin Books, 1995, p. 396.

105 "When Peggy Lee": Julia Blackburn, *With Billie: A New Look at the Unforgettable Billie Holiday*, New York: Vintage Books, 2006, p. 194.

106 "She was always": Dona Harsh Hutchinson to JG, Feb. 9, 2011.

106 "Miss Lee sees": *Life*, Mar. 29, 1948.

106 "from a very": Kathy Levy to JG, June 12, 2013.

106 "I never fly": Ross MacDonald, "Peggy Lee," *New Liberty* (Canada), 1948.

106 "Dave was drunk": Dona Harsh Hutchinson to JG, Feb. 9, 2011.

107 "Glenn Wallichs didn't": Kay Starr to JG, Nov. 15, 2010.

107 "Contrary to the belief": Glenn Wallichs, "Looking Backward Means Little, Next Ten Years Offer Challenge," *Billboard*, Aug. 2, 1952.

109 "like a mountain lake . . . success": Dona Harsh Hutchinson to JG, Feb. 9, 2011.

109 "morose": Kirtley Baskette, "Peggy Lee: She Can't Stop Giving."

109 "Peggy said, 'no, no'": Hal Schaefer to JG, Feb. 11, 2011.

110 "I had to be": Dona Harsh Hutchinston to JG, May 17, 2011.

110 "I never knew": Steve Allen to JG, Mar. 19, 1999.

110 "out of her element": Jack Gould, "Programs in Review," *New York Times*, Jan. 4, 1950.

110 "this little": Dona Harsh Hutchinson to JG, Feb. 9, 2011.

111 "Objection . . . stress": "Schnozzle's 1-Man Show in Court as Song Suit Witness," *Variety*, Nov. 15, 1950.

CHAPTER FIVE

113 "She didn't tell you": Robert W. Richards to JG, Feb. 15, 1999.

113 "Teabags": Steve Allen to JG, Mar. 19, 1999.

113 "When you see": George T. Simon, "Hooray for Love," *Metronome*, Dec. 1948.

113 "a very demanding": Harold Jovien to JG, Nov. 16, 2010.

114 "I think I was": Kay Starr to JG, Nov. 15, 2010.

114 "Dave used to": Dona Harsh Hutchinson to JG, Feb. 9, 2011.

114 "Miss Lee . . . rich food": Letter, Dave Barbour to Dona Harsh, c. 1950.

114 "i suppose now": Ibid.

114 "Dave's a modest man": "Peggy Lee Heads Opening Program at State Theater," *Hartford Courant*, Sept. 11, 1948.

114 "big ambition": George T. Simon, "Hooray for Love."

115 "breaking into": "Dave Barbour Bags Massey Skein Show," May 1948.

115 "It occurred": Charles Emge, "Mel Ferrer Adds Fresh Slant to Music in Pix," *Down Beat*, Dec. 30, 1949.

115 "Peggy Lee's husband": Hedda Hopper, "Looking at Hollywood," *Chicago Daily Tribune*, Nov. 5, 1949.

115 "After the first": "Peggy Lee Goes South of the Border, and Dave Barbour Takes a Shine to Crewcut," *Metronome*, Oct. 1950.

115 "I don't think": Hal Schaefer to JG, Feb. 11, 2011.

115 "cheap and lurid twaddle": Bosley Crowther, "The Screen in Review," *New York Times*, June 22, 1950.

116 "He was beaten": Glen Egstrom to JG, June 6, 2011.

116 "much time": "Mexican Tune Spells Success for Peggy Lee," *Minneapolis Sunday Tribune*, Mar. 14, 1948.

116 "I saw her": Artis Conitz Tranmer to JG, Jan. 8, 2012.

117 "Her appearance": Lee Ringuette to JG, June 28, 2011.

117 "glamorous Hollywood": "Peggy Lee Leaves by Truck for Bedside of Sick Father," unknown Valley City newspaper, Mar. 8, 1950.

117 "It was like": Dean McConn to JG, Nov. 27, 2011.

118 "because the": Earl Wilson, "Farmerette Makes Hay," *New York Post*, Apr. 26, 1953.

118 "within me": *Miss Peggy Lee*, p. 136.

118 "father of": *Jamestown Sun*, Apr. 27, 1950.

119 "Screw Louella": Dick LaPalm to JG, June 17, 2011.

119 "You're fired! . . . owe you": Virginia Wicks to JG, Jan. 14, 2013.

120 "Whether this is true": Magda Katz to JG, May 4, 2011.

121 "didn't find their": "Legion's 'Red, White and Blue' Folding Jan. 20; $500,000 Loser," *Variety*, Jan. 9, 1951.

122 "Peggy Lee plans": Sheilah Graham, "Flashes from Filmland," *Cleveland Plain Dealer*, Dec. 31, 1950.

122 "told her": *Boston Globe*, May 16, 1951.

122 "little or": "'Red, White, Blue' Folds Next Week; Legion Loss May Reach $600,000," *Variety*, Jan. 9, 1951.

122 "limping": "Legion's 'Red, White and Blue' Folding Jan. 20; $500,000 Loser."

122 "The actors": Claudia Cassidy, "On the Aisle," *Chicago Tribune*, Jan. 2, 1951.

122 "the second": "'Red, White, Blue' Folds Next Week."

122 "her": Dick LaPalm to JG, Oct. 21, 2010.

122 "was tired": Ibid.

122 "It was just": Dona Harsh Hutchinson to JG, Feb. 9, 2011.

123 "Getting along": Liz Nichols, "Old-Fashioned Girl in Sequins," *TV Show*, Aug. 1953.

123 "I loved him dearly": John M. Cathcart, "After 4 Broken Marriages My Career Has Cost Me Enough, Says Peggy Lee," *National Enquirer*, 1974.

123 "friendly": "Singer Peggy Lee to Ask Divorce," *Los Angeles Times*, Apr. 7, 1951.

123 "cruelty": "Seeks Divorce," *Chicago Tribune*, Apr. 29, 1951.

123 "He said he didn't": "Peggy Lee Wins Divorce," *New York Times*, May 16, 1951.

124 "shortly lead": The Associated Press, July 14, 1951.

124 "Roger": *Miss Peggy Lee*, p. 140.

124 "and when I first": Ibid.

124 "By now": Ibid., p. 140.

124 "sent him home": Magda Katz to JG, Feb. 12, 2011.

125 "For her latest": "Capitol Hunts Lee Backing," *Billboard*, Feb. 24, 1951.

126 "*very* difficult": Dick LaPalm to JG, Oct. 21, 2010.

126 "Nobody could be": "Life of a Canary," Louis Berg, *New York Herald Tribune*, Nov. 4, 1951.

127 "had these séances": Hal Schaefer to JG, Feb. 11, 2011.

127 "rays of love": Dick LaPalm to JG, Oct. 21, 2010.

127 "stay here forever": "Where's That Car I Wasn't Driving?," *High Point (NC) Enterprise*, May 21, 1952.

127 "Here is a guy": Leonard Feather, "Feather's Nest," *Down Beat*, Nov. 19, 1952.

127 "I also decided": Alan Jackson, "That's Not All There Is, Says Miss Lee," *Times* (U.K.), June 15, 1994.

128 "They just . . . went crazy": PL to Alan Dell, BBC Radio 2 interview, rec. 1992.

CHAPTER SIX

131 "years of romance": *Miss Peggy Lee*, p. 159.

131 "He said he didn't": "Peggy Lee Wins Divorce," *New York Times*, May 16, 1951.

131 "He did say": Kirtley Baskette, "Peggy Lee: She Can't Stop Giving," *Redbook*, Apr. 1955.

131 "easily one of": PL, notes to William Luce for musical *Peg*, 1982.

131 "She was *always*": Dona Harsh Hutchinson to JG, Feb. 9, 2011.

132 "I tried to bury": Liz Nichols, "Old-Fashioned Girl in Sequins," *TV Show*, Aug. 1953.

132 "She was restless": Dona Harsh Hutchinson to JG, Feb. 9, 2011.

132 "It could be Billie": Leonard Feather, "More 'Yeas' Than 'Nays' from Dick," *Down Beat*, June 17, 1953.

132 "I even went": Edward (Sonny) Murrain, "Front and Center," *New York Age*, Aug. 9, 1952.

133 "They couldn't hear": Aida Pavletich, "Thrushing with PL," *Los Angeles Free Press*, May 10, 1974.

133 "Oh, it's just": PL to Alan Dell, BBC Radio 2 interview, rec. 1992.

134 "*What time?*": Recorded interview, U.K., source unknown, c. 1982.

134 "orgiastic": Philip K. Scheuer, "Peggy Lee's Heart Lies in Song Writing," *Los Angeles Times*, May 9, 1954.

134 "I suppose": Ralph J. Gleason, "Take It Easier on Our Tunes, Fellas, Richard Rodgers Asks of Arrangers," *Down Beat*, July 15, 1953.

134 "I don't know": David Lehman, *A Fine Romance: Jewish Songwriters, American Songs*, New York: Schocken, p. 140.

134 "By the way": Phoebe Jacobs to JG, Feb. 11, 1999.

134 "In the years": Recording, "The Heyday of Rodgers and Hart," Philharmonic Hall, New York, Nov. 16, 1969.

135 "I do not remember": Mary Rodgers Guettel to JG, May 11, 2011.

135 "Peggy is not": Eddie Gallaher, "On Records," *Washington Post*, May 25, 1952.

135 "Chesterfield": *Radio-TV Mirror*, June 1953.

135 "My beer is Rheingold": unknown magazine, c. 1953.

135 "Peggy puts more sex": Warner Brothers press release, 1955.

136 "They were intrigued . . . her anymore": Arthur Hamilton to JG, Mar. 11, 1999.

137 "I've tried": Tape, Peggy Lee, The Ballroom, New York, Mar. 25, 1990.

137 "People say": Whitney Balliett, "Still There," *New Yorker*, Aug. 5, 1985.

137 "I start": Martin Burden, "Peggy Lee Gives It All That There Is," *New York Post*, Dec. 7, 1983.

137 "It was a very": Gene DiNovi to JG, Dec. 19, 2010.

137 "You'd have two . . . she got": George Schlatter to JG, Apr. 20, 2011.

137 "It seemed to me": "Peggy Lee's Progress Shows Flair of Ferrer," *Down Beat*, Jan. 28, 1953.

138 "She is in": Sidney Skolsky, "Hollywood Is My Beat," *New York Post*, Oct. 12, 1952.

138 "I sometimes like": Doris Day with A.E. Hotchner, *Doris Day—Her Own Story*, New York: Bantam Books, 1975, p. 102.

138 "wasn't up to": Gwynn, *New York Daily Mirror*, June 26, 1952.

138 "I felt that": Gene Handsaker, The Associated Press, Sept. 12, 1952.

139 "scared to death": James Bacon, " 'Refrain from Acting,' Says Mike Curtiz, 'That's Best Way to Become Movie Star,' " *Boston Globe*, Oct. 19, 1952.

139 "great actress . . . biggest stars": "Mike Curtiz Says Peggy Lee Will Be 'One of Biggest Stars,' " *Brooklyn Daily Eagle*, July 28, 1953.

139 "He's still mad": Graham, *Variety*, Oct. 2, 1952.

139 "When I saw": Hedda Hopper, "Doris Day 'Grows Up' in Etting Role," *Chicago Tribune*, June 12, 1955.

139 "Peggy Lee is gonna": *Hollywood Reporter*, Connelly, Aug. 1, 1952.

139 "Doris is": Warner Bros. press release for *The Jazz Singer*, 1952.

140 "I thanked him": "Lee Surrenders; Thus Peggy Begins Singing Film Career," *Los Angeles Times*, Sept. 7, 1952.

140 "inner sadness": *Miss Peggy Lee*, p. 156.

141 "Peggy was typical": Dona Harsh Hutchinson to JG, Feb. 9, 2011.

141 *"She's so wise"*: Peggy Lee, *Softly—with Feeling*, Los Angeles: private publication, 1953.

142 "Whenever I go": Jack Smith, "Peggy Lee Tells How She Reached Heights," *Los Angeles Times*, Aug. 16, 1959.

142 "a charming man": PL to Alan Dell, BBC Radio 2 interview, rec. 1992.

142 "He liked": Ibid.

143 "sudden glandular illness": Erskine Johnson, *New York Daily News*, Sept. 29, 1952.

143 "She moves": "Capitol, Wash.," *Variety*, Dec. 10, 1952.

143 "Papa": Dona Harsh Hutchinson to JG, Feb. 9, 2011.

143 "He wasn't a great": Betty Jungheim to JG, Feb. 9, 2011.

144 "Brad's wonderfully kind": Liz Nichols, "Old-Fashioned Girl in Sequins," *TV Show*, Aug. 1953.

144 "modernized": Jesse Zinser, "New Films," *Cue*, Jan. 24, 1953.

145 "Peggy Lee performed": Redelings, *Citizen*, Jan. 6, 1953.

145 "one of the handsomest": Betty Craig, "Life Singing Love Song for Peggy Lee," *Denver Post*, Feb. 12, 1953.

145 "says his mother": Louella Parsons, newspaper unknown, Dec. 1952.

145 "I think I": Dona Harsh Hutchinson to JG, May 17, 2011.

145 "It was a storybook": Unidentified newspaper, Jan. 1953.

145 "Either that!": Nicki Lee Foster to JG, Jan. 30, 1999.

146 "sometimes tense": Unidentified newspaper, Jan. 1953.

146 "Brad said": Betty Jungheim to JG, Feb. 9, 2011.

146 "I write in": Gene Handsaker, The Associated Press, Sept. 12, 1952.

146 *"We have a new . . . breathe upon me"*: Peggy Lee, *Softly—with Feeling*, Los Angeles: private publication, 1953.

147 "Oh, my God . . . pages for me": Lea Sullivan to JG, July 7, 2012.

147 "I'll be a ghost": Recording, Peggy Lee, "New York City Ghost," Hollywood Bowl, Los Angeles, Sept. 5, 1953.

147 "It came up": Ibid.

147 "successfully established": Albert Goldman, "'Pop' Concert Writes Bowl Season Finish," *Los Angeles Times*, Sept. 7, 1953.

148 "hypnotizing": Mark Murphy to JG, Mar. 7, 1999.

148 "She was dressed": Susan Sherman, *America's Child: A Woman's Journey Through the Radical Sixties*, Willimantic, CT: Curbstone Press, 2007, pp. 95–96.

148 "Warner's decided": Connolly, *Hollywood Reporter*, Mar. 13, 1953.

149 *"Of course!"*: Dick LaPalm to JG, Oct. 21, 2010.

149 "knew what": Charles Solomon, "Peggy Lee Bangs Out Jazz in 'Lady and the Tramp,'" *Los Angeles Times*, Dec. 26, 1986.

149 "Walt, please . . . rat stays": PL to Alan Dell, BBC Radio 2 interview, rec. 1992.

150 "make phonograph records": Contract, PL and Walt Disney Productions, Oct. 20, 1952.

151 "an elegant nightclub": Virginia Wicks to JG, Apr. 12, 2012.

151 "I wanted to": Recorded interview, PL to Ken Bloom and Bill Rudman, June 1993.

152 "not just musically": PL, magazine interview, source unknown, c. 1954.

152 "Rowles could": Dave Frishberg, *Written Word*, davefrishberg.net, Dec. 2006.

152 "Wait till": Ed Shaughnessy to JG, Dec. 8, 2010.

152 "Being very cautious": "At La Vie en Rose Peggy Rates Raves," *Down Beat*, May 6, 1953.

153 "a kind of scrim": Charlie Cochran to JG, Aug. 9, 2011.

154 "sprinkle a little": Ed Shaughnessy to JG, Dec. 8, 2010.

154 "It must be": Leonard Feather, "Raymond Scott on a Hi-Fi Kick," *Down Beat*, Oct. 21, 1953.

154 "I would make": Recorded interview, U.K., source unknown, c. 1982.

155 "That record": Mark Murphy to JG, Mar. 7, 1999.

155 "Here, we suspect": *Down Beat*, Sept. 23, 1953.

155 "my Bible": Petula Clark to JG, Mar. 5, 2013..

155 "virtuoso": *Paul McLoone Show Today*, FM Ireland, June 17, 2010.

155 "The problem arose": David Noh, "Gifts from Down Under," *Gay City News*, Mar. 27, 2013.

155 "pretty well perfect": Lorraine Feather to JG, May 9, 2011.

156 "I really loved": Ed Shaughnessy to JG, Dec. 8, 2010.

156 "It was a big": Kirtley Baskette, "Peggy Lee: She Can't Stop Giving," *Redbook*, Apr. 1955.

156 "I liked Brad": Dona Harsh Hutchinson to JG, Feb. 9, 2011.

156 "I don't have time": Liz Nichols, "Old-Fashioned Girl in Sequins," *TV Show*, Aug. 1953.

156 "With such disregard": Kirtley Baskette, "Peggy Lee: She Can't Stop Giving."

156 "because it was . . . tell you": Dona Harsh Hutchinson to JG, Feb. 9, 2011.

157 "Dave's business mistakes": *Miss Peggy Lee*, p. 161.

157 "husband to help": Lee Ringuette to JG, June 28, 2011.

157 "didn't like": "Singer Peggy Lee Wins Divorce in California," *Hartford Courant*, Nov. 4, 1953.

CHAPTER SEVEN

159 "One day my": "Jon Whitcomb Visits Peggy Lee," *Cosmopolitan*, Feb. 1955.

159 "walk": *Miss Peggy Lee*, p. 172.

159 "tripped": *Miss Peggy Lee*, p. 173.

160 "She wanted": Jack Larson to JG, Sept. 30, 2012.

160 "Egyptian": *Person to Person*, CBS-TV, Oct. 20, 1960.

160 "was like Pekingese": Lorraine Feather to JG, May 9, 2011.

160 "I get my ideas": "Peggy's Pitch is for People," *New York Journal-American*, Apr. 3, 1961.

160 "She hates": Jimmy Rowles, unpublished memoir, 1999.

161 "I was more or less": Gene DiNovi to JG, Dec. 19, 2010.

161 "Aunt Peg": Lee Ringuette to JG, June 28, 2011.

161 "Peggy could swing": Stella Castellucci to JG, Nov. 26, 2010.

161 "She's a complete": PL to Alan Dell, BBC Radio 2 interview, rec. 1992.

162 "wrote three": "Yvonne De Carlo Will Be Star in Latin Musical Made in Berlin," *Chicago Tribune*, Dec. 15, 1953.

162 "torrid romance": Dorothy Kilgallen, "Voice of Broadway: Station Wagon Set," *Washington Post and Times-Herald*, Apr. 1, 1954.

162 "Why would they book . . . is full.": Don Cherry with Neil Daniels, *Cherry's Jubilee*, Chicago: Triumph Books, 2006, p. 81.

163 "Nobody in . . . been her": Don Cherry to JG, July 31, 2012.

163 "take them . . . lettuce": *Cherry's Jubilee*, p. 82.

163 "I am simply mad": "Mr. Coward Dissects Las Vegas," *New York Times*, June 26, 1955.

164 "Vegas was a": George S. Jacobs with William Stadiem, *Mr. S: My Life with Frank Sinatra*, New York: It Books, 2003, p. 89.

164 "She didn't adjust": George Schlatter to JG, Apr. 20, 2011.

164 "I don't remember": Jack Costanzo to JG, Apr. 17, 2012.

165 "She struck me": Polly Bergen to JG, Dec. 22, 2010.

165 "wonderful yet": PL, notes to William Luce for musical *Peg*, 1982.

165 "She drinks": *The Colgate Variety Hour*, NBC-TV, July 24, 1955.

166 "It was like meeting": Arthur Hamilton to JG, Mar. 11, 1999.

166 "a beautiful woman": Ibid.

166 "a kind of hit": Mark Murphy to JG, Mar. 7, 1999.

167 "illness that befell": *Chicago Defender*, Nov. 20, 1954.

167 "major surgery": *Boston Globe*, Dec. 18, 1954.

167 "Zenlike peace": Lee Ringuette to JG, June 28, 2011.

167 "a New Age": Bill Rudman to JG, Apr. 2, 2013.

168 "I had never": Gene DiNovi to JG, Dec. 19, 2010.

168 "Peggy said, 'You know'": Stella Castellucci to JG, Nov. 26, 2010.

169 "You pick up": Peggy Lee, *Softly—with Feeling*, Los Angeles: private publication, 1953.

169 "Marianne was": Dona Harsh Hutchinson to JG, Feb. 9, 2011.

169 "which is unlike": Sidney Skolsky, "Hollywood Is My Beat," *New York Post*, Oct. 12, 1952.

169 "Peggy Lee doll": Mark Murphy to JG, Mar. 7, 1999.

170 "somebody was": Dona Harsh Hutchinson to JG, Feb. 9, 2011.

170 "I did not": Press release, *Pete Kelly's Blues*, Warner Bros., 1955.

171 "The only time": Janet Leigh, Warner Bros. press release, 1955.

172 "Reva": Betty Jungheim to JG, Feb. 9, 2011.

173 "I remember that": Nicki Lee Foster to JG, Jan. 30, 1999.

173 "with that stepmother": Stella Castellucci to JG, Aug. 22, 2012.

173 "I was bothered": Press release, *Pete Kelly's Blues*, Warner Bros., 1955.

173 "like a friendly cat": *Miss Peggy Lee*, p. 167.

173 "Our conversations": *City Lights* (Brian Linehan, host), Citytv, Toronto, 1984.

174 "He really started": Gene DiNovi to JG, Dec. 19, 2010.

174 "Sing a rainbow . . . she cried": Arthur Hamilton to JG, Mar. 11, 1999.

175 "I got so": *Dick Biondi & Friends*, WCFL-AM, Chicago, 1970.

175 "She was playing": Arthur Hamilton to JG, Mar. 11, 1999.

175 "Peggy Lee has always": Paul Pines to JG, Jan. 5, 2012.

175 "as manly as . . . 1955 picture": Henry McLemore, *Altoona (PA) Tribune*, May 23, 1955.

176 "below par": Bosley Crowther, *New York Times*, June 24, 1955.

177 "Few contemporary figures": John Tynan, "Peggy Lee—In Which a Multi-Talented Singer Discusses a Many-Faceted Career," *Down Beat*, Mar. 21, 1957.

177 "remarkable assignment": Randy Newman to JG, Jan. 14, 2013.

177 "I'm still not . . . implied sadness": John Tynan, "Peggy Lee."

177 "severe abdominal pains": "Singer III," *Chicago Tribune*, June 28, 1953.

177 "Peggy Lee's losing weight": Dorothy Kilgallen, "Eddie Fisher, Manage, Revamp Financial Deal," *Washington Post*, Apr. 12, 1956.

178 "You could tell . . . for them": Jack Larson to JG, Sept. 30, 2012.

178 "outstanding": Edwin Schallert, "Jack Webb Gets Tough with Music," *Los Angeles Times*, Aug. 11, 1955.

179 "no fewer": Edwin Schallert, "Chief Romantic Idol of Germany Contracted; Middleton Again Henry," *Los Angeles Times*, Sept. 12, 1955.

180 "I was an alcoholic . . . with me": Shaun Considine, "Miss Peggy Lee: ' . . . quite simply the finest singer in the history of popular music,' " *After Dark*, June 1974.

180 "They had me": PL, notes to William Luce for musical *Peg*, 1982.

180 "She *did*": Nicki Lee Foster to JG, Jan. 30, 1999.

180 "Peggy Lee has": Dorothy Kilgallen, "Bullfighter Luis Dating Ava Gardner," *Washington Post and Times-Herald*, Aug. 25, 1955.

180 "begun": Dorothy Kilgallen, "Rudy Calls Names, Vice Versa," *Washington Post and Times-Herald*, Aug. 9, 1955.

180 "she saw me": George Schlatter to JG, Apr. 20, 2011.

180 "I would have liked": PL to Alan Dell, BBC Radio 2 interview, rec. 1992.

181 "but I've never": George Christy, "Peggy Lee: Still at Fever's Pitch," *Interview*, Oct. 1984.

CHAPTER EIGHT

183 "It's orange": Newspaper column, source unknown, c. 1954.

183 "I can't seem": Ibid.

185 "You should cry": Stephen Citron, *Noel & Cole: The Sophisticates*, New York: Oxford University Press, p. 283.

185 "Are you a": Mark Murphy to JG, Dec. 20, 2011.

185 "My mom told me": Nancene Cohen to JG, May 16, 2011.

185 "was like the bouncer": Jack Costanzo to JG, Apr. 18, 2012.

185 "She's after me": Angela Levey to JG, Dec. 5, 2010.

186 "When the night": Max Bennett to JG, Oct. 28, 2010.

186 "There was no": Jack Costanzo to JG, Apr. 18, 2012.

186 "Give me a": John Tynan, "Peggy Lee: In Which a Multi-Talented Singer Discussed a Many-Faceted Career," *Down Beat*, Mar. 21, 1957.

186 "She'd say, 'I'd like": Lou Levy to JG, Feb. 2, 1999.

186 "I played": "Lou Levy talks to Steve Voce, Part 2," 1981–1982.

187 "I didn't get": PL to Alan Dell, BBC Radio 2 interview, rec. 1992.

187 "She was way up": Nicki Lee Foster to JG, Jan. 30, 1999.

187 "artistic gift": Mark Murphy to JG, Mar. 7, 1999.

187 "this group of": Nicki Lee Foster to JG, Jan. 30, 1999.

187 "She makes": Dick Kleiner, "Peggy Lee Wants to Quit the Road," *New York World-Telegram & Sun*, Nov. 5, 1955.

188 "If it becomes": Kirtley Baskette, "Peggy Lee: She Can't Stop Giving," *Redbook*, Apr. 1955.

188 "the thighs": Richard Lamparski to JG, June 22, 2013.

188 "He was spectacular looking": Jack Larson to JG, Sept. 30, 2012.

188 "a huge flirt": Charlie Cochran to JG, Aug. 9, 2011.

188 "I've been in love . . . flipped": "Peggy Lee and Dewey Martin: Their Love Story," *Modern Screen*, June 1957.

188 "There were two": Nicki Lee Foster to JG, Jan. 30, 1999.

188 "He was kind": Dona Harsh Hutchinson to JG, Feb. 9, 2011.

188 "She was one": Stella Castellucci to JG, Aug. 22, 2012.

190 "There, praying . . . our friends": "Peggy Lee and Dewey Martin: Their Love Story."

190 "He seemed utterly": Lee Ringuette to JG, June 28, 2011.

190 "Sometimes I feel": Walter Winchell, "The Broadway Beat," *Washington Post*, July 15, 1956.

191 "The House": "About Nat King Cole," *American Masters*, pbs.org, May 17, 2006.

192 "get Peggy back": Margaret Whiting to JG, Mar. 13, 1999.

192 "Let's do an album": PL to Harry Boswell, Magic 61, KFRC-FM, San Francisco, 1989.

192 "He conducted": Stella Castellucci to JG, Aug. 22, 2012.

193 "A lot of times": Jess Rand to JG, Aug. 29, 2011.

193 "Debussy meets": Gary Schocker to JG, Aug. 13, 2012.

193 "Frank wanted": PL to Alan Dell, BBC Radio 2 interview, rec. 1992.

194 "I don't remember": Dona Harsh Hutchinson to JG, Feb. 9, 2011.

194 "Dewey ran out": George Schlatter to JG, Apr. 20, 2011.

194 "insanely": Max Bennett to JG, Oct. 28, 2010.

194 "No. Let's just": Nicki Lee Foster to JG, Jan. 30, 1999.

194 "one instance": Stella Castellucci to JG, Aug. 22, 2012.

194 "He tried": Fred Apollo to JG, May 16, 2012.

194 "She had a joke": William Luce to JG, Nov. 8, 2011.

195 "I never heard": Lee Ringuette to JG, June 28, 2011.

195 "detested": Stella Castellucci to JG, Aug. 22, 2012.

197 *perfect for Peggy:* Max Bennett to JG, Oct. 28, 2010.

199 "The eternal struggle": Leonard Feather, "Peggy Lee": An Open Mind and Eager Ear for Today," *Los Angeles Times,* Mar. 7, 1971.

199 "effect of belting": Henry Pleasants, *The Great American Popular Singers,* New York: Simon & Schuster, 1974, p. 351.

199 "those provocatively": Don Bailer, "Peggy Sets a Feverish Pace!" *New York Daily Mirror,* Aug. 20, 1958.

199 "The young people": Ibid.

200 "free the sexual slaves": "Burning Desire," *The Fifties,* History Channel, 1997.

200 "a definite danger": Nick Redfern, *Celebrity Secrets: Official Government Files on the Rich and Famous,* New York: Simon & Schuster, 2007, p. 97.

200 "unacceptably light": Chris Fujiwara, *The World and Its Double: The Life and Work of Otto Preminger,* New York: Faber & Faber, Inc., 2008, p. 144.

200 "truly a composite": George Metalious and June O'Shea, *The Girl from Peyton Place,* New York: Dell, 1965.

201 "People were outraged": "Burning Desire," *The Fifties.*

201 "My mother was": Sidney Myer to JG, Jan. 2, 2013.

201 "A year ago": "Flynn Replaces Martin in 'Cavalry Patrol,'" *Hartford Courant,* May 26, 1957.

202 "Peggy would wake": Joe Harnell to JG, Mar. 13, 1999.

202 "exaggerated": Fred Apollo to JG, May 16, 2012.

202 "infectious": "Peggy Lee, III, May Be Sent to Hospital Today," *Los Angeles Times,* July 26, 1958.

202 "glandular fever": Don Bailer, "Peggy Sets a Feverish Pace!"

202 "a truckload of things": PL to Alan Dell, BBC Radio 2 interview, rec. 1992.

202 "grievous mental suffering": "Singer Peggy Lee Sues to Divorce Third Mate," *Los Angeles Times,* Sept. 11, 1958.

202 "hostile and moody": "Singer Divorces Actor," source unknown, June 18, 1959.

202 "extremely jealous": "Peggy Sings Blues, Exes 3d," *New York Daily News,* June 18, 1959.

203 "vile language": "Third Mate Divorced by Singer Peggy Lee," *Los Angeles Times,* June 17, 1959.

203 "he always tried": "Singer Divorces Actor."

203 "Nobody wanted": Max Bennett to JG, Oct. 28, 2010.

CHAPTER NINE

205 "They were her family": Fred Apollo to JG, May 16, 2012.

205 "Mary told me": Max Bennett to JG, Oct. 28, 2010.

206 "occasional beneficiary . . . the block": George S. Jacobs with William Stadiem, *Mr. S: My Life with Frank Sinatra,* New York: It Books, 2003, p. 75.

206 "an acute virus": "Peggy Lee Stricken," *Washington Post and Times-Herald,* Mar. 15, 1959.

207 "She stopped": Video, Joe Williams, *Society of Singers* tribute to Peggy Lee, 1994.

207 "He wasn't": André Previn to JG, Nov. 30, 2012.

207   "She owned": William Harbach to JG, Dec. 1, 2010.

207   "*Oh*, she was": André Previn to JG, Nov. 30, 2012.

208   "very reclusive": Clark Burroughs to JG, Apr. 2, 2012.

209   "worship of mediocrity": Sean O'Neal, "R.I.P. 'Sing Along with' Mitch Miller," avclub
.com, Aug. 2, 2010.

209   "one step from fascism": "Pop Goes the Little Old Music Maker," *New York Daily
News*, Sept. 20, 2004.

209   "one of the largest": William Barlow, *Voice Over: The Making of Black Radio*, Philadelphia: Temple University Press, 1998, p. 187.

210   "There we were": Yahoo! Latin jazz group, date unknown.

210   "because George": Will Friedwald, liner notes for CD reissue of *Beauty and the Beat!*,
1992.

210   "We had": Fred Hall, *Dialogues in Swing: Intimate Conversations with the Stars of the
Big Band Era*, Pathfinder Publisher of California, 1989.

211   "I was so exhausted": Will Friedwald, *Beauty and the Beat!*

211   "I never had": Eleanor Fuerst to JG, Oct. 26, 2010.

212   "The whisper": Column item, 1959; source unknown.

214   "We had a crush . . . thoughts": William Harbach to JG, Dec. 1, 2010.

214   "She was *funny* . . . riot": Ibid.

215   "went over": Dona Harsh Hutchinson to JG, May 17, 2011.

216   "The kids consider": John Crosby, "Dreadful Popular Music Hasn't a Monopoly Yet,"
Washington Post and Times-Herald, Aug. 17, 1959.

216   "She cost us": Lennie Green to JG, Dec. 11, 2010.

217   "Back then": Mike Melvoin to JG, Dec. 14, 2010.

217   "He was so": Barbara Carroll to JG, Dec. 4, 2010.

217   "Moe will be": Lennie Green to JG, Oct. 11, 2010.

217   "with earrings . . . dark room": Ibid.

218   "huge crowd": Bob Rolontz, "Benny Gasses Old and Young Anew," *Billboard*, Nov. 16,
1959.

219   "the queen": "Peggy Lee: The Life, the Songs," Kathy Larkin, *New York Daily News*,
Nov. 28, 1983.

219   "homely": Jess Rand to JG, Oct. 21, 2010.

219   "the rugged face": Larry L. King, "Rappin' with Peggy Lee," *Cosmopolitan*, Sept. 1971.

219   "I can take": Larry Townsend, "Night Scene: Perfect Light Man for a Perfectionist,"
Chicago Tribune, Feb. 19, 1971.

219   "Peggy, I can't . . . from the piano": Lou Levy to JG, Feb. 2, 1999.

219   "She looked like": Sheldon Roskin to JG, Nov. 4, 2010.

219   "She was loud": Lennie Green to JG, Dec. 11, 2010.

219   "Smitten by Peggy's": Phoebe Jacobs to JG, Feb. 11, 1999.

220   "If Peggy": Betty Jungheim to JG, Feb. 9, 2011.

220   "Perfection": Alan Jackson, "That's Not All There Is, Says Miss Lee," *Times* (London),
June 15, 1994.

220   "ravishing beauty": Phoebe Jacobs to JG, Feb. 11, 1999.

220   "No eyebrows": Bruce Vanderhoff to JG, Oct. 17, 2010.

220   "She made up . . . on that stage": Phoebe Jacobs to JG, Feb. 11, 1999.

221   "lima beans": Stella Castellucci to JG, Aug. 22, 2012.

221   "Clouds raised": Nicki Lee Foster to JG, Jan. 30, 1999.

221   "Power.' 'Burn.'": Lou Levy to JG, Feb. 2, 1999.

221   "This was not": William Harbach to JG, Dec. 1, 2010.

222   "In all her": Nick Lapole, "Peggy Lee Soars to Heights," *New York Journal-American*,
Mar. 8, 1960.

222   "Peggy Lee is one": Letter, Arthur Godfrey to Louis Sobel, Apr. 5, 1963; from Sobel's *The Longest Street*, New York: Crown Publishers, 1968, pp. 355–356.

223   *"Dear Peggy"*: Ronald William Towe, "Basin Street East and Miss Peggy Lee," source unknown, Jan. 1961.

223   "Basin Street": Bob Rolontz, "Can't Beat That Gal Peggy Lee," *Billboard*, Mar. 28, 1960.

223   "People of intelligence": Stella Castellucci to JG, Aug. 22, 2012.

223   "he took me . . . old friends": *City Lights* (Brian Linehan, host), Citytv, Toronto, 1984.

224   "Mousse of Salmon": Peggy Lee menu, date unknown.

224   "She did wonderful": Lee Ringuette to JG, June 28, 2011.

224   "that unique": Steve Allen to JG, Mar. 19, 1999.

225   "Singer Peggy Lee's Aim": *Boston Globe*, Sept. 20, 1959.

225   "to gain control": Kirtley Baskette, "Peggy Lee: She Can't Stop Giving," *Redbook*, Apr. 1955.

225   "I would far": Ibid.

225   "We are living" Ernest Holmes, *The Science of Mind*, New York: Penguin Putnam, p. 140.

225   "She always spoke . . . other person": Stella Castellucci to JG, Aug. 22, 2012.

226   "the most exercise": Max Bennett to JG, Oct. 28, 2010.

227   "Like the pretty . . . miserable": Mark Murphy to JG, Mar. 7, 1999.

CHAPTER TEN

229   "putting together": Lou Levy to JG, Feb. 2, 1999.

229   "They were the kind": Stefanie Powers to JG, Oct. 1, 2012.

229   "It is not": Larry L. King, "Rappin' with Peggy Lee," *Cosmopolitan*, Sept. 1971.

230   "All the big": Bart Howard to JG, Aug. 11, 1984.

231   "When I realized . . . tell me about": Gavin McLeod to JG, Apr. 18, 2011.

232   "Well, Charles . . . dogs": *Person to Person*, CBS-TV, Oct. 20, 1960.

233   "I was just . . . with laughter": Mart Crowley to JG, May 20, 2011.

234   "breaking up": Alex Freeman, "M.M. Gives Haley Headache," *Hartford Courant*, Mar. 13, 1963.

234   "This is the house": Leonard Harris, "Peggy Lee's Evening," *New York World-Telegram & Sun*, Mar. 1965.

234   "sizzling": "An Unrehearsed Performance," Arthur Gelb, *New York Times*, Feb. 3, 1961.

234   "When Peggy": Lou Levy to JG, Feb. 2, 1999.

234   "Miss Lee is late . . . herself onstage": "Jim Bishop, Reporter, Raves About: Peggy Lee," *Toronto Telegram*, Nov. 14, 1961.

234   "As one would": Richard Lamparski, *Manhattan Diary*, Albany, GA: Bear Manor Media, 2006, p. 9.

235   *"terribly* good-looking": Recording, Peggy Lee, Central Park, New York, July 27, 1970.

235   "His relationship": Steve Blum to JG, Sept. 6, 2011.

235   "she sagged": "Jim Bishop, Reporter, Raves About: Peggy Lee."

235   "Miss Lee comes out": Ann Geracimos, "Peggy Lee Leaves Nothing to Chance," *Toledo Blade*, May 16, 1965.

236   "was absolutely perfect": *Miss Peggy Lee*, p. 216.

236   "She was mad": Betty Jungheim to JG, Feb. 9, 2011.

236   "His skills": Bob Freedman to JG, Oct. 3, 2012.

236   "She wouldn't": Betty Jungheim to JG, Feb. 9, 2011.

236   "Quincy and I": Dona Harsh Hutchinson to JG, Feb. 9, 2011.

236 "prerecords": "Star-Gazing," *Pittsburgh Courier*, Sept. 25, 1965.

237 "uniformly good": John A. Tynan, *Down Beat*, July 19, 1962.

237 "provocative": Arthur Gelb, "An Unrehearsed Performance," *New York Times*, Feb. 3, 1961.

237 "the hub": Ronald William Towe, "Basin Street East and Miss Peggy Lee."

237 "I've never known . . . hear me?": Max Jones, "And Here's What Happens at a Miss Lee Rehearsal," *Melody Maker* (U.K.), July 22, 1961.

238 "diamond-studded gathering": *Evening News* (London), July, 17, 1961.

238 "Big hunks": "Nightbeat: PL," *Stage* (London), July 20, 1961.

238 "a singer with": "Happy Singer," *Evening Standard* (London), July 13, 1961.

238 "Oh, it must": Paula Ringuette to JG, Aug. 28, 2012.

238 "painfully self-conscious": Richard Lamparski, *Manhattan Diary*, Albany, GA: Bear Manor Media, 2006, p. 9.

238 "How I Wish": "How I Wish I Were Like My Mum—Says Nicki," *Daily Mirror* (London), July 4, 1961.

238 "Nicki could do": Phoebe Jacobs to JG, Feb. 11, 1999.

238 "I shall never": "How I Wish I Were Like My Mum—Says Nicki."

239 "majesty": Frank Quinn, "Peggy Lee Has SRO at BSE," *New York Mirror*, Nov. 11, 1961.

239 "*Why can't they*": Earl Wilson, "Peggy Lee Stages a Comeback," *New York Post*, Nov. 24, 1961.

239 "Peggy's more than": Ibid.

239 "I came so close": J.D. Reed, "Peggy Lee's Broadway Debut Was a Bust, but the Lady Has Lived Through Hard Times Before," *People*, Jan. 9, 1984.

240 "Most people": Martin Burden, "Peggy Lee Gives It All That There Is," *New York Post*, Dec. 7, 1983.

240 "take the scare": Charles Champlin, "Peggy, Benny in the Swing of It," *Los Angeles Times*, Apr. 28, 1965.

240 "I wanted desperately": Marshall Berges, "Peggy Lee: Is That All There Is? A Lady of Many Moods Finds There's Much More," *Los Angeles Times Home Magazine*, Oct. 19, 1975.

241 "I did only": Bob Thomas, "Peggy Lee Hopes Music by Big Bands Will Come Back," *Reading* (PA) *Eagle*, Mar. 4, 1960.

241 "I have to": Mike Melvoin to JG, Dec. 14, 2010.

242 "the funkiest": Jerry Leiber and Mike Stoller with David Ritz, *Hound Dog: The Leiber & Stoller Autobiography*, New York: Simon & Schuster, 2010, p. 234.

243 "too correct": Ibid.

243 "an impatient gal": Ibid.

244 "I don't want": Arthur Hamilton to JG, Mar. 11, 1999.

245 "a sweetheart": Dona Harsh Hutchinson to JG, Feb. 9, 2011.

245 "That was just . . . I left": Jack Sheldon to JG, Dec. 13, 2010.

246 "Peggy hardly": Jack Jones to JG, Feb. 6, 2013.

246 "just as volatile": Alex Freeman, "Peggy Lee Ends Another Marriage," *Hartford Courant*, June 25, 1964.

247 "Quincy made": Dona Harsh Hutchinson to JG, Feb. 9, 2011.

247 "The door was open": Lou Levy to JG, Feb. 2, 1999.

248 "loneliness": Nicki Lee Foster to JG, Jan. 30, 1999.

248 "Who is *that*?": Lou Levy to JG, Feb. 2, 1999.

248 "marry this chick": *Hartford Courant*, June 25, 1964.

248 "quietly hitched": Herb Lyon, "Tower Ticker," *Chicago Tribune*, Feb. 17, 1964.

248 "chronic": "Clerk Takes Marriage License to Peggy Lee," *Los Angeles Times*, Feb. 22, 1964.

249 "I think she": Nicki Lee Foster to JG, Jan. 30, 1999.

249 "All this": Lou Levy to JG, Feb. 2, 1999.

249 "Peggy introduced": Lynn Ringuette to JG, June 29, 2011.

249 "He told me": Dona Harsh Hutchinson to JG, May 17, 2011.

249 "I think the sand": Betty Jungheim to JG, Nov. 15, 2012.

249 "the man I love. . . . singing": John M. Cathcart, "After 4 Broken Marriages My Career Has Cost Me Enough, Says Peggy Lee," *National Enquirer*, 1974.

250 "It was a barn": Vince Mauro to JG, Jan. 2, 2013.

250 "Say it . . . cute": Richard Lamparski, *Manhattan Diary*, p. 9.

250 "I want you": Lou Levy to JG, Feb. 2, 1999.

250 "She really needed": Emilio Palame to JG, May 19, 2013.

251 "Father, if you": Thomas C. Wheeler, "The Timeless Charm of Peggy Lee," *Saturday Evening Post*, Oct. 10, 1964.

251 "figuring how": Martin Burden, "Peggy Lee Gives It All That There Is."

251 "We were a little": "True Love Hits Bumps for 3 Film Couples," *Los Angeles Times*, June 18, 1964.

251 "forced to go": "Peggy Lee Gets Divorce, Claiming Husband Lazy," *St. Joseph (MO) Gazette*, Nov. 5, 1964.

251 "You have the same . . . knew you": Hal Schaefer to JG, Feb. 7, 2011.

CHAPTER ELEVEN

253 "grandma": Lou Levy to JG, Feb. 2, 1999.

253 "The place is": "Joan to Take It Slower This Time," *Washington Post and Times-Herald*, Aug. 11, 1964.

253 "Pink makes me": Arlene Dahl, "Attitude, Voice and in Beauty," *Chicago Tribune*, Nov. 2, 1964.

253 "piercing scream . . . let us know": Paul Coates, "Ex-Landed Gentleman Relaxes Back Where the Livin' Is Noisy," *Los Angeles Times*, Apr. 21, 1965.

255 "She looks like . . . Cary Grant": Thomas C. Wheeler, "The Timeless Charm of Peggy Lee," *Saturday Evening Post*, 1964.

255 "spiritual": Phoebe Jacobs to JG, Feb. 11, 1999.

255 "Without explaining": Peggy Lee, "And Then I Wrote," *Record World*, Mar. 8, 1969.

255 "When this scene": Johnny Mandel to JG, Nov. 14, 2010.

256 "I see you": John Pisano to JG, Dec. 8, 2010.

256 "panhandlers": *Hy Gardner's Offbeat Guide to New York*, New York: Grosset & Dunlap, 1964, p. 99.

256 "aim for": *Billboard*, July 10, 1965.

256 "They started": PL to Ken Bloom and Bill Rudman, June 1993.

257 "crowded to the": Nick Lapole, "Peggy Makes Magic," *New York Journal-American*, Mar. 2, 1965.

257 "Whenever she's on": *The Dean Martin Show*, NBC-TV, Nov. 13, 1969.

257 "a cigar-store Indian": Bob Spitz, "The Beatles Invasion, 50 Years Ago: Sunday, Feb. 9, 1964," *Time*, Feb. 9, 2014.

257 "I think I'm": *The Andy Williams Show*, NBC-TV, Sept. 27, 1962.

257 "looked like": Lou Levy to JG, Feb. 2, 1999.

257 "Peggy wasn't": Robert W. Richards to JG, Feb. 15, 1999.

258 "this huge": Doak Roberts to JG, Apr. 14, 2011.

258 "You see the garden": PL, *Monitor*, NBC radio, May 10, 1970.

258 "about twice": Eugene Boe, "Peggy Lee: An Artist Tunes Up for the Waldorf," *Cue*, Apr. 5, 1969.

259   "was everyone's idea": Bruce Vanderhoff to JG, Nov. 13, 2010.

259   "endless": Lou Levy to JG, Feb. 2, 1999.

259   "Guys who played": Grady Tate to JG, Feb. 13, 1999.

259   "She explained": Bill Holman to JG, June 21, 2011.

260   "airy sounds": Vince Mauro to JG, Jan. 2, 2013.

260   "She didn't have": Walter Willison to JG, June 22, 2011.

260   "was the pinnacle . . . earshot": Mel Tormé, "A Farewell to the Old Hotel Night Spots," *New York Times*, Jan. 30, 1977.

261   "*Move your*": Sheldon Roskin to JG, Nov. 4, 2010.

261   "triumph": Nick Lapole, "Peggy Scores a Kayo," *New York Journal-American*, Nov. 12, 1965.

261   "She needed people . . . projects": Sheldon Roskin to JG, Nov. 4, 2010.

261   "I must": "Parsimonious Peggy," *Time*, Nov. 3, 1967.

261   "woman of": Thomas C. Wheeler, "The Timeless Charm of Peggy Lee."

262   "God will not": Kathy Larkin, "Peggy Lee: The Life, the Songs," *New York Daily News*, Nov. 28, 1983.

262   "I'm a Woman": PL lighting chart, c. 1975.

262   "down almost": Eugene Boe, "Peggy Lee: An Artist Tunes Up for the Waldorf."

262   "She'd hire . . . helpful to me": Kathy Levy to JG, June 11, 2013.

263   "She poured": Kathy Levy to JG, Feb. 3, 1999.

263   "Most of the time": Bruce Vanderhoff to JG, Oct. 24, 2012.

263   "She had a": Doak Roberts to JG, Apr. 14, 2011.

263   "If she'd worn": Bruce Vanderhoff to JG, Oct. 24, 2012.

263   "pretty goofy": Jack Sheldon to JG, Dec. 13, 2010.

264   "She would just . . . nonreality of it": Kathy Levy to JG, Feb. 3, 1999.

264   "She seems almost": Peper, "Peggy Lee Back at Basin Street," *New York World-Telegram & Sun*, Apr. 17, 1962.

264   "Each time": Larry L. King, "Rappin' with Peggy Lee," *Cosmopolitan*, Sept. 1971.

264   "everything she did": Peter Levinson to JG, Mar. 12, 1999.

265   "Age has done": Norman J. O'Connor, "Peggy Lee Manufacturers Smooth Nightclub Performance," *Boston Globe*, Mar. 31, 1963.

265   "When Marian": Angela Levey to JG, Dec. 5, 2010.

265   "After being": Kathy Levy to JG, June 12, 2013.

265   "David and I": Dona Harsh Hutchinson to JG, Feb. 9, 2011.

266   "She just fled": Nancy Olson Livingston to JG, May 26, 2011.

266   "She's sitting": Marian Collier to JG, Mar. 1, 2012.

266   "former husband": "Dave Barbour Dies; Guitarist Was 53," *New York Times*, Dec. 13, 1965.

266   "Recent reports": "Song Writer Barbour, 53," *Washington Post–Times Herald*, Dec. 14, 1965.

266   "My father": Nicki Lee Barbour to JG, Jan. 30, 1999.

266   "There's no way": Marian Collier to JG, Mar. 1, 2012.

267   "Peg, what do": Robert W. Richards to JG, Feb. 15, 1999.

267   "three A.M.": Peter Reilly, "Peggy Lee: Ready to Begin Again," *Stereo Review*, Mar. 1976.

267   "A couple of days": Steve Blum to JG, Sept. 6, 2011.

268   "I'm quite nutty": Donal Henahan, "Cary Grant Records Holiday Lullaby for Daddies," *New York Times*, Dec. 19, 1967.

269   "Plump": "Miss Peggy Lee a Hit at Copa," Doug McClelland, source unknown, Oct. 14, 1967.

269   "thin at the top": "Parsimonious Peggy," *Time*, Nov. 3, 1967.

269 "For one": *The Joe Franklin Show*, WOR-AM, June 24, 1968.

269 "so many": Rex Reed, "Somethin' Groovy," *Stereo Review*, Jan. 1968.

270 "not impressed": "A Confidential Report Covering 1956–1964 to Alan W. Livingston from Dave Dexter, Jr., International A&R Director," Oct. 1, 1964.

270 "just a bunch": Neil McCormick, "Nearly 50 Years Ago Today, The Beatles Taught the U.S. to Play," *Telegraph* (U.K.), Jan. 21, 2014.

270 "the hottest thing": "A Confidential Report . . ."

270 "Music Executive": Dennis McLellan, "Alan Livingston, 1917–2009: Music Executive Signed the Beatles to Capitol Records," *Chicago Tribune*, Mar. 15, 2009.

271 "exclusionary": Vince Mauro to JG, Jan. 14, 2013.

271 "When you feel": Judy Klemesrud, "Peggy Lee Is Still on Top—Is That All There Is?" *New York Times*, Apr. 26, 1970.

271 "a job with": Dave Dexter, Wikipedia.org.

271 "To Gortikov": Dave Dexter, Jr., *Playback*, New York: Billboard Press, 1976, p. 212.

272 "We have to": "Cap. A&R Staffers Hit 17; Wright Is Added," *Billboard*, Dec. 7, 1968.

272 "I want to move": Leonard Feather, "Peggy Lee Turns to the Now Sound," *Los Angeles Times*, May 19, 1968.

273 "tough broad . . . recording her": Charles Koppelman to JG, Oct. 17, 2012.

274 "pinky rings . . . fans of Peggy Lee": Ibid.

274 "For some years now": Peter Reilly, "Peggy Lee . . . and That Old Vocal Eroticism," *Stereo Review*, Oct. 1973.

275 "all of you": Peggy Lee, *2 Shows Nightly*, Capitol, 1968.

275 "was vintage": Charles Koppelman to JG, Oct. 17, 2012.

275 "Peggy Lee Turns to the Now Sound": Leonard Feather, "Peggy Lee Turns to the Now Sound."

275 "weren't gonna": Don Rubin to JG, Oct. 24, 2012.

275 "Working with": Leonard Feather, "Peggy Lee Turns to the Now Sound."

276 "At that time": Charles Koppelman to JG, Oct. 17, 2012.

276 "From the time": Brian Panella to JG, Oct. 11, 2012.

276 "about as relaxing": Larry L. King, "Rappin' with Peggy Lee."

276 "The minute": Betty Jungheim to JG, Feb, 9, 2011.

277 "I had come . . . Adela": Brian Panella to JG, Oct. 11, 2012.

277 "You know, Betty": Betty Jungheim to JG, Nov. 15, 2012.

277 "Trust the divine": Brian Panella to JG, Oct. 11, 2012.

277 "the curse": Dennis McLellan, "Writer Adela Rogers St. Johns Dies at 94," *Los Angeles Times*, Aug. 11, 1988.

277 "And she would": Brian Panella to JG, Oct. 11, 2012.

278 "She was the biggest": Grady Tate to JG, Feb. 13, 1999.

278 "sustained herself": Albert Goldman, "A Queen on a Lonely Peak," *Life*, Oct. 19, 1971.

278 "Aggressive females": Ernest Leogrande, "Here's Peggy," *New York Daily News*, Apr. 18, 1970.

278 "I've always been": "Peggy Lee Still Sings Way Across Country," *Hartford Courant*, Jan. 26, 1972.

278 "I'd like to . . . nameless something": Unedited interview with Shirley Eder for *Monitor*, NBC radio, Dec. 1967.

281 "Well, gentlemen . . . *Everything*": Jerry Leiber to JG, Feb. 22, 1999.

CHAPTER TWELVE

283 "I've lived": Eugene Boe, "Peggy Lee: An Artist Tunes Up for the Waldorf," *Cue*, Apr. 5, 1969.

283 "There are two": PL, *Monitor*, NBC radio, Dec. 14, 1969.

283 "That movie": Sidney Myer to JG, Jan. 2, 2013.

283 "As hard as": Brian Panella to JG, Oct. 11, 2012.

284 "a put-on": Ben Ratliff, "Gravel-Voiced Portraits of a Gallery of Rogues," *New York Times*, Sept. 21, 2008.

284 "I really consider": Recording, Peggy Lee, Central Park, New York, July 27, 1970.

284 "I'd seen her . . . attainment": Randy Newman to JG, Jan. 14, 2013.

285 "some pseudo": Mike Stoller to JG, Dec. 17, 2012.

286 "We're playing": Mike Barone to JG, Oct. 18, 2012.

286 "something a little": Mike Stoller to JG, Dec. 17, 2012.

286 "weren't great": Jerry Leiber to JG, Feb. 22, 1999.

286 "Listen, I": Mike Stoller to JG, Dec. 17, 2012.

286 "I was always": Tony Terran to JG, Jan. 20, 2013.

286 "hallucinatory": Albert Goldman, "A Queen on a Lonely Peak," *Life*, Oct. 19, 1971.

286 "I almost": Jerry Leiber to JG, Feb. 22, 1999.

287 "What's wrong?": Jerry Leiber and Mike Stoller, *Hound Dog: The Leiber and Stoller Autobiography*, New York: Simon & Schuster, 2009, p. 244.

287 "Either he": Jerry Leiber to JG, Feb. 22, 1999.

287 "Guess I'll have": *Hound Dog*, p. 245.

287 "nothing short": Ibid.

288 "somber": Jerry Leiber to JG, Feb. 22, 1999.

288 "She had a . . . glasses": Phil Wright to JG, Jan. 12, 2013.

289 "She was not": Mike Melvoin to JG, Dec. 14, 2010.

289 "I could": Nat Hentoff, "Cosmo Listens to Records," *Cosmopolitan*, 1969.

289 "I fell in love": Vermettya Royster to JG, Apr. 9, 2013.

289 "It is cold . . . Ribbit!": John Hallowell, "Peggy Lee Is Very Different from You and Me," *Los Angeles Times*, Apr. 12, 1970.

289 "She knew": Phil Wright to JG, Jan. 12, 2013.

289 "There's no": Nat Hentoff, "Cosmo Listens to Records."

290 "I think she": Mike Melvoin to JG, Dec. 14, 2010.

290 "a stunning": Nat Hentoff, "Cosmo Listens to Records."

290 "a bundle": "Peggy Lee Gives a Music Lesson," Cliff Smith, source unknown.

291 "fool's assumption": Mike Melvoin to JG, Dec. 14, 2010.

292 "Remember Peggy?": Joyce Haber, "Improvement in Barbra's 'Concert,'" *Los Angeles Times*, July 17, 1969.

292 "Naturally I": Judy Klemesrud, "Peggy Lee Is Still on Top—Is That All There Is?" *New York Times*, Apr. 26, 1970.

292 "If the truth": Bruce Vanderhoff to JG, Oct. 24, 2012.

293 "She screamed": Betty Jungheim to JG, Feb. 9, 2011.

293 "crown jewel": Press release, Waldorf-Astoria Hotel, 1969.

293 "It *was* intimidating": Sidney Myer to JG, Jan. 2, 2013.

294 "Honey-dripping singing": Marlene Dietrich, *Marlene Dietrich's ABC*, New York: Doubleday, 1962, p. 93.

294 "Hugo would be": Bruce Vanderhoff to JG, Nov. 13, 2010.

295 "I helped": Doak Roberts to JG, Apr. 14, 2011.

295 "She wings": Peter Reilly, "Peggy Lee . . . and That Old Vocal Eroticism," *Stereo Review*, Oct. 1973.

296 "So many things": Sidney Myer to JG, Jan. 2, 2013.

296 "with open": Albert Goldman, "A Queen on a Lonely Peak," *Life*, Oct. 19, 1971.

297 "today's trends": *Variety*, Apr. 16, 1969.

297 "Peggy, you've . . . never open!": *Miss Peggy Lee*, WNET, 1969.

299 "Peggy was the eye": Robert Foshko to JG, June 28, 2011.

299 "planned for": Cecil Smith, "Peggy Lee, Singer for All Seasons," *Los Angeles Times*, July 2, 1969.

299 "government work": Peter Levinson to JG, Mar. 12, 1999.

299 "got it in her head": Lou Levy to JG, Feb. 2, 1999.

299 "You're not . . . century": Betty Jungheim to JG, Feb. 9, 2011.

300 "the toughest": Norma Lee Browning, "Streisand in Vegas," *Chicago Tribune*, June 30, 1969.

300 "curious . . . to learn": Charles Champlin, *Los Angeles Times*, July 1969.

300 "The acclaim": *Cue*, July 1969.

300 "suffused the room": Charles Champlin, *Los Angeles Times*.

300 "the old pro": John Hallowell, "Peggy Lee Is Very Different from You and Me."

301 "But if you": Brian Panella to JG, Oct. 17, 2010.

301 "too long": Peter Levinson to JG, Mar. 12, 1999.

301 "apocalypse": Jann Wenner, "Jagger Remembers," *Rolling Stone*, Dec. 14, 1995.

301 "some kind": Franklin Bruno, " 'Is That All There Is?' and the Uses of Disenchantment," *Listen Again: A Momentary History of Pop Music* (Eric Weisbard, ed.), Durham, NC: Duke University Press, p. 139.

301 "It was unlike": Randy Newman to JG, Jan. 14, 2013.

302 "The principal thrust": "New Artist Development Keys Cap to Be No. 1," *Billboard*, June 13, 1970.

302 "sullen, cold-steel": Dave Dexter, Jr., *Playback*, New York: Billboard Press, 1976, p. 214.

303 "a moment of muddy": Jon Pareles, "Woodstock: A Moment of Muddy Grace," *New York Times*, Aug. 5, 2009.

303 "one of the greatest": *The Joey Bishop Show*, ABC-TV, Aug. 21, 1969.

304 "the phones at ABC": "Insider Tribute," *TV Guide*, Feb. 23, 2002.

304 "old woman": Rob Hoerburger, "The Lives They Lived: Is That All There Is?," *New York Times*, Dec. 29, 2002.

305 "I think most": Sidney Myer to JG, Jan. 2, 2013.

305 "Maybe the world": Jerry Leiber to JG, Feb. 22, 1999.

305 "extremely pessimistic": Neil Simon, *Desert Island Discs* (BBC), May 14, 1995.

305 "They still refused": Brian Panella to JG, Oct. 17, 2010.

305 "Some people": *Monitor*, NBC radio, Dec. 14, 1969.

306 "When you've reached": Paul Pines to JG, July 18, 2012.

306 "very liberating": Mike Stoller to JG, Dec. 17, 2012.

306 "When she went": Brian Panella to JG, Oct. 17, 2010.

306 "She kept calling": Betty Jungheim to JG, Feb. 9, 2011.

306 "He was gone . . . Sills": Kathy Levy to JG, June 12, 2013.

306 "may have": Brian Panella to JG, Feb. 9, 2011.

307 "Peggy Lee, I used": Bruce Vanderhoff to JG, Oct. 17, 2010.

309 "the most gracious . . . feel it": Brian Panella to JG, Feb. 9, 2011.

CHAPTER THIRTEEN

311 "an obstinate volcano": John Hallowell, "Peggy Lee Is Very Different from You and Me," *Los Angeles Times*, Apr. 12, 1970.

312 "because she is": "Pompidou Dinner, Leaders Trade Praise," *New York Times*, Feb. 25, 1970.

312 "One of the reasons": Judy Klemesrud, "Peggy Lee Is Still on Top: Is That All There Is?" *New York Times*, Apr. 26, 1970.

312 "You're not gonna": Peter Levinson to JG, Mar. 12, 1999.

312 "pinnacle of success . . . *Miss* Peggy Lee.": Recording, PL, White House, Feb. 24, 1970.

313 "I'm very fond . . . Indians!" Ibid.

313 "I was thinking": Mundell Lowe to JG, Dec. 2, 2010.

313 "I had a pet . . . along with me?": Recording, PL, White House.

314 "*I don't know . . . all right!*": Ibid.

314 "a disaster": Vera Glaser, "Peggy's Act Tests Nixon's Tact," newspaper unknown, Feb. 26, 1970.

314 "was in such": Betty Beale, "Letter from Washington," *Washington Star*, Mar. 7, 1970.

314 "sexy routines": "Peggy's Act Tests Nixon's Tact."

314 "We made a": Earl Wilson, "It Happened Last Night," *New York Post*, Mar. 2, 1970.

314 "totally inaccurate": Judy Klemesrud, "Peggy Lee Is Still on Top."

315 "*Miss Peggy Lee! . . . very* much." Ibid.

316 "like the phoenix": Nicki Lee Foster to JG, Jan. 30, 1999.

316 "What a remarkable": Marilyn Beck, "Peggy Lee Must Limit Engagements," *Hartford Courant*, Apr. 13, 1970.

317 "It was so": *City Lights* (Brian Linehan, host), Citytv, Toronto, 1984.

317 "She had that . . . as I was": Petula Clark to JG, Mar. 5, 2013.

318 "She was born": *Petula*, ABC-TV, Dec. 9, 1970.

318 "I can't say": Brian Panella to JG, Oct. 17, 2010.

319 "It was so": Judy Collins to JG, Feb. 12, 2013.

319 "*WE LOVE YOU! . . .* always": Recording, Peggy Lee, Central Park, New York, July 27, 1970.

319 "She led with that": William Luce to JG, Aug. 17, 2012.

320 "I think a big": Robert Strom to JG, Jan. 8, 2012.

320 "If Peggy had": Robert W. Richards to JG, Feb. 15, 1999.

320 "She played everybody": Angela Levey to JG, Dec. 5, 2010.

320 "*Don't* mention": Peter Levinson to JG, Mar. 12, 1999.

320 "I don't think": Brian Panella to JG, Oct. 17, 2010.

320 "How old": Angela Levey to JG, Dec. 5, 2010.

321 "We used to": Betty Jungheim to JG, Feb. 9, 2011.

321 "I don't think": Betty Jungheim to JG, Feb. 9, 2011.

321 "Oh, no, honey": Leata Galloway to JG, Mar. 30, 2013.

321 "My kids need me": Patricia Bernard to JG, May 5, 2011.

322 "I think Nicki": Dona Harsh Hutchinson to JG, Feb. 9, 2011.

322 "a direct input": Nancy Liebler and Sandra Moss, *Healing Depression the Mind-Body Way: Creating Happiness with Meditation, Yoga, and Ayurveda*, Hoboken, NJ: John Wiley & Sons, 2009, p. 103.

322 "At some point": Earl Wilson, "It Happened Last Night," *New York Post*, Oct. 30, 1976.

323 "Oh, that's the . . . furious": Betty Jungheim to JG, Nov. 15, 2012.

323 "I was watching": *Tonight*, NBC-TV, Oct. 29, 1979.

323 "I think I've died": Jim Bailey to JG, Aug. 19, 2011.

323 "Friends were calling": Shaun Considine, "Miss Peggy Lee: ' . . . quite simply the finest singer in the history of popular music,'" *After Dark*, June 1974.

323 "What was I . . . in a way": Jim Bailey to JG, Aug. 19, 2011.

324 "She's burned . . . every night": Brian Panella to JG, Oct. 17, 2010.

324 "I'm thinking . . . that basket": Ibid.

325 "It's no wonder . . . better job": "Miss Peggy Lee," *New Yorker*, Mar. 18, 1972.

325 "The way she smokes": Mary Daniels, "Peggy Keeps Going, Still Glowing," *Chicago Tribune*, Feb. 19, 1971.

325 "It was a dress": Jim Bailey to JG, Aug. 19, 2011.

326   "There are different": Bob Mardesich to JG, June 30, 2011.

326   "vanilla-whip-'N-Chill": Mary Daniels, "Peggy Keeps Going, Still Glowing."

326   "We touched it": Bruce Vanderhoff to JG, Oct. 17, 2010.

327   "He looked like Hercules": Leata Galloway to JG, Mar. 30, 2013.

327   "demented queen": Robert W. Richards to JG, Feb. 15, 1999.

327   "Oh, you want": Bob Mardesich to JG, June 30, 2011.

327   "She's the best": Joan Rattman Heilman, "Fringe Benefits for Jet-Set Hairdressers," *Australian Women's Weekly*, Dec. 6, 1972.

328   "This is the way . . . over here": Larry L. King, "Rappin' with Peggy Lee," *Cosmopolitan*, Sept. 1971.

328   "I went to": Brian Panella to JG, Jan. 27, 2013.

328   "Sing 'Fever.' . . . *enough!*": Larry L. King, "Rappin' with Peggy Lee."

328   "Are you all right? . . . went nuts": Ibid.

329   "the queen": Bruce Vanderhoff to JG, Oct. 17, 2010.

329   "She was a sneak": Phoebe Jacobs to JG, Feb. 11, 1999.

329   "I don't understand": Betty Jungheim to JG, Dec. 15, 2012.

330   "Oh, I take": Bill Burrus, "Peggy Lee: At Fever Pitch," *New York Post*, Apr. 12, 1969.

330   "I want to live": Alfred G. Aronowitz, "Miss Peggy Lee (III)," *New York Post*, Mar. 23, 1972.

331   "Now he's broke . . . *it's mine!*": "Smiles from Yesterday," *Owen Marshall, Counselor at Law*, ABC-TV, Feb. 17, 1972.

332   "I helped *start*": Betty Jungheim to JG, Apr. 15, 2011.

332   "His ego": Brian Panella to JG, Oct. 17, 2010.

332   "a little pisher . . . applauded": Artie Butler to JG, Mar. 20, 1999.

334   "I'm watching her": Brian Panella to JG, Oct. 17, 2010.

334   "Whatever the craziness": Artie Butler to JG, Mar. 20, 1999.

334   "*Has he lost*": Brian Panella to JG, Oct. 17, 2010.

335   "sort of": Tom Von Malder, *Chicago Herald*, Aug. 4, 1972.

335   "three or four": Peter Reilly, "Peggy Lee . . . and That Old Vocal Eroticism," *Stereo Review*, Oct. 1973.

336   "Peggy was great": Spider Saloff to JG, July 13, 2013.

336   "Last night": Leonard Feather, "The Pleasures and Pains of Peggy Lee," *Los Angeles Times*, Dec. 10, 1972.

337   "He *made* me . . . about this": *This Is Your Life*, Mar. 11, 1973.

337   "Betty and I": Doak Roberts to JG, Apr. 14, 2011.

338   "completely made up": Robert W. Richards to JG, Feb. 15, 1999.

338   "I slipped": Shaun Considine, "Miss Peggy Lee: ' . . . quite simply the finest singer in the history of popular music,'" *After Dark*, June 1974.

338   "the richest girl": Rob Haskell, "Doris Duke: The Richest Girl in the World," *Harper's Bazaar*, Aug. 29, 2012.

339   "Is everything OK": Paul Horner to JG, Apr. 28, 2013.

340   "sexy act": Larry L. King, "Rappin' with Peggy Lee."

340   "It was going": Robert W. Richards to JG, Feb. 15, 1999.

341   "Gail said . . . spiritual": Walter Willison to JG, June 22, 2011.

342   "beneath her . . . periphery . . .": Brian Panella to JG, Oct. 17, 2010.

343   "Peggy didn't fall": Bruce Vanderhoff to JG, Nov. 3, 2010.

343   "They did not": Brian Panella to JG, Oct. 17, 2010.

343   "I want you": Betty Jungheim to JG, Nov. 15, 2012.

343   "I learned": Brian Panella to JG, Oct. 17, 2010.

CHAPTER FOURTEEN

345 "It was very . . . done for me": Nicki Lee Foster to JG, Jan. 30, 1999.

345 "The conversations": Robert W. Richards to JG, Feb. 15, 1999.

346 "There was the . . . you ain't!": Doak Roberts to JG, Apr. 14, 2011.

348 "He sat down": Betty Jungheim to JG, Nov. 15, 2012.

348 "If she looked": Doak Roberts to JG, Apr. 14, 2011.

348 "for no reason": Peggy Lee, "The Miracle That Saved My Career," *National Enquirer*, July 28, 1974.

349 "started eating them": Doak Roberts to JG, June 23, 2011.

349 "turned to God": Peggy Lee, "The Miracle That Saved My Career."

349 "some fantastic": Bruce Vanderhoff to JG, May 15, 2013.

349 "It's so marvelous": Shaun Considine, "Miss Peggy Lee."

350 "simply because . . . minute of it": Doak Roberts to JG, June 23, 2011.

351 "Success is": Press release, "Peggy Lee Comments on Assorted Subjects."

351 "My favorite color": Ibid.

351 "An English butler": Colin Dangaard, " 'Miss Standing Ovation' Mellows with Age," *Washington Star*, Mar. 16, 1975.

351 "a flowing gown . . . Weird": Scarth Flett, "Meeting People: What Man Would Stand for His Wife Writing Songs in the Middle of the Night?," *Sunday Express* (London), Nov. 25, 1973.

351 "By the way . . . go back": Bruce Vanderhoff to JG, Oct. 17, 2010.

352 "crushing pain": *One Christmas*, Truman Capote, New York: Random House, 1983, p. 39.

352 "Oh, my God! . . . protective of her": George Plimpton, *Truman Capote: In Which Various Friends, Enemies, Acquaintances and Detractors Recall His Turbulent Career*, New York: Doubleday, 1997, pp. 373–376.

353 "I wanna do": Christopher Andersen, *Barbra: The Way She Is*, New York: Harper Entertainment, p. 220.

354 "disastrous": Shaun Considine, "Not All Pop Legends Are Indestructible," *New York Times*, Oct. 27, 1974.

354 "minor surgery": "Peggy Lee Recovering After Minor Surgery," *Hartford Courant*, Apr. 6, 1974.

354 "I'm either": Len Epand, "The Generation Bridge," *Zoo World: The Music Magazine*, July 18, 1974.

354 "long-term contract": "Peggy Lee Contract," *Los Angeles Times*, May 10, 1974.

354 "I am so . . . an inspiration": Len Epand, "The Generation Bridge."

355 "He said, 'Peggy' ": Betty Jungheim to JG, Apr. 15, 2011.

355 "No, that's": Len Epand, "The Generation Bridge."

355 "Rock music tore": Shaun Considine, "Miss Peggy Lee: ' . . . quite simply the finest singer in the history of popular music,' " *After Dark*, June 1974.

356 "keeps on happening": Morgan Ames, *High Fidelity*, 1974.

356 "first-rate": Shaun Considine, "Not All Pop Legends Are Indestructible."

356 "He's not contemporary": Betty Jungheim to JG, Feb. 9, 2011.

357 "I was way . . . leave holes": Frank Fiore to JG, Feb. 23, 2013.

357 "Back then . . . to move": Leata Galloway to JG, Mar. 30, 2013.

357 "When I was . . . precious": Recording, Peggy Lee, North Dakota State University, Fargo, May 23, 1975.

358 "To criticize her": David Tipmore, "Wanted: The Real Miss Peggy Lee," *Village Voice*, Sept. 26, 1974.

358 "because we were . . . per se": Frank Fiore to JG, Feb. 23, 2013.

359 "When I first": John Whitfield to JG, Apr. 16, 2013.

359 "Once she": Leata Galloway to JG, Mar. 30, 2013.

359 "We would get . . . silly": Frank Fiore to JG, Feb. 23, 2013.

359 "I remember a time": Leata Galloway to JG, Mar. 30, 2013.

360 "It was the": Frank Fiore to JG, Feb. 23, 2013.

360 "*I don't want* . . . not talk": Betty Jungheim to JG, Feb. 9, 2011.

360 "seemed to run": Mike Stoller to JG, Mar. 2, 1999.

360 "Everybody's sick": Robert W. Richards to JG, Feb. 15, 1999.

360 "North Dakota's": Recording, Peggy Lee, North Dakota State University.

361 "Lou divorced": John Pisano to JG, Dec. 8, 2010.

361 "What do you": Kathy Levy to JG, Feb. 3, 1999.

361 "PEGGY LEE SANG HERE": George Christy, "Peggy Lee: Still at Fever's Pitch," *Interview*, Oct. 1984.

361 "tremendous contribution . . . back again": Recording, Peggy Lee, North Dakota State University.

362 "Just where": Alec Wilder, *Letters I Never Mailed*, New York: Little, Brown & Co., 1975, p.164.

362 "She loved cold": Lou Levy to JG, Feb. 2, 1999.

362 "She kept putting . . . current": Jerry Leiber to JG, Feb. 22, 1999.

362 "by singing covers": Mike Stoller to JG, Dec. 17, 2012.

363 "wanted a lot": Phil Wright to JG, Jan. 12, 2013.

363 "Peggy, we've": Jerry Leiber to JG, Feb. 22, 1999.

363 "Those purchases": Jerry Leiber and Mike Stoller (with David Ritz), *Hound Dog: The Leiber & Stoller Autobiography*, New York: Simon & Schuster, 2010, p. 252.

364 "They just wanted": David McMacken to JG, June 18, 2011.

364 "To have an album . . . advantage of": Jerry Moss to JG, June 21, 2010.

365 "as a backup": Peter Stoller to JG, May 11, 2014.

366 "That's really": Mike Stoller to JG, Dec. 17, 2012.

366 "She was completely": Kathy Levy to JG, Feb. 3, 1999.

367 "I couldn't breathe": Jerry Moss to JG, June 21, 2010.

367 "I won't record": Mike Stoller to JG, Mar. 2, 1999.

367 "she suddenly got": Robert W. Richards to JG, Feb. 15, 1999.

367 "some bitter . . . beautiful performance": Mike Stoller to JG, Mar. 2, 1999.

368 "unstable tonality": Liner notes, William Bolcom, A&M CD reissue of *Mirrors*, 1989.

368 "It brings back": David McGee, "Peggy Lee: A Consummate Artist," *Record World*, Dec. 27, 1975.

368 "the recordings worked": Johnny Mandel to JG, Nov. 14, 2010.

369 "Like a mirror": Freeman Gunter, "Visiting Miss Peggy Lee," *Mandate*, Dec. 1975.

369 "just a sultry . . . should look": David McMacken to JG, June 18, 2011.

370 "Peggy made": John Pisano to JG, Dec. 8, 2010.

370 "I saw she . . . other hotel": Kathy Levy to JG, Feb. 3, 1999.

370 "frozen in time": Ron Powers, "Peggy Lee Sings, Time Stands Still in Empire Room," *Chicago Sun-Times*, Sept. 17, 1975.

371 "corny comedy": Will Leonard, "Peggy Lee: Miss Perfect," *Chicago Tribune*, Sept. 12, 1975.

371 "There's a verse . . . nails": *Tonight*, NBC-TV, Oct. 10, 1975.

372 "disappointingly": John S. Wilson, "Peggy Lee Sings Old Songs of Success," *New York Times*, Oct. 27, 1975.

372 "dreck": Stephen Holden, *Rolling Stone*, Dec. 18, 1975.

372 "These guys": Mike Stoller to JG, Dec. 17, 2012.

372 "failure": Mikal Gilmore, *Down Beat*, Apr. 8, 1976.

372 "at times pretentious": Peter Reilly, " . . . one would have thought she had already scaled all the peaks . . . ," *Stereo Review*, Mar. 1976.

372 "I was embarrassed": Jerry Leiber to JG, Feb. 22, 1999.

372 "more than disliked": Morgan Ames to JG, May 10, 2012.

373 "didn't last . . . warhorses": Byron Olson to JG, May 24, 2011.

373 "I'm not going": Max Jones, "Purrfect Peggy," *Melody Maker* (U.K.), Mar. 19, 1977.

373 "People believed": Freeman Gunter, "Visiting Miss Peggy Lee."

373 "It looks like": Paul Horner to JG, Apr. 28, 2013.

373 "It's all of a piece": Robert W. Richards to JG, Feb. 15, 1999.

373 "these new": Johnny Mandel to JG, Nov. 14, 2010.

373 "fine wine": Liner notes, William Bolcom, A&M CD reissue of *Mirrors*, 1989.

374 "slander, fraud": "Peggy Lee Names Former Manager in $6 Million Suit," *Los Angeles Times*, Aug. 27, 1975.

374 "I want to put": Betty Jungheim to JG, Nov. 15, 2012.

374 "It's the dumbest": Dona Harsh Hutchinson to JG, Feb. 9, 2011.

374 "If there were": Brian Panella to JG, Oct. 18, 2010.

374 "If Betty Jungheim": Bruce Vanderhoff to JG, Sept. 29, 2012.

374 "gross negligence . . . a friend": Betty Jungheim to JG, Feb. 9, 2001.

CHAPTER FIFTEEN

377 "Miss Lee . . . expensive": Magda Katz to JG, May 4, 2011.

378 "always first-class": John Whitfield to JG, Apr. 16, 2013.

378 "She went . . . the creeps": Magda Katz to JG, May 4, 2011.

378 "a living legend": Freeman Gunter, "Visiting Miss Peggy Lee," *Mandate*, Dec. 1975.

378 "She seemed to": Wendy Glickstein to JG, May 4, 2011.

379 "She was in": Lee Horwin to JG, Mar. 15, 2014.

379 "Mm-hmm": Walter Willison to JG, June 22, 2011.

379 "It shrinks . . . *did to me!*": Magda Katz to JG, May 4, 2011.

380 "because her great": Bob Thomas, "Peggy Taking U.S. Flag to Land of Rising Sun," *Tennessean Showcase*, Aug. 8, 1976.

381 "He hated it . . . to do well": Larry Grossman to JG, Feb. 4, 2013.

382 "She grew up": John Culhane, "The Muppets in Movieland; Muppets Moving Muppets," *New York Times*, June 10, 1979.

382 "I often wonder": Marshall Berges, "Peggy Lee: Is That All There Is? A Lady of Many Moods Finds There's Much More," *Los Angeles Times Home Magazine*, Oct. 19, 1975.

383 "the magic was gone": Mel Tormé, "A Farewell to the Old Hotel Night Spots," *New York Times*, Jan. 30, 1977.

383 "It was an": Robert W. Richards to JG, Feb. 15, 1999.

383 "The cost of": Jack O'Brian, *Gloversville-Johnston Leader-Herald*, Sept. 25, 1974.

383 "one of her": John S. Wilson, "Miss Lee a Hit at the Waldorf," *New York Times*, Oct. 16, 1976.

384 "No Peggy": Spider Saloff to JG, Apr. 16, 2013.

384 "She was just": Robert W. Richards to JG, Feb. 15, 1999.

385 "delighted": PL, telegram to William Morris Agency, Oct. 22, 1976.

385 "In two minutes": Robert W. Richards to JG, Feb. 15, 1999.

385 "I said to myself . . . find you!": Recording, Peggy Lee, Empire Room, Waldorf-Astoria, New York, Oct. 23, 1976.

386 "Look for me": Ibid.

386 "Especially . . . wrong with her": Magda Katz to JG, May 4, 2011.

386 "He got so": Doak Roberts to JG, Apr. 14, 2011.

387 "What she has": Rick Kogan, "Peggy Lee Still Has Some of the Ol' Magic Left," *Chicago Daily News*, Oct. 5, 1977.
387 "They are, indeed": Letter, Shigeru Okada to PL, Feb. 1, 1977.
387 "Ro-bair . . . for months": Robert W. Richards to JG, Feb. 15, 1999.
389 "He has a quality": George Christy, "Peggy Lee: Still at Fever's Pitch," *Interview*, Oct. 1984.
389 "I just don't . . . coma": Robert W. Richards to JG, Feb. 15, 1999.
391 "People had . . . in the past": Ken Barnes to JG, Feb. 24, 2013.
392 "I'm very": Max Jones, "Purrfect Peggy," *Melody Maker* (UK), Mar. 19, 1977.
393 "That's out . . . Stoller": Ken Barnes to JG, Feb. 24, 2013.
393 "I've revived": "Peggy Lee: Is That All There Is?"
393 "I've never seen": Shaun Considine, "Miss Peggy Lee: ' . . . quite simply the finest singer in the history of popular music,'" *After Dark*, June 1974.
393 "the impersonal": Ray Coleman, *Melody Maker* (UK), Mar. 19, 1977.
394 "The albums were": Ken Barnes to JG, Feb. 24, 2013.
394 "Why hasn't . . . the party": Robert W. Richards to JG, Feb. 15, 1999.
395 "She had to be": Dona Harsh Hutchinson to JG, Feb. 9, 2011.
395 "cracked rib": "The Midnight Earl . . . ," *Milwaukee Sentinel*, Apr. 13, 1977.
395 "toppled spittoon": PL, notes to William Luce for musical *Peg*, Aug. 12, 1982.
395 "left her with": Marilyn Beck, "Her Day in Court Nears for Injured Peggy Lee," *New York Daily News*, May 24, 1982.
395 "cracked skeleton": PL, notes to William Luce for musical *Peg*, 1982.
395 "I literally": Kathy Larkin, "Peggy Lee: The Life, The Songs," *New York Daily News*, Nov. 28, 1983.
395 "nearly died": Bob Thomas, "Peggy Lee Credo: Go Back to Work," *Chicago Tribune*, Aug. 29, 1984.
396 "calming effect": Phoebe Jacobs to JG, Feb. 11, 1999.
396 "very selective . . . offensive song": Leonard Feather, "Peggy Lee Casts a Vote for Class," *Los Angeles Times*, Feb. 19, 1978.
396 "subculture of": "Three Profiles of Heavy Metal Fans: A Taste for Sensation and a Subculture of Alienation," *Journal Qualitative Sociology*, Netherlands: Springer, 1993, p. 423.
396 "outsider": Rob Zombie, *Metal: A Headbangers Journey* (documentary), 2005.
397 "sticking": Cynthia Kirk, "Scandals Opens with Minimum Drama," source unknown, Aug. 1978.
397 "all-out elegance": *Tonight*, NBC-TV, Aug. 3, 1978.
398 "acute viral": "Peggy Lee to Stay Hospitalized Longer," *Variety*, Aug. 17, 1978.
398 "Peggy Lee Still": Rick Kogan, *Chicago Daily News*, Oct. 5, 1977.
398 "She wasn't": Max Bennett to JG, Oct. 28, 2010.
399 "walking calamity": Michael Musto, "Miss Manners," *Village Voice*, Apr. 25, 1989.
399 "What was the . . . a friend": PL, notes to William Luce for musical *Peg*, 1982.
399 "Something is": Transcript of session with psychic Don Torres, c. 1980.

CHAPTER SIXTEEN

401 "It would shimmer": PL, notes to William Luce for musical *Peg*, 1982.
401 "I've found": Maggie Daly, "Peggy Lee Finds Dream House in Bel Air," *Chicago Tribune*, Mar. 24, 1980.
402 "The colors": Newspaper interview, c. 1982, source unknown.
402 "was so thick": Ken Bloom to JG, Apr. 2, 2013.
402 "which we call": *CBS This Morning*, 1990.

402   "When I watch": Elaine St. Johns, "A Presence in My Life: Recollections by Peggy Lee," *Science of Mind*, May 1987.

402   "Some people": Dennis Hunt, "Peggy Lee: A Legend Making a Comeback," *Los Angeles Times*, Feb. 26, 1981.

402   "I've already done": Shaun Considine, "Miss Peggy Lee: ' . . . quite simply the finest singer in the history of popular music,' " *After Dark*, June 1974.

403   "She couldn't keep": Kathy Levy to JG, June 11, 2013.

403   "She was very": Teri Ralston to JG, Jan. 18, 2013.

403   "She was a": Greg MacKellan to JG, Jan. 25, 2013.

403   "As the hostess": Lawrence DeVine, "Peggy's on Outside of Sondheim's Revue," *Detroit Free Press*, June 26, 1980.

404   "What's that, Paul? . . . our lives": Paul Horner to JG, Nov. 16, 2010.

405   "I was down": "Peggy Bounces Back," *New York Daily News*, Sept. 12, 1980.

405   "my life would": William Luce to JG, Nov. 8, 2011.

405   "life or death . . . million dollars": Marilyn Beck, "Her Day in Court Nears for Injured Peggy Lee," *New York Daily News*, May 24, 1982.

406   "run up": Paul Horner to JG, Nov. 16, 2010.

406   "very nasty": Robert W. Richards to JG, Feb. 15, 1999.

406   "our kids": Irving Cowan to JG, May 30, 2013.

407   "the now-famous": Liz Smith, *New York Daily News*, 1982.

407   "connected": Zev Bufman to JG, May 21, 2013.

408   "one of the great": Jon Wilner to JG, July 1, 2012.

408   "She was a dream": Zev Bufman to JG, May 21, 2013.

408   "Everyone told me": Bob Thomas, "Peggy Lee Coming to Broadway," *Gannett Westchester Newspapers*, Sept. 6, 1982.

408   "I KISS YOUR ": Telegram, Zev Bufman to PL, June 14, 1982.

409   "If you had": Paul Horner to JG, Apr. 28, 2013.

409   "bring a friend": Zev Bufman to JG, May 21, 2013.

409   "Do you know": Bruce Vanderhoff to JG, May 15, 2013.

409   "something long": Paul Horner to JG, Nov. 16, 2010.

409   "It was off . . . break it": William Luce to JG, Nov. 8, 2011.

410   "These were business": Paul Horner to JG, Nov. 16, 2010.

410   "Peggy went": William Luce to JG, Nov. 8, 2011.

410   "At the door": Ibid.

410   "I knew there . . . that woman": Zev Bufman to JG, May 21, 2013.

411   "Marge and Zev": Irving Cowan to JG, May 30, 2013.

411   "This was . . . on Broadway": Jon Wilner to JG, July 1, 2012.

411   "a side of Peggy": Bob Thomas, "Peggy Lee Coming to Broadway," *Gannett Westchester Newspapers*, Sept. 6, 1982.

411   "This is one": Ibid.

411   "It'll be my": Lawrence Christon, "Peggy Lee Set for 'Personal' Musical," *Los Angeles Times*, Aug. 19, 1982.

411   "like a rock": Zev Bufman to JG, May 21, 2013.

412   "needed support": Marilyn Beck, "Her Day in Court Nears for Injured Peggy Lee," *New York Daily News*, May 24, 1982.

412   "We hoped": Marilyn Beck, "Does Lee's Suit Fit B'way Plans?," *New York Daily News*, Aug. 19, 1982.

412   "Peggy deserved nothing": Bruce Vanderhoff to JG, May 15, 2013.

412   "I've been around": Kathy Larkin, "Peggy Lee: The Life, The Songs," *New York Daily News*, Nov. 28, 1983.

412   "quiet intensity": Susan Heller Anderson, "Peggy Lee Is Set to Star in a Musical She Wrote," *New York Times*, Aug. 18, 1982.

412   "You have some": Transcript of session with psychic Don Torres, May 20, 1982.

413   "He was gentle": Zev Bufman to JG, May 21, 2013.

413   "He reeled off . . . my life": William Luce to JG, Nov. 8, 2011.

413   "I'm diabetic . . . *first-class?*": Ibid.

414   "eerie": Stephen Holden: Stephen Holden, "Reunion in Tribute to Capitol," *New York Times*, Sept. 13, 1982.

414   "I felt . . . new bond": William Luce to JG, Nov. 8, 2011.

418   "dearly loved her": Paul Horner to JG, Nov. 16, 2010.

419   "You look outrageous!": *Tonight*, NBC-TV, June 25, 1984.

419   "something wonderful": *London Night Out*, Thames TV, Feb. 9, 1983.

419   "We're going": Susan Heller Anderson, "Peggy Lee Is Set to Star in a Musical She Wrote."

419   "I know the value": George Christy, "Peggy Lee: Still at Fever's Pitch," *Interview*, Oct. 1984.

419   "Look": Kathy Larkin, "Peggy Lee: The Life, The Songs."

420   "I took it": Paul Horner to JG, Nov. 16, 2010.

420   "This is bullshit!": Ibid.

420   "We seemed": William Luce to JG, May 10, 2013.

420   "Somebody's got": Paul Horner to JG, Apr. 28, 2013.

420   "Our star": William Luce to JG, Nov. 8, 2011.

420   "Peggy Lee will": Paul Horner to JG, Apr. 28, 2013.

420   "I chose not": Zev Bufman to JG, May 21, 2013.

421   "I was like": Holly Foster-Welles to JG, Jan. 30, 1999.

421   "I think that": Zev Bufman to JG, May 21, 2013.

421   "She fit a . . . lovefest": Andrew Sarewitz to JG, July 2, 2011.

422   "creative consultant": Clive Barnes, "Peg's Broadway Debut: A Strange Triumph," *New York Post*, Dec. 15, 1983.

423   "like Lena . . . her way": William Luce to JG, Nov. 8, 2011.

423   "You are upsetting": Ibid.

423   "I look like . . . GORILLA": Andrew Sarewitz to JG, July 2, 2011.

424   "came out like . . . respect": William Luce to JG, Apr. 28, 2013.

424   "We were all": Zev Bufman to JG, May 21, 2013.

425   "and boldly . . . *my* life!": William Luce to JG, May 10, 2013.

425   "How dare you": Letter, PL to Paul Horner, May 26, 1983.

425   "The music for": Liz Smith, "Musical 'Peg': Background Disharmony?," *New York Daily News*, 1983.

425   "Already they": Ibid.

426   "somewhere an": Letter, Abraham Marcus to Ralph Roseman, Nov. 17, 1983.

426   "revised the libretto": Letter, William Luce to Zev Bufman and Irving Cowan, Nov. 11, 1983.

426   "sabotage . . . do that?": Andrew Sarewitz to JG, July 2, 2011.

426   "It was just . . . of *him!*": Paul Horner to JG, Apr. 28, 2013.

427   "What is this": William Luce to JG, May 10, 2013.

427   "I kept looking": Jane Harvey to JG, Oct. 31, 2010.

427   "Everybody was saying": Paul Horner to JG, Apr. 28, 2013.

427   "sweet": Jon Wilner to JG, July 1, 2012.

428   "But in my": Andrew Sarewitz to JG, July 2, 2011.

428   "Bobby . . . eight-year-old girl": Ibid.

429 "The world knows": PL to Ken Bloom and Bill Rudman, recorded interview, June 1993.

429 "What we see": Martin Burden, "Peggy Lee Gives It All That There Is," *New York Post*, Dec. 7, 1983.

429 "beyond salvation . . . postponement": Zev Bufman to JG, May 21, 2013.

429 "ridiculous": Irving Cowan to JG, May 30, 2013.

429 "I had no": Zev Bufman to JG, May 21, 2013.

430 "David leaked it": Jon Wilner to JG, July 1, 2012.

430 "was so guarded": Zev Bufman to JG, May 21, 2013.

430 "through typesetters": Frank Rich to JG, May 22, 2013.

430 "During previews": Irving Cowan to JG, May 30, 2013.

430 "They said": Zev Bufman to JG, May 21, 2013.

430 "He never said . . . wasn't me": Sharon Churcher, *New York Confidential: The Low-down on the Big Town*, New York: Random House, 1986.

430 "They wanted": Zev Bufman to JG, May 21, 2013.

430 "I'd say": Sharon Churcher, *New York Confidential*.

431 "laughing": Paul Horner to JG, Nov. 16, 2010.

431 "I was done": Zev Bufman to JG, May 21, 2013.

431 "Soul . . . *strange* child": All *Peg* quotes from audio recordings of the show.

432 "This was supposed": Mike Renzi to JG, Nov. 3, 2010.

433 "feeling mildly": Jacques le Sourd, "Peggy Lee Tells Her Story," *Gannett Westchester Newspapers*, Dec. 15, 1983.

434 "I was really": Vince Mauro to JG, Jan. 14, 2013.

434 "I was so": Bruce Vanderhoff to JG, Oct. 17, 2010.

434 "My heart sank": Artie Butler to JG, Mar. 20, 1999.

434 "Somehow, Peggy": Mary Young to JG, Nov. 3, 2010.

434 "revenge": Paul Horner to JG, Apr. 28, 2013.

434 "Peggy Lee swept": Arthur Bell, "Bell Tells," *Village Voice*, Dec. 20, 1983.

434 "Oh, aren't . . . fabulous": Paul Horner to JG, Apr. 28, 2013.

434 "Yes, indeed . . . concert": Arthur Bell, "Bell Tells."

435 "takes to the stage": Frank Rich, "Stage: Peggy Lee Self-Portrait," *New York Times*, Dec. 15, 1983.

435 "If this had": Transcript, Joel E. Siegel, review, *Eyewitness News*, ABC-TV, Dec. 14, 1983.

435 "They didn't like it!": Paul Horner to JG, Nov. 16, 2010.

435 "What went on": Irving Cowan to JG, May 30, 2013.

436 "The heaviest": Arthur Bell, "Bell Tells."

436 "Have you paid": John Simon, *New York*, Dec. 26–Jan. 2, 1984.

436 "somewhere between": Linda Winer, "Peg Strikes a Maudlin Note," *Chicago Tribune*, Dec. 16, 1983.

436 "virtually flawless": Richard Humm, "Show on Broadway: *Peg*," *Variety*, Dec. 1983.

436 "The unanimous opinion": Irving Cowan to JG, May 30, 2013.

436 "She kept saying": D. Michael Heath to JG, Nov. 7, 2011.

437 "People feel": Jon Wilner to JG, July 1, 2012.

437 "You get to": Mary Campbell, "That's Not All There Is," *Los Angeles Daily News*, Oct. 8, 1992.

437 "this particular . . . *PEGGY!*": Recording, *Peg*, Lunt-Fontanne Theatre, New York, Dec. 17, 1983.

437 "I began to feel": *On Stage America*, Sept. 9, 1984.

437 "People were": George Christy, "Peggy Lee: Still at Fever's Pitch," *Interview*, Oct. 1984.

438 "If my life": Mary Campbell, "Peggy Lee: No Hard Feelings," The Associated Press, July 12, 1985.

438 "She stamped": Paul Horner to JG, Nov. 16, 2010.

438 "She was a nice": Jon Wilner to JG, July 1, 2012.

438 "minor league": Zev Bufman to JG, May 21, 2013.

438 "The orchestra": D. Michael Heath to JG, Nov. 7, 2011.

439 "The Peggy Lee flop": Liz Smith, "I'M Pei's Artistic Plans for the Louvre," *New York Daily News*, Dec. 1983.

439 "Zev never": Jon Wilner to JG, July 1, 2012.

CHAPTER SEVENTEEN

441 "This has": Michael Kearns, "Miss Peggy Lee," *Drama-Logue*, June 21–27, 1984.

441 "reminiscences": Leonard Feather, "From Peggy Lee, a Message of Less Is More," *Los Angeles Times*, June 21, 1984.

441 "The audience": Lee Ringuette to JG, June 28, 2011.

442 "Look at those": Recording, Peggy Lee, The Ballroom, New York, June 13, 1986.

442 "Boudoir . . . benefit": *CBS This Morning*, July 20, 1990.

442 "Being associated": Emilio Palame to JG, May 19, 2013.

442 "extraordinary": Stephen Holden, "Jazz Duets, Onstage and in Spirit," *New York Times*, Aug. 10, 2010.

443 "It's gonna blow": Emilio Palame to JG, May 19, 2013.

443 "I just stood . . . bugged me again": Mike Renzi to JG, Nov. 3, 2010.

443 "There were three . . . the fact": John Chiodini to JG, Mar. 20, 1999.

444 "Most of our": Emilio Palame to JG, May 19, 2013.

444 "Let us consider": Mary Strong, *Letters of the Scattered Brotherhood*, Louisville, KY: House of Light, p. 59.

444 "For years": Betty Jungheim to JG, Apr. 15, 2011.

445 "She had that": Emilio Palame to JG, May 19, 2013.

446 "more of an": Neal Karlen, "Ladies and Gentlemen, Miss Peggy Lee," *7 Days*, Feb. 22, 1989.

446 "I thought . . . We'll see": Greg Dawson to JG, Feb. 1999.

447 "Ladies and . . . hel-*LO*!": Recording, Peggy Lee, The Ballroom, New York, July 18, 1985.

448 "It all came": Greg Dawson to JG, Feb. 1999.

448 "upbeat show": Mary Campbell, "Peggy Lee: No Hard Feelings," *Asbury Park* (NJ) *Press*, July 12, 1985.

448 "She was tired": Emilio Palame to JG, May 19, 2013.

448 "Can you imagine": Recording, PL, The Ballroom, New York, July 30, 1985.

448 "Don't get any": Recording, PL, The Ballroom, New York, July 18, 1985.

448 "I've come to love": Ibid.

448 "It got to": Greg Dawson to JG, Feb. 1999.

448 "hip cool": Charlotte Curtis, "Peggy Lee, Regal as Ever," *New York Times*, July 23, 1985.

449 "She was a": Greg Dawson to JG, Feb. 1999.

449 "She was having . . . almost died": Holly Foster-Welles to JG, Jan. 30, 1999.

450 "called all": PL to Alan Dell, BBC Radio 2 interview, rec. 1992.

450 "Miss Lee's spirits": "Peggy Lee 'Gracious,'" *Santa Monica* (CA) *Sumter Daily Item*, Dec. 10, 1985.

450 "I came": Don Heckman, "Is That All There Is? No Way, Says Peggy Lee," *Los Angeles Times*, Apr. 8, 1986.

450 "I'm in tune": John Chiodini to JG, Mar. 20, 1999.

451 "For any": Recording, Peggy Lee, The Ballroom, New York, June 13, 1986.

451 "Maxine just": Ted Ono to JG, July 13, 2012.

451 "too filled": Vince Mauro to JG, Jan. 2, 2013.

451 "She was": Robert W. Richards to JG, Feb. 15, 1999.

452 "*What was*": Greg Dawson to JG, Feb. 1999.

452 "Please don't": Michael Musto, *Village Voice*, Feb. 9, 1983.

452 "a little like": Patrick Pacheco, "Like a Statue Rising Above the Ruins," *New York Daily News*, Feb. 7, 1989.

453 "I can see": Sheryl Connolly, "Miss Peggy Lee," *New York Daily News*, Jun, 15, 1986.

453 "I used to call": Phoebe Jacobs to JG, Feb. 11, 1999.

453 "Frankly": Mary Campbell, "Peggy Lee Records Again," The Associated Press, Feb. 10, 1988.

453 "Some people . . . do this": Emilio Palame to JG, May 19, 2013.

454 "and overdid it": Mary Campbell, "Peggy Lee Records Again."

454 "She never really": Nicki Lee Foster to JG, Jan. 30, 1999.

454 "Your part": Joseph McLellan, "On with the Show," *Washington Post*, Apr. 6, 1987.

454 "Everywhere": Emilio Palame to JG, May 19, 2013.

454 "through that door": Recording, *Peg*, Lunt-Fontanne Theatre, New York, Dec. 4, 1983.

455 "She was into": Emilio Palame to JG, May 19, 2013.

455 "She was completely": Robert W. Richards to JG, Feb. 15, 1999.

456 "five times": *Today*, NBC-TV, Oct. 15, 1986.

456 "a little joke": Stephen Silverman, "She's Got the Fever," *New York Post*, Feb. 2, 1988.

457 "insulting": Matthew Flamm, "Peggy Sues," *New York Post*, Nov. 17, 1988.

457 "Pull my contract": John Saulle to JG, Oct. 24, 2011.

457 "Nothing in": Contract, PL and Walt Disney Productions, Oct. 20, 1952.

458 "within a week": Letter, Alvin Deutsch to Michael Eisner, June 17, 1988.

458 "granted Disney": Letter, John J. Reagan to Alvin Deutsch, July 11, 1988.

458 "just acted": James Ulmer, "Lee Lawsuit Over Disney 'Lady' Vid May Set Precedent," *Hollywood Reporter*, Nov. 17, 1988.

458 "All I received": "Video Battle," *New York Daily News*, Nov. 17, 1988.

458 "Mouse-schwitz . . . ironclad": Lee Ringuette to JG, June 28, 2011.

458 "*no* respect": Nancy Olson Livingston to JG, May 26, 2011.

459 "When it comes": *Barron's*, quoted in *Video Age International*, Oct. 1, 1991.

459 "Such a large . . . Oscar telecast": *Video Age International*, Oct. 1, 1991.

459 "Sure, I thought": James Ulmer, "Lee Lawsuit Over Disney 'Lady' Vid May Set Precedent."

459 "Numerous licenses . . . stretch": Tom Bierbaum, "Lee Sues Disney for $25 Million Over 'Lady' Vid," *Variety*, Nov. 17, 1988.

460 "He explained": Cheech Marin to JG, June 6, 2013.

460 "seated on": Matthew Flamm, "Peggy Sues," *New York Post*, Nov. 17, 1988.

460 "I'm not being": Glenn Collins, "Peggy Lee is Suing Disney," *New York Times*, Nov. 17, 1988.

461 "Do you think . . . gonna win": John Saulle to JG, Oct. 24, 2011.

461 "unfair competition": "TV Creator Sues Over 'Addams Family,'" *San Francisco Chronicle*, Jan. 17, 1992.

461 "This is the": David Blasband to JG, Apr. 6, 2014.

461 "She did": David Blasband to JG, Apr. 13, 2014.

461 "I saw her get": John Chiodini to JG, Mar. 20, 1999.

462 "I can't stop": Bob Harrington, "Profile in Courage," *New York Post*, Jan. 31, 1989.

462 "She didn't get . . . person ever": John Saulle to JG, Oct. 24, 2011.

462   "I didn't come": Betty Jungheim to JG, Feb. 9, 2011.

463   "thoughtful . . . talking with you": Rebecca Freligh, "A Peggy Lee Valentine," *Cleveland Plain Dealer*, Feb. 14, 1989.

463   "When I sing": Neal Karlen, "Ladies and Gentlemen, Miss Peggy Lee," *7 Days*, Feb. 22, 1989.

463   "Jennifer Holliday": Chris Albertson, *Stereo Review*, Dec. 1988.

464   "a center core": Rebecca Freligh, "A Peggy Lee Valentine."

464   "You know dear": Bill Rudman to JG, Apr. 2, 2013.

464   "Miss Peggy Lee": Neal Karlen, "Ladies and Gentlemen, Miss Peggy Lee," *7 Days*, Feb. 22, 1989.

464   "Are you": Recording, PL, The Ballroom, New York, Feb. 2, 1988.

464   "the story of . . . *the soul*": Recording, PL, The Ballroom, New York, Feb. 16, 1989.

465   "left more": Stuart Troup, "Peggy Lee in White and Blues," *New York Newsday*, Jan. 1989.

465   "To us": Rob Hoerburger, "The Lives They Lived: Is That All There Is?" *New York Times*, Dec. 29, 2002.

465   "I believe": Letter to the editor, PL to *Los Angeles* magazine, 1983.

466   "Sometimes life": *Miss Peggy Lee*, p. 264.

466   "morass": "On the Town with Rex Reed," *New York Observer*, Feb. 13, 1989.

466   "I sang": *Miss Peggy Lee*, p. 202.

466   "has always been": *Miss Peggy Lee*, p. 221.

466   "gloppy": Michael Musto, "Miss Manners," *Village Voice*, Apr. 25, 1989.

467   "I told her": Phoebe Jacobs to JG, Feb. 11, 1999.

467   "No one": Jane David to JG, Nov. 12, 2010.

467   "She was tired": Emilio Palame to JG, May 19, 2013.

467   "No! I think": *CBS This Morning*, July 20, 1990.

468   "I really hate": Patricia Morrisroe, "Cabaret: Miss Peggy," *New York*, Apr. 30, 1990.

469   "This power held": Mary Strong, *Letters of the Scattered Brotherhood*, Louisville, KY: House of Light, p. 91.

CHAPTER EIGHTEEN

471   "evil empire": Peter Burke to JG, May 7, 2013.

471   "I thought": David Blasband to JG, Apr. 6, 2014.

472   "what could be": "Singer Lee Gets Judge's Nod in 'Tramp' Dispute," *Hollywood Reporter*, Apr. 3, 1990.

472   "Stars are": *Entertainment Weekly*, Apr. 12, 1991.

472   "a dear, sweet man": PL to Mike Rapchak, WGN-AM (Chicago), c. 1988.

473   "Maybe that's": Nicki Lee Foster to JG, Jan. 30, 1999.

473   "as long as": *Wogan*, BBC, Jan. 18, 1990.

473   "more than . . . blanket": Robert Strom to JG, Jan. 8, 2012.

475   "That story is": Bruce Vanderhoff to JG, Nov. 13, 2010.

475   "Someone was": Dona Harsh Hutchinson to JG, Feb. 9, 2011.

475   "She had": Robert Strom to JG, Sept. 6, 2011.

476   "Hi, little": PL to Alan Dell, BBC Radio 2 interview, rec. 1992.

476   "Now here": PL to Ken Bloom and Bill Rudman, June 1993.

476   "That bell": PL to Alan Dell, BBC Radio 2 interview, rec. 1992.

476   "prize-winning": Joseph McLellan, "On with the Show," *Washington Post*, Apr. 6, 1987.

476   "a distant": Glenn Plaskin, "Lee's Triumph of Spirit," *New York Daily News*, Aug. 17, 1992.

476 "I almost drowned . . . coincidence": PL to Alan Dell, BBC Radio 2 interview, rec. 1992.

477 "very much . . . wanted to": George Christy, "Peggy Lee: Still at Fever's Pitch," *Interview*, Oct. 1984.

477 "my melodies": Mary Campbell, "That's Not All There Is," *Los Angeles Daily News*, Oct. 8, 1992.

477 "After she'd": Bruce Vanderhoff to JG, Oct. 24, 2012.

477 "knew that": Robert Strom to JG, Jan. 8, 2012.

477 "don't realize": PL to Alan Dell, BBC Radio 2 interview, rec. 1992.

478 "He was proud": Mary Campbell, "Despite Her Ailments, Peggy Lee Is Still Going Strong," *Gannett Suburban Newspapers*, Sept. 27, 1992.

478 "There were . . . abandonment thing": Robert Strom to JG, Sept. 6, 2011.

478 "It's a drain": PL to Alan Dell, BBC Radio 2 interview, rec. 1992.

478 "and to a program": Sharon Bernstein, "The Lady and the Lawsuit," *Los Angeles Times*, Feb. 19, 1991.

478 "She suffers": "Jury Tramps on Disney, Awards Millions to Lady," *Ocala Star-Banner*, May 21, 1991.

478 "Sitting up . . . still here": Sharon Bernstein, "The Lady and the Lawsuit," *Los Angeles Times*, Feb. 19, 1991.

479 "control freaks": *Barron's*, quoted in *Video Age International*, Oct. 1, 1991.

479 "confident . . . sympathetic": Stephen M. Lachs to JG, June 7, 2013.

480 "dear Walt": PL, notes to William Luce for musical *Peg*, 1982.

480 "They were rapt": David Blasband to JG, Apr. 6, 2014.

480 "What a lovely": David Blasband to JG, Apr. 13, 2014.

481 "expert witness": Marc Berman, "Lee's Claim Scaled to $9 Mil," *Variety*, Mar. 18, 1991.

481 "I honestly": Court transcript, Peggy Lee vs. Walt Disney Productions, Mar. 11, 1991, p. 776.

481 "Where do": Marc Berman, "Lee's Claim Scaled to $9 Mil," *Variety*, Mar. 18, 1991.

482 "Did Mr. Reardon . . . bizarre conduct": "Disney Lawyer Demands Mistrial in Lawsuit," *Bowling Green* (KY) *Daily News* Mar. 13, 1991.

482 "big mistake . . . Peggy herself": David Blasband to JG, Apr. 6, 2014.

482 "big Peggy Lee fan": Cheech Marin to JG, June 6, 2013.

482 "a character reference . . . That's cool!": Ibid.

483 "Any inference": Marc Berman, "Lee's Claim Scaled to $9 Mil."

483 "in a way": Holly Foster-Welles to JG, Jan. 30, 1999.

484 "wanted to": Dan Boyle, "Peggy Lee Asks of Disney Royalties to Tune of $9M," *Los Angeles Daily News*, Mar. 16, 1991.

484 "She retained": Marc Berman, "Lee's Claim Scaled to $9 Mil."

485 "victory": "Disney Must Pay Peggy Lee," *San Francisco Chronicle*, Mar. 21, 1991.

485 "To take . . . understand them": "Lee Gets $2.3 Mil in Dis Video Ruling," *Hollywood Reporter*, Apr. 17, 1993.

485 "The message of": "Disney Must Pay Peggy Lee," *San Francisco Chronicle.*

485 "I think she": Dan Boyle, "Peggy Lee Wins Big Against Disney," *Los Angeles Daily News*, Mar. 22, 1991.

486 "Lawyers are": Stephen M. Lachs to JG, Apr. 15, 2014.

486 "I accept": Dan Boyle, "Peggy Lee Wins Big Against Disney."

486 "a compromise": "Lee Gets $2.3 Mil in Dis Video Ruling," *Hollywood Reporter*, Apr. 17, 1991.

486 "People are": Sharon Bernstein, "The Lady and the Lawsuit," *Los Angeles Times*, Feb. 19, 1991.

486 "If they didn't": Ed Shaughnessy to JG, Dec. 8, 2010.

487 "worst quarter": Alan Citron and Nina J. Easton, "Disney Adjusts to Fallibility," *Los Angeles Times*, May 24, 1991.

487 "As the company": *Video Age International*, Oct. 1, 1991.

487 "When it comes": Alan Citron and Nina J. Easton, "Disney Adjusts to Fallibility."

487 "that can possibly": Cheech Marin to JG, June 6, 2013.

487 "Then they . . . after that": David Blasband to JG, Apr. 6, 2014.

487 "That battle": Jane David to JG, Nov. 12, 2010.

488 "She was abusive": Jane David to JG, June 10, 2013.

488 "I'm kinda glad": Recording, PL, Pasadena Playhouse, CA, May 10, 1991.

488 "I'd be sitting": Jane David to JG, Nov. 12, 2010.

489 "they were still": Bob Harrington, "Bistro Bits: Miss Peggy Lee: The Event," *Back Stage*, Aug. 7, 1992.

489 "It was like": David Rothenberg to JG, June 24, 2011.

490 "When she sang": Jacques le Sourd, "Valiant Peggy Lee: She Lives to Sing," *Gannett Suburban Newspapers*, Aug. 2, 1992.

490 "I used to have": Recording, PL, Club 53, New York Hilton, July 28, 1992.

490 "The smoke detector": Ibid.

490 "Even when": Howard Kissel, "A 'Fever'-Pitch Comeback," *New York Daily News*, July 31, 1992.

490 "will power": Stephen Holden, "The Peggy Lee Charisma That Withstands the Years," *New York Times*, Aug. 3, 1992.

490 "She just couldn't": Jane David to JG, Nov. 12, 2010.

491 "Like Madonna": Rob Hoerburger, "The Lives They Lived: Is That All There Is?" *New York Times*, Dec. 29, 2002.

491 "lonely girl": J. Randy Taraborrelli, *Madonna: An Intimate Biography*, New York: Simon & Schuster, 2002, p. 14.

491 "I can't figure": Rebecca Freligh, "Peggy Lee Still Rates 'Miss Standing Ovation,'" *Cleveland Plain Dealer*, Feb. 4, 1993.

491 "just wasn't . . . the words": *Erotica Diaries*, Shep Pettibone, sheppettibone.com.

492 "quite shy . . . impeccably": Rebecca Freligh, "Peggy Lee Still Rates 'Miss Standing Ovation.'"

492 "beautiful cabbage roses": "Peggy Lee: Singing Legend Finds Madonna's Her Newest Fan," source unknown, 1992.

492 "Stein understood . . . over Miss Lee": David Munk, "Torch Song Elegy, Volume 5: (N)e(u)rotica: The unbelievably Bitchy Thing Madonna Said to k.d. lang," *stargayzing.com*, Mar. 12, 2014.

493 "based, I'm sure": Robert W. Richards to JG, Feb. 15, 1999.

494 "I was learning": Gilbert O'Sullivan to JG, Dec. 9, 2010.

495 "because the Peggy": Ibid.

495 "Her voice sounds": Jon Pareles, "k.d. lang: A Torch Singer for Modern Times," *New York Times*, Aug. 28, 1992.

495 "profoundly . . . And she did": k.d. lang to JG, Feb. 22, 1999.

496 "Finally": Ibid.

496 "Miss Lee . . . occasion": Jane David to JG, Nov. 12, 2010.

496 "far-out subjects": newspaper interview, source unknown, ca. 1992.

496 "a lot of": Mike Renzi to JG, Nov. 3, 2010.

497 "Mel Tormé was": Eleanor Fuerst to JG, Oct. 26, 2010.

497 "The Hollywood Bowl": Jay Mohr to JG, Sept. 5, 2013.

497 "this wonderful": Recording, Mel Tormé, Hollywood Bowl, July 17, 1992.

497 "She was able": Leonard Feather, "Lee, Tormé Team at Bowl," *Los Angeles Times*, July 20, 1992.

497 "hurtful things": Holly Foster-Welles to JG, Jan. 30, 1999.

497 "What she really . . . in the house": Jane David to JG, Nov. 12, 2010.

498 "makes me want": Ray Rogers, "The Goddess of Pop," *Interview*, Sept. 1997.

498 "on her successes": Jane David to JG, Nov. 12, 2010.

499 "This is incredible!": *Los Angeles Times*, May 11, 1994.

500 "what she truly": Video, Society of Singers salute to PL, May 11, 1994.

500 "It's been said": Ibid.

500 "*leveza*": Zuza Homem de Mello to JG, Mar. 10, 2014.

501 "Then we'd": Jane David to JG, Nov. 12, 2010.

502 "Do you think": PL, press conference, Le Parker Meridien hotel, New York, June 22, 1995.

502 "Mel has really . . . Pocahontas": Ibid.

502 "Peggy hit": Phoebe Jacobs to JG, Nov. 17, 2011.

502 "She was worried": Phoebe Jacobs to JG, Feb. 11, 1999.

502 "You're not gonna": Jane David to JG, Nov. 12, 2010.

503 "One didn't know": Gene Seymour, "Jazz Pop Lives with Lee, Tormé," *New York Newsday*, June 27, 1995.

503 "*WE LOVE YOU*": Recording, PL, Carnegie Hall, New York, June 23, 1995.

504 "She stopped": Sidney Myer to JG, Jan. 2, 2013.

504 "You will never": Phoebe Jacobs to JG, June 23, 1995.

504 "Her ballads": Stephen Holden, "Peggy Lee and Mel Tormé Offer Mystery and Precision," *New York Times*, June 26, 1995.

504 "They said": Robert W. Richards to JG, Feb. 15, 1999.

504 "completely ignored": Stella Castellucci to JG, Aug. 22, 2012.

504 "She cared": Emilio Palame to JG, May 19, 2013.

505 "which no doubt": Tony Gieske, "Mel, Peggy and George," *Hollywood Reporter*, Aug. 4–6, 1995.

505 "endless . . . last time": Stella Castellucci to JG, Aug. 22, 2012.

506 "I intend to . . . over your body": "The Goddess of Pop."

506 "On the way": Jane David to JG, June 10, 2013.

506 "In the case": *Baby, That's Rock and Roll: The Story of Leiber and Stoller*, Bravo TV, 1997.

506 "I did it": Glenn Plaskin, "Lee's Triumph of Spirit," *New York Daily News*, Aug. 17, 1992.

507 "I never thought": Nicki Lee Foster to JG, Jan. 30, 1999.

507 "What is it": PL to Alan Dell, BBC Radio 2 interview, rec. 1992.

507 "I'm having problems . . . been to her": Kathy Levy to JG, June 1, 2013.

508 "Did I . . . been to her": Kathy Levy to JG, June 11, 2013.

508 "Didn't necessarily": Nicki Lee Foster to JG, Jan. 30, 1999.

508 "Virginia would say": Jane David to JG, Nov. 12, 2010.

508 "She had different": Kathy Levy to JG, June 11, 2013.

509 "*Who picked*": Kathy Levy to JG, Mar. 2000.

509 "and just sat": Jane David to JG, Nov. 12, 2010.

509 "Dear Peggy": Kathy Levy to JG, Sept. 28, 1999.

510 "It's very strange": Kathy Levy to JG, Sept. 28, 1999.

510 "which Peggy never . . . who's that?": Letter, Kathy Levy to Cy Godfrey, Apr. 11, 1999.

510 "I'm not leaving . . . I'm here now": Kathy Levy to JG, June 11, 2013.

511 "She seems peaceful": Kathy Levy to JG, Mar. 7, 2000.

511 "I don't want this": Stella Castellucci to JG, Aug. 22, 2012.

511 "Oh, she's gonna . . . always does": Kathy Levy to JG, June 11, 2013.

511 "She had a little": Lee Ringuette to JG, June 28, 2011.

511 "She hugged me": Dona Harsh Hutchinson to JG, Feb. 9, 2011.

512 "I touched her": Kathy Levy to JG, June 11, 2013.

EPILOGUE

513 "Peggy Lee's last . . . was bad . . .": "One Last Goodbye," *Los Angeles Times*, Feb. 5, 2002.

514 "While other singers": Justin Green, "Norma Egstrom (Peggy Lee) The Ageless Miss," *Pulse*, Nov. 1993.

515 "I love everything": Jon Thurber, "Peggy Lee, Sultry Jazz and Pop Singer, Dies at 81," *Los Angeles Times*, Jan. 23, 2002.

515 "atrocity": Jerry Leiber to JG, Feb. 22, 1999.

515 "It wasn't a parody": Jeff McLaughlin, "Rock's Cristina: What You Hear Isn't All There Is," *Boston Globe*, May 12, 1980.

516 "could conjure": Stephen Holden, "Paying Homage to a Departed Jewel, a Single Facet at a Time," *New York Times*, June 25, 2003.

516 "symbol of": Jon Pareles, "Iggy Pop Flaunts His Energy," *New York Times*, Apr. 10, 1996.

516 "Peggy was a": Iggy Pop to JG, June 17, 2013.

517 "I do Pilates": Video, Chuck Sweeney, B.B. King Blues Club & Grill, New York, May 4, 2010.

517 "She'll be turning": Meredith Deliso, "It's a Peggy Lee Impersonation Festival," *Brooklyn Paper*, Mar. 30, 2011.

517 "all about how": Richard Barone to JG, Nov. 27, 2012.

518 "She was a": Paul Pines to JG, Jan. 5, 2012.

518 "Through all": Emilio Palame to JG, May 19, 2013.

518 "I was in agreement": CNN obituary, Jan. 21, 2002.

Discography

The following is a listing of Peggy Lee's original albums and selected compilations, including years of recording. For anyone seeking additional information, Iván Santiago-Mercado's website, peggyleediscography.com, offers comprehensive details about Lee's recorded history.

ALBUMS

Black Coffee (1953/1956)
Selections from Irving Berlin's White Christmas (with Bing Crosby, Danny Kaye, Trudy Erwin) (1954)
Songs from Walt Disney's Lady and the Tramp (1954)
Songs from the Warner Bros. Film Pete Kelly's Blues (with Ella Fitzgerald) (1955)
Sea Shells (1955)
Dream Street (1956)
Miss Wonderful (1956)
The Man I Love (1957)
Jump for Joy (1957–1958)
Things Are Swingin' (1958)
I Like Men! (1958)
Beauty and the Beat! (1959)
Latin ala Lee! (1959)
Christmas Carousel (1959–1960)
Pretty Eyes (1960)
Olé ala Lee! (1960)
Basin Street East Proudly Presents Miss Peggy Lee (1961)
Peggy at Basin Street East (recorded by Capitol in 1961 and first issued in 2002)
Blues Cross Country (1961)
If You Go (1961)
Sugar 'n' Spice (1962)
Mink Jazz (1962–1963)
I'm a Woman (1962–1963)
In Love Again! (1963)
In the Name of Love (1964)

Pass Me By (1964-1965)

Then Was Then, Now Is Now! (1964–1965)

Happy Holidays (1959–1965)

Big Spender (1965–1966)

Guitars a là Lee (1966)

Extra Special! (1960–1966)

Somethin' Groovy! (1967)

2 Shows Nightly (1968)

A Natural Woman (1969)

Is That All There Is? (1969)

Bridge Over Troubled Water (1970)

Make It with You (1970)

Where Did They Go (1971)

Norma Deloris Egstrom from Jamestown, North Dakota (1972)

Let's Love (1974)

Mirrors (1975)

Peggy (1977)

Live in London (1977)

Close Enough for Love (1979)

Miss Peggy Lee Sings the Blues (1988)

Love Held Lightly: Rare Songs by Harold Arlen (1988)

There'll Be Another Spring: The Peggy Lee Songbook (1989)

Moments Like This (1992)

COMPILATIONS

Peggy Lee & Benny Goodman: The Complete Recordings 1941–1947

Miss Peggy Lee (Capitol anthology 1944–1972)

The Lost '40s & '50s Capitol Masters (1944–1952)

Rendezvous with Peggy Lee (Capitol singles, 1945–1947)

The Complete Peggy Lee & June Christy Capitol Transcription Sessions (1945–1949, Mosaic Records)

Peggy Lee Collectors Series (Capitol singles, 1945–1950)

Rare Gems and Hidden Treasures (Capitol singles and previously unissued tracks, 1946–1962)

Classics & Collectibles (Decca tracks, 1952–1956)

The Best of Peggy Lee (Decca tracks, 1952–1956)

All Aglow Again (Capitol singles, 1952–1959)

Peggy Lee Sings for You (World radio transcriptions, mid-1950s)

Index